Advances in Signal Processing and Artificial Intelligence:

Proceedings of the 2nd International Conference on Advances in Signal Processing and Artificial Intelligence

18 - 20 November 2020
Berlin, Germany

Edited by Sergey Y. Yurish

Sergey Y. Yurish, *Editor*
Advances in Signal Processing and Artificial Intelligence
ASPAI' 2020 Conference Proceedings

E-mail (for orders and customer service enquires): ifsa.books@sensorsportal.com

Visit our Home Page on http://www.sensorsportal.com

ISBN: 978-84-09-21931-5
e-ISBN: 978-84-09-21930-8
BN-20200705-XX
BIC: UYQ

Contents

Foreword

On behalf of the ASPAI’ 2020 Organizing Committee, I introduce with pleasure these proceedings devoted to contributions from the 2nd International Conference on Advances in Signal Processing and Artificial Intelligence (ASPAI' 2020).

Advances in artificial intelligence (AI) and signal processing are driving the growth of the artificial intelligence market as improved appropriate technologies is critical to offer enhanced drones, self-driving cars, robotics, etc. Today, more and more sensor manufacturers are using machine learning to sensors and signal data for analyses. The machine learning for sensors and signal data is becoming easier than ever: hardware is becoming smaller and sensors are getting cheaper, making Internet of things devices widely available for a variety of applications ranging from predictive maintenance to user behavior monitoring. Whether we are using sounds, vibrations, images, electrical signals or accelerometer or other kinds of sensor data, we can build now richer analytics by teaching a machine to detect and classify events happening in real-time, at the edge, using an inexpensive microcontroller for processing - even with noisy, high variation data.

According to recent study, the artificial intelligence market is expected to reach USD 202.57 billion by 2026, at a CAGR of 33.1 % during the forecast period. Artificial intelligences currently transforming the manufacturing industry. Virtual reality, automation, Internet of Things (IoT), and robotics are some important features of AI that are benefitting the manufacturing industry. AI has been one of the fastest-growing technologies in recent years. The market growth is mainly driven by factors such as the increasing adoption of cloud-based applications and services, growing big data, and increasing demand for intelligent virtual assistants. The major restraint for such market is the limited number of AI technology experts.

The Series of ASPAI Conferences have been launched to fill-in this gap and to provide a forum for open discussion and development of emerging artificial intelligence and appropriate signal processing technologies focused on real-word implementations by offering Hardware, Software, Services, Technology (Machine Learning, Natural Language Processing, Context-Aware Computing, Computer Vision and Signal Processing). The goal of the conference is to provide an interactive environment for establishing collaboration, exchanging ideas, and facilitating discussion between researchers, manufacturers and users. The first ASPAI conference has taken place in Barcelona, Spain in 2019.

The conference is organized by the International Frequency Sensor Association (IFSA) - one of the major professional, non-profit association serving for sensor industry and academy more than 20 years, in technical cooperation with media partners – IOS Press (journal *‘Integrated Computer-Aided Engineering’*) and World Scientific (*International Journal of Neural Systems*). The conference program provides an opportunity for researchers interested in signal processing and artificial intelligence to discuss their latest results and exchange ideas on the new trends.

I hope that these proceedings will give readers an excellent overview of important and diversity topics discussed at the conference. Selected, extended papers will be submitted to the media partners’ journals and IFSA’s open access ‘*Sensors & Transducers*’ journal based on the proceeding’s contributions.

We thank all authors for submitting their latest work, thus contributing to the excellent technical contents of the Conference. Especially, we would like to thank the individuals and organizations that worked together diligently to make this Conference a success, and to the members of the International Program Committee for the thorough and careful review of the papers. It is important to point out that the great majority of the efforts in organizing the technical program of the Conference came from volunteers.

Prof., Dr. Sergey Y. Yurish
ASPAI’ 2020 Conference Chairman

(003)

Dwelling Detection on VHR Satellite Imagery of Refugee Camps Using a Faster R-CNN

L. Wickert [1], M. Bogen [1] and M. Richter [1]
[1] Fraunhofer IAIS, Schloss Birlinghoven, 53757 Sankt Augustin, Germany
Tel.: +49 2241 14-3415
E-mail: lorenz.wickert@iais.fraunhofer.de

Summary: The management of humanitarian operations in highly intense situations like migration movements happening at borders often lack current and sufficient information. Satellites do provide large-scale information fast. When dealing with a migration situation, satellite images now can give information about where refugees are before they arrive at a border, giving first responders urgently needed lead time for contingency and capacity planning. Dwelling Detection, a method conducted on satellite images of refugee camps, is able to count the dwellings in a camp. From that, the number of inhabitants in a camp can be estimated for forecasting purposes. To count the dwellings, object detection machine learning methods can be used. In this paper, a dwelling detection workflow using a Faster R-CNN is described. To train the Faster R-CNN, a fast training data annotation workflow was developed. The Faster R-CNN outputs an estimate of people living in a camp and a confidence factor, giving a global evaluation metric about the quality of the analysis of the image and by that of the calculation itself. This workflow yields results that can be used in humanitarian operations. So our related proposal is to get satellite images fast, evaluate them with our method, and have better numbers for contingency and capacity planning. By this, stress for all people involved in a humanitarian (crisis) situation can be reduced.

Keywords: Artificial intelligence (AI), Machine learning (ML), Convolutional neural network (CNN), Faster R-CNN, Remote sensing (RS), Dwelling detection, Object detection, Pattern recognition.

---

1. Introduction

Forced Migration is one of the most pressing issues of society today. The United Nations High Commissioner for Refugees reported that in 2018 the worlds forcibly displaced population remained yet again at a record high [1]. This leads to highly intense humanitarian operations like the migration movements in Europe in 2015/16, where humanitarian operations were challenging to all people involved because of a short reaction time and a lack of sufficient information. Satellite data allows the monitoring of large areas of the earth in a short time. Together with machine learning technology, satellite data can be used to yield large-scale information almost immediately, supporting decision making in humanitarian operations. In this paper, advances in satellite sensors [2, p. 187ff] and object detection using machine learning [3] are used to speed up the task of Dwelling Detection [4]. This is a fast method to get information on the number of inhabitants of camps when those information are hard to get otherwise, either because those numbers are not available or there is no communication among the different parties, authorities and organization engaged in a humanitarian situation.

The research described in this paper was conducted in the context of the HUMAN+[1] project. In the HUMAN+ project, a real-time situational awareness system for efficient management of migration movements was developed. Besides the dwelling detection module, camera streams from cameras located at borders are analyzed, social media platforms are evaluated concerning migration movement and reports from operators in the field are collected and included in the situational awareness system.

2. Methodology

2.1. Dwelling Detection

Due to the fact that individual humans cannot be seen on commercially available satellite images a method for extracting valuable information about humans from satellite imagery had to be defined. Dwelling Detection offers a fitting method. It is conducted on very high resolution (VHR) satellite images of refugee camps. Those satellite images are available as a result of regular satellite operations and recordings. Dwellings are counted and multiplied with an average, size-based factor of how many people live in one dwelling, giving an estimate over how many people may live in a camp. This information can be used in medium-term planning of humanitarian operations during migration situations. Reasons why these information are not available for humanitarian operators can be that camps are run by private companies [5], that camps do not develop as planned because of a rapid growth of inhabitants [6] or because camps are makeshift camps which are created arbitrarily, sometimes called jungles [5, 7].

---

[1] https://giscience.zgis.at/human/

2.2. Deep Learning Object Detection

Dwelling Detection is traditionally done by experts by hand, taking a lot of time which is not available in crisis situations. Recent advantages in image classification and object detection on images using Convolutional Neural Networks (CNN) allow first approaches to automate this task [8, 9]. A Faster R-CNN [10] offers a state-of-the-art CNN architecture for object detection to eventually develop a Dwelling Detection Workflow. To do so, a complete machine learning workflow (see Fig. 1) was created, following a framework of preparing input data, defining the expected output data and building a core network which constructs the intrinsic and natural relationship of the input-output pair [11].

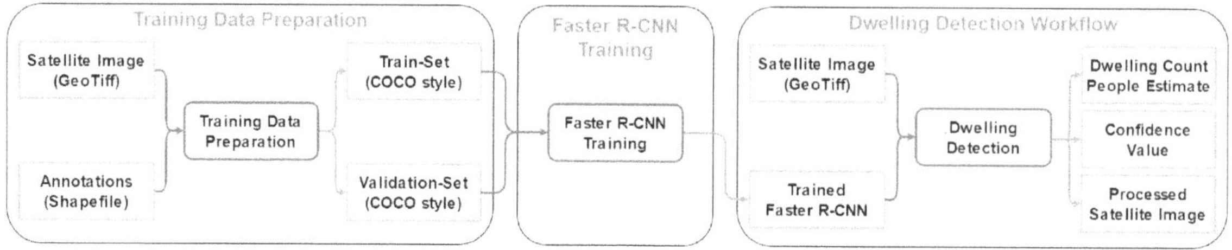

Fig. 1. The machine learning workflow.

The workflow consists of three main steps. In the first step, satellite images which are annotated by hand are used to prepare ground truth training data consisting of a train- and a validation-set. Those sets are used to train a Faster R-CNN. In the last step, the trained Faster R-CNN is used to analyze a new satellite image of a camp. The classifier outputs a dwelling count and a people estimate, a confidence value concerning the Faster R-CNN analysis and the processed input satellite image with found dwellings marked.

2.3. Training Data Preparation

The input data in a dwelling detection task is VHR satellite imagery of refugee camps identified at this point in time by a human being. In this work, images were taken from Google Earth (Google Inc.) as examples and due to the fact that free satellite images were not available. On those, the dwellings forming a camp have to be found by an object detection algorithm like Faster R-CNN and marked with a bounding box.

A Faster R-CNN is trained using supervised learning. The ground truth data required to train the network consists of bounding boxes around each dwelling. Further, the size of the input images needs to be small enough to be efficiently handled by a Faster R-CNN. Therefore, the input satellite image is split up into 300 pixel × 300 pixel tiles. For speeding up the annotation process, a workflow building up on a seeded region growing algorithm [12], was developed (see Fig. 2). Each dwelling needs to be point-annotated by a human, then each annotation is used by the region growing algorithm as a seed to estimate the extent of one dwelling. The results of the region growing algorithm are then filtered to eliminate bad regions. Around each region, a bounding box is defined and stored in the MS COCO-annotation format [13].

Fig. 2. To create training data, the initial tile containing point annotations (a) is analyzed using a region fill algorithm (b), resulting in ground truth bounding boxes (c) around dwellings.

2.4. Faster R-CNN Training

Refugee settlements inhabit a huge degree of variety due to their characteristics discussed in Section 2.1. To achieve a network generalizing well, this variety has to be represented in the training data [8]. Therefore, annotations for the training set were made on satellite images of nine different refugee camps. The images have a huge variation in the landscape surrounding the camps, the organization form of the camps, the size of the camps and the quality of the images as a result of the recording distance from the satellite and the satellites optical sensors. On each image, annotations on the upper 50 % of the input image were added to the training set, annotations on the lower 50 % of the input image were added to the validation set.

For implementation and training of the Faster R-CNN an open source implementation was used[2]. A Faster R-CNN consists of a pre-trained backbone network for feature extraction, a Regional Proposal Network (RPN) for generating object proposals and a classification network outputting bounding boxes around found objects and a class vector for each bounding box. As a backbone, ResNet50 [14] was used. The network was trained on one GPU for 36,000 iterations.

2.5. Dwelling Detection Workflow

To analyze a satellite image using the trained Faster R-CNN, a copy of the input image, which is cut in various 300 pixel × 300 pixel tiles to handle its size, is made. Each tile is analyzed separately. Found objects are accepted as a dwelling if their class security for being a dwelling is higher than a defined threshold. The Dwelling Detection workflow has two outputs: The first output is a copy of the input satellite image with all found dwellings marked with a bounding box (see Fig. 3). The second output consists of the number of found dwellings and the estimated number of inhabitants in a camp. The number of inhabitants is estimated with regard to the size of the found bounding boxes. Problematic is that the spatial resolution of one pixel can change from image to image and is not always known. Therefore, the estimation algorithm has to be independent of this information. This is achieved by assigning a fixed number of inhabitants to the smallest and the largest dwelling found by the Faster R-CNN. For the dwellings with sizes between those anchor points, the number of inhabitants in a tent is interpolated linearly.

Further, a confidence metric indicating the certainty of the network about the results of the analysis is calculated. The metric is the ratio of the number of found objects $O_{cls \geq 0.85}$ with a class security higher or equal than 0.85 divided by the number of objects $O_{cls \geq 0.5}$ with a class security higher or equal than 0.5:

$$\text{Confidence} = \frac{O_{cls \geq 0.85}}{O_{cls \geq 0.5}} \tag{1}$$

3. Results

A complete machine learning workflow was implemented. For training data creation an annotation method using point annotations which are processed using a seeded region growing algorithm to generate ground-truth data was developed. This method allows creating a sufficient amount of ground-truth bounding boxes in a short amount of time.

3.1. Machine Learning Results

The Faster R-CNN was trained and tested on nine satellite images of refugee camps with different sizes from different parts of the world on different landforms and with varying image quality. On the validation set, comprising of ground truth data from all of the nine used satellite images, a mean Average Precision (mAP) of 68.2 % and a mean Average Recall (mAR) of 72.0 %, determined using the COCO detection evaluation metrics [15], was achieved. It can be concluded, that the network was able to construct the relationship between the input-satellite image and the dwellings appearing on the image. This holds true for the huge variety of camps the network was trained on.

3.2. Dwelling Detection Results

The trained Faster R-CNN finds objects on the analyzed image. To estimate the number of inhabitants in a camp the workflow described in Section 2.5, which is independent of the spatial resolution of the input satellite image and therefore works without image-specific configurations, is used. For the estimation, the number of inhabitants in the smallest dwelling was set to three and the number of inhabitants in the largest dwelling was set to twelve while the threshold for a found object being accepted as a dwelling was set to a class security of 0.85, following [9].

To evaluate the estimate numbers, real-world numbers of inhabitants for each camp, measured at around the time the satellite image was shot, were researched in newspaper articles. It has to be noted that these numbers are not official numbers and are therefore fuzzy. Further, the estimations are based on no concrete knowledge of an individual camp. Therefore the absolute numbers cannot be assumed as the real numbers but function as an early warning system, stating an order of magnitude of the number of inhabitants.

Consequences from the result of the workflow have to be taken in accordance to the computed confidence metric and the visual output of the network. A look on the annotated satellite image produced by the workflow can give a first impression on how successful the analysis was. Further, the confidence metric makes a statement about how well the Faster R-CNN could work with the input image. A low confidence means, that there were a lot of objects the network didn't discard in the first place, but is also not sure about the objects being a dwelling. In that case, it is recommended for humanitarian operators to gather more information from different sources concerning the camp and the area around it. A higher confidence indicates, that humanitarian operators can include the order of magnitude of displaced peoples in their medium-term planning.

[2] https://github.com/facebookresearch/Detectron

4. Discussion

The workflow was developed with the goal of fast applicability. This goal was reached successfully by using open software and data, speeding up the slow and cumbersome process of ground-truth generation and annotation and building convenient workarounds when information about the data was missing. Nevertheless, trade-offs between accuracy and applicability had to be made.

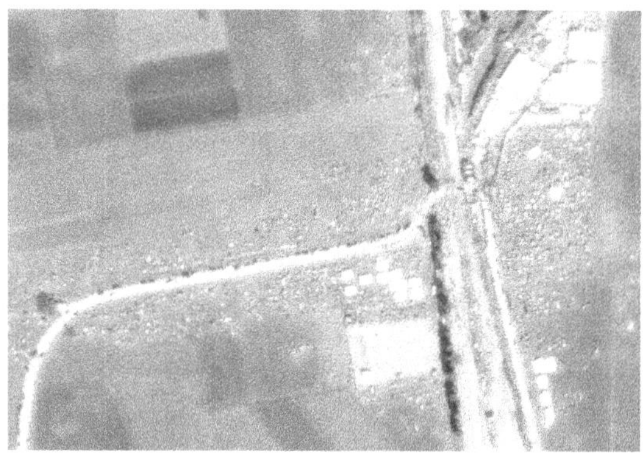

Fig. 3. The output of the Faster R-CNN. The input satellite image of a refugee camp located in Idomeni (Greece) was analyzed. The red bounding boxes mark the dwellings found by the Faster R-CNN.

The seeded region growing algorithm used for speeding up annotating ground truth data is rather simple. Plenty of improved image segmentation algorithms that are existing today [16] could improve the ground truth generation. A more accurate ground truth segmentation would also allow switching the deep learning architecture from a Faster R-CNN to a Mask R-CNN [17]. Mask R-CNN builds up on the Faster R-CNN architecture and allows image segmentation on top of object detection in images. Using segmentations of dwellings can yield more accurate estimates for the inhabitant estimation. Further accuracy can be achieved by using georeferenced satellite imagery where the spatial resolution of a pixel is known. Combining the extend or the footprint of a dwelling with the spatial resolution of a pixel allows to accurately determine the size of a dwelling which can be used for inhabitant estimation based on a parameter taking the actual size of a tent into account.

If accuracy or fast applicability is more important is nevertheless context dependent. For operators managing one specific camp, more accurate results are essential. For humanitarian operators working on broader migration situations, fast information giving insights about the magnitude of the situation are important. In this context, the presented workflow is a good enhancement: Actual workflow results were presented in September 2019 to professionals in migration management like the Red Cross as part of an international exercise carried out in the HUMAN+ project. The additional information about people in the refugee camps generated through Dwelling Detection was appreciated unanimously. Though those professionals wanted to have absolute numbers, this is not doable due to the uncertainties described in this paper. The number of people in a refugee camp has to be seen in context with the confidence value generated. Those numbers have to combined and merged with other information gathered in the HUMAN+ project. Only then a meaningful picture of the situation can be achieved to help first responders to make the right decisions in crisis management and refugees to be taken care of.

5. Conclusion

A machine learning based dwelling detection classifier was built using modern object detection techniques, a classifier which yields results almost immediately helpful in humanitarian operations. An important step for doing so is the developed training data preparation workflow, which is fast and convenient for annotations.

The workflow outputs results in the magnitude of the real numbers of inhabitants in a migrant camp. It works on the image without the need of adjustments by the user, thus generating rapid and useful information. The generated information are best combined with other information about the migration situation from different sources. The visual representation of the results with bounding boxes drawn on the input image as well as the calculated confidence factor increase the interpretability of the results. The results were deemed to be useful by experts in the field.

Acknowledgements

The authors acknowledge the financial support by the German Federal Ministry of Education and Research (BMBF) and the Austrian Bundesministerium Klimaschutz, Umwelt, Energie, Mobilität, Innovation und Technologie (BMVIT) in the framework of the HUMAN+ project (funding code 13N14716 to 13N14723)

References

[1]. Global Trends – Forced Displacement in 2018, *UNHCR*, Switzerland, 2018.

[2]. J. B. Campbell, R. H. Wynne, Introduction to Remote Sensing, 5th Ed., *Guilford Press*, 2011.

[3]. Z.-Q. Zhao, P. Zheng, S.-T. Xu, X. Wu, Object detection with deep learning: A review, *IEEE Transactions on Neural Networks and Learning Systems*, 2019, pp. 1-21.

[4]. K. Spröhnle, D. Tiede, E. Schoepfer, P. Füreder, A. Svanberg, T. Rost, Earth observation-based dwelling detection approaches in a highly complex refugee camp environment – A comparative study, *Remote Sensing*, Vol. 6, Issue 10, Sep. 2014, pp. 9277-9297.

[5]. I. Katz, A network of camps on the way to Europe, *Forced Migration Review*, Issue 51, 2016, p. 17.

[6]. A. Dalal, A. Darweesh, P. Misselwitz, A. Steigemann, Planning the ideal refugee camp? A critical interrogation of recent planning innovations in Jordan and Germany, *UP*, Vol. 3, Issue 4, Dec. 2018, p. 64.

[7]. B. Beznec, M. Speer, M. S. Mitrović, Governing the Balkan route: Macedonia, Serbia and the European border regime, *Rosa Luxemburg Stiftung Southeast Europe*, 2016.

[8]. J. A. Quinn, M. M. Nyhan, C. Navarro, D. Coluccia, L. Bromley, M. Luengo-Oroz, Humanitarian applications of machine learning with remote-sensing data: review and case study in refugee settlement mapping, *Philosophical Transactions of the Royal Society A: Mathematical, Physical and Engineering Sciences*, Vol. 376, Issue 2128, Sep. 2018, 20170363.

[9]. O. Ghorbanzadeh, D. Tiede, Z. Dabiri, M. Sudmanns, S. Lang, Dwelling extraction in refugee camps using CNN – First experiences and lessons learnt, *ISPRS – International Archives of the Photogrammetry, Remote Sensing and Spatial Information Sciences*, Vol. XLII–1, Sep. 2018, pp. 161-166.

[10]. S. Ren, K. He, R. Girshick, J. Sun, Faster R-CNN: Towards real-time object detection with region proposal networks, *IEEE Transactions on Pattern Analysis and Machine Intelligence*, Vol. 39, Issue 6, Jun. 2017, pp. 1137-1149.

[11]. L. Zhang, L. Zhang, B. Du, Deep learning for remote sensing data: A technical tutorial on the state of the art, *IEEE Geoscience and Remote Sensing Magazine*, Vol. 4, Issue 2, Jun. 2016, pp. 22-40.

[12]. R. Adams, L. Bischof, Seeded region growing, *IEEE Transactions on Pattern Analysis and Machine Intelligence*, Vol. 16, Issue 6, Jun. 1994, pp. 641-647.

[13]. T.-Y. Lin, *et al.*, Microsoft COCO: Common Objects in Context, in *Proceedings of the European Conference on Computer Vision (ECCV'14)*, Vol. 8693, 2014, pp. 740-755.

[14]. K. He, X. Zhang, S. Ren, J. Sun, Deep residual learning for image recognition, in *Proceedings of the IEEE Conference on Computer Vision and Pattern Recognition (CVPR'16)*, 2016, pp. 770-778.

[15]. The COCO Consortium, Common Objects in Context, Detection Evaluation, http://cocodataset.org/#detection-eval.

[16]. H. Zhu, F. Meng, J. Cai, S. Lu, Beyond pixels: A comprehensive survey from bottom-up to semantic image segmentation and cosegmentation, *Journal of Visual Communication and Image Representation*, Vol. 34, Jan. 2016, pp. 12-27.

[17]. K. He, G. Gkioxari, P. Dollar, R. Girshick, Mask R-CNN, in *Proceedings of the IEEE International Conference on Computer Vision (ICCV'17)*, 2017, pp. 2961-2969.

(006)

Automatic Thresholding Methods for Diabetic Retinopathy's Detection

Moumena Salah Alhadithi
Department of Computer Science, Education College for Pure Science, University of Mosul, Mosul, Iraq
Moumena.alhadithi@yahoo.com

Summary: In general, diabetic destroys the small blood vessels in the retinal. This is called Diabetic retinopathy. It is causing blindness. The aim of this work is to test five thresholding methods for detection diabetic retinopathy. These methods will extract the blood vessels of the retina.

Keywords: Diabetic retinopathy (DR), Thresholding, Segmentation, Between class variance.

1. Introduction

The body cells need the sugar to do their functions. Pancreas produces insulin to organize the sugar in the blood. If the pancreas does not produce enough insulin, or the cells do not respond to the insulin that is produced; the blood sugar will be increased causing diabetes. The world health organization declares that about 347 million of people suffer from diabetes worldwide [3, 4]. Usually diabetes increases the number of blood vessels in the retina; also it damages the old vessels. This is called diabetic retinopathy [1]. Early detection can decrease the risk of diabetic retinopathy and vision loss. Therefore, there is a need to improve computer-aided diagnosis (CAD) systems to help a clinician in his diagnosis for the diabetic retinopathy.

In our work, we will apply five accurate thresholding methods. These methods will show the vessels of the retina in a clear way. All the blood vessels will be extracting from the retina images.

This paper is presented as follows: Section 2 presents the introduction of thresholding. Section 3 describes the formulation. Section 4 shows the work of between class variance and all the methods that are depended on it. Section 5 presents the thresholding evaluation method. In section 6, the experimental results will be explained. Finally, Section 7 has the conclusion of the study.

2. Thresholding

Segmentation can solve many problems in pattern recognition and computer vision. In medical images, we suffer from high noise and low contrast between the blood vessels and the background [1, 3]. Therefore, one of the most effective used methods for segmenting images is thresholding. It is simple, but effective in isolation the objects from the background [7].

Fig. 1(a) displays the original image; (b) the histogram shows the threshold that isolates the blood vessels from the background; (c) the segmented image.

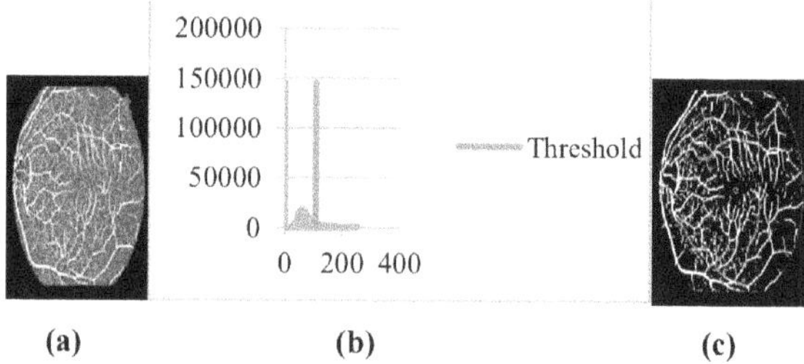

Fig. 1. Image of the retina, (a) Original image, (b) histogram, (c) segmented image.

Many researchers wrote in this subject. For example [2] (Mehmet Burak 2019) applied bottom hat filtering, [6] (Jiang K., Zhou Z., Wu H. and Geng X. 2015) presented isotropic un decimated wavelet transform fuzzy to extract retinal blood vessel, [7] (Hassan G., El-Bendary N., Hassanian A.E., Fahmy A., and Snasel V., 2015) used mathematical morphology to show the blood vessels in the retina images [8] (Nogol Memari, Abd Ruhman Ramli and Mehrdad Moghbel) implemented matched filtering and fuzzy C means clustering to extract the vessels in the retinal images. In our work, we will split the blood vessels by increasing the separate factor between the classes.

3. Formulation

To analyze and study any image we have to realize that the image has a group of pixels known as$n$; for every image level there are a group of pixels denoted asn_i. The total number of pixels is known as:

$$n = \sum_{i=0}^{L-1} n_i \qquad (1)$$

Gray level histogram is normalized as a probability distribution:

$$h_i = \frac{n_i}{n} \qquad (2)$$

The gray level of an image is [0… L-1]. Gray level 0 is the black while the gray level L-1 is the lightest.

The probability of occurrence of the two classes can be known as the following:

$$w_1(t) = \sum_{i=0}^{t} h(i) \qquad w_2(t) = \sum_{i=t+1}^{L-1} h(i) \tag{3}$$

The mean and variance of the object and background are known as the following:

$$\mu_1(t) = \sum_{i=0}^{t} i\, h(i), \sigma_1^2(t) = \sum_{i=0}^{t} (i - \mu_1(t))^2 h(i), \tag{4}$$

$$\mu_2(t) = \sum_{i=t+1}^{L-1} i\, h(i), \sigma_2^2(t) = \sum_{i=t+1}^{L-1} (i - \mu_2(t))^2 h(i) \tag{5}$$

Every image has a thresholding algorithm used to select an optimal threshold. The selected threshold will separate the object from the background.

A. Between Class Variance (Otsu Method)

It assumed the segmented image as two classes (background and object) or bimodal histogram. The optimal threshold should maximize inter-class variance [9].

$$\sigma_W^2(t) = \omega_1(t)\sigma_1^2(t) + \omega_2(t)\sigma_2^2(t), \tag{6}$$

$$\sigma_B^2(t) = \omega_1(t)(\mu_1(t) - \mu_T(t))^2 + \omega_2(\mu_2(t) - \mu_T(t))^2, \tag{7}$$

$$\sigma_B^2(t) = \omega_1(t)\omega_2(t)\big(\mu_2(t) - \mu_1(t)\big)^2, \tag{8}$$

B. Valley Emphasis Method

A method succeeded in selected both big and tiny objects. The new method implements a new weight to ensure that the best threshold located at the deepest point between two peaks for (bimodal histogram), or at the bottom rim of a single peak for (unimodal histogram); also it should increase the variance between the classes to the maximum [10].

$$t_{opt} = \arg \underset{0 \le t \le L-1}{\text{Max}} \{(1 - h(t)(\omega_1(t)\mu_1^2(t) + \omega_2(t)\mu_2^2(t))\} \tag{9}$$

C. Neighborhood Valley Emphasis Method

This method calculates between class variance for both the threshold point and it's neighbourhood. This method is used to obtain the best threshold for images have big diversity between object variance and background variance. The sum of neighborhood gray level value $\bar{h}(i)$ refers within the interval n = 2m + 1 for gray level i, n refers to the number of neighborhood.

If the image has one dimensional histogram hi the neighborhood gray value $\bar{h}(i)$ of the grey level i is as the following:

$$\bar{h}(i) = [h(i-m) + \ldots + h(i-1) + h(i) + h(i+1) + \ldots + h(i+m)] \tag{10}$$

The method is as the following:

$$\xi(t) = (1 - \bar{h}(t))((\omega_1(t)\mu_1^2(t) + \omega_2(t)\mu_2^2(t)) \tag{11}$$

In Eq. (12) the first group refers to the maximum weight of the valley point and its neighborhood, while the second the group refers to the maximum between class variance [11].

The best threshold is:

$$t_{opt} = \arg \underset{0<t<L-1}{\text{Max}} \{(1 - \bar{h}(t)(\omega_1(t)\mu_1^2(t) + \omega_2(t)\mu_2^2(t))\} \tag{12}$$

D. Thresholding Based on Variance and Intensity Contrast

The best threshold is selected by the computing of the weighted sum of within class variance and the intensity contrast between the object and background.

$$J(\lambda, t) = (1 - \lambda)\,\sigma_W(t) - \lambda|\,\mu_1(t) - \mu_2(t)| \tag{13}$$

Within class variance $\sigma_W(t)$ refers to the intensity of the object and background, and the intensity contrast $|\mu_1(t) - \mu_2(t)|$ is no n as the different in mean' intensitiesbetween them. λ is a critical item in the method. It is a weight that calculates the contribution of (within class variance and the intensity contrast) in the method. λ Within [0, 1).

1) λ = 0 decreases within class variance to the minimum.
2) λ = 1 increases the intensity contrast to the maximum.

The best threshold will be selected by the intensity contrast [12].

The optimal threshold t_{opt} is chosen by minimizing the following.

$$J(\lambda, t_{opt}) = \underset{t}{\min}\, J(\lambda, t) \tag{14}$$

E. Variance Discrepancy Method

It used to threshold images have big variance discrepancy between the object and background. Variance discrepancy method used both class variance sum and variances discrepancy to determine the best threshold.

$$J(\alpha, t) = \alpha(\sigma_1^2(t) + \sigma_2^2(t)) + (1 - \alpha)\sigma_D(t), \tag{15}$$

where $\sigma_D(t) = \sigma_1(t)\,\sigma_2(t)$ and $\sigma_1^2(t) <= \sigma_D(t) <= \sigma_2^2(t)$ or $\sigma_2^2(t) <= \sigma_D(t) <= \sigma_1^2(t)$. $\sigma_D(t)$ is the measurement of variance discrepancy of the two classes (the object and background). While $\sigma_1(t)$ and $\sigma_2(t)$ are the standard deviation of them. In this method the smaller number of $\sigma_D(t)$ means there is bigger variance disrepancy in the image α is an important item; it calculates the contributions of variance sum and variance discrepancy in the method. α values will be within the range [0,1]. If α is zero or near to zero the method will be depended on variance discrepancy, and the effect of variance sum will be so small. But if α is one or near to one the variance discrepancy method will be based on class variance sum. This leads the class variance discrepancy to have small effect [13].

The best threshold is determined by minimizing the new equation.

$$J(\alpha, t_{opt}) = \text{Arg Min}_{0 \le t \le L-1} J(\alpha, t) \quad (16)$$

4. Thresholding Evaluation Method

The work of the thresholding method is very important. It based on the kind of the thresholding method and the type of image. In our study, we will implement evaluation metric (region non uniformity (NU)).

- **Region Non-Uniformity (NU)**

This method measures the ability to determine the different between the background and object in the segmented image. A good segmented image should have larger intra region uniformity, which is related to the similarity attribute about region element. In NU Equation (17): $\sigma^2(t)$ refers to the variance of the image, while $\sigma_o^2(t)$ refers to the variance of the object. $w_o(t)$. This refers to the probability of occurrence of the object. NU = zero refers to good segmented image, but NU = 1 means we have bad segmented image [15].

$$NU = \frac{w_o(t)\,\sigma_o^2(t)}{\sigma^2(t)} \quad (17)$$

5. Gaussian Distribution

Gaussian distribution is known as a continuous probability distribution. Its shape is focused in the center, and then it minimized on either side taking a shape like a bell. This kind of distribution is very simple analytically. Moreover, it is easy to implement mathematically. The equation is known as the following:

$$f(x, \mu, \sigma^2) = \frac{1}{\sigma\sqrt{2\pi}} e^{-\frac{(x-\mu)}{2\sigma^2}} \quad (18)$$

$\Pi = 3.14$; $e = 2.71828$.

The following form describes the shape of Gaussian distribution.

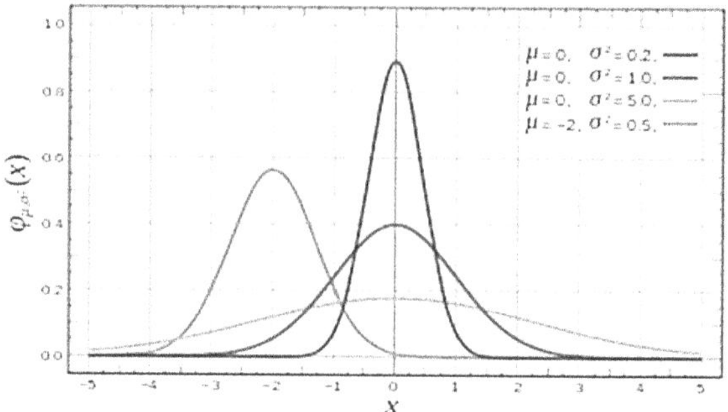

Fig. 2. Gaussian distribution.

6. Experimental Results

Commonly, for diagnosis diabetic retinopathy the clinician demonstrates that there are a large number of blood vessels in the retina and many damaged vessels. This means the disease is in the final stage. We made our test for huge number of retinal images; especially for people have diabetic retinopathy. Then as seen in Fig. 3(a-f); Fig. 3(b) Otsu method detects the blood vessels with optimal threshold T = 109. Fig. 3(c) valley emphasis method also isolates the blood vessels from the background with optimal threshold T = 125. As we see neighborhood valley emphasis method shows the blood vessels with optimal threshold T = 137. This method is the best in present all the blood vessels the damaged one and the new one. Variance and intensity contrast method gives bad results. The segmented image did not show all the blood vessels. It is threshold T = 203. Variance discrepancy method failed in extraction the blood vessels; it did not get all the details of the.

Table 1 presents the outcomes of the five thresholding methods including the optimal threshold, region non uniformity. The best segmented image should have NU near to zero; and as we see the neighborhood valley method is the best in separate the blood vessels from the background with NU = 0.500064 threshold T = 137.

7. Conclusion

The Segmentation of the blood vessel of the retinal can play an important role in diagnosis the retinal disorders. Automatic thresholding is a well-known method in medical image segmentation. In our work we used five thresholding methods on a huge data of medical images. Then we found the methods showed the blood vessels in the retina, but one of them displays the blood vessels in a clear way. It is neighborhood valley emphasis method. It gave the good segmented image with small value of region non uniformity.

Table 1. Show the values of (T, NU) of the five thresholding methods in Fig. 3.

		Example
Otsu (Gaussian)	T	109
	NU	0.730197
Valley (Gaussian)	T	125
	NU	0.660064
Neighborhood valley (Gaussian)	T	**137, n = 3**
	NU	**0.500064**
Variance and intensity contrast (Gaussian)	T	302 λ = 0.35
	NU	0.890364
Variance discrepancy technique (Gaussian)	T	189, α = 1
	NU	0.950779

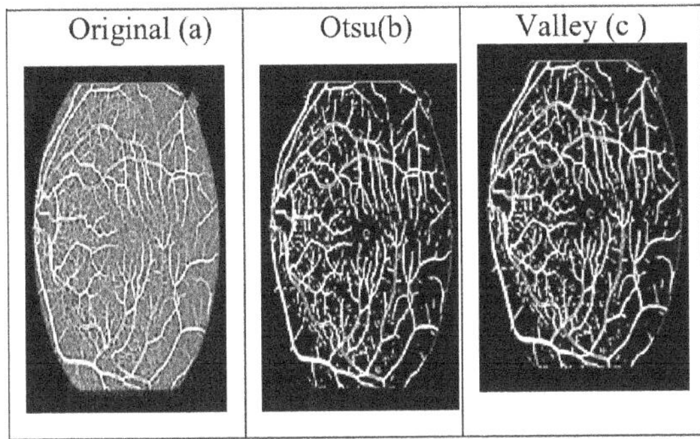

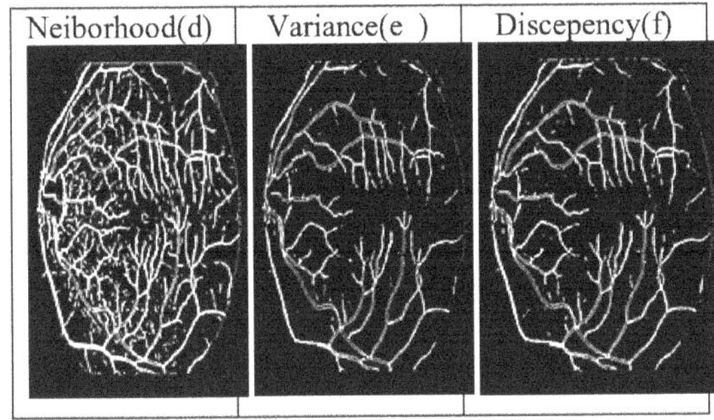

Fig. 3. Original (a), Otsu (b), Valley (c), Neiborhood (d), Variance (e), Discepency (f).

References

[1]. C. Hima, An improved medical image segmentation algorithm using OTSU method, *International Journal of Recent Trends in Engineering*, Vol. 2, Issue 3, November 2009.

[2]. M. Burak Eker, Diabetic Retinopathy Detection with Image Thresholding Technique, April 2019. https://www.researchgate.net/publication/332683947_Diabetic_Retinopathy_Detection_with_Image_Thresholding_Technique

[3]. National Eye Institute, National Institutes of Health, US, Department of Health and Human Services. Diabetic Retinopathy: What You Should Know, https://www.nei.nih.gov/sites/default/files/2019-06/Diabetic-Retinopathy-What-You-Should-Know-508.pdf

[4]. Diabetic Retinopathy's Detection, https://www.kaggle.com/c/diabetic-retinopathy-detection

[5]. K. Kipli, C. Jiris, S. Kudnie Sahari, N. Junaidi, M. Sawawi, K. Hong Ping, T. Zulcaffle, Morphological an Otsu's thresholding base retinal blood vessel segmentation for detection of retinopathy, *International Journal of Engineering & Technology*, Vol. 7, Issue 3, 2018, pp. 15-20.

[6]. K. Jiang, Z. Zhou, H. Wu, X. Geng, Isotropic un decimated wavelet transform fuzzy to extract retinal blood vessel, *Journal of Medical Imaging and Health Informatics*, Vol. 5, 2015, pp. 1524-1527.

[7]. G. Hassan, N. El-Bendary, A. E. Hassanian, A. Fahmy, Snasel, Retina blood vessels segmentation approach based on mathematical morphology, *Procedia Computer Science*, Vol. 65, 2015, pp. 612-622.

[8]. N. Memari, A. Ramli, M. Moghbel, Implemented matched filtering and fuzzy C means clustering with integrated level set method for diabetic retinopathy assessment, *Journal of Medical and Biological Engineering*, 2018.

[9]. N. Ots, A threshold selection method from gray level histograms, *IEEE Transactions on Systems, Man and Cybernetics*, Vol. SMC-9, Issue 1, 1979, pp. 62-66.

[10]. H.-F. Ng, Automatic thresholding for defect detection, *Pattern Recognition Letters*, Vol. 27, 2006, pp. 1644-1649.

[11]. J. Fan, B. Lei, A modified valley-emphasis method for automatic thresholding, *Pattern Recognition Letters*, Vol. 33, 2012, pp.703-708.

[12]. Y. Qiaoa, Q. Hua, G. Qiana, S. Luob, W Nowinskia, Thresholding case on variance an intensity contrast, *Pattern Recognition*, Vol. 40, 2007, pp. 596-608.

[13]. Z. Li, C. Liu, G. Liu, Y. Cheng, X. Yang, C. Zhao, A novel statistical image thresholding method, *International Journal of Electronics and Communications*, Vol. 64, Dec. 2010, pp. 1137-1147.

[14]. S. Stahl, The evolution of the normal distribution, *Mathematics Magazine*, Vol. 79, Issue 2, April 2006, pp. 96-113.

[15]. Y. J. Zhang, A survey on evaluation methods for image segmentation, *Pattern Recognition*, Vol. 29, Issue 8, August 1996, pp. 1335-1346.

(009)

Predicting Heart Disease Stage by Tuning Convergence and Cross Validation

Dibakar Sinha [1] **and Dr. Ashish Sharma** [2]
[1] Department of Computer Science &Engineering, Shri Vaishnav Vidyapeeth Vishwavidyalaya, Indore (MP), India,
[2] Department of Computer Engineering & Applications,
GLA University, NH#2, Delhi Mathura Highway, Post Ajhai, Mathura (UP), India
E-mails: dibakar.sinha_phd18@gla.ac.in, ashishs.sharma@gla.ac.in

Summary: Heart ailments are an important major terminal illness in most parts of the planet. The acute limitation of no medical professionals, experts and shortage of machines and technology which can detect vital symptoms is a big challenge which is the prime reason of mortality and injury for a patient. So there is a requirement of intelligent and efficient model and technology which is able to lead early detection of heart disease stage. Here in the current article, a new experience-based system is proposed in order to predict heart diseases and heart attack stage detection using a modified logistic regression algorithm, and prediction techniques. The proposed algorithm used inverse regularization strength as an independent object that keeps the strength modification of Regularization. Various up-gradation are done in logistic regression to create the proposed model. The suggested method was tested on various public health care data sets. Results on those data sets [12] show that the suggested method extraordinarily improves the accuracy for the system for the prediction of disease. The results display that the mixture of enhanced logistic regression techniques with hyper parameter optimization and noise removal can be useful in disease prediction by using current medical data sets. The experience-based system can be useful health care professionals in the medical practice as an efficient method for analysis.

Keywords: Machine learning, Classification, Cardio vascular, Logistic regression.

1. Introduction

The coronary disease is known as one of the major killers in the whole world, WHO declared that around 31 % of the total world population died in 2015 which is going to be increased very rapidly in 2020. Approximately 20 million people die each year showing it is the strong reason for death in the world. Cardio Vascular Disease (CVD) is an illness that is caused mainly by blood vessels taking the blood, oxygen, etc. to the heart leading to the blockage in the vessels for various reasons. Coronary Heart Disease (CHD) or Coronary Artery Disease (CAD) is part of CVD which mainly caused by the veins which take blood and oxygen to the heart. These types of illnesses are known as lifestyle diseases such as diabetes, high blood pressure which is mainly caused by lifestyle changes in today's fast-paced modern world. Another terminology is atherosclerosis which depicts the accumulation of fatty production on the border wall of arteries. Due to this, the amount of blood gets block throws the arteries, blocking smooth action of heart which ultimately causes angina or heart attack. Angina is usually known as angina pectoris is chest pain in the heart which typically starts with pain in the limbs then jaws and then ultimately in the heart. Some of the names heart attacks are myocardial infarction (MI), cardiac or myocardial infarction, and coronary thrombosis or occlusion. It occurs either when the arteries are torn apart or unable to take blood to the heart due to the narrowness of the arteries. A blood clot formed partially or completely during the repair of blood vessels which rupture reduces the blood flow to the heart muscles causing heart attacks [18]. Some pains which also radiate to the left are also one type of heart attack. Some of the causes for such kind of illness are the use of nicotine, family history, diabetes, high cholesterol, high blood pressure, older age, less physical activity or stress. Congestive heart failure is also known as a heart attack where both the side of the heart wall, valve and arteries are damaged and once it is damaged cannot be repaired due to such reason, the heart arteries get damaged on both part of the side and it is not able to supply the required amount of blood which is required by the heart which makes it a serious health concern for the person [9].

In another way, the chest trouble compared to a heart attack or different heart problem which may be denied by or amalgamated with one or more of the following symptoms:

- Cool perspirations;
- Brevity of inhalation;
- Dizziness or faintness;
- Queasiness or vomiting;
- Uneasiness in the chest;
- A pain which comes back after it goes down again and again;
- The severe pain that spreads starting from hand to most part of the body.

The heart became so weak that the heart was unable to pump the blood to the heart. Another type of heart disease is peripheral artery disease (PAD) which makes the side of arteries narrower of arms, legs, stomach, head, legs and stomach. Some other abnormalities are venous thrombosis which is the clotting of blood in the vein, and aortic aneurysms which allow the artery to widen suddenly which is already weakened enough to do so [2, 3]. So from the above all the statistics we can safely conclude that it is very difficult to diagnose heart disease just from the visual perspective because it has many risk factors and usually the heart diseases or heart attack doesn't come with prominent noticeable symptoms. Some important signs of the patient suffering in heart disease are triglyceride, cholesterol, diabetes, heartbeat, blood pressure and then measurement from ECG, EEG, EMG which are very important and represent an important role in diagnosing and detecting the stages of heart attack and whether in future the patient will suffer a cardiac arrest or not. Some devices like WBAN (Wireless body area network) are used for detecting such vital signs of the patient which is due to the advancement in wireless technology. These technologies used some very tiny chip or devices which the patient can wear most of the time and it will continuously sense the vital signs of the patient regularly and if there is any abnormality it can immediately inform the patient or the doctor or the relatives via the digital communication mode.

In the proposed system the primary data set [12] contains 14 different health attributes of 108 and 90 patients for training and testing purposes respectively and 2 features (patient_id and heart_disease_present) for predicting patient disease.

Brief details of the features used in the data sets are as below:

1. Age;
2. Sex;
3. Chest pain type;
4. Blood Pressure;
5. Cholesterol;
6. Electrocardiogram Data;
7. Heart Rate;
8. Exercise related pain;
9. Exercise after rest;
10. Slope of exercise and work hours;
11. Fluoroscope results of major veins;
12. Thalesemia symptoms;
13. Diagnosis of heart disease Value 0: < 50 % and Value1:> 50 % diameter narrowing.

Originally, various ML algorithms are examined to understand what degree their forecast results estimated or enhanced upon the outcomes achieved in the initial Framingham model, a very significant cardiovascular hazard forecast reports from the purpose of design of clinical training. The reports are discussed in the forthcoming section of this paper. The proposed system is dependent on the cardiovascular situation of the patients, i.e., a time-dependent record of previous days. Although recently scholars have attempted to enhance upon the Framingham model's imminent value, the centre of the existing research is completely procedural, considering the goal of examining the usefulness of ML patterns in well-being. Precisely, the prime purpose was to match in order to inner-city and correctness, numerous supervised Machine Learning algorithms tied to the forecast of medical situations, applying structured data; the trivial intention was to resemble the efficacy, usability, and outcomes attained employing two software instruments, Python (Programming Language) and Anaconda (IDE for ML development).

The major benefactions of this paper are: An enhanced model is inducted in the paper for the need of a patient health attribute and machine learning process to detect and guess the cardiac diseases at a very premature stage. HSPUCD (Heart Stage Prediction Using Clinical Data) is judged by using actual life time-varying attributes or data. The proposed prediction system is very much useful for the medical professional to detect heart diseases. It is particularly influential in the sense that it helps the medical professional to make a correct prediction in terms of detecting the patient heart attack stage. If a medical professional is aware of the chances of the patient is going to suffer a heart attack than it is very easy for him/her to take necessary precautionary measures to avoid or minimize the loss in terms of death or any other physical disability. Its Detail working principle is discussed in the Methodology section of this paper.

The experimental outcome shows the accuracy or correctness of the proposed prediction system comparing to the previously used models by a different researcher has a huge improvement with 82.5 % accuracy [12].

The remaining section of the current article is modelled into various parts: Literature reviews are explained in Section 2. In Section 3 where the previous lessons have been evaluated. The suggested heart disease prediction system is delivered in Section 4. Results and discussions have been explained in Section 5. At last, the conclusion of this paper is discussed in Section 6.

2. Related Work

Extraordinary growth has been done in the way of various machine learning algorithms utilized to the rape tic data sets for exposing various disorders, e.g. disclosure of different kinds of cancer. The chief clinical systems for evaluation of heart illness involve an electrocardiogram (ECG) [26], echo cardiogram [27], cardiac computer-assisted tomography (CT) scan [28], Holter monitoring [29], cardiac magnetic resonance imaging (MRI) [30], blood tests [31], including cardiac categorization [32]. In this segment, heart-related research is appraised, with a centre on CAD, applying data mining and machine learning procedures.

Sellappan Palaniappan et al. [33] suggested Naive Bayes, Neural Network, and also Decision Trees. Notwithstanding proper results, each procedure has its extremely personal character. Shrouded cases and relationships among them are employed to create this structure. It is simple to learn, expand able and automatic. Niti Guru et. al. [35] suggested the estimate of Blood Pressure, Sgar and Heart ailment including the design of neural systems. The history of 13 fields in all was employed in the data set for fitting and measuring of data, the managed systems. Heon Gyu Lee et. al. [36] introduced a different method, to produce the several parametric components including through and nonlinear properties of HRV (Heart Rate Variability) rare classifiers for standard Bayesian Classifiers, CMAR (Classification dependent on Multiple Association Rules), C4.5 (Decision Tree) and SVM (Support Vector Machine) has been employed by them to assess the polluting impact of a section or faction of developing tuples [34]. Shu et al. [37] suggested foretelling heart disease (HD) practicing quantitative computer-assisted classical Chinese medication and representation-based approaches. The implemented classifiers (11 algorithms) were optimized utilizing the probabilistic collaborative representation-based passageway. Following utilizing to pre-processing including normalization and characteristic wrenching, the recommended practice was connected to a heart disorder data set utilizing four principal classifiers: SVM, KNN, PNN, and RBFNN. The outcomes symbolized that the evolutionary-neural practice with logistic regression had the biggest achievement with 90 % efficiency for a data set [12] with 17 classes. Alizadehsani et al. implemented various machine learning algorithms on CAD examination from 2012 to 2017 [38-40]. The most important efficiency achieved among all these investigations was 94.08 %, which was achieved by utilizing the Information Gain-SMO algorithm [41].

It has been shown that cognitive machine learning can be utilized for precise phenol typing of high volume electrocardiograph data sets. The machine learning algorithm is also applied to understand various features driving patient satisfaction. Our collective experience in large-scale, automated mining of EMR data suggests that such approaches are useful for both discovery research and the identification of actionable clinical parameters driving diseases or outcomes. In the course of a larger study, it will be important to evaluate the impact of glucose in different organs maintaining viscosity and oxygen flow to able to counteract Cardiac illness and also to predict it.

3. Proposed Method

3.1. Methodology

Numerous thoughts on cardiovascular disease disclosure have been supervised using AI algorithms and various data sets [20, 21]. The contemporary investigation examines CAD (Coronary Artery Disease) apprehension practicing a different strategy. This division renders more aspects of the insinuated methodology. The explanation of the proposed system employed is bestowed beneath. It is perceived that though the proposed model has been examined depending on Correctness and F1-score metrics, we impersonated the best outcomes according to Correctness. To examine Heart Disease data [12], different AI algorithms were examined. The research focuses on one central area: optimization of the classifier. The foregoing methodology employed in the algorithm is beneficial for fore-telling heart disease by measuring the patient prevailing heart maladies and explaining it minutely to make the prognostication, so the recommended practice can be designated as Heart Stage Prediction Using Clinical Data (HSPUCD).

3.2. Flow Diagram of Proposed Model

A procedure flow diagram of the suggested process is shown below.

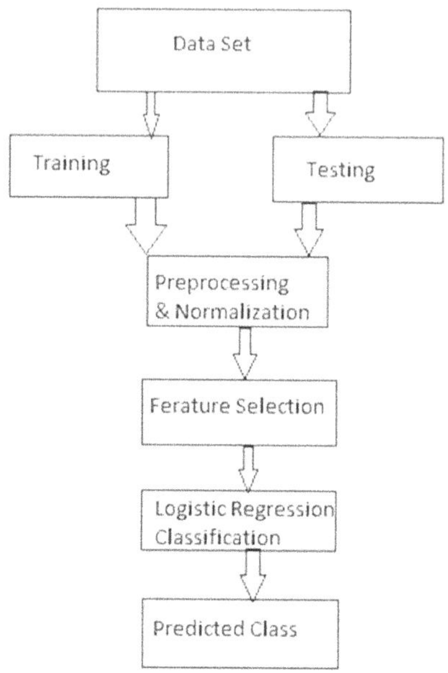

Fig. 1. Flow chart of proposed algorithm.

As explained above, pre-processing is utilized for both definite and digital properties with a normalization procedure. While choosing characteristic unnecessary samples were excluded. Therefore, parameters are linked to the feature modification including cross validation procedures. Hence, both cross-validation and convergence approaches were employed on the feature modification scene. Therefore to assess the achievement, two conventional metrics were adopted: Accuracy (ACC) and F-measure (F1-score) [23, 24].

$$\frac{\sum_{I}^{N} \frac{TP+TN}{TP+FP+TN+FN}}{N}, \tag{1}$$

$$F1\ Score = \frac{\sum_{I}^{C} \frac{\sum_{I}^{N} \frac{2TP+}{2TP+FP+FN}}{N}}{C}, \tag{2}$$

where N is the set no used in the cross-validation (i.e. scaled 100-fold cross-validation), TP is the True Positives units, TN is the True Negatives units, FP is the False Positives units, FN is the False Negatives units, C expresses the abundance of sources.

The recommended model has been strengthened by taking patient health histories obtained utilizing WBAM and machine learning technology to provide health practice to the people in common or disease tramped, who are under-going pain formed from the cardiac complications. In the aforementioned part, HSPUCD is discussed in detail.

In HSPUCD, the health test studies of cardiac sufferers are split into several standards, which are scrutinized and treated using the earlier stated methodology as document review or record pre-processing. Then those pre-processed report extricated from the data set [12] has been established within the earlier specified suggested prototype for extricating the analytical properties or specialties. This output info is utilized for decision-making arrangements for the foretelling heart attack scaffold of a cardiac patient.

In the proposed model the hyper parameter of logistic regression is modified to make more efficient for prediction of heart disease, for better understanding below explanation is described.

3.3. Over Fitting

In the case of most of the previous models, they are usually trained on smaller data known as training data. The aim of those models is to calculate the result of each training example from the training data.

Sometimes those models acquires signal as well as turbulence in the training data and notable to work on the data which it was not trained onto solve this, a penalty is applied to the training data equation. All entities are penalized excluding intercept so that pattern convinces the data and will not over fit.

$$J(\theta) = \frac{1}{2m}\left[\sum_{i}^{m}\left(h_{\theta}(x^{i}) - y^{(i)}\right)^{2} + \lambda\sum_{j=1}^{n}\theta_{j}^{2}\right] \quad (3)$$

As the complexity of training data is grows, a penalty will be applied for more important object. It will reduce the attention provided to more eminent object, and pattern will be produced for a less complex equalization. This penalty terminology can be explained as Regularization which is basically of two types L2 and L1.

L2 regression sum squared magnitude as a penalty term coefficient derived to the cost function as per below figure.

$$\sum_{i=1}^{n}\left(y_{i} - \sum_{j=1}^{p}x_{ij}\beta_{j}\right)^{2} + \lambda\sum_{j=1}^{p}\beta_{j}^{2} \quad (4)$$

Lasso Regression sums absolute value of magnitude as a penalty term coefficient derived to the cost function.

$$\sum_{i=1}^{n}\left(Y_{i} - \sum_{j=1}^{p}X_{ij}\beta_{j}\right)^{2} + \lambda\sum_{j=1}^{p}|\beta_{j}| \quad (5)$$

Eq. (5) is a L1Regression model, n is the Number of Samples, p is the Number of Independent Variables or Features, X is a Feature, Y is the Actual Target or Dependent Variable, f(x) is the Estimated Target, β is a Coefficient or Weight Corresponding to each Feature or Independent Var.

Also in the previous models features and turbulence are determined as a part of training data to the degree that it influences wrongly to the achievement of the model on fresh data. That indicates the turbulence or irregular variations in the training data is selected up and studied as theories by those models.

The difficulty is that these theories unfit for fresh data and influence negatively the capability of model's to generalize. So a penalty is induced for increasing the impact of the values of the parameter. So parameters are chosen in such a way which gives the data that suits best for the model. This way the error is reduced which is generated during the model prediction for the dependent variable.

The problem comes when there are a lot of parameters/features but not too much data available for training purpose. So naturally the model will often tailor the parameter values to fits the data almost perfectly. However because those perfect fit data don't reappear in future, so the model predicts poorly.

For the suggested model L2 remains practiced because by changing the state of Lambda under fitting or over fitting intricacy is resolved. L1 can be practiced if there are huge no of characteristics in the data set by flinching few significant features' coefficients to nothing therefore, eliminating some feature. To accomplish Regularization, the proposed algorithm will transform the Cost function by totalling a penalty to RSS (sum of squared residuals).

$$SS_{(residuals)} = \sum_{i=1}^{n}\left(y_{i} - \widehat{y_{i}}\right)^{2} \quad (6)$$

Eq. (6) is a sum of squared residuals, y_i is the ith value of the variable to be predicted, $\widehat{y_i}$ is the predicted value of y_i.

By combining a penalty to the cost Function, the contents of the parameters would decline and therefore the over fitted model slowly begins to attend out depending on the extent of the penalty combined.

The'L2 Regularization', sum up penalty equal to the square to the coefficients magnitude. Thus, it optimizes:

$$Objective = RSS + \alpha \star (sum\ of\ square\ coefficients) \quad (7)$$

Eq. (7) is a sum of squared residuals.

Here, α (alpha) is the tuning parameter which matches the quantity of importance given to reducing RSS vs reducing the whole of the square of coefficients.

3.4. C (Inverse of Regularization Strength)

A most useful parameter is chosen while preparing a model for the prediction purpose. Which means depreciating the failure within what the model foretells for the subordinate variable provided the data resembled what the subordinate variable is? The dilemma occurs if a data set has several parameters (a lot of autonomous variables) but no significant data. In this proposed solution, the pattern will usually tailor the parameter states to characteristics in the data which suggests it implements the data virtually flawlessly. Nevertheless, because these peculiarities don't resemble in later training data of the proposed model, the chance that the proposed model will prophesy badly. To resolve this, also for overcoming the failure, in the proposed model a function is reduced that penalizes high contents to the parameters.

Most regularly the function is $\lambda*\Theta j2$ where θj = sum of squared values.

The more substantial l is the less possible it is that the parameters will be raised in quantity simply to settle for tiny disorders in the data. Most of the cases, nevertheless, somewhat than designating l, researchers designate C = 1.

As discussed previously, regularization is used as a penalty for reducing complexity and also for maximizing the regularization strength to penalize large weight coefficients, which is a goal of the proposed model. The escorts are given to reduce the loss function, i.e. to look out the for the feature weights which relate to the global cost minimum, this purpose lambda as a hyper parameter is used, to get hold of the regularization strength. That's why this article offers inverse regularization strength which is a key variable that holds intensity adjustment of Regularization by being inversely placed to the Lambda regulator ranging from 0.0001,001, 0.01, 0.1, 1, 10, 100, 1000, 10000.

4. Result

4.1. Issues in Earlier Model

Previous researcher has not much used logistic algorithm because:
1. To avoid over fitting;
2. Improper presentation of data where there is a requirement of presidential implication of the important independent variable;
3. Outcome requirement is non categorical;
4. Problem is non-linear.

The first and second issue is solved by using proper pre-processing and regularization function by applying a penalty to cost function which is discussed in Section 3.

In the proposed model categorical output is required so that the model can identify and represent different stages of heart disease and also most of the time the cardiac data is pre-processed and cleaned to make it linear separable.

4.2. Advantages of the Proposed Algorithm

Among most of the other algorithm (Gradient Boosting Classier, Decision Tree, Logistic Regression, Naive Bayes, Random Forest, Nearest Neighbours, Linear SVM, Neural Net etc.) Proposed algorithm works very well for the data set [12] mainly because:
1. The data set, it can produce a discrete binary result within 0 and 1 for better prediction of heart disease present or not.
2. It covers the connection among the subordinate variable and the one or more autonomous variables, by evaluating possibilities using its carrying own function
3. The proposed algorithm has data set which doesn't require much of the computational resources, so it perfectly fits here [15, 16].

The advantages of these algorithms can be developed using optimization methods. So, an information normalization procedure [17-19] and pre-processing approach were also carried out. From the above crucial points, it can be easily understood that the proposed model works perfectly fine for the data set and considering the complex nature of it and the environment where the prediction is done.

4.3. Comparison with Other Algorithm

Initially eight machine learning algorithms were tested against the data set [12] for finding out their performance. The result has been demonstrated using a small table below.

Table 1. Performance Chart of ML algorithm for the data set [12].

S. No	Classifier	Training Score	Testing Score	Training Time
1.	Gradient Boosting Classier	1	0.814815	0.576464
2.	Decision Tree	1	0814815	0.003336
3.	HSPUCD	0.880952	0.796296	0.017176
4.	Naïve Bayes	0.849206	0.796296	0.00537
5.	Random Forest	1	0.777778	1.120774
6.	Nearest Neighbors	0.722222	0.62963	0.007363
7.	Linear SVM	1	0.462963	0.007136
8.	Neural Net	0.587302	0.444444	0.149942

The experiment has been applied to the data set [12]. This data set contains 14 features and 108 records for training and 1 target features and 108 records for target data set and 14 features and 90 records for testing dataset. The training and test data set contains major feature like Age, Sex, Chest pain type, Blood Pressure, Cholesterol, Electrocardiographic Data, Heart Rate, Exercise-related pain, Exercise after rest, Slope of exercise and work hours, Flurosopy results of major veins, Thalassemia symptoms, Diagnosis of heart disease (target label) and target data set have only two features patient id and heart disease present identifier. This data set is provided by the data-driven website for actually winning a competition for prediction heart disease which later on used by the various researchers because of its errorless and noise fewer data and very minimum pre-processing is required.

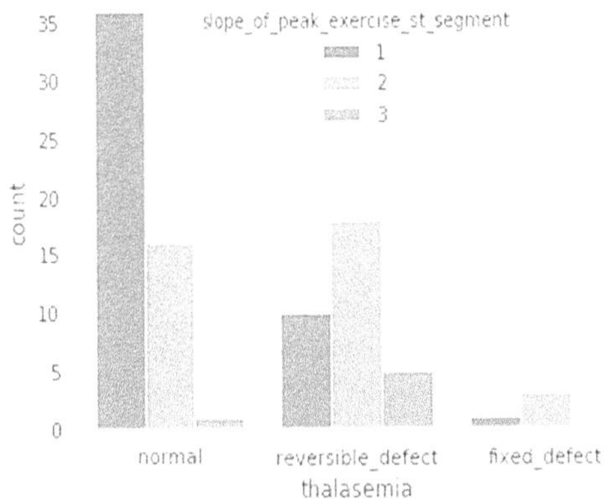

Fig. 2. Count Plot graph for blood pressure with increasing level of exercise.

It can be noted that the proposed algorithm training time is very less and but the training score is very high. On the contrary, other classification techniques can increase time but accuracy will be much more improved in the proposed algorithm.

Nevertheless, Hybridization approach is required as the different algorithm has a different process to get the result of a particular problem and this approach take the strength of the entire algorithm and use it for finding the proper accuracy of a model. In the second phase of our model some analysis is executed which displays that though time performance will impact by using multiple classification techniques accuracy will be significantly improved. The model which we proposed can be used by the doctor and all types of medical professionals to detect heart disease diagnose them properly and possible cure them before and accidental death happens. A learner in all types of medical professionals can use this model to improve their detection skills and save patients' lives.

The above graph (Fig. 2) shows the variation of propensity of thalasemia attack towards heart disease with the variation of the exercise. Thalassemia attack is at mild stage (normal) when a person is physically active, on the contrary, it changes from reversible(more prone to heart attack) to red (severe cardiac arrest) when the person has reduced his/her physical exercise which ultimately causes CVD (cardiovascular disease).

5. Conclusion & Future Work

The final results show that the proposed model obtains important results in the prediction of mortality and on the onset of cardiovascular diseases in cardiac patients. The different score developed and validated in the general population, and once validated in a wider context, will allow predicting the individual risk of mortality and/or CV (cardio vascular) events starting from a denied, minimal set of variables. Interestingly, the performance of our model was similar in a real setting (i.e. in models including only patients without missing data) and in databases with missing data recovered, thus demonstrating its robustness. Furthermore, our model was tested in a diverse data set [12], to compare the performance of the model in a different setting. Further analyses in different settings will allow us to implement to the general populations in which our model could be applied.

The main strength of the study derives from the quality of datasets used to test the prediction models. The driven data set comes from a regional, well-consolidated registry, in which data quality check was extensively performed during the entire duration of the study.

One limitation of the study is the observational design of the driven data dataset, which cannot exclude the presence of bias. Also, a large data set such as the driven data one showed a certain number of missing values, which could introduce a bias in our results. However, as previously reported, even when the model was tested in the data set after recovering missing data the performance remained virtually unchanged.

Some of the limitations can be the involvement of only heart disease. Additionally, very less number of parameters is analyzed to analyze the heart disease. Nevertheless, the coming work of this article is to produce a composite classification design based on an added number of characteristics to distinguish heart disease more accurately.

References

[1]. N. Reddy, Satish Chandra, et al., Classification and feature selection approaches by machine learning techniques: Heart disease prediction, *International Journal of Innovative Computing*, Vol. 9, Issue 1, 2019.

[2]. M. Thiyagaraj, G. Suseendran, Survey on heart disease prediction system based on data mining techniques, *Indian Journal of Innovations and Developments*, Vol. 6, Issue 1, 2017, pp. 1-9.

[3]. S. Narayan, E. Sathiyamoorthy, A novel recommender system based on FFT with machine learning for predicting and identifying heart diseases, *Neural*

Computing and Applications, Vol. 31, Issue 1, 2019, pp. 93-102.

[4]. C.-Y. Joanne Peng, K. L. Lee, G. M. Ingersoll, An introduction to logistic regression analysis and reporting, *The Journal of Educational Research*, Vol. 96, Issue 1, 2002, pp. 3-14.

[5]. D. Maclaurin, D. Duvenaud, R. Adams, Gradient-based hyperparameter optimization through reversible learning, in *Proceedings of the International Conference on Machine Learning (ICML'15)*, 2015.

[6]. W. Sun, Z. Cai, Y. Li, F. Liu, S. Fang, G. Wang, Data processing and text mining technologies on electronic medical records: A review, *Journal of Healthcare Engineering*, 2018, 4302425.

[7]. Y. Lin, S. Zhu, B. Qi, P. Zhang, M. Huang, Z. Rong, The recognition of dissolved gas abnormality based on high di-mensional support vector machine, in *Proceedings of the IEEE Conference on Electrical Insulation and Dielectric Phenomenon (CEIDP'17)*, 2017, pp. 724-727.

[8]. P. Pawiak, An estimation of the state of consumption of a positive displacement pump based on dynamic pressure or vibrations using neural networks, *Neurocomputing*, Vol. 144, 2014, pp. 471-483.

[9]. O. Yildirim, R. San Tan, U. R. Acharya, An efficient compression of ECG signals using deep convolutional autoencoders, *Cognitive Systems Research*, Vol. 52, 2018, pp. 198-211.

[10]. M. Abdar, et al., A new machine learning technique for an accurate diagnosis of coronary artery disease, *Computer Methods and Programs in Biomedicine*, 2019, 104992.

[11]. F. Pedregosa, et al., Scikit-learn: Machine learning in Python, *Journal of Machine Learning Research*, 2011, pp. 2825-2830.

[12]. A. P. Davie, C. M. Francis, M. P. Love, L. Caruana, I. R. Starkey, T. R. D. Shaw, J. J. V. McMurray, Value of the electrocardiogram in identifying heart failure due to left ventricular systolic dysfunction, *BMJ: British Medical Journal*, Vol. 312, Issue 7025, 1996, 222.

[13]. D. Y. Leung, P. M. Davidson, G. B. Cranney, W. F. Walsh, Thromboembolic risks of left atrial thrombus detected by transesophageal echocardiogram, *The American Journal of Cardiology*, Vol. 79, Issue 5, 1997, pp. 626-629.

[14]. S. Rajpal, L. Alshawabkeh, A. R. Opotowsky, Current role of blood and urine biomarkers in the clinical care of adults with congenital heart disease, *Current Cardiology Reports*, Vol. 19, Issue 6, 2017, 50.

[15]. T. Shu, B. Zhang, Y. Y. Tang, Effective heart disease detection based on quantitative computerized traditional Chinese medicine using representation based classifiers, *Evidence-based Complementary and Alternative Medicine*, 2017.

[16]. R. Alizadehsani, J. Habibi, Z. A. Sani, H. Mashayekhi, R. Boghrati, A. Ghandeharioun, B. Bahadorian, Diagnosis of coronary artery disease using data mining based on lab data and echo features, *Journal of Medical and Bioengineering*, Vol. 1, Issue 1, 2012, pp. 26-29.

[17]. R. Alizadehsani, M. J. Hosseini, R. Boghrati, A. Ghandeharioun, F. Khozeimeh, Z. A. Sani, Exerting cost-sensitive and feature creation algorithms for coronary artery disease diagnosis, *International Journal of Knowledge Discovery in Bioinformatics (IJKDB)*, Vol. 3, Issue 1, 2012, pp. 59-79.

[18]. R. Alizadehsani, M. J. Hosseini, Z. A. Sani, A. Ghandeharioun, R. Boghrati, Diagnosis of coronary artery disease using cost-sensitive algorithms, in *Proceedings of the IEEE 12th International Conference on Data Mining Workshops (ICDMW'12)*, 2012, pp. 9-16.

[19]. R. Alizadehsani, J. Habibi, M. J. Hosseini, R. Boghrati, A. Ghandeharioun, B. Bahadorian, Z. A. Sani, Diagnosis of coronary artery disease using data mining techniques based on symptoms and ECG features, *European Journal of Scientific Research*, Vol. 82, Issue 4, 2012, pp. 542-553.

[20]. R. Alizadehsani, J. Habibi, Z. A. Sani, H. Mashayekhi, R. Boghrati, A. Ghandeharioun, F. Alizadeh-Sani, Diagnosing coronary artery disease via data mining algorithms by considering laboratory and echocardiography features, *Research in Cardiovascular Medicine*, Vol. 2, Issue 3, 2013, 133.

[21]. R. Alizadehsani, J. Habibi, M. J. Hosseini, H. Mashayekhi, R. Boghrati, A. Ghandeharioun, Z. A. Sani, A data mining approach for diagnosis of coronary artery disease, *Computer Methods and Programs in Biomedicine*, Vol. 111, Issue 1, 2013, pp. 52-61.

[22]. R. Alizadehsani, M. H. Zangooei, M. J. Hosseini, J. Habibi, A. Khosravi, M. Roshanzamir, S. Nahavandi, Coronary artery disease detection using computational intelligence methods, *Knowledge-based Systems*, Vol. 109, 2016, pp. 187-197.

[23]. Z. Arabasadi, R. Alizadehsani, M. Roshanzamir, H. Moosaei, A. A. Yarifard, Computer aided decision making for heart disease detection using hybrid neural network-genetic algorithm, *Computer Methods and Programs in Biomedicine*, Vol. 141, 2017, pp. 19-26.

[24]. R. D'Agostino, R. S. Vasan, M. J. Pencina, et al., General cardiovascular risk prole for use in primary care the framingham heart study, *Circulation*, Vol. 117, 2008, pp. 743-753.

[25]. C. Brotons Cuixart, et al., Grupo de Prevencion Cardiovascular del PAPPS. Recommendations preventives cardiovasculares, Actualizacion PAPPS *Aten Primaria*, Vol. 50, Suppl. 1, 2018, pp. 4-28.

[26]. J.-J. Beunza, et al., Comparison of machine learning algorithms for clinical event prediction (risk of coronary heart disease), *Journal of Biomedical Informatics*, 2019, 103257.

[27]. M. M. McDermott, Functional impairment in peripheral artery disease and how to improve it in 2013, *Current Cardiology Reports*, Vol. 15, Issue 4, 2013, 347.

[28]. H.-B. Park, et al., Clinical feasibility of 3D automated coronary atherosclerotic plaque quantification algorithm on coronary computed tomography angiography: comparison with intravascular ultrasound, *European Radiology*, Vol. 25, Issue 10, pp. 3073-3083.

[29]. V. Salvatori, et al., Holter monitoring to detect silent atrial fibrillation in high-risk subjects: the Perugia General Practitioner Study, *Internal and Emergency Medicine*, Vol. 10, Issue 5, 2015, pp. 595-601.

[30]. A. Splendiani, et al., Magnetic resonance imaging (MRI) of the lumbar spine with dedicated G-scan machine in the upright position: a retrospective study and our experience in 10 years with 4305 patients, *La Radiologia Medica*, Vol. 121, Issue 1, 2016, pp. 38-44.

[31]. R. Sun, et al., Congenital heart disease: causes, diagnosis, symptoms, and treatments, *Cell Biochemistry and Biophysics*, Vol. 72, Issue 3, 2015, pp. 857-860.

[32]. C. Broberg, et al., Accuracy of administrative data for detection and categorization of adult congenital heart disease patients from an electronic medical record, *Pediatric Cardiology*, Vol. 36, Issue 4, 2015, pp. 719-725.

[33]. S. Palaniappan, R. Awang, Intelligent heart disease prediction system using data mining techniques, in *Proceedings of the IEEE/ACS International Conference on Computer Systems and Applications*, 2008, pp. 108-115.

[34]. K. Koperski, J. Han, Discovery of spatial association rules in geographic information databases, in *Proceedings of the International Symposium on Spatial Databases (SSD'95)*, 1995, pp. 47-66.

[35]. N. Guru, A. Dahiya, N. Rajpal, Decision support system for heart disease diagnosis using neural network, *Delhi Business Review*, Vol. 8, Issue 1, 2007, pp. 99-101.

[36]. S. H. Koo, K. Y. Lee, H. G. Lee, Effect of cross-linking on the physicochemical and physiological properties of corn starch, *Food Hydrocolloids*, Vol. 24, Issues 6-7, 2010, pp. 619-625.

[37]. A. J. Collins, et al., Chronic kidney disease and cardiovascular disease in the Medicare population: Management of comorbidities in kidney disease in the 21st century: Anemia and bone disease, *Kidney International*, Vol. 64, 2003, pp. S24-S31.

[38]. R. Alizadehsani, et al., A data mining approach for diagnosis of coronary artery disease, Computer Methods and Programs in Biomedicine, Vol. 111, Issue 1, 2013, pp. 52-61.

[39]. DrivenData: https://www.drivendata.org/competitions/54/machine-learning-with-a-heart/data/

[40]. M. Abdar, et al., A new machine learning technique for an accurate diagnosis of coronary artery disease, *Computer Methods and Programs in Biomedicine*, Vol. 179, 2019. 104992.

[41]. J. López, Á. Barbero, J. R. Dorronsoro, On the equivalence of the SMO and MDM algorithms for SVM training, in *Proceedings of the Joint European Conference on Machine Learning and Knowledge Discovery in Databases (ECML PKDD'08)*, 2008, pp. 288-300.

(010)

Acoustic Room Impulse Response Simulation with GPUs

David Diaz-Guerra, Antonio Miguel and Jose R. Beltran
Department of Electronic Engineering and Communications, University of Zaragoza, Zaragoza, Spain
E-mail: ddga@unizar.es

Summary: Room acoustics simulations have been widely employed to test acoustic and speech signal processing algorithms and, more recently, they have also been used as a data augmentation technique for training machine learning systems which deal with acoustic signals. One of the most common Room Impulse Response (RIR) simulation algorithms is the Image Source Method (ISM), which allows us to get the Impulse Response between two points of a room as the sum of the reflections in its walls; however, the computational complexity of the ISM grows cubically with the length of the reverberation. We present a parallel implementation of the ISM that uses Graphic Processing Units (GPUs) to reduce the simulation time in more than a factor 100 compared with state of the art CPU libraries. We have also included our implementation in a Free and Open Source Python library.

Keywords: Room impulse response (RIR), Image source method (ISM), Room acoustics, Graphic processing units (GPUs).

1. Introduction

Datasets of speech (and other acoustic signals) recorded in different and realistic acoustic conditions are hard to obtain, especially if we want to control the actual acoustic properties of the environment, such as the reverberation time, or we need to accurately label the position of the microphones and the sound sources. To deal with this problem, acoustic and speech algorithms have been traditionally tested using simulated environments [1]. Similarly, in order to train machine learning systems that use acoustic signals as inputs, simulated Room Impulse Responses (RIRs) are typically employed as data augmentation technique to make them more robust against reverberation effects [2]. This is a topic of increasing popularity due to the need for far-field speech recognition systems in home virtual assistants such as the smart speakers, but these applications require huge datasets which would need an unfeasible amount of time to be simulated. In addition, new Virtual or Augmented Reality applications also could benefit from fast RIR simulations, allowing us to simulate room acoustics in real time.

In this paper, we present a new implementation of the well-known Image Source Method (ISM) that parallelizes most of the computations of the original algorithm to be able to exploit the computing power of Graphics Processing Unites (GPUs). Using this implementation, we are able to simulate more than one thousand times more RIRs per second than other state of the art implementations. The reminder of this document is structured as follows: Section 2 reviews the original ISM and some of the improvements that have been proposed in the past years and that we have included in our implementation, we explain our GPU implementation in Section 3, Sections 4 and 5 present the Free and Open Source Python library that we made to encapsulate this implementation and the results we obtained with it, and finally, Section 6 concludes the paper.

2. The Image Source Method (ISM)

The image source method [3] is one of the most common techniques employed for RIR simulation since it models the delay and the amplitude of each wall reflection with high accuracy and allows us to modify several parameters such as the position of the sound source and the receiver, the size of the room, or the absorption coefficients of the walls (and therefore the reverberation time). It models each wall reflection as an equivalent (image) source and computes the RIR as the sum of all of them:

$$h(t) = \sum_{i=1}^{N_x} \sum_{j=1}^{N_y} \sum_{k=1}^{N_z} A_{ijk} \delta\left(t - \tau_{ijk}\right), \quad (1)$$

where $h(t)$ is the simulated RIR, N_x, N_y, and N_z are the number of images to compute in each dimmension and A_{ijk} and τ_{ijk} are the amplitude and the delay with which each one of these sources arrives to the receiver. In order to compute A_{ijk} and τ_{ijk}, we model each image source as specular reflections of the original sound source in each wall; see Fig. 1 for an example simplified to 2D.

For a desired RIR length, we need to include all the image sources whose contribution arrives in the desired reverberation time. The number of sources to compute for each dimension is proportional to the length of the RIR and, consequently, for the simulation of a 3D room, the whole number of image sources grows cubically. Several techniques have been proposed to reduce the complexity of the ISM and to improve its accuracy, but it is still too slow for some applications, such as modeling a moving sound source recorded with a microphone array.

We have included in our implementation some of these proposals. For example, we use negative reflection coefficients [4] in order to avoid low frequency artefacts and the need for a high-pass filter. Since we are simulating a sampled RIR and the values of τ_{ijk} will not be multiples of the sampling period, we use, as proposed in [5], windowed sinc functions instead of deltas in (1) to model the fractional delays of each image source:

$$\delta'(t) = \\ = \begin{cases} \frac{1}{2}\left(1+\cos\left(\frac{2\pi t}{T_\omega}\right)\right)\operatorname{sinc}(\pi f_s t) & if \frac{-T_\omega}{2} < t < \frac{-T_\omega}{2}, \\ 0 & otherwise \end{cases} \quad (2)$$

where T_ω is the window length (typically about 4 ms), f_s is the sampling frequency and the sinc function is defined as $\operatorname{sinc}(x) = \sin(x)/x$. Using this technique instead of rounding τ_{ijk} to the nearest sample highly increases the accuracy of the simulations, but also has a huge impact on the computational cost of the algorithm due to the high number of nonlinear operations that we need to compute.

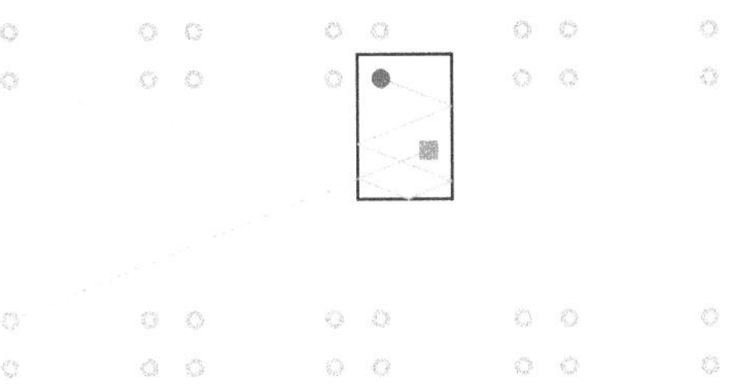

Fig. 1. Example of image sources for a two dimensional room. The red square and the blue dot represents the receiver and the source and the blue circumferences represents the image sources. The solid green line represents one of the multiple reflection paths and the dashed green line the direct path of the equivalent image source.

In addition, in order to reduce the number of images that need to be computed, we included the option of modeling the last part of the RIR as a noise tail with the proper energy envelope as proposed in [6]. However, for the sake of computational efficiency, we replaced the power envelope model employed in [6] by an exponential envelope following the popular Sabine formula [7].

3. Parallel GPU Implementation

In order to reduce the simulation times, we propose a parallel CUDA implementation which runs in Graphics Processing Units (GPUs). It allows us to parallelize the computation of the contribution of each image source and also the simulation of several RIRs.

To the best of our knowledge, only [8] propose to implement the ISM in GPUs. Unfortunately, they did not provide the code of their implementation and they used an overlap-add strategy with atomic operations to combine the contributions of each image source, which strongly reduces the level of parallelism. Our implementation has a higher degree of parallelism, which allows us to achieve higher speed-ups with cheaper GPUs and, more importantly, we publish it under an open-source license.

Table 1 shows the kernels in which our implementation is divided: `calcAmpTau_kernel` computes the amplitude and the delay with which the contribution of each image source arrives at the receiver, `generateRIR_kernel` computes the sinc of each image source contribution and `reduceRIR_kernel` perform the sum of every contribution to get the RIR. Finally, `envPred_kernel` predicts the power envelope that the late reverberation of the RIR is going to follow, `generate_seed_pseudo` and `gen_sequenced` are cuRAND functions that we use to generate a random noise and then `diffRev_kernel` transform this uniform distributed noise to a logistic distributed one [6] and apply the predicted power envelope.

Table 1. CUDA kernels.

Kernel name	Time (%)
calcAmpTau_kernel	0.68
generateRIR_kernel	90.34
reduceRIR_kernel	1.07
envPred_kernel	0.03
generate_seed_pseudo	7.78
gen_sequenced	0.01
diffRev_kernel	0.01

Most parts of the ISM algorithm are quite straightforward to parallelize since the computations for each image source are independent of each other. The most complex part is the sum of the sinc functions generated by each source to the final RIRs since a direct parallelization would lead to several threads writing in the same memory position. To avoid this issue, we use `reduceRIR_kernel` recursively to pairwise sum the contribution of each group of images until we get the final RIRs.

Parallelizing the computation of several RIRs is also straightforward, but we restricted it to work only with RIRs from the same room. We did this due to the fact that we need to use the same number of image sources for all the RIRs in the batch, and using the worst case scenario (higher reverberation and smaller room) would be inefficient.

As an example, Table 1 shows the time employed in each kernel to compute a standard case of 6 RIRs with T_{60} = 1 s with an NVidia GTX 980Ti. We can see how the main bottleneck is at `generateRIR_kernel`, which contains the sinc calculations. This also happens in the CPU implementations, but by using GPUs we can perform many sinc computations in parallel.

Refer to [9] for more information about the parallel implementation of each kernel.

4. Python Library

We have encapsulated the CUDA implementation in a Free and Open Source Python library, so it can be used to simulate RIRs without needing any knowledge of CUDA programming. It is available in our GitHub page (https://github.com/DavidDiazGuerra/gpuRIR) and can be installed using the Python package manager pip.

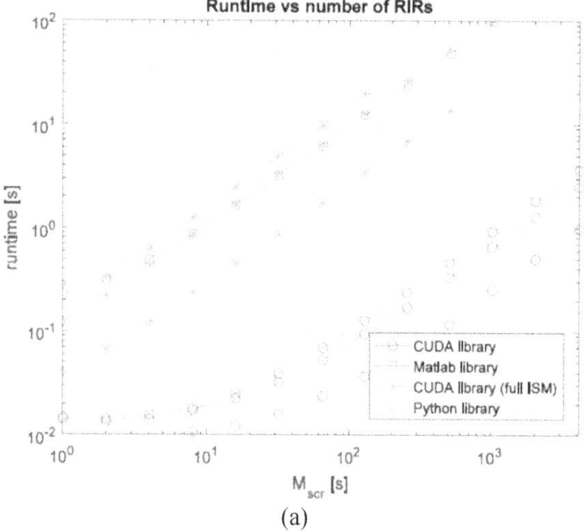

(a)

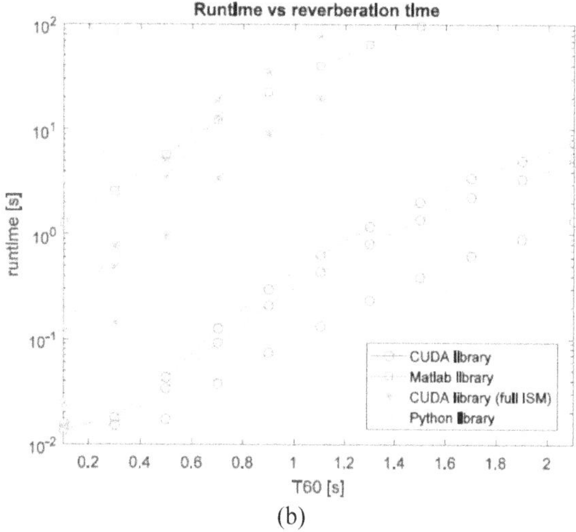

(b)

Fig. 2. Runtime of each library for computing (a) different numbers of RIRs in a room with size 3×4×2.5 m and T_{60} = 0.7 s and (b) 128 RIRs with different reverberation times. The solid lines were obtained using an NVidia GTX 980Ti GPU, the dashed with an NVidia Tesla P100 and the dotted with an NVidia Tesla V100.

The library provides a function to simulate RIRs tacking as input parameters the size of the room, the absorption coefficients of the walls, the positions of the source and the receivers, the number of images to simulate in each dimension, and the duration of the RIR. This function is able to simulate in parallel several RIRs for different source and receiver positions in the same room.

We also included a function to perform the convolution of an audio signal with the RIRs in GPU. If several source positions are provided, the function interprets it as the trajectory points of a moving sound source and uses the overlap-add method to simulate the movement.

In addition to the GPU simulation function, we included some useful functions to compute the absorption coefficients needed to match the desired reverberation time for a given room dimensions or to get the number of images that need to be simulated to avoid losing accuracy in the simulation. Due to the low computational cost of these functions, we implemented them in plain python without any use of the GPU.

5. Results

We conducted several simulations to compare the performance of our library with other state of the art CPU libraries that are commonly used by the signal processing and the machine learning communities. Specifically, we used the Matlab library presented in [6] and the Python library presented in [10]. It is worth saying that the Python library does not implement the diffuse model of the late reverberation so, for a fair comparison with it, we must compute the full RIR using the ISM. For a fairer comparison, we also replaced the power envelope model of the original Matlab library by an exponential power envelope like the one used in our library.

The simulations with the sequential libraries and the ones with the NVidia GTX 980Ti (solid line in Fig. 1) were performed in a computer with an Intel Core i7-6700 CPU and 16 GB of RAM, while the simulations with the NVidia Tesla P100 (dashed line) and the Tesla V100 (dotted lines) were performed in a n1-highmem-4 instance in the Google Cloud Platform with 4 virtual CPUs cores and 26 GB of RAM.

As we can see in Fig. 2, our implementation is about two orders of magnitude faster than CPU libraries even with a 5 years old gaming GPU like the NVidia GTX 980 Ti and, using more modern GPUs such as the Tesla V100, we can increase even more the number of RIRs simulated per second. Simulating large reverberation times using only the ISM without any kind of diffuse reverberation model is not feasible in CPU, but with our library, we get results in GPU similar to the ones obtained by using diffuse models in CPU.

Since we are not including any new modification in the ISM that has not been previously studied in the literature, we did not perform any simulation campaign to analyze the acoustical accuracy of our implementation, but we checked it against the other CPU libraries to confirm that it had not any bug.

5. Conclusions

We have presented a new GPU implementation of the ISM that can simulate more than 100 times more

RIRs per second than other state of the art CPU libraries and we have included this implementation in a Free and Open Source Python library so anyone can use it without the need of any knowledge about GPU programming. This library might be extremely useful for applications that need a huge number of acoustic simulations, such as training far-field speech recognition systems, or for real-time acoustic simulations in Virtual or Augmented Reality applications.

Acknowledgements

This work was supported in part by the Regional Government of Aragon (Spain) with a grant for postgraduate research contracts (2017-2021) co-funded by the Operative Program FSE Aragon 2014-2020.

This material is based upon work supported by Google Cloud.

References

[1]. X. Dang, Q. Cheng, H. Zhu, Indoor multiple sound source localization via multi-dimensional assignment data association, *IEEE/ACM Transactions on Audio, Speech, and Language Processing*, Vol. 27, Issue 12, 2019, pp. 1944-1956.

[2]. C. Kim, A. Misra, K. Chin, T. Hughes, A. Narayanan, T. Sainath, M. Bacchiani, Generation of large-scale simulated utterances in virtual rooms to train deep-neural networks for far-field speech recognition in Google Home, in *Proceedings of the Annual Conference of the International Speech Communication Association (Interspeech'17)*, Stockholm, Sweden, 20-24 August 2017, pp. 379-383.

[3]. J. B. Allen, D. A. Berkley, Image method for efficiently simulating small-room acoustics, *The Journal of the Acoustical Society of America*, Vol. 65, Issue 4, 1979, pp. 943–950.

[4]. J. Antonio, L. Godinho, A. Tadeu, Reverberation times obtained using a numerical model versus those given by simplified formulas and measurements, *Acta Acustica United with Acustica*, Vol. 88, 2002, pp. 252–261.

[5]. P. M. Peterson, Simulating the response of multiple microphones to a single acoustic source in a reverberant room, *The Journal of the Acoustical Society of America*, Vol. 80, Issue 5, 1986, pp. 1527-1529.

[6]. E. A. Lehmann, A. M. Johansson, Diffuse reverberation model for efficient image-source simulation of room impulse responses, *IEEE Transactions on Audio, Speech, and Language Processing*, Vol. 18, Issue 6, 2010, pp. 1429-1439.

[7]. W. C. Sabine, Collected Papers on Acoustics, *Harvard University Press*, 1922.

[8]. Z.-H. Fu, J.-W. Li, GPU-based image method for room impulse response calculation, *Multimedia Tools and Applications*, Vol. 75, Issue 9, 2016, pp. 5205-5221.

[9]. D. Diaz-Guerra, A. Miguel, J. R. Beltran, GPURIR: A Python library for room impulse response simulation with GPU acceleration, *arXiv Preprint*, arXiv:1810.11359, 2018.

[10]. P. M. Peterson, Simulating the response of multiple microphones to a single acoustic source in a reverberant room, *The Journal of the Acoustical Society of America*, Vol. 80, Issue 5, 1986, pp. 1527-1529.

(011)

Hybrid Feature-based Approach for Face Shape Identification

Theiab Alzahrani and Waleed Al-Nuaimy
Department of Electrical Engineering and Electronics, University of Liverpool, UK
E-mail: {pstalzah, wax}@liverpool.ac.uk

Summary: Face shape classification is a vital process to choose an appropriate eyelashes, hairstyle and facial makeup, and section of a suitable glasses' frames according to the guidelines from experts. Measuring face characteristics by experts manually costs time and efforts. Therefore, developing automated face shape identification system could alleviate the need for additional time and efforts made by experts. This paper presents a deep convolutional neural network method (CNN) approach for classifying face shape into five types. The proposed method which is based on merging the features learnt by CNN with hand crafted features has proven to be efficient in identification of facial shape. The obtained results demonstrate that the proposed method is promising in identifying the shape of face by achieving accuracy of 81.1 % and suggest further improvements to address the limitations of data.

Keywords: Face shape, Convolutional neural networks, Cosmetics, Hand-crafted features, Engineered features.

1. Introduction

Identifying of person's face shape plays important role in recommending the suitable hairstyle, eyelashes, makeup, and glasses by fashion stylists. The process of determining facial shape manually by beauty experts can be carried out in several stages such as capturing pictures, outlining the face, measuring the width and length of the face, jaw, forehead, cheekbones, and finally determination the face shape. According to the beauty experts, the face shape can be recognised as five categories: oval, square, round, oblong, and heart shapes.

With a noticeable growth of computer aided design systems, automation of the process of face classification based on image processing and computer vision strategies can help in decreasing time and efforts achieved by experts. In the literature, many automated face shape classification systems were presented. Many published face classification methods consider extracting the face features manually then passing them for a classifier for classification. Others use features extracted automatically by convolutional neural networks.

Face shape classification is challenging task due to the complexity of face and the variations in the rotation, size, illumination, age and expressions. Furthermore, the existence of face occlusion like hats and glasses also adds difficulties to the classification process. Therefore, the existing face classification systems require more efforts for achieving a better performance. In this work, we propose deep learning-based approach for automated face shape classification into heart, oblong, oval, round, and square. The developed method combines the features engineered manually such as histogram of oriented gradients (HOG) and facial landmarks with the features extracted automatically by convolutional neural network to identify the face shape.

2. Materials and Method

A publicly available dataset has been used in this work [1]. This database comprises of 500 female celebrity images which has been labelled into five face shapes namely heart, oval, oblong, square and round. The block diagram of proposed framework shown in Fig. 1 includes three main stages which can be explained as follows.

Fig. 1. Block Diagram of proposed face shape classification system.

2.1. Face Detection and Cropping

In this stage of face shape classification framework, face is detected and cropped from an image. The face detection is carried out using a widely applied face detection model trained on histogram of oriented gradients (HOG) features with Linear Support Vector Machine model [2]. The dataset used for training, consists of 2825 images which are obtained from LFW dataset.

2.2. Landmark Detection and Alignment

In this stage, the detected and cropped face is aligned by firstly detecting the face landmarks (68 landmarks) by ensemble of regression tree method (ERT) [3] then use them to align the faces. Face alignment is a form of data normalisation. The face alignment is similar to feature vectors normalisation done via scaling to unit norm or zero centring prior to learning a machine learning algorithm. It is common to align the faces in dataset before training a face recogniser. The detected facial landmarks coordinates (68 landmarks) help to align the faces by making all faces in the dataset centred in the image, scaled such that the size of the faces is almost identical, and rotated such that the eyes locate on a horizontal line (the face is rotated such that the eyes locate along the same y-axis). ERT for landmark detection is trained on 300W dataset which contains more than 4000 in the wild images.

2.3. Classification by Inception Convolutional Neural Network

In the last stage, the aligned images are split into 80 % training and 20 % testing. The training images are fed to the pre-trained Inception V3 convolutional neural network [4] along with HOG features and landmarks to classify face shape into five classes. To train the networks, stochastic gradient descent SGD with the momentum optimisation algorithm is used with learning rate of 0.016 and momentum parameter 0.95. The dense layers of pre-trained Inception network are trained with 200 epochs.

3. Results and Discussions

The obtained results from developed system are shown in Table 1. From the table, it can be noticed that face shape classification using features extracted by CNN, CNN features combined with HOG features, CNN features combined with face landmarks, CNN features combined with HOG and face landmarks achieve accuracy of 75.2 %, 76.9 %, 78.2 %, and 81.1 %, respectively.

The obtained results reveal that combining hand crafted features with automatically extracted features can improve the overall performance of the face shape classification system. It also shows that our approach outperforms the other methods in the literature. Author in [1], who developed system based on features extracted automatically, reported accuracy of 84.4 % on the same data that we used for training and testing. However, he tested his method on the all data including data used for training which results in overfitting. Furthermore, testing on the data used for training is not an indicator for the system performance. In our system, 80 % of data was used for training while the remaining 20 % of unseen data was used for testing.

Finally, it is worth mentioning that the results obtained from our proposed system require more improvement. This is due to the small number of training and testing images used to train and test the model which are only 500 labelled images. It also needs more verification for the generalisation capabilities of the proposed system when it comes to test images outside this dataset. Therefore, we are aiming to increase the labelled data and consider building learning system which is able to classify face shape effectively.

Table 1. The performance of proposed method compared to methods in literature.

Method	Acc.	Dataset
Inception V3[1]	84.4 %	500 images [1]
Region Similarity, Correlation and Fractal Dimensions	80 %	Caltech 450 Cuhk 260 Lfw 200
Active Appearance Model (AAM), segmentation, and SVM	72 %	1000 image
Hybrid approach VGG and SVM	70.3 %	500 images
3D data and SVM	73.68 %	209 3D image
Geometric features	80 %	400 images
Probability Neural Network and Invariant Moments.	80 %	120 images
Inception3 CNN	75.2 %	500 images
Inception3 CNN+HOG	76.9 %	
Inception3 CNN+LMs	78.2 %	
Inception3 CNN+HOG+LMs	**81.1 %**	

4. Conclusions

In this paper, a framework for face shape classification has been presented and evaluated. The proposed method has proven that merging the features extracted manually with features learned by CNN can boost the classification performance. The results obtained from the proposed model comparing to the existing method proved the efficiency of presented system for face shape classification. This work can be extended, and results can be improved by providing more labelled data for study as well as testing more handcrafted features and more complicated CNN architectures.

References

[1]. A. E. Tio, Face shape classification using inception v3, *ArXiv*, arXiv:1911.07916, 2019

[2]. N. Dalal, B. Triggs, Histograms of oriented gradients for human detection", in *Proceedings of the International Conference on Computer Vision & Pattern Recognition (CVPR'05)*, Vol. 1, 2005, pp. 886-893.

[3]. V. Kazemi, J. Sullivan, One millisecond face alignment with an ensemble of regression trees, in *Proceedings of the IEEE Conference on Computer Vision and Pattern Recognition (CVPR'14)*, 2014, pp. 1867-1874.

[4]. C. Szegedy, V. Vanhoucke, S. Ioffe, J. Shlens, Z. Wojna, Rethinking the inception architecture for computer vision, in *Proceedings of the IEEE Conference on Computer Vision and Pattern Recognition (CVPR'16)*, 2016, pp. 2818-2826.

(013)

The Strategy of Service Recommendation to Bank Customers Using Machine Learning Algorithm

A. Sharifihosseini
Department of Mathematics and Computer Scince, Leipzig University, Germany
E-mail: farhang@sharifi.ws

Summary: Bank are trying to digitalizing their business process and tend to use recent cutting-edge technology in online business models. The main core of bank business involve customer relations management resulting in decision-making for customer investment. In recent years, use of recommender systems has changed into an indispensable part of customer-oriented organizations including bank. Bank try to introduce their services and products to their customers, thereby extracting the customers who can potentially use the recommendations. Use of machine learning in recommender systems results in enhanced accuracy recommendation and thus increased application. In this paper, a method is used based on matrix factorization, which is one of the best algorithm in collaborative filtering method. The initial data are in the form of a customer-service interaction matrix developed through RFM (one of the marketing methods for determining the customer significance) via clustering method. The method utilized Regularized General Singular Value Decomposition solution for recommendation.

Keywords: Recommender systems, Electronic banking, RGSVD, Collaborative filtering, Machine learning.

1. Introduction

Recommender systems are a group of machine learning algorithms dealing with offering a proper product to users [1]. Recommender systems are crucial for some industries, as they can both generate a lot of revenue and create a competitive environment. Since the 1990s, electronic banking as a product distribution channel has created the greatest potential for financial institutions. Most banks and financial institutions are now offering their customers access to many services through this [2].

Due to the spread of information technology, many banks are facing enormous amounts of accumulated data. Analyzing this data can help managers make the right marketing decisions [3]. One of the areas of computer science that can support banking innovation is the recommendation system [4].

Since banks provide customers with a variety of services, it is difficult for customers to choose a service. Therefore, a system that can help customers refine information is essential

The main paradigms of machine learning in recommender systems include collaborative filtering and content based [5]. In CF, algorithms such as user-based CF, item-based CF and matrix factorization are used [5, 6]. In this paper, one of the MF-based methods is described.

In MF-based methods, which are a model-based method [7, 8], a sparse user-product interaction matrix is divided into two smaller and dense matrices known as user and product specific matrices. Through their multiplication by a smaller dimensional space, the values of user-product interactions are reproduced [9]. In this text, user is same as customer, while product is bank services, whereby regularized generalized singular value decomposition is used. It deals with the recommendation through a gradient descent based classical approach [10]. This recommendation is indeed introduction of a service of a product to the customers of that product.

2. The Data Set

The data utilized in this research include customers applying the services of the mobile-based product of one of the private banks in Iran. The Services of this product include charging, paying bills, tracking bills, etc.

Meanwhile, other data are also used in this paper including the customers of this mobile product who use other terminals to utilize similar services. To create the customer-service matrix in each group of data, a marketing technique (RFM) and K-means clustering are used.

The author intends to use the two data to recommend services that the customer has not yet used on this mobile-based product. Information on successful customer transactions is: customer mobile number, customer number, type of service (these include: charging, bill payment, bill tracking, etc.), amount, transaction date

3. The Proposed Algorithm

CF problem in this method is defined as follow: a set of customers of mobile-based product C and a set of services on this product T. The priorities of customers with regards to services are represented as matrix W with $|T|\times|C|$ dimensions, in which the row vector represents the services and every column vector denotes a special customer. Meanwhile, this method also benefits from other data including set of customers C and set of similar services of this product utilized in other terminals B ; the priorities of customers in using the services is represented as matrix A with $|B|\times|C|$ dimension. If w_i and a_i represent the available data in matrices W and A.

The goal is to create an exploratory estimator, which is recommender; it can estimate the missing raings with minimum cumulative error based on available ratings in the Train Set.

As with SVD and GSVD method, the goal of RGSVD method is to create a low rank matrix from matrices of W and A. The first step of this algorithm is performing the following calculation:

$Y = \begin{bmatrix} A \\ W \end{bmatrix}$ and we assume the rank(Y) = c. The orthogonal matrics $V \in \mathbb{R}^{txt}$ and $U \in \mathbb{R}^{bxb}$, a nonsongular matrix $X \in \mathbb{R}^{cxc}$, where:

$$A = U\Sigma_1 Q^{-1} \qquad W = V\Sigma_2 Q^{-1}, \tag{1}$$

$\Sigma_1 \in \mathbb{R}^{b\times c}$ and $\Sigma_2 \in \mathbb{R}^{t\times c}$ are diagonal matrices, define as follows:

$$\begin{aligned} \Sigma_1 &= diag(\delta_{11},...,\delta_{1c}) \\ \Sigma_2 &= diag(\delta_{21},...,\delta_{2\min\{t,c\}}) \end{aligned}, \tag{2}$$

where $0 \le \delta_{11} \le ... \le \delta_{1c} \le 1$ and $1 \ge \delta_{21} \ge ... \ge \delta_{2\min\{t,c\}} \ge 0$. Thus, $\Sigma_{2j}^2 + \Sigma_{1j}^2 = 1 \quad forj = 1,...,\min\{t,c\}$.

$\delta_j = \dfrac{\Sigma_{1j}}{\Sigma_{2j}}$ is the generalized singular values of $\{A, W\}$ pair. Thus, for prediction through RGSVD method for customer i and service j, the following steps are taken:

$$\hat{a}_{ij} = u_i q_j^T, \tag{3}$$

where u_i and q_j are k-dimensional vector parameters. The k_{th} layer of parameters of all vectors of u_i and q_j is called the k_{th} feature.

Generally, parameters are estimated through minimization of the Regularized Squared Error (RSE) on test set (ts) as well as gradient descent method via regularization and determining the stop point.

Hence, the goal is a proper estimation of parameters U and Q .RSE calculation is as follows:

$$\begin{aligned} RSE &= \sum (a_{ij} - u_i q_j^T - bp_i - bu_j) - avg + \\ &+ \frac{\lambda}{2}(\|u_i\|^2 + \|q_j\|^2), \end{aligned} \tag{4}$$

where $\|.\|$ is the standard Euclidean norm and λ shows the Tikhonov regularization coefficient used for preventing overfitting. To obtain the local minimum of the above equation, SGD method is used, which improves through creating a loop for all variables present in the test set and altering the involved parameters against the gradient direction (slope). Considering the method used for updating the feature matrices here, the values of U and Q are initialized with the same values obtained from matrix A factorization, which are updated simultaneously.

$$\begin{aligned} &(U,Q) = \arg\min RES \Rightarrow \\ &\begin{cases} \dfrac{\partial}{\partial u_i} RSE = -2(a_{ij} - u_i q_j) q_j + \lambda u_i \\ \dfrac{\partial}{\partial q_j} RSE = -2(a_{ij} - u_i q_j) u_i + \lambda q_j \end{cases} \\ &\Rightarrow \begin{cases} u_i \leftarrow u_i + \eta(a_{ij} - u_i q_j) q_j - \lambda u_i \\ q_j \leftarrow q_j + \eta(a_{ij} - u_i q_j) u_i - \lambda q_j \end{cases}, \end{aligned} \tag{5}$$

where η coefficient is called learning rate.

The training process is iterated several times. In this method, typically several training epochs are required so that the model would converge. The number of epochs is usually dependent on the value of η and λ as well as the trainset data.

The linear bias bu_j and bp_i are trained alongside the missing features u_i and q_j, where the general average avg is estimated by the average of the available data of the trainset. The average is generally affected by the available statistical data.

It is generally proven that Regularized Matrix Factorization methods are highly accurate and scalable. But since this method is part of batch learning methods, it essentially requires batch processing based on the fixed training dataset.

Therefore, it is recommended that the customer-service set is not variable and as soon as the rating dataset is expanded, the only way to discover new patterns from the new dataset is to rebuild the entire recommender system.

4. The Experimental Results

4.1. Evaluation Metric

Cross-validation is used to validate the model as well as convert the data into two categories of testing and training for validation. Recommendation model tries to predict the ratings of test set using the training data.

In the K-fold cross validation, which is K = 5 in this study, the data are randomly used as a test set and the rest as a training set. This process is repeated with K and the prediction model is evaluated.

In recommender systems, the prediction accuracy is calculated using Root Mean Square Error criterion [11]:

$$RMSE = \sqrt{\sum_{b,c\in ts} (a_{bc} - \hat{a}_{bc})^2 \Big/ |\tau|}, \qquad (6)$$

where a_{bc} represent the real rating and $\hat{a}_{bc}$ shows the predicted rating and τ denotes the set for data validation.

In general, the evaluation process is schematically described in Table 1.

Table 1. K-Fold Cross Validation Description.

K-Fold CV: This approach involves randomly dividing the set of observations into *k* groups, or folds, of approximately equal size.
1. The first fold is treated as a validation set, and the method is fit on the remaining k – 1 folds. 2. The root mean squared error, RMSE, is then computed on the observations in the held-out fold. 3. This procedure is repeated k times: – Each time, a different group of observations is treated as a validation set. – This process results in k estimates of the test error, RMSE, …, RMSEk. 4. The k-fold CV estimate is computed by averaging these values: $CV_{(k)} = \frac{1}{K}\sum_{i=1}^{k} RMSE_i$

4.2. Results

As discussed in the previous sections, the RGSVD method uses two matrices to propose, while the model is trained alternatively in different steps. One of the marketing techniques (RFM) and K means clustering is used to form the customer-service interaction matrix in each data set. The author intends to use the two data to recommend services that the customer has not yet used on this mobile-based product.

Implementation of RGSVD algorithm on the data that categorized into training and test sets on 5-fold cross validation method show in Table 2.

In the implementation of RGSVD algorithm, matrix cutting dimensions are 2, learning rate 0.0001, Tikhonov coefficient 0.00002 and iterative algorithm for convergence 100 times. The results show that the least error occurred in fold-2. The RMSE error for the RGSVD method is 0.79.

Comparison of proposed algorithm with SVD and GSVD method per different fold shows in Fig. 1.

Table 2. The Result of RGSVD Algorithm.

Fold	RMSE
1	1.11
2	0.79
3	1.15
4	0.96
5	0.96

The X-axis represents Fold 1-5 and the Y-axis represents the RMSE error value for each algorithm. In general, RGSVD method is better than GSVD and SVD method. The lowest error in all three algorithms occurred in Fold-2 and the RMSE for RGSVD is 0.79, GSVD is 1.048 and SVD is 2.41.

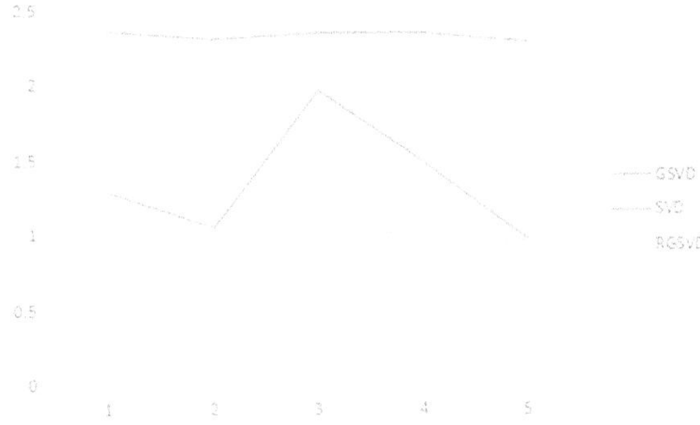

Fig. 1. Comparison of GSVD, RGSVD and SVD.

Table 3 compares the proposed algorithms in this study with two methods proposed in the collaborative refinement algorithm [12, 13] (user-based collaborative filtering, item-based collaborative filtering).

Table 3. Comparison of RGSVD Technique with User-based Collaborative Filtering and Item-based Collaborative Filtering.

Method	RMSE
RGSVD	0.788
User based CF algorithm	1.1213
Item based CF algorithm	1.1396

5. Conclusions

Recommender systems are an essential component of many industries and have recently attached a great deal of attention. In this paper, a well-known method in collaborative filtering called matrix factorization was investigated. RGSVD method was used for recommending the services of the bank mobile based product to customers.

This algorithm is model-based and one of the dimensionality reduction methods. The starting point in the RGSVD algorithm is the rating matrix. The rows of this matrix are the customers and the columns of those services. The columns with value indicate the customer interest rate and of a service using a mobile based product, and Missing Value means that we do not know whether the customer is willing to use that service on a mobile based product.

The RGSVD method uses two rating matrices to predict the rating and estimate the missing values in the data. In addition, this method uses the SGD method for model convergence and error reduction. The implementation steps of the algorithm are such that the process of executing it is repeated alternatively to reduce the prediction error and to provide an accurate estimation of the data values.

The error value obtained from this method indicated that this algorithm enjoys a good accuracy for recommendation; it had lower error values compared to SVD, GSVD and the traditional methods of collaborative filtering techniques such as the item-based method and the user-based method.

References

[1]. I. Portugal, P. Alencar, D. Cowan, The use of machine learning algorithms in recommender systems: A systematic review, *Expert Systems with Applications*, Vol. 97, 2018, pp. 205-227.

[2]. G. Nie, W. Rowe, L. Zhang, Y. Tian, Y. Shi, Credit card churn forecasting by logistic regression and decision tree, *Expert Systems with Applications*, Vol. 38, Issue 12, 2011, pp. 15273-15285.

[3]. F. Liébana-Cabanillas, R. Nogueras, L. J. Herrera, A. Guillén, Analysing user trust in electronic banking using data mining methods, *Expert Systems with Applications*, Vol. 40, Issue 14, 2013, pp. 5439-5447.

[4]. A. Gigli, F. Lillo, D. Regoli, Recommender system for banking and financial service, in *Proceedings of the 11th ACM Conference on Recommender System (RecSys'17)*, Como, Italy, 28 August 2017.

[5]. G. Adomavicius, A. Tuzhilin, Toward the next generation of recommender systems: A survey of the state-of-the-art and possible extensions, *IEEE Transactions on Knowledge and Data Engineering*, Vol. 17, Issue 6, 2005, pp.734-749.

[6]. P. Thakkar, K. Varma, V. Ukani, S. Mankad, S. Tanwar, Combining user-based and item-based collaborative filtering using machine learning, *Information and Communication Technology for Intelligent Systems*, Vol. 107, 2019, pp 173-180.

[7]. S. Kant, T. Mahara, Merging user and item based collaborative filtering to alleviate data sparsity, *International Journal of System Assurance Engineering and Management*, Vol. 9, Issue 1, 2018, pp. 173-179.

[8]. S. R. Kuche and Prof. S. R. Dinge, A novel approach of collaborative filtering using singular value decomposition, *International Journal of Advanced Research in Science, Communication and Technology*, Volume 4, Issue 4, April 2020, pp.1-8.

[9]. M. Nasiri, Z. Sharifi, B. Minaei, Alleviate sparsity problem using hybrid model based on spectral co-clustering and tensor factorization, in *Proceedings of the International Conference on Computer and Knowledge Engineearing (ICCKE'15)*, Mashhad, Iran, 29 October 2015, pp. 285-289.

[10]. K. Davagdorj, K. H. Park, K. H. Ryu, A collaborative filtering recommendation system for rating prediction, in Advances in Intelligent Information Hiding and Multimedia Signal Processing. Smart Innovation, Systems and Technologies (J. S. Pan, J. Li, P. W. Tsai, L. Jain, Eds.), Vol. 156, *Springer*, Singapore, 2020.

[11]. J. Herlocker, J. Konstan, L. Terveen, J. Riedl, Evaluating collaborative filtering recommender systems, *ACM Transaction on Information Systems*, Vol. 22, Issue 1, 2004, pp. 5-53.

[12]. C. Aggarwal, Neighborhood-based collaborative filtering, in Recommender Systems, *Springer*, 2016, pp. 29-70.

[13]. B. Sarwar, G. Karypis, J. Konstan, J. Riedl, Item-based collaborative filtering recommendation algorithms, in *Proceedings of the ACM 10th International Conference on World Wide Web (WWW'01)*, New York, NY, USA, 2001, pp. 285-295.

(017)

An Ensemble of Transparent Models to Predict Car Parking Occupancy

L. Pfeiffer [1], G. Bologna [1], Y. Rekik [1], M. Bénard [2] and N. Foukia [1]
[1] University of Applied Sciences and Arts, 4 Rue de la prairie, 1204 Geneva, Switzerland
[2] IEM Group, 109 Chemin du Pont du centenaire, 1228, Plan-Les-Ouates, Geneva, Switzerland
Tel.: + 41 22 5462551, fax: + 41 22 5462410
E-mail: guido.bologna@hesge.ch

Summary: One goal of our on-going *PreGIS* project is to assess car parking occupancy predictions using several supervised learning models. A dataset related to this prediction problem has been collected from sensors located in the city of Geneva (Switzerland). In this work, we focus on special ensembles of neural networks trained on data predictions by bagging. A remarkable characteristic of our trained ensembles is that their predictions can be explained by means of propositional rules. We have accurately predicted car parking occupancy up to one hour in the future; the closer the prediction the better the results. Specifically, for a 30 minutes prediction in the future the predictive accuracy reaches an average of 87.6 %.

Keywords: Ensembles, Prediction, Rule extraction, Transparent models, Supervised learning.

1. Introduction

In many cities, the imbalance between limited supply and growing demand for parking zones poses enormous problems, such as traffic growth. Increasing the number of on-street parking areas is often unworkable. Cities therefore should optimize operations of existing places by improving their management.

Car parking occupancy prediction is at the core of intelligent services, such as predictive visualization of parking occupancy, intelligent control routing and dynamic price adjustment. The goal of our on-going *PreGIS* project is to assess car parking prediction by several supervised learning models. The prediction area is the city of Geneva in Switzerland. We collected a dataset there with the use of sensors that detect metallic bodies of vehicles. Here, we focus on ensembles of neural networks trained with temporal series of car parking occupancy rates that can be explained by propositional rules. On one hand, the prediction response explanation is useful to make decisions at the managerial level. On the other hand, it is also possible to provide users with a confidence measure of the activated rules.

1.1. Related Work

Statistical learning models were used to predict the occupancy rate of car parking. Dan described one of the first attempts to use statistical learning for this type of problem [3]. His approach is based on the use of cameras. He used support vector machines (SVMs) on characteristic color vectors to distinguish between car-occupied and unoccupied regions.

Zheng et al. used public historical data that have been learned from three models: decision trees, neural networks and SVMs [6]. Their results show that decision trees using time attributes (hours and days of the week) work better than the other two models. In [5], a sensor network is segmented into four different areas. Then, neural networks were developed for each region. More precisely, multi-layer, genetically optimized Perceptrons have accurately predicted car parking occupancy up to one hour in the future, using only the time data from the last five minutes. Their results showed that the short-term prediction of available places is reliable. In [4], six models were compared for predicting the car parking occupancy rate in the city of Birmingham. The authors argue that there was no better model among those studied.

2. Experiments

In our current work, we use ensembles of *Discretized Interpretable Multi Layer Perceptrons* (DIMLPs) to generate symbolic rules from ensembles of 25 DIMLPs trained by Bagging, as in [1]. We performed the experiments in two parts. In the first one, we have embraced the view of the manager who may be interested in offering reduced prices to customers when occupancy rate predictions yield low values. In the second part, we have adopted the customer's interest to know whether in the near future she will be able to park her car.

2.1. Dataset Description

Very low power sensors developed by IEM Ltd. gathered our dataset. Each sensor detects the car metallic body. In the current study, we focus on a particular parking area including 50 sensors. Each data of our dataset includes a temporal series of 30 inputs, with each input representing parking occupancy rate every two minutes. Furthermore, we added to each input vector the occupancy rate observed one and two weeks earlier. The intuitive reason is that the prediction at the current time could correspond to that of one or two weeks earlier. The whole dataset includes

159046 samples collected in 2018 in the city of Geneva. We defined three prediction problems: 14 minutes in the future; 30 minutes; and 60 minutes. With the first prediction problem (14 min. in the future), we generated a training set including the first 139883 samples, the last 19163 samples representing a testing set. A very similar number of samples is assigned in the other two prediction problems. For each problem and for each model we performed ten trials, the provided results being based on their average.

2.2. Neural Network Architecture

DIMLP differs from a standard Multi Layer Perceptron in the number of connections between the input layer and the first hidden layer. Specifically, a hidden neuron receives only a connection from an input neuron and the bias neuron [1]. All layers above the first hidden layer are fully connected. This special architecture allows us to precisely determining discriminatory boundaries corresponding to axis-parallel hyperplanes.

Usually, we define DIMLP architectures with two hidden layers, the size of the first hidden layer being the same as the input layer. The number of neurons in the input layer is 35, with 30 neurons representing the temporal series of the occupation rate, and the other neurons indicating the prediction one week and two weeks before the current prediction.

For the second hidden layer, in order to avoid overtraining, the number of neurons is chosen so that the total number of connections is less than the number of training samples. Specifically, for this layer we defined 40 neurons. Finally, the output layer size is two for a problem with two classes and three for three classes (see below).

We trained ensembles of DIMLPs by bagging [2], which is based on resampling techniques. Specifically, assuming a training set of size p, bagging selects for each classifier included in an ensemble p samples drawn with replacement from the original training set. Note that those samples left out represent a subset of the training set that is used to avoid over-training. In practice, as soon as the sum squared error starts to increase on this subset the training phase is stopped. Finally, each DIMLP is trained by back-propagation with default parameters. Specifically, the learning parameter is equal to 0.1 and the momentum is equal to 0.6.

2.3. Predictions for the Manager

We defined a prediction problem of three classes. In the first class, the occupancy rate is between 0 % and 60 %. The second class lies between 60 % and 90 % and the last deals with the interval between 90 % and 100 %. Experiments being based on ten trials, Table 1 illustrates the obtained average predictive accuracy (Acc. on the testing set), average fidelity (Fid. on the testing set), which is the degree of matching between extracted rules classifications and ensembles responses [1], and average number of extracted rules (#Rules). Note that the proportion of the dominant class on the testing set is 55.5 %.

Table 1. Average predictive accuracy of the rules, fidelity and average number of rules obtained by DIMLP ensembles.

	Acc.	Fid.	#Rules
14 (min.)	87.4 %	99.7 %	816.5
30 (min.)	84.0 %	99.6 %	932.0
60 (min.)	80.2 %	99.5 %	1073.3

Table 2 shows in the first column the predictive accuracy provided by an intuitive decision rule yielding the same classification a week earlier at the same time. Then follows the predictive accuracies provided by the K-nearest neighbor classifier with K = 1 and K = 20.

Table 2. Average predictive accuracies obtained by a simple classification rule and K-nearest neighbor classifiers with K = 1 and K = 20.

	Naive	K-NN (1)	K-NN (20)
14 (min.)	76.5 %	83.5 %	86.1 %
30 (min.)	76.5 %	79.0 %	83.1 %
60 (min.)	76.5 %	75.2 %	78.5 %

Tables 3, 4, and 5 present the average confusion matrices of the three prediction problems.

Table 3. Average confusion matrix obtained by DIMLP ensembles for 14 min. predictions.

	True 0-60	True 60-90	True 90-100
Ens. 0-60	10343.2	300.9	0
Ens. 60-90	292.8	7473.6	1414.9
Ens. 90-100	0	1032.5	3345.1

Table 4. Average confusion matrix obtained by DIMLP ensembles for 30 min. predictions.

	True 0-60	True 60-90	True 90-100
Ens. 0-60	10229.1	390.1	0
Ens. 60-90	406.9	7340.1	2007.1
Ens. 90-100	0	1068.8	2752.9

Table 5. Average confusion matrix obtained by DIMLP ensembles for 60 min. predictions.

	True 0-60	True 60-90	True 90-100
Ens. 0-60	10074.6	537.4	5.2
Ens. 60-90	561.4	7448.1	2881.4
Ens. 90-100	0	798.5	1873.4

2.4. Predictions for the Customer

We defined a prediction problem of two classes. The positive class is defined with an occupancy rate between 0 % and 90 %, while the negative class is defined with an occupancy rate between 90 % and 100 %. The proportion of the negative class is equal to 12.2 % in the training set, while it is 20.6 % in the testing set. Table 6 and Table 7 provide similar results with respect to the first two tables.

Table 6. Average predictive accuracy of the rules, fidelity and average number of rules obtained by DIMLP ensembles.

	Acc.	Fid.	#Rules
14 (min.)	90.1 %	99.6 %	675.0
30 (min.)	87.6 %	99.5 %	805.3
60 (min.)	84.9 %	99.6 %	679.7

Table 7. Average predictive accuracies obtained by a simple naïve classification rule and K-nearest neighbor classifiers with K = 1 and K = 20.

	Naive	K-NN (1)	K-NN (20)
14 (min.)	81.8 %	86.3 %	88.9 %
30 (min.)	81.8 %	83.6 %	83.7 %
60 (min.)	81.8 %	81.5 %	83.1 %

Tables 8, 9, and 10 present the average confusion matrices for the three prediction problems.

Table 8. Average confusion matrix obtained by DIMLP ensembles for 14 min. predictions.

	True Pos. Cls	True Neg. Cls.
Ens. Pos. Cls.	14377.1	1071.6
Ens. Neg. Cls.	832.9	2881.4

Table 9. Average confusion matrix obtained by DIMLP ensembles for 30 min. predictions.

	True Pos. Cls	True Neg. Cls.
Ens. Pos. Cls.	14348.4	1529.7
Ens. Neg. Cls.	853.6	2423.3

Table 10. Average confusion matrix obtained by DIMLP ensembles for 60 min. predictions.

	True Pos. Cls	True Neg. Cls.
Ens. Pos. Cls.	14437.5	2151.5
Ens. Neg. Cls.	749.5	1801.5

Fig. 1 illustrates the averaged Receiver Operating Characteristic (ROC) curves for the three prediction problems. Finally, Table 11 shows the Area Under Curve (AUC) measure, the optimal False Positive Rate (FPR) and the optimal True Positive Rate (TPR) determined from the ROCs.

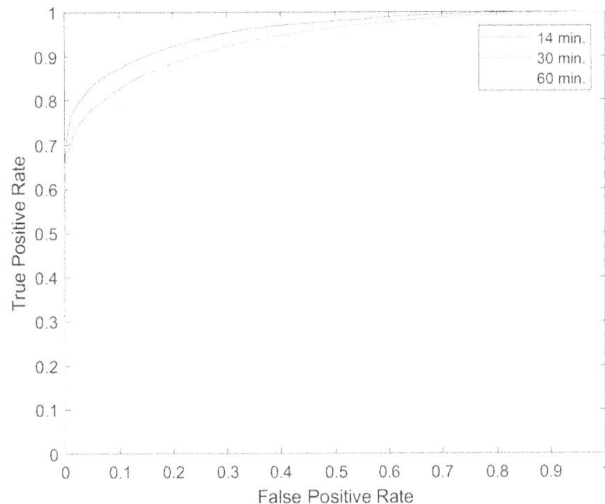

Fig. 1. Average ROC curves obtained on the prediction problems.

Table 11. AUC, optimal FPR and optimal TPR obtained from the ROC curves.

	AUC	FPR	TPR
14 min.	95.6 %	28.8 %	95.1 %
30 min.	93.6 %	31.0 %	92.5 %
60 min.	91.1 %	43.1 %	92.6 %

2.5. Examples of Extracted Rules

Fig. 2 shows the characteristics of the first twenty rules extracted from a DIMLP ensemble that predicts car parking occupancy (cf. Section 2.4). From left to right we have: the rule number; the number of covered examples in the testing set; the number of correctly classified examples; the number of wrongly classified examples; and the accuracy of the rule on the testing set.

```
--------------------------------------------------------------
          #Ex    #Corr  #Wrong    Accuracy

Rule   1:13768 13321   447       0.967533       Class = POS.
Rule   2:13818 13373   445       0.967796       Class = POS.
Rule   3:13671 13228   443       0.967596       Class = POS.
Rule   4:13700 13280   420       0.969343       Class = POS.
Rule   5:13543 13135   408       0.969874       Class = POS.
Rule   6:13389 13048   341       0.974531       Class = POS.
Rule   7:13296 12954   342       0.974278       Class = POS.
Rule   8:13220 12900   320       0.975794       Class = POS.
Rule   9:13092 12731   361       0.972426       Class = POS.
Rule  10:13179 12815   364       0.972380       Class = POS.
Rule  11:12828 12504   324       0.974743       Class = POS.
Rule  12:12792 12536   256       0.979988       Class = POS.
Rule  13:11846 11582   264       0.977714       Class = POS.
Rule  14:11831 11687   144       0.987829       Class = POS.
Rule  15:10392 10346    46       0.995574       Class = POS.
Rule  16: 5297  4838   459       0.913347       Class = POS.
Rule  17: 4717  4367   350       0.925800       Class = POS.
Rule  18: 4757  4431   326       0.931469       Class = POS.
Rule  19: 4765  4513   252       0.947114       Class = POS.
Rule  20: 4796  4472   324       0.932444       Class = POS.
```

Fig. 2. Characteristics of the first twenty rules extracted from a DIMLP ensemble.

The first rule of the positive class appears at rank 80. Fig. 3 shows the characteristics of several rules belonging to the positive class.

```
------------------------------------------------------
           #Ex   #Corr #Wrong    Accuracy

Rule   80: 1864  1589   275      0.852468          Class = NEG.
Rule   82: 1842  1574   268      0.854506          Class = NEG.
Rule   83: 1820  1560   260      0.857143          Class = NEG.
Rule   84: 1886  1618   268      0.857900          Class = NEG.
Rule   85: 1759  1505   254      0.855600          Class = NEG.
Rule   86: 1870  1608   262      0.859893          Class = NEG.
Rule   87: 1808  1552   256      0.858407          Class = NEG.
Rule   88: 1761  1503   258      0.853492          Class = NEG.
Rule   90: 1684  1431   253      0.849762          Class = NEG.
Rule   92: 1676  1445   231      0.862172          Class = NEG.
Rule   93: 1781  1528   253      0.857945          Class = NEG.
Rule   94: 1607  1376   231      0.856254          Class = NEG.
Rule   95: 1612  1398   214      0.867246          Class = NEG.
Rule   96: 1670  1452   218      0.869461          Class = NEG.
Rule   97: 1545  1323   222      0.856311          Class = NEG.
Rule   99: 1569  1335   234      0.850860          Class = NEG.
Rule  103: 1643  1432   211      0.871576          Class = NEG.
Rule  104: 1473  1270   203      0.862186          Class = NEG.
Rule  105: 1480  1259   221      0.850676          Class = NEG.
Rule  106: 1461  1249   212      0.854894          Class = NEG.
Rule  107: 1625  1411   214      0.868308          Class = NEG.
Rule  108: 1431  1206   225      0.842767          Class = NEG.
Rule  109: 1386  1177   209      0.849206          Class = NEG.
Rule  110: 1619  1447   172      0.893762          Class = NEG.
```

Fig. 3. Characteristics of a number of rules belonging to the negative class.

Fig. 4 depicts the first five rules. Symbol x_{30} designates the actual occupancy rate, while x_1 corresponds to the occupancy rate 58 minutes earlier. For each condition in a rule between round parentheses, we have a logical "and".

```
------------------------------------------------------

Rule 1:  (x1 < 0.978416)   (x27 < 0.919903)
         (x28 < 0.919815)  (x30 < 0.899947)   Class = POS.

Rule 2:  (x20 < 0.979972)  (x26 < 0.979798)
         (x28 < 0.939833)  (x29 < 0.899649)
         (x30 < 0.899947)                     Class = POS.

Rule 3:  (x5 < 0.956737)   (x26 < 0.939938)
         (x28 < 0.919815)  (x30 < 0.899947)   Class = POS.

Rule 4:  (x28 < 0.898555)  (x30 < 0.899947)   Class = POS.

Rule 5:  (x5 < 0.956737)   (x20 < 0.938794)
         (x28 < 0.919815)  (x30 < 0.899947)   Class = POS.
```

Fig. 4. Examples of positive rules.

Fig. 5 illustrates five positive rules among the rules with highest support in this class. Note that x_{35} represents the occupancy rate at the same time as x_{30}, but one week earlier.

3. Conclusions

In the on-going *PreGIS* project, we assessed the accuracy of DIMLP ensembles. We have accurately predicted car parking occupancy up to one hour in the future. The closer the prediction the better the results. Specifically, for a prediction of 14 minutes in the future the average true positive rate is equal to 95.1 %, with the average true negative rate being equal to 71.2 %. This is encouraging, especially by considering that the number of samples will increase. Furthermore, by examining the extracted rules, we noticed that an attribute representing the occupancy rate at the time of the prediction, but exactly one week earlier, appears in many rules. In the future we will compare the current results with those provided by deep learning models, such as LSTM (*Long Short Term Memory*).

```
------------------------------------------------------

Rule 80: (x24 > 0.899262) (x28 > 0.898555)
         (x29 > 0.899649) (x30 > 0.939639)
         (x35 > 0.859414)                   Class = NEG.

Rule 82: (x26 > 0.899952) (x28 > 0.919815)
         (x30 > 0.939639) (x35 > 0.859414)  Class = NEG.

Rule 83: (x24 > 0.919662) (x29 > 0.919657)
         (x30 > 0.939639) (x35 > 0.839857)  Class = NEG.

Rule 84: (x23 > 0.919561) (x28 > 0.919815)
         (x30 > 0.939639) (x35 > 0.819875)  Class = NEG.

Rule 85: (x19 > 0.838019) (x27 > 0.899931)
         (x28 > 0.919815) (x29 > 0.939782)
         (x30 > 0.939639) (x35 > 0.839857)  Class = NEG.
```

Fig. 5. Examples of negative rules.

References

[1]. G. Bologna, Is it worth generating rules from neural network ensembles ?, *Journal of Applied Logic*, Vol. 2, Issue 3, 2004, pp. 325-348.

[2]. L. Breiman, Bagging predictors, *Machine Learning*, Vol. 24, Issue 2, 1996, pp. 123-140.

[3]. N. Dan, Parking Management System and Method, US Patent App. 10/066, 215, *USA*, 2003.

[4]. D. H. Stolfi, E. Alba, X. Yao, Predicting car park occupancy rates in smart cities, in *Proceedings of the International Conference on Smart Cities (ICSC'17)*, 2017, pp. 107-117.

[5]. E. I. Vlahogianni, K. Kepaptsoglou, V. Tsetsos, M. G. Karlaftis, Exploiting new sensor technologies for real-time parking prediction in urban areas, in *Proceedings of the Transportation Research Board 93rd Annual Meeting Compendium of Papers*, 2014, pp. 1614-1673.

[6]. Y. Zheng, S. Rajasegarar, C. Leckie, Parking availability prediction for sensor-enabled car parks in smart cities, in *Proceedings of the IEEE 10th International Conference on Intelligent Sensors, Sensor Networks and Information Processing (ISSNIP'15)*, 2015, pp. 1-6.

(019)

Identification of the Ultra Short Laser Parameters during Irradiation of Thin Metal Films Using the Interval Lattice Boltzmann Method and Evolutionary Algorithm

M. Paruch, A. Piasecka-Belkhayat and A. Korczak
Silesian University of Technology, Department of Computational Mechanics and Engineering,
18A Konarskiego Str., 44-100 Gliwice, Poland
Tel.: +48322372203, fax: +48322371282
E-mail: marek.paruch@polsl.pl

Summary: In the paper the one-dimensional numerical modelling of heat transfer in thin metal films irradiated by ultra-short laser pulses is considered. In the mathematical description the relaxation times and the boundary conditions for phonons and electrons are given as interval numbers. The direct problem has been solved by means of the interval lattice Boltzmann method using the rules of directed interval arithmetic, while at the stage of the inverse problem solution, the evolutionary algorithm is applied. In the final part of the paper the examples of numerical computations are presented.

Keywords: Interval Boltzmann transport equation, Interval lattice Boltzmann method, Directed interval arithmetic, Evolutionary algorithm, Inverse problem.

1. Introduction

Heat transfer problems in thin metal films irradiated by the ultra-short laser pulses frequently encountered in many fields of technical engineering are usually described by means of govering equations for phonons and electrons with deterministic thermophysical parameters [1, 2]. However, in most cases, the values of these parameters cannot be defined precisely, and in such cases it is convenient to define these parameters as intervals numbers. The direct problem has been solved using the interval lattice Boltzmann method assuming the interval relaxation times and the interval boundary conditions [3, 4].

The inverse problem discussed in this paper consists of the three parameters identification, in particular the peak power intensity of the laser pulse, absorption coefficient and the laser pulse parameter occurring in the source term in the energy equation. The task formulated in this way is solved using the evolutionary algorithm (EA) [5, 6].

2. Interval Boltzmann Transport Equation

The interval Boltzmann transport equations for the coupled problem with two relaxation times can be written in the following form

$$\frac{\partial \overline{e}_k}{\partial t} + \mathbf{v}_k \cdot \nabla \overline{e}_k = \frac{\overline{e}_k^{\,0} - \overline{e}_k}{\overline{\tau}_k} + \overline{Q}_k , \qquad (1)$$

where k = 'e' or 'ph' corresponds to the successive energy carriers as electrons or phonons, $\overline{e}_e$, $\overline{e}_{ph}$ are the interval values of carrier energy densities, $\overline{e}_e^{\,0}$, $\overline{e}_{ph}^{\,0}$ are the interval equilibrium carrier energy densities and $\overline{\tau}_e$, $\overline{\tau}_{ph}$ are the interval relaxation times, $\overline{Q}_e$ is the interval electron energy source and $\overline{Q}_{ph}$ is the interval phonon energy source defined as

$$\overline{Q}_e = Q' - G(\overline{T}_e - \overline{T}_{ph}),\ \overline{Q}_{ph} = G(\overline{T}_e - \overline{T}_{ph}) , \qquad (2)$$

where Q' is the external source associated with the laser irradiation

$$Q'(x,t) = I_0 \delta e^{-\delta x - \beta t} , \qquad (3)$$

while G is the electron-phonon coupling factor which characterizes the energy exchange between electrons and phonons, $\overline{T}_e$ and $\overline{T}_{ph}$ are the interval temperature values of electrons and phonons.

3. Inverse Problem

The aim of investigations is to determine the peak power intensity of the laser pulse I_0, absorption coefficient δ and laser pulse parameter β, see Eq. (3). The functional (fitness function) S is defined as follows

$$S(I_0, \delta, \beta) = \sum_{f=1}^{F} \sum_{k=1}^{K} \left(T_k^f - T_{dk}^f \right)^2 \rightarrow \text{MIN} , \qquad (4)$$

where T_k^f are the temperatures at the internal control points, resulting from the numerical solution of the direct problem for assumed values of I_0, δ and β, in turn the T_{dk}^f are the 'postulated' temperatures, K is a number of internal nodes, F is a number of time steps. The minimum of functional (4) is found using the evolutionary algorithm (using floating point coding). It is an algorithm belonging to the group of artificial intelligence methods, which does not require the analysis of the impact of design variables on the identification criterion, and allows one to obtain an optimal solution with a low risk of error.

In Table 1, the parameters of evolutionary algorithm used in computations are collected.

Table 1. Evolutionary algorithm parameters.

EA parameter	Value
Number of generations	150
Number of chromosomes	75
Probability of uniform mutation	15 %
Probability of nonuniform mutation	30 %
Probability of arithmetic crossover	40 %
Probability of cloning	100 %

4. Results of Computations

As a numerical example of the direct problem, the heat transport in a gold thin film of the thickness 200 nm has been analysed. The following interval input data with the 5 % perturbation have been introduced: boundary temperature at non-irradiated edge $\overline{T}_b = [285, 315]$K, relaxation times for phonons and for electrons: $\overline{\tau}_{ph} = [0.76, 0.84]$ps and $\overline{\tau}_e = [0.038, 0.042]$ps. The other adequate laser properties are defined in Table 2 (cf. exact value). Solution of direct problem is presented in Fig. 1.

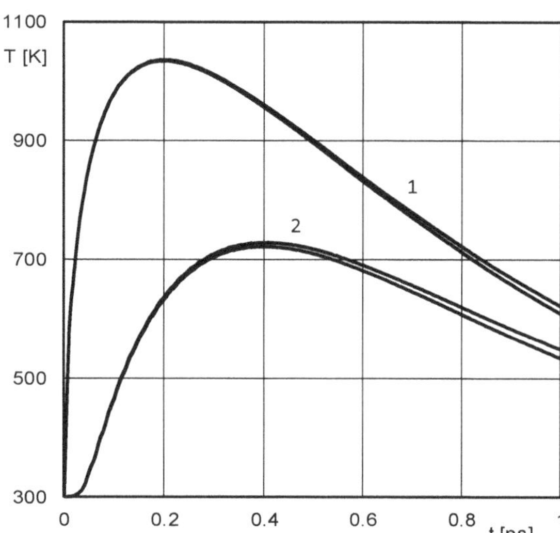

Fig. 1. Solution of the direct problem (1: x = 0, 2: x = L/2).

To solve the inverse problem, the evolutionary algorithm has been used. The solutions is presented in Table 2.

Table 2. Results of computations using the EA.

Design variable	Exact value	Found value	Error %	Fitness function value
I_0, (W/m^2)	$2\cdot10^{13}$	$2.11\cdot10^{13}$	5.5	$1.173\cdot10^{-1}$
δ, (1/m)	$7.55\cdot10^{7}$	$7.87\cdot10^{7}$	4.24	
β, (1/s)	$0.5\cdot10^{13}$	$0.553\cdot10^{13}$	10.6	

5. Conclusions

The main goal of the direct problem solution is to obtain the interval temperatures in thin metal film assuming the interval values of the relaxation times and the boundary conditions. The inverse problem is to identify the three laser parameters occurring in the external source function. The application of EA for the solutions of identification problems is (from the numerical point of view) essentially time-consuming. The reduction of the identification time can be obtained by the computations parallelizing. Summing up, the solution of the inverse problem discussed in this paper is very satisfactory.

Acknowledgements

Publication is supported under the Rector's grant in the area of scientific research and development works, Silesian University of Technology, grant number 10/040/RGJ19/0082.

References

[1]. M. Kaviany, A. J. H. McGaughey, Integration of molecular dynamics simulations and Boltzmann transport equation in phonon thermal conductivity analysis, in *Proceedings of the ASME International Mechanical Engineering Congress and Exposition (IMECE'03)*, Washington, DC, USA, 15-21 November 2003, pp. 277-287.

[2]. J. B. Lee, K. Kang, S. H. Lee, Comparison of theoretical models of electron-phonon coupling in thin gold films irradiated by femtosecond pulse lasers, *Materials Transactions*, Vol. 52, Issue 3, 2011, pp. 547-553.

[3]. A. Piasecka-Belkhayat, A. Korczak, Modelling of transient heat transport in metal films using the interval lattice Boltzmann method, *Bulletin of the Polish Academy of Science*, Vol. 64, Issue 3, 2016, pp. 599-606.

[4]. A. Piasecka-Belkhayat, A. Korczak Modeling of thermal processes proceeding in 1D domain of crystalline solids using the lattice Boltzmann method with interval source function, *Journal of Theoretical and Applied Mechanics*, Vol. 55, Issue 1, 2017, pp. 167-175.

[5]. M. Paruch, Identification of the degree of tumor destruction on the basis of the Arrhenius integral using the evolutionary algorithm, *International Journal of Thermal Sciences*, Vol. 130, 2018, pp. 507-517.

[6]. B. Mochnacki, E. Majchrzak, M. Paruch, Soft tissue freezing process. Identification of the dual phase lag model parameters using the evolutionary algorithms, *AIP Conference Proceedings*, Vol. 1922, 2018, 060001.

(025)

Enhanced Error Estimation of Robot Path Accuracy Using Artificial Neural Networks as an Approach to Increase the Robots Accuracy

M. Neitmann [1], **M. Brysch** [1], **S. Meyer** [1] **and M. Sinapius** [1]
[1] Technische Universität Braunschweig, Institute of Adaptronics and Function Integration, Langer Kamp 6, 38126 Braunschweig, Germany
Tel.: +49 531 391-2697, fax: +49 531 391-8110
E-mail: m.neitmann@tu-braunschweig.de

Summary: This article proposes a new approach to use artificial neural networks for increasing the accuracy of industrial robots. A large part of the error in a robot path origins in simplifications in the formulation of the robot's inverse kinematics. Theses simplifications are necessary to allow an analytical solution, which is needed to enable real-time calculations of the inverse kinematics. To overcome this limitation an artificial neural network is used to model the deviation between the simplified analytically solution and experimental data. It is shown, that small feed-forward networks are capable of modelling the path deviation between the setpoint and real path measurements with 6 % accuracy. Thus, the applicability of artificial neural networks to increase the accuracy of industrial robots is demonstrated.

Keywords: Robot calibration, Feed forward, Inverse kinematics, Deep learning, Modelling, Mechanical systems, Real time.

---

1. Introduction

In robotics there is a big discrepancy between repeatability and accuracy. Accuracy describes the difference between the robot's set point and the real position of the robots Tool Center Point (TCP). The repeatability is defined as the difference between the average path and the maximum path deviation in 30 path iteration [1].

Commonly robots show very good repeatability and poor accuracy. As an example, the robot used in this study has a guaranteed repeatability of 60 µm, whereas literature shows that robot accuracies are generally in the range of 1 to 2 cm [2].

Further analysis shows that the poor accuracy is mainly caused by two effects. Since robots are long and slender structures, they are prone to bending. The bending is caused by the robots own weight, process loads and thermal expansion. The second source of errors is the simplification in the calculation of the robots inverse kinematic. The kinematic of robots is highly nonlinear [3]. Since robot kinematics have to be calculated in real-time, only modelling approaches with very short computation time are feasible. Thereby the modelling approaches are usually limited to modeling approaches with analytical solutions.

These and more effects, which cause path deviation in robotics, are well studied in the field of robot calibration. But the approaches to encounter theses effects commonly suffer from two problems. One is the use of differential or even nonlinear equations which leads to long computation time, the other is a complicated experimental setup to find parameters for the models.

This study proposes a way of robots calibration facilitating Artificial Neural Network (ANN). It is shown, that feed-forward networks can be used to calculate the inverse kinematic of robotic systems [3]. Since it is barely possible to change the inverse kinematics in commercial available industrial robots, this study proposes a new method to compensate modelling errors with minimal changes in the robot's software architecture through ANN.

2. Concept

The overall concept is best explained using a control loop like representation of the robot as shown in Fig. 1. The operating principle of current robotics is shown in blue. The Cartesian path setpoint is defined by the robot's programmer and calculated from the Cartesian space to axis angles using inverse kinematics. The calculated angles are then used to move the robot's joints accordingly, resulting in a robot position due to the physical kinematics.

Fig. 1. Industrial mobile robot used in this paper with Etalon LaserTRACER measurement system.

In order to minimize the changes in the robot's software, no changes will be made to the inverse kinematics and the robot's kinematic control. Instead, an ANN, depicted in green in Fig. 2, compensates for the errors in the Cartesian space before the calculation of the inverse kinematics. This approach has two main advantages. Compared to changing the whole inverse kinematics of existing commercial robots, it is possible to use interfaces provided by the robot's manufacturer for sensor guided movements. Furthermore, this approach possesses a significantly lower safety risk. Considering the fact that neural networks can show unexpected behavior, the presented approach offers the possibility to limit the correction to a couple of Millimeters, thus prohibiting large unexpected robot movements.

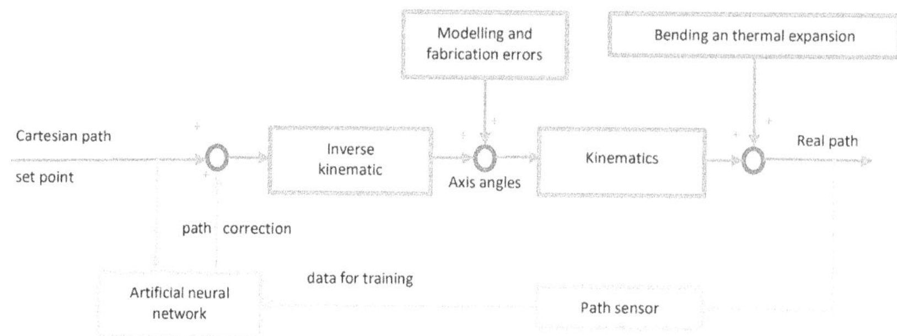

Fig. 2. Robot architecture described as control loop with proposed artificial neural network.

In order to train the neural network, a path sensor is used to provide the training data. Since the sensor is only needed for training, the ANN training can be done in the factory before the installation of the industrial robot. Hence, the cost per robot will be much cheaper than using a sensor for path control.

3. Experimental Setup and Data Processing

The experimental setup consists of a Kuka KMR Quantec KR150 mobile robot and an Etalon LaserTRACER Measuring system (see Fig. 2). The measuring system is capable to measure the position of the robots tool-center-point with accuracies up to 10 µm [4]. Both systems are connected with a programmable logic controller (PLC). This setup allows saving both the robot's set point and the measured position in real-time.

Unfortunately the robot uses a different sampling time than the PLC and the measuring system. The latter two use sampling times of 1 ms, while the robot has slightly varying sampling times around 50 ms (see Fig. 3). This leads to high noise when calculating the path error as the difference of set point and measurement. Therefore all the data acquired from the robots is interpolated quadratic within the robot's sampling intervals to simulate a higher sampling frequency of the robot.

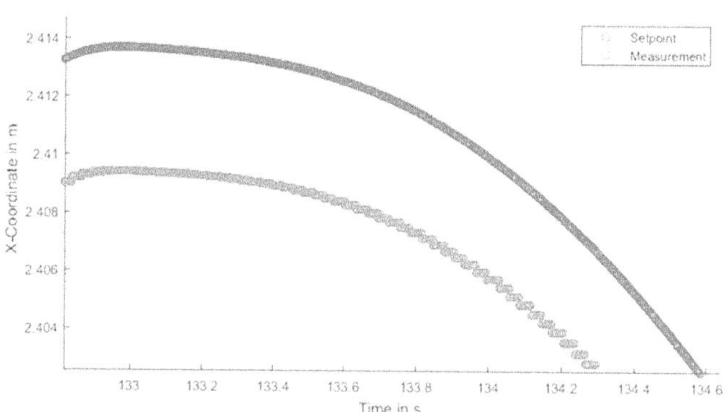

Fig. 3. Sampled Raw Data.

One of the later discussed ANN needs the robot's velocity and acceleration as input. These values are acquired through differentiation of the robot's pose. To reduce noise, a Butterworth low pass filter was applied.

4. Robot Moments for Training

In order to train an ANN, which is able to model the robot comprehensively, the robot movement used for training has to contain various paths within the whole workspace at different speeds and accelerations. Since these requirements will lead to an enormous measurement and training time, and since the main goal of this paper is also to provide a proof of concept and an outline for further work, a certain simplification was made in the path definition for the training data. First of all the orientation, maximum speed and maximum acceleration of the TCP are kept constant and low level throughout the whole measurements. In order to define a subsection of the workspace, the ISO 9283 is used. The ISO suggests defining a cube with one meter length in a place where the robot does most of its work. Therefore, a position in front of the robot was chosen as the center of the cube. The path of the robot consists of 100 randomly chosen points within this cube. These points are interconnected with movements along straight lines. Because it is common to approximate sharp edges in robotics to avoid excitation by high accelerations, the standard approximation setting of the Kuka robot was used. Since the approximation is done in path planning, the measured setpoints already contain the approximations.

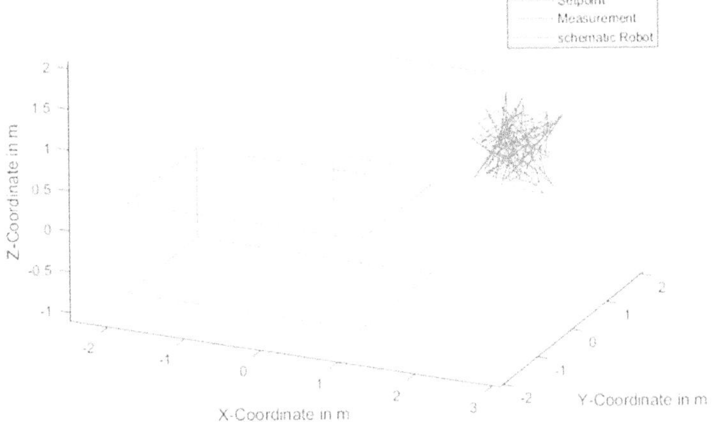

Fig. 4. Randomly generated path for training and schematic representation of the robot.

5. Design of the Artificial Neural Network

The primary goal of the neuronal network design is to minimize the number of layers and neurons. This is a requirement for the long-term goal of this work, which consists of the implementation of the neuronal network on a PLC to perform real-time robot path adjustments.

As shown in Fig. 2, the ANN is intended to model the deviation of the robot position based on the values of the robot controller. In a first attempt, a data set containing only the target position as input and the path deviation as output is used. The training experiments of an ANN using this dataset showed poor performance in modelling and predicting the path deviations.

Our investigation revealed that the reasons for the bad modelling performance are dynamic forces and the resulting deflection of the robot's structure.

This effect becomes even more apparent with increasing the speed of the robot. Therefore, it is evident that the dynamic behaviour of the robot has a large influence on the robot's path deviations.

Unlike a simple feed-forward approach, handling of time series and sequential data usually requires a recurrent network or long-term short-term memory (LSTM) network architecture [5]. This type of ANN poses a very challenging task with respect to the implementation on a PLC.

The training data for the ANN is therefore extended by dynamic and time-related data sets in place of using an LSTM Network. For this purpose, an investigation with two datasets and two neural network architectures is conducted.

The dataset for the first network contains the robot's position, velocity and acceleration. As shown in Fig. 5, it contains an input layer with 9 neurons and linear activation function. The first input layer is followed by two hidden dense layers with 30 neurons each and bias neurons in the first hidden layer. The neurons in the hidden layers have ReLu activation functions. For the prediction of the robot path error in x-, y- and z-direction the output layer contains 3 neurons, with linear activation functions.

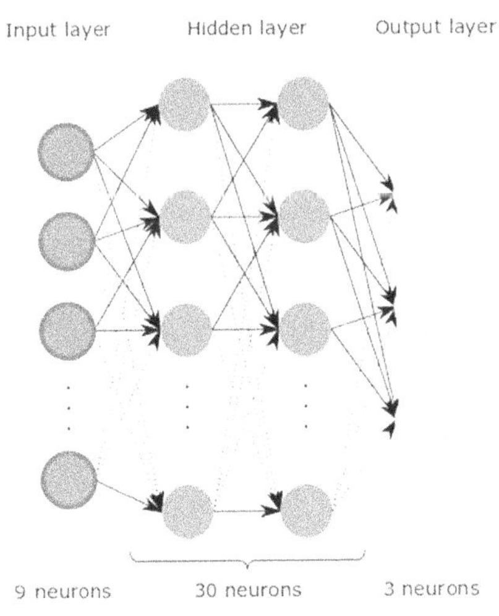

Fig. 5. Network 1 works with dynamic input variables of the target position, velocity and acceleration at the respective time step. It is assembled of an input layer with 9 neurons, followed by two dense layers with 30 neurons each and an output layer with 3 neurons. The hidden layer neurons have ReLu activation functions while the input and output neurons contain linear activation functions.

The second networks dataset consists of the current- and past positions of the robot. Therefore, the second network, shown in Fig. 6, uses the time steps of the current target position and 9 past time steps, each at intervals of 5 ms.

The resulting input layer has 3×10 input neurons with linear activation functions. It is followed by a single hidden layer with 30 neurons, with ReLu function and a bias neurons. The output layer is the same with 3 neurons and linear activation functions. Thus, the current robot position error is predicted by the network from the last 9 position observations.

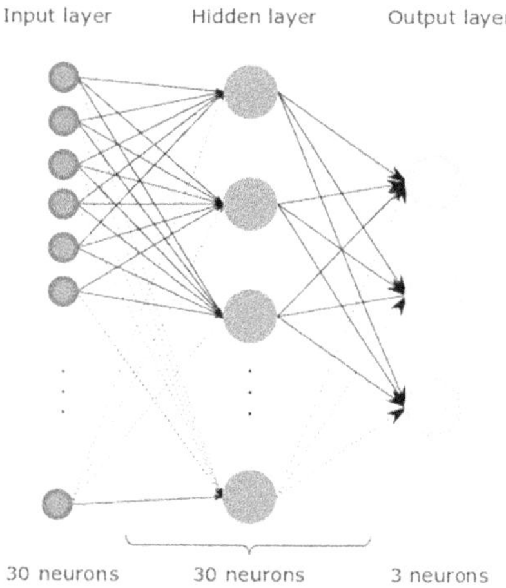

Fig. 6. Network 2 has an input layer of 30 neurons which takes the current target position and 9 past time steps. It is followed by one dense layer with 30 neurons and ReLu activation function. The output layer contains 3 neurons. Input and output neurons have linear activation functions.

The training of both networks is performed with an Adam optimizer. For the regression problem a mean squared error (mse) loss is applied with metrics of mean absolute percentage error (mape) and mean absolute error (mae).

6. Numeric Results

The ANN models have been trained with recoded measurements taken from the robot during operation.

Network one showed fast learning progress without signs of over-fitting. As shown in Fig. 7, the learning process length is 50 epochs. The data set consists of approximately 300000 measurements. The ratio between the training and testing dataset was 25 %. After the training, the performance of each network is evaluated with an unknown dataset. The result for network one can be seen in Fig. 8.

In general, network two shows a larger validation loss compared to network one. This can be attributed to the bigger amount of input data as the input layer takes 9 past time steps. A convergence of a validation loss of 0.0009 is reached after 100 epochs as shown in Fig. 9. Training and validation data are the same as mentioned for network one.

Both networks show a similar performance in the qualitative and quantitative modelling of the robots path error. Both model the path error with an average deviation from the measured path error of 6 %. Therefore the dynamic values velocity and acceleration, as well as past time steps, are suitable to model path errors in robotics due to inertia.

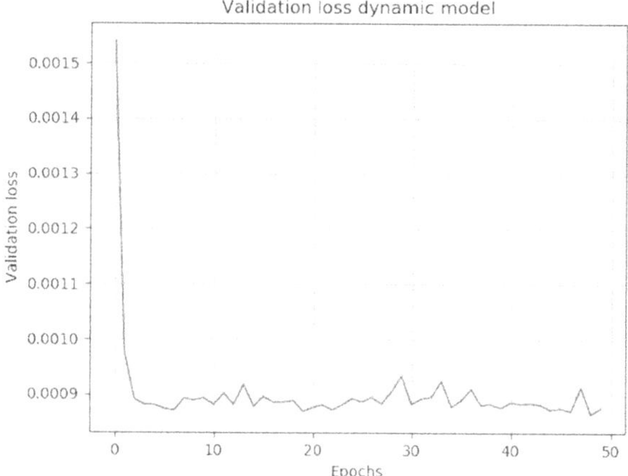

Fig. 7. Validation loss of network 1 with dynamic state variables.

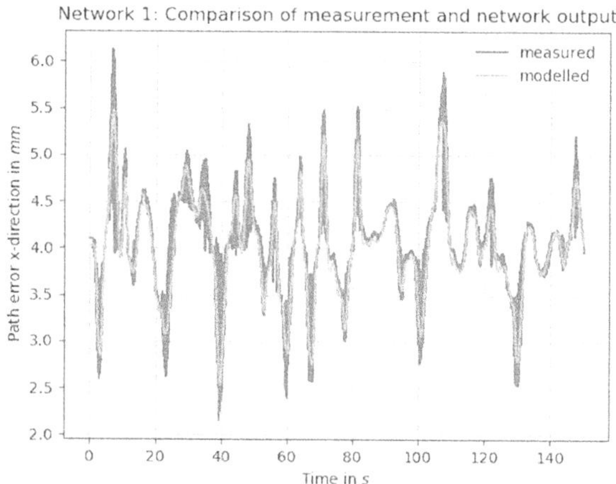

Fig. 8. Comparison of measured path deviation in x-direction to the response of network one with dynamic variables.

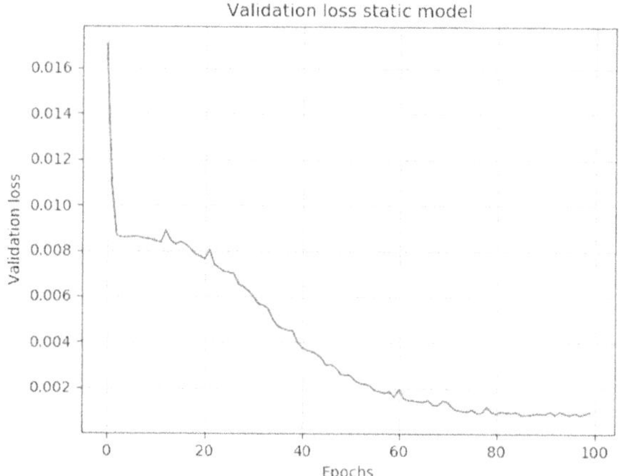

Fig. 9. Validation loss of network 1 with static time steps.

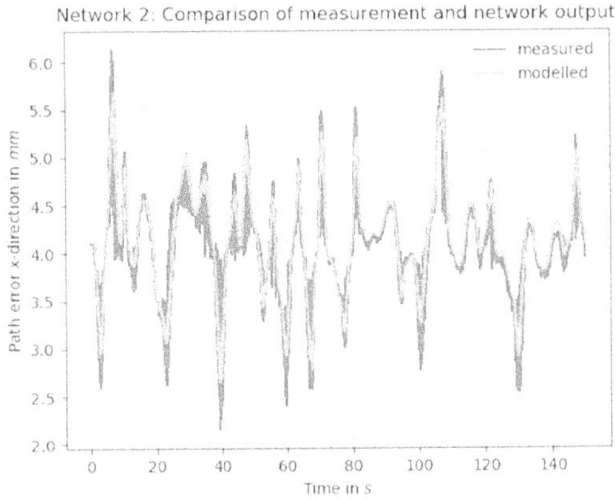

Fig. 10. Comparison of measured path deviation in x-direction to the response of network two with time steps.

7. Conclusions and Further Work

The results show that neural networks are able to describe path errors of robots with high accuracy. Therefore, they have the potential to increase the accuracy of robots.

Since both proposed neural network architectures perform similarly, further investigations are required to decide which architecture is suited best. For such investigations, it makes sense to use the Keras tuner [6] and challenging paths with high accelerations resulting in high path deviations. If, after further investigation, there is still no clearly better approach, it is suggested to implement the network with the time steps, since this approach does not require any additional differentiation in the PLC, which facilitates implementation.

All the presented networks have been trained with a constant robot loading. In real robot applications like pick and place tasks and even more challenging tasks like milling there are significantly varying process loads. Similar to the dynamic forces due to the robot's inertia, it is expected that the networks needs to be extended in order to model the additional process load. Therefore, it is suggested to use a force and a torque sensor between the robot and the end-effector and to use the data as additional inputs for the network.

Once the performance of the network is satisfactory, the next step is to implement the neural network on the PLC and investigate the improvement in path accuracy in the application of industrial robot.

References

[1]. Leistungskenngrößen und zugehörige Prüfmethoden hd., *Europäisches Komitee für Normung*, Berlin, 1998.

[2]. O. Rösch, Steigerung der Arbeitsgenauigkeit bei der Fräsbearbeitung metallischer Werkstoffe mit Industrierobotern, *Herbert Utz Verlag*, 2015.

[3]. B. Karlik, S. Aydin, An improved approach to the solution of inverse kinematics problems for robot manipulators, *Engineering Applications of Artificial Intelligence*, Vol. 13, 2000, pp. 159-164.

[4]. K. Wendt, M. Franke, F. Härtig, Measuring large 3D structures using four portable tracking laser interferometers, *Measurement*, Vol. 45, 2012, pp. 2339-2345.

[5]. S. Hochreiter, J. Schmidhuber, Long short-term memory, *Neural Computation*, Vol. 9? Issue 8, 1997, pp. 1735-1780.

[6]. F. Chollet, et.al., Keras, https://keras.io

(026)

Exposure Time Simulation Thanks to the LIP (Logarithmic Image Processing) Model with Noise Reduction by Deep Convolutional Neural Networks

M. Carré [1] **and M. Jourlin** [2]
[1] NT2I Company, 20 rue du Pr Lauras, 42000 Saint-Etienne, France
[2] Hubert Curien Laboratory, 18, rue du Pr Lauras, 42000 Saint-Etienne, France
E-mails: m.carre@nt2i.fr, michel.jourlin@univ-st-etienne.fr

Summary: The LIP (Logarithmic Image Processing) model is recognized as an efficient framework to process images acquired in transmitted and reflected light, and to take into account the human visual system. An important property of the LIP model consists of simulating exposure time variations. Applied to very low light images, our LIP algorithms enhance not only the signal, but also the noise and lead to quantized grey levels. In order to overcome such a drawback, we perform a noise reduction based on deep convolutional neural networks.

Keywords: LIP model, Exposure time simulation, Low light images, Noise reduction, Deep convolutional neural networks.

1. Context of the Paper

The LIP framework ([1-3], and more recently [4]) was first dedicated to images acquired in transmission. If f and g represent grey level images defined on a same spatial support D, the Transmittance Law permits to define:

- The addition $f \triangle\!\!\!\!\!+\, g$ of two images, according to:

$$f \triangle\!\!\!\!\!+\, g = f + g - \frac{f.g}{M} \tag{1}$$

- The product $\lambda \triangle\!\!\!\!\!\times\, f$ of f by a real number λ, according to:

$$\lambda \triangle\!\!\!\!\!\times\, f = M - M(1 - \frac{f}{M})^{\lambda} \tag{2}$$

These two laws possess strong mathematical properties giving a structure of Vector Space to the set I(D, [0,M[) of images defined on D with values in the grey scale [0,M[.

Remark: Brailean ([5]) demonstrated that the Model is consistent with Human Vision, which means that the LIP tools are successfully applicable to images acquired in reflection, particularly when we want to interpret those images as a human eye would do.

One of the most significant properties of the LIP model consists of simulating exposure time variations ([6]). Fig. 2 presents an example of such a simulation.

Moreover, the LIP Model has been extended to Color Images ([7]), for which the exposure time simulation remains true ([8]).

2. Problem: Noise and Quantization

When we apply the exposure time simulation to low-light images in order to enhance them, we classically observe that the algorithm enhances not only the signal, but also the noise.

On Fig. 2, we apply on a sequence of images acquired at different exposure times (Fig. 1) a brightness stabilization algorithm based on LIP exposure time simulation ([9]). In this example, each image is stabilized to a reference brightness corresponding to the image acquired with the higher exposure time, here 50 ms. Obviously, the noise level increases as the exposure time decreases.

Fig. 1. Images acquired at different exposure time, from left to right: 0.75 ms, 2.22 ms, 6.67 ms, 20 ms, 50 ms.

Fig. 2. LIP stabilization applied on Fig. 1 images.

Such a problem damages the quality of the enhanced image and necessitates the application of a noise filtering more or less adapted to the considered class of images.

Another issue concerns the quantization of the grey level scale. Since the original dark image presents a compressed histogram, our enhancement leads to a quantized histogram (Fig. 2). In the case of strong exposure time correction, this quantization can be visible by a human observer.

3. Proposed Solution

To overcome those drawbacks, we decided to apply a Deep Learning approach, according to [10]. This approach consists in restoring noisy images by training a convolutional neural network. The proposed network is based on a U-network shape ([11]) and the particularity of [10] lies in the use of only corrupted couples of images in the training phase, instead of classical couples constituted of a noisy image and a clean one.

In our situation, this particularity greatly facilitates the preparation of images databases required in machine learning methods. Generating thousands of noisy/clean images would require an acquisition system able to switch quickly between two exposure times (a low exposure time for the noisy image, and a higher one for the clean target). Creating sequences of noisy images acquired in the same conditions is much easier and makes the solution adaptable to many acquisition systems.

In order to process enhanced images presenting different noise intensities as described in Fig. 2, we train the network with images acquired under different brightness conditions, with variable exposure times.

Fig. 3 shows the application of the trained network on the images of Fig. 2. In each situation, the noise has been significantly reduced.

In our case, the benefits of the network are twofold: as expected the noisy signal is cleaner, and in addition, the quantization of the signal is corrected. Indeed, due to the last layer of the neural network presenting a linear activation, the output signals get continuous values, while every trained ones were quantized. This point appears clearly on the histograms of Fig. 2 and Fig. 3.

Fig. 3. Noise and quantization correction on Fig. 2 images.

4. Applications

The proposed solution, LIP brightness stabilization and noise reduction with DCNN, can be directly applied to color images by learning RGB noisy images. An example is shown on Fig. 4.

The adaptation of the network to different noise intensities allows its application on images enhanced by another LIP algorithm about brightness spatial stabilization ([9]). This algorithm consists of simulating local variations of exposure time in order to process high dynamic images. The brightness is locally adjusted in order to enhance only the dark areas. This local correction leads to different noise intensities within a single image. Since the network has been trained under different brightness conditions, its application in this situation is well adapted (Fig. 5).

Fig. 4. Application on a color image, top left: low exposure acquisition (2 ms), top right: higher exposure acquisition (50 ms), bottom left: LIP stabilization applied on the low exposure image, bottom right: noise reduction applied on the enhanced image.

Fig. 5. Brightness spatial stabilization, top left: low exposure acquisition (5 ms), top right: higher exposure exposition (50 ms) leading to burned areas, bottom left: LIP local stabilization applied on the low exposure image, bottom right: noise reduction applied on the enhanced image.

Other low light imaging applications can be processed by the proposed solution. For example, if we plan to acquire images of moving objects using standard exposure times, we will get blurred results. This is regularly the case for sports meetings, traffic surveillance and for industrial control when objects are transported by means of a conveyor. In such situations, the solution to acquire clear images consists of drastically reducing the exposure time, which produces low-light images.

We have already mentioned ([8]) the ability of the LIP Model to enhance such images. Nevertheless, at this time we had not applied the denoising step.

Considering the efficiency of the LIP/DCNN solution, we plan to write an extended paper dedicated to this subject in a near future.

References

[1]. M. Jourlin, J.-C. Pinoli, Logarithmic Image Processing, *Acta Stereologica*, Vol. 6, Issue 3, 1987, pp. 651-656.

[2]. M. Jourlin, J.-C. Pinoli, A model for Logarithmic Image Processing, *Journal of Microscopy*, Vol. 149, Issue 1, 1988, pp. 21-35.

[3]. M. Jourlin, J.-C. Pinoli, Logarithmic Image Processing: The mathematical and physical framework for the representation and processing of transmitted images, *Advances in Imaging and Electron Physics*, Vol. 115, 2001, pp. 129-196.

[4]. M. Jourlin, Logarithmic Image Processing: Theory and Applications, *Advances in Imaging and Electron Physics*, Vol. 195, *Elsevier*, 2016.

[5]. J. Brailean, B. Sullivan, C. Chen, M. Giger, Evaluating the EM algorithm for image processing using a human visual fidelity criterion, in *Proceedings of the International Conference on Acoustics, Speech, and Signal Processing (ICASSP'91),* Vol. 4, 1991, pp. 2957-2960.

[6]. M. Carre, M. Jourlin, LIP operators: Simulating exposure variations to perform algorithms independent of lighting conditions, in *Proceedings of the International Conference on Multimedia Computing and Systems (ICMCS'14)*, 2014, pp. 122-126.

[7]. M. Jourlin, J. Breugnot, F. Itthirad, M. Bouabdellah, B. Closs, Logarithmic image processing for color images, *Advances in Imaging and Electron Physics*, Vol. 168, 2011, pp. 65-108.

[8]. V. Deshayes, P. Guilbert, M. Jourlin, How simulating exposure time variations in the LIP model. Application: moving objects acquisition, in *Proceedings of the 14th International Congress for Stereology and Image Analysis (ICSIA'15)*, 2015.

[9]. M. Carre, M. Jourlin, Brightness spatial stabilization in the LIP framework, in *Proceedings of the 14th International Congress for Stereology and Image Analysis (ICSIA'15)*, 2015.

[10]. J. Lehtinen, J. Munkberg, J. Hasselgren, S. Laine, T. Karras, M. Aittala, T. Aila, Noise2Noise: Learning image restoration without CleanData, in *Proceedings of the 35th International Conference on Machine Learning (ICML'18),* Stockholm, Sweden, Vol. 80, 2018, pp. 2965-2974.

[11]. O. Ronneberger, P. Fischer, T. Brox, U-net: Convolutional networks for biomedical image segmentation, *Medical Image Computing and Computer-Assisted Intervention (MICCAI*), Vol. 9351, 2015, pp. 234-241.

(027)

Low Cost Quality Metric for DCT Domain

G. Spampinato, A. Bruna, A. Buemi and G. Messina
ST Microelectronics, System Research and Innovation, Stradale Primosole, 50, 95121, Catania, Italy
E-mails: {giuseppe.spampinato, arcangelo.bruna, antonio.buemi, giuseppe.messina}@st.com

Summary: Digital video sequences may lead to visible degradation due to blur, commonly caused by the object motion, camera shake or out of focus. To avoid this kind of distortion, also due to video compression, quality metrics for measuring sharpness are important to suppress worst images, to obtain better looking video for the final user. In this paper, we present a low cost DCT-based single step algorithm, which requires no additional memory, so it is suitable for real time processing. It is a simple but robust method and it obtains similar visual results compared to more complicated algorithm (also not DCT-based). Moreover, the measure proposed takes into consideration not only blurring, but also other visual quality attributes, like brightness and orientation.

Keywords: Discrete cosine transform, Image quality, Blurring, Sharpness.

1. Introduction

Image based algorithms performances usually depend on the quality of the processed shot. When sequences of images are acquired by a generic device (e.g. digital still camera, mobile phone, smart glasses, etc.), it is important to take the best one to obtain a more pleasant shot and to help further steps (video quality post-processing, classification, etc.). One of the most unpleasant artefact for final user is the blurring, which affects salient features like contours and results in a drastic quality degradation.

Moreover, in low memory devices, if the video has to be stored too, it is important to acquire directly compressed images to reduce memory occupancy. Almost all compression algorithms (for both video and still images) use Discrete Cosine Transform (DCT). We propose a quality metrics working in the DCT domain. It allows selecting the best shot in a burst of frames. In this field, different quality measures have been proposed: exponential probability density function [1], scale tree with sub-band decomposition [2], non-linear operation [3], average and standard deviation [4].

The proposed algorithm is partially inspired by a two-steps DCT algorithm [5]. Our contribution consists in reducing memory requirements (histogram is not more needed) and reducing computation time, reaching at the same time better results.

2. Proposed Algorithm

The proposed DCT based algorithm can be inserted before or after the Quantizer step of the standard JPEG. At the end of the encoding process, the proposed measures are available to make proper decisions. Our solution is applied just on Luma *DC* and *AC* coefficients of all 8×8 DCT blocks of the whole image. Position of *DC* coefficient and indexes of *AC* coefficients in each block are indicated in Table 1.

Table 1. Indexes of AC coefficients.

DC	1	2	3	4	5	6	7
8	9	10	11	12	13	14	15
16	17	18	19	20	21	22	23
24	25	26	27	28	29	30	31
32	33	34	35	36	37	38	39
40	41	42	43	44	45	46	47
48	49	50	51	52	53	54	55
56	57	58	59	60	61	62	63

The algorithm calculates efficiently (i.e., in a single step) several quality measures for each 8×8 block of the whole image:

$$OQ = OQ + \sum_{i=1}^{63} w_i : (\mathrm{AC(i)} \neq 0), \quad (1)$$

$$DC\_mean = DC\_mean + DC, \quad (2)$$

$$HQ = HQ + \sum_{i=1}^{7} w_i : (\mathrm{AC(i)} \neq 0), \quad (3)$$

$$VQ = VQ + \sum_{i=8}^{56\,(step=8)} w_i : (\mathrm{AC(i)} \neq 0), \quad (4)$$

where *OQ* is the overall quality (higher values means better quality); *DC_mean* (at the end divided by the number of blocks) is the mean of DC coefficients of the whole image (values near to central value e. g. 128 means better quality); *HQ* is the horizontal quality and *VQ* is the vertical quality (higher values means better quality); w_i are weights as indicated in Table 2.

It is easy to note that the system is really fast and no extra memory is required: just seven weights (w_i) are required. A good choice for them, experimentally validated, is the following:

$$w_i = 2^{i-1}, i = 1..7 \quad (5)$$

Table 2. Weights used for AC coefficients.

	w1	w2	w3	w4	w5	w6	w7
w1	w1	w2	w3	w4	w5	w6	w7
w2	w2	w2	w3	w4	w5	w6	w7
w3	w3	w3	w3	w4	w5	w6	w7
w4	w4	w4	w4	w4	w5	w6	w7
w5	w5	w5	w5	w5	w5	w6	w7
w6	w6	w6	w6	w6	w6	w6	w7
w7	w7	w7	w7	w7	w7	w7	w7

The proposed quality measures are incrementally considered. The first measure *OQ* is considered. If the two *OQ* measures are similar, the second measure *DC_mean* is considered. If two *DC_mean* measures are similar, the best *HQ* and *VQ* measures are considered. In this way, best quality image is chosen between two or more images.

3. Experimental Results

Lots of tests have been executed in different conditions: simulated sequences with increasing blurring, brightness and rotation; real sequences, acquired with smart glasses. In all tested conditions the proposed algorithm reaches good performances.
An example is shown in Fig. 1 and Fig. 2. As reference, we choose *FSWM* [6], pixel-based algorithm using a weighted median 5×5 filter, so computational heavier than the proposed one. The best two images of a real sequence are well detected by *FSWM* and the *proposed* algorithm through the two peaks (frames 4 and 14), while *Prior Art* algorithm [5] does not distinguish well the two best images and the frame 14 is not chosen.

4. Conclusions

A really fast single-step DCT-based quality metric has been developed, so easily used for real-time processing in low cost devices, with the characteristic to not use any further memory for the whole processing. In addition, apart to take into consideration the more relevant effect of blurring, the proposed solution considers also other important visual attributes, that is brightness and orientation of the pictures. It achieves significant improvements in a subjective manner compared to other simple DCT-based metrics and it reaches similar results compared to a good reference (not DCT domain) metric.

References

[1]. F. Kerouh, D. Ziou, A. Serir, A multiresolution DCT-based blind blur quality measure, in *Proceedings of the International Conference on Image Processing Theory, Tools and Applications (IPTA'17)*, 2017, pp. 1-6.

[2]. Z. Zhang, Y. Liu, X. Tan, M. Zhang, Robust sharpness metrics using reorganized DCT coefficients for auto-focus application, in *Proceedings of the Asian Conference on Computer Vision (ACCV'14)*, 2014, pp. 172-187

[3]. S. Jiao, H. Qi, W. Lin, No-reference perceptual image sharpness index using normalized DCT-based representation, in *Proceedings of the 7th International Symposium on Computational Intelligence and Design (ISCID'14)*, 2014, pp. 150-153.

[4]. V. Tuba, M. Beko, DCT based algorithm for blurred regions determination in digital images, in *Proceedings of the 23rd Telecommunications Forum Telfor (TELFOR'15)*, 2015, pp. 815-818.

[5]. X. Marichal, W. Y. Ma, H. J. Zhang, Blur determination in the compressed domain using DCT information, in *Proceedings of the IEEE International Conference on Image Processing*, Vol. 2, 1999, pp. 386-390.

[6]. K. Choi, J. Lee, S. Ko, New autofocusing technique using the frequency selective weighted median filter for video cameras, *IEEE Transactions On Consumer Electronics*, Vol. 45, Issue 3, 1999, pp. 820-827.

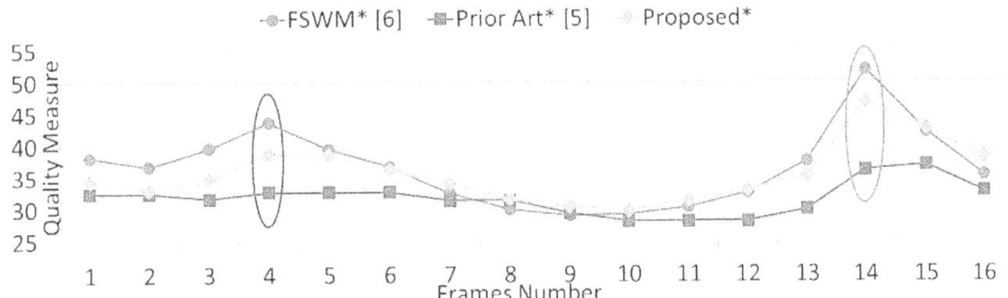

Fig. 1. Normalized output of reference (FSWM), Prior Art and proposed quality measures for images taken by smart glasses.

Fig. 2. Frames number 13, 14 and 15 of the analized sequence of images taken by smart glasses.

(028)

Modifying Gradient of a Loss Function to Tackle Class Imbalance

I. Kilbas [1], **R. Paringer** [1,2], **N. Ilyasova** [1,2] **and A. Kupriyanov** [1,2]
[1] Samara National Research University, Moskovskoye Shosse, 34, 443086, Samara, Russia
[2] IPSI RAS – Branch of the FSRC "Crystallography and Photonics" RAS, Molodogbardeyskaya 151, 443001, Samara, Russia
Tel.: + 79021540443
E-mail: whitemarsstudios@gmail.com

Summary: Advances in the field of deep neural networks led to highly accurate object detectors. Yet, training such object detectors comes with several challenges. The performance of the deep learning models relies not only on the network architecture but also on the choice of training objective. Cross-entropy loss found to be the most common choice for the classification problem. But its main downside is that it can not handle data with huge class imbalance which arises during training of object detectors. In order to improve this issue, the Focal loss has been proposed. In this paper we investigate the reasons behind its good performance. We find several properties of the Focal loss' gradient and apply them to modify the gradient of the cross-entropy loss. We propose new loss functions and provide an experimental evidence of their validity.

Keywords: Convolutional network, Computer vision, Object recognition, Class imbalance, Focal loss, Object detection, Single shot detector.

1. Introduction

Development of deep convolutional neural networks has led to a series of breakthroughs in the object detection field [1-5]. Though the accuracy of the models is high, it is still a huge challenge to train such neural networks [7].

For the present there are two types of object detection models: one stage and two stage detectors. Two stage detectors [1-3] are based on region proposal approach. In this approach the first neural network extracts regions of interest from the input image which are then classified by a pretrained convolutional neural network. In contrast, one stage detectors [4, 5] already have a default set of possible object locations (usually called anchors) that are being classified in one run.

1.1. Class Imbalance

In both models the training data is inherently unbalanced since most of the object locations belong to the class of background. Huge class imbalance leads to pure performance or even divergence of the training procedure. Several approaches were proposed to tackle the class imbalance: OHEM (Online Hard Example Mining) [6], adaptive loss function [8].

Hard examples are the image locations that have objects, easy examples are the image locations that do not have any object. In OHEM the number of easy examples is manually controlled during training. This allows the network to concentrate on the hard example and learn useful representations.

The authors of [8] proposed the focal loss, an adaptive loss function. An important feature of this loss is that its value becomes very small for well classified examples ($p > 0.5$). Thus, at certain point the loss for the easy example becomes smaller than the loss for the hard examples and the network starts to focus on the hard ones.

In this paper we investigate the focal loss and try to answer the question why the focal loss is superior to the vanilla cross-entropy in cases with class imbalance. We find several properties of its gradient and propose new loss functions that follow these properties. Performance of the proposed loss functions is shown experimentally.

2. Gradient Scale Term

2.1. Training Objective

The following reasoning considers Single Shot Multibox Detector [5]. Since the detector performs classification of the anchors and regression of the coordinates of the objects in these anchors the training objective is composed of two terms: the classification loss and the localization loss.

$$Objective = CL + \lambda * LL, \tag{1}$$

where CL is the classification loss, λ is the hyperparameter and LL is the localization loss.

The objective loss is then minimized using the gradient descent algorithm [9]. Thus, the behavior of the training process is highly dependent on the form of the gradient of the training objective.

2.2. Classification Loss Gradient

Classification result is usually formed by the softmax function. The errornes of the result is then measured with the cross-entropy loss or the focal loss:

$$CEL = -\log(p), \quad (2)$$

$$FL = -(1-p)^{\gamma}\log(p), \quad (3)$$

where p is the softmax output, CEL is the cross-entropy loss, FL is the focal loss and γ is the hyperparameter.

In general the gradient of the classification loss is

$$\frac{dCL}{dW} = \frac{dCL}{dp}\frac{dp}{dW}, \quad (4)$$

where W is the weights of the object detector and p is the softmax output.

The second term in the formula (4) does not depend on the loss function and always remains the same. Thus, the first term fully defines the behavior of the training procedure. It will be referred later as the gradient scale term (GST).

2.3. Gradient Scale Term of the Focal Loss and Cross-entropy Loss

GSTs of the focal loss and the cross-entropy loss are

$$\frac{dFL}{dp} = \gamma(1-p)^{\gamma-1}\log(p) - \frac{(1-p)^{\gamma}}{p}, \quad (5)$$

$$\frac{dCEL}{dp} = -\frac{1}{p}, \quad (6)$$

GST of the focal loss has the following properties:

- Tends to zero as p tends to one;
- Increase monotonically as p tends to zero.

The GTS of the focal loss in comparison to the GTS of the cross-entropy loss is shown in the Fig. 1.

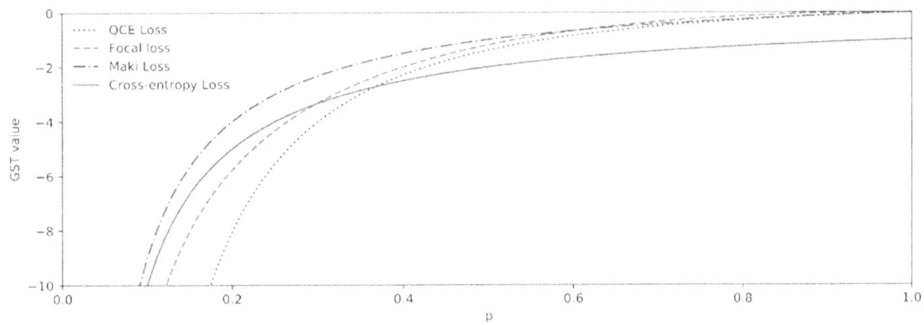

Fig. 1. GST value of the QCE loss, the focal loss, the maki loss and the cross-entropy loss. Values of the focal loss are computed for $\gamma = 2.0$, values of the maki loss are computed for $\gamma = 1$.

3. Modifying GST of the Cross-entropy Loss

3.1. Maki Loss

GST of the cross-entropy loss does not follow the first property. We propose a simple modification that solves this issue:

$$\frac{dCEL}{dp} = -\frac{1}{p} + 1 = -\frac{1-p}{p} \quad (7)$$

We generalize this new GST as

$$\frac{dCEL}{dp} = -\frac{(1-p)^{\gamma}}{p} \quad (8)$$

Loss function that corresponds to this GST is called maki loss and is written as

$$ML = -(\log(p) + \sum_{k=1}^{\gamma}\frac{C_{\gamma}^{k}(-p)^{k}}{k} - \\ - \sum_{k=1}^{\gamma}\frac{C_{\gamma}^{k}(-1)^{k}}{k}), \quad (9)$$

where γ is the natural number and C_{γ}^{k} is the binomial coefficient.

3.2. Quadratic Cross-entropy Loss

Another simple modification for the cross-entropy's GST can be

$$\frac{dCEL}{dp} = \frac{\log(p)}{p} \quad (10)$$

With such formulation this expression can be easily integrated as

$$QCE = \frac{\log^{2}(p)}{2} \quad (11)$$

This new loss function is called quadratic cross-entropy (QCE) loss.

The values of all the GSTs for all the losses are shown in the Fig. 1.

3.3. Implementation Details

All the losses were implemented in the MakiFlow machine learning framework [10]. Following [5] values of the maki loss, the focal loss and the cross-entropy loss are normalized by the number of hard examples in the batch. In contrast, value of the

QCE loss is normalized by the total number of examples in the batch, i.e. the mean value is taken. It was decided to implement this loss in a way to make it simple not only analytically, but in the implementation regard as well.

4. Experiment

A single shot detector was trained using the proposed losses in order to assess them. The model was built using the MakiFlow framework [10]. Pretrained MobileNetV2 was used as a feature extractor. The object detector was trained and tested on the PascalVOC2007 and the PascalVOC2012 datasets. The accuracy during training was measured using a separate test set and is shown in the Fig. 2.

4.1. Training Details

The hyperparameters such as learning rate, γ and λ were chosen individually for each of the loss functions. The object detector was trained for 35000 iterations on each loss. The batch size was set to 128. The training was done using the Adam optimizer.

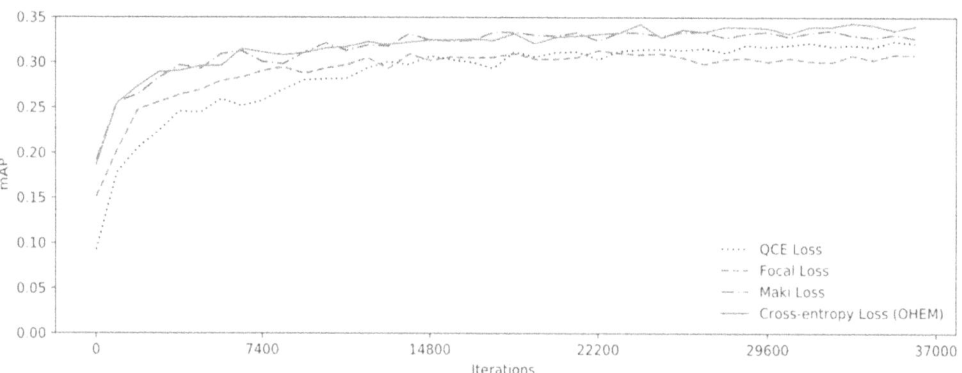

Fig. 2. Test mAP value during training.

4.2. Data Preparation

Each image in the datasets was resized to the size of 300 by 300 pixels. The pixel values were normalized by division by 255. In order to increase the amount of the training data it was augmented in several ways: Gaussian noise, horizontal and vertical flip, contrast and brightness adjustments.

5. Discussion of the Results

Results of the experiment show that by modifying GST of the cross-entropy according to the focal loss' GST we can make it immune to the class imbalance problem.

It can be seen that the QCE loss has a slower convergence in the beginning compare to other losses. We relate it to the way of the normalization of the loss value during training. Even with such implementation the loss produces comparable results.

In addition, the proposed losses are not constrained by training only the object detectors and therefore can be applied to other problems where a severe class imbalance appears.

6. Conclusions

In this paper we investigated the reasons behind the good performance of the focal loss. We found several properties of the focal loss gradient and proposed new QCE loss and maki loss that follow these properties. We showed experimentally that the proposed losses are able to tackle the class imbalance problem. The proposed losses can be applied to problems with severe class imbalance, such as training an object detector or a fully convolutional neural network for biomedical image segmentation.

Acknowledgements

The research was carried out within the state assignment theme FSSS-2020-0017, was partly financially supported by the Russian Foundation for Basic Research under grant # 19-29-01135.

References

[1]. R. Girshick, J. Donahue, T. Darrell, J. Malik, Rich feature hierarchies for accurate object detection and semantic segmentation, in *Proceedings of the IEEE Conference on Computer Vision and Pattern Recognition (CVPR'14)*, 2014, pp. 580-587.

[2]. R. Girshick, Fast R-CNN, in *Proceedings of the IEEE International Conference on Computer Vision (ICCV'15)*, 2015, pp. 1440-1448

[3]. S. Ren, K. He, R. Girshick, J. Sun, Faster R-CNN: Towards real-time object detection with region proposal networks, *Advances in Neural Information Processing Systems*, 2015, pp. 91-99.

[4]. J. Redmon, S. Divvala, R. Girshick, A. Farhadi, You only look once: Unified, real-time object detection, in *Proceedings of the IEEE Conference on Computer Vision and Pattern Recognition (CVPR'16)*, 2016, pp. 779-788.

[5]. W. Liu, D. Anguelov, D. Erhan, C. Szegedy, S. Reed, C. Y. Fu, A. C. Berg, SSD: Single shot multibox detector, in *Proceedings of the European Conference on Computer Vision (ECCV'16)*, 2016, pp. 21-37.

[6]. A. Shrivastava, A. Gupta, R. Girshick, Training region-based object detectors with online hard example mining, in *Proceedings of the IEEE Conference on Computer Vision and Pattern Recognition (CVPR'16)*, 2016, pp. 761-769.

[7]. R. Zhu, S. Zhang, X. Wang, L. Wen, H. Shi, L. Bo, T. Mei, ScratchDet: Training single-shot object detectors from scratch, in *Proceedings of the IEEE International Conference on Computer Vision (ICCV'19)*, 2019, pp. 2268-2277.

[8]. T. Y. Lin, P. Goyal, R. Girshick, K. He, P. Dollár, Focal loss for dense object detection, in *Proceedings of the IEEE International Conference on Computer Vision (ICCV'17)*, 2017, pp. 2980-2988.

[9]. S. Ruder, An overview of gradient descent optimization algorithms, https://arxiv.org/pdf/1609.04747.pdf

[10]. MakiFlow Machine Learning Framework, GitHub, https://github.com/MakiResearchTeam/MakiFlow

(029)

Algorithm for Data Balancing Based on Gradient Descent

A. V. Mukhin [1], **I. A. Kilbas** [1], **R. A. Paringer** [1,2], **N. Yu. Ilyasova** [1,2] **and A. V. Kupriyanov** [1,2]
[1] Samara National Research University, Moskovskoye Shosse, 34, 443086, Samara, Russia
[2] IPSI RAS – Branch of the FSRC "Crystallography and Photonics" RAS, Molodogbardeyskaya 151, 443001, Samara, Russia
Tel.: + 79272151817
E-mail: artemmukhinssau@gmail.com

Summary: Deep learning models are very sensible to the data imbalance. Predominance of some classes in the data during training makes neural network inaccurate on the rare classes. In this paper we propose an algorithm for data balancing to address this issue. One of the features of the proposed algorithm is that it allows to balance the data which data points contain multiple classes. It was formulated as the multiclass data balancing problem. We have experimentally shown the influence of the data balancing by the proposed algorithm on the convolutional neural network accuracy built for biomedical image segmentation. Recommendations on how to use the proposed algorithm are also formulated.

Keywords: Gradient descent, Unbalanced data, Convolution, Neural networks, Convolutional network, Fundus, Biomedical data, Semantic segmentation.

1. Introduction

The semantic segmentation problem has become very relevant nowadays [1, 2]. The most difficult and specific is the biomedical image segmentation [3, 4]. Neural networks found to be the most common approach to solve this problem. Inherently, there is always a class imbalance in the biomedical image segmentation problems [5-7].

The class imbalance is a situation when some of the classes in the data appear more rarely than the others. Due to this problem the classification rate of the rare classes is very low.

The existing data balancing methods [8] can be summarized by two common techniques: the undersampling and the oversampling. In the undersampling the data points that belong to the predominant classes are being removed, in oversampling the data points that belong to the rare classes are being copied.

These techniques can be easily applied to binary problems. However, the data balancing becomes challenging when one data point belongs to multiple classes. Due to this fact copying or deleting any data points leads to change in the distribution of all classes. Consequently, it is very problematic to change the percentage of one class in the dataset without changing the percentages of all the other classes. Let us denote it as the multiclass data balancing problem.

In order to address this issue we have developed a new algorithm for the multiclass data balancing based on the gradient descent.

2. Biomedical Data

The data consists of 115 images of fundus. Each image pixel is labeled by experts into 8 classes: the optic disk (class 1), the macula (class 2), the blood vessels (class 3), the solid exudate (class 4), the soft exudate (class 5), the new coagulates (class 6), the pigmented coagulates (class 7), the retinal hemorrhage (class 8).

Not all of the classes appear on all the images. The classes 6 and 7 are the rarest – they appear in less than 20 % of all the images. The Fig. 1 shows this.

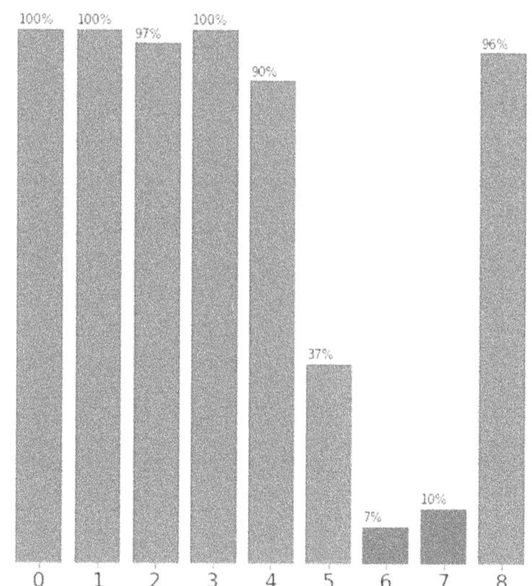

Fig. 1. Percent of images that contains i^{th} class.

3. The Proposed Data Balancing Algorithm

3.1. The Algorithm Definition

The algorithm comes to semiautomatic data balancing using oversampling and undersampling performed by gradient descent.

Each image in the dataset can be described by a vector λ that consists of zeros and ones. This vector is constructed in such way that its ith element is 1 if the corresponding image contains i[th] class and 0 otherwise. Thus, the dataset can be represented by a set of such vectors, let us denote it as Ω.

The sum of all the vectors in the Ω will be denoted as $\sum(\Omega)$. Then, the ith element of this sum equals to the number of the images in the Ω that contain the ith class.

Let π be the distribution vector (or the objective vector). Its ith element equals to the number of images that contain the ith class divided by the total number of images. Let us call these values the default one if they are set according to the dataset. This vector must be set manually because it represents the desired distribution.

The problem formulation: from the vector set Ω create a vector set Ω' such that it satisfies the following condition

$$\frac{\sum|\Omega_i`|}{|\Omega`|} = \pi, \quad (1)$$

where $|\Omega`|$ is a total number of the elements in the $\Omega$`. In other words, the set Ω' consists of vectors λ_i duplicated α_i times.

In order to find the set Ω' we define the following objective function:

$$L = \left|\frac{\sum_i \alpha_i \lambda_i}{\sum_i \alpha_i} - \pi\right|, \quad (2)$$

where λ_i is the unique vectors from the Ω, α_i is the number of copies of the vector λ_i.

We then minimize the defined objective function (2) by changing the α_i parameters (weights) using gradient descent. This procedure allows us to find the solution Ω'.

Unfortunately, it often results in a set with a large number of duplicates that can affect the segmentation accuracy. To address this issue, we have formulated a regularization function. Let us denote ω_i as the number of appearances of the vector λ_i in the Ω. The regularization function is then formulated as

$$RL = \sum_{i=1}^{N}\left(\frac{\omega_i}{\sum_{j=1}^{N}\omega_i} - \frac{\alpha_i}{\sum_{j=1}^{N}\alpha_j}\right)^2 \quad (3)$$

This regularization function prevents the α_i parameters from large changes what results in a more optimal solution with a smaller number of duplicates.

The final objective function is formulated as

$$Objective = L + \gamma RL, \quad (4)$$

where γ is the hyperparameter.

3.2. Applying the Proposed Algorithm

The proposed algorithm was implemented in the MakiFlow framework [9]. This algorithm has several parameters that have to be controlled in order to get the best data balancing result.

A special attention must be paid to the initial values of the distribution vector π. In our experiments values for the rare classes were set to one, for the predominant classes the default values were left. We stop the algorithm when the resulted distribution values for the rare classes were increased by around 10 to 15 percents. This interval may be different for the other datasets. However, we do not recommend to increase the distribution of a certain class by a large amount since it will lead to a big number of duplicates for that class.

In our experiments we investigated two ways of the weights α_i initialization. The first way is to initializate the weights with a single constant value. The second one is to initialize the weights with the ω_i multiplied by some constant θ. Both of them gave us similar results. However, with constant initialization the algorithm convergence is slower and more careful γ regularization parameter tuning is needed. Therefore, we recommend the second way of the weights initialization. In our experiments the θ was set to the numbers greater than 1. It guarantees that all the images from the dataset will be used and also gives the algorithm a margin of freedom to change the weights values.

As for the γ regularization parameter, in our experiments it was set to 0.0004. Since the regularization function values and the objective function values are normalized, the value for the γ used in our experiment must be applicable to other cases.

4. vDice Metric

In order to measure the quality of the multiclass semantic segmentation we generalize the Dice coefficient [10]. This generalized metric is called "vDice". First, the Dice coefficient for each class is calculated. Then, the vDice value is obtained by averaging the individual Dice coefficient values.

5. Experiment

In order to do the image segmentation, we have built and trained a convolutional neural network using the MakiFlow framework [9]. The U-Net [11] neural network was chosen as the base architecture. The Xception-65 [12] pre-trained on the ImageNet dataset [13] was used as the feature extractor. The network was trained using the Adam optimizer [14], with learning rate 8e-3. We used the FocalLoss [15] as the loss functions. The network was trained for 10 epochs, the batch size was set to 8 images.

The significance of the obtained results is provided by cross-validation. Each of the cross-validation sets were balanced separately. An example of the balancing results is shown in the Table 1. We compare our algorithm to oversampling. The distribution of the data balanced with oversampling is shown in the Table 1 as well.

6. Results

The Table 2 shows that training on the data balanced by the proposed algorithm results in a higher Dice values compare to the training on the unbalanced data. In the case of the oversampling the accuracy drops significantly. We relate it to the overfitting on the large number of the duplicates for the rare classes.

In the case of the balancing without regularization a sudden drop in accuracy on the class 5 is observed. Similar to the oversampling, we relate it to the overfitting caused by a large number of the duplicates of this class. In fact, the percentage of this class is even higher than the one in the case of the oversampling.

Table 1. An example of the obtained data distribution.

Class	Without balancing (original)	Balanced by oversampling	Balanced (without regularization)	Balanced (with regularization)
1	100 %	100 %	100 %	100 %
2	97 %	99 %	98 %	98 %
3	100 %	100 %	100 %	100 %
4	90 %	95 %	81 %	93 %
5	37 %	43 %	56 %	36 %
6	7 %	41 %	31 %	16 %
7	10 %	31 %	44 %	20 %
8	96 %	99 %	95 %	97 %

Table 2. Maximum test accuracy values averaged over all the cross-validation sets.

Class	Without balancing	Balanced by oversampling	Balanced (without regularization)	Balanced (with regularization)
1	0.9130	0.7667	0.9198	**0.9266**
2	0.6287	0.4665	**0.7364**	0.7049
3	0.7346	0.6678	0.7416	**0.7425**
4	0.3786	0.2669	0.5639	**0.5892**
5	0.3060	0.2150	0.1899	**0.3132**
6	0.0801	0	0.0857	**0.1031**
7	0.0929	0	0.0895	**0.1808**
8	0.5728	0.5106	0.6182	**0.6491**
vDice	0.4511	0.3060	0.4762	**0.5050**

7. Conclusions

In this paper we proposed a multiclass data balancing algorithm based on the gradient descent. The proposed algorithm is able to tackle the multiclass data balancing problem. In order to assess the proposed algorithm, we used it to balance the data with an extreme class imbalance and trained a convolutional neural network on this data. It is experimentally shown that the data balancing using the algorithm leads to improved accuracy. Considering the results, we can conclude that the proposed algorithm allows to decrease the influence of the data imbalance on the accuracy of a convolutional neural network.

Acknowledgments

The research was carried out within the state assignment theme FSSS-2020-0017, was partly financially supported by the Russian Foundation for Basic Research under grant # 19-29-01135.

References

[1]. R. Girshick, J. Donahue, T. Darrell, J. Malik, Rich feature hierarchies for accurate object detection and semantic segmentation, in *Proceedings of the IEEE Conference on Computer Vision and Pattern Recognition (CVPR'14)*, 2014, pp. 580-587.

[2]. H. Noh, S. Hong, B. Han, Learning deconvolution network for semantic segmentation, in *Proceedings of the IEEE International Conference on Computer Vision (ICCV'15),* 2015, pp. 1520-1528.

[3]. Y. Zhang, L. Yang, J. Chen, M. Fredericksen, D. P. Hughes, D. Z. Chen, Deep adversarial networks for biomedical image segmentation utilizing unannotated images, *Medical Image Computing and Computer-Assisted Intervention – MICCAI*, 2017, pp. 408-416.

[4]. L. Yang, Y. Zhang, J. Chen, S. Zhang, D. Z. Chen, Suggestive annotation: A deep active learning framework for biomedical image segmentation, *Medical Image Computing and Computer-Assisted Intervention – MICCAI,* 2017, pp. 399-407.

[5]. H. Haibo, E. A. Garcia. Learning from imbalanced data, *IEEE Transactions on Knowledge and Data Engineering*, Vol. 21, Issue 9, 2009, pp. 1263-1284.

[6]. M. Mostafizur Rahman, D. N. Davis, Addressing the class imbalance problem in medical datasets, *International Journal of Machine Learning and Computing*, Vol. 3, Issue 2, 2013, pp. 224-228.

[7]. R. Longadge, S. Dongre. Class imbalance problem in data mining review, *ArXiv Preprint*, arXiv:1305.1707, 2013.

[8]. B. W. Yap, K. A. Rani, H. A. A. Rahman, S. Fong, Z. Khairudin, N. N. Abdullah, An application of oversampling, undersampling, bagging and boosting in handling imbalanced datasets, in *Proceedings of the 1st International Conference on Advanced Data and Information Engineering (DaEng'13)*, Singapore, 2013, pp. 13-22.

[9]. Framework MakiFlow, https://github.com/MakiResearchTeam/MakiFlow

[10]. L. R. Dice, Measures of the amount of ecologic association between species, *Ecology*, Vol. 26, Issue 3, 1945, pp. 297-302.

[11]. O. Ronneberger, P. Fischer, T. Brox, U-net: Convolutional networks for biomedical image segmentation, in *Proceedings of the International Conference on Medical Image Computing and Computer-assisted Intervention (MICCAI'15)*, Cham, 2015, pp. 234-241.

[12]. F. Chollet, Xception: Deep learning with depthwise separable convolutions, in *Proceedings of the IEEE Conference on Computer Vision and Pattern Recognition (CVPR'17)*, 2017, pp. 1251-1258.

[13]. O. Russakovsky, J. Deng, H. Su, J. Krause, S. Satheesh, S. Ma, A. C. Berg. Imagenet large scale visual recognition challenge, *International Journal of Computer Vision*, Vol. 115, Issue 3. 2015, pp. 211-252.

[14]. D. P. Kingma, J. Ba, Adam: A method for stochastic optimization, *ArXiv Preprint*, arXiv:1412.6980, 2014.

[15]. T. Y. Lin, P. Goyal, R. Girshick, K. He, P. Dollár, Focal loss for dense object detection, in *Proceedings of the IEEE International Conference on Computer Vision (ICCV'17)*, 2017, pp. 2980-2988.

(031)

Sample-Efficient Covariance Matrix Adaptation Evolutional Strategy via Simulated Rollouts in Neural Networks

H. Xue [1], **S. Böttger** [1], **N. Rottmann** [1], **H. Pandya** [2], **R. Bruder** [1], **G. Neumann** [3], **A. Schweikard** [1] **and E. Rueckert** [1]

[1] University of Luebeck, Institute of Robotics and Cognitive Systems, Luebeck, Germany
[2] University of Lincoln, School of Computer Science, College of Science, Lincoln, UK
[3] Karlsruhe Institute of Technology, Bosch Center for Artificial Intelligence, University of Tuebingen, Germany

Abstract: Gradient-free reinforcement learning algorithms often fail to scale to high dimensions and require a large number of rollouts. In this paper, we propose learning a predictor model that allows simulated rollouts in a rank-based black-box optimizer Covariance Matrix Adaptation Evolutional Strategy (CMA-ES) to achieve higher sample-efficiency. We validated the performance of our new approach on different benchmark functions where our algorithm shows a faster convergence compared to the standard CMA-ES. As a next step, we will evaluate our new algorithm in a robot cup flipping task.

Keywords: CMA-ES, Reinforcement learning, Dynamic movement primitives, Cup flipping

1. Introduction

Reinforcement Learning (RL) has become a popular approach in robotics [2], where an agent learns a policy from scratch based on the cost. In this paper, we investigate an episodic reinforcement learning problem. Several approaches have been proposed. One categorization of these learning approaches is whether it is a gradient-based approaches or a gradient-free approach. Gradient-based approaches are efficient but sensitive to the design of the cost function, whereas gradient-free approaches remained less affected by the cost function design but less efficient. In this work, we focus on one state-of-the-art gradient-free algorithm, Covariance Matrix Adaptation Evolutional Strategy (CMA-ES) [5].

However, one problem of the CMA-ES is its limited performance in high feature dimensions, leading to larger number of rollouts or convergence in local optima. In real robot control tasks, fast convergence to optimal policies is essential [6, 7]. The goal of this paper is to enhance the sample-efficiency of the original CMA-ES algorithm to achieve faster convergence.

In order to enhance of the performance of CMA-ES, several variants have been proposed on top of that. CMA-ES with Active Update [16] adapts the covariance matrix by considering all the offsprings. Some other approaches, e.g., Mirrored Sampling [17], Orthogonal Sampling [18] and Quasi-Gaussian Sampling [21] introduce new ways of proposing offsprings. In Mirrored Sampling, two offsprings are generated symmetrically with one random vector so that the samples spread evenly in the sampling space. Orthogonal Sampling bases itself on Mirrored Sampling, where offspring vectors are orthnormalized by Gram-Schimdt process. In Quasi-Gaussian Sampling, a uniform sampling in unit ball instead of Gaussian distribution is performed so that trust-region effect is enabled. CMA-ES with Increasing Population Size [24] schemes an increasing population size after restart to achieve a more global search. [15] introduces a computationally efficient CMA-ES for large scale optimization by applying Cholesky decomposition into covariance matrix to reduce time and memory. Another work is close relation is [22], where they replaced the original ranking of the candidate solutions in CMA-ES by an approximate ranking using local weighted regression. Some other approaches suggest online selection strategy to search for the best variant fit into the current optimization function [19, 20]. In these approaches, the best variant is chosen via automatic machine learning.

Our approach is categorized as a variant of changing the sampling scheme of the offsprings. However, distinct from the above variants, where some adaptations are only valid under the inherent uni-modal Gaussian distribution, our approach can theoretically be applied to any other black-box optimizers with arbitrary sampling distribution. Moreover, our approach can be easily combined with previous variants. In this work, we validate this idea in one black-box optimizer CMA-ES. The idea arises from the observation that the samples in previous iterations only contribute indirectly to the update of Gaussian covariance and mean, causing low data-efficiency. One way to improve it is to learn a global predictor model based on all of the tested samples. The idea of learning a predictor model and proposing candidate solutions is also closely related to [12], where they address the problem of automatic machine learning by learning a predictor model mapping the current configuration of the algorithm and the dataset feature to the performance score.

The main contributions of this paper are as follows:

(i) Integration of a predictor model into standard CMA-ES for further performance enhancement with no extra efforts on tuning predictor model hyper-parameters.

(ii) Formulation of the cup flipping task as an RL problem, introducing proper objective function considering the arm constraints.

(iii) Evaluation of CMA-ES with active update and Mirrored Sampling on the flipping task.

2. Methods

In this section, we give a brief overview on our new algorithm CMA-ES with Simulated Rollouts (CMA-ES-SR) and the trajectory formulation using dynamic movement primitives.

2.1. Covariance Matrix Adaptation Evolutional Strategies with Simulated Rollouts (CMA-ES-SR)

CMA-ES is an optimizer that searches for the optimal parameters θ_{opt} that minimizes the cost C. In standard CMA-ES, a multi-variate Gaussian distribution is used to characterize the distribution of candidate solutions (samples). In each generation, N_{pop} candidate solutions are drawn such that $\theta_{1:N_{pop}} \sim \mu + \sigma\mathcal{N}(0, \Sigma)$, where the mean vector $\mu \in \mathbb{R}^D$ and D represents the dimension of θ, the step size $\sigma \in \mathbb{R}^1$ determines the degree of exploration and $\Sigma \in \mathbb{R}^{D\times D}$ is the covariance matrix. After each sample is tested, μ, σ and Σ get updated to increase the sampling probability of better candidate solutions. A detailed explanation on the update rule is listed in [25].

However, the standard CMA-ES only uses the previous samples for updating μ, σ and Σ, which is data-inefficient. We suggest integrating a predictor model $\mathcal{M}$, such that

$$\mathcal{M}: \boldsymbol{\theta} \rightarrow C \text{ with } \boldsymbol{\theta} \in \mathbb{R}^D, C \in \mathbb{R}^1. \quad (1)$$

The predictor $\mathcal{M}$ is fit to all the tested candidate solutions in each iteration of CMA-ES. With an available model, more promising candidate solutions can be proposed than random samples, leading to faster convergence [12]. In this paper, we use a multi-layer perceptron as it is a universal function approximator [13]. However, any arbitrary predictor model can be used in general.

The algorithm is shown in Fig. 1. With a learned predictor model, N samples are drawn $\theta_{1:N} \sim \mu + \sigma\mathcal{N}(0, \Sigma)$, with $N \gg N_{pop}$. The best N_{best} solutions are picked according to the model prediction. The final N_{pop} candidate solutions θ_{pop} consist of the N_{best} predictor-proposed solutions θ_{model} and $N_{pop} - N_{best}$ samples θ_{random} randomly drawn from the Gaussian distribution. The value of N_{best} adjusts itself based on the quality of θ_{model} and θ_{random}. Meanwhile, we also design a heuristic determining to which extent we trust the model. It is measured by the quality of θ_{model} and θ_{andom}, where the mean and variance of cost values from both are calculated. We use the optimistic bound similar to the acquisition function in Gaussian process. Since CMA-ES minimizes the objective function, the optimistic bound is calculated by subtracting the variance. When the quality of θ_{model} is better than that of θ_{random}, we trust the model more by incrementing N_{best} by one.

Algorithm 1 CMA-ES-SR

Let N be the number of samples drawn from the current distribution and passed to the model, D be the input dimension. N_{best} is the number of the best samples according to model.

```
Initialize N = min(4096, N_pop^d), N_best = 2, Model M      ▷ Can increase 4096
repeat(for each training episode)
    Draw N samples Θ = {θ_1, ..., θ_n} under current Gaussian distribution
    Pass Θ to M to get the predicted cost (Θ, Ĉ) = {(θ_1, ĉ_1)..., (θ_n, ĉ_n)}
    Take the N_best highest ranking samples Θ_model from Θ based on C
    Θ_model = {θ_1, ..., θ_N_best}
    Take the N_pop − N_best samples Θ_random randomly from Θ \Θ_model
    Θ_pop = Θ_model ∪ Θ_random
    Evaluate Θ_model and Θ_random, get C_pop = C_model ∪ C_random
    Save (Θ_pop, C_pop) to replay buffer B
    Update M for all samples in B
    Compute μ_model, σ_model, μ_random, σ_random from C_model, C_random
    if μ_model − σ_model < μ_random − σ_random then ▷ Trust the predictor more
        N_best+ = 1
    else                                          ▷ Trust the random samples more
        N_best− = 1
    end if
    N_best = max(2, min(N_best, N_pop/2))
    Update all parameters in standard CMA-ES algorithm
until max iteration or target value is reached
return (θ_best, c_best)
```

Fig. 1. CMA-ES-SR algorithm.

Additionally, we set an upper bound for N_{best} to avoid the dominance of the predictor-proposed solutions over the random solutions. Without this upper bound, one potential consequence is that the final candidate solution contains mainly predictor-proposed solutions, i.e., over-trust on the predictor. In the case where the predictor fails to fit the cost landscape but happens to render better solutions than random samples, the algorithm will converge to local optima. For small input dimensions, we also restrict the upper bound of N_{best} and N so that the final set of candidate solutions still follow the Gaussian distribution. Otherwise, the final offsprings can cluster due to the model-fitted landscape especially in low dimension, and no longer follow the original Gaussian distribution. This can cause less exploration and a non-desired update in μ, σ and $\sum$. In high dimensions, N samples remain sparse in space and the final offspring distribution will not be affected by the model-fitted landscape. In short, one advantage of our algorithm is the preservation of the Gaussian distribution on both θ_{model} and θ_{random}. Therefore, it does not affect the Gaussian parameter update.

The hyperparameters of this algorithm are the boundaries of N and N_{best}. Typically, a batch forward is computationally cheap. One can increase the upper bound of N to exceed 4096 if sufficient computation power is available. The lower bound of N (N_{pop}^D) scales exponentially with the number of dimensions D, the base can be chosen as values other than N_{pop} as long as the number of model proposed samples N_{best} remains sparse in low dimensions. The default setting of $N_{pop}/2$ takes into account that half of the offsprings affect the update.

The details of model learning are presented in Supplementary Information, Section 5.

2.2. Dynamic Movement Primitives (DMP)

DMPs is an approach to characterize smooth trajectory profiles of a robot [9-11]. The trajectory expressiveness is achieved by combining a second-order spring-damper system with a learnable external forcing function $f(t)$.

$$\ddot{y} = \alpha(\beta(g - y) - \dot{y}) + f(t), \quad (2)$$

$$f(t) = \frac{\sum_{i=1}^{N} \Psi_i(t) w_i}{\sum_{i=1}^{N} \Psi_i(t)}. \quad (3)$$

The system describes the trajectory in terms of the position y, velocity $\dot{y}$ and acceleration $\ddot{y}$ given the goal position g and the damping coefficients α and β. Forcing function $f(t)$ adds to the trajectory complexity by incorporating a set of weighted sum of N basis functions $\Psi_i(t)$, which can either be stroke-based or rhythmic-based. Variable t denotes the discrete time. For a cup flipping task, we applied stroke-based basis functions

$$\Psi_i(t) = \exp[(t - b_i)^2 / 2h_i]. \quad (4)$$

It is characterized as a set of Gaussian Basis Functions (GBFs) with pre-defined mean b_i and width h_i.

3. Results and Discussion

We evaluated the performance of CMA-ES-SR on different benchmark optimization problems using the same neural network with no additional tuning. In addition, we started to investigate an episodic RL problem [7] where the goal for a 7-DoF robot arm is to flip a cup filled with liquid around 360 degrees while achieving minimal spillage.

3.1. Benchmarks

For the same benchmark function, we are also interested in the performance enhancement of CMA-ES-SR in different input dimensions. And the detailed settings of benchmarks are shown in Supplementary Information, Table 3.

3.2. Performance of CMA-ES-SR on Benchmarks

In order to evaluate the performance of CMA-ES-SR compared to the standard CMA-ES, we quantified the following metrics:
(i) The convergence acceleration rate P;
(ii) The best cost value found within a fixed number of iterations;
(iii) The number of predictor-proposed samples N_{best} w.r.t. the number of generations (iterations) and the number of predictor-proposed samples used for mean and covariance update.

The convergence acceleration P is defined as $(I_1 - I_2)/\min(I_1, I_2)$, where I_1 and I_2 refer to the minimal number of generations required to achieve a certain threshold in cost value respectively from CMA-ES and CMA-ES-SR.

The learning curve of CMA-ES-SR on some exemplary benchmarks are shown in Fig. 2. It can be observed that our algorithm achieves faster convergence than the original CMA-ES in cases where the learned model is capable of generalizing the cost landscape. Under the circumstance where the model fails to learn the cost landscape, it does not affect the overall optimization process and behaves similarly as the standard CMA-ES. This corresponds to the case of Rosenbrock function, where the cost value is of large magnitude. This poses challenges on regression using MLP and the predictor fails to fit or generalize with our current configuration. Nonetheless, a similar learning curve as the standard CMA-ES can still be observed. Detailed statistics on the convergence acceleration rate P on all tested benchmarks are illustrated in Table 1. If one compare the same benchmark of different input dimensions, a consistent performance boost with increasing input dimension can be observed on average.

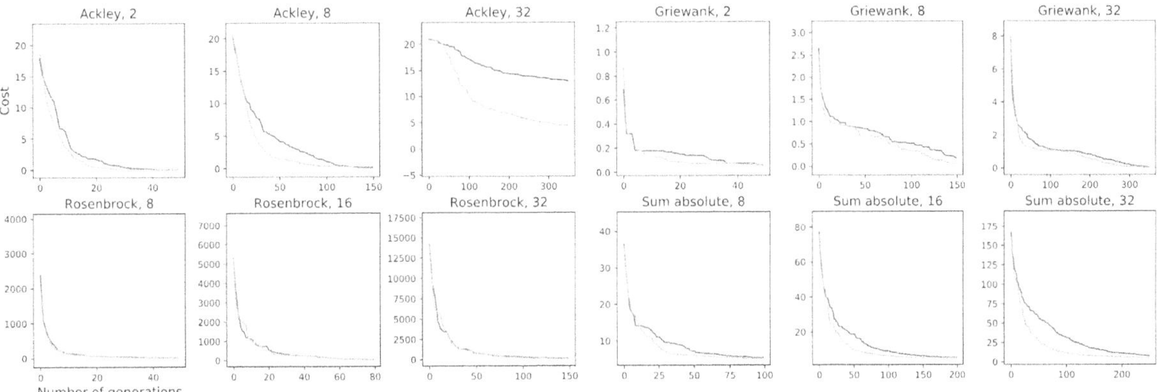

Fig. 2. Learning curves on exemplary benchmarks: The tasks are specified by a function and the feature dimension, and the incumbent settings (the best solutions found so far) are shown. The population size is $\lfloor 4 + 3\ln(D) \rfloor$. For each problem, we ran our algorithm CMA-ES-SR and standard CMA-ES algorithm five times, the mean and variance of the learning curves are shown.

Table 1. Performance of CMA-ES-SR on different benchmarks, where the mean and variance of final converged value in the given iteration are shown. The columns P_{50}, P_{75}, P_{90} refers to the convergence acceleration rate with the threshold set as 50 %, 75 %, 90 % percentile of the final convergence value of standard CMA-ES.

Benchmark Function, Dimension	**Iterations**	**CMA-ES**		**CMA-ES-SR (NN)**				
		Mean	**Var**	**Mean**	**Var**	P_{50} **(%)**	P_{75} **(%)**	P_{90} **(%)**
Ackley, 2	50	0.018	0.01	**0.012**	0.01	75	22	43
Ackley, 8	150	0.080	0.04	0.254	0.48	14	71	108
Ackley, 32	350	12.963	9.83	4.408	8.32	91	161	261
DejongsF5, 2	100	**0.399**	0.49	**0.399**	0.49	29	7	13
DejongsF5, 8	100	**1.402**	1.29	2.747	2.41	-300	0	62
DejongsF5, 20	200	1.408	0.74	**0.896**	0.61	0	-33	160
Griewank, 2	50	**0.061**	0.02	0.062	0.03	0	-25	114
Griewank, 8	150	0.181	0.10	**0.049**	0.05	100	32	33
Griewank, 32	350	0.064	0.01	**0.031**	0.00	-29	95	14
Michalewicz, 2	50	-1.841	0.06	**-1.866**	0.01	-50	-67	-75
Michalewicz, 10	100	-4.415	0.87	**-4.491**	1.64	107	16	30
Michalewicz, 20	200	-6.875	1.24	**-7.417**	0.94	467	1343	178
Rosenbrock, 2	50	**0.031**	0.04	0.547	0.85	100	-50	-25
Rosenbrock, 8	100	**5.977**	0.91	6.346	0.84	0	0	17
Rosenbrock, 16	150	**14.999**	0.56	16.238	1.81	0	-14	5
Rosenbrock, 32	250	53.157	42.57	**33.594**	1.63	40	-21	3
Sphere, 8	100	0.022	0.01	**0.010**	0.00	50	50	70
Sphere, 16	150	0.167	0.06	**0.031**	0.01	25	40	94
Sphere, 32	200	1.693	0.51	**0.277**	0.08	25	47	131
Sum absolute, 8	100	5.376	0.11	**5.139**	0.02	-25	46	72
Sum absolute, 16	200	5.398	0.11	**5.104**	0.01	-11	33	67
Sum absolute, 32	250	8.023	0.52	**5.672**	0.11	33	146	125
Averaged Performance	/	4.467	/	**3.093**	/	**33**	**86**	**68**

We also show metric (iii) for one benchmark in Fig. 3 as an example. Most of the benchmarks also register similar patterns. It can be observed that the number of predictor-proposed solutions N_{best} nearly reaches its upper bound, and the number of accepted solutions proposed by the model takes similar value as N_{best}. This shows predictor-proposed samples are of higher quality than random samples. It can be concluded that the model indeed contributes to higher-quality solutions than random samples when N_{best} reaches its upper bound. At this stage, a faster convergence. The quality of proposed samples is highly dependent on the current step size, mean vector, data distribution and trained model. In the later phase, random samples are at least as good as model-proposed samples, CMA-ES-SR behaves similarly as standard CMA-ES and the algorithm starts to converge.

3.3. Performance of CMA-ES on Flipping Task

For the flipping task, we used the package Pycma [4]. The trajectories are trained from scratch on two robot arms Franka Panda and KUKA-iiwa R820 in V-REP simulator [14]. All the settings are the same except for the joint constraints, where KUKA-iiwa has stricter joint constraints. Hence, the performance on KUKA-iiwa is restricted. We demonstrated one learned trajectory of Panda in Fig. 4. It can be illustrated that the robot arm learns to flip the cup vertically down and finally stopped at an upright pose, with no spillage. We validated the performance five times with a Gaussian noise of zero-mean and variance of 0.2 applied on each joint, shown in Table 2.

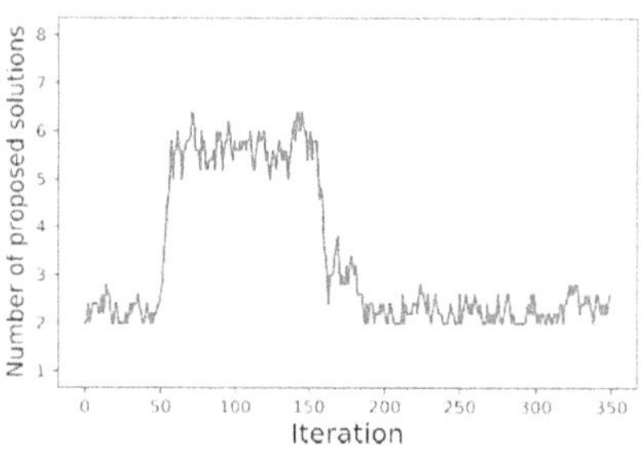

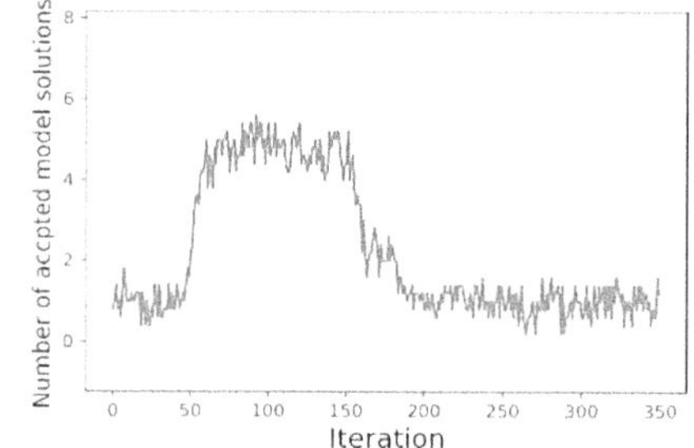

Fig. 3. MLP Model contribution on Ackley with input dimension of 32. N_{pop} is 14.

Fig. 4. Illustration of cup flipping task performed on Franka Panda robot in V-REP simulator.

Table 2. Learned trajectory performance per robot type.

Robot Type	Spillage (%)	$\varphi_{\mathbf{max}}$ (°)	$\varphi_{\mathbf{end}}$ (°)
Franka Panda	0±0	179.89±0.04	0.18±0.06
KUKA iiwa R820	23±6	136.01±0.07	1.39±0.08

4. Conclusions

Reducing the number of required rollouts in robot tasks requires sample-efficient RL algorithms. The popular RL algorithm CMA-ES fails to scale to high dimensions. To improve the sample efficiency, we extended the standard CMA-ES by learning a predictor to propose high-quality samples. We tested our new algorithm CMA-ES-SR on different benchmark optimization functions and showed that CMA-ES-SR outperforms the standard CMA-ES by at least 50 % in terms of convergence speed. With the increasing dimension, the performance gain is higher. The limitation is the additional overhead in fitting the model. In addition, we demonstrated how to learn a cup flipping task in 7-DoF robot arms which features fast robot motion and fulfils the joint angle and angular velocity constraints. The future work is to evaluate the performance of CMA-ES-SR on the flipping task and extend to different predictor models.

Acknowledgements

The project receives funding from the Deutsche Forschungsgemeinschaft (DFG, German Research Foundation) – No 430054590 (TRAIN).

References

[1]. M. Jamil, X. S. Yang, A literature survey of benchmark functions for global optimization problems, *ArXiv Preprint*, arXiv:1308.4008, 2013

[2]. J. Kober, J. A. Bagnell, J. Peters, Reinforcement learning in robotics: A survey, *The International Journal of Robotics Research*, Vol. 32, Issue 11, 2013, pp. 1238-1274.

[3]. A. R. Conn, K. Scheinberg, L. N. Vicente, Introduction to Derivative-free Optimization, *Siam*, 2009.

[4]. N. Hansen, Y. Akimoto, P. Baudis, CMA-ES/pycma on Github, *Zenodo*, February 2019.

[5]. N. Hansen, A. Ostermeier, Adapting arbitrary normal mutation distributions in evolution strategies: The covariance matrix adaptation, in *Proceedings of the IEEE International Conference on Evolutionary Computation*, 1996, pp. 312-317.

[6]. M. P. Deisenroth, G. Neumann, J. Peters, A survey on policy search for robotics, *Foundations and Trends in Robotics*, Vol. 2, Issues 1-2, 2013, pp. 1-142.

[7]. A. Kupcsik, M. P. Deisenroth, J. Peters, A. P. Loh, P. Vadakkepat, G. Neumann, Model-based contextual policy search for data-efficient generalization of robot skills, *Artificial Intelligence*, Vol. 247, 2017, pp. 415-439.

[8]. S. Ioffe, C. Szegedy, Batch normalization: Accelerating deep network training by reducing internal covariate shift, *ArXiv Preprint*, arXiv:1502.03167, 2015.

[9]. S. Schaal, Dynamic movement primitives-a framework for motor control in humans and humanoid robotics, in Adaptive Motion of Animals and Machines, *Springer*, 2006, pp. 261-280.

[10]. E. Rückert, A. d'Avella, Learned parametrized dynamic movement primitives with shared synergies for

controlling robotic and musculoskeletal systems, *Frontiers in Computational Neuroscience*, Vol. 7, 2013, 138.

[11]. A. J. Ijspeert, J. Nakanishi, H. Hoffmann, P. Pastor, S. Schaal, Dynamical movement primitives: learning attractor models for motor behaviors. *Neural Computation*, Vol. 25, Issue 2, 2013, pp. 328-373.

[12]. F. Hutter, H. H. Hoos, K. Leyton-Brown, Sequential model-based optimization for general algorithm configuration, in *Proceedings of the International Conference on Learning and Intelligent Optimization (LION'11)*, 2011, pp. 507-523.

[13]. T. Chen, H. Chen, Universal approximation to nonlinear operators by neural networks with arbitrary activation functions and its application to dynamical systems, *IEEE Transactions on Neural Networks*, Vol. 6, Issue 4, 1995, pp. 911-917.

[14]. E. Rohmer, S. P. Singh, M. Freese, CoppeliaSim (formerly V-REP): A versatile and scalable robot simulation framework, in Proceedings of *the International Conference on Intelligent Robots and Systems (IROS'13)*, 2013.

[15]. I. Loshchilov, A computationally efficient limited memory CMA-ES for large scale optimization, in *Proceedings of the Annual Conference on Genetic and Evolutionary Computation (GECCO'14)*, 2014, pp. 397-404.

[16]. D. V. Arnold, N. Hansen, Active covariance matrix adaptation for the (1+1)-CMA-ES, in *Proceedings of the 12th Annual Conference on Genetic and Evolutionary Computation (GECCO'10)*, 2010, pp. 385-392.

[17]. D. Brockhoff, A. Auger, N. Hansen, D. V. Arnold, T. Hohm, Mirrored sampling and sequential selection for evolution strategies, in *Proceedings of the International Conference on Parallel Problem Solving from Nature (PPSN'10)*, 2010, pp. 11-21.

[18]. H. Wang, M. Emmerich, T. Bäck, Mirrored orthogonal sampling with pairwise selection in evolution strategies, in *Proceedings of the 29th Annual ACM Symposium on Applied Computing (SAC'14)*, 2014, pp. 154-156.

[19]. D. Vermetten, S. van Rijn, T. Bäck, C. Doerr, Online selection of CMA-ES variants, *in Proceedings of the Genetic and Evolutionary Computation Conference (GECCO'19)*, 2019, pp. 951-959.

[20]. S. van Rijn, H. Wang, B. van Stein, T. Bäck, Algorithm configuration data mining for CMA evolution strategies, in *Proceedings of the Genetic and Evolutionary Computation Conference (GECCO'17)*, 2017, pp. 737-744.

[21]. B. Bischl, O. Mersmann, H. Trautmann, M. Preuß, Algorithm selection based on exploratory landscape analysis and cost-sensitive learning, in *Proceedings of the 14th Annual Conference on Genetic and Evolutionary Computation (GECCO'12)*, 2012, pp. 313-320.

[22]. Z. Bouzarkouna, A. Auger, D. Y. Ding, Local-meta-model CMA-ES for partially separable functions, in *Proceedings of the 13th Annual Conference on Genetic and Evolutionary Computation (GECCO'11)*, 2011, pp. 869-876.

[23]. I. Loshchilov, F. Hutter, Fixing weight decay regularization in Adam, 2018, https://openreview.net/forum?id=rk6qdGgCZ

[24]. A. Auger, N. Hansen, A restart CMA evolution strategy with increasing population size, in *Proceedings of the IEEE Congress on Evolutionary Computation (CEC'05)*, 2005, pp. 1769-1776.

[25]. A. Auger, N. Hansen, Tutorial CMA-ES: evolution strategies and covariance matrix adaptation, in *Proceedings of the 14th Annual Conference Companion on Genetic and Evolutionary Computation (GECCO'12)*, 2012, pp. 827-848.

Supplementary Information

5. Algorithm Details

The network architecture we used is a three-layer MLP with 1024 nodes on each layer. We added two batch normalization layers [8] after non-linear activation layer PReLU. We used AdamW [23] as the optimizer with the default learning rate of 10^{-3}. Loss Metric is mean square error with mean reduction. In order to prevent overfitting, we conducted early stopping with a tolerance of nine iterations and performed train-test split on the experience in the replay buffer. The validation dataset consists of the samples collected from the last optimization iteration. Since CMA-ES updates the Gaussian mean and variance in an accumulative manner, we assume the query points in current iteration are not far away from the query points in the last iteration. A small error in validation set infers similar error for the query points in current iteration given the trained network. In the first iteration, we did not perform any training as no dataset from previous iterations is available. In the second iteration, only samples from the first iteration are available, hence, we defined the validation set to be one-fifth of the samples retrieved in the first iteration. The remaining samples serve as training samples. From the third iteration on, the training and validation dataset were chosen as explained above. In each iteration, we retrained MLP from scratch. All of the samples were pre-processed to have zero-mean and unit-variance in each dimension.

6. Experiment Details

We validated the performance of CMA-ES and CME-ES-SR on different benchmark optimization problems suggested in [1]. The problem settings differ from each other in the domain for each input feature. The details of the problem setting are shown in **Table 3**. The initial mean vector μ_0 passed to CMA-ES(-SR) was chosen uniformly from the input domain, while the initial variance σ_0 passed to CMA-ES optimizer to be $0.3(\mu_{max} - \mu_{max})$. For each benchmark and each input dimension, we ran the experiment five times respectively for CMA-ES, CMA-ES-SR with two models.

Table 3. The settings of benchmark optimization functions.

Optimization Problems	**Domain μ_0**
Ackley	[-32,32]
DeJong F5	[-65,65]
Griewank	[-50,50]
Michalewicz	[0, π]
Rosenbrock	[-2,2]
Sphere	[-10,10]
Sum of absolute value	[-10,10]

In the cup flipping task, the learnable parameters θ describe the robot trajectories τ in joint space. The parameters θ consist of 10 weight parameters w_i for GBFs, two meta-parameters α and g. We characterized each of the seven joint trajectory profiles with one DMP so that the total number of learnable parameters is 84. β is chosen as $\alpha/4$, so that the system is critically-damped [9]. The trajectory time is fixed as five seconds. The cost function is defined as

$$\begin{aligned} C_1 &= a_1 C_{spi} + a_2(180 - \varphi_{max}) + \\ &a_3 \varphi_{end} + a_4 \delta_{col} C_{col}, \\ C_2 &= C_{worst} + a_5 \delta_{con} C_{con}, \end{aligned} \tag{6}$$

where C_1 is the case when joint angle and angular velocity constraints are satisfied and C_2 corresponds to the case of violation. The term φ_{max} is the largest difference of the cup normal vector to the vector (0,0,1) in 3D space throughout the whole trajectory, while the term φ_{end} refers to the same angle difference but at the end of the trajectory. Initially, cup normal vector is (0,0,1). C_{worst} denotes the worst possible of C_1. δ_{col} and δ_{con} are indicator functions telling whether collision happens and robot constraints are met. The cost maximizes the rotation angle of the cup φ_{max} while achieving minimal spillage C_{spi} and the upright final pose φ_{end}. When the constraints are not satisfied, the cost is C_{worst} plus an extra cost for exceeding the joint angle and joint velocity constraints. With such design, the robot arm constraints must be first satisfied so that it can learn to perform flipping.

(034)

Determination of Psychotic Behaviour Using a Network of Chemical Oscillators

Ashmita Bose and Jerzy Gorecki
Institute of Physical Chemistry, Polish Academy of Sciences, Kasprzaka 44/52, 01-224 Warsaw, Poland
E-mail: abose@ichf.edu.pl

Summary: Schizophrenia is the most common form of psychotic behaviour where patients experiences hallucination, dillusion or chaotic speech. Schizophrenia is difficult to detect and easily go undetected for years. Here we propose the idea of detecting schizophrenia by a network of interacting chemical oscillators. We optimized a classifier based on six interacting oscillator using genetic algorithm and obtained 82 % accuracy of schizophrenia detection on a selected training dataset.

Keywords: Schizophrenia, EEG signal, Chemical computing, Oscillatory network, Oregonator model, Genetic optimization.

1. Introduction

The modern information processing has been dominated by semiconductor technology and the binary information coding in electric potentials. Semiconductor logic gates are reliable, fast and inexpensive. Moreover, they can be concatenated into large structures. As the result the bottom-up approach is used to make more complex information processing devices as a combination of the simple ones [1].

Living organisms use chemistry for information processing. Experiments with man-made chemical information processing media shows that the maximum processing power can be achieved if different parts of the medium process information in parallel [2]. It can be expected that the top-down design strategy is more appropriate to reveal the computing power of a chemical medium than the bottom-up approach. The results presented below are continuation of the previous studies on top-down design of chemistry based classifiers [3-5]. We consider a chemical system that works as a classifier of a selected dataset containing records in a form of (n + 1) tuples, where the first n elements are predictors and the last one is a discrete data type. Our computing medium is supposed to return the correct data type if the predictor values are used as the input. Problems of such structure are common in medical applications [4], where one is supposed to determine if a patient is healthy or not (data type) on the basis of medical tests performed (the predictor values).

In our approach a computing medium made of interacting chemical oscillators is studied in-silico. The numerical model of a chemical oscillator is inspired by the two-variable Oregonator model [6, 7] of the Belousov-Zhabotinsky (B-Z) reaction [8]. This reaction is probably the most studied chemical process where the nonlinear phenomena, like oscillations, excitability, wave propagation or chaotic behavior, are clearly manifested [9]. The interest in BZ-reaction as a medium for chemical information processing has been motivated by the fact that its properties are similar to that observed for the nerve system [2, 10]. One can form channels in which propagation of concentration pulses is observed. These pulses interact (annihilate) one with another and can change their frequency on the junctions between channels [11]. The output information is usually coded in the presence of excitation (a high concentration of a selected reagent) at a given point of the medium and at the specific time.

For a specific choice of the catalyst BZ-reaction becomes photosensitive and it can be inhibited by illumination [12-14]. If a high intensity illumination is applied to an oscillatory medium then excitations are rapidly damped and the system reaches a stable, steady state. On the other hand, the oscillatory behaviour re-appears immediately after the illumination is switched off [15]. The existence of such external inhibiting factor is very important for information processing applications because it allows to control the medium evolution by inhibiting its selected parts. Moreover, we can input digital information into the computing medium by inhibiting specific reactions for times functionally related to the input value.

Our recent results suggest that reasonably accurate database classifiers can be constructed with a network of interacting chemical oscillators [3-5], like the one illustrated in Fig. 1(b). The output information is extracted from the network evolution, for example from the number of concentration maxima observed within a fixed time interval. The network is made of two types of oscillators. There are input oscillators that are used to input predictor values. Oscillators assigned as inputs of predictor #1 are inhibited for time related to this predictor value. There are also so called "normal oscillators", which are inhibited for a fixed time that is not related to the predictor value. These normal oscillators are supposed to moderate interactions in the medium and optimize them for a specific problem. In order to find a classifier for a given problem we need to specify the number of oscillators and their interactions. Also, such parameters as locations of input and normal droplets, inhibition of normal droplets, method for inputting the predictor values or the type of interactions between droplets have to be optimized. To do it we can use the top-down strategy

[3-5]: First we specify the function that should be performed by the considered system. Next, we search for possible factors that can modify the system evolution and increase its information processing ability. Finally we combine all these factors and apply them to achieve the optimum performance. We have found [3-5] that evolutionary optimization oriented on obtaining the best classifier for a representative training dataset of the problem can lead to the desired computing medium.

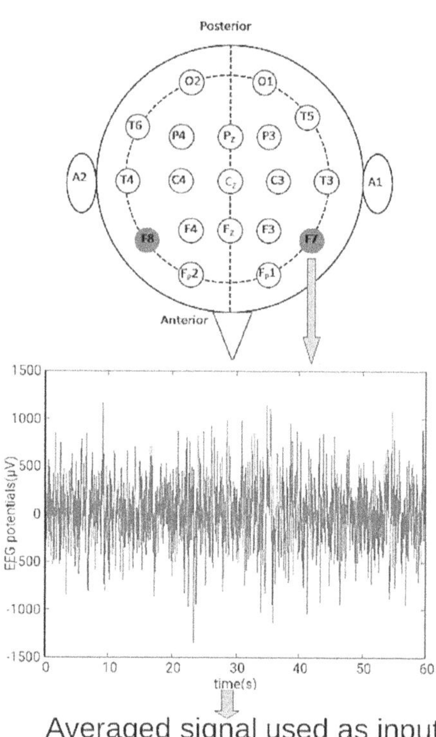

(a)

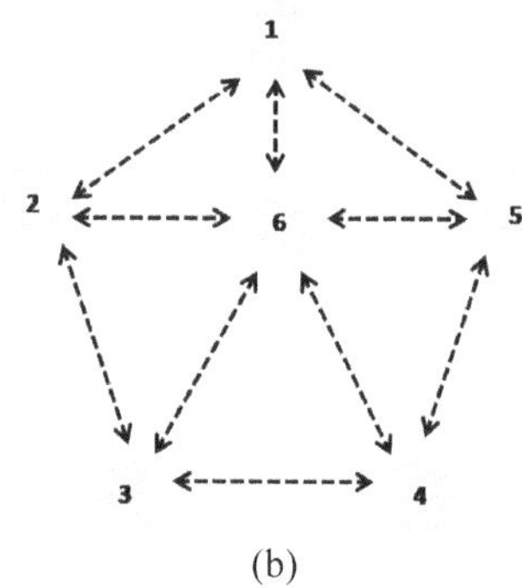

(b)

Fig. 1. (a) The location of electrodes and EEG signals used as inputs. (b) The schematic representation of the network of oscillators used to determine a schizophrenic patient.

In this report we concentrate on design of a classifier that is supposed to determine if a patient has schizophrenia or not. Schizophrenia is the most common form of psychotic behavior where patients experiences hallucination, delusion, chaotic speech. However, schizophrenia is difficult to detect and easily go undetected for years. We postulate that the detection of schizophrenia can be done by a network of interacting chemical oscillators that process information extracted from brain activity of a patient. There are two aspects of using the concepts of Artificial Intelligence in the presented study. First the network parameters are optimized using an evolutionary algorithm without a human involvement. Second, the resulting network can be seen as an example of Artificial Intelligence, that can predict if a patient is ill or not.

2. Results

We postulate that information necessary to detect schizophrenia can be extracted from the EEG signals recording brain activity [16]. Signals (the time dependent potential values) were recorded from electrodes placed in different parts of the scalp (see Fig. 1(a)). For the analysis we used signals received from F7 and F8 channels marked red in Fig. 1(a). The signal dataset available on the web [17] containing signals recorded on 84 patients, out of which 45 were schizophrenic and 39 were healthy controls, was used as our training dataset.

The time dependent potentials were time averaged over 60 second interval and next standardized in the following way:

$$p_{7,m} = \frac{x_{7,m}^1 - \mu_7}{\sigma_7} \quad p_{8,m} = \frac{x_{8,m}^2 - \mu_8}{\sigma_8}$$

Here the index m $(0 < m < 85)$ numbers patients in the considered database. The values $x_{7,m}$ and $x_{8,m}$ are the averaged potentials from F7 and F8 channels, μ_7 and μ_8 are the mean values of $x_{7,m}$and $x_{8,m}$averaged over all patients and σ_7 and σ_8 are the standard deviations of $x_{7,m}$ and $x_{8,m}$. A record of the considered training database has a form of 3-tuple: $(p_{7,m}, p_{8,m}, z)$ where the record type $z = 0$ for schizophrenic patients and $z = 1$ for healthy ones.

We assumed that a classifier that can distinguish between schizophrenic and healthy subject was formed of just 6 oscillators arranged in geometry shown in Fig 1(b). The broken arrows illustrate interactions between the oscillators. Following the analogy with Belousov Zhabotinsky reaction as a computing medium we used the same two-variable Oregonator model [6, 7] to simulate the time evolution of each oscillator:

$$\frac{\partial u}{\partial t} = \frac{1}{\varepsilon}\left(u - u^2 - (\mathrm{f}v + \varphi(t))\frac{u-q}{u+q}\right), \quad (1a)$$

$$\frac{\partial v}{\partial t} = u - v, \quad (1b)$$

where u and v denote concentrations of activator U and inhibitor V of Belousov-Zhabotinsky reaction respectively. In our simulations we used the following values of model parameters: $q = 0.0002$, $\varepsilon = 0.2$, $f = 1.1$. The parameters of the Oregonator model were fixed and did not undergo optimization. In the

Equation (1a) the function $\varphi(t)$ represents time dependent illumination of the medium. We used illumination to control the time evolution of an oscillator and considered $\varphi(t)$ in the form:

$$\varphi_k(t) = 0.1 * (1.001 + +\tanh(-10 * (t - t_{osc}(k)))), \quad (2)$$

where: $t_{osc}(k)$ is the time when illumination of oscillator #k was terminated. At the beginning the value of $\varphi_k(t = 0) = 0.2$ and the Oregonator model predicts a stable steady state corresponding to $u = 0.0002$ and $v = 0.0002$. For long times $\varphi_k(t)$ goes to 0.0001 what correspond to an oscillator with the period of approximately 10.8 time units. In an oscillator #k is a normal one than the value of $t_{osc}(k)$ is the same for all processed records of the training dataset. If the oscillator #j functions as the input of the predictor p_l ($l = 7$ or 8) than:

$$t_{osc}(j) = t_{start} + (t_{end} - t_{start}) * p_l \quad (3)$$

The coupling between the oscillators #k and #j is described by additional reactions involving the activators U_k and U_j of these oscillators: $U_k + A_j \rightarrow$ products with the reaction rate α and:

$$U_j + B_j \rightarrow U_k + C_k,$$
$$U_k + B_k \rightarrow U_j + C_j,$$

with the reaction rate β.

The time evolution of the network is described by the following kinetic equation:

$$\frac{\partial u_j}{\partial t} = \frac{1}{\varepsilon}(u_j - u_j^2 - (\mathrm{f}v_j + \varphi(t))\frac{u_j - q}{u_j + q}) - -(\alpha + \beta\sum_{k=1}^{6} s_{j,k}) + \beta(\sum_{k=1}^{6} s_{j,k}u_k), \quad (4a)$$

$$\frac{\partial v_j}{\partial t} = u_j - v_j, \quad (4b)$$

where u_j and v_j denote concentrations of activator and inhibitor in the oscillator #j. The last terms in Eq. (4a) represent the coupling between oscillators #j and #k. The values of symbols $s_{j,k}$ are equal to 1 if oscillators #j and #k interact and $s_{j,k} = 0$ if they do not.

In order to get information if a patient characterized by the predictors p_7 and p_8 is healthy or ill we simulated numerically Eqs. (4a, b) the network evolution within the time interval $[0, t_{max}]$ using Cash-Karp R-K45 method [18] with $\Delta t = 10^{-3}$ time steps. We postulate that information about patient's health can be extracted from the number of activator maxima recorded on a selected oscillator of the network, during the time interval $[0, t_{max}]$.

Following the idea of cancer classification described in [3] we optimized the system parameters to maximize the mutual information [19] between the number of oscillations received from the output droplet and the health of a patient represented by records of the training database. It can be expected that the value of mutual information increases with the classifier accuracy. An evolutionary algorithm covering all parameters of the network, i.e.:

- The time during which network evolution is studied t_{max} ($t_{max} < 100$ time units);
- Locations and illumination times (t_{osc} (i)) for all normal oscillators;
- Locations of input oscillators and times t_{end}, t_{start} in the Eq. (3);
- The rate constants α, β describing interactions between oscillators, was applied.

The quality (fitness) of a specific classifier was calculated as the mutual information between the list of types in the training database and the list of numbers of activator maxima observed on the output droplet [3]. As the output droplet we select the one for which the mutual information was the maximum one. The network optimization was performed using an evolutionary optimization algorithm presented in [5]. We considered 740 optimization generations over the population of 200 classifiers. The progress of optimization is illustrated in Fig. 2(a). When the optimization was terminated the mutual information between the list of types in the training database and the number of activator maxima observed on the output droplet was 0.416. The most fit network we obtained is illustrated in Fig. 2(c). The symbols In_1 and In_2 mark locations of inputs for predictors p_7 and p_8 respectively. The normal oscillators are represented by pie-charts. The ratio between the surface of the red area and the area of disk representing an oscillator represents the value of $t_{osc}(\#)/ t_{max}$. The optimized network is characterized by: $t_{max} = 79.5$, $t_{start} = 72.1$, $t_{end} = 4.9$, $\alpha = 0.46$, $\beta = 0.65$, $t_{osc}(1) = 52.3$, $t_{osc}(5) = 52.3$.

Fig. 2(b) illustrates the mutual information between the list of numbers of activator maxima observed on a specific oscillator and the list of types of the training database. As seen the highest values of mutual information are observed for oscillators that are also the inputs of predictor p_8. The maximum mutual information is for the oscillator #2. It can be expected the classifier accuracy increases with the mutual information, thus using the number of maxima of the activator for the oscillator #2 we should obtain the most accurate diagnosis. The number of cases corresponding to a given number of activator maxima observed on the oscillator #2 for healthy and schizophrenic patients is shown in Fig. 2(c). Using these results we can postulate the classification rule: if 1,3 or 4 maxima of activator are observed during the time evolution on the oscillator #2 then the patient is healthy. If the number of observed maxima is different than the patient is schizophrenic. This rule gives the accuracy of 82 % in determination of schizophrenic patients in the considered database.

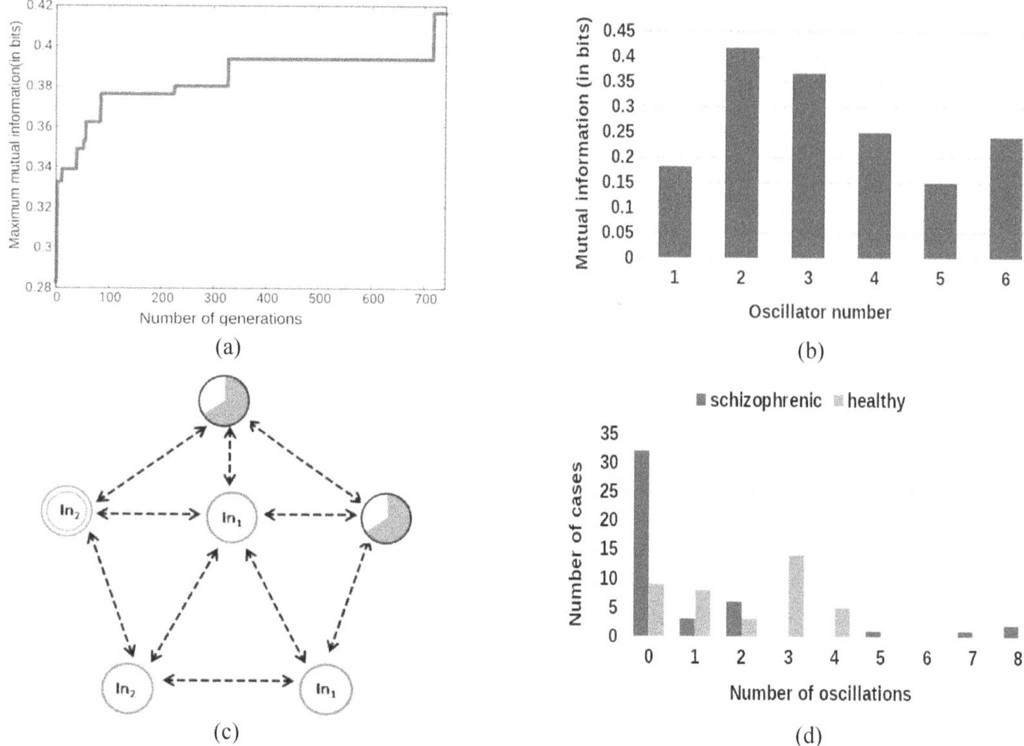

Fig. 2. The optimization of a schizophrenia classifier. (a) The maximum mutual information between the list of record types and the list of numbers of activator maxima as a function of the evolutionary step. (b) The mutual information between the list of record types and the list of numbers of activator maxima measured for different oscillators of the optimized network. The oscillator #2 gave the maximum mutual information and it was selected as the output one. (c)The structure of optimized schizophrenia classifier. In_1 and In_2 represent inputs for p_7 and p_8. The green ringed droplet represents the output droplet. (d) The numbers of cases in the considered training database for which a given number of activator maxima is observed on the oscillator #2.

3. Conclusions and Discussions

In the presented study we assumed that schizophrenia can be detected by an Artificial Intelligence program that analyses EEG signals recorded from electrodes located on a patient scalp. Using a limited dataset we demonstrated that an interacting system of chemical oscillators can be trained to perform as a classifier and it has a potential to distinguish a schizophrenic patient. We considered a network of 6 coupled oscillators and optimize it to diagnose correctly 82 % of cases in the considered dataset. We tested a number of combinations of two signals and, within the available data, the highest accuracy was obtained for F7 and F8 channels (cf. Fig. 1(a)). We think the result is promising and encourage future research in this field. Having access to much larger databases we could generalize the presented results. A larger network would allow to combine information from a large number of channels which should increase the diagnosis accuracy.

Acknowledgements

This publication is part of a project that has received funding from the European Union's Horizon 2020 (H2020-EU.1.3.4.) research and innovation program under the Marie Skłodowska-Curie Actions (MSCA-COFUND ID 711859) and from the Polish Ministry of Science and Higher Education for the implementation of an international co-financed project.

References

[1]. R. Feynman, T. Hey, R. Allen, Feynman Lectures on Computation, *CRC Press*, Boulder, Colorado, USA, 2000.

[2]. J. Gorecki, K. Gizynski, J. Guzowski, J. N. Gorecka, P. Garstecki, G. Gruenert, P. Dittrich, Chemical computing with reaction-diffusion processes, *Philosophical Transactions of the Royal Society A: Mathematical, Physical and Engineering Sciences*, Vol. 373, Issue 2046, 2015.

[3]. K. Gizynski, G. Gruenert, P. Dittrich, J. Gorecki, Evolutionary design of classifiers made of droplets containing a nonlinear chemical medium, *MIT Evolutionary Computation*, Vol. 25, Issue 4, 2017, pp. 643-671.

[4]. K. Gizynski, J. Gorecki, Cancer classification with a network of chemical oscillators, *Physical Chemistry Chemical Physics*, Vol. 19, Issue 42, 2017, pp. 28808-28819.

[5]. K. Gizynski, J. Górecki, A chemical system that recognizes the shape of a sphere, *Computational Methods in Science and Technology*, Vol. 22, Issue 4, 2016, pp. 167-177.

[6]. R. J. Field, R. M. Noyes, Oscillations in chemical systems. IV. Limit cycle behavior in a model of a real chemical reaction, *The Journal of Chemical Physics*, Vol. 60, Issue 5, 1974, pp. 1877-1884.

[7]. M. Kuze, M. Horisaka, N. J. Suematsu, T. Amemiya, O. Steinbock, S. Nakata, Chemical wave propagation in the Belousov-Zhabotinsky reaction controlled by electrical potential, *The Journal of Physical Chemistry A*, Vol. 123, Issue 23, 2019. pp. 4853-4857.

[8]. I. R. Epstein, J. A. Pojman, An Introduction to Nonlinear Chemical Dynamics: Oscillations, Waves, Patterns, and Chaos, *Oxford University Press*, New York, NY, USA, 1998.

[9]. A. Adamatzky, B. De Lacy Costello, T. Asai, Reaction-diffusion Computers, *Elsevier*, New York, NY, USA, 2005.

[10]. H. Haken, Brain Dynamics: Synchronization and Activity Patterns in Pulse-coupled Neural Nets with Delays and Noise, *Springer*, Berlin, Germany, 2002.

[11]. J. Sielewiesiuk, J. Gorecki, Logical functions of a cross junction of excitable chemical media, *The Journal of Physical Chemistry A*, Vol. 105, Issue 35, 2001, pp. 8189-8195.

[12]. L. Kuhnert, A new optical photochemical memory device in a light-sensitive chemical active medium, *Nature*, Vol. 319, 1986, pp. 393-394.

[13]. L. Kuhnert, K. I. Agladze, V. I. Krinsky, Image processing using light-sensitive chemical waves, *Nature*, Vol. 337, 1989, pp. 244-247.

[14]. N. G. Rambidi, A. V. Maximychev, Towards a biomolecular computer. Information processing capabilities of biomolecular nonlinear dynamic media, *BioSystems*, Vol. 41, Issue 3, 1997, pp. 195-211.

[15]. K. Gizynski, J. Gorecki, Chemical memory with states coded in light controlled oscillations of interacting Belousov-Zhabotinsky droplets, *Physical Chemistry Chemical Physics*, Vol. 19, Issue 9, 2017, pp. 6519-6531.

[16]. J. G. Byeon, A. Y. Kaplan, S. F. Timashev, G. V. Vstovskii, B. W. Park, Variability of the EEG autocorrelation structure in adolescents with schizophrenia spectrum disorders, *Human Phsysiology*, Vol. 33, Issue 1, 2007, pp. 122-124.

[17]. EEG of healthy adolescents and adolescents with symptoms of schizophrenia, http://brain.bio.msu.ru/eeg_schizophrenia.htm

[18]. W. H. Press, S. A. Teukolsky, W. T. Vetterling, B. P. Flannery, Numerical Recipes in C: The Art of Scientific Computing, 2nd Ed., *Cambridge University Press*, USA, 1992.

[19]. T. M. Cover, J. A. Thomas, Elements of Information Theory, *Wiley-Interscience*, New York, 2006.

(035)

Binary Pattern Descriptor Based Face Recognizer for Access Control System with Real-time Dataset Generation

Sarthak Srivastava [1], Narendra Kumar Shukla [2] and Himanshu Ujjawal Singh [3]
Madan Mohan Malaviya University of Technology, India
Prithvi AI Lab Pvt Ltd, India [3] Algo8 Pvt Ltd, India
E-mails: sarthak.srivastava14apr@gmail.com, narendra.shukla@ieee.org, himanshu@algo8.ai

Summary: State-of-the-art biometric based access control systems like fingerprint and retina scan systems are becoming ubiquitous. In this novel-work, we propose to use a common camera to generate user-data in real-time and store it on cloud for access control of the user to any premise by face recognizer working on the principles of Computer vision, Image Processing and Artificial Intelligence. It may seem tedious and challenging to gather the large set of data which could train our model for better accuracy but in this work, we have generated the training data in an efficient way by using the concept of real-time data set generation. We have used the frontal face Haar-Cascade classifier to detect the object for which it has been trained for, from the source. The Haar-Cascade is trained by superimposing the positive image over a set of negative images. For training we have used Local Binary Pattern (LBP) algorithm which is a simple yet very efficient texture operator which labels the pixels of an image by thresholding the neighbourhood of each pixel and saves the result as a binary number in a CSV file. Once we have the dataset in structured (CSV format), we apply the AI algorithms to detect the current face by naming them (multiclass classification). If some unknown person (no training data available) happens to be in the frame, he is labelled as 'unknown'. Thus, a trigger is created by comparing names of objects and names in our data set to grant access.

Keywords: LBP, Haar Cascade classifier, Face recognition, Access Control, Real-time dataset generation, Artificial Intelligence.

1. Introduction

Face recognition-based access control systems are becoming ubiquitous for granting access to office premises, unlocking your smartphone to gain access and also to maintain database management systems by considering your frontal face data as the primary key of the ER model. In this work we implement a face recognition system where image acquisition is done in real-time for access control to a premise. This technique helps us to overcome the challenging problem of gathering the large set of data which could train our model for better accuracy. Computer vision and machine learning is used to train a model and which is used to classify the query image. The class in which the image is classified is then used to generate the trigger and then result in binary value (1- access granted, 0-access not granted).

This system will also be replacing the use of Radio Frequency ID cards, Quick Response code cards and other tedious techniques of access control systems. Thus the frontal face data of humans will become the uniquely identifying feature in the incoming future.

1.1. Related Work

Zhao et al summarized the research work in the area of face recognition in 2003 in their seminal paper [1]. Local binary pattern (LBP) based descriptor was proposed by authors in [2] for face recognition. Access control and spoof detection for face recognition based smartphone unlocking was considered by authors in [3]. We implemented the LBP method proposed in [2].

Abate et al has done the face recognition work using the feature extraction process of fractal based techniques [5] Kosov et al has worked on Rapid stereo-vision enhanced face recognition [6].

Yin S, Dai X, Ouyang P, Liu L, Wei S et al has worked on A Multi-Modal Face Recognition Method Using Complete Local Derivative Patterns and Depth Maps [7].

1.2. LBP Descriptors

To find the image that matches the query image we just need to compare two histograms and return the image with the closest histogram.

Local Binary Pattern (LBP) is a powerful texture operator which labels the pixels of an image by thresholding the neighborhood of each pixel and considers the result as a binary number. This relatively new approach was introduced in 1996 by ojala LBP and combined with histograms of oriented gradients (HOG) descriptor, improves the detection performance considerably on facial image datasets. Using the LBP combined with histograms we can represent the face images with a simple data vector. The first computational step of the LBPH is to create an intermediate image that describes the original image in a better way, by highlighting the characteristics of faces. To do so, the algorithm uses a concept of a sliding window, based on the parameters radius and neighbors as shown in Fig. 1.

We used the Euclidean distance based on the following equation given in eq. (1):

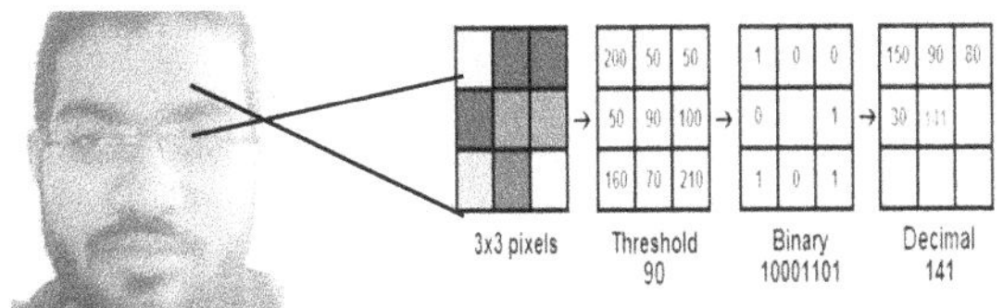

Fig. 1. LBP Procedure for an image acquired.

$$D = \sqrt{\sum_{i=1}^{n} (hist1i - hist2i)^2} \tag{1}$$

where D = Distance, hist n= the nth histogram obtained.

We already know about using facial points as features descriptors which indicates whether there's a facial expression or not. They are very powerful, but they can't decode everything for instance, if you have a little dimple or scar because in this case there is no movement of the facial points. We don't get a geometric variation but we do get a change in appearance. To encode such features/variations and maximize the variation or features that are relevant to facial expressions we will use highly successful feature i.e. Local Binary Pattern. Local Binary pattern looks at 9 pixels at a time. It is a 3 x 3 block of pixels and we derive LBP Pattern starting from central pixel e.g. as shown in Fig. 2(a) that central pixel value is '8' and there are 8 pixels around it.

12	15	18
5	8	3
8	1	2

(a)

1	1	1
0		0
1	0	0

(b)

Fig 2.

Local binary pattern is now going to turn this set of 3 x 3 pixels into binary values. We compare value of central pixel with every neighbouring pixel. If the neighbouring pixel's value is greater than or equal to the central pixel thn its going to assign 1 and if smaller, then it is going to assign 0 as shown in Fig. 2(b). Further we convert set of 8-binary digits to a byte by reading the matrix in Fig. 2B clockwise as shown in Fig. 3.

1	1	1	0	0	0	1	0

The byte thus obtained is converted to decimal for training our system. The most important feature of LBP is being illumination invariant i.e. a change the lighting conditions changes intensity value of all these pixel values in a frame but the relative difference between them will remain the same.

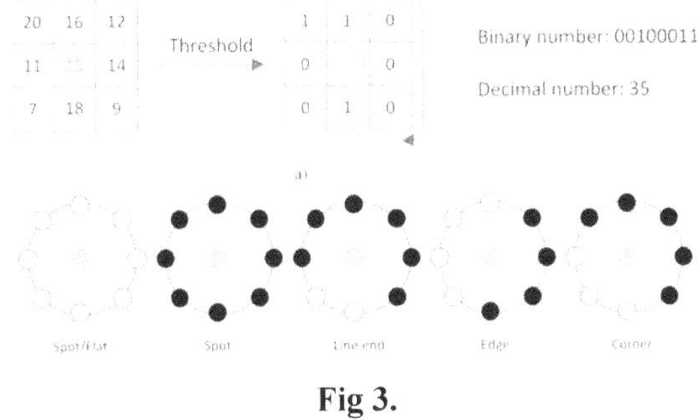

Fig 3.

So, our binary pattern will remain the same irrespective of illumination in general. For a face extracted by Haar-cascade classifier we are going to divide the face into a number of blocks and this local binary pattern is centred on a single pixel and then compares with its neighbors, so we have to do this for every pixel in each block and each of them will result in a different decimal number. If there are enough pixels in a block i.e. if a block is big enough, we will actually turn these values into a histogram.

1.3. Proposed Methodology

The local binary pattern uses four parameters namely 'Radius', 'Neighbors','Grid X' and 'Grid Y'. The radius is used to build the circular local binary pattern. Neighbors refer to the number of sample points to build the circular local binary pattern. Grid X and Grid Y are the number of cells in the horizontal and vertical directions respectively. The more cells, the finer the grid, the higher the dimensionality of the resulting feature vector.

With LBP it is possible to describe the texture and shape of a digital image. This is done by dividing an image into several small regions from which the features are extracted. We divide the image into small regions and features are extracted from it. These features consist of binary patterns that describe the vicinity of pixels in the regions. Thus, the obtained features from the regions are concatenated into a single feature histogram, which forms a representation of the query image. Images then can be compared by measuring the similar aspects between relative histograms.

Earlier LBP operators worked with the eight neighbors of a pixel, using the value of this center pixel as a threshold. If a neighbor pixel has a greater than or equal to value than the center pixel then [1] is assigned to that pixel, else it gets a 0. The LBP code for the center pixel is then produced by concatenating the eight ones or zeros to a binary code.

The LBP operator was later on extended to use neighborhoods of a variety of shapes and sizes. In this case a circle is made with radius R from the center pixel. P sampling points on the edge of this circle are taken into consideration and then compared with the value of the center pixel. To get the values of all sampling points in the neighborhood for any length of radius and for any number of pixels, bilinear interpolation is applied.

If the coordinates of the center pixel are (x_c, y_c) then the coordinates of his P neighbors (x_p, y_p) on the edge of the circle with radius R can be calculated with the sine and cosines:

$$x_p = x_c + R \cos (2 \pi p / P) \quad (2)$$

$$y_p = y_c + R \sin (2 \pi p / P) \quad (3)$$

If the matrix value of the center pixel is g_c and the matrix values of their neighbors are g_p, with $p = 0, ..., P - 1$, then the texture T in the local neighborhood of pixel (x_c, y_c) can be defined as

$$T = \tau(\gamma_\chi, \gamma_0, \ldots, \gamma_{\Pi-1}) \quad (4)$$

Once these values of the points are obtained is it also possible do describe the texture in another way, i.e. by subtracting the value of the center pixel from the values of the points on the circle. In this way the local texture is represented as a joint distribution of the value of the center pixel and the differences.

$$T = t(g_c, g_0 - g_c, \ldots, g_{P-1} - g_c) \quad (5)$$

Since $t(g_c)$ describes the overall luminance of an image, which is unrelated to the local image texture as explained above in this paper, it does not provide useful information for texture analysis. Therefore, much of the information about the textural characteristics in the original joint distribution (Eq. 3) is preserved in the joint difference distribution:

$$T \approx (g_0 - g_c, \ldots, g_{P-1} - g_c) \quad (6)$$

Although invariant against gray scale shifts, the differences are affected by scaling. To achieve invariance with respect to any monotonic transformation of the gray scale, only the signs of the differences are taken into consideration. This means that in the case a point on the circle has a higher gray value than the center pixel (or the same value), a one is assigned to that point, and else it gets a zero:

$$T \approx (s(g_0 - g_c), \ldots, s(g_{p-1} - g_c) \quad (7)$$

where

$$s(x) = \{1, \ x \geq 0 \ x, \ x < 0$$

In the last step to produce the LBP for pixel (x_c, y_c) a binomial weight 2^p is assigned to each $sign(g_p - g_c)$. These binomial weights are summed:

$$LBP_{P,}(x_{c,} y_c) = \Sigma_{P=0}^{p-1} \, s \, (g_p - g_c) 2^p \quad (7)$$

The Local Binary Pattern characterizes the local image texture around (x_c, y_c). The original LBP operator in figure 1.3 is very similar to this operator with P = 8 and R = 1, thus LBP8,1. The main difference between these operators is that in $LBP_{8,1}$ the pixels first need to be interpolated to get the values of the points on the circle.

Concept of Feature Vectors:

Once we have the Local Binary Pattern for every pixel, the feature vector of the image can be constructed easily. For an efficient representation of the face, first the image is divided into K^2 regions. For every region a histogram with all possible labels is constructed. This means that every bin in a histogram represents a pattern and contains the number of its appearance in the region. The feature vector is then constructed by concatenating the regional histograms to one big histogram.

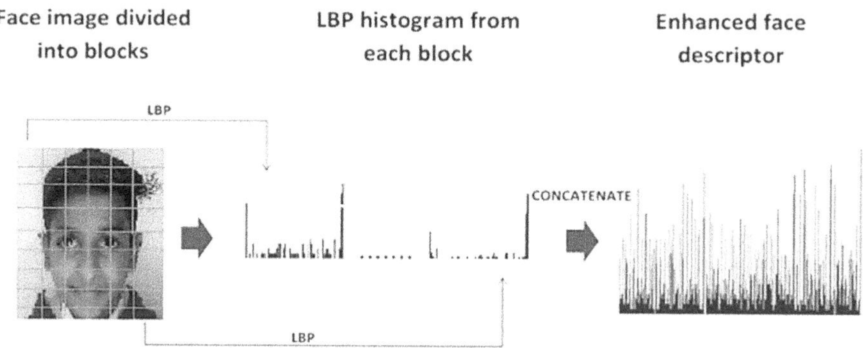

Fig. 4. Face image divided into 64 regions, with for every region a histogram.

For every region all non-uniform patterns (more than two transitions) are labeled with one single label. This means that every regional histogram consists of $P (P - 1) + 3$ bins: $P (P - 1)$ bins for the patterns with two transitions, two bins for the patterns with zero transitions and one bin for all non-uniform patterns. The total feature vector for an image contains $K^2 (P (P - 1) + 3)$ bins. So, for an image divided into 64 regions and eight sampling points on the circles. The LBP code cannot be calculated for the pixels in the area with a distance R from the edges of the image.

This means that, in constructing the feature vector, a small area on the borders of the image is not used. For an $N \times M$ image the feature vector is constructed by calculating the LBP code for every pixel (x_c, y_c) with x_c Ɛ{R + 1, . . . ,N − R} and y_c Ɛ{R + 1, . . . , M − R}. If an image is divided into k × k regions, then the histogram for region (k_x, k_y), with k_x {1, . . . , k} and k_y {1, . . . , k}, can be defined as:

$$H_i(K_x , K_y) = \sum_{x,y} I\{LBP_{P,R(x,y)} = L(i)\},$$
$$i = 1, \ldots\ P(P - 1) + 3$$

$$x \in \{\{R+1, \ldots \ldots \ldots ,N/K\}\ K_x = 1$$
$$\{(K_x - 1)\ (N/K) + 1, \ldots, N = R \quad K_x = K$$
$$\{(K_x - 1)(N/K) + 1, \ldots, K_x(N/K)\}\}\ else$$

$$\in\ \{\{R+1, \ldots \ldots \ldots ,M/K\}\ K_y = 1$$
$$\{(K_y - 1)(M/K) + 1, \ldots\ ,M - R\}\ K_y = K$$
$$\{(K_y - 1)(M/K) + 1, \ldots\ \ ,K_y(M/K)\}\}\ else$$

in which L is the label of bin i and

$$I(A) = \{1,\ A\ is\ True\ \ 0,\ \ A\ is\ False$$

N X M is the dimension of the image matrix.

The feature vector is effectively a description of the face on three different levels of locality: the labels contain information about the patterns on a pixel-level; the regions, in which the different labels are summed, contain information on a small regional level and the concatenated histograms give a global description of the face.

2. LBP Based Training and the Classifier

A block diagram of the proposed approach is shown in Fig. 5. We have implemented the system as 3 sub parts viz.

1. Creation of dataset: - We create a dataset of users from their captured video frames by segregating them on basis of a unique id and name. The dataset consists only of facial image and not the full body pose. The images from the acquired video are stored after converting them into grayscale. We used frontal face Haar-Cascade OpenCV library classifier [4] to detect and store facial images in the dataset. While creating the dataset we should make sure that there should only be a single person in the frame otherwise it may cause anomalies in data.
2. Training of Model: We used Local Binary Pattern (LBP) algorithm to train our model and save its yml file. This yml file is used further for detection. LBP descriptors are simple yet very efficient texture operators which label the pixels of an image by thresholding the neighborhood of each pixel and considers the result as a binary number.
3. Detecting and Granting/Denying access: - For classifying a query image of the person in front of the camera and mark his presence on the data frame we use a classifier on the trained model obtained in step 2 above.

We used a frontal face Haar Cascade classifier to detect the object for which it has been trained for, from the source. The Haar Cascade is trained by superimposing the positive image over a set of negative images. We use conditional '==' operator to check is the object I the camera is to be given access or not and thus we generate a trigger and display out as 0/1 (binary number).

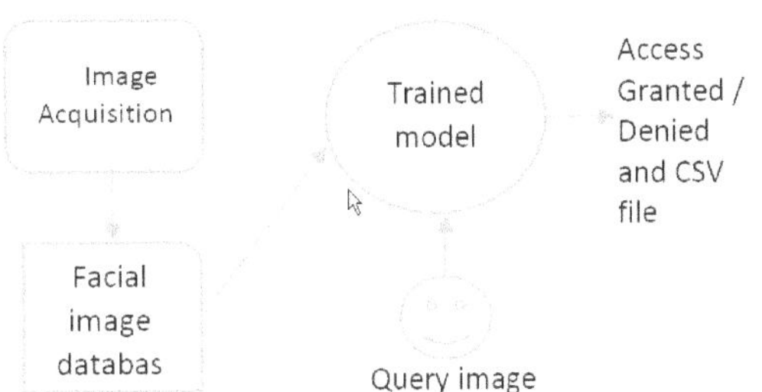

Fig. 5. Block Diagram representation of our method.

3. Results and Discussions

Our preliminary database contained facial image dataset of 21 persons sequentially acquired in real-time from the camera and model was trained to generate yml file as described in Section 2. Access was granted to the persons having their facial image in the grabbed video frame at the time of querying the system.

Fig. 6. Sample facial images from database of person A (left) and person B (right) and Unknown.

Left image in the result shown in Fig. 7 shows correct classification and access granted scenario while right image is for access denied to the person on extreme right in the image. It illustrates the classification accuracy of our system.

When a user is correctly identified and granted access it is marked as 1 in the daily log of access control in our system while access denied scenario is marked as 0 in the log file.

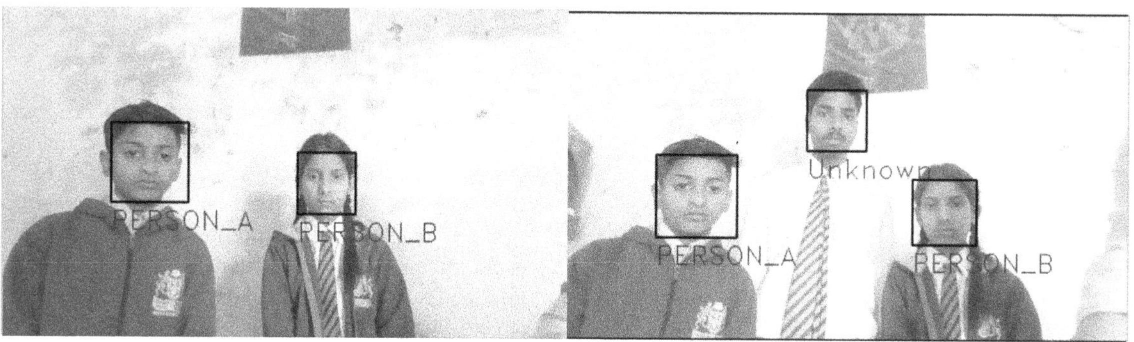

Fig. 7. Classification of granted access (L) and Restricted access (R) for two persons in a video feed.

The output in Fig. 8 shows that the people who are in the grabbed video frame as access granted i.e. '1' and access denied ones are marked as '0' under the Day column.

One limitation of the work which needs further investigation is to include liveness detection of captured images. Presently the system sometimes grants access to static images of the person in real-time instead of the actual person being present at the time of query. Spoof detection method described in [3] will be applicable here.

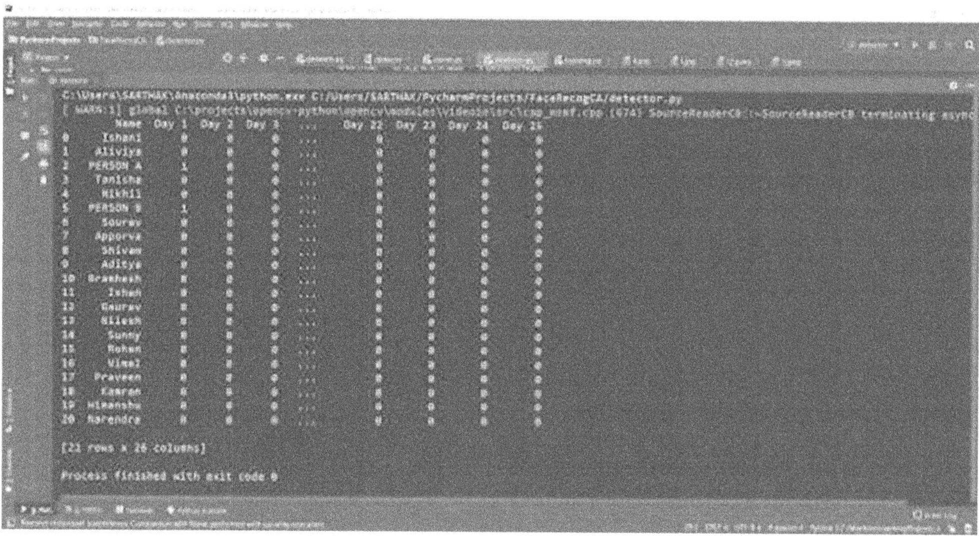

Fig. 8. CSV File of Access Control List.

4. Conclusions

We have implemented and tested an access control system based on LBP for training the model on the images acquired in real-time. High classification accuracy (~98%) is observed in testing the system for known and unknown faces.

Acknowledgements

Authors would like to thank Mr. Saurabh Gupta and Nandan Mishra of Algo8.ai for their necessary guidance in carrying out this work.

References

[1]. W. Zhao, R. Chellappa, P. J. Phillips, A. Rosenfeld, Face recognition: A literature survey, *ACM Computing Surveys*, Vol. 35, Issue 4, December 2003, pp. 399-458.

[2]. T. Ahonen, A. Hadid, M. Pietikainen, Face description with local binary patterns: Application to face recognition, *IEEE Transactions on Pattern Analysis and Machine Intelligence*, Vol. 28, Issue 12, 2006, pp. 2037-2041.

[3]. K. Patel, H. Han, A. K. Jain, Secure Face Unlock: Spoof Detection on Smartphones, *IEEE Transactions on Information Forensics and Security*, Vol. 11, Issue 10, October 2016, pp. 2268-2283.

[4]. OpenCV on Wheels, https://pypi.org/project/opencv-python

[5]. Abate A. F., Nappi M., Riccio D. and Sabatino G., 2D and 3D face recognition: A survey, *Pattern Recognition Letters*, 28, 14, 2007, pp. 1885-1906.

[6]. Kosov S., Scherbaum K., Faber K., Thormahlen T. and Seidel H.-P., Rapid stereo-vision enhanced face detection, in *Proceedings of the 16th IEEE International Conference on Image Processing (ICIP)*, 2009, pp. 1221-1224.

[7]. Yin S., Dai X., Ouyang P., Liu L., Wei S., A multi-modal face recognition method using complete local derivative patterns and depth maps, *Sensors (Basel)*, 14, 10, 2014, pp. 19561-19581.

Using Deep Learning for Sonar Targets Localization

Q. Bruel [1], **F. Heitzmann** [2], **D. Morche** [2], **J. Huillery** [3], **E. Blanco** [3] **and L. Bako** [3]
[1] Univ. Grenoble Alpes, CEA, List, 17 Avenue des Martyrs, F-38000, Grenoble, France
[2] Univ. Grenoble Alpes, CEA, Leti, 17 Avenue des Martyrs, F-38000, Grenoble, France
[3] Ecole Centrale de Lyon, Laboratoire Ampère, 36 Avenue Guy de Collongue, 69134, Ecully, France
Tel.: +33 4 38 78 97 69
E-mail: quentin.bruel@cea.fr

Summary: This paper addresses the problem of target localization in sonar signal in a 2D (range-azimuth) scene. The aim is to propose an approach based on an artificial neural network that outputs a binary occupancy grid. A dataset is generated using a sonar simulator and used to train and validate a deep neural network based on a U-net architecture. A pre-processing chain converts analog data to a form that can be passed through the neural network, in this case a (range-azimuth) 2D map with power received. Finally, the performances of the network are compared to those of an approach built around on a CFAR-based range estimation and a MUSIC-based direction of arrival estimation. The results show that the network is able to provide at least similar performances than the reference approach, without the algorithmic calibration currently required by the latter.

Keywords: Sonar, Deep learning, Mapping, Detection, Occupancy grid.

1. Introduction

When it comes to autonomous driving and robotic navigation in general, knowing where the agents can move without touching an obstacle is a crucial matter. This information can be displayed as a 2D occupancy grid (OG) of the environment indicating the probability for a region of space to be free or occupied (i.e. containing an obstacle). An example is provided in Fig. 1. These grids – here called "probabilistic" – are popular due to their ability to quantify uncertainty and the possibility to fuse sensor measurements [1, 2]. The sensors whose measurements are used to build OG can be separated into two categories according to their field-of-view (FOV), i.e. the area of space where they are able to detect obstacles. A sensor is considered to have either a narrow FOV that we model as a line, or a large one. In this case a large part of the environment is seen, that we can model as being between two boundaries forming a cone. These notions are illustrated in Fig. 2.

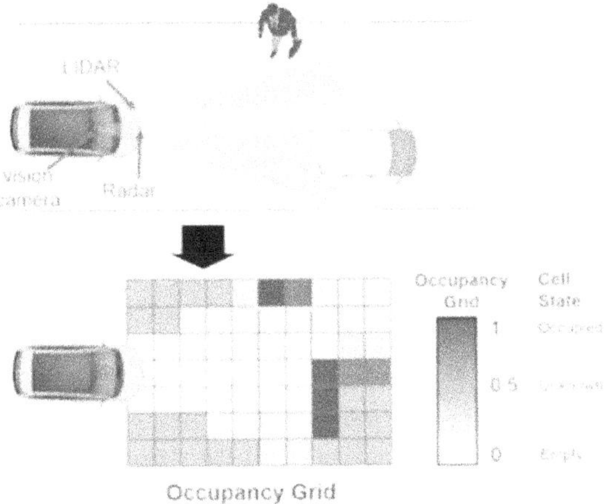

Fig. 1. Building an occupancy grid from sensor measurements in an automotive context [1].

If both explicit and efficient methods already allow to compute OG for narrow FOV sensors [1], problems arise when the FOV is large [3]. It is a problem since sensors with large FOV can bring significant advances in autonomous driving and robotic navigation. A first advantage is the larger area covered by a sensor measurement. Another advantage is the fact that the main sensors having a narrow FOV are Lidar ones, and suffer from a heavy cost and inefficiency in scenes presenting optical occlusion. Radar can be seen as a potential answer [4], as well as sonar in certain scenarios. These large FOV sensors present several similarities in the principles behind their signal processing techniques [5]. For these reasons, alongside others, multimodal sensor fusion is seen as a key component for autonomous driving and efficient methods computing OG from large FOV sensors are needed. The existing methods, based on Bayesian filtering, are currently either too costly to compute or relying on restrictive hypothesis. To deal with these latter scenarios, the use of deep neural networks has been recently proposed in the literature [6]. Neural networks may provide a suitable approximation of an OG computation model at a reasonable cost.

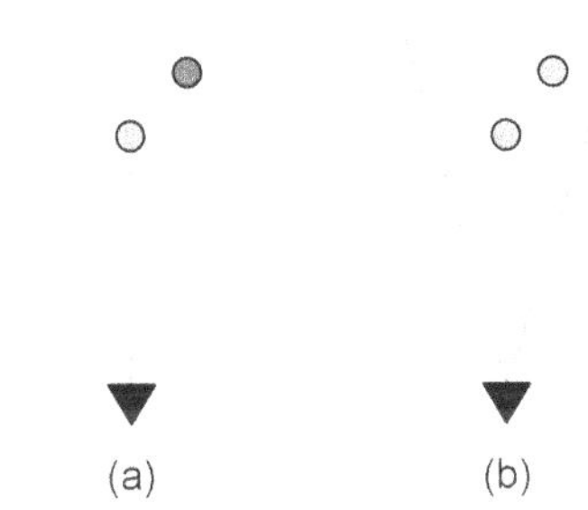

Fig. 2. An illustration of the difference between narrow (left) and large (right) field of view sensors. The blue dots represent the sensor's field of view. The circles are targets and the ones in green are seen by the sensor.

Taking benefit from an analogy between 2D range-azimuth maps, OG and images, networks initially intended for image segmentation problems were used for building OG. To do so, the previous works as in [6] use U-net architectures [7] for this type of task. These networks convert the output of the sensor signal processing chain into an OG. The original work used a radar that has a beam too narrow to match our work, even though it produced probabilistic OG. Others have been applied to radar post target detection data (the range and azimuth, as depicted in Fig. 3) with ternary OG (the cell can be "free", "occupied" but also "unknown") [8, 9].

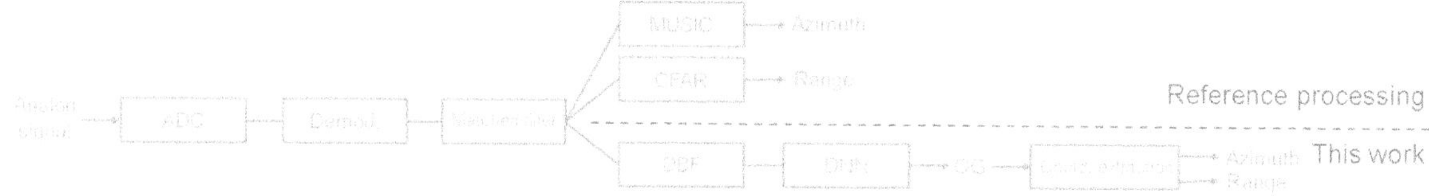

Fig. 3. A typical sonar signal processing chain and the one used in this work.

All these works use metrics that do not give a clear indication of the accuracy of the targets localization. This metric, the Intersection-over-Union (IoU) is the reference in image segmentation. Yet it does not give a direct estimation of the localization accuracy. On top of that, these approaches use "high level" data that have gone through several signal processing algorithms (like those given in Fig. 3 as references) that already realize localization tasks. These algorithms have limitations like the need of a complex calibration for the CFAR used as reference [5, 10]. Other references of radar target localization using deep learning exist. They addressed this problem in terms of accuracy for the range, azimuth and elevation estimations [11]. However, they do not output occupancy grids.

This work is a continuation of these approaches [6, 8, 9], using a sonar as a large FOV sensor. A neural network has been trained to generate an OG from sonar signal before target detection. As a preliminary work, the OG only contains binary states: occupied or free. In the mono-target case, accuracy of the target's range and azimuth estimates is evaluated and compared with the estimation accuracy of a reference approach, based on MUSIC and CFAR [10].

2. Reference Sonar Signal Processing Chain

This work aims to evaluate the precision of the target localization performed by the network in a 2D context. A target has two main characteristics: its range in the sensor centered referential (in this work in cm) and its azimuthal orientation (in degrees). The comparison is limited to mono-target scenario. This avoids problems such as occlusion that would complicate the evaluation. Concerning the approach used as reference, the range is obtained using a CFAR detection [10] and time-of-flight calculation. An Order Statistic (OS) CFAR [10], a common version of the algorithm, is implemented and calibrated. This algorithm is the reference when it comes to target detection in radar and sonar, but it suffers some flaws. One of them is the range resolution: if two targets are too closed, it is not possible to separate them. Another is the complicated calibration of the algorithm which is to be used in a specific configuration of noise. As for the direction of arrival (DOA) estimation, the MUSIC algorithm is chosen due to its high resolution [10]. Note that MUSIC needs a priori knowledge of the number of targets present in the scene. The goal is to compare the network's performances to those of the reference. Since the network products OG as output, the range and azimuth are extracted from this OG using image processing tools as depicted in Fig. 3. For this purpose, a binary OG is sufficient.

3. Deep Learning Based Processing Chain

The network's architecture is described in this section, followed by the dataset generation.

3.1. Neural Network Architecture

Similarly with [6, 8, 9], the network's architecture is a U-net due to its performances in general image segmentation problems. The loss used is the standard binary crossentropy. The network, depicted in Fig. 4, acts as an encoder-decoder. A first half extracts features from the input signal and the second converts the feature maps extracted into a signal with the same dimensions as the input one. More specifically, the network is composed of 5 "levels" – not to be confused with "layers" – that can be represented so that it has the "U" shape that gives it its name. The four first levels are present in both encoder and decoder half while the 5th is the feature map. An encoder block, as well as the feature map, is composed of two convolutions layers and a max pooling. The same goes for the decoder except that it also comprises a concatenation layer connected to the output of the last convolution layer of the encoder block in the same level in order to "remap" the features at the right pixels. This way, each pixel of the output image is a cell of the grid associated to the class "free" or "occupied".

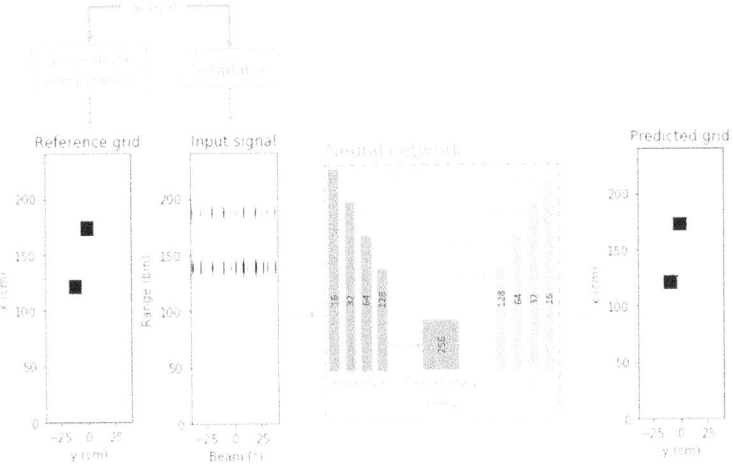

Fig. 4. The workflow of the DL-based approach. Each rectangle represents 2 convolution layers and a max pooling one. The numbers of convolution kernels for each layer are given in the corresponding rectangles.

3.2. Dataset Generation

The perception task that this work is tackling consists in converting a sonar signal into a representation of the environment in front of the sensor. The training of the network needs an input and the output that the network is supposed to produce given such input. It is a supervised learning handling an image segmentation problem [12]. Considering this, the dataset must consist of a sonar signal and the occupancy grid of the environment that induced this signal as groundtruth. It is the output that we expect the network to produce given this sonar signal.

A dataset has to be generated since there is no – to the best of our knowledge- public dataset suitable for the problem addressed in this paper. Automotive datasets already tend to rarely contain radar data [13]. Existing datasets containing radar data are however not fit for this work. The main problem is that the data available only contain signals that have passed through a CFAR detector [14]. This would not allow to test the potential of replacing the algorithm with a neural network. Considering the need of fine tuning the scenes for an evaluation accuracy purpose, simulation is chosen for providing a sufficient dataset with a reasonable cost.

A sonar simulator is used to compute the signal received by the sensor after propagation within a scene containing arbitrarily positioned obstacles. In order to focus on the localization and since it is to be performed on an OG, the targets are as large as a cell and placed so that they perfectly fit into one. The region of interest (ROI) is the 80×240 cm rectangle in front of the sensor (with it at the center of the x-axis). This rectangle is partitioned into a grid with the same dimensions (each cell is a 1 cm square). A scene consists of between one and three 1 cm wide planes. The planes are randomly placed on cells considering a margin of 10 cells on the x-axis and between 35 and 220 cm. 3000 scenes are generated. A problem arises with groundtruth grids computation. It is difficult for a neural network to output an image with a segmentation of only one pixel. Thus, the targets on the groundtruths are not represented as a single cell but rather as a 7×7 square as shown in Fig. 5. The square's center of mass represents the coordinates of the detected target.

A sonar is then simulated in order to obtain an input signal to the network. The sensor consists of one emitter so that the emission beam is the widest possible. It also has 5 transducers for reception that allow direction of arrival (DOA) estimation for the echoes. This way, it is possible to estimate the azimuth of the detected targets. The sonar emits a sine pulse and the simulator computes the acoustic wave received at each transducer after reflection on target(s). The signal is amplified and converted into the digital domain. The common processing to both reference and deep learning approaches includes a signal demodulation followed by a matched filter. Since a 2D signal is required, a Digital Beamforming (DBF) algorithm is used for obtaining a 2D polar map representing the power received from each point of space in front of the sensor [15]. The process is illustrated in Fig. 3. An example of input signal is also depicted in Fig. 4.

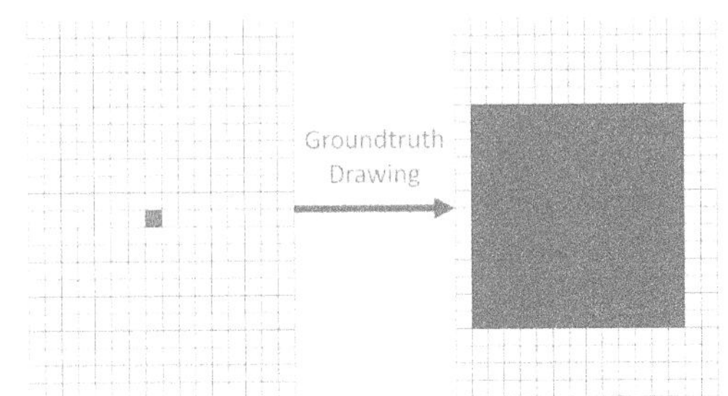

Fig. 5. In order to provide a groundtruth that allows to train the network, we represent each cell by a bigger square.

4. Simulation Results

Both the reference and neural network's implementations were evaluated in terms of range and azimuth accuracy using the Root Mean Squared Error (RMSE) as a metric:

$$RMSE(y, \tilde{y}) = \sqrt{\frac{\sum_{i=1}^{N}(y_i - \tilde{y}_i)^2}{N}}, \quad (1)$$

where y_i is the groundtruth and $\tilde{y}_i$ is the value predicted by the model for a validation test of N samples for vectors y and $\tilde{y}$. Since this metric is used for evaluating estimation, we do not count the cases where the target is not detected or where a non-existing target is, which can happen when the SNR drops too low. Results obtained for each cell on the left half of the ROI (miss detections not taken into account) are displayed in Table 1.

Table 1. Performances of both approaches on the validation data (RMSE).

Approach	Range (cm)	Azimuth (°)
CFAR + MUSIC	4,463	0.424
Neural network	**0.820**	**1.465**

4.1. Results Analysis

The network achieved a better accuracy than the reference approach for the range estimation. On the contrary, MUSIC achieved a better result on azimuth estimation, even though the network provided encouraging results. An example of scene reconstruction (in a multi-target scenario) is given in Fig. 4. In order to obtain a richer information than the global performance displayed in Table 1, a set of 20 simulations was run where the error is evaluated at every possible cell of the grid (this time, a miss detection gives a maximum error). Thanks to the symmetrical RMSE distribution over the x-axis, only the left half of the map was computed. It allows to draw an image containing in each pixel the RMSE for each corresponding cell in the grid. For each approach, an error map is drawn for each of the two estimated parameters. The resulting maps are displayed in Fig. 6.

As expected, the reference approach has trouble detecting targets that are at the extremities of the emission diagram, where it ensues failures. The phenomenon is less pronounced with the neural network, which suffers less miss detections in this area. This aside, the reference approach performs a pinpoint accuracy regarding the azimuth estimation on the rest of the region. The network has trouble with the extremities of the ROI, where the SNR drops. Observing the grids computed for targets in this area show that the network does not draw perfect 7×7 squares. This adds another source or error since the center of mass of the square does not correspond to the target location. This is not observed for range estimation, where the network keeps giving better results than CFAR and shows a pretty uniform error.

4.2. Discussion

These results must be regarded in the light of limitations in the possibilities offered by the simulator. The absence of reflective elements besides the targets clearly eases their localization and cannot be considered "realistic". In a concrete sonar situation a lot of constraints such as clutter would considerably complicate the problem and thus reduce the implementations performances [5]. Nevertheless, this work aimed to provide a proof-of-concept for computing occupancy grids from low level sonar data with satisfying performances, which the results tend to infer. These results must now be consolidated by conducting experiments on real world data or more complex simulation scenarios.

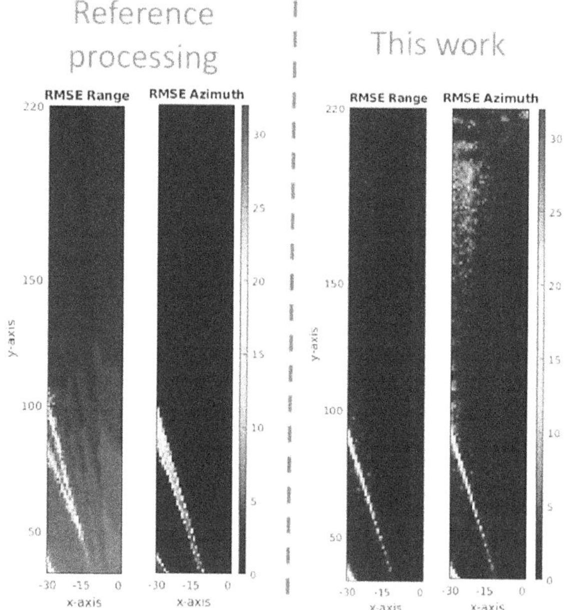

Fig. 6. The errors observed for each approach estimations of range and azimuth. The errors above 12 are caused by more or less frequent miss detections.

5. Conclusions

A deep neural network converting pre-processed sonar data into occupancy grids indicating the location of the targets has been successfully trained. To do so, simulated scenes and associated sonar outputs were used for training and testing the artificial neural network. This network has shown encouraging results for range and azimuth estimation on single target scenario. It holds the comparison with a CFAR and MUSIC combination. Future works shall focus on the robustness of this approach to more challenging conditions in terms of noise, by using real world data. Alongside a certain consolidation, it would also allow to study if it keeps performing well in situations where CFAR and MUSIC show their limitations. It is also intended to work on the generation of probabilistic occupancy grids for sensor fusion purposes.

References

[1]. T. Rakotovao Andriamahefa, Integer Occupancy Grids: A probabilistic multi-sensor fusion framework for embedded perception, PhD Thesis, *Université Grenoble Alpes*, CEA Grenoble, February 2017.

[2]. S. Thrun, W. Burgard, D. Fox, Probabilistic Robotics, *MIT Press*, 2005.

[3]. R. Dia, General inverse sensor model for proba-bilistic occupancy grid maps using multi-target sensors, in *Proceedings of the 23rd International Symposium on Mathematical Theory of Networks and Systems (MTNS'18),* Hong Kong, 2018, pp. 941-948.

[4]. I. Bilik, O. Longman, S. Villeval, J. Tabrikian, The rise of radar for autonomous vehicles: Signal processing solutions and future research directions, *IEEE Signal Processing Magazine*, Vol. 36, Issue 5, September 2019, pp. 20-31.

[5]. F. LeChevalier, Principles of Radar and Sonar Signal Processing, *Artech House Publishers*, 2002.

[6]. R. Weston, S. Cen, P. Newman, I. Posner, Probably unknown: Deep inverse sensor modelling radar, in *Proceedings of the International Conference on Robotics and Automation (ICRA'19)*, Montreal, QC, Canada, 2019, pp. 5446-5452.

[7]. O. Ronneberger, P. Fischer, T. Brox, U-Net: Convolutional Networks for Biomedical Image Segmentation, in *Proceedings of the International Conference on Medical Image Computing and Computer-assisted Intervention (MICCAI'15)*, 2015, pp. 234-241.

[8]. L. Sless, et al., Self supervised occupancy grid learning from sparse radar for autonomous driving, *arXiv:1904.00415*, 2019.

[9]. D. Bauer, L. Kuhnert, L. Eckstein, Deep, spatially coherent Inverse Sensor Models with Uncertainty Incorporation using the evidential Framework, in *Proceedings of the IEEE Intelligent Vehicles Symposium (IV'19)*, 2019, pp. 2490-2495.

[10]. M. I. Skolnik, Radar Handbook, 3rd Ed., *McGraw-Hill Education*, 2008.

[11]. D. Brodeski, I. Bilik, R. Giryes, Deep radar detector, in *Proceedings of the IEEE Radar Conference (RadarConf'19)*, 2019, pp. 1-6.

[12]. J. Long, E. Shelhamer, T. Darrell, Fully convolutional networks for semantic segmentation, in *Proceedings of the IEEE Conference on Computer Vision and Pattern Recognition (CVPR'15)*, 2015, pp. 3431-3440.

[13]. D. Feng, *et al.*, Deep multi-modal object detection and semantic segmentation for autonomous driving: Datasets, methods, and challenges, *arXiv:1902.07830*, 2019.

[14]. H. Caesar, *et al.*, nuScenes: A multimodal dataset for autonomous driving, *arXiv:1903.11027*, 2019.

[15]. B. D. V. Veen, K. M. Buckley, Beamforming: A versatile approach to spatial filtering, *IEEE ASSP Magazine*, Vol. 5, Issue 2, 1988, pp. 4-24.

(037)

A Study of Cardiac Contractility Estimations from Single-beat Pressure Volume Loop Data

Edward Marcus
Cardiology Department, Children's Hospital Boston, 9 Hope St., Waltham, Massachusetts, USA
Tel: (001) 781-216-2532
E-mail: ed.marcus@cardio.chboston.org

Summary: Cardiac contractility can be estimated from one beat of pressure volume loop (PV loop) data. In this study, single-beat estimation effectiveness is examined with contractility defined by maximum elastance (Emax), isovolumic mode pressure (Piso), pressure volume area (PVA), and pressure volume area of the isovolumic mode (PVAiso). All estimates were based on approximations to volume equilibrium (Vo) provided as a calculation input. Results from approximated Vo input were then compared to direct measures of contractility from a multiple-beat sequence of PV loops. Digitizing 23 published datasets, the single-beat estimates yielded these percent differences to multi-beat results: PVAiso (4 ± 4 %), Piso (8 ± 6 %), PVA (9 ± 6 %), Emax (22 ± 17 %); $p<.0001$ one way ANOVA. The PVAiso results demonstrated the minimum differences, and it appears the PVAiso measure of contractility can reliably estimate contractility and streamline the process of its measurement.

Keywords: Pressure volume loop, Single-beat processing, Pressure volume area, Isovolumic contracting mode, Contractility methods.

1. Introduction

The PV loop is a graph which displays the heart's cyclical pattern of chamber pressure (P) vs. chamber volume (V). Indices of cardiac contractility measured from the PV loop can include developed elastance, pressure, stroke work, and mechanical potential energy [1, 2]. To measure these parameters, hemodynamic responses are recorded when the chamber filling pattern (preload) or the arterial impedance to outflow (afterload) becomes altered by an intervention. Yet, these procedures to adjust the natural functioning load are not always feasible for human subjects, and a load alteration may not yield a hemodynamic pattern which allows for contractility to be accurately measured. For these reasons, different techniques to apply data collected at natural load can be examined – with the goal to confidently measure contractility when load adjustment may not be feasible or effective.

2. Methods

2.1. Physiology Basis of Contractility Measures

The methods to be studied for single-beat contractility effectiveness are properties of the cardiac pressure volume (PV) relationship outlined by Suga and Sagawa [1] in this mathematical equation.

$$\text{PV relationship: } P(t) = E(t)*(V(t)-Vo) \qquad (1)$$

The PV relationship's E(t) property is a time varying elastance, and defines the chamber's cyclical pattern of dP/dV mechanical modulus variation. The Vo property of Eq. (1) is termed the "equilibrium volume", and Vo measures minimum chamber size if experimentally depressurized to $P = 0$ equilibrium.

Applying the PV relationship, four measures of contractility are implemented for the single-beat estimation effectiveness study: *Emax elastance* is defined as the maximum of the time-varying E(t) property from Eq. 1, and is calculated from measures of Vo and PV loop samples of V(t), P(t).

$$\begin{aligned} Emax &= \text{maximum } E(t) = \\ &= \text{maximum } P(t)/(V(t)-Vo), \end{aligned} \qquad (2)$$

P_{iso} pressure defines peak pressure if aortic clamping were applied to maintain the chamber size at a constant end-diastolic volume (EDV). In this paper, it is assumed Emax and Vo properties measured from the ejecting beat remain in effect for isovolumic conditions [3]. From this assumption, the isovolumic contracting mode's maximum pressure P_{iso} can be calculated from Eqs. (1-2).

$$P_{iso} = Emax * (EDV-Vo), \qquad (3)$$

PVA energy is a measure of the combined work by contracting cells to provide ejected stroke work (SW) delivered for arterial consumption, and mechanical elastic potential energy (EPE) which remains within the chamber structure [2]. The ejecting heart's PVA measure of contractility is an energy sum of SW and EPE.

$$PVA = SW + EPE, \qquad (4)$$

PVA_{iso} energy is a special case of the PVA energy measured in the isovolumic mode. As ejected stroke

work is absent (SW = 0) in the isovolumic mode, all contractile mechanism energy measured by PVA_{iso} is comprised of EPE elastic potential energy.

$$PVA_{iso} = \text{EPE of the isovolumic mode (SW = 0)} \quad (5)$$

2.2. Single-beat Estimation Modeling

To estimate the Eqs. (2-5) contractility definitions from single-beat inputs, the Vo equilibrium property of Eq. 1 was first approximated by a zero-bias linear regression model. A volume difference between end-diastolic volume (EDV), and end-systolic volume (ESV) was computed as a cardiac stroke volume quantity SV = EDV-ESV, and SV was applied as the regression's independent variable. From digitized measures [4] of EDV, ESV, and Vo collected from 23 multi-beat right ventricle diagrams [5-20], a regression model of EDV-Vo based on SV was formulated into this result.

$$\text{Regression model: EDV-Vo} = 1.91*SV, \quad R^2=.966 \quad (6)$$

The slope factor was rounded to a nearest whole number of 2, and applied to approximate the Vo inputs provided to single-beat estimate calculations.

$$\text{Approximated Vo input: Vo} \sim \text{EDV}-2*\text{SV} \quad (7)$$

2.3. Single-beat and Multi-beat Calculations

Each estimate calculated from the input of a single-beat Vo approximation was compared to the corresponding calculated result from Vo input that was directly measured from multi-beat data. Fig. 1 illustrates the direct measure of Vo from multiple beats, or the approximation to Vo from a single-beat, was combined with digitized PV loop samples to calculate Emax and P_{iso} for both input types. Ejecting PVA = SW+EPE energies were computed from area planimetry of SW and EPE regions in the PV diagram. The diagram's planimetry included energy difference measurements of $\Delta PVA = PVA_{iso} - PVA$, such that $PVA_{iso} = PVA + \Delta PVA = SW + EPE + \Delta PVA$.

Both diagrams outline fundamental components of calculation. Baseline beat sample 'tmax' is the time point of Emax = maximum P(t)/(V(t)-Vo) and P_{iso} = Emax *(EDV-Vo). SW energy is a red region area enclosed by baseline beat samples, and EPE is a blue region area forming an energy component of PVA = SW+EPE. The gray region area specifies the $\Delta PVA = PVA_{iso} - PVA$ energy difference between isovolumic and ejecting mode pressure volume area measurement. The figure is adapted from Bellofiore and Chesler [21] with permission from Springer Nature.

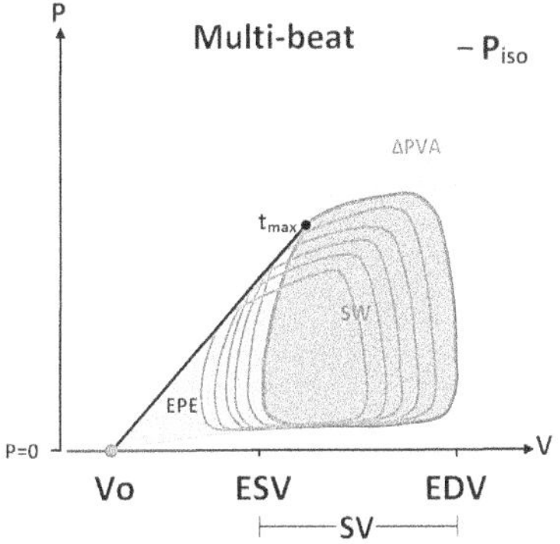

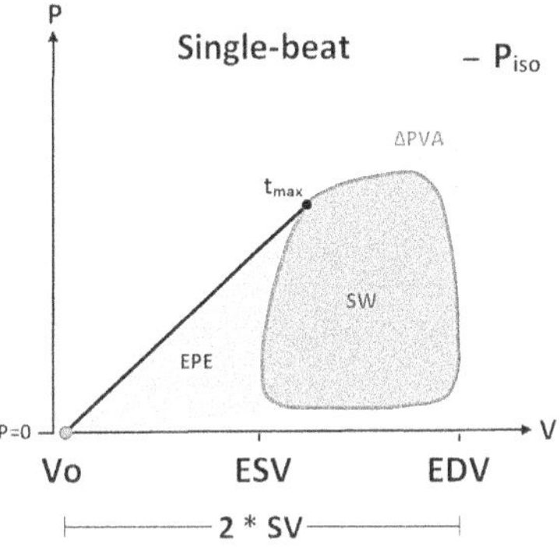

Fig. 1. Contractility can be calculated from a multi-beat measure or a single-beat estimate of Vo. Multiple PV loops recorded during a preload reduction from baseline function (PV loop shown in red) form a gradual trend of depressurization to a limiting Vo equilibrium volume. With single-beat data at baseline, the depressurization response cannot be measured, and Vo input to calculation is estimated as Vo = EDV – 2*SV.

3. Results

Outcomes of the calculation differences between single-beat and multi-beat provided inputs are summarized in Table 1. Percent errors between the estimates and multi-beat results were between 4 ± 4 % for the PVA_{iso} method and 22 ± 17 % for the Emax method. One way ANOVA with repeated measures yielded a p<.0001 result across the method defined groups.

Table 1. Differences between single-beat (sb) and multi-beat (mb) calculation results from 23 datasets.

Method	% Difference	Slope	R^2
E_{max}	22 ± 17 %	sb = 1.189 * mb	.904
PVA	9 ± 6 %	sb = 1.047 * mb	.991
P_{iso}	8 ± 6 %	sb = 1.002 * mb	.924
PVA_{iso}	4 ± 4 %	sb = 1.015 * mb	.999

Details of individual PVA_{iso} datapoints are shown in Fig. 2 to demonstrate the PVA_{iso} estimations were effective through the entire range of studied chamber energies. These results suggested the PVA_{iso} measures might be similarly correlated to chamber size variations forming this energy range.

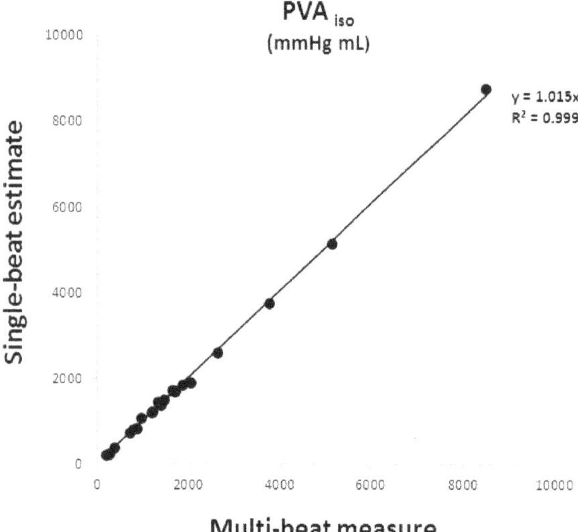

Fig. 2. Estimates of PVA iso contractility from single-beat data were effective over a range of contractile energy outputs.

The chamber size influence on measures of PVA_{iso} (and PVA) was confirmed by the positive EDV correlations shown in Table 2. E_{max} results were observed to be inversely EDV dependent, and the P_{iso} results were not EDV correlated.

Table 2. Variation of estimates with end-diastolic volume.

	R^2
E_{max} = – 0.016 * EDV + 2.485	.400
PVA = 27.52 * EDV – 794.13	.791
P_{iso} = 0.032 * EDV + 45.02	.007
PVA_{iso} = 34.72 * EDV -1024.6	.775

4. Discussion

Effective estimation is a convenient initial step to interpret contractile function. A second, and vital component of contractility diagnosis is to determine whether a measured outcome is within a normal range for a patient's age, height, or weight. For pediatric patients, understanding the normal value progressions expected during stages of physical development [22] becomes a critical factor to interpret whether a contractility measurement is within or outside of a normal limit.

From the results of calculation, and the need to interpret with normal ranges, there are two benefits realized by the studied PVA_{iso} method. As the PVA_{iso} estimate from a single-beat reliably reflects its multi-beat counterpart, a need for load adjustment during the PV loop procedure might be circumvented. It was also observed, that the PVA_{iso} measurement had a positive correlation to the EDV measure of chamber size. This compelling result suggests the PVA_{iso} index can facilitate forming pediatric contractility normal range charts.

As these benefits are based on computing factors, it is noted Emax and P_{iso} methods have established records of application to experimental research, and that Emax measurement is a proven tool for modeling purposes. Given a unique computing or experimental benefit realized by any given method, it is anticipated that future research might address which methods most effectively gauge a clinical intervention. Procedures such as the enhancement to contractility by a drug, an alteration to pacing, or a surgical change to the heart's structure might produce some change to measured contractility which is of interest to record and assess. Estimation effectiveness in these scenarios will need to be weighed with a method's ability to provide needed diagnostic sensitivity.

In the context of mechanics, the PVA_{iso} measurement is interpreted as an energy quantity defining an ejecting heart's *potential* to generate a maximum measured PVA. As an upper limit, the PVA_{iso} measure always exceeds the ejecting PVA measure, and supplemental $\Delta PVA = PVA_{iso} - PVA$ energy might reflect physical influences of more than one mechanism. For example, after some latency to introduced isovolumic conditions, contractile energy outputs may experience a natural gain from adaptation. Also, the energy dissipated by the ejecting heart's motions (such as viscous energy and kinetic energy) will reduce the ejecting PVA measure in relation to the isovolumic PVA_{iso} measure. In this way, the ΔPVA supplement to ejecting PVA might represent natural adaptations of energy output, or improvements to the PVA measurement accuracy in the absence of motion mechanism losses, or some combination of both these factors.

A limitation is realized by the method of V(t), P(t) data acquisition from PV diagram charts, and the possibility of error introduced to calculated results. While manually acquired data would generate some error, these effects were considered to be very limited in comparison to the larger effects of generating error by approximating Vo.

To summarize, the right ventricle's natural capability to develop PVA_{iso} energy is reliably estimated from single-beat PV loop data. The PVA_{iso} estimate is effective over a significant range of energy, and is correlated to chamber size variation. These versatile features might be considered with future efforts to simplify the PV loop procedure, or to form charts of normal ranges anticipated during pediatric growth.

References

[1]. H. Suga, K. Sagawa, Instantaneous pressure-volume relationships and their ratio in the excised, supported canine left ventricle, *Circulation Research*, Vol. 35, Issue 1, Jul 1974, pp. 117-126.

[2]. H. Suga, Total mechanical energy of a ventricle model and cardiac oxygen consumption, *American Journal of*

Physiology, Vol. 236, Issue 3, March 1979, pp. H498-H505.

[3]. S. Brimioulle, *et al.*, Single-beat estimation of right ventricular end-systolic pressure-volume relationship, *American Journal of Physiology: Heart and Circulatory Physiology*, Vol. 284, Issue 5, May 2003, pp. H1625-H1630.

[4]. A. Rohatgi, WebPlotDigitizer, 4.2 Ed., San Francisco, California, USA, https://automeris.io/WebPlotDigitizer

[5]. M. L. Dickstein, O. Yano, H. M. Spotnitz, D. Burkhoff, Assessment of right ventricular contractile state with the conductance catheter technique in the pig, *Cardiovascular Research*, Vol. 29, Issue 6, June 1995, pp. 820-826.

[6]. F. S. de Man, *et al.*, Bisoprolol delays progression towards right heart failure in experimental pulmonary hypertension, *Circulation: Heart Failure*, Vol. 5, Issue 1, January 2012, pp. 97-105.

[7]. S. Rex, C. Missant, P. Claus, W. Buhre, P. F. Wouters, Effects of inhaled iloprost on right ventricular contractility, right ventriculo-vascular coupling and ventricular interdependence: A randomized placebo-controlled trial in an experimental model of acute pulmonary hypertension, *Critical Care (London, England)*, Vol. 12, Issue 5, 2008, R113.

[8]. W. L. Maughan, A. A. Shoukas, K. Sagawa, M. L. Weisfeldt, Instantaneous pressure-volume relationship of the canine right ventricle, *Circulation Research*, Vol. 44, Issue 3, March 1979, pp. 309-315.

[9]. B. Schmitt, *et al.*, Integrated assessment of diastolic and systolic ventricular function using diagnostic cardiac magnetic resonance catheterization: validation in pigs and application in a clinical pilot study, *Journal of American College of Cardiology: Cardiovascular Imaging*, Vol. 2, Issue 11, November 2009, pp. 1271-1281.

[10]. A. Vonk-Noordegraaf, *et al.*, Right heart adaptation to pulmonary arterial hypertension: physiology and pathobiology, *Journal of the American College of Cardiology*, Vol. 62, Issue 25 Suppl., December 24 2013, pp. D22-D33.

[11]. T. Kuehne, *et al.*, Combined pulmonary stenosis and insufficiency preserves myocardial contractility in the developing heart of growing swine at midterm follow-up, *Journal of Applied Physiology*, Vol. 99, Issue 4, October 2005, pp. 1422-1427.

[12]. R. G. Axell, *et al.*, Ventriculo-arterial coupling detects occult RV dysfunction in chronic thromboembolic pulmonary vascular disease, *Physiological Reports*, Vol. 5, Issue 7, April 2017, e13227.

[13]. J. C. Grignola, F. Gines, D. Guzzo, Comparison of the Tei index with invasive measurements of right ventricular function, *International Journal of Cardiology*, Vol. 113, Issue 1, October 26 2006, pp. 25-33.

[14]. K. A. Brown, R. V. Ditchey, Human right ventricular end-systolic pressure-volume relation defined by maximal elastance, *Circulation*, Vol. 78, Issue 1, July. 1988, pp. 81-91.

[15]. C. Yerebakan, *et al.*, Acute and chronic response of the right ventricle to surgically induced pressure and volume overload – An analysis of pressure-volume relations, *Interactive Cardiovascular and Thoracic Surgery*, Vol. 10, Issue 4, April 2010, pp. 519-525.

[16]. M. Alaa, *et al.*, Right ventricular end-diastolic stiffness heralds right ventricular failure in monocrotaline-induced pulmonary hypertension, *American Journal of Physiology: Heart and Circulatory Physiology*, Vol. 311, Issue 4, October 1 2016, pp. H1004-H1013.

[17]. D. Boulate, Pulmonary circulatory – right ventricular uncoupling: New insights into pulmonary hypertension pathophysiology, in Pulmonary Hypertension: Basic Science to Clinical Medicine, *Springer*, Cham, 2016, pp. 241-253.

[18]. H. Latus, W. Binder, G. Kerst, M. Hofbeck, L. Sieverding, C. Apitz, Right ventricular-pulmonary arterial coupling in patients after repair of tetralogy of Fallot, *Journal of Thoracic and Cardiovascular Surgery*, Vol. 146, Issue 6, December 2013, pp. 1366-1372.

[19]. S. Rain, Right ventricular diastolic dysfunction in pulmonary arterial hypertension, PhD Thesis, Pulmonology and Physiology, *Free University Amsterdam*, 2015.

[20]. B. Lambermont, *et al.*, Comparison between single-beat and multiple-beat methods for estimation of right ventricular contractility, *Critical Care Medicine*, Vol. 32, Issue 9, September 2004, pp. 1886-1890.

[21]. A. Bellofiore, N. C. Chesler, Methods for measuring right ventricular function and hemodynamic coupling with the pulmonary vasculature, *Annals of Biomedical Engineering*, Vol. 41, Issue 7, July 2013, pp. 1384-1398.

[22]. S. D. Colan, Normal echocardiographic values for cardiovascular structures, in Echocardiography in Pediatric and Congenital Heart Disease (W. Lai, M. Cohen, T. Geva, L. Mertens, Eds.), *Wiley-Blackwell*, West Sussex, UK, 2009, pp. 765-785.

(038)

The Concept of a Control System Shell for Autonomous Mobile Robots

M. Kosior [1], P. Przystałka [1] and W. Panfil [1]
[1] Silesian University of Technology, Department of Fundamentals of Machinery Design, 18A Konarskiego Street, 44-100 Gliwice, Poland
E-mail: mateusz.kosior@polsl.pl, piotr.przystalka@polsl.pl, wawrzyniec.panfil@polsl.pl

Summary: The paper presents the concept of a control system shell that features different knowledge representations including shallow or deep neural networks, fuzzy neural networks, Boolean and fuzzy logic rules, Bayesian networks, etc. Such a system can be re-configured for different tasks performed by a variety of mobile platforms without changing its base architecture. In the first part the authors explain the architecture of a universal control system based on the idea of system shells commonly used in expert systems. The second part describes a use case of the system deployed on Nvidia's autonomous educational mobile robot. The knowledge base of the shell-based control system has been implemented using publicly available AlexNet convolutional neural network, MobileNet V2 deep neural network and Boolean logic rules. It was done in order to re-implement basic functionalities presented in Nvidia's exemplary code such as object following and obstacle avoidance. Then the system performance was examined on a simple use case.

Keywords: Autonomous robots, Control system shell, Knowledge representations, Deep neural networks.

1. Introduction

A general concept of an expert system shell emerged in 1980 when EMYCIN was created by emptying the knowledge base of MYCIN medical expert system [1]. Since then many examples of expert system shells featuring different knowledge representations have been designed. For example, the DEX system which operates on purely qualitative attributes is able to explain its reasoning. Depending on supplied knowledge, DEX evaluates technology or performs as a staff or an enterprise manager [2]. Other examples include JESS, the project written entirely in Java and based on CLIPS expert system [3, 4] and HUGIN which utilizes Bayesian belief networks [5]. Some systems integrate fundamentally different approaches of neural network and rule-based reasoning. An example of such a system is used as an operators' aid in the diagnosis of faults in large-scale chemical process plants [6].

The idea of an expert system shell used as a control system has been introduced to rule-based reasoning e.g. in [7]. However, conventional symbolic-based systems shells lack performance at processing large amounts of data. While still viable for basic applications, their use in vision systems, lidars and radars common in advanced mobile robotics applications results in high latency. The required performance can be achieved by migrating to parallel computing techniques and neural networks.

A plenty of control systems architectures with different approaches exist. Many of them are behavior-based such as R. Brooks's subsumption architecture [8] or motor schemes proposed by R. Arkin [9]. Introduction of model-based design [10] and unified communication systems such as the Robot Operating System (ROS) [11] has reduced the time to deploy a control system. Nevertheless, migrating of a mostly unchanged control system between different robotic platforms is still uncommon. By introducing the concept of a system shell to the domain of mobile robotics it is expected to further reduce amount of work required to design and implement full-fledged systems.

2. Control System Shell

An architecture of a control system shell is shown in Fig. 1. The system consists of base components required for its operation and optional components. The signals could be transferred online during the system's operation or offline when it is shut down. The online part of the shell consists of data converters, a knowledge base, two databases and a computation module. The components as shown in Fig. 1 could be implemented e.g. as interconnected ROS nodes [11].

A **static data base** stores parameters known *a priori* by the system, such as a path and a map supplied by an external mission planner or configuration settings supplied by the operator. The base is modified only outside the operation of the control system, so only the reading speed is meaningful to its performance. The static data base could be implemented e.g. as a relational database such as PostgreSQL or as a configuration file such as an XML or a JSON. This form is preferred to allow the operator to fine-tune the parameters directly on the target platform.

A **temporal data base** serves as the system's short-time memory and stores is previous states. Since it works on a principle of a two-way data transmission, both read and write speeds are equally important and have to be minimal. An implementation example includes POSIX shared memory or Windows paging files.

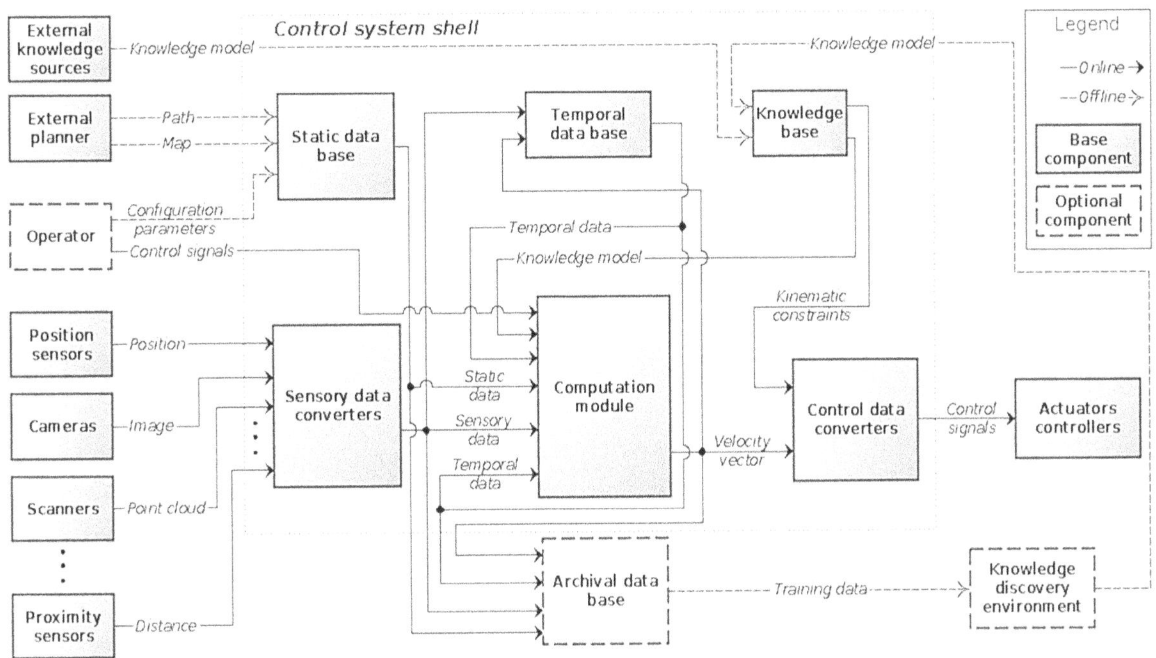

Fig. 1. A concept of a control system shell.

A **knowledge base** holds knowledge models acquired during the machine learning phase or directly from external sources of knowledge such as human experts. It is able to process a variety of different knowledge models as: (1) Boolean logic rules, (2) neural networks (NNs) including convolutional (CNNs), recurrent (RNNs) and deep (DNNs), (3) fuzzy logic models, (4) Bayesian networks and (5) finite automaton models with a possibility to extend the support to other representations as they emerge. The base is a collection of configuration files for initializing and linking building blocks of the computation module. It also contains actual models referenced by the computation module.

A **computation module** could be understood as a network of interconnected sub-models taken from the knowledge base. The models are independent agents (e.g. ROS nodes) or classes cooperating as a single application (both further referred to as computation nodes). Each computation node includes a collection of inputs and outputs. An input can be linked to an output of another node. Inputs and outputs also could be connected with data converters or databases. If required, control signals from a human operator can be included as an additional data source. The computation node also contains a processing function defined according to the type and configuration of the specific knowledge model. The final output of the module for positioning tasks is a single velocity vector. It is then stored in the temporal data base for subsequent iterations.

A variable set of sensors provides data to corresponding **sensory data converters**. The converters standardize the data format to be consistent for all data sources. Since they act similarly to drivers, it should be assumed that each type of a sensor would require its own data converter.

Control data converters are the opposite of the above. Their role is to gather the standardized data output of the computation module (a velocity vector in positioning tasks). They transform it using kinematic constraints to control signals used by the final low-level hardware actuator controllers. Like sensors, each type of an actuator also requires a unique data converter.

Optional components that further enhance the performance of the control system shell include an **archival data base** and a **knowledge discovery environment**. Both are used offline during the machine learning phase. The base stores the system states during its operation and the discovery environment extracts knowledge from the data. New knowledge models are inserted into the knowledge base. Components used for machine learning as well as the machine learning phase itself will be the subject of further research.

3. Implementation Example

A minimal working example of a control system shell was deployed on a modified Nvidia's JetBot educational platform (Fig. 2) [12]. JetBot is a differential steered two-wheeled platform with a supporting ball at its rear. The robot measures $137 \times 112 \times 98$ mm³ and weighs about 0.5 kg. As its on-board computer JetBot uses Jetson Nano Developer Kit that features a quad core 64-bit ARM A57 CPU and a 128-core MAXWELL GPU. Other hardware includes two 5 V DC motors with integrated reduction gear and open-loop control, a Raspberry Pi V2 NoIR camera with 160° FoV lens, a TB6612 motor driver, an Intel Wireless AC 8265 card and an OLED display. JetBot is powered by a built-in powerbank with capacity of 10 Ah and current output of 2×3 A.

The software is based on ROS Melodic Morenia compiled from source to support Python 3. Additional resources include: Nvidia's JetPack v. 4.3, TensorFlow GPU v. 2.0.0+nv20.1.tf2, PyTorch v. 1.0.0a0+18eef1d with torchvision v. 0.2.2.post3, Keras-Applications v. 1.0.8, Keras-Preprocessing v. 1.0.5. and slightly modified source code from the JetBot repository [12].

Fig. 2. Custom 3D-printed JetBot platform.

Control principle of the robot is as follows: the robot moves forward at a constant speed, while detecting objects and looking for obstacles. If the camera sees objects of given class, JetBot drives towards the center of the object closest to the center of the image. When an obstacle is detected, the robot turns left until no obstacle is visible and resumes the detection phase.

Collision avoidance is accomplished by AlexNet CNN [13, 14]. The final layer of the network has been modified to include only two outputs. The weights were downloaded from the official repository [12]. Object detection part is realized using a generic MobileNet V2 DNN [15, 16] trained on the COCO data set [17]. The network is able to detect 90 different common objects.

Due to simplicity of the task only a subset of the control system shell components was used. Each component has been implemented as a ROS node as depicted in Fig. 3. A knowledge base is a JSON file internally parsed by the computation module during startup, so it is not present on the ROS graph. The computation module itself is a single node built of classes. The module dynamically selects, configures and links the classes at startup according to the knowledge base. Fig. 4 presents the classes used in the example. The computation module uses image data only and outputs a single velocity vector expressed by topics: */jetbot_camera/bgr8* and */jetbot_motors/cmd_vel*, respectively.

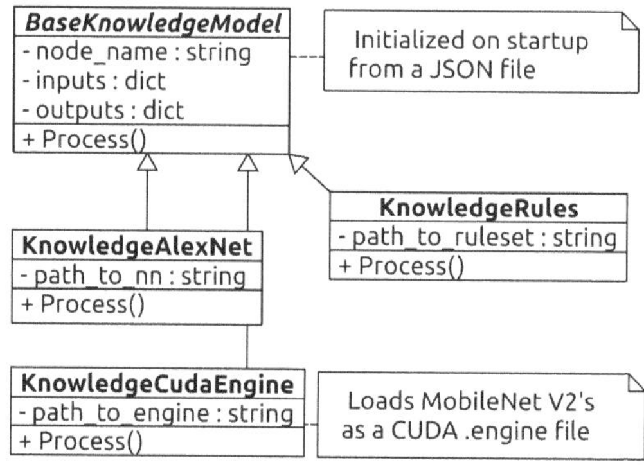

Fig. 4. The classes of the computation module.

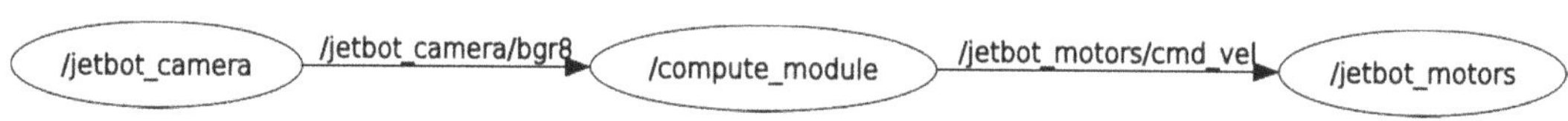

Fig. 3. The ROS nodes and topics used in the example

4. Verification Study

The purpose of the verification study was to test performance of the shell-based control system deployed on a JetBot mobile platform [12]. The tests covered two basic robotic tasks presented in Nvidia's exemplary code: (1) collision avoidance and (2) object detection. The tasks were verified separately. Apart from the node-based data transmission layer and the lack of user interface the implemented code was effectively identical to Nvidia's reference.

In the **collision avoidance** task as in Fig. 5 the robot had to continuously move across closed square area of 2×2 m² while simultaneously avoiding static obstacles including a bottle of water (19 liters), a stack of books, two cardboard boxes, a tape roll and paper walls. Performance of the system was measured by counting total amount of collisions within 5 minutes. The test was repeated four times with a different initial placement of JetBot ($JB_1 \div JB_4$, respectively). Obstacles used during the verification are summarized in Table 1 and the results in Table 2.

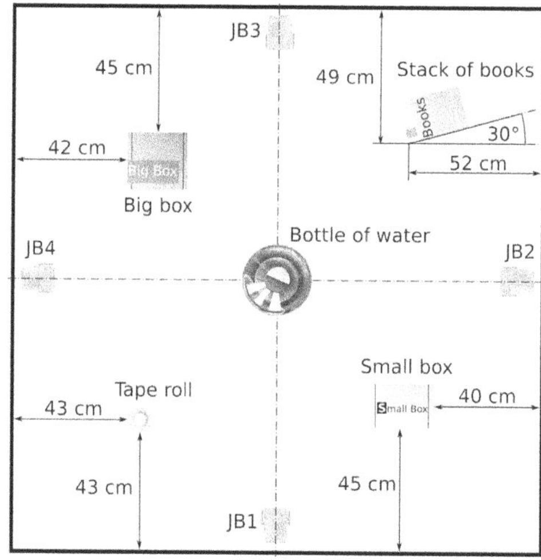

Fig. 5. Collision avoidance testing environment.

Table 1. Obstacles used during the collision avoidance.

No.	Obstacle type	Simplified shape	Dimensions [cm]	Material
1.	Bottle of water	Cylinder	$\phi 26\times 36$	PET
2.	Big box	Box	$23\times 21\times 14$	Cardboard
3.	Tape roll	Cylinder	$\phi 9\times 5$	PP
4.	Small box	Box	$24\times 16\times 7$	Cardboard
5.	Stack of books	Box	$23\times 16\times 11$	Paper

Table 2. Results of the collision avoidance test

Pos.	Number of collisions within 5 minutes						
	Walls	Bottle	Big box	Tape	Sm. box	Books	Total
JB1	3	1	0	0	0	2	**6**
JB2	3	0	0	0	0	1	**4**
JB3	2	1	0	0	0	1	**4**
JB4	1	0	1	0	0	0	**2**

The **object detection** task shown in Fig. 6 was performed by placing an object at a distance of about 1.5 m in front of the robot and shifting it to the left or right side. The robot had to detect the object and approach it (solid green line). In the case of unsuccessful detection the robot simply drove forward passing the object (dotted red line). The test was repeated ten times for each of the four different objects, i.e. a bottle of water (1.5 liters), a backpack, a computer mouse and an orange. The results are given in Table 3.

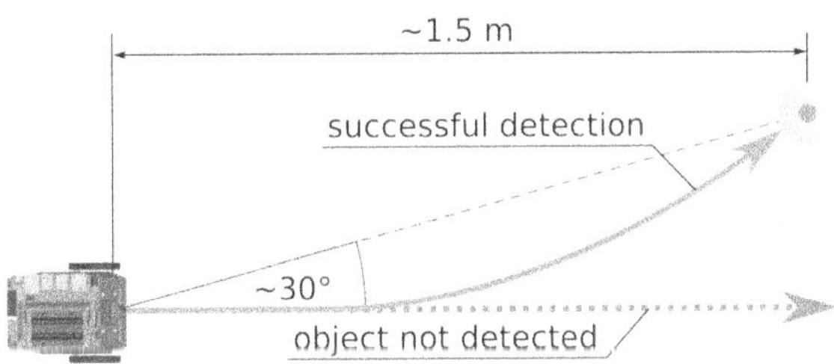

Fig. 6. Object detection test.

Table 3. Results of the object detection test.

No.	Detected object	COCO class	Detection rate
1.	Bottle of water	44	10 / 10
2.	Backpack	27	9 / 10
3.	Computer mouse	74	6 / 10
4.	Orange	55	7 / 10

5. Conclusions

It has been proven that the proposed shell-based control system architecture is able to conduct basic robotic tasks shown in Nvidia's sample code. When assessing system performance, it should be noted that the NNs used during verification were generic and not trained in the test environment.

In the further research the authors intend to expand the idea of the control system shell and proof-test it on more complex use cases. This includes cooperation of more varied knowledge models, implementation of the databases and an alternative concept of computation module as a sub-network of ROS computation nodes that could act in parallel.

References

[1]. T. Sitek, Technologie informatyczne wykorzystywane w projektowaniu i implementacji systemów inteligentnych, *Zarządzanie Technologiami Informatycznymi: Stan i Perspektywy Rozwoju*, 2006, pp. 69-82 (in Polish).

[2]. M. Bohanec, V.Rajkovič, DEX: An expert system shell for decision support, *Sistemica*, Vol. 1, 1990, pp. 145-157.

[3]. E. J. Friedman-Hill, Jess, The Java expert system shell, No. SAND-98-8206, *Sandia Labs*, Livermore, CA USA, 1997.

[4]. JESS Web Portal, https://www.jessrules.com

[5]. S. Andersen, et al., HUGIN – A Shell for Building Bayesian Belief Universes for Expert Systems, in *Proceedings of the 11th International Joint Conference on Artificial Intelligence (IJCAI'89)*, Vol. 2, 1989, pp. 1080-1085.

[6]. S. Ginsburg, Model-based Design for Embedded Systems, *MathWorks*, 2008.

[7]. W. R. Becraft, P. L. Lee, An integrated neural network/expert system approach for fault diagnosis, *Computers & Chemical Engineering*, Vol. 17, Issue 10, 1993, pp. 1001-1014.

[8]. R. Brooks, A Robust layered control system for a mobile robot, *IEEE Journal of Robotics and Automation*, Vol. RA-2, Issue 1, 1986, pp. 14-23.

[9]. R. C. Arkin, Behavior-based Robotics, *MIT Press*, 1998.

[10]. R. A. Oyen, et al., An expert system shell embedded in the control system, in Artificial Intelligence in Real-Time Control, *Elsevier*, 1988, pp. 61-66.

[11]. M. Quigley, et al., ROS: An open-source Robot Operating System, in *Proceedings of the ICRA Workshop on Open Source Software*, Vol. 3, Issue 3.2, 2009.

[12]. JetBot Github Repository, https://github.com/Nvidia-AI-IOT/jetbot

[13]. A. Krizhevsky, et al., ImageNet classification with deep convolutional neural networks, *Advances in Neural Information Processing Systems*, Vol. 25, Issue 2, 2012, pp. 1097-1105.

[14]. A. Krizhevsky, One weird trick for parallelizing convolutional neural networks, *ArXiv Preprint*, arXiv:1404.5997, 2014.

[15]. A. G. Howard, et al., MobileNets: Efficient convolutional neural networks for mobile vision applications, *ArXiv Preprint*, arXiv:1704.04861, 2017.

[16]. M. Sandler, et al., MobileNet V2: Inverted residuals and linear bottlenecks, in *Proceedings of the IEEE Conference on Computer Vision and Pattern Recognition (CVPR'18)*, 2018, pp. 4510-4520.

[17]. T.-Y. Lin, et al., Microsoft COCO: Common Objects in Context, in *Proceedings of the European Conference on Computer Vision (ECCV'14)*, 2014, pp. 740-755.

(039)

An Efficient Method for Voice to Voice Recognition and Synthesizer

Naeem Hadiq [1], Nibras Nazar [2], Sumeena Salam [2], Neha Parveen, [2] Sobin C. C. [3] and Rohit Chivukula [4]

[1] Innovation Incubator Advisory, Technopark, Trivandrum, Kerala, India
[2] 4notfour LPP, Kuttippuram, Kerala, India
[3] Dept. of CSE, SRM University AP, Andhra Pradesh, India
[4] School of Computing and Engineering, University of Huddersfield, Huddersfield, UK
Tel.: +91-866-2429299
E-mail: sobin.c@srmap.edu.in

Summary: Speech recognition is the ability of a machine or program to identify words and phrases in spoken language and convert them to a machine-readable format. One of the main difficulties in speech recognition is the immense variations among people in pronouncing words. Background noise can also cause a whole system to fail. As a result, speech recognition fails in many cases due to noises that are out of the user's control. In this paper, we developed a method to synthesize natural synthetic speech as processed output from input voice. The input speech is converted to text which is then syntactically and semantically processed to analyse the requirement and then the output is converted back to synthetic speech. The proposed method outperforms some of the existing methods on the Switchboard Hub 500 corpus, achieving less than 16 percent error, and performs better than commercial systems in noisy speech recognition tests.

Keywords: Speech recognition, Recurrent neural network, Lexical analysis, Syntactic analysis.

1. Introduction

Speech recognition technology, which can recognize human speech and change to text, or to perform a command, has emerged as the next big thing of the IT industry. Speech recognition is a technology that uses desired equipment and a service which can be controlled through voice without using items such as mouse or keyboard. It also appeared as part of ongoing research in progress in 1950's, but was not popularized until the mid of 2000, with low voice recognition. Presently, related speech recognition technologies, which have been previously used limited for special purposes, have been rapidly evolving because of the proliferation of portable computing terminals such as smartphones interconnected with the expansion of the cloud infrastructure.

One of the most prominent examples of a mobile voice interface is *Siri*, the voice activated personal assistant that comes built into the latest iPhone. But voice functionality is also built into Android, the Windows Phone platform, and most other mobile systems, as well as many applications. While these interfaces still have considerable limitations, we are inching closer to machine interfaces we can talk to. Top speech recognition systems rely on sophisticated pipelines composed of multiple algorithms and hand-engineered processing stages.

In this paper, we describe an end-to-end speech system, where deep learning supersedes these processing stages. Combined with a language model, and a response generator, the proposed approach achieves higher performance than traditional methods on hard speech recognition and processing tasks while also being much simpler. These results are made possible by training a large recurrent neural network (RNN) using multiple GPUs and thousands of hours of data for recognition and processing alongside a DNN trained for speech synthesis. As the proposed system learns directly from data, we do not require specialized components for speaker adaptation or noise filtering. In fact, in many of the cases robustness to speaker variation and noise are critical. The proposed system outperforms some of the existing techniques in literature, by achieving less error, and performs better than commercial systems in noisy speech recognition tests while also being able to generate speaker embedded high quality modulate synthetic speech outputs.

2. Related Work

Related approaches to speech recognition system introduced in the existing systems is briefly discussed in this section. The most commonly used approaches are listed below.

2.1. Automatic Speech Recognition (ASR)

The main focus of Automatic Speech Recognition (ASR) is to analyze the performance of in different emotional environments using prosody modification. The majority of ASR systems are trained using neutral speech and the performance of such systems degrade when tested with the emotional speech. The various components of speech that contribute to the emotion characteristics are studied. The prosody features of the source emotional utterances are modified according to the target neutral utterances using Flexible Analysis Synthesis Tool (FAST). In the FAST, Dynamic Time Warping (DTW) is used to align the source emotional and target neutral utterances. Components of the prosody such as intonation, duration and excitation source are manipulated to incorporate the desired features into the source utterance. The modified (source emotional) utterances are then used for testing the ASR system which is trained using neutral speech. Three emotions (compassion, happiness and anger) are considered for the analysis. Experimental results indicate an average improvement in the speech recognition system performance by considering prosody modified speech.

Automatic Speech Recognition (ASR) involves the process of considering the machine driven transcription of the language spoken by the speaker and converting them to a readable text. The goal of an ASR system is to accurately convert a speech signal into sequence of symbols. ASR in the presence of different emotion conditions is one of the research problems in natural human-machine interaction. Emotional environments may be viewed as a state where speakers produce speech in different emotions such as compassion, anger and happiness.

The majority of ASR systems are trained on the neutral speech. The performance of the ASR system is degraded in different emotions. The naturalness of the human-machine interaction mainly depends on the ASR system's ability to recognize speech under emotional conditions. In the literature, it is stated that the ASR system performance can be improved in three different levels namely pre-processing level, robust feature representation level and model-based adaptation level. The prosody modification is done at the pre-processing level to convert the emotional utterance into neutral utterance and the MFCC features are extracted later for ASR system [1].

2.2. Support Vector Machine (SVM)

One of the powerful tools for pattern recognition that uses a discriminative approach is a SVM. SVMs use linear and non-linear separating hyper-planes for data classification.

However, since SVM can only classify fixed length data vectors, this method cannot be readily applied to task involving variable length data classification. The variable length data has to be transformed to fixed length vectors before SVM can be used. It is a generalized linear classifier with maximum-margin fitting functions. This fitting function provides regularization which helps the classifier generalized better. The classifier tends to ignore many of the features.

Conventional statistical and neural network methods control model complexity by using a small number of features. SVM controls the model complexity by controlling the VC dimensions of its model. This method is independent of dimensionality and can utilize spaces of very large dimensions spaces, which permits a construction of very large number of on-linear features and then performing adaptive feature selection during training. By shifting all non-linearity to the features, SVM can use linear model for which VC dimensions is known.

2.3. Acoustic Models

Research in speech processing and communication for the most part, was motivated by people desire to build mechanical models to emulate human verbal communication capabilities. Speech is the most natural form of human communication and speech processing has been one of the most exciting areas of the signal processing. Speech recognition technology has made it possible for computer to follow human voice commands and understand human languages. The main goal of speech recognition area is to develop techniques and systems for speech input to machine. Speech is the primary means of communication between humans. For reasons ranging from technological curiosity about the mechanisms for mechanical realization of human speech capabilities to desire to automate simple tasks which necessitates human machine interactions and research in automatic speech recognition by machines has attracted a great deal of attention for sixty years.

Based on major advances in statistical modeling of speech, automatic speech recognition systems today find widespread application in tasks that require human machine interface, such as automatic call processing in telephone networks, and query based information systems that provide updated travel information, stock price quotations, weather reports, data entry, voice dictation, access to information: travel, banking, commands, avionics, automobile portal, speech transcription, handicapped people (blind people) supermarket, railway reservations etc. Speech recognition technology was increasingly used within telephone networks to automate as well as to enhance the operator services. This report reviews major highlights during the last six decades in the research and development of automatic speech recognition, so as to provide a technological perspective. Although many technological progresses have been made, still there remains many research issues that need to be tackled. Fig. 1 shows a mathematical representation of speech recognition system in simple equations which contain front end unit, model unit, language model unit, and search unit. The recognition process is shown below (Fig. 1).

The standard approach to large vocabulary continuous speech recognition is to assume a simple probabilistic model of speech production whereby a specified word sequence, W, produces an acoustic observation sequence Y, with probability P(W,Y). The goal is then to decode the word string, based on the acoustic observation sequence, so that the decoded string has the maximum a posteriori (MAP) probability [2].

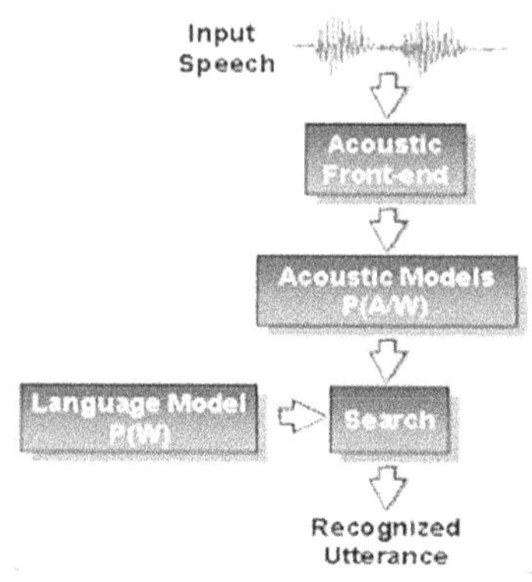

Fig. 1. Basic model of speech recognition.

3. Proposed Method

Speech recognition is the ability of a machine or program to identify words and phrases in spoken language and convert them to a machine-readable format [3]. The proposed system create a completely offline (Low Inference Compute) vocal recognition and response system capable of understanding the context of speech and differentiate between tones of speech. The system can be used as critical responses for computer controlled devices including robots and war equipment.

3.1. Speech to Text Conversion

The complete RNN model is illustrated in Fig. 2. Its structure is considerably simpler than related models used in this domain – we have limited ourselves to a single recurrent layer (which is the hardest to parallelize) and we do not use Long-Short-Term-Memory (LSTM) circuits. One disadvantage of LSTM cells is that they require computing and storing multiple gating neuron responses at each step.

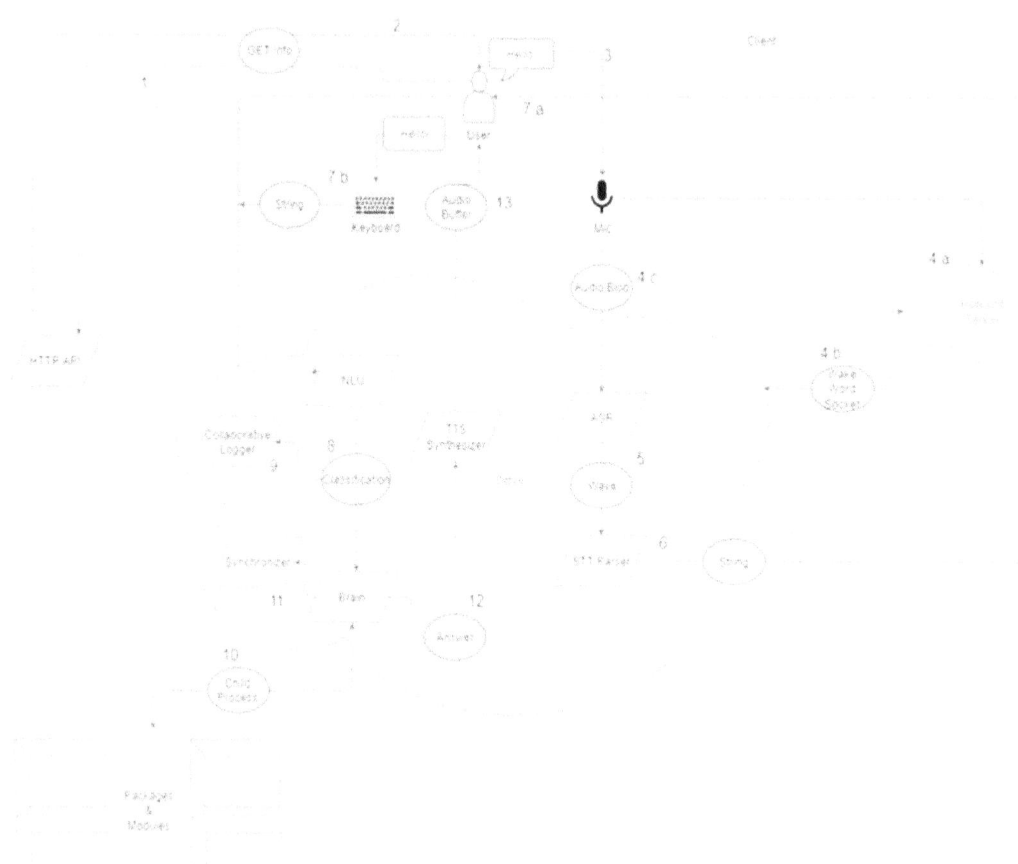

Fig. 2. Basic model of speech recognition.

Since the forward and backward recurrences are sequential, this small additional cost can become a computational bottleneck. By using a homogeneous model we have made the computation of the recurrent activations as efficient as possible: computing the ReLu outputs involves only a few highly optimized BLAS operations on the GPU and a single point-wise nonlinearity.

3.2. Query Analyzer

The system performs Natural Language processing on the input string. Fig. 3 shows the steps involved in the process. This model consist of combination of analysis like lexical analysis, Query Analysis, Morphological Analysis, Syntactic Analysis, Semantic

Analysis. The output obtained is a JSON data which is then Fed into a Response generator.

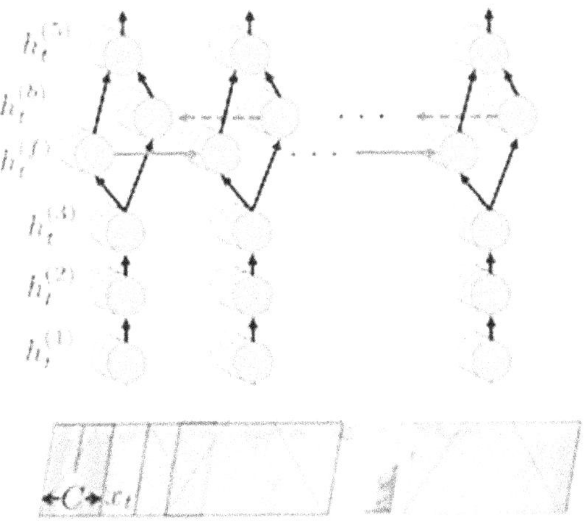

Fig. 3. Structure of RNN model and notation.

3.2.1. Lexical Analysis

Lexical Analyzer is the first state in translation. It is called by parser to fulfill the demand of word's type. It generates the tokens for the requested words as their types and then handover to the parser for further processing converts sequence of characters into a sequence of tokens. A lex file contains, mainly, set of regular expressions or word patterns that will be applied on each word to recognize the words as a valid token. These regular expressions are written according to the language we are using. So Lexical Analyzer performs two things, mapping of source language words to target language words and returns the appropriate token of target language word to the parser.

3.2.2. Morphological Analysis

Identifies, analyzes, and describes the structure of a given language's linguistic units. It analysis shape of the text which defers by the positioning of different words in it. It provides a primary source of evidence of facilitation between words formed from the same morpheme (i.e. Morphological relatives). Generally, target (second presentation) decision latency's and error rates are reduced in the context of morphological related primes (first presentation).

3.2.3. Syntactic Analysis

Syntactic parser analyze sentences in terms of a grammar and parts of speech. This analysis does not attempt to identify constituents that represent similar or related meanings. It analyzes texts, which are made up of a sequence of tokens, to determine their grammatical structure. Syntax analyser validates the English Text query whether the input query is syntactically correct.

3.2.4. Semantic Analysis

Relates syntactic structures from the levels of phrases and sentences to their language-independent meanings semantic analysis, attempts to analyze sentences based on constituents that represent concepts or meaning.

3.3. Response Generator

The system accepts a JSON code from the previous module and then processes it to perform the required action. Fig. 4 shows the various steps involved in the process.

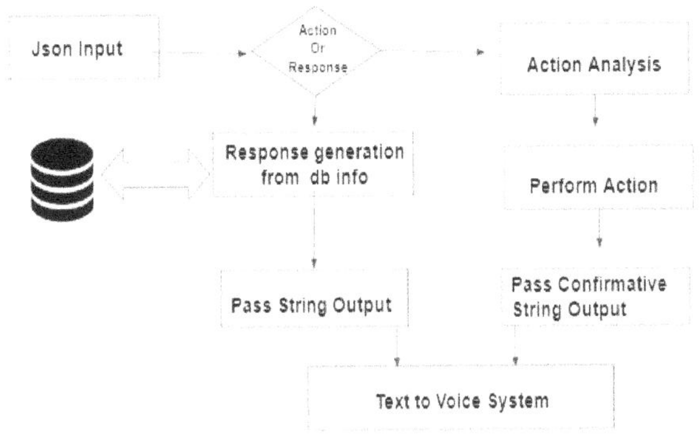

Fig. 4. Response Generator.

3.3.1. Action or Response Analyzer

Analyses if the given JSON is an action command or a question and diverts the control flow to action block user expects an action or response block if it is a response accordingly. Implemented using a desicive tree logic that analyse the Noun,Verb combinations.

3.3.2. Action Block

Analyses the action command from JSON and initiates the action performance that is most appropriate and passes a confirmation string when action is complete.

3.3.3. Response block

Analyses the question from JSON and generates a response that is most appropriate from data in Database or earlier question buffer using n dimensional search RNN and passes a generated string response to the next module. The response generated is a syntactically correct language expression having meaningful intents in the given language and are valuable information in the context of the question.

3.4. Text to Voice System

Encoder: A fully-convolutional encoder, which converts textual features to an internal learned representation.

Decoder: A fully-convolutional causal decoder, which decodes the learned representation with a multi-hop convolutional attention mechanism into a low-dimensional audio representation (mel-scale spectrograms) in an autoregressive manner.

Converter: A fully-convolutional post-processing network, which predicts final vocoder parameters (depending on the vocoder choice) from the decoder hidden states. Unlike the decoder, the converter is non-causal and can thus depend on future context information.

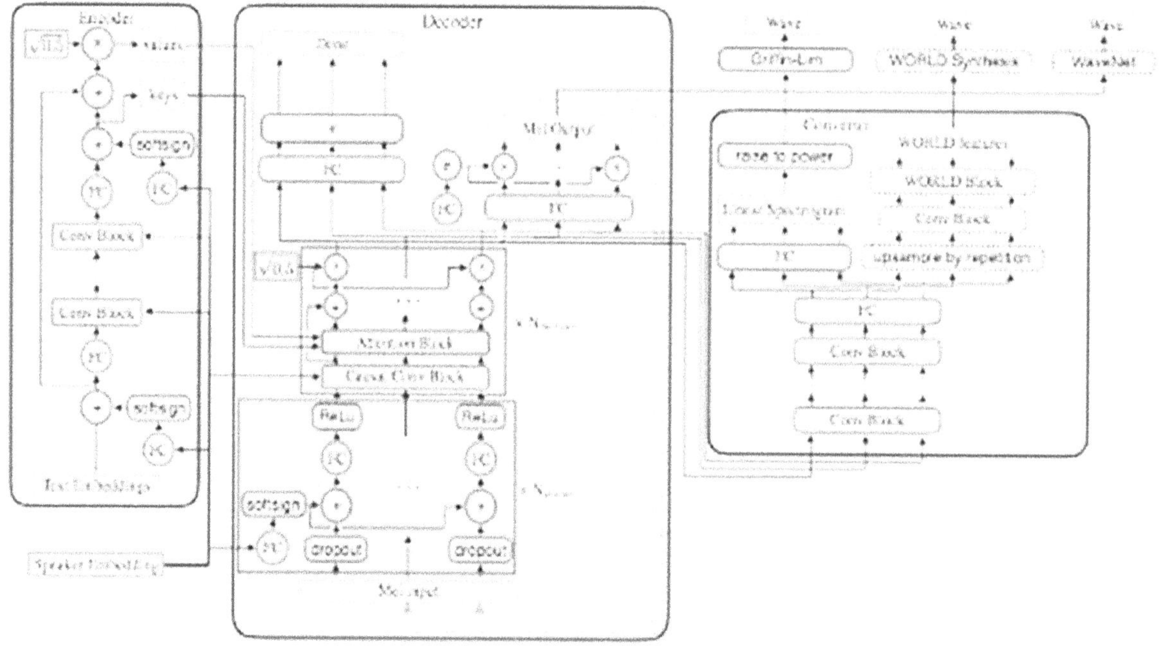

Fig. 5. Text to Voice System.

3.4.1. Text Processing

Text pre-processing is crucial for good performance. Feeding raw text (characters with spacing and punctuation) yields acceptable performance on many utterances. However, some utterances may have mispronunciations of rare words, or may yield skipped words and repeated words. We alleviate these issues by normalizing the input text as follows:

1. Change to uppercase all characters in the input text;
2. Removed all intermediate punctuation marks;
3. Ended every utterance with a period or question mark;
4. Replaced spaces between words with special separator characters.

The duration of pauses inserted by the speaker between words. We use four different word separators, indicating (i) slurred-together words; (ii) standard pronunciation and space characters; (iii) a short pause between words; and (iv) a long pause between words.

3.4.2. Encoder

The encoder network begins with an embedding layer, which converts characters or phonemes into trainable vector representations, *he*. These embeddings *he* are first projected via fully-connected layer from the embedding dimension to a target dimensionality. Then, they are processed through a series of convolution blocks described to extract time-dependent text information. Lastly, they are projected back to the embedding dimension to create the attention key vectors *hk*. The attention value vectors are computed from attention key vectors and text embeddings, hv = 0.5 (*hk* + *he*), to jointly consider the local information in *he* and the long-term context information in *hk*. The key vectors are used by each attention block to compute attention weights, whereas the final context vector is computed as a weighted average over the value vectors *hv*.

3.4.2. Decoder

The decoder generates audio in an auto regressive manner by predicting a group of future audio frames conditioned on the past audio frames. Since the decoder is auto regressive, it must use causal convolution blocks. We choose mel-band log-magnitude spectrogram as the compact low-dimensional audio frame presentation. We empirically observed that decoding multiple frames together (i.e. having r greater than 1) yields better audio quality. The decoder network starts with multiple fully-connected layers with rectified linear unit (*ReLU*) nonlinearities to pre-process input mel-spectrograms (denoted as *PreNet*). Then, it is followed by a series of causal convolution and attention blocks. These convolution blocks generate the queries used to attend over the encoders hidden states. Lastly, a fully-connected layer output the next group of *r* audio frames and also a binary final frame prediction (indicating whether the last frame of the utterance has been synthesized). Dropout is applied before each fully-connected layer prior to the attention blocks, except for the first one. L1 loss 6 is computed using the output mel-spectrograms and a binary cross-entropy loss is computed using the final-frame prediction.

3.4.2. Attention Block

A dot-product attention mechanism is used. The attention mechanism uses a query vector (the hidden states of the decoder) and the per-time step key vectors from the encoder to compute attention weights, and then outputs a text vector computed as the weighted average of the value vectors. Empirical benefits from introducing an inductive bias where the attention follows a mono-tonic progression in time is observed. Thus, we add a positional encoding to both the key and the query vectors. These positional encodings hp are chosen as $hp(i) = sin\ (si/10000\ k/d)$(for even *i*) or cos $(si/10000\ k/d)$(for odd *i*), where *i* is the time step index, *k* is the channel index in the positional encoding, *d* is the total number of channels in the positional encoding, andsis the position rate of the encoding.

The position rate dictates the average slope of the line in the attention distribution, roughly corresponding to speed of speech. For a single speaker, *Omega s* is set to one for the query, and be fixed for the key to the ratio of output timesteps to input timesteps (computed across the entire data set). For multi-speaker datasets,sis computed for both the key and query from the speaker embedding for each speaker. As sine and cosine functions form an orthonormal basis, this initialization yields an attention distribution in the form of a diagonal line. We initialize the fully-connected layer weights used to compute hidden attention vectors to the same values for the query projection and the key projection. Positional encodings are used in all attention blocks. We use context normalization as a fully-connected layer is applied to the context vector to generate the output of the attention block. Overall, positional encodings improve the convolutional attention mechanism.

3.4.5. Converter

The converter network takes as inputs the activations from the last hidden layer of the decoder, applies several non-causal convolution blocks, and then predicts parameters for downstream vocoders. Unlike the decoder, the converter is non-causal and non-autoregressive, so it can use future context from the decoder to predict its outputs. The loss function of the converter network depends on the type of the vocoder used.

- **Gri□n-Lim Vocoder**: Gri□n-Lim algorithm converts spectrograms to timedomain audio waveforms by iteratively estimating the unknown phases. We find raising the spectrogram to a power parameterized by a sharpening factor before waveform synthesis is helpful for improved audio quality, as suggested. L_1 loss is used for prediction of linear-scale log-magnitude spectrograms.
- **WORLD Vocoder:** The WORLD vocoder is based on [6]. As vocoder parameters, we predict a Boolean value (whether the current frame is voiced or unvoiced), an F0 value (if the frame is voiced), the spectral envelope, and the periodicity parameters. We use a cross-entropy loss for the voiced unvoiced prediction, and L1 losses for all other predictions as shown in Fig. 6.

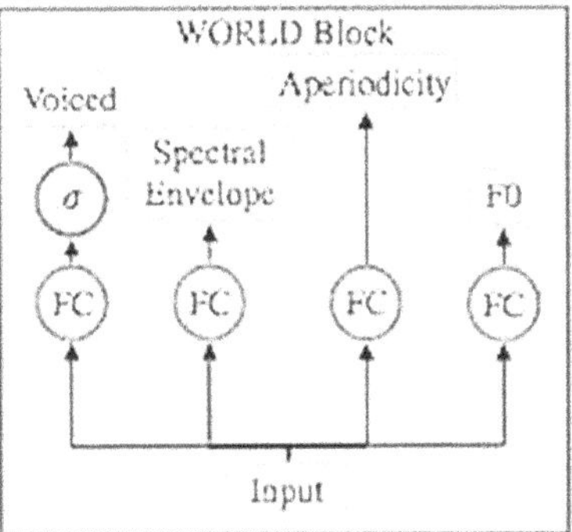

Fig. 6. Generated WORLD vocoder parameters with fully connected (FC) layers.

- **WaveNet Vocoder:** We separately train a WaveNet to be used as a vocoder treating mel-scale log-magnitude spectrograms as vocoder parameters. These vocoder parameters are input as external conditioners to the network. The WaveNet is trained using ground-truthmel-spectragrams and audio wave forms. The architecture besides the conditioner is similar to the WaveNet. While the WaveNet is conditioned with linear-scale log-magnitude spectrograms, we observed better performance with mel-scale spectrograms, which corresponds to a more compact representation of audio. In addition to L_1 loss on mel-scale spectrograms at decode, L_1 loss on linear-scale spectrogram is also applied as Gri□n-Lim vocoder.

2. Results

In this section, the performance evaluation of the proposed method. When trained on the combined 2300 hours of data the Deep Speech [4] system improves upon this baseline by 2.4 percent absolute WER (Word Error Rate) and 13.0 percent relative. The model from Maas et al. (DNN-HMM FSH) achieves 19.9 percent WER (Word Error Rate) when trained on the Fisher 2000 hour corpus. Graph of this comparison is given in Fig. 7.

The results of the evaluation of WER for 5 systems on original audio is given in Fig. 8. Scores are reported only for utterances with predictions given by all systems.

The MOS ratings with 95 % confidence intervals for audio clips from neural TTS systems on multi-speaker datasets is listed in Fig. 9. Deep voice [5] and Tactron [7] are used for the analysis.

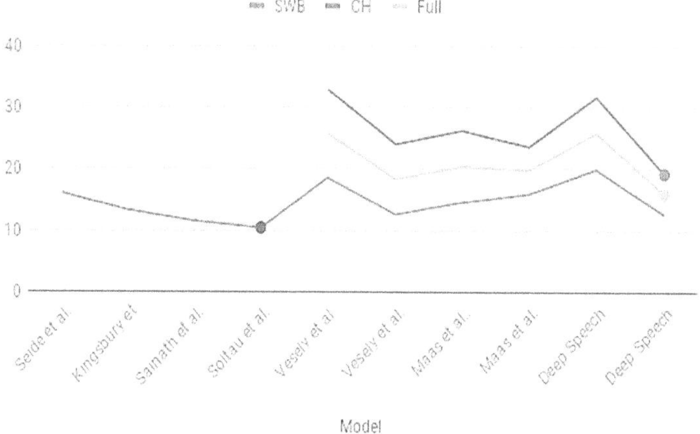

Fig. 7. Compared WER on Switchboard dataset splits.

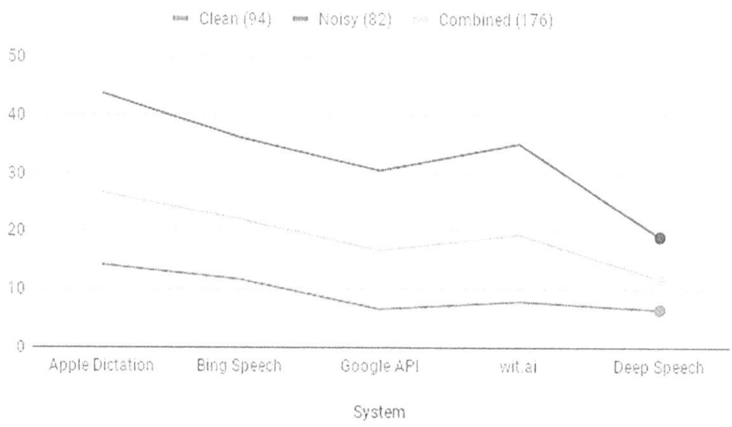

Fig. 8. Results WER for 5 systems.

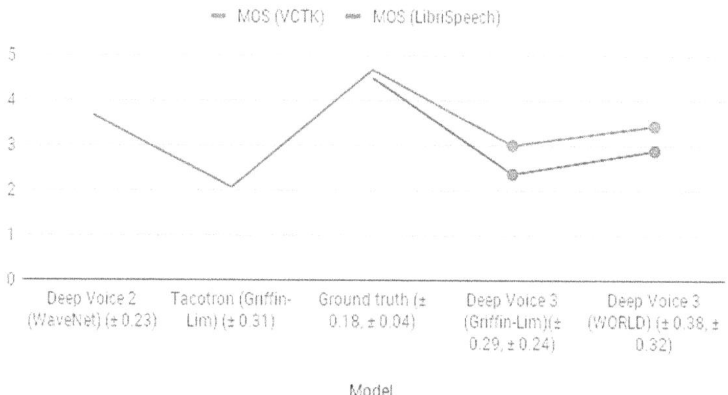

Fig. 9. MOS ratings with 95 % confidence intervals.

4. Conclusions

In this paper, we have proposed a system where the input is taken and processed through a multi microphone array and processed to generate an intermediate noise free audio signal which is then passed to an end-to-end speech system, where deep learning super sedes the processing stages. Combined with a language model, this approach achieves higher performance than traditional methods on hard speech recognition tasks while also being much simpler. These results are made possible by training a large recurrent neural network (RNN) using multiple GPUs and thousands of hours of data. Because this system learns directly from data, we do not require specialized components for speaker adaptation or noise filtering. In fact, in settings where robustness to speaker variation and noise are critical, it produces a higher accuracy on output.

References

[1]. M. Anusuya, S. Katti, Speech recognition by machine, A review, *ArXiv Preprint*, arXiv:1001.2267, 2010.

[2]. V. V. Raju, P. Gangamohan, S. V. Gangashetty, A. Kumar Vuppala, Application of prosody modification for speech recognition in different emotion conditions, in *Proceedings of the Conference on IEEE Region 10 Conference (TENCON'16)*, 2016, pp. 951-954.

[3]. B. Pendharkar, P. Ambekar, P. Godbole, S. Joshi, S. Abhyankar, T. R. Moore, Twenty things we still don't know about speech proc. CRIM, in *Proceedings of the FORWISS Workshop on Progress and Prospects of Speech Research and Technology*, 1994.

[4]. A. Hannun, C. Case, J. Casper, B. Catanzaro, G. Diamos, E. Elsen, A. Y. Ng, Deep speech: Scaling up end-to-end speech recognition, *ArXiv Preprint*, arXiv:1412.5567, 2014.

[5]. W. Ping, K. Peng, A. Gibiansky, S. O. Arik, A. Kannan, S. Narang, J. Miller, Deep voice 3: Scaling text-to-speech with convolutional sequence learning, *ArXiv preprint*, arXiv:1710.07654, 2018.

[6]. M. Morise, F. Yokomori, K. Ozawa, WORLD: A vocoder-based high-quality speech synthesis system for real-time applications, *IEICE Transactions on Information and Systems*, Vol. 99, Issue 7, 2016, pp. 1877-1884.

[7]. Y. Wang, R. J. Skerry-Ryan, D. Stanton, Y. Wu, R. J. Weiss, N. Jaitly, Q. Le, Tacotron: Towards end-to-end speech synthesis, *ArXiv Preprint*, arXiv:1703.10135, 2017.

(042)

Quantum Low Entropy Based Associative Reasoning

M. Jankovic [1,2] and A. Exadaktylos [1]
[1] Department of Emergency Medicine, Bern University Hospital "Inselspital", 3010 Bern, Switzerland
[2] ARTORG Center for Biomedical Engineering Research, University of Bern, 3008 Bern, Switzerland
Tel.: +41 31 632 7592, fax: +41 31 632 7576
E-mail: marko.jankovic@artorg.unibe.ch

Summary: In this paper, the classification method based on a learning paradigm, we are going to call Quantum Low Entropy based Associative Reasoning (QLEAR learning), has been proposed. The approach is based on the idea that classification can be understood as supervised clustering, where a quantum entropy in the context of the quantum probabilistic model, will be used as a "capturer" (measure) of the "natural structure" of the data. By using quantum entropy we don't make any assumption about linear separability of the data that are going to be classified. The basic idea is to find close neighbours to a query sample and then use relative change in the quantum entropy as a measure of similarity of the newly arrived sample with the representatives of interest. In other words, method is based on calculation of quantum entropy of the referent system and its relative change with the addition of the newly arrived sample. Effectivness of the method has been demonstrated on several classification problems.

Keywords: Classification, Clustering, Quantum probability model, Quantum entropy.

1. Introduction

The field of pattern recognition, as well as some fileds of artificial intelligence are concerned with the automatic discovery of regularities in data through the use of computer algorithms and with the use of these regularities to take actions such as classifying the data into different categories (see e.g. [1]). Generally, most of the algorithms are applied in areas like classification, regression or change point detection.

Recently, it has been shown that a probabilistic model based on two of the main concepts in quantum physics – a density matrix and the Born rule, can be suitable for the modeling of learning algorithms in biologically plausible artificial neural networks framework. It has been shown that the proposed probabilistic interpretation is suitable for modeling on-line learning algorithms for Independent /Principal/Minor Component Analysis [2-5], which could be realized on parallel hardware based on very simple computational units. Also, it has been shown that the quantum entropy of the system, related to that model, can be successfully used in the problems like change point or anomalies detection [6, 7] as well as simple classification problems [7].

Here another application of the proposed quantum probabilistic model is going to be presented. A general paradigm called QLEAR learning (Quantum Low Entropy based Associative Reasoning) would be presented and tested in classification context. Proposed method potentially can overcome the problem that classifier performance depends greatly on the characteristics of the data to be classified. The proposed method automatically adjusts its performance according to characteristics of the data on which it is applied. An interesting aspect is that proposed method inherently solves the problem of unbalanced classes. The proposed paradigm can be applied in any area in which standard classification techniques are applied.

We'll analyze only the case in which data is represented by vectors while generalization toward multiway data would not be discussed here. Also, some modification of the existing quantum probabilistic model, that have no ground in temporary quantum mechanics, that were used to improve the quality of the model in the classification context, will not be discussed here.

2. QLEAR Learning

In this section we are going to introduce a Quantum Low Entropy based Associative Reasoning – or QLEAR learning in classification context. In the Subsection 2.1 a brief recapitulation of quantum probability model has been presented. In the Subsection 2.2, a simplified approach in several simple examples where proposed method gives good results, is going to be presented. In the Subsection 2.3 we are going to present a more complex idea that overcomes few drawbacks of the simplified approach.

The approach is based on the idea that classification can be understood as supervised clustering. Clusters analysis divides data into groups (clusters) that are meaningful, useful, or both. If meaningful groups are the goal, then the clusters should capture the natural structure of the data. Classes, or conceptually meaningful groups of objects that share common characteristics, play an important role in how people analyze and describe the world. Human beings (even very small kids) are skilled at dividing objects into groups (clustering) and assigning particular objects to these groups (classification). In the context of understanding data, clusters are potential classes. It is well known that people can quite well generalize the concepts and perform classification based on a few examples. This actually represent the starting point of the method that is going to be analyzed in this paper The basic intention is to "imitate" the principles that are used by humans, and to improve them using some mathematical models that are "not implemented" in the brain, since the brain has the basic function of supporting human survival. In this project, a quantum entropy in the context of the recently proposed probabilistic model (that is going to be presented in the Subsection 2.1), will be used as a "capturer" (measure, or external index) of the "natural structure" of the data.

2.1. Quantum Probability Model and Quantum Tsallis' Entropy

In quantum mechanics the transition from a deterministic description to a probabilistic one is done using a simple rule termed the Born rule. This rule states that the probability of an outcome ($\boldsymbol{a}$) given a state ($\boldsymbol{\Psi}$) is the square of their inner product $(\boldsymbol{a}^{\mathrm{T}}\boldsymbol{\Psi})^2$. This section is based on a similar section in [8, 3].

In quantum mechanics the Born rule is usually taken as one of the axioms. However, this rule has well established foundations. Gleason's theorem [9] states that the Born rule is the only consistent probability distribution for a Hilbert space structure. Wooters [10] has shown that by using the Born rule as a probability rule, the natural Euclidean metrics on a Hilbert space coincides with a natural notion of a statistical distance. Short review for some other justifications of the Born rule can be seen in [8].

The quantum probability model takes place in a Hilbert space H of finite or infinite dimension. A state is represented by a positive semidefinite linear mapping (a matrix ρ) from this space to itself, with a trace of 1, i.e. $\forall \boldsymbol{\Psi} \in$ H $\boldsymbol{\Psi}^{\mathrm{T}}\boldsymbol{\rho}\boldsymbol{\Psi} \geq 0$, $\mathrm{Tr}(\boldsymbol{\rho}) = 1$. Such $\boldsymbol{\rho}$ is self adjoint and is called a density matrix.

Since $\boldsymbol{\rho}$ is self adjoint, its eigenvectors $\boldsymbol{\Phi}_i$ are orthonormal and since it is positive semidefinite its eigenvalues p_i are real and nonnegative $p_i \geq 0$. The trace of a matrix is equal to the sum of its eigenvalues, therefore $\sum_i p_i = 1$.

The equality $\boldsymbol{\rho} = \sum_i p_i \boldsymbol{\Phi}_i \boldsymbol{\Phi}_i^{\mathrm{T}}$ is interpreted as "the system is in state $\boldsymbol{\Phi}_i$ with probability p_i". The state $\boldsymbol{\rho}$ is called the pure state if $\exists i$ s.t. $p_i = 1$. In this case, $\boldsymbol{\rho} = \boldsymbol{\Psi}\boldsymbol{\Psi}^{\mathrm{T}}$ for some normalized state vector $\boldsymbol{\Psi}$, and the system is said to be in state $\boldsymbol{\Psi}$.

A measurement M with an outcome $\boldsymbol{x}$ in some set $\boldsymbol{X}$ is represented by a collection of positive definite matrices $\{\boldsymbol{m}_z\}_{z\in Z}$ such that $\sum_{z\in} \boldsymbol{m}_z = \mathbf{1}$ ($\mathbf{1}$ being the identity matrix in H). Applying measurement M to state $\boldsymbol{\rho}$ produces an outcome $\boldsymbol{x}$ with probability

$$p_x(\boldsymbol{\rho}) = \mathrm{trace}(\boldsymbol{\rho}\boldsymbol{m}_x)$$

This is the Born rule. Most quantum models deal with a more restrictive type of measurement called the von Neumann measurement, which involves a set of projection operators $\boldsymbol{m}_a = \boldsymbol{a}\boldsymbol{a}^{\mathrm{T}}$ for which $\boldsymbol{a}^{\mathrm{T}}\boldsymbol{a}' = \delta_{aa'}$. In a modern language, von Neumann's measurement is a conditional expectation onto a maximal Abelian subalgebra of the algebra of all bounded operators acting on the given Hilbert space. As before, $\sum_{a\in M} \boldsymbol{a}\,\boldsymbol{a}^{\mathrm{T}} = \mathbf{1}$. For this type of measurement the Born rule takes a simpler form: $p_a(\boldsymbol{\rho}) = \boldsymbol{a}^{\mathrm{T}}\boldsymbol{\rho}\boldsymbol{a}$. Assuming $\boldsymbol{\rho}$ is a pure state this can be simplified further to

$$p_a(\boldsymbol{\rho}) = (\boldsymbol{a}^{\mathrm{T}}\boldsymbol{\Psi})^2$$

So, we can see that the probability of the outcome of the measurement will be $\boldsymbol{a}$, if the state is $\boldsymbol{\rho}$, is actually the cosine square of the angle between vectors $\boldsymbol{a}$ and $\boldsymbol{\Psi}$, or $p_a(\boldsymbol{\rho}) = \cos^2(\boldsymbol{a}, \boldsymbol{\Psi})$.

Tsallis' entropy [11] is non-extensive entropy measure proposed in 1988. Given a discrete set of probabilities $\{p_i\}$ and any real number q, the Tsallis entropy is defined by the following equation:

$$E_{TS} = \frac{1 - \sum_{k=1}^{K} p_i^q}{q-1},$$

while quantum Tsallis' entropy is defined as (for $q = \boldsymbol{r}$)

$$S_q(\rho) = S^r(\rho) = (1-r)^{-1}(\mathrm{tr}(\rho^r) - 1), r > 0, r \neq 1$$

2.2. Simple Classification Problems

Here, it will be shown how proposed quantum probabilistic model can be used to solve some classification problems (already presented in [7]). It will be shown how we can solve XOR problem using quantum entropy. We define input vectors as

$$a_1 = \begin{bmatrix} 1 \\ 1 \end{bmatrix}, \quad a_2 = \begin{bmatrix} -1 \\ -1 \end{bmatrix}, \quad b_1 = \begin{bmatrix} 1 \\ -1 \end{bmatrix} \text{ and } b_2 = \begin{bmatrix} -1 \\ 1 \end{bmatrix}$$

Matrix A which describes the system in the plane z = 1 (the vectors are presented in 3-D system x-y-z) is defined as $A = a_1 * a_1^{\mathrm{T}} + a_2 * a_2^{\mathrm{T}}$, while the system in plane z = -1 is defined as $B = b_1 * b_1^{\mathrm{T}} + b_2 * b_2^{\mathrm{T}}$. Then we can calculate the entropy of the individual systems E_a and E_b. Overall entropy of the unified system is calculated as $E = E_a + E_b$. Then, for any x and y coordinate, we can calculate how it affects the entropy of the overall system, by adding it to the system A or the system B. We will label it in such a way that addition of the individual point to one of the system creates a minimum change in the overall entropy. The result of such calculation is shown in Fig. 1. From the figure we can see that the problem is successfully solved.

The logical AND problem could be solved in a similar way. However, since the system is unbalanced, it is necessary to define four subclasses and to evaluate the overall entropy for the four possibilities – meaning that any point can potentially belong to any of the four subclasses. The result of classification is shown on Fig. 2.

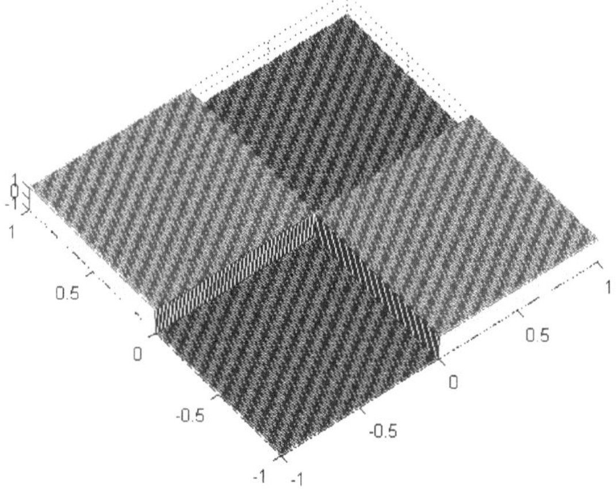

Fig. 1. XOR problem classification.

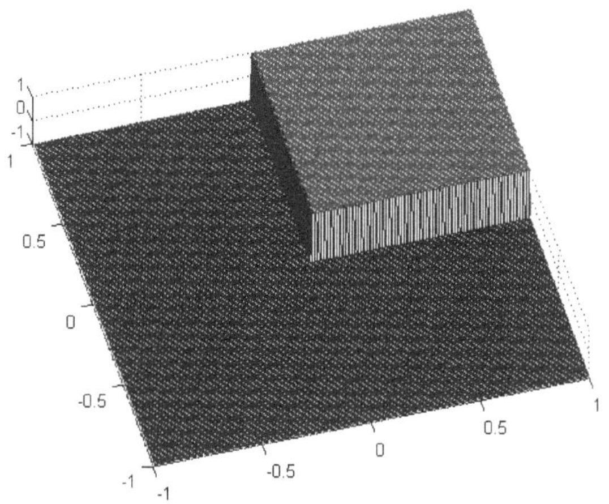

Fig. 2. AND problem classification.

Similar method could be used in the famous IRIS classification problem. Taking some points as characteristic representatives (in this case points numbered (20-34) from each group) we can correctly classify the rest of the points. As was the case in the logical AND classification problem, here we have 45 subclasses, and we have to evaluate the entropy for 45 cases – for every point we wont to classify, we can assume that it can belong to any of the 45 subclasses. Although it can look time consuming, we actually have 45 simple independent processes that could be easily realized on parallel hardware, like GPU. For illustration we can use the following Fig. 3, where we used only attributes 3 and 4 for classification (we can see that this classification is not 100 % correct – it is necessary to add attribute 1 too, but we cannot present it graphically).

2.3. More Complex Problems Approach

The approach proposed in the Subsection 2.2 cannot be easily and successfully implemented on more complex classification problems. There are two obvious drawbacks in that approach – one is, with the exception of XOR problem, representative of the classes were used individually and they were not correlated in any way (they do not 'cooperate') and second is that we are only interested about the similarity with the class representative, but we do not use the opportunity to check what is the level of dissimilarities with the other class representatives, and in a such way we discard potentially useful information.

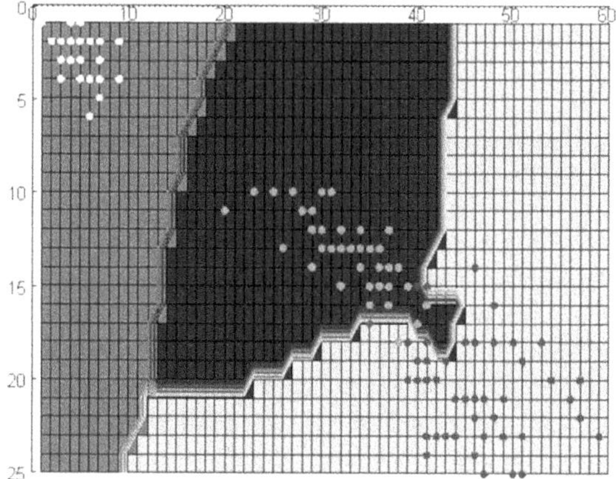

Fig. 3. Classification of IRIS data if we use only the data specified by attributes 3 and 4.

Here, the category recognition problem represents modification of the approach proposed in [12]. It is done in the framework of measuring similarities to prototype examples of categories, while this approach is quite flexible. While nearest neighbour classifiers are natural in this setting, they suffer from the problem of high variance (in bias-variance decomposition) in the case of limited sampling. Alternatively, one could use some machine learning techniques (like support vector machine), but they usually involve time-consuming optimization, and frequently assume that data could be linearly separated in the hyper plane of proper dimension. We propose a hybrid of these two methods which deals naturally with the multiclass setting, and at the same time has reasonable computational complexity both in training and at run time, and yields excellent results in practice. The basic idea is to find close neighbours to a query sample and then use change in the quantum entropy as a measure of similarity of the newly arrived sample with the representatives of interest. By using quantum entropy we don't make any assumption about linear separability of the data that are going to be classified. At the same time we calculate the dissimilarities with the "most similar" class representatives of the all other groups, and by this, we use most of the information that is available.

The original motivation comes from studies of human perception by Rosch and collaborators [13] who argued that categories are not defined by lists of features, rather by similarity to prototypes. From a machine learning perspective, the most important aspect of this framework is that the emphasis on similarity, rather than on feature spaces, gives us a more flexible framework.

The algorithm of the proposed method could be presented as:

1. Choose a pool of representatives of the N classes represented by sets of vectors $S_1, S_2, \ldots, S_N$ (they do not have necessarily to contain same number of elements).
2. For a given sample, choose the proper value q for the calculation of the Tsallis' entropy, choose a number N_s of the most similar vectors (class representatives) from each pool S_i, that are going to form matrix ρ_s that represent the state of the current class. Also, chose a number N_{ns} (usually smaller than N_s) of the "most similar" class representatives from all other pools S_j, $j\neq i$, that are going to form matrix ρ_{ns} that represent the state of the "complementary" class. Then calculate the entropy of the state ρ_s and state ρ_{ns}, and its relative changes dE_s and dE_{ns}, by addition of the current sample. Then find for which class the term

$$dE_s - \alpha * dE_{ns}$$

is minimized, and label new sample as a member of that class. The α is a positive real number, usually smaller than 1.
3. Repeat the process for all samples that should be analyzed.

In our case, proper values for q, N_s, N_{ns} and α were selected from 2-fold cross validation (CV) process that is implemented on training data represented by the union of sets S_i.

3. Experiments and Results

In this section we are going to present results for several classification problem. Classification results were based on the method proposed in Section 2.3. In all examples the maximum size of the pool of the representatives was the half of the data from that class.

Sets that were analyzed (taken from [14]), together with classification results were presented in the following Table 1. We will stress that results are improved by application of several techniques, that could be understood as engineering of the proposed theoretical model, and which are not going to be analyzed here.

From the Table 1 we can see, that results of the classification could be considered satisfactory. Here must be stressed that values for most of the parameters are probably not optimal, since the goal of this research was to explore the potential of the proposed paradigm, and not to find optimal values for the parameters.

The Table 2 contains results for face recognition task on ORL database, in the leave one out setup. In this case, two dimensional data has been represented by the vector that contains Tsallis' entropy for raws and columns of the
[original image,
vertical halves of the image,
horizontal halves of the image,
quarters of the image],
together with the entropies of the numerical derivatives of those vectors. It has to be said that the values of the entropies of the derivatives were multiplies with values smaller than 1 (in concrete case 0.2), while the values of the entropies of the raws and columns of the quarters of the image were multiplied by the values bigger than 1 (in the concrete case 1.7).

Table 1. Results of classification for several publically available data sets.

	Max pool size	N_s	N_{ns}	Q	Error [%]
Appendix	35	7	4	0.03	0
Australian Credit	195	7	5	0.11	0
Banana	1500	26	1	1.78	3.2
Contra-Captive	320	29	1	1.5	9.7
Glass	38	5	2	1.22	2.8
German Credit	265	25	1	0.5	0
Parkinson	40	14	5	0.03	0.003
Pima	230	13	1	0.95	0
Wine	25	9	6	0.03	0

Table 2 shows that the proposed method is superior to many other machine learning techniques in the proposed setup [15].

Table 2. Results of classification for several algorithms on ORL database.

Leave-one-out	
Method	**Error[%]**
Fisherfaces	1.5
ICA	6.2
Eigenfaces	2.5
Kernel Eigenfaces	2.0
2DPCA	1.7
Proposed method	0.0

4. Conclusions

In this paper new learning paradigm, called QLEAR learning was introduced and applied on classification problem where data is represented by vectors. Based on presented results, we can conclude that proposed paradigm has some potential in application where classification of vectors is required.

Since the proposed paradigm is generic in nature, it is clear that full potential of the proposed learning method requires further analyses. There are several aspects of the proposed method that could be improved and some of them are quite obvious. For instance, it could be possible to create an on-line adaptive method that search for optimal number of the class representatives that is optimized after every sample (or every few samples). Also, it could be analyzed is the Euclidean distance the optimal choice of the similarity measure or is the Tsallis' entropy the optimal choice of quantum entropy measure.

Extension of the proposed learning method to the data represented with matrices and higher-order multiway arrays could be also analyzed and it would represent the direction of future research.

References

[1]. C. M. Bishop, Pattern Recognition and Machine Learning, *Springer Science+Busines Media*, 2006.

[2]. M. V. Jankovic, M. Manic, B. Reljin, Probabilistic model for minor component analysis based on Born rule, in *Proceedings of the 11th Symposium on Neural Network Applications in Electrical Engineering (NEUREL'12)*, Belgrade, Serbia, 2012, pp. 85-88.

[3]. M. V. Jankovic, M. Sugiyama, Probabilistic principal component analysis based on JoyStick Probability Selector, in *Proceedings of the International Joint Conference on Neural Networks (IJCNN'09)*, Atlanta, USA, 2009, pp 1414-1421.

[4]. M. V. Jankovic, N. Rubens, A new probabilistic approach to independent component analysis suitable for on-line learning in artificial neural networks, *Lecture Notes in Computer Science*, Vol. 7665, 2012, pp. 552-559.

[5]. M. V. Jankovic, Probabilistic approach to neural networks computation based on quantum probability model – Probabilistic principal subspace analysis example, *Tech. Rep.*, arXiv:1001.4301v1, 2010.

[6]. N. L. Georgijevic, M. V. Jankovic, S. Srdic, Z. Radakovic, The detection of series arc fault in photovoltaic systems based on the arc current entropy. *IEEE Transactions on Power Electronics*, Vol. 31, Issue 8, 2016, pp. 5917-5930.

[7]. M. V. Jankovic, N. L. Georgijevic, Applications of probabilistic model based on joystick probability selector, in *Proceedings of the International Joint Conference on Neural Networks (IJCNN'14)*, Atlanta, USA, 6-9 July 2014, pp. 1028-1035.

[8]. L. Wolf, Learning using the Born rule, *Tech. Rep.*, MIT-CSAIL-TR-2006-036, 2006.

[9]. A. M. Gleason, Measure on the closed subspaces of a Hilbert space, *J. Math. & Mechanics*, Vol. 6, 1957, pp. 885-893.

[10]. W. K. Wooters, Statistical distance and Hilbert space, *Physical Review D*, Vol. 23, 1981, pp. 357-362.

[11]. C. Tsallis, Possible generalization of Boltzmann-Gibbs statistics, *J. Statistical Physics*, Vol. 52, 1988, pp. 479-478.

[12]. H. Zhang, A. C. Berg, M. Maire, J. Malik, SVM-KNN: Discriminative nearest neighbor classification for visual category recognition, in *Proceedings of the IEEE Conference Computer Vision and Pattern Recognition (CVPR'06)*, 2006, pp. 2126-2136.

[13]. E. Rosch, Natural categories, *Cognitive Psychology*, Vol. 4, 1973, pp. 328-350.

[14]. M. Lichman, UCI Machine Learning Repository, http://archive.ics.uci.edu/ml

[15]. J. Yang, D. Zhang, A. F. Frangi, J. Yang, Two-dimensional PCA: A new approach to appearance-based face representation and recognition, *IEEE Transactions on Pattern Analysis and Machine Intelligence*, Vol. 26, Issue 1, 2004, pp. 131-137.

(043)

On Improving the Accuracy of Visible Light Positioning System Using Deep Autoencoder

Lina Shi [1], Xun Zhang [1], Yanqi Huang [1,2], El-Hassane Aglzim [2], Andrei Vladimirescu [1]

[1] Laboratory LISITE, Institut supérieur d'électronique de Paris, Paris, France

[2] Laboratory DRIVE, Université Bourgogne, Nevers, France

E-mail: lina.shi@isep.fr

Summary: Visible light positioning (VLP) technology has been paid more and more attention recently because of its many attractions such as the centimeter level positioning accuracy. DC-biased optical orthogonal frequency division multiplexing (DCO-OFDM) is widely used in VLP systems to reduce the effects of intersymbol interference (ISI) and to achieve high-speed data transmission. However, DCO-OFDM suffer from high peak-to-average power ratio (PAPR) issue which affects the system performance, especially the degradation of positioning accuracy. In this paper, we investigate the deep autoencoder based PAPR reduction scheme for DCO-OFDM used in VLP systems. A trilateration positioning algorithm based on received signal strength (RSS) is used to estimate the receiver's coordinates. The positioning errors in all reference points of a room is further calculated and compared with the conventional PAPR reduction scheme, i.e., Selected Mapping (SLM). We demonstrate that in terms of improving positioning accuracy the deep autoencoder based PAPR reduction scheme outperforms its conventional counterpart.

Keywords: VLC, VLP, indoor positioning system, DCO-OFDM, autoencoder, deep learning, PAPR, SLM.

1. Introduction

Visible light communication (VLC) has been widely studied in recent years and it is considered as an appealing alternative of radio frequency (RF) technology because of its attractive features, such as worldwide availability, radiation-free, high transmission capacity, potential huge unlicensed bandwidth to cope with radio interference and network congestion, especially in indoor environment [1-5]. Besides that, due to its ability to achieve centimeter level positioning accuracy, visible light positioning (VLP) system is discussed in plenty of studies [6-9]. In these studies, the DC-biased optical orthogonal frequency division multiplexing (DCO-OFDM) modulation scheme is widely used for two reasons: 1) generating the real and non-negative positioning signals to satisfy the intensity modulation with direct detection (IM/DD) requirement in VLC system; 2) reducing the effects of intersymbol interference (ISI) and achieving high-speed data transmission in VLC system.

However, the high peak-to-average power ratio (PAPR) is the inherent disadvantage in DCO-OFDM. High PAPR of positioning signal is very sensitive to the LED nonlinear devices, which imposes the nonlinear distortion and leads to the change of transmitted positioning signal power. It will directly affect the positioning accuracy in the VLP systems.

As far as we know, the present conventional PAPR reduction schemes used in VLC system have been classified into three categories: clipping [10, 11], signal scrambling [12, 13], and coding schemes [14]. For example, the amplitude clipping is one of the simplest schemes to reduce PAPR thanks to its low algorithm complexity, but the distorted original signal leads to a higher bit error rate (BER). The partial transmission sequence (PTS) and the selective mapping (SLM) are more favorable PAPR reduction schemes of signal scrambling techniques, but additional information (side information) need to provide in order to reconstruct the transmitted signal properly. The transmission performance is greatly influenced by the quality of side information [15].

Within this context, in this paper, we consider a deep autoencoder based PAPR reduction scheme for DCO-OFDM to address high PAPR issue and to mitigate the effect of PAPR on positioning accuracy. The deep learning as an emerging technique to solve the problem of high PAPR in OFDM-based VLC system becomes more and more attractive in recent years because of its strong auto-adaptive ability [10][15]. A successful case by using an autoencoder network combined with extended SLM methods to reduce the PAPR for the DCO-OFDM has been realized by [16]. In [17], a PAPR reduction scheme by using the weighted autoencoder along with amplitude clipping method is proposed for asymmetrically Clipped Optical OFDM (ACO-OFDM) VLC system. But to the best of our knowledge, few work considers applying deep learning method to reduce the effect of PAPR on positioning accuracy for DCO-OFDM in the VLP. Thus, the objective of this paper is to study the PAPR effect on positioning accuracy by training a deep autoencoder network for DCO-OFDM VLP systems.

The main contributions of this paper are summarized in two aspects as follows:

- The effect of PAPR on positioning accuracy in VLP is investigated. A PAPR reduction scheme by combining a deep autoencoder architecture is proposed to minimize this effect while maintaining an acceptable positioning error.

- We comparatively evaluate the positioning performance of the proposed scheme with the conventional PAPR reduction scheme: SLM. The simulation results show that the deep autoencoder based PAPR reduction scheme outperforms its conventional counterpart.

The remainder of this paper is organized as follows. Section II gives an overview of proposed autoencoder and presents the detailed information of the system model as well as used positioning algorithm. Section III contains the simulation results and a discussion of the proposition compared to the conventional methods. Finally, conclusions are reported in Section IV.

2. Autoencoder, System Model and Positioning Algorithm

2.1. Autoencoder Architecture for DCO-OFDM

Autoencoder is widely used for denoising corrupted data and is suitable to dealing with the non-linear distortions such as high PAPR. The proposed deep autoencoder architecture is illustrated in Fig. 1. The general autoencoder architecture mainly consists two components: encoder and decoder. Both the encoder and the decoder consists of the identical hidden layers, each hidden layer includes Dense layer, Activation function and Dropout. It can be seen from Fig. 1, s, $f(x)$, $g(x)$ and $\hat{s}$ is the input, encoder, decoder and reconstruction of the original positioning data s respectively.

To adapt the output power constraint at transmitter in a communication system, a normalization layer is added into the traditional autoencoder. Moreover, we add a noise layer to simulate the influence of noise (mostly the ambient and natural light) in VLC system [20] [21].

In the proposed scheme, we assume that there are $2N$ subcarriers are used to generate DCO-OFDM symbols s. It can be seen from Fig. 1 that after serial to parallel operation, the parallel mapping data $x = [x_1, x_2, \dots x_N]^T$ is used as the input of encoder. The encoded symbols $f(x_{k\ (k\in[1,N])})$ are constrained to have Hermitian symmetric in order to obtain a real signal after the 2N-IFFT operation. After DC bias, the positive real DCO-OFDM symbols in time domain $s = [s_1, s_2, \dots s_{2N}]^T$ are generated for VLC transmission.

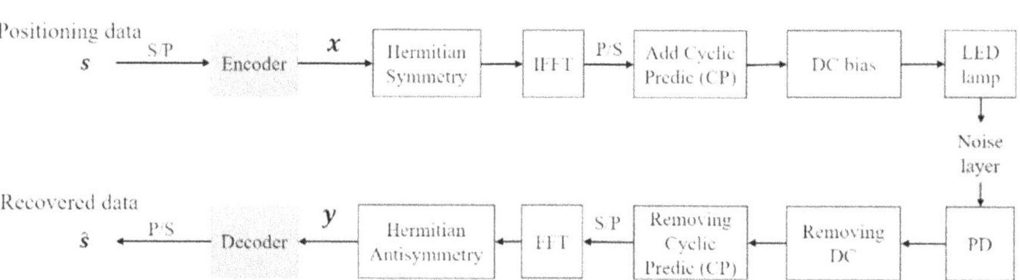

Fig. 1. Proposed deep autoencoder architecture for DCO-OFDM.

After passing through a wireless channel and DCO-OFDM demodulation processes, the reconstructed symbol at the receiver $g(f(x_k))$ can be written as follows:

$$\widehat{x_k} = g\big(h \circ IFFT \circ H \circ FFT \circ h^{-1} \circ f(x_k)\big), \qquad (1)$$

where $k \in [1, N]$, h is Hermitian symmetric operation, h^{-1} is inverse Hermitian symmetric operation, H is a VLC wireless channel model.

The training process is simply described for minimizing the joint loss function $\mathcal{L}$ defined in equation (2). $\mathcal{L}$ consists two loss functions $\mathcal{L}_1$ and $\mathcal{L}_2$, where λ is weight parameter to decide which loss function is dominant. We initially set λ to 0.001. The function of $\mathcal{L}_1$is to enable BER do not deteriorate and reconstruct the transmitted signals form the received data. The function of $\mathcal{L}_2$is to minimize PAPR. Through the training of σ_g and σ_f , the joint loss function is minimized.

$$\mathcal{L}(x_k, \widehat{x_k}) = \mathcal{L}_1(x_k, \widehat{x_k}) + \lambda\mathcal{L}_2(x_k) \qquad (2)$$

$$\mathcal{L}_1(x_k, \widehat{x_k}) = MSE(x_k - g(h \circ IFFT \circ H \circ FFT \circ h^{-1} \circ f(x_k) + n); \sigma_g) \qquad (3)$$

$$\mathcal{L}_2(x_k) = PAPR\{f(x_k);\ \sigma_f\}, \qquad (4)$$

where n is the noise. $\sigma = \{W, b\}$, W is the weight matrix and b is the bias vector of autoencoder. The stochastic gradient descent (SGD) method is used to update W and b. The PAPR is defined as below:

$$PAPR\{s\} = \frac{\max\limits_{1\le k\le 2N} s_k^2}{mean(|s_k^2|)} \qquad (5)$$

Its denominator is the average power of DCO-OFDM symbols. The detailed parameters of the autoencoder network will be introduced in Section 3.

2.2. System Model and Positioning Algorithm

Fig. 2 depicts the proposed VLP system model, where three transmitters and one receiver are placed in a room of $2m \times 1m \times 2.11m$. The coordiantes of

transmitters are namely LED1 (-0.5, 0.6, 2.195); LED2 (-0.5,0.25,2.195); LED3 (0.6,0.25,2.195).
In order to acquire the position of receiver (Rx), different position information should be transmitted from the respective LEDs. Moreover, only the line of sight (LOS) link is considered in this work because the influence of the directed light is large and greatly depends on the performance of the system [18].

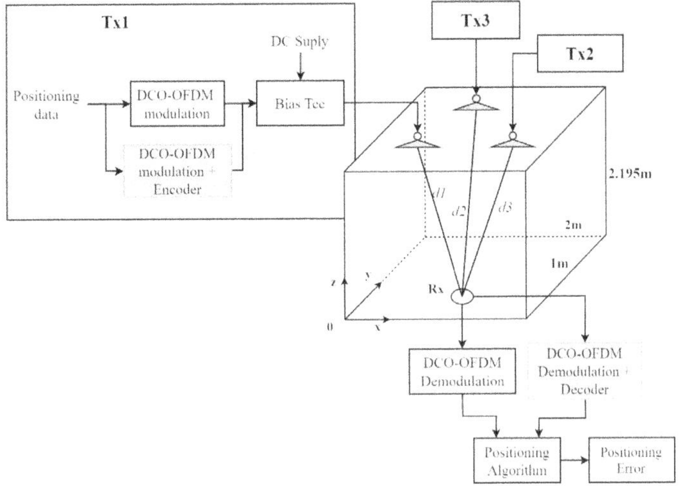

Fig. 2. VLP system model.

We defined LED's ID as the positioning data which are encoded into DCO-OFDM symbols. The basic Received Signal Strength (RSS) algorithm for trilateration positioning is used to estimate Rx's position. Provided the Rx is within the triangle areas, see Fig. 2, the whole calculation process is as follows:

The distance d_1, d_2 and d_3 between different transmitters and receiver are calculated by eq. (6).

$$d = \sqrt[(m+3)]{\left(\frac{(m+1)A_r h^{(m+1)}}{2\pi}\right)\frac{P_T}{P_R}}, \quad (6)$$

where A_r is the effective area of the receiving surface of the receiver. h is the known constant about the vertical distance between the receiver and the LED. m is the order of Lambertian emission, which is relative to the semi-angle at half power of the LED denoted as $\varphi_{1/2}$.

$$m = \frac{-ln2}{ln(cos(\varphi_{1/2}))} \quad (7)$$

The received power P_R can be represented as:

$$P_R = H(0) * P_T, \quad (8)$$

where P_T is the transmitted light power of LED. $H(0)$ is VLC channel gain between the LED and Rx which can be shown as:

$$H(0) = \frac{(m+1)A_r cos^m(\varphi) cos(\theta)}{2\pi d^2} \quad (9)$$

where φ is the radiation angle between the LED and the Rx, and θ is the angle of light incident to the receiving surface of the Rx. Thus, the distance d_1, d_2 and d_3 can be obtained respectively

The projection distance r_1, r_2, and r_3 between LED and receiver is expressed as shown below:

$$r = \sqrt{d^2 - h^2} \quad (10)$$

The estimated coordinates of Rx: X_e (x_e, y_e) thus can be calculated as follows:

$$\begin{cases} (x_e - x_1)^2 + (y_e - y_1)^2 = r_1^2 \\ (x_e - x_2)^2 + (y_e - y_2)^2 = r_2^2 \\ (x_e - x_3)^2 + (y_e - y_3)^2 = r_3^2, \end{cases} \quad (11)$$

where, (x_1, y_1), (x_2, y_2) and (x_3, y_3) are the known coordinates of three LED respectively. (11) can be formed in a matrix format as (12)

$$\boldsymbol{B}X_e = \boldsymbol{C} \quad (12)$$

where $\boldsymbol{B}$, $\boldsymbol{C}$ and X_e are defined as

$$\boldsymbol{B} = \begin{bmatrix} x_2 - x_1 & y_2 - y_1 \\ x_3 - x_1 & y_3 - y_1 \end{bmatrix}, X_e = \begin{bmatrix} x_e \\ y_e \end{bmatrix} \quad (13)$$

$$\boldsymbol{C} = \begin{bmatrix} \frac{d_1^2 - d_2^2 + x_2^2 + y_2^2 - x_1^2 - y_1^2}{2} \\ \frac{d_1^2 - d_3^2 + x_3^2 + y_3^2 - x_1^2 - y_1^2}{2} \end{bmatrix} \quad (14)$$

The estimated X_e can then be obtained by the linear least squares [19].

$$\widehat{X_e} = (\boldsymbol{B}^T\boldsymbol{B})^{-1}\boldsymbol{B}^T C \quad (15)$$

3. Simulation Results and Discussion

In our simulation three commercial 3.6 W LED lamps and a Silicon avalanche photodetector (Hamamatsu APD C5331-11) are used as transmitter and receiver respectively. Their detailed parameters are listed in the Table 1.

For the configuration of the proposed autoencoder network, we initially set the number of hidden layers to three ($L_f = L_g$=3). The rectifier linear unit (ReLU) is used as the activation function. The dropout is used for addressing the overfitting problem [23]. The parameters of the autoencoder network are summarized in Table 2.

Table 1. Parameters of transmitter and receiver.

Transmitter	Receiver
Lambertian mode (m): 1 Elevation : -90° Azimuth : 0°	Effective area : Φ 7.00 mm Elevation : +90 ° Azimuth : 0 ° FOV : 60 ° Photosensitivity : 0.42 A/W

Table 2. Parameters of the proposed autoencoder network.

Layer (type)	Output shape
Input layer	128
Dense (ReLU)	1024
Dense (ReLU)	512
Dense (ReLU)	128
Encoder (BatchNormalization)	128
Noise layer	128
Dense (ReLU)	512
Dense (ReLU)	1024
Dropout	1024
Decoder	128

We considered a DCO-OFDM with 128 subcarriers and QPSK modulation, 640000 independent random bits for training, 128000 bits for validation and 128000 bits for testing, respectively. In particular, 100000 DCO-OFDM symbols are used to generate all simulation results.

The positioning error (PE) is adopted to represent the positioning performance. The PE is given by

$$PE = \sqrt{(x - x_e)^2 + (y - y_e)^2}, \qquad (16)$$

where (x, y) and (x_e, y_e) are the coordinates of reference and estimated points, respectively.

The preliminary simulation results are compared in three cases: (a) original; (b) with SLM scheme (U = 4); (c) with the proposed deep autoencoder based PAPR reduction scheme. As shown in Fig. 3, the red sign * represents the estimated points and the blue sign * represents the reference points, respectively. There are 6 × 11 reference points are selected in total. In the case of original, a mean PE of 22.11 cm with a maximum PE of 40.26 cm and a minimum PE of 0.80 cm are obtained. In case of SLM scheme, a mean PE of 15.30 cm with the maximum PE of 28.8 cm and the minimum PE of 0.54 cm are achieved. By using the SLM, the positioning accuracy (mean PE) can be improved around 6.81 cm compared with original case. In the case of proposed autoencoder, a mean PE of 10.67 cm with the maximum PE of 21.01 cm and the minimum PE of 0.36 cm are achieved. The positioning accuracy (mean PE) can be improved around 11.44 cm compared with original case. The simulation results demonstrated that the positioning performance of proposed scheme is much better than the others.

Fig. 4 depicts the cumulative distribution function (CDF) curves of the simulation results shown in Fig. 3. It can be found that after using proposed scheme PE is improved around 17.5 cm compared to the original case at the confidence of 90 %.

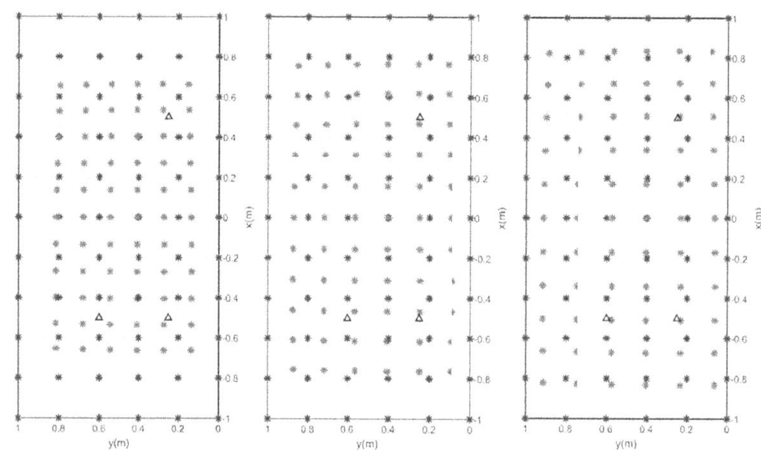

Fig. 3. Estimated points and reference points distribution: (a) original; (b) with SLM scheme; (c) proposed scheme.

4. Conclusions

In this paper, a novel deep autoencoder-based PAPR reduction scheme for DCO-OFDM VLP is proposed. The autoencoder could improve the positioning accuracy while maintaining a low PAPR for VLP system. Based on the positioning performance comparison results, the mean PE can be improved around 11.44 cm compared to the original case.

The topic of this paper is to present the feasibility and the first simulation results to address PAPR issue by using deep learning method, the improvement of the proposed autoencoder network is not discussed in this paper. However, in the near future, we hope to explore this network and compare performance of different deep learning models, more comprehensive analysis will be obtained and reported in the future.

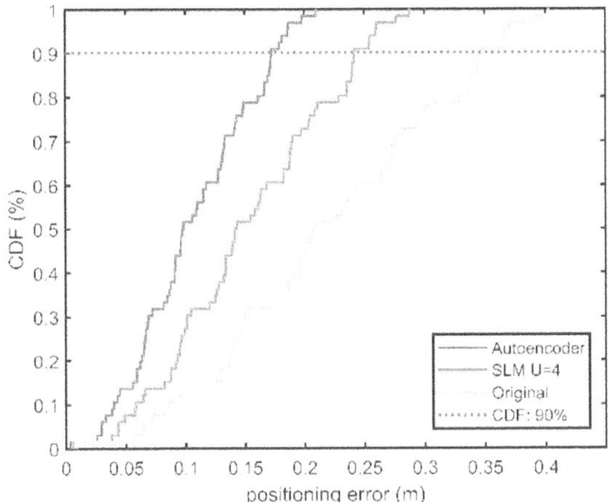

Fig. 4. CDF of PE.

Acknowledgements

The authors gratefully acknowledge the financial support of the EU Horizon 2020 program towards the Internet of Radio Light project H2020-ICT 761992 and the Bourgogne-Franche-Comté Region (Robassist project).

References

[1] L. Shi, W. Li, X. Zhang, Y. Zhang, G. Chen, and A. Vladimirescu, Experimental 5G New Radio integration with VLC, in *Proceedings of the 25th IEEE International Conference on Electronics, Circuits and Systems (ICECS)*, 2018, pp. 61–64.

[2] H. Elgala, R. Mesleh, and H. Haas, Indoor optical wireless communication: potential and state-of-the-art, *IEEE Commun. Mag.*, Vol. 49, No. 9, pp. 56–62, 2011.

[3] L. Feng, R. Q. Hu, J. Wang, P. Xu, and Y. Qian, Applying VLC in 5G networks: Architectures and key technologies, *IEEE Netw.*, Vol. 30, No. 6, pp. 77–83, 2016.

[4] H. Elgala, R. Mesleh, H. Haas, and B. Pricope, OFDM Visible Light Wireless Communication Based on White LEDs, 2007, pp. 2185–2189.

[5] W. Shieh and I. Djordjevic, OFDM for optical communications. Amsterdam: *Elsevier, Acad. Press*, 2010.

[6] B. Lin, X. Tang, Z. Ghassemlooy, C. Lin, and Y. Li, Experimental demonstration of an indoor VLC positioning system based on OFDMA, *IEEE Photonics J.*, Vol. 9, No. 2, pp. 1–9, 2017.

[7] L. Shi, X. Zhang, and A. Vladimirescu, "Experimental testbed for VLC-based localization framework in 5G Internet of Radio Light, in *Proceedings of the 26th IEEE International Conference on Electronics, Circuits and Systems (ICECS)*, 2019.

[8] J. Song, W. Ding, F. Yang, H. Yang, B. Yu, and H. Zhang, An indoor broadband broadcasting system based on PLC and VLC, *IEEE Trans. Broadcast.*, Vol. 61, No. 2, pp. 299–308, 2015.

[9] S. D. Dissanayake and J. Armstrong, Comparison of ACO-OFDM, DCO-OFDM and ADO-OFDM in IM/DD systems, *J. Light. Technol.*, Vol. 31, No. 7, pp. 1063–1072, 2013.

[10] Y. He, M. Jiang, X. Ling, and C. Zhao, A Neural Network Aided Approach for LDPC Coded DCO-OFDM with Clipping Distortion, in Proceedings of the *IEEE International Conference on Communications (ICC' 19)*, 2019, pp. 1–6.

[11] S.-K. Deng and M.-C. Lin, OFDM PAPR reduction using clipping with distortion control, in Proceedings if the *IEEE International Conference on Communication (ICC 2005)*, Vol. 4, pp. 2563–2567.

[12] Y.-C. Wang and Z.-Q. Luo, Optimized iterative clipping and filtering for PAPR reduction of OFDM signals, *IEEE Trans. Commun.*, Vol. 59, No. 1, pp. 33–37, 2010.

[13] T. Jiang and G. Zhu, Nonlinear companding transform for reducing peak-to-average power ratio of OFDM signals, *IEEE Trans. Broadcast.*, Vol. 50, No. 3, pp. 342–346, 2004.

[14] Y. Jiang, New companding transform for PAPR reduction in OFDM, *IEEE Commun. Lett.*, Vol. 14, No. 4, pp. 282–284, 2010.

[15] L. Shi *et al.*, PAPR reduction based on deep autoencoder for DCO-OFDM VLC system, in *Proceedings of the IEEE International Symposium on Broadband Multimedia Systems and Broadcasting (BMSB)*, 2019.

[16] L. Hao, D. Wang, Y. Tao, W. Cheng, J. Li, and Z. Liu, The Extended SLM Combined Autoencoder of the PAPR Reduction Scheme in DCO-OFDM Systems, *Appl. Sci.*, Vol. 9, No. 5, p. 852, 2019.

[17] L. Hao, D. Wang, W. Cheng, J. Li, and A. Ma, Performance enhancement of ACO-OFDM-based VLC systems using a hybrid autoencoder scheme, *Opt. Commun.*, Vol. 442, pp. 110–116, 2019.

[18] T. Komine and M. Nakagawa, Fundamental analysis for visible light communication system using LED lights, *IEEE Trans. Consum. Electron.*, Vol. 50, No. 1, pp. 100–107, February 2004.

[19] Mousavi H. S., Monga V., Tran T. D., Iterative convex refinement for sparse recovery, *IEEE Signal Processing Letters*, Vol. 22, Issue 11, 2015, pp. 1903-1907.

[20] T. Wang, C.-K. Wen, H. Wang, F. Gao, T. Jiang, and S. Jin, Deep learning for wireless physical layer: Opportunities and challenges, *China Commun.*, Vol. 14, No. 11, pp. 92–111, 2017.

[21] Lin B., Tang X., Ghassemlooy Z., Lin C., Li Y., Experimental demonstration of an indoor VLC positioning system based on OFDMA, *IEEE Photonics Journal*, Vol. 9, Issue 2, 2017, pp. 1-9.

[22] S. Ioffe and C. Szegedy, Batch normalization: Accelerating deep network training by reducing internal covariate shift, *ArXiv Prepr. ArXiv150203167*, 2015.

[23] Srivastava N., Hinton G., Krizhevsky A., Sutskever I., Salakhutdinov R., Dropout: a simple way to prevent neural networks from overfitting. *The Journal of Machine Learning Research*, Vol. 15, Issue 1, 2014, pp. 1929-1958.

(045)

Deep Learning Model for Upper-body Action Recognition Using Body-worn Sensors

M. Martinez-Zarzuela [1], S. Saez-Bombín [1], F. J. Díaz-Pernas [1], D. González-Ortega [1] and M. Antón-Rodríguez [1]
[1] University of Valladolid, ETSI Telecomunicación, Paseo de Belén, 15 Valladolid, Spain
Tel.: +34 983 423 000
E-mail: mario.martinez@tel.uva.es

Summary: We compare different Deep Learning proposals for upper-body human activity recognition using body-worn sensors. The evaluated models have been designed so that they need only quaternion data as input and provide results in real-time, with the aim of being potentially included on a wearable system to monitor daily activities in medical applications. Among other contributions, we propose using Fast Fourier Transform feature engineering to significantly improve recognition results and introduce a new technique for data augmentation that helps the models to learn the activities with independence of subject orientation. The proposed models were evaluated using the REALDISP dataset and overcome previous methods or achieve comparative results using 30 times less features and 110 times less training instances. The winning model achieves an accuracy of 97.7 % in a subject-wise classification and of 99.5 % in a 10-fold evaluation.

Keywords: Deep learning, Human action recognition, Inertial measurement units, Wearables, Real-time.

1. Introduction

1.1. Motivation and Contribution

Deep learning based methods are being widely adopted for Human Activity Recognition (HAR) using different sensor modalities, including ambient, object, and body-worn sensors [1].

Wearable sensors like those that can be found on smartwatches have the potential of continuous monitoring human motion in daily environment, providing valuable information [2]. It is indeed a developing trend to apply HAR to health and disease issues. However, for many applications in the medical field, the simultaneous tracking of the movement of different body joints is needed, using a larger number of body-worn sensors [3, 4]. At least 9 IMU (Inertial Measurement Unit) sensors are required to track the full body and typical configurations for only single upper or lower body monitoring need at least 5 of them.

Increasing the number of sensors introduces new opportunities, but also influences patients discomfort and systems complexity. In our opinion, the requirements of an embedded, comfortable, and portable system should include wireless communication among body-worn sensors and ubiquitous HAR recognition for feedback interaction. This requirements introduce restrictions on the data collected by the sensors that can be wirelessly transferred and processed in real-time.

On the other hand, most of the solutions for HAR using IMUs that can be found in the literature do not take these restrictions into account. Those machine learning approaches tend to use as much input data as possible, in their search to maximize the performance of the recognition.

In this paper we introduce an upper-body activity recognition model using 5 IMUs and a data-driven network that can provide real-time high-accuracy recognition rates while minimizing the required sensors data size. The contributions of this work are: (1) Robust Deep Learning models using only Quaternion data from IMUs, (2) Fast Fourier Transform feature engineering to significantly improve models performance, (3) New data augmentation technique to introduce rotation invariance of the subject and high accuracy using a very small number of training examples.

1.2. Previous Works

Deep Neural Networks have been recently used to classify limbs movements in combination with IMU sensors, with the aim of monitoring the clinical progress of subjects under rehabilitation. An interesting contribution proposed a light-weight Convolutional Neural Network (CNN) model for arm movement classification on 3 different types of gestures and targeting stroke rehabilitation. It uses tri-axial acceleration to monitor the progress of rehabilitated subjects under ambulatory settings [5]. The authors achieved an accuracy of 97.89 % on semi-naturalistic data and 88.87 % on naturalistic data, from not public databases.

Our work follows a similar philosophy, but considering the classification of activities in which both limbs and the back participate. The chosen dataset is REALDISP [6], containing raw data (accelerometer, gyroscope, and magnetometer) and quaternion data of 33 activities and 17 subjects. The authors of REALDISP [7] explored the use of classical Machine

Learning algorithms (*K-nearest neighbors*, *Decision Trees*, and *Naïve-Bayes*) for classification and obtained a classification accuracy of 97 %, but not considering a *subject-wise* decomposition of samples for training and testing. In a more recent study [8], the authors achieved a *subject-wise* 99.4 % accuracy, using feature engineering to generate up to 4,086 features.

Only those activities from the previous dataset related to upper-body movements were considered in our proposal. The reason is that we aim to develop a system for continuous monitoring of human motion of upper body in daily environment, providing valuable and complementary information to that obtained in clinical tests.

The challenges we faced during our development were a small number of data examples to train the model and a self-imposed limitation on the number of inputs and features that should be fed into the network. These restrictions are related to the final objective of potentially embedding the designed network models on a portable device in the near future.

2. Methods

2.1. Quaternions

Quaternions are hypercomplex numbers that define an element in $\mathbb{R}^4$ as shown in Eq. (1).

$$q = q_0 + \boldsymbol{q} = q_0 + \boldsymbol{i}q_1 + \boldsymbol{j}q_2 + \boldsymbol{k}q_3, \quad (1)$$

where $\boldsymbol{i} = (1,0,0), \boldsymbol{j} = (0,1,0)$ and $\boldsymbol{k} = (0,0,1)$ are the orthonormal bases of $\mathbb{R}^3$ and q_0, q_1, q_2, q_3 are real numbers that define the quaternion.

The main interest of using quaternions in the HAR problem comes from their potential to represent the movements by using a parametrized skeleton. In contrast to Euler Angles, they do not suffer from gimbal lock.

In addition, quaternions can represent body orientations with less data, which make them ideal for an embedded system. Actually, even while working with datasets that include 3D absolute joint positions, some researchers propose computing and using quaternions for short-term movement prediction and long-term movement generation [9].

2.2. Dataset Movement Reconstruction

First of all, we used REALDISP quaternion information for movement reconstruction using a 3D avatar. To this end, we self-developed a program from scratch using a *Game Engine*. This step was crucial to determine data that would be fed into the neural network, detect small time series of wrong labelled data in the dataset and generate augmented data for networks training, as explained in the next subsection. Fig. 1 shows different time steps of an activity reconstructed using this program.

Fig. 1. Movement reconstruction using a 3D avatar of activity 9 "Trunk twist (arms outstretched)" from REALDISP dataset.

2.3. Data Preparation and Proposed Models

We selected data from 11 upper-body activities contained in the dataset. The selected activities were: (L9) Trunk twist (arms outstretched), (L10) Trunk twist (elbows bent), (L11) Waist bends forward, (L12) Waist rotation, (L13) Waist bends (reach foot with opposite hand), (L19) Lateral elevation of arms, (L20) Frontal elevation of arms, (L21) Frontal hand claps, (L24) Shoulders low-amplitude rotation, (L25) Arms inner rotation, (L31) Rowing. Activities that could not be recognized independently using only the upper body were discarded (e.g. walking, cycling ...).

We manually examined the 3D reconstruction of these activities and followed a data consistency and input data balancing criteria for data curation. In addition, five subjects in which data for at least one activity could not be found, were discarded (subjects 4, 6, 7, 12, and 15). At the end of this process, we selected 12 subjects to be used in our experiments.

In order to reduce the number of features as much as possible, only quaternion data is used as an input to the network. Instances of 128 time samples at 50 Hz were used for training and testing, containing activity windows of 2.56 seconds. Each time sample includes the quaternion data of the 5 upper-body sensors (back, arms, and forearms), for a total of 20 raw features.

Remarkably, we observed an improvement in the accuracy of the results by increasing the inputs using a feature engineering approach. For every activity instance, we concatenated the raw features with their 2D Discrete Fourier Transform (2D-DFT), computed using the Fast Fourier Transformation (FFT). Intuitively, this adds frequency of movement information to the network.

Deep Neural Networks are usually considered pure data driven models. However, a network able to model a FFT would require $O(n^2)$ multiplies instead of $O(n\log(n))$ operations required by the FFT. In addition, a much larger number of examples would be needed so that the network could be able to learn to model the Fourier Transform. Since one of our objectives is to keep the number of computations as small as possible, using a classical pre-processing stage is the optimal strategy to follow. The final number of inputs for the 5 upper-body sensors when the input includes de 2D-DFT is 40.

For preventing network overfitting, we propose a new Data Augmentation technique. As explained before, we were able to reconstruct on an avatar the movements in the dataset. For data augmentation, we reoriented all the subjects heading towards the Earth's north direction and then generated ×24 times more data by rotating subjects in the dataset every 15 degrees.

Six different data pre-processing strategies were considered and tested on the network models explained in Subsection 2.4: (1) Raw data, (2) Raw data with Data Augmentation, (3) Raw data with Data Augmentation and 2D-DFT features, (4) Normalized data with Data Augmentation, (5) Normalized data with Data Augmentation and 2D-DFT computed, (6) 2D-DFT.

All those pre-processing strategies were tested on six different deep network models based on Convolutional Neural Networks (CNN) and Recurrent Neural Networks (RNN). Table 1 subsumes the architecture of these models in terms of number of *layers*, number of *feature maps* per layer and recurrent *units*. Two CNN and four CNN+RNN models were evaluated. The number of *trainable parameters* for those models when input data features are of size 40 is in the range of 91,851 to 232,651.

Table 1. Neural network models proposed and accuracy obtained on each evaluation method. C stands for Convolutional layer, DR stands for Dropout, RG stands for GRU, Sm stands for Softmax.

Model Type	Architecture	Number of parameters	10-Fold *random-partitioning*	12-Fold *subject-wise*
CNN	C(16)-C(32)-S_m	121,179	97.5%	93.3%
	C(16)-C(32)-C(64)-C(128)-DR(0.5)- S_m	206,811	98.5%	95.7%
CNN+RNN	C(32)-C(64)-C(32)-DR(0.5)-RG(64)- S_m	91,851	97.1%	95.7%
	C(32)-C(64)-C(32)-DR(0.5)-RG(96)- S_m	123,083	98.1%	96.3%
	C(64)-C(64)-C(64)-DR(0.5)-RG(64)- S_m	158,155	**99.5%**	**97.7%**
	C(64)-C(64)-C(64)-DR(0.5)-RG(128)- S_m	232,651	99.1%	97.5%

3. Results and Discussion

3.1. Network Models Performance

The accuracy of every model has been obtained using two evaluation methods, consisting in two different *K-Fold cross-validation* approaches, as in [8]: (1) *10-Fold random-partitioning* and (2) *12-Fold subject-wise*. In the first case one tenth of the instances are left out during training and results are the average of 10 different evaluations. In the second case, instances of one of the subjects are left out during training and 12 different trainings are conducted to obtain the average accuracy of the network for classification of the 11 different activities.

The best results for every network were obtained with pre-processing methods (3) and (5) explained in Section 2.2. Table 1 contains the accuracy obtained using (3) Raw data with Data Augmentation and 2D-DFT features.

The first model consists in a two-layer CNN of 16 and 32 feature maps. In the second model, the number of layers is increased up to four and the number of feature maps rises up to 128 for the last convolutional layer, which is connected to a 0.5 dropout layer. Last model achieves a better performance, at the expense of increasing the number and complexity of layers.

The four CNN+RNN networks were proposed with the aim that both spatial and temporal relationships of the data could be learned. In the first two CNN+RNN models, we explored the idea of using a smaller convolutional network in terms of feature maps and adding a RNN with 64 GRU or 96 GRU units.

The third CNN+RNN proposal was the winning model in terms of accuracy. It consists in a three-layer CNN of 64 feature maps, a dropout layer and a RNN of 64 GRU units. The output comes from a *Softmax* layer of 11 units, one per activity class. In this network, the number of feature maps is greater than in previous models, but after each convolutional layer, the dimensionality reduction is greater using a larger stride, so that we can connect it also to 64 GRU units. Finally, in the fourth CNN+RNN proposal, the number of GRU units was increased, but this did not provide an improvement in performance.

In addition to measuring the performance of the winning model in terms of accuracy, we measured its performance in terms of running time on a CPU Intel® Core™ i54690 and a not-last-generation commodity GPU NVIDIA GeForce GTX 1060. Feature engineering takes $t_{DFT+concat} = 196\,\mu s \pm 230\,ns$ and inference time in the winning model takes $t_{inference} = 248\,\mu s$ for a total time $t_{TOTAL} = 444\,\mu s \pm 230\,ns$.

Data acquisition from IMUs occurs every 20 ms (50 Hz) and the proposed model deployed on a not optimized TensorFlow implementation takes less than 450 µs to pre-process data and perform the classification. For the above reasons, we consider that our model meets real-time restrictions and could be potentially embedded in a portable system in a near future.

3.2. Discussion

Table 2 compares the results of this work against previous works [7, 8]. It includes the total number of IMUs, the sensors info used as input (ACC: accelerometer, GYR: gyroscope, MAG: magnetometer and QUAT: quaternions), the number of features per IMU, the number of activities classified in the work, the number of subjects used for that classification, the evaluation method, the number of instances extracted from the dataset and the accuracy obtained for the classification problem. In our work we only classify 11 activities. On the other hand we use only data from 12 subjects and 5 IMUs instead of 9. It is important to highlight that our results are relevant and should be compared in terms of the achieved performance using only a fraction of input features and training instances.

Table 2. Classification results.

Network	#IMUs	Sensors	#features (per IMU)	#features (total)	#activities	#subjects	Evaluation Method	Number of instances	Accuracy
Oresti [6]	9	ACC+GYR+MAG+QUAT	-	-	33	17	1	-	97.0 %
Zhu [7]	9	ACC+GYR+MAG+QUAT	106	4086	33	17	2	130000	99.4 %
		QUAT		1224					93.0 %
Our work	5	QUAT	8	40	11	12	1	1176	**99.5 %**
							2		**97.7 %**

In the *random-partitioning* evaluation method we overtake the results obtained in [7], with a 99.5 % of accuracy against 97 %. In the *subject-wise* evaluation method, we improve or have similar results than those obtained in [8]. Using only quaternion data and 40 features we obtain a 97.7 % of accuracy, while previous work achieved a 93 % using 30 times more features. We also had 110 times less features: only 1,176 data instances instead of 130,000. Finally, we are only 1.7 % below from the best result obtained in [7], using 100 times less input features.

5. Conclusions

This paper introduces and evaluates six Deep Neural Networks for Human Activity Recognition (HAR) of upper-body movements. The winning CNN+RNN model is able to classify 11 different activities with an accuracy of 99.5 % or 97.7 %, depending on the evaluation method. Remarkably, it has been trained using a very small set of input features and training examples. We propose using 2D Fast Fourier Transform features and a new data augmentation method to increase the networks performance.

Our research is driven by the feel that in the next years there would be a growing interest for developing technologies for low-cost human motion analysis using wearable technology. Deep Neural Networks combined with wireless IMU sensors have many potential applications in the areas of healthcare, fitness, and entertainment. The work presented here is the first step towards developing a system that in the future could be used to track patients during their activities of daily living (ADL).

Acknowledgements

We would like to specially thank Professor Oresti Banos for his help and explanations related to the REALDISP dataset.

References

[1]. J. Wang, Y. Chen, S. Hao, X. Peng, L. Hu, Deep learning for sensor-based activity recognition: A survey, *Pattern Recognit. Lett.*, Vol. 119, March 2019, pp. 3-11.

[2]. I. H. Lopez-Nava, A. Munoz-Melendez, Wearable Inertial Sensors for Human Motion Analysis: A Review, *IEEE Sens. J.*, Vol. 16, Issue 22, November 2016, pp. 7821-7834.

[3]. N. Jalloul, Wearable sensors for the monitoring of movement disorders', *Biomed. J.*, Vol. 41, Issue 4, August 2018, pp. 249-253.

[4]. C. J. Newman, *et al.*, Measuring upper limb function in children with hemiparesis with 3D inertial sensors, *Childs Nerv. Syst.*, Vol. 33, Issue 12, December 2017, pp. 2159-2168.

[5]. M. Panwar, *et al.*, Rehab-Net: Deep learning framework for arm movement classification using wearable sensors for stroke rehabilitation, *IEEE Trans. Biomed. Eng.*, Vol. 66, Issue 11, November 2019, pp. 3026-3037.

[6]. UCI Machine Learning Repository: REALDISP Activity Recognition Dataset Data, https://archive.ics.uci.edu/ml/datasets/REALDISP+Activity+Recognition+Dataset

[7]. O. Banos, M. Toth, M. Damas, H. Pomares, I. Rojas, Dealing with the effects of sensor displacement in wearable activity recognition, *Sensors*, Vol. 14, Issue 6, June 2014, pp. 9995-10023.

[8]. J. Zhu, R. San-Segundo, J. M. Pardo, Feature extraction for robust physical activity recognition, *Hum.-Centric Comput. Inf. Sci.*, Vol. 7, Issue 1, December 2017, 16.

[9]. D. Pavllo, C. Feichtenhofer, M. Auli, D. Grangier, Modeling human motion with quaternion-based neural networks, *Int. J. Comput. Vis.*, Special Issue, October 2019.

(046)

Fine-grained Vision-based Vehicle Classification

K. Zahn[1], A. Caduffl, J. Hofstetter[1], M. Rechsteiner[1] and P. Bucher [2]
[1] Lucerne University of Applied Sciences and Arts, Technikumstr. 21, 6048 Horw, Switzerland
[2] SICK System Engineering, Flurhofstr. 15, 6374 Buochs, Switzerland
Tel.: +41 41 349 3573, fax: +41 41 349 3311
E-mail: klaus.zahn@hslu.ch

Summary: The detection and classification of vehicles by suitable monitoring systems is an integral part of Intelligent Transportation Systems (ITS). We report results on fine-grained vehicle classification based on video images obtained from roadside based cameras. A new dataset of more than 100'000 samples allowing for a total of 36 fine-grained vehicle categories is introduced and classification results based on convolutional neural networks (CNN) are presented. We show, that simple CNN architectures suitable for real-time applications lead to surprisingly good results. As a practical outcome applicable to ITS we illustrate that – to our knowledge – for the first time a vision system fulfils the challenging traffic norm TLS 8+1 A1.

Keywords: Intelligent Transportation, Vehicle Classification, Image Processing, Machine Learning, Deep Learning.

1. Introduction

Traffic monitoring systems play an important role for Intelligent Transportation Systems (ITS) in order to supply reliable real-time data on vehicle frequencies and categories. This data is an important basis for private or public transportation agencies to manage toll operation, optimize traffic flow and improve road safety.

Over the last decade, considerable progress in vision sensor hardware and image processing algorithms – in particular machine learning – was achieved and camera-based system are increasingly used for ITS applications [1]. However, despite the considerable amount of work performed, results on fine-grained vehicle classification above 10 categories is still scarce [1], because no suitable database is available. In fact, the only relevant work in this context is the classification of vehicles in different brands due to the existence of an appropriate dataset [2].

Our contributions to this problem context are the following. First, a new – and in this form – unique database is presented, which consists of more than 100'000 samples of 36 fine-grained vehicle categories. Second, different CNN architectures for fine-grained vehicle classification are evaluated on this set. Based on these results we will finally show, that – to our knowledge for the first time – a vision system is able to fulfil the challenging traffic norm TLS 8+1 A1 [3].

2. Approach

The following analysis is based on images from cameras installed roadside with a similar perspective as shown in Fig. 1. We will furthermore limit the discussion to the classification task only and assume, that the bounding boxes as shown in Fig 1 are already given. In fact, the complete application, which will be presented in its full extend elsewhere, performs first vehicle detection based on Faster R-CNNs [4] with a subsequent tracking to improve the overall detection accuracy.

Fig. 1. Typical camera perspective used in the project.

2.1. Data Acquisition

The major challenge in creating an appropriate data set for fine-grained vehicle classification is the fact, that few categories (car, van, bus ...) dominate and sufficient numbers for the "rare" classes are difficult to obtain. This leads to the currently available very unbalanced data sets having only a limited amount of categories [1]. An efficient way to solve this problem is online preselection of vehicles. For this purpose, overhead Laser scanners installed at the test site were used, which immediately rule out the frequent classes and trigger the cameras to save only the rare ones. The resulting images were manually classified/corrected and in total, the numbers of class-specific samples given in Table 1 were obtained. Overall, 18 fine-grained vehicle categories, with a minimum 200 samples each, plus a trailer class were used. With these overall 36 classes consisting of 18 basic types with or without a trailer can be formed. This covers most of the internationally existing category systems and as one practical example we will show, how to fulfil the German norm TLS 8+1 A1 by a merge of suitable fine-grained subclasses.

We are not aware of any other existing database coming close to our number of categories and/or samples.

Table 1. Class-specific samples in the vehicle data set.

Category	Sample Images
ArticTruck	6588
ArticTruckDumptor	1318
ArticTruckLowLoaded	621
ArticTruckTanker	766
ArticVan	548
Bike	4115
Bus	3548
CamperVan	4729
Car	44480
TractorTruck	270
Truck	5036
TruckCarTransporterEmpty	229
TruckCarTransporterLoadeded	193
TruckDumptor	5141
TruckLowLoaded	2403
TruckTanker	3389
Van	5455
VanPickup	4581
Trailer	7246
Total	**100656**

2.2. Classification Approach

For the classification, a CNN (convolutional neural network) was used. As the final application is running in real time on an embedded processing platform an architecture as simple as possible was preferred. Iterative trials lead to a CNN with input size 128x128 and 4 convolutional layers, each of a size 3x3, stride 1 and of numbers 32, 64, 128 and 256 respectively. Activation function was ReLU. Each convolutional layer is followed by a max-pooling layer of size 2x2 and stride 2. Finally, a single hidden layer with 256 neurons and output to the 18 + 1 vehicle classes of Table 1 is chosen. Single image inference requires 7 ms on a Core i7-6820EQ @ 2.8 GHz.

3. Results

Fig. 2 (bottom) shows the results for the validation and test sets obtained with the discussed CNN on the full 18+1 classes from Table 1. Despite the simple architecture, the results of the test set are all close to or well above 80 %. A closer look to the confusion matrix reveals, that misclassifications are mainly within similar classes, which will fall into the same class of the norm TLS 8+1 (Fig. 2, top).

Thus, when the fine-grained classes are merged to the reduced set of TLS 8+1 classes, the true positive rates as given in Fig. 3 result. In addition, the limits for the most challenging norm TLS 8+1 A1 are drawn in red. As required by TLS the lower limit of the 95% confidence interval lie all well above the TLS limits. To our knowledge, this is currently the only vision system fulfilling TLS 8+1 A1.

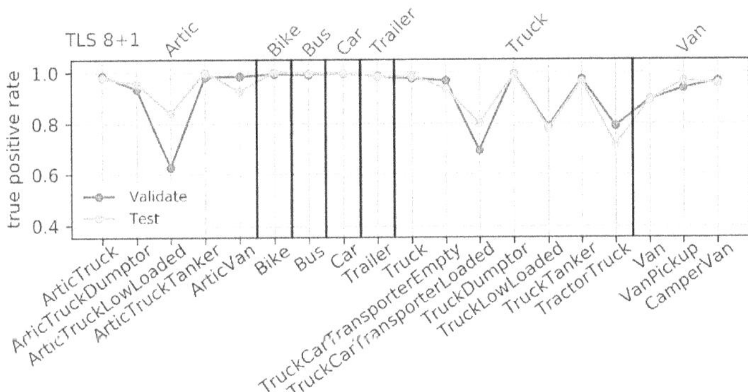

Fig. 2. True positive rate for the 18+1 classes obtained with a simple 6-layer CNN architecture.

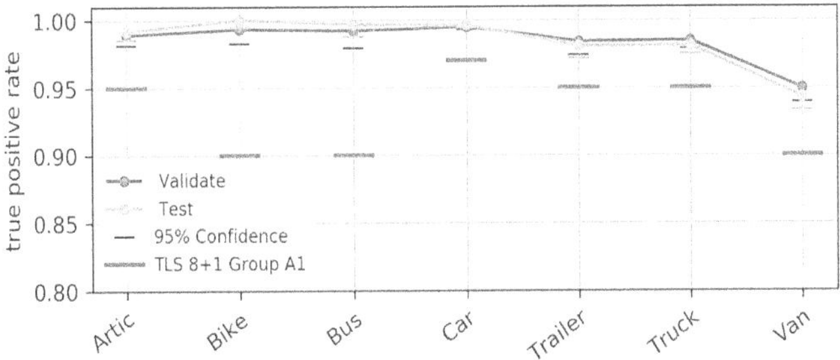

Fig. 3. True positive rate of validation and test data sets for the merged categories allow to fulfil TLS 8+1 A1.

4. Conclusions

In summary, we present a new vehicle dataset of more than 100'000 images consisting of 36 fine-grained categories. Classification with a simple 6-layer CNN shows overall good result and a merge to the 8+1 classes of the norm TLS allows to fulfil the most challenging limit TLS 8+1 A1 in real time on state-of-the art PC hardware, even without GPU.

Acknowledgements

This project was supported by the Swiss Innovation Agency Innosuisse.

References

[1] Won, M. Intelligent Traffic Monitoring Systems for Vehicle Classification: A Survey, preprint, http://arxiv.org/abs/1910.04656

[2] Liao, L., et al., Exploiting effects of parts in fine-grained categorization of vehicles, in *Proceedings of the International Conference on Image Processing (ICIP)*, 2015.

[3]. https://www.bast.de/BASt_2017/DE/Publikationen/Regelwerke/Verkehrstechnik/Unterseiten/V5-tls-2012.html

[4]. Ren, S., et al., Faster R-CNN: Towards Real-Time Object Detection with Region Proposal Networks, *IEEE Transactions on PAMI*, Vol. 39, Issue 6, 2016, pp. 1137–1149.

[5]. Adu-Gyamfi, et al., Automated vehicle recognition with deep convolutional neural networks, *Transportation Research Record: Journal of the Transportation Research Board*, No. 2645, 2017, pp. 113–122.

(047)

Training of a cycleGAN Net by the use of Air/water Images Dataset Obtained by Taking Pictures of Colored Plastic Bricks Submerged in an Ad-hoc Pool

M. Guarneri [1], **P. Castellini** [2], **M. Ciaffi** [1] **and E. P. Tomasini** [2]
[1] ENEA R.C. Frascati, FSN-TECFIS-DIM Laboratory, Via E. Fermi 45 Frascati (RM), Italy
[2] Marche Polytechnic Univ., Mechanical Engeneering, Ancona, Italy
Tel.: + 390694005553
E-mail: massimiliano.guarneri@enea.it

Summary: In the last years the application of Artificial Intelligence algorithms has grown drastically in different sectors and aspects of our lives. One of the major successful sectors is the treatment of images, not only in terms of classification, but also in terms of processing and data improvements: one of the most diffuse examples are the mobile camera software, which uses neural-networks-based algorithms for obtaining high quality pictures from lenses with a reduced resolving power, if compared with professional optical ones. The present work aims to use unsupervised Convolutional Neural Networks for underwater images processing, so to try to obtain air-quality images and reduce all the effects caused by the interaction between light and water particles. Nowadays several works are presented for the correction of low contrast and blurriness effects, but most of them generate synthetic images obtained by applying complementary algorithms used for water effects correction. The present work aims to create a real dataset composed by air/water images by the use of an ad-hoc experimental setup for training an unsupervised Generative Adversarial Network (GAN). Because of their nature to be generative models of data, GANs can learn to estimate the underlying probability distribution of the data and the unsupervised GAN can make it without a one-to-one mapping.

Keywords: CNN, Underwater, LEGO, Colorimetry, Corals.

1. Introduction

In the last years the application of Artificial Intelligence algorithms has grown drastically in different sectors and aspects of our lives. One of the major successful sectors is the treatment of images, not only in terms of classification, but also in terms of processing and data improvements: one of the most diffuse examples are the mobile camera software, which uses neural-networks-based algorithms for obtaining high quality pictures from lenses with a reduced resolving power, if compared with professional optical ones; other examples are the image enhancement of photos captured in low-light conditions, where the neural network algorithms are trained for balancing the colors by processing pairs of input/output images [1].

This work was born few years ago approaching the problem to document and monitor marine bioindicators like corals [2, 3] for following the evolutions of climate changes, especially in terms of water temperature. The first approach of the research group was to select the best approach for obtaining colored 3D models, passing from the standard photogrammetry to the most sophisticated laser scanning techniques [4]. The choice to use at the end the photogrammetry was preferred to other 3D digitalization methods, like described also in [5], especially because of their complexities without a significative improvements respect the photogrammetry itself. However, also if the results presented in [4] satisfied the minimum requirements of the problem, the method presented a too manual approach especially in terms of preprocessing of the single images. Most of the preprocessing approach was oriented to correct the different ambient illuminations occurred in every case study approached during the research.

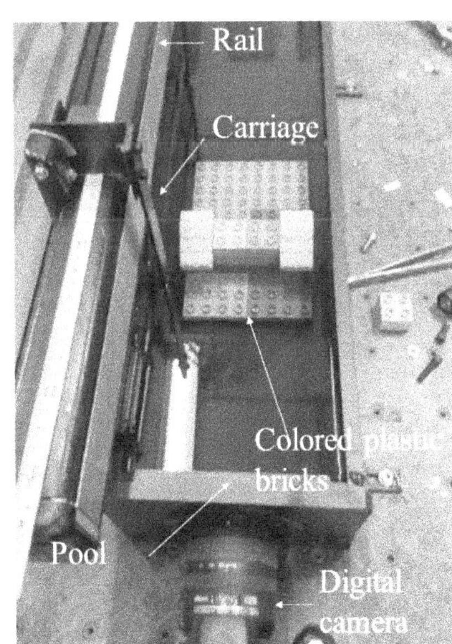

Fig. 1. Laboratory setup for data acquisition.

The idea to start a completely different approach derived also by simplifying both the data processing and information access to the researchers who operate in the marine ecosystem monitoring: for example, a rapid approach to determine benthic population modifications is to observe the growth and color changes on time [6]. Another scope of the present work was to calibrate the images coming from a standard digital camera in a controlled underwater environment, so to extract the information mentioned above, minimizing the effects caused by the presence of the water. For this purpose, an ad-hoc pool has been built, with the facility to move the samples along 1200mm from the chosen sensor, for simulating also the effects caused by the light absorptions versus the distance. For creating simply air/water pairs datasets, several plastic bricks with different colors and shapes and with the possibility to be dovetailed together have been chosen.

The approach adopted in this work is to use the resulting dataset for training a Convolutional Neural Network for discriminating the optical/physical components that affect an underwater picture respect a same image obtained without the presence of the water.

Nowadays several works are presented for the correction of low contrast and blurriness effects [7, 8], but most of them generate synthetic images [9] obtained by applying complementary algorithms used for water effects correction. Also for this work an unsupervised Generative Adversarial Network (GAN) was used: because of their nature to be generative models of data, GANs can learn to estimate the underlying probability distribution of the data and the unsupervised GAN can make it without a one-to-one mapping.

2. Acquisition and CNN Training Workflow

2.1. Laboratory Setup

As mentioned before, the training and testing datasets for training a Convolutional Neural Network were created acquiring couples of air/underwater images of the same subject placed at different distances inside an ad-hoc pool. The pool has a shape of a parallelepiped with dimensions of (WxHxD) 250×250×1200 mm; the upper side of the parallel pool is open, while the rest of the walls are painted with opaque black paint. One of the small squared faces accommodates a coated window with a diameter of 200 mm for reducing the rays-of-light's refraction caused by the different air/water index. The samples are placed on a carriage, which can translate along one of the longest sides of the parallelepiped.

In a first approach the samples came from typical objects, which can easily find in a laboratory, but the difficulty to position them in the same place at different time steps and the limitation of the variety of colors – most of the object are black or gray – were the main reasons for changing the targets.

Starting from a preliminary and hypothetical idea that training a Neural Network is like to train a fresh brain, like the brain of a kid, the choice to use the plastic colored brick (LEGO Duplo©) was quite natural. However, in a second step, the choice resulted winning for several reasons: the possibility to arrange the same scene several times and also in different temporal moments, with a tolerance of few hundreds microns, compatible with the scopes of this work; the bricks present different shapes and colors and can be dovetailed together, creating almost new infinite shapes; the choice to use the biggest version of the famous plastic bricks facilitated also the possibility to easily measure scene dimensions, colors and distances from the sensor. In particular for the color information, also if several online sources are available [10, 11], the possibility to measure directly this parameter by a colorimeter or spectrophotometer opens the scenario to train the CNN for producing images colorimetrically corrected also in presence of different light sources and without the use of colored checkboards.

The volume of the pool was completely filled with clean water and emptied by the use of a small electronic pump. In a second stage of the experiment, several different concentrations of milk were diluted in the water.

The bricks composition was fixed on the bottom of the carriage by a double-side tape. Outside the pool, with the lenses matching the coated window, a Nikon D90 camera was placed. The camera parameters have been fixed, for simulating a real condition in underwater case, and set so to keep a sufficient depth of field for covering all the range traveled by the carriage, corresponding to a total distance of 1140 mm. Fig. 1 shows the experimental setup used for creating the air/water dataset.

2.2. Dataset Creation and CNN Training Pipeline

The acquisition of the dataset composed by couples of air/water images was made by following this pipeline: several blocks were assembled together in a random configuration and the base fixed at the bottom of the carriage; at the beginning of the acquisition, the pool was empty; the carriage was placed at a distance of 240 mm from the camera and a picture captured; the next pictures were collected moving the carriage at a distance of 10mm from the previous position; when the carriage reached the end of the rail, the pool was filled with the water and the same procedure, before mentioned, was completed again. Fig. 2 shows an example of images composing the air/water dataset: the images (b, c, d) show also the reflection caused by the air/water interface. For increasing the samples of the dataset and removing the undesired portions of the collected images, a Python script was developed for limiting the area used for creating several 256x256 pixels random crops, compatible with the input layer of the GAN.

The chosen GAN network was the cycleGAN [12] composed by two Generators, which respectively map the X to the Y domain and the Y to the X, and two Discriminators, which attempt to differentiate the synthetized images from the original ones. The cycleGAN objective function is composed by two components:

$$Loss_{full} = Loss_{adv} + \lambda \cdot Loss_{cycle}, \quad (1)$$

where $Loss_{adv}$ is the adversarial loss, the measure of how much efficient are the generators to fool the discriminators: in other words, how much the generators images belong to the destination domain, without giving any measure about how much they are consistent; on the other side, $Loss_{cycle}$, weighted by the λ parameter, usually set at 10, is the cycle consistency loss, needed for estimating how much consistent are the generated images by the Generators. For the reasons mentioned above, this particular GAN is classified as an unsupervised neural network, which means that it doesn't need of pairs of corresponding images for solving the problem: however, the possibility to have also pairs of corresponding images simplify the comparison between the originals and the generated images. Especially in an advanced phase of this research, the pairs of the corresponding images will allow to determine colorimetric differences (ΔE) and make considerations about which coordinates in a determined color space are more affected by the neural network [13].

The PyTorch [14] version of the cycleGAN was trained with more than 7000 air+water samples and tested with more than 700 images.

3. Results and Conclusions

The present work shows the preliminary results obtained by training and testing the cycleGAN network with the dataset built as described before. Fig. 2(a, b) show an example of the images collected in different air/water conditions; Fig. 2c shows an example of image obtained mixing 0.75 ml of milk in 25l of water. The water and milk images (Fig. 2d) were scaled of a factor 1.3, equivalent to the water refraction index: at this stage of the research no further corrections are needed for the presence of the milk. Fig. 3 and Fig. 4 show respectively some preliminary results (columns d) obtained by the Underwater-cycleGAN, which received as input water and water+milk images. Columns (c) show a correction obtained applying the histogram equalization algorithm [15] between air and water/water+milk images. It's important to highlight that, at this stage of the work, the GAN wasn't trained also with the water+milk samples, so the results shown in Fig. 4 are obtained with the weights coming from the air/water dataset training.

The present work is still at an early stage of the research and further improvements of the training and testing phases have to be adopted. The possibility to work with controlled environment and samples have a dual important aspect: on one side, it is possible to follow and better control all the phases of the train and test of a neural network, studying how it reacts by modifying easily the dataset creation and selection; on the other side, it is possible also to control the quality of the network output, so to analyze and inspect the data for the estimation of colorimetric and structural information, needed especially in the marine research sector for benthic population modifications. Another aspect of the choice to train a cycleGAN network is, due to its nature to be composed by two Generators and two Discriminators, it can be used also for generating synthetic underwater images, useful in other research sectors.

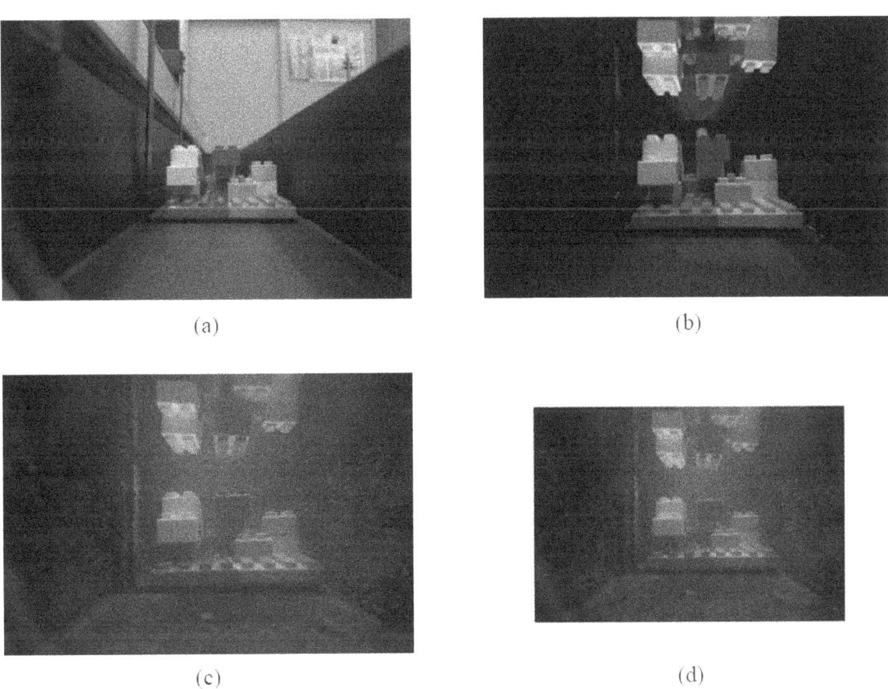

Fig. 2. Some examples of the collected dataset (a) an example of image collected with the empty pool; (b) shows the same sample submerged in 25l water; (c) inside the pool filled by the water, 0.75 ml of milk were added; (d) the previous image scaled of the water refraction index (1.3).

(a) (b) (c) (d)

Fig. 3. A crop of air/water+milk images. (a) image acquired inside the empty pool; (b) the same sample collected inside 25l of water where 0.75ml of milk were added; (c) histogram equalization algorithm applied to the image (b); (d) the result obtained by processing the (b) with the cycleGAN.

(a) (b) (c) (d)

Fig. 4. A crop of air/water images. (a) image acquired inside the empty pool; (b) the same sample collected inside the water; (c) histogram equalization algorithm applied to the image (b); (d) the result obtained by processing (b) with the cycleGAN.

References

[1]. M. Gharbi, J. Chen, J. T. Barron, S. W. Hasinoff, and F. Durand, Deep bilateral learning for real-time image enhancement, in *ACM Transactions on Graphics*, Vol. 36, No. 4, 2017.

[2]. L. Gutierrez-Heredia, F. Benzoni, E. Murphy, and E. G. Reynaud, End to End Digitisation and Analysis of Three-Dimensional Coral Models, from Communities to Corallites, *PLoS One*, Vol. 11, No. 2, 2016.

[3]. T. F. Cooper, J. P. Gilmour, and K. E. Fabricius, Bioindicators of changes in water quality on coral reefs: Review and recommendations for monitoring programmes, *Coral Reefs*, Vol. 28, No. 3, 2009, pp. 589–606.

[4]. R. Napolitano, M. Guarneri, M. C. Gambi, and E. P. Tomasini, Evaluation and comparison of non-contact measurement techniques for the observation and shape reconstruction of sessile benthic organisms, in *Proceedings of the IMEKO TC19 Workshop on Metrology for the Sea, MetroSea 2017: Learning to Measure Sea Health Parameters*, 2017, Vol. 2017-October, pp. 62–67.

[5]. M. Massot-Campos and G. Oliver-Codina, Optical sensors and methods for underwater 3D reconstruction, *Sensors (Switzerland)*, Vol. 15, No. 12, 2015, pp. 31525–31557.

[6]. G. Winters, R. Holzman, A. Blekhman, S. Beer, and Y. Loya, Photographic assessment of coral chlorophyll contents: Implications for ecophysiological studies and coral monitoring, *J. Exp. Mar. Bio. Ecol.*, Vol. 380, No. 1–2, November 2009, pp. 25–35.

[7]. Y. Y. Schechner and N. Karpel, Recovery of underwater visibility and structure by polarization analysis, *IEEE J. Ocean. Eng.*, Vol. 30, No. 3, July 2005, pp. 570-587.

[8]. M. Block, B. Gehmlich, and D. Hettmanczyk, Automatic Underwater Image Enhancement using Improved Dark Channel Prior, *Stud. Digit. Herit.*, Vol. 1, No. 2, p. 566, 2017.

[9]. J. Li, K. A. Skinner, R. M. Eustice, and M. Johnson-Roberson, WaterGAN: Unsupervised generative network to enable real-time color correction of monocular underwater images, *IEEE Robot. Autom. Lett.*, Vol. 3, No. 1, 2018, pp. 387–394.

[10]. Understanding the LEGO Color Palette - BRICK ARCHITECT., https://brickarchitect.com/color/

[11]. BrickLink Color Guide., [Online]. Available: https://www.bricklink.com/catalogColors.asp

[12]. J. Y. Zhu, T. Park, P. Isola, and A. A. Efros, Unpaired Image-to-Image Translation Using Cycle-Consistent Adversarial Networks, in *Proceedings of the IEEE International Conference on Computer Vision*, 2017, Vol. 2017-Octob, pp. 2242–2251.

[13]. C. H. Chen, L. F. Pau, P. S. P. Wang, and Q.-T. Luong, Color in Computer Vision, *World Scientific*, 1993.

[14]. PyTorch., [Online] https://pytorch.org/

[15]. M. A. Al Wadud, M. H. Kabir, M. A. A. Dewan, and O. Chae, A dynamic histogram equalization for image contrast enhancement, *IEEE Transactions on Consumer Electronics,* Vol. 53, Issue 2, May 2007, pp. 593 - 600.

(049)

Chinese Short Text Classification Based on Interactive Attention Mechanism

Qinyu Bian [1,2,3], **Yuan Rao** [1,2,3], **Leipeng Wang** [1,2,3], **Fan Yang** [1,2,3], **and Shipeng Dong** [1,2,3]
[1] Shenzhen Research Institute of Xi'an Jiaotong University, 518057, Shenzhen, China
[2] Lab of Social Intelligence and Complex Data Processing, Software School, Xi'an Jiaotong University, 710049, Xi'an, China
[3] Shannxi Joint Key Laboratory for Artifact Intelligence (Sub-Lab of Xi'an Jiaotong University), 710049, Xi'an, China
Tel.: +8618829284609
E-mail: 1260042017@qq.com

Summary: With the explosive growth of social media, millions of Chinese short texts are produced every day. However, these short texts is exactly short, so the machine can not extract features accurately from short texts for classification learning. In this paper, we propose an effective semantic enhancement model that not only combines character-level features, word-level features and sentence-level features as additional features for Chinese short text, but also removes noise by introducing Interactive Attention Mechanism to measure the semantic similarity between the i-th character and short text representation. Experiments on the open dataset Chinese news headlines classification task (190,000 news headlines/18 tags) show that our model achieves 84.53 %, 84.32 % and 84.36 % in macro-averaged precision, recall, F1, which boosts 1.26 % F1, 1.22 % recall and 1.3 % precision and achieves the state-of-the art performance.

Keywords: Short text classification, Semantic enhancement, Interactive attention mechanism.

1. Introduction

With the rapid development of internet technology, millions of Chinese short texts are produced every day, in the form of search queries, Weibo, etc. Compared with paragraphs or documents, one of the most notable characteristics of these short text is that they just consist of several dozens of words, for instance the length of a Weibo message is limited to 140 characters. It is very necessary to mine valuable information from short texts, so our work is to organize and classify these massive fragmented short texts effectively, and generate a large amount of available structured data for the research and processing of data mining, recommendation, knowledge network construction and other work. Furthermore, unlike English and other western languages, Word segmentation is the first step in Chinese natural language processing, and the error caused by word segmentation can be transmitted to the whole system. In order to reduce the impact of word segmentation and improve the overall performance of Chinese short text classification system, we propose a hybrid model of character-level and word-level features based on Interactive Attention Mechanism.

At present, the main research works for short text classification focus on text representation and classification model, Jin Wang et al. [1] proposed a framework based on words and relevant concepts vectors, but when an entity is missing in a knowledge base, we cannot obtain any feature of it and thus we will get error classification, to reduce the bad influence of some improper concepts introduced due to the ambiguity of entities or the noise in KBs. Jindong Chen et al. [2] proposed Concept towards Short Text (C-ST) attention and Concept towards Concept Set (C-CS) attention to acquire the weight of concepts from two aspects. And Jingwen Li et al. [3] took word-level vectors and character-level vectors as inputs simultaneously, and encoded sentence semantics by two Long Short-Term Memory (LSTM) or bi-directional Long Short-Term Memory (BiLSTM). Based on the above analysis, this paper will also propose an effective method to combine character-level features as additional features and word-level features for Chinese short text representation. We introduce Char towards Short Text (C-ST) attention mechanisms based on vanilla attention [4] to measure the semantic similarity between the i-th char and short text representation. Meanwhile, we introduce Char towards Char Set attention (C-ST) mechanisms to assign a larger weight to the key character. We introduce a soft switch to combine two attention weights into one and produce the final attention weight of each character.

2. Our Model

Our model is a Word-Level and Character-Level Mixed Features deep neural network shown in Fig. 1. We provide a brief overview of our model before detailing it. The input of the network is a short text *s*, which is a sequence of words. The output of the network is the probability distribution of class labels.

We present a joint model called Bert joint Word2vec GRU Attention (BW_GA), using two sub-networks to extract the word and character features. Our model contains three modules. Word Embedding Encoding Module encodes the word level features of the short text by self-attention and produces short text representation q. Char Embedding Encoding Module applies two attention mechanisms on char vectors to obtain the character-level short text representation p and get sentence-level short text representation S. Next, we concatenate p, q and S to fuse the word-level short text, char-level short text and sentence-level short text, which is fed into a fully connected layer. Finally, we use an output layer to acquire the probability of each class label.

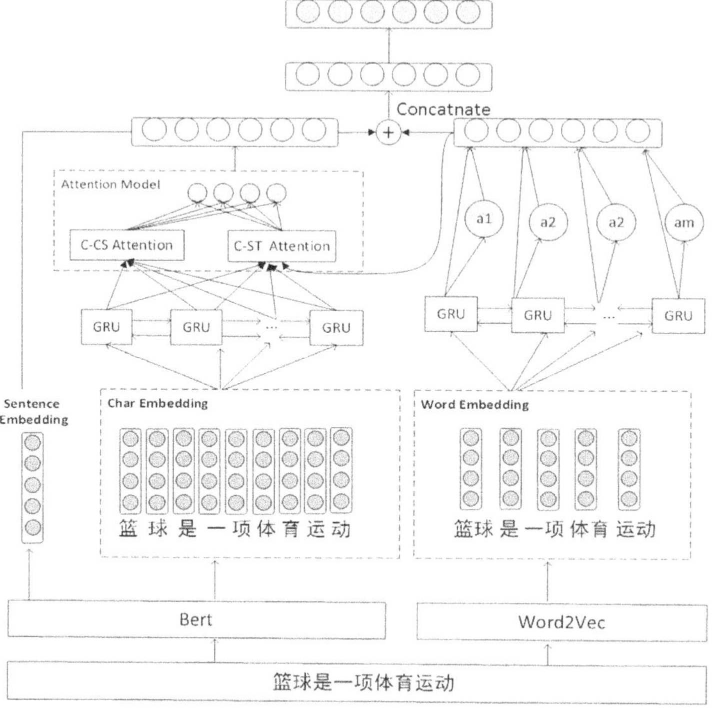

Fig. 1. Model Architecture.

2.1. Word Embedding Encoding

The first step of our work is to transform the short text into a matrix of embedding. We complete word segmentation before any processing short text and use the tool word2vec [5] to train word. If a word is not long enough, we will use 0 as padding. Therefore, an input word sequence will be mapped into a series of word vectors v(x1, x2, xn), where n is the length of the input sequence. The post is then encoded by Bi-directional Gated Recurrent Unit [6] (Bi-GRU), the reasons is that GRU not only maintains the effects of LSTM while making the structure simpler, reducing training parameters and increasing the rate of model training, but also captures long−term dependencies, and obtain effectively context information. We put vectors v into a BiGRU neural network, the calculation strategy of a BiGRU at the step t is listed as follows:

$$Z_t = \sigma(W_z x_t + U_{z\ t-1}), \quad (1)$$

$$r_t = \sigma(W_r x_t + U_r {}_{t-1}), \quad (2)$$

$$g_t = \tanh(W_h x_t + U_r(r_t \odot h_{t-1})), \quad (3)$$

$$_t = (1 - z_t) \odot h_{t-1} + z_t \odot g_t, \quad (4)$$

where x_t denotes the input data at time t. h_t and h_{t-1} are the hidden units at time t and t-1, respectively. Z_t is update gate. r_t is reset gate. σ, tanh, ⊙ denote the sigmod activation function, the tanh activation function and element wise multiplication. In bidirectional GRU, the forward and backward outputs of the hidden layer are aggregated together for uniform definition about the output of text sequence features.

Attention mechanism learns which input word is important by calculating the weight between the input sequence and target. Attention can be described as mapping a query and a set of key-value pairs to an output, attention is computed like equation (5).

$$\text{Similarity}(\text{Query}, \text{Key}_i) = \text{Query}\cdot \text{Key}_i, \quad (5)$$

$$a_i = Softmax(Sim_i) = \frac{e^{Sim_i}}{\sum_{j=1}^{L_x} e^{Sim_j}}, \quad (6)$$

$$\text{Attention(Query,Source)} = \\ =\sum_{i=1}^{L_x} a_i \cdot Value_i \quad (7)$$

We put the last hidden units vectors $t-1$ from GRU as queries and GRUs' hidden units at time i.

Key_i. Next, we acquire the short text representation q by equation (7).

The sentence representation generated by combining outputs of the last step hidden state of the two LSTM/BiLSTM is regarded as a document representation.

2.2. Char Embedding Encoding

Considering that the single character of Chinese also contains important semantic information. In this paper, we select a public pre-training deep representation language model, named BERT-Base [7], to represent char embedding. Therefore, an input word sequence will be mapped into a series of word vectors v (y_1, y_2, ... ,y_n) and the sentence vector S by BERT, where n is the length of the input sequence. Then we put vectors v into a BiGRU neural network by the equations (1-5), which can capture long-term dependencies, and obtain effectively context information. So we can obtain the hidden units H(h_1, h_2, h_3, ..., h_n), where h_i is the hidden units at time *i*. We aim at producing Sentence vector representation p by Char Vector, So We first introduce two attention mechanisms to pay more attention to important character. To reduce the bad influence of some improper Semantic information from Character, we propose Char towards Short Text(CST) attention based on vanilla attention [4] to measure the semantic similarity between the i-th char and short text representation. We use the following formula (8) to calculate the C-ST attention, and we introduce Char towards Char Set (C-CS) attention mechanism to assign a larger weight to the key char. We use the following formula (9) to calculate the C-CS attention:

$$\alpha_i = softmax\ (w_1^T f(W_1[h_i;q]) + b_1), \qquad (8)$$

$$\beta_i = softmax\ w_2^T f(W_{2\ i} + b_2) \qquad (9)$$

Here α_i denotes the weight of attention from i-th character towards the short text, β_i denotes the weight of attention from the i-th character towards whole character set. f(·) is a non-linear activation function such as hyperbolic tangent transformation, and softmax is used to normalize attention weight of each character. W_1,W_2 are weight matrix and b_1 is the offset.

We combine α_i and β_i by the following formula to obtain the final attention weight of each concept:

$$a_i = \text{softmax}(\gamma\alpha_i + (1-\gamma)\beta_i) \qquad (10)$$

Here a_i denotes the final attention weight from the i-th character towards the short text. $\gamma \in [0,1]$ is a soft switch to adjust the importance of two attention weights a_i and i. We treatγ as a hyper-parameter and manually adjust to obtain the best performance.

In the end, the final attention weights are employed to calculate a weighted sum of the character vectors, resulting in a sentence vector *p*.

$$\text{p} = \sum_{i=1}^{m} a_i\, h_i \qquad (11)$$

2.3. Text Classifier

In order to expand the semantic information of the short text, the sentence vector p generated by char embedding, the sentence vector q generated by word embedding, and the sentence vector S generated by BERT were combined to obtain a vector with rich semantic information. Finally, we employ Softmax activation function to obtain the classification label.

3. Experiments and Results

3.1. DataSet

We use NLPCC 2017 Shared Task 2 [8]: News Headlines Categorization as experimental corpus. The dataset contains 192000 news headlines with 18 classes, such as social, educational, economic and historical. 156,000 headlines are used as train set, 36,000 headlines are used as test set. The maximum length of text is 42. After segment, all the titles in the corpus, the maximum length of text is 30.

3.2. Baselines

LSTM[8]: A bidirectional LSTM network with pretraining language models by GloVe for word embedding.

CNN[8]: A deep CNN networks with convolution coresize of different scales.

NBOW[8]: a neural Bag-of-Words model containing the task specific word importance weights.

Fasttext[9]: A FastText network combined with pretraining language models to enhance semantic representation.

Expand System[9]: A semantic enhancement method for extending keywords in domain-specific datasets.

Mixed embedding CNN-LSTM[10]: Takes wordlevel vectors and character level vectors as inputs simultaneously, and encodes sentence semantics.

Fusion System[11]: A text classification method based on GRU and multimode binary classification voting mechanism.

3.3. Results and Analysis

In order to verify the effectiveness of our proposed model, in Table 1, the results of the comparison experiments show that our model, our model obtains 84.53 %, 84.32 % and 84.36 % in macro-averaged precision, recall, F1.

Compared to the best method of benchmark, our method boosts 1.26 % F1, 1.22 % recall and 1.3 % precision and achieves the state-of-the-art performance.

Table 1. Comparison of experimental results.

Model	Marco P	Marco R	Marco F1
LSTM	0.775	0.768	0.771
CNN	0.79	0.784	0.787
NBOW	0.797	0.790	0.787
Fasttext	0.81	0.805	0.808
Fusion System	0.8141	0.8114	0.8116
Mixed embedding CNN-LSTM	0.81575	0.8165	0.8165
Expand System	0.8320	0.8310	0.8310
BW_GA (our model)	0.8453	0.8432	0.8436

From the above results, we can observe that most existing work relied on either explicit or implicit text representation to address this problem. The value of evaluation index of different model is shown in Table 1. Compared with traditional methods, convolutional neural network approach achieve better results, the main reason is that CNN is able to capture richer features with various filter, sizes in the convolution layer and select more discriminative features from pooling layers. Since NBOW model considered the statistical information of words, the performance of classification is greatly improved than the traditional models of LSTM and CNN. But, these models with shallow network can not represent the deep semantic information, so it only widely can be used as basic module for extracting text features. Furthermore, Mixed embedding CNN-LSTM combined word-level vectors and character-level vectors, which effectively solves the problem of insufficient representation of single character level features or word-level features. Expand System adds some keywords extracted from the most similar news to expand the word features. While the external knowledge introduced some noise, so our model not only combine word-level vectors and character-level vectors, but also remove noise by introducing Char towards Short Text(C-ST) attention mechanism to measure the semantic similarity between the i-th char and short text representation and Char towards Char Set(C-CS) attention mechanisms to assign a larger weight to the key character.

5. Conclusions

In this paper, we propose our model which is a Word-Level and Character-Level Mixed Features deep neural network. We present a joint model using two sub-networks to extract the word and character features. Our model contains three modules. Word Embedding Encoding module encodes the word level features of the short text by self-attention. Char Embedding Encoding module applies two attention mechanisms on char vectors to obtain the short text representation. Next, we combine character-level features, word-level features. Finally, we use an output layer to acquire the probability of each class label.

Acknowledgements

The research work is supported by "Shenzhen Science and Technology Project" (JCYJ20180306170836595); "National key research and development program in China" (2019YFB2102300); "the World-Class Universities (Disciplines) and the Characteristic Development Guidance Funds for the Central Universities of China" (PY3A022); "Ministry of Education Fund Projects" (No. 18JZD022 and 2017B00030); "Basic Scientific Research Operating Expenses of Central Universities" (No.ZDYF2017006); "Xi'an Navinfo Corp.& Engineering Center of Xi'an Intelligence Spatial-temporal Data Analysis Project" (C2020103); "Beilin District of Xi'an Science & Technology Project" (GX1803).

References

[1]. J. Wang, et al., Combining knowledge with deep convolutional neural networks for short text classification, in *Proceedings of the International Joint Conference on Artificial Intelligence (IJCAI'17)*, Melbourne, Australia, 2017.

[2]. J. Chen, Y. Hu, J. Liu, Y. Xiao, H. Jiang, Deep short text classification with knowledge powered attention, *ArXiv Preprint*, arXiv:1902.08050, 2019.

[3]. J. Li, X. Wan, S. Qin, Word-level and character-level mixed features for Chinese short text classification, in *Proceedings of the International Conference on Computer and Communications (ICCC'18)*, Chengdu, 2018, pp. 2344-2348.

[4]. D. Bahdanau, K. Cho, Y. Bengio, Neural machine translation by jointly learning to align and translate, *Computer Science*, Vol. 1409, 2014. https://arxiv.org/pdf/1409.0473.pdf

[5]. T. Mikolov, K. Chen, G. Corrado, J. Dean, Efficient estimation of word representations in vector space, *ArXiv Preprint*, arXiv:1301.3781, 2013.

[6]. J. Chung, C. Gulcehre, K. Cho, Y. Bengio, Empirical evaluation of gated recurrent neural networks on sequence modeling, in *Proceedings of the NIPS 2014 Workshop on Deep Learning*, 2014.

[7]. J. Devlin, M.-W. Chang, K. Lee, K. Toutanova, Bert: Pre-training of deep bidirectional transformers for language understanding, *ArXiv Preprint*, arXiv:1810.04805, 2018.

[8]. X. Qiu, J. Gong, X. Huang, Overview of the NLPCC 2017 shared task: Chinese News headline categorization, in *Proceedings of the National CCF Conference on Natural Language Processing and Chinese Computing*, 2017, pp. 948-953.

[9]. Z. Yin, J. Tang, C. Ru, W. Luo, Z. Luo, X. Ma, A semantic representation enhancement method for

Chinese news headline classification, in *Proceedings of the National CCF Conference on Natural Language Processing and Chinese Computing*, 2017, pp. 318-328.

[10]. M. Zhang, CNN-LSTM short text classification based on word mixture vector, *Computer Application Technology*, 2019, Vol. 1, pp. 77-80.

[11]. X. Dong, R. Song, F. Zhu, Q. Zhu, Multi-model based news headline classification, *Journal of Chinese Information Processing*, Vol. 32, Issue 10, 2018, pp. 73-81.

(050)

Temporarily Activated Patterns for Multi-trial Functional Connectivity Data

Gaëtan Frusque [1], **Julien Jung** [2], **Pierre Borgnat** [3] **and Paulo Gonçalves** [2]
[1] Univ. Lyon, Inria, CNRS, ENS de Lyon, UCB Lyon 1, LIP UMR 5668, F-69342, Lyon, France
[2] HCL, Neuro. Hosp., Functional Neurology and Epileptology Dept. & Lyon Neurosc. Res. Cent., INSERM, CNRS, Lyon, France
[3] Univ. Lyon, ENS de Lyon, UCB Lyon 1, CNRS, Laboratoire de Physique, F-69342 Lyon, France
E-mail: frusque.gaetan@ens-lyon.fr

Summary: Functional connectivity is a graph-like data structure commonly used by neuroscientists to study the dynamic behaviour of brain activity. We address the problem of decomposing multi-trial functional connectivity data, with potential duration heterogeneity, into a set of common patterns contributing to each trial and their associated trial specific temporal activations. We apply our method on iEEG recording from different epileptic seizures of the same patient.

Keywords: Matrix decomposition, Tensor decomposition, Parafac2, Fused Lasso, iEEG, Functional connectivity.

1. Introduction

Epilepsy is one of the most common neurological disorder in the world population. iEEG electrodes are used to exhibit the stages of a seizure characterized by similar patterns in different areas of the brain. Functional Connectivities (FC) that quantify along time, these similarities are calculated between all pairs of signals, usually through the spectral coherence or the Phase Locking Value [1].

1.1. Problem

The patient stays in the hospital for several days with electrodes implemented in the brain to record multiple epileptic seizures. Since the number of FC to be studied is quadratic with the number of electrodes, the analyses of these FC become complicated and time-consuming. Hence, there is a need in the epileptologic community to use automatic methods to extract the FC dynamic global to all seizures.

Since the stages of seizures distinguish themselves by similar evolution of FC patterns, but with possibly different temporal activation, the joint analysis of these records should ease the identification of dynamical FC patterns common to all seizures but with specific temporal activation for each seizure.

1.2. Notation and Existing Propositions

Let N be the number of recorded seizures and $\boldsymbol{X}(n)$ the FC measures along time for the nth seizure. $\boldsymbol{X}(n)$ is of dimension $I*T(n)$, with I the number of FC and $T(n)$ the number of time samples (which can vary for each seizure n).

In [2], a constrained tensor decomposition method is used to infer FC patterns common to all seizures. However, this method does not exhibit the temporal activations to each seizure. Moreover, seizures time series must have the same number of ($T(n) = T$ for all n), which is sometimes impossible.

The usual tensor decomposition to deal with duration heterogeneity and producing a trial-specific activation matrix is Parafac2 [3], which allows the following approximation:

$$\mathbf{X}(n) \approx \mathbf{F}\mathbf{D}(n)\mathbf{V}(n)^t \quad \forall n \in 1, ..., N$$

$\boldsymbol{F}$ is the pattern matrix of dimension $I*K$ and K the number of FC pattern in the seizure. $\boldsymbol{V}$(n) is the time activation matrix is of dimension T*K and $\boldsymbol{D}$(n) is a diagonal matrix characterising the contribution of each pattern in the seizure. The principal default of this decomposition is the difficulty to add structural constraints on matrices $\boldsymbol{F}$ and $\boldsymbol{V}$(n) simultaneously, to get interpretable results.

2. Proposed Decomposition

We propose a modification of the Parafac2 problem. First, a sparse regularization on $\boldsymbol{F}$ is added, this is important in the context of epileptic data where a large number of FC measurements can be passively implied in a neurological process (during the discharge of the seizure, for example). Secondly, a Fused lasso constraint is imposed on the columns of $\boldsymbol{V}$(n), noted $\boldsymbol{v}(n)_{:k}$, to get few consistent and interpretable temporal activation for each pattern in all seizures. $\boldsymbol{F}$ and $\boldsymbol{V}$(n) are also imposed to be non-negative since FC are generally positive measures. Thus, the decomposition consists to find matrices $\boldsymbol{V}$(n) and $\boldsymbol{F}$ minimizing:

$$\underset{\mathbf{F}\geq 0, \mathbf{V(n)}\geq 0}{\text{argmin}} \sum_{n=1}^{N} || \mathbf{X}(n) - \mathbf{F}\mathbf{V}(n)^t ||_F^2 + a_1 || \mathbf{F} ||_1$$
$$s.t. \quad b_1 || \mathbf{v}(n)_{:k} ||_1 + b_2 TV(\mathbf{v}(n)_{:k}) + || \mathbf{v}(n)_{:k} ||_F^2 \leq 1$$

With a_1, b_1 and b_2 hyperparameters, *TV(.)* is the total variation function. The norms are entrywise and correspond to the Frobenius and the 1-norm respectively.

Here the diagonal matrices $\boldsymbol{D}(n)$ are imposed to be identity, which constitutes the principal difference with the Parafac2 model. In addition to simplify the implementation, identity matrices $\boldsymbol{D}(n)$ prompts to reveal only FC patterns contributing in each seizure.

The algorithm of our proposed decomposition consists to alternate two steps, first we fix and concatenate matrices $\boldsymbol{V}(n)$, and a lasso regression is done to estimate $\boldsymbol{F}$. Then knowing $\boldsymbol{F}$, a constrained regression for each seizure estimates the matrices $\boldsymbol{V}(n)$. We can show that this procedure ensures convergence of the loss function.

3. Application on iEEG Data

3.1. Data

We use the same dataset as in [2]: it consists of four FC measures $\boldsymbol{X}(n)$ (N = 4), computed employing Phase Locking value from iEEG recording of different seizures of the same patient (read [2] for more details).

Here, $T(n) = T$ for all n because the temporal activations of each FC pattern are similar through all seizures, which is an essential condition to use the methodology from [2]. We expect the proposed decomposition to produce similar FC patterns as in [2], and in addition specific and coherent temporal activation for each seizures.

3.2. Results

From matrices $\boldsymbol{X}(n)$, we compute the FC patterns $\boldsymbol{F}$ and their temporal activations $\boldsymbol{V}(n)$ using the proposed decomposition. We empirically fix K = 5 patterns, and $a_1 = 2$, $b_1 = 1$ and $b_2 = 1$. Fig. 1 shows the temporal activation profile of each FC patterns for all seizures. For each seizure, patterns activate in the same order, showing a succession of temporally coherent states.

Fig. 2 shows the position of the 33 electrodes projected on the transverse plane (according to the Tailarach coordinate). For each pattern, the FC i such that $\boldsymbol{F}_{ik} > 0$ is displayed by a link between involved pairs of electrodes. We recover FC patterns very similar to the four patterns found in [2], we also find another pattern (k = 2), which gives supplementary information on the seizure dynamic.

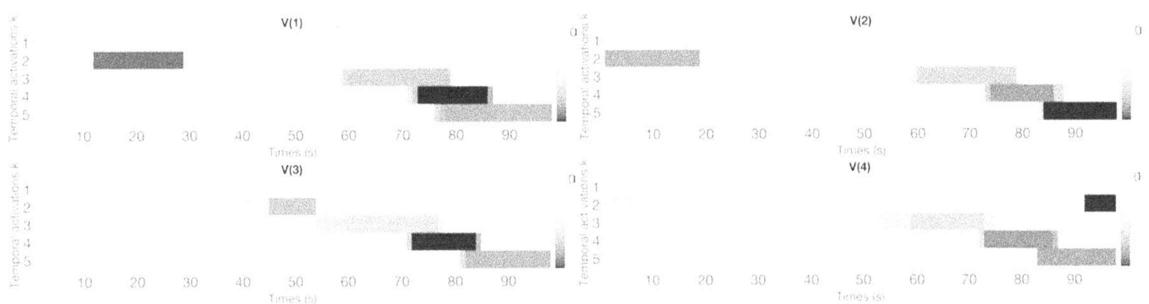

Fig. 1. Temporal activation matrices $\boldsymbol{V}(n)$ for the four studied seizures.

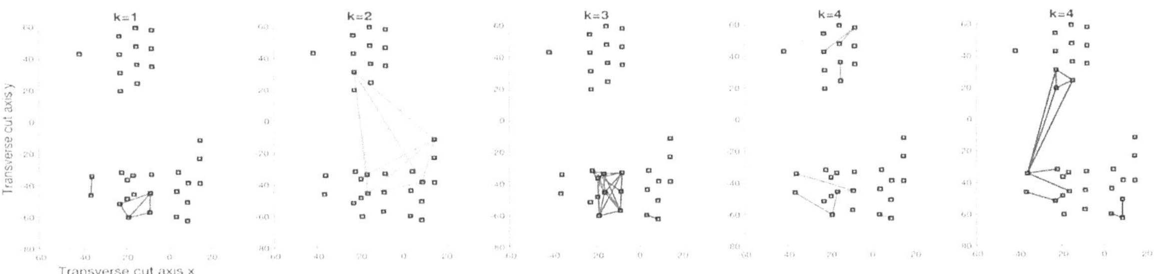

Fig. 2. Five common patterns $\boldsymbol{F}_{:k}$, FC i is displayed as a link when $\boldsymbol{F}_{ik}>0$.

4. Conclusions

In this work, we propose a method decomposing a multi-trial dynamic graph of functional connectivity, with potential duration heterogeneity. The application of our method on iEEG recording reveals the patterns common to all seizures, and identifies their specific temporal activation relevant to each seizure.

Acknowledgements

This work was supported by the ANR-14-CE27-0001 GRAPHSIP grant, and by the ACADEMICS grant of the IDEXLYON, project of the Université de Lyon, PIA operated by ANR-16-IDEX-0005.

References

[1]. P. van Mierlo, et al. Functional brain connectivity from EEG in epilepsy: Seizure prediction and epileptogenic focus localization, *Progress in Neurobiology*, Vol. 121, 2014, pp. 19-35.

[2]. G. Frusque, et al., Multiplex network inference with sparse tensor decomposition for functional connectivity, *IEEE Transaction T-SIPN*, Special Issue on Topological Network Inference, 2020.

[3]. H. A. L. Kiers, et al., PARAFAC2 Part I. A direct fitting algorithm for the PARAFAC2 model, *Journal of Chemometrics: A Journal of the Chemometrics Society*, Vol. 13, Issues 3-4, pp. 275-294.

(051)

Bot Detection in Social Networks Based on Machine Learning Techniques, User Information and Activities

Sandeep Singh Sengar [1], **Sanjay Kumar** [2], **Pradyot Raina** [2] **and Mukul Mahaliyan** [2]
[1] Department of Computer Science and Engineering, SRM University-AP, Andhra Pradesh, India-522 502
[2] Department of Computer Science and Engineering, Delhi Technological University, Shahbad Daulatpur, Main Bawana Road, New Delhi-110042, India
E-mails: sandeep.iitdhanbad@gmail.com, sanjay.kumar@dtu.ac.in, pradyotrainaout@gmail.com, mukulmahaliyan@gmail.com

Summary: With the swift rise of social networking sites, they have now come to hold tremendous influence in the daily lives of millions around the globe. The value of one's social media profile and its reach has soared highly. This has invited the use of fake accounts, spammers and bots to spread content favourable to those who control them. Thus, in this project we propose using a machine learning approach to identify bots and distinguish them from genuine users. This is achieved by compiling activity and profile information of users on Twitter and subsequently using natural language processing and supervised machine learning to achieve the objective classification. Finally, we compare and analyse the efficiency and accuracy of different learning models in order to ascertain the best performing bot detection system.

Keywords: Bot detection, Machine learning, Natural language processing, Social network, Text classification.

1. Introduction

Today, social networking sites have acquired an integral position in the daily lives of almost every person with access to the internet around the globe. The amount of time the average user spends on social media apps has also been increasing at an almost alarming rate for some time. Nowadays, users don't just use social networks like Facebook, Twitter, Instagram, etc. for interacting within their social circles but also for getting news updates, multimedia entertainment, political discussions, business and even shopping. All this points to the fact that social media has a massive hold on a significant part of the world's population and can thus be used, or misused, for influencing them. With people increasingly resorting to the social media profiles to judge and make views of the people around them, it has become increasingly important to have an impressive social media following. This is particularly a cause of concern for celebrities, politicians and others with similar public careers. Moreover, social media has the tendency to broadcast content to millions of people in a matter of minutes and thus all prominent organizations, from political parties to corporations, have started using it to push their own narratives and sway public opinion one way or another. And so, the use of fake accounts and bots in an organized manner on a massive scale has recently become a short cut to becoming 'viral' and inflating one's social media presence. 'Bots' are simply computer programs that automatically produce or repost content and interact with humans on social networks. When used on a large enough scale, such bots have had significant impact on the real world – from spreading fake news during elections, influencing stock prices, swaying opinion about a company or a product, hacking and cybercrimes, data stealing and also promoting and distorting the popularity of individuals and groups. Thus, with our project we aim to identify and distinguish bots from genuine humans in order to curb the menace caused by them. To achieve this, we have proposed a layered machine learning approach. Starting with a labelled dataset, we perform feature extraction based on established tests and correlation analysis. Then, text attributes are processed using feature engineering followed by initial classification that produces a vector of predictions for each text attribute. We further provide a comparative analysis of the performance of various well-known classification algorithms based on their prediction accuracy on the testing dataset. This evaluation also includes a comparison of two popular feature engineering techniques for text attributes i.e. Bag-of-Words and n-gram model.

1.1. Dataset

Our project has been implemented on a Twitter dataset which contains information about more than 5000 different Twitter users and nearly 200,000 tweets. The user information is across attributes including their *handle, name, location, followers count, profile description or bio, favourites count, tweets count, sample tweets* etc. which we compiled together to build our model. Out of these 20 attributes, 16 attributes are either numerical or categorical while the remaining 4 i.e. *description, status, name* and *screen_name,* have text values. Also, the dataset includes labels for each of its instances, classifying a user as a bot(1) or a genuine user(0) which enabled us to take a supervised learning approach and train classifier algorithms over it.

The approach proposed in this paper generates predictions based entirely on a user's public data and information which can be easily extracted from Twitter itself in real-time.

2. Methodology

Before performing the actual learning on our data, we analyse our dataset in a comprehensive manner in order to better identify strongly correlated attributes, highlight weak correlations and determine which features are most significant in the prediction of the target variable i.e. *bot* status. Due to the variance in attribute types we proceed in steps towards our aim of generating a smaller set of strong features to train our learning algorithm on.

First, we separate the 4 text valued attributes and perform feature engineering on each of them in a subsequent step. Of the remaining non-text attributes, by elementary analysis tools and intuition, we are able to eliminate some like *location, created_at* etc. as these contain either majority NaN, have a single repeated value, are completely random or strongly correlated with another attribute in the dataset. Thus, on the remaining numerical/categorical attributes and 4 text attributes, we perform feature engineering. For the non-text attributes, we obtain the following correlation matrix, as shown in Fig. 1 that provides an approximate idea about the relation between the attributes and the target variable i.e. *bot.*

However, feature selection based purely on correlation is not always reliable. Thus, we apply the chi^2 test to determine the 5 best or strongest features and the resulting dataset with reduced dimensionality includes the attributes *id, followers_count, friends_count, listed_count* and *statuses_count.*

Having previously separated the 4 text attributes, we proceed with feature engineering for these by observing the correlation between them and the target variable one by one. To achieve this, we employ two feature extraction methods i.e. Bag-of-Words model and the n-gram model and then compare results for the two. Once we derive the 'features' or 'vectors', which are simply the frequency of words appearing in the text after the appropriate transformations, we train a classifier on each of these 4 vectorized attributes and use it to make predictions for the training samples which are then recorded in a column. The resulting 4 prediction columns, one for each text attribute, are then added to the selected features.

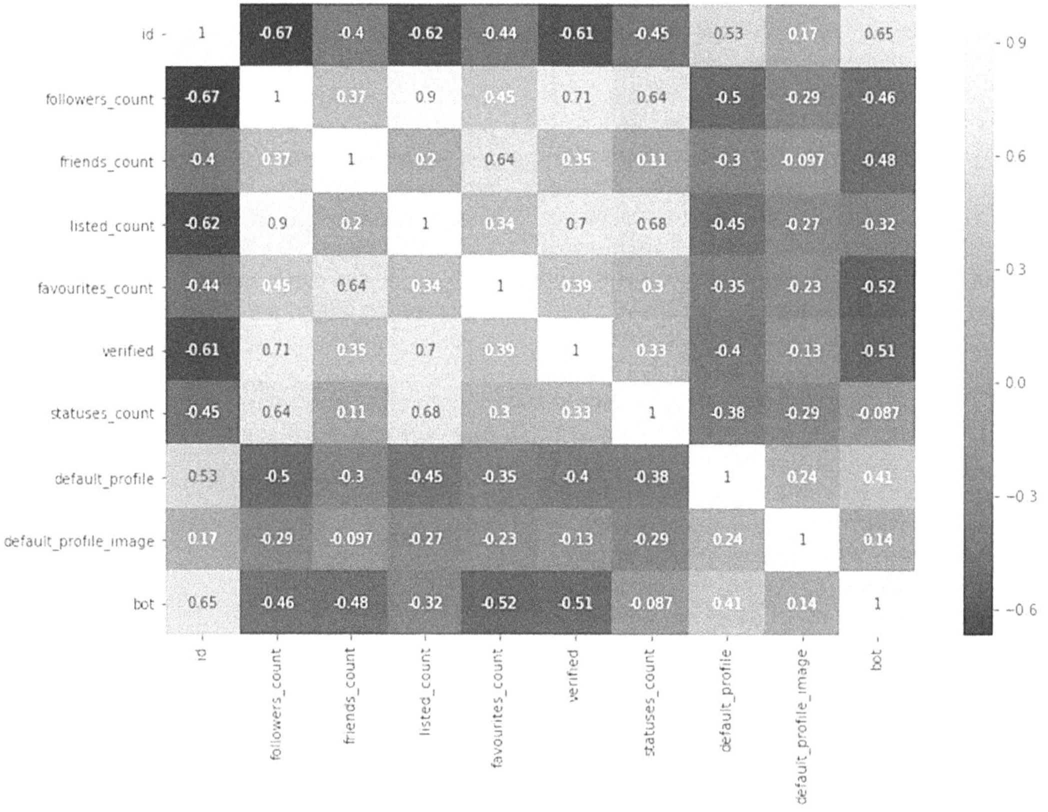

Fig. 1. Correlation Matrix for non-text features.

In the final step, we perform the final classification using the extracted feature set and the *bot* labels by training different classification models and then comparing their accuracy scores. This step is performed for two feature sets i.e. one obtained from Bag-of-Words extraction and the other from n-gram extraction technique.

As stated earlier, we follow a supervised learning approach to learn how a bot and human differ in the behaviour on social networks. First, we load the data into a *pandas* dataframe to make it usable in the Python environment. By analysis we find that there are some missing values throughout the dataset so we proceed by filling these values in order to prevent errors. This leads us to the feature selection and extraction step where we separate the text attributes beforehand. On the remaining dataset consisting only of numerical and categorical attributes, we select a few best performing attributes based on the chi^2 test. Now, we turn our focus to extracting useful features from the text attributes. The text attributes to be analysed are *screen_name, name, description* and *status.* The *status* attribute contains nearly 200k tweets grouped by the user id of the user who sent them. Now, we employ two different feature engineering techniques i.e. Bag-of-Words and n-gram. These methods work by analysing how frequently each word occurs and how this relates to the target attribute. Once this 'vectorization' is achieved, we perform term frequency-inverse document frequency transformation in order to normalize the 'vectors' and pre-empt bias towards higher frequency words. The result after this is a sparse matrix of transformed word frequencies which we then convert to pandas dataframes for all the four attributes and then concatenate them together to perform classification for all four together. Also, the feature sets resulting from the Bag-of-Words model and the one resulting from the n-gram model are maintained separately in order to allow comparisons at a later stage.

The flowchart of the methodology followed in the implementation of this research paper is elaborated in Fig. 2.

Once the two step feature extraction process is finished and the final training dataset is generated, we perform the actual learning using several different established machine learning algorithms in order to compare and analyze their performance and determine the best suited model for our problem. The machine learning algorithms thus used and analyzed for performing the classification in this paper are:

- K Nearest Neighbours Classifier;
- Decision Tree Classifier;
- Random Forest Classifier;
- Ada Boost Classifier;
- Gradient Boosting Classifier;
- Gaussian NB Classifier;
- Multinomial Naïve Bayes Classifier;
- Multilayer Perceptron.

3. Findings

The accuracy scores for different classifiers on both the textual feature extraction models are detailed in Table 1 and Table 2 below.

As seen, the multilayer perceptron and multinomial bayes classifiers show the best results when the bag-of-words model is used to extract features from the textual data.

As is evident from the table of accuracy scores above, the n-gram model of feature extraction offers significantly better accuracy on average over different classifiers with 89.7 % average accuracy than the Bag-of-Words model with average accuracy score of 87.3 %.

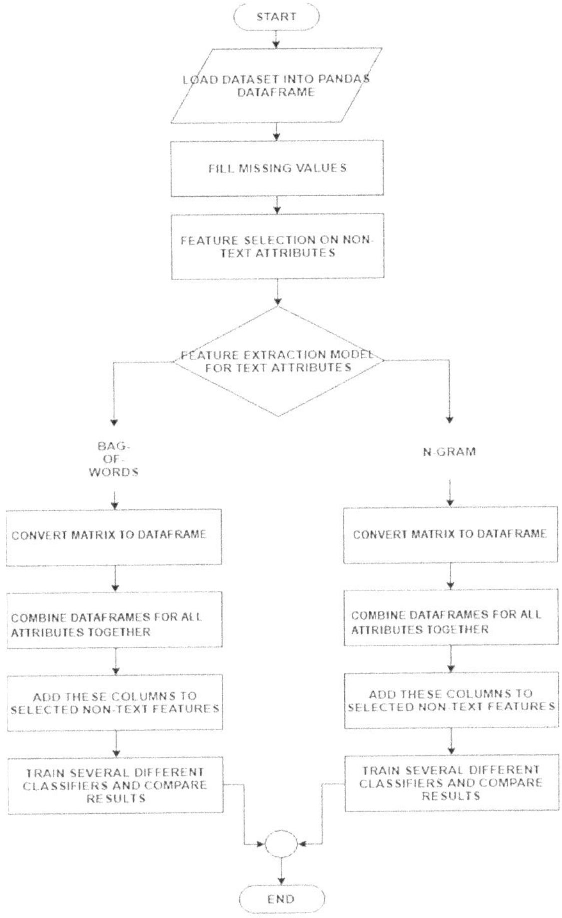

Fig. 2. Flowchart representing the methodology of the proposed method.

Table 1. Accuracy Scores for bag-of-words model.

K Neighbors Classifier	57.1019%
Decision Tree Classifier	92.9699%
Random Forest Classifier	86.8006%
Ada Boost Classifier	91.1047%
Gradient Boosting Classifier	91.6069%
Gaussian Naïve Bayes	89.3113%
Multinomial Naïve Bayes	94.7633%
Multilayer Perceptron	94.7633%
	87.3027%

Table 2. Accuracy scores for n-gram model (n = 2).

K Neighbors Classifier	79.5552%
Decision Tree Classifier	92.8264%
Random Forest Classifier	92.6112%
Ada Boost Classifier	90.6026%
Gradient Boosting Classifier	90.0287%
Gaussian Naïve Bayes	87.7331%
Multinomial Naïve Bayes	89.3831%
Multilayer Perceptron	95.4089%
	89.7685%

Table 3 below details an analysis of the performance of each classifier.

Table 3. Accuracy scores (%) of each classifier model.

S.No	Classifier	Bag of Words Accuracy	[illegible]	Average Accuracy
1.	K Neighbors	57.10%	79.55%	**68.32%**
2.	Decision Tree	92.96%	92.82%	**92.89%**
3.	Random Forest	86.80%	92.61%	**89.70%**
4.	Ada Boost	91.10%	90.60%	**90.85%**
5.	Gradient Boosting	91.60%	90.02%	**90.81%**
6.	Gaussian Naïve Bayes	89.31%	87.73%	**88.52%**
7.	Multinomial Naïve Bayes	94.76%	89.38%	**92.07%**
8.	Multilayer Perceptron	94.76%	95.40%	**95.08%**
	Overall Average			***88.53%***

4. Conclusions

This research paper lays emphasis on the identification, detection and eradication of bots that populate social networks today. We focus on Twitter to determine which user is a bot and which is a human based on their activity and profile information. By taking a machine learning approach for such distinction, we are not only able to detect bots with sufficient accuracy but this also enables us to define the behaviour and activity patterns exhibited by bots. Apart from the mechanism to detect bots, we also offer a comparative analysis of the performances of various established machine learning techniques and algorithms in our project. We evaluate the accuracy of several classification algorithms when applied after two different feature engineering techniques. The results show that neural networks based Multilayer Perceptron algorithm gives the most accurate predictions. We find that our proposed technique results in an average accuracy of 88.5 % across several established tools.

References

[1]. R. J. Oentaryo, A. Prasetyo, K. Murdopo, E.-P. Philips Lim, On profiling bots in social media, in *Proceedings of the International Conference on Social Informatics*, 2016.

[2]. M. Fazil, M. Abulaish, A Hybrid approach for detecting automated spammers in twitter, *IEEE Transactions on Information Forensics and Security*, Vol. 13, Issue 11, 2018, pp. 2707-2719.

[3]. R. Aswani, A. Kar, I. Vigneswara, Detection of spammers in twitter marketing: A hybrid approach using social media analytics and bio inspired computing, *Information Systems Frontiers*, Vol. 20, 2017, pp. 1-16.

[4]. P. G. Efthimion, S. Payne, N. Proferes, Supervised machine learning bot detection techniques to identify social twitter bots, *SMU Data Science Review*, Vol. 1, Issue 2, 2018, 5.

[5]. A. H. Wang, Machine learning for the detection of spam in twitter networks, in *Proceedings of the International Conference on E-Business and Telecommunications (ICETE'10)*, 2010, pp. 319-333.

[6]. A. Mostrous, M. Bridge, K. Gibbons, Russia used Twitter bots and trolls 'to disrupt' Brexit Vote, https://www.thetimes.co.uk/edition/news/russia-used-web-posts-to-disrupt-brexitvote-h9nv5zg6c

[7]. A. Bessi, E. Ferrara, Social Bots Distort the 2016 U.S. Presidential Election Online Discussion by Alessandro Bessi and Emilio Ferrara, http://firstmonday.org/ojs/index.php/fm/article/view/7090

[8]. S. Kramer, Identifying Viral Bots and Cyborgs in Social Media, https://www.oreilly.com/ideas/identifying-viral-bots-and-cyborgs-in-social-media

[9]. S. S. Sengar, S. Mukhopadhyay, Moving object detection using statistical background subtraction in wavelet compressed domain, *Multimedia Tools and Applications*, 2019, Vol. 79, pp. 5919–5940.

[10]. S. Cresci, R. Di Pietro, M. Petrocchi, A. Spognardi, M. Tesconi, The paradigm-shift of social spambots: Evidence, theories, and tools for the arms race, in *Proceedings of the 26th Int. Conference World Wide Web Companion (WWW)*, Geneva, Switzerland, 2017, pp. 963-972

[11]. P. Suárez-Serrato, M. E. Roberts, C. Davis, F. Menczer, On the influence of social bots in online protests, in *Proceedings of the Int. Conference Social Informat. (SocInfo'16)*, Cham, Switzerland, 2016, pp. 269-278.

[12]. S. S. Sengar, S. Mukhopadhyay, Motion segmentation-based surveillance video compression using adaptive particle swarm optimization, *Neural Computing and Applications*, 2019, pp. 1-15.

[13]. S. S. Sengar, S. Mukhopadhyay, Motion detection using block based bi-directional optical flow method, *Journal of Visual Communication and Image Representation*, Vol. 49, 2017, pp. 89-103.

(053)

Gender Differences in EEG Features While Driving

I. Stančin [1], K. Friganović [1], M. Zelenika Zeba [2], A. Jović [1] and M. Cifrek [1]

[1] University of Zagreb, Faculty of Electrical Engineering and Computing, Unska 3, Zagreb, Croatia

[2] Polyclinic SUVAG, Ul. Kneza Ljudevita Posavskog 10, Zagreb, Croatia

Tel.: + 38516129-554

E-mail: igor.stancin@fer.hr

Summary: Gender differences in traffic are generally analyzed through the number of accidents reported to the police. Our research aims to observe gender differences in electroencephalographical signals (EEG) while participants are driving. Time-frequency domain features and recurrence quantification analysis (RQA) features are calculated in order to analyze the differences. To compare male and female drivers, we used Mann–Whitney U test and compared correlations between features and brain regions. Female drivers showed significantly higher beta relative power in the occipital right region and significantly higher alpha relative power in the frontal regions, while male drivers showed significantly higher theta relative power in all regions except in the front right region. Most RQA features show a significant difference between male and female drivers. Also, male drivers showed significantly higher correlations between the RQA features, especially between different brain regions. These results could reflect the differences in the information processing strategies of male and female drivers, e.g. they tend to focus on different information when performing the task. That could account for reported gender differences in the number of traffic accidents and traffic behavior.

Keywords: Gender difference, EEG features, Driving, Recurrence quantification analysis.

1. Introduction

Gender differences in traffic are generally analyzed through the number of accidents reported to the police [1]. In Ireland, in 2001, it was ten times more likely for a male driver to be killed in an accident than for a female driver [2]. Although the number of female drivers is still increasing, this difference in the number of accidents is still large [3]. The argument used against gender difference in driving performance is that male drivers drive more often and more kilometers [4], while other research concludes that even with taking that into account, there are still more accidents involving male drivers [5].

Behavioral and neurophysiological differences between genders should also be examined. International Transportation Forum reports that, in 2018, male drivers still run higher risks while driving [6]. Another indirect reason for this kind of gender difference is that spatial orientation tasks are harder for women [7], which makes them more careful in traffic. Additionally, other researchers concluded that female drivers are involved in accidents due to errors of perceptual nature and judgment error [8].

Gender differences based on the traffic statistics [2, 3, 5, 6] and from experiments while participants performing simple tasks [7], [9-12] are obvious. With our research, we aim to observe gender differences in electroencephalographical signals (EEG) while participants perform a complex task – drive a car, in order to provide a deeper understanding of differences between genders while driving, and in general.

2. Methodology

2.1. Experiment Design

In our study, we used a research-grade EEG recorder with 32 channels for recording signals from 14 healthy participants (seven males and seven females) during a driving simulation. Although we used 32-channel EEG, we wanted to describe dependencies and differences between certain brain regions – front left (FL), front right (FR), occipital left (OL), and occipital right (OR) regions. We calculated the mean value for each feature calculated from five electrodes in that region (shown in Table 1). In addition to channels from these four regions, we also used Oz, Pz and Cz channels in our analysis.

Table 1. Electrodes in brain region.

Region	Electrodes
Front left (FL)	F7, F3, FC5, FC1, T7
Front right (FR)	F8, F4, FC6, FC2, T8
Occipital left (OL)	O1, P7, P3, CP5, CP1
Occipital right (OR)	O2, P4, P8, CP6, CP2

Simulation scenario was shown on the screen. Steering the car was done using a professional steering wheel joystick. All participants were instructed to drive following traffic regulations. Male participants were 27.14 years old on average with a standard deviation of 2.94 years, while female participants were 26.0 years old on average with a standard deviation of 3.66 years. The driving scenario was the same for all participants and consisted of driving on both state and highway roads, and in an urban city environment, for around 40 minutes. The recording sessions were held in the afternoon.

EEG features were calculated based on 10 seconds epochs with five seconds of overlap between epochs. To represent differences in EEG features between male and female drivers, we averaged the values of each feature in each epoch for all male and female drivers, respectively, thus constructing time-series of each feature for both genders.

For each feature, we calculated the Mann-Whitney U test between the time-series of both genders, with the usage of $\alpha_0 = 0.001$. Since we repeated our test 105 times, we also used Bonferroni correction to reduce the chances for type I error, which gave us $\alpha = 9.26*10^{-6}$. Also, the correlation for the time-series of each feature between the two genders was calculated and compared.

2.2. Filtering and EEG features

The first step of pre-processing was to filter raw EEG signals in order to remove unwanted artefacts from the signal. For filtering, we used a bandpass filter from 0.5 Hz to 40 Hz. In this way, we filtered out line noise (50 Hz). Independent component analysis (ICA) was also used for removing artefacts like eye movements.

We calculated basic time-frequency domain features: relative power of alpha (8-12 Hz), beta (12-30 Hz), theta (4-8 Hz), delta (0.5-4 Hz) and gamma (30-50 Hz) frequencies. They were calculated with the usage of the Thomson multitaper method [13] for obtaining power spectral density. We also used recurrence quantification analysis (RQA) features: determinism (Det), laminarity (Lam), recurrence rate (RR), trapped time (TT), determinism divided by recurrence rate (Det/RR), longest diagonal (Lmax), longest vertical line (Vmax), average diagonal line length (Adll), divergence (Div) and entropy (Ent). RQA features were calculated from the recurrence plot (RP) of the signal. RP is a 2D representation of the phase space trajectory of the signal [14]. It is a matrix of dimensions N x N, where N is the length of the signal. Position (i, j) in the matrix is marked with one if i-th and j-th point in the signal are close to each other.

The total number of features extracted was 15 per channel/region. We used three channels and four regions, which gave us a total of 105 features.

3. Results

Although we used the conservative $\alpha_0 = 0.001$ with Bonferroni correction, we still got 93 features with a p value smaller than α. Table 2 shows p values for all features. Among 12 features that have p value larger than α, eight are from the occipital regions (six from the Oz channel); 10 of them are from Oz, Pz or Cz channels; and only one is from the frontal regions of the brain. Among 50 features with the smallest p values, there are mostly RQA features, with a few exceptions – five relative beta powers, one relative alpha power, and one relative theta power. Among the first nine features with equal (and smallest) p value, four of them are Lam and three of them are RR. Fig. 1 shows two RQA features with the smallest p values and two time-frequency domain features with the smallest p values. We can see that relative beta power is higher for female drivers than for male drivers on the Pz channel and in the OR region, which is also true for all other channels and regions. Female drivers also have significantly larger values for relative alpha power in the FR region, FL region and on the Cz channel, while all other channels and regions have similar values. Male drivers have significantly larger values for relative theta power in all regions, except on the Oz channel and in the FR region. Male drivers have higher values for the RR on all channels and in all regions, except for Cz, where female drivers have higher values (RR on the Pz channel shown in Fig. 1).

Fig. 2 shows all correlations for male and female drivers. Female drivers have a lot more white color present in Fig. 2, which represents weak correlations (correlation between -0.4 and 0.4). Male drivers, in general, show much stronger correlations between different features than female drivers, especially between different regions of the brain. Even in cases where female drivers show some correlations between different channels and regions of the brain, male drivers, in general, have stronger correlations on these same channels and in the same regions. Fig. 3 shows an example of a strong correlation between Det in the FR region and Lam in the FL region for male drivers, together with a weak correlation of the same features for female drivers.

4. Discussion

Brain electrical activity, as assessed by relative power and RQA features, was significantly different between male and female drivers. Female drivers showed significantly higher beta relative power in the OR region and significantly higher alpha relative power in the frontal regions, while male drivers showed significantly higher theta relative power in all regions, except in the FR region. In addition, male drivers showed significantly higher correlations between the RQA features.

The higher alpha and beta relative power reported for women in other studies [10, 15] was confirmed by the present results. In addition, observed relative alpha power in our sample was the largest for the FR and FL regions, and Cz channel. Obtained results are in line with an fMRI study which found that females showed activation in frontal and parietal regions as they performed the spatial-cognition performance task, while men showed distinct activation of the left hippocampus [16]. Furthermore, the absence of a reduction in relative alpha power has been related to information processing differences between men and women in spatial tasks [10].

Table 2. *p* values for all features.

Feature	*p* value	Feature	*p* value	Feature	*p* value	Feature	*p* value
Pz_RR	1.15E-89	Pz_Det/RR	3.42E-89	Oz_Lam	3.04E-72	Cz_Adll	8.09E-25
Pz_Beta	1.15E-89	OR_Det	5.46E-89	OR_Theta	6.71E-72	Pz_Delta	1.67E-23
FL_Lam	1.15E-89	FL_Det/RR	1.42E-88	Cz_Theta	2.52E-70	Oz_Det	2.21E-23
Pz_Lam	1.15E-89	OL_Adll	1.90E-88	Cz_Alpha	1.22E-69	Oz_Alpha	5.45E-23
OL_Lmax	1.15E-89	Pz_Div	3.64E-88	FR_Beta	8.22E-69	Oz_Vmax	2.41E-21
OL_RR	1.15E-89	OR_Div	4.44E-88	Pz_Ent	1.33E-68	FL_Gamma	2.30E-17
OL_Lam	1.15E-89	OL_Ent	5.70E-88	Cz_Div	8.81E-68	FR_Div	8.22E-17
OR_RR	1.15E-89	FR_Vmax	5.87E-88	Cz_Delta	2.57E-65	FR_Gamma	4.93E-16
OR_Lam	1.15E-89	OL_Det/RR	8.22E-88	FR_Det	3.62E-64	FL_Delta	7.96E-15
FL_Vmax	1.16E-89	OR_Det/RR	8.49E-88	Pz_TT	9.11E-61	Oz_Theta	3.51E-08
OL_Div	1.16E-89	OL_TT	2.76E-87	FR_Adll	6.37E-59	Oz_Det/RR	6.42E-08
OR_Beta	1.17E-89	OR_Adll	4.95E-87	OR_Delta	1.56E-58	Oz_Delta	4.91E-06
FL_RR	1.18E-89	FL_Adll	1.37E-86	OL_Delta	1.15E-51	OL_Gamma	2.12E-04
FL_TT	1.19E-89	FL_Div	3.14E-86	FR_TT	2.93E-51	Oz_Div	1.03E-03
FL_Lmax	1.23E-89	Cz_Det/RR	6.43E-86	Cz_Lam	1.45E-50	OR_Gamma	2.21E-03
OR_Lmax	1.28E-89	OR_TT	1.42E-85	Oz_Lmax	4.43E-50	Oz_Beta	2.48E-03
OL_Det	1.29E-89	FL_Ent	6.69E-85	Cz_Lmax	7.31E-45	Oz_Ent	3.33E-03
OL_Beta	1.30E-89	OR_Ent	1.02E-84	FR_Delta	3.57E-42	Cz_Vmax	4.79E-03
Cz_Beta	1.33E-89	FL_Beta	1.49E-84	FL_Theta	5.45E-41	Oz_Gamma	4.92E-03
OL_Vmax	1.33E-89	Cz_RR	1.31E-82	Cz_Gamma	3.93E-38	Oz_Adll	1.00E-02
OR_Vmax	1.52E-89	Oz_RR	1.57E-82	FR_Det/RR	5.04E-34	Cz_TT	1.23E-02
FR_Lam	1.65E-89	FL_Alpha	8.39E-81	OR_Alpha	7.68E-34	Pz_Alpha	2.65E-01
FL_Det	1.74E-89	Pz_Theta	6.07E-80	OL_Alpha	2.72E-33	FR_Theta	5.86E-01
Pz_Det	2.02E-89	Pz_Vmax	1.27E-77	Oz_TT	8.58E-33	Cz_Ent	6.76E-01
FR_RR	2.27E-89	FR_Alpha	3.41E-76	Pz_Gamma	3.99E-28		
FR_Lmax	2.37E-89	OL_Theta	4.12E-74	FR_Ent	4.71E-28		
Pz_Lmax	3.15E-89	Pz_Adll	6.64E-73	Cz_Det	5.81E-27		

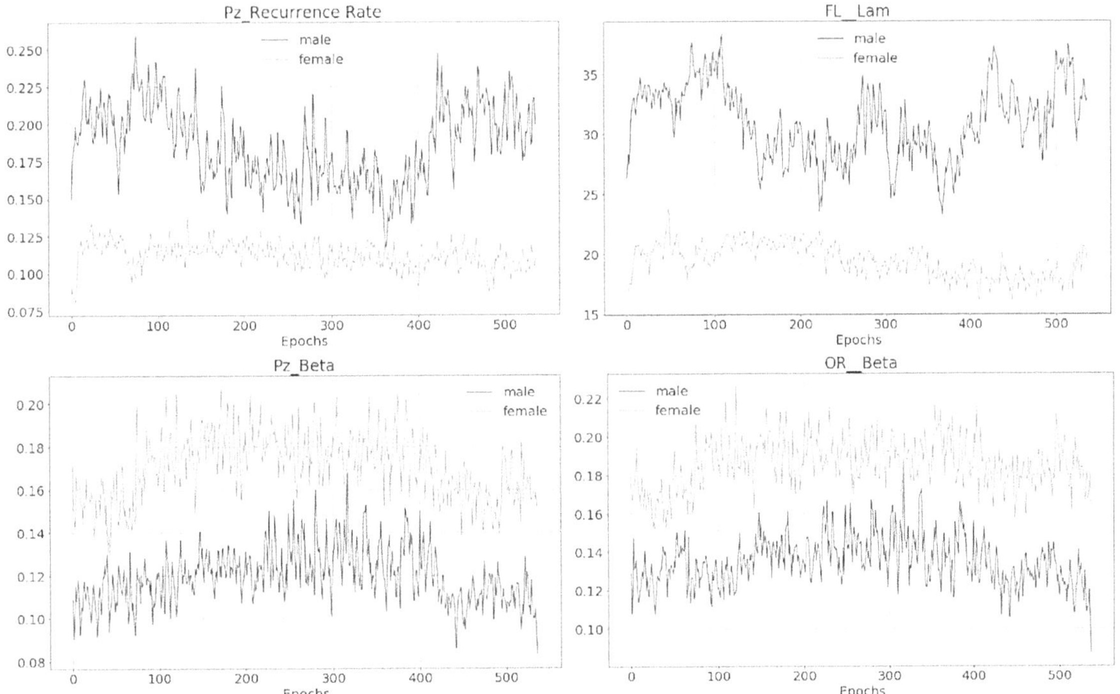

Fig. 1. Difference between male and female drivers: recurrence rate from Pz channel, laminarity (Lam) from FL region, relative alpha power from FR region and relative beta power from the Pz channel. Y-axis shows values of observed features.

Our results showed a higher contribution of theta relative power only in men. Increased relative theta power has been related to more active task-related processing [17-21]. Observed theta power was the largest for the FL region and Cz channel, which is in line with the previous results [11].

Neuroanatomical studies have shown that the hippocampus, the parietal lobes, and the right prefrontal areas are activated by visuospatial working memory tasks and are implicated in complex navigation [22, 23]. Also, all centric or world-centered representation of the environment has been linked to the functioning of the hippocampus, while the posterior parietal cortex is involved in egocentric or body-centered spatial cognition [24]. Therefore, observed differences between men and women in our sample could be related to different strategies used to perform the task, where men tend to focus more on the global-spatial information from the environment when performing the task, while women tend to use analytic information processing when performing the task [9].

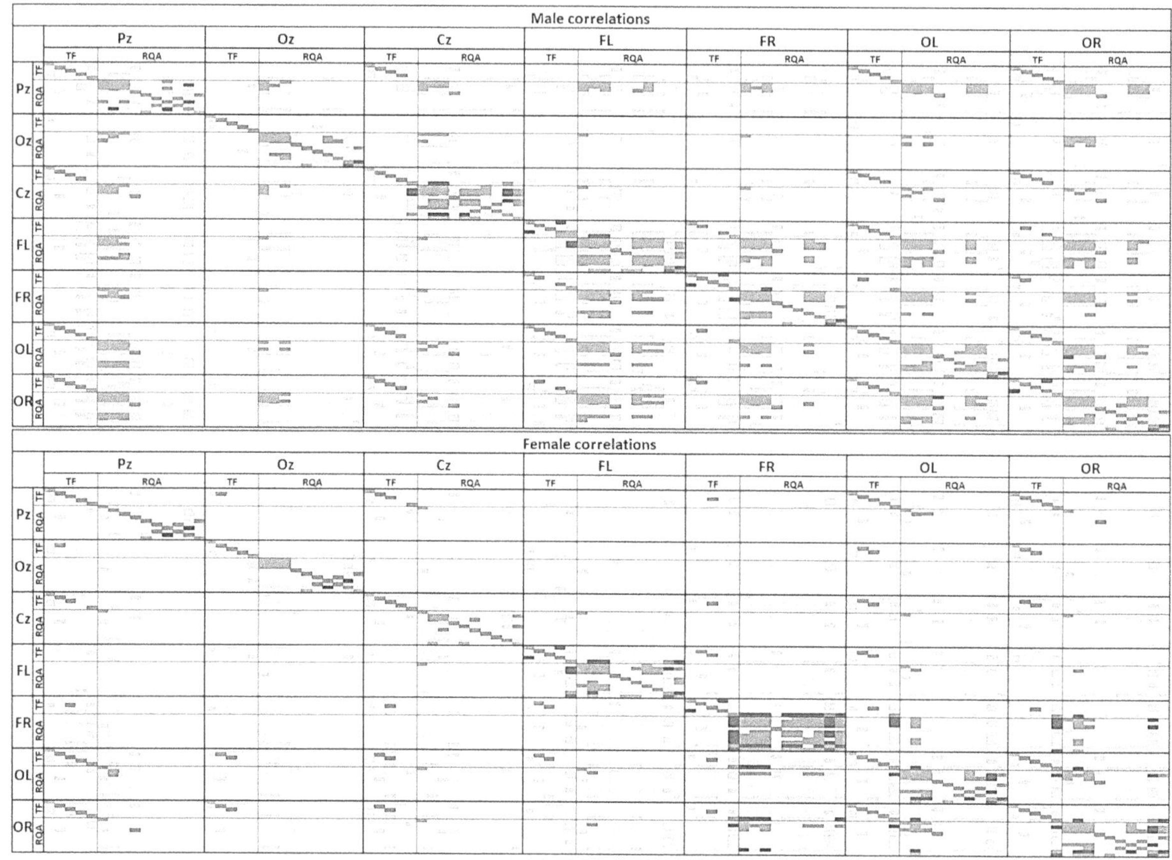

Fig. 2. Correlations for males and females with color-coded values. White – correlation between -0.4 and 0.4, light green – correlation between 0.4 and 0.7, dark green – correlation between 0.7 and 1, light red – correlation between -0.4 and -0.7 and dark red – correlation between -0.7 and -1. TF represents time-frequency domain features and RQA represents features from recurrence quantification analysis.

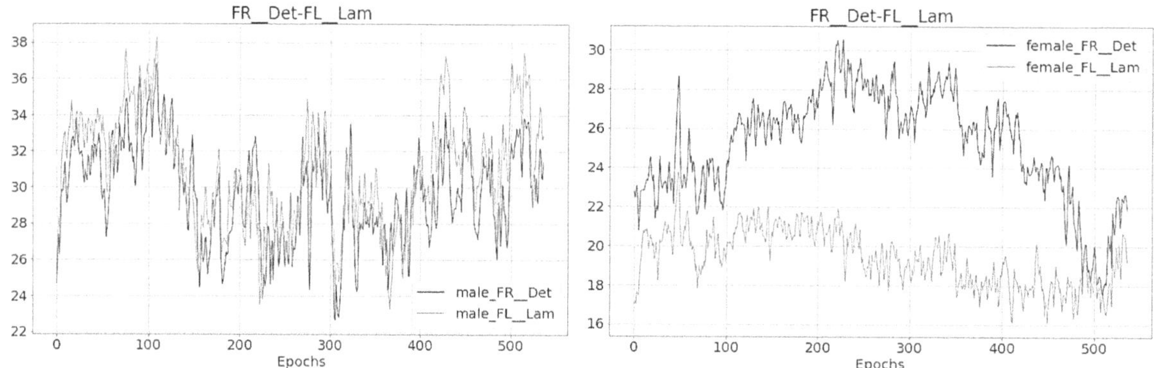

Fig. 3. On the left: highly correlated determinism (Det) from the FR region and laminarity (Lam) from the FL region for male drivers; on the right: weakly correlated determinism from the FR region and laminarity from the FL region for female drivers. Y-axis shows values of observed features.

Analysis of correlations between features points to the similar behavior of two signals. Therefore, higher correlations between different channels and regions could indicate shared neuronal processes. In our results, male drivers showed significantly higher correlations between the RQA features with respect to female drivers. This could indicate stronger synchronization of neuronal activity for male drivers that are in line with the active task-related processing which has been reflected by increased relative theta power in men.

RQA features are used to analyze non-linear relation between the recurrences of states $x(i)$ in phase space [25]. They do not need assumptions about stationarity or length of signal and are not too sensitive to noise in the signal. These are all favorable characteristics for describing EEG signals, which are non-stationary and are often susceptible to noise [14]. The flaw of using RQA features is that they are harder to interpret.

RR represents the density of recurrence points on the RP. Recurrence plot of white noise consists of many single dots, while RP of deterministic signal consists of many long diagonals. Det is the ratio of points forming diagonal lines with all points and can be interpreted as predictability of signal. Like Det, Lam is the ratio of points forming vertical lines and represents the number of laminar states in the dynamical system. Long vertical lines mean that the dynamical system has slow changes. TT is the mean length of vertical lines and indicates that changes of states are slow. Ent measures the complexity of the signal.

Unfortunately, there are not many reliable studies including RQA features, especially related to gender differences. Therefore, it is hard to compare these features and results based on them directly with the existing studies about gender differences. Despite that, studies like ours are necessary for further expansion and acceptance of different kinds of features that show significant differences between the inspected groups.

5. Conclusion

The present results show that male and female drivers differ significantly in many ways in EEG features. Observed differences of the time-frequency domain features and RQA features, together with the strength of correlations between different features and brain regions, for male and female drivers, could reflect the differences in their information processing strategies during driving. Furthermore, these results could suggest that men and women tend to focus on different information when driving. Therefore, observed results could account for reported gender differences in the number of traffic accidents and traffic behavior.

This conclusion, with further research, may lead to improvements in a better understanding of gender differences in brain functions during different cognitive tasks and to a better understanding of brain functions in general. There is a large number of applications that could benefit from a better understanding of gender differences in brain functions (better understanding of inter-gender behavior in traffic; improved quality of disease detection; understanding of learning, memory, and emotions; and similar).

In our further work, we plan to record more participants and implement more features, the ones that have already been used in studies related to gender differences in EEG signals, as well as the ones that have not yet been used in this field. With a larger number of features that can be related to existing studies, we hope that we will be able to provide better interpretations and explanations of differences between male and female drivers. At the same time, we would strive to lay the foundations for future studies that would analyze features which have not been inspected in the field of gender differences.

References

[1]. B. A. Jonah, Accident risk and risk-taking behaviour among young drivers, *Accid. Anal. Prev.*, Vol. 18, Issue 4, August 1986, pp. 255-271.

[2]. Young Driver Accidents, *National Roads Authority*, 2000.

[3]. S. Laapotti, E. Keskinen, S. Rajalin, Comparison of young male and female drivers' attitude and self-reported traffic behaviour in Finland in 1978 and 2001, *J. Safety Res.*, Vol. 34, Issue 5, January 2003, pp. 579-587.

[4]. P. Cordellieri, F. Baralla, F. Ferlazzo, R. Sgalla, L. Piccardi, and A. M. Giannini, Gender effects in young road users on road safety attitudes, behaviors and risk perception, *Front. Psychol.*, Vol. 7, September 2016, 1412.

[5]. S. J. Wylie, Young female drivers in New Zealand, *Accid. Anal. Prev.*, Vol. 27, Issue 6, December 1995, pp. 797-805.

[6]. Road safety: Annual Report 2018, *International Transportation Forum*, 2018.

[7]. D. Kimura, Sex and Cognition, *The MIT Press*, 1999.

[8]. V. J. Storie, Male and female car drivers: Differences observed in accidents, *Transp. Res. Int. Doc.*, Vol. 761, 1977.

[9]. J. Ramos-Loyo, L. M. Sanchez-Loyo, Gender differences in EEG coherent activity before and after training navigation skills in virtual environments, *Hum. Physiol.*, Vol. 37, Issue 6, November 2011, pp. 700-707.

[10]. M. Corsi-Cabrera, J. Ramos, M. A. Guevara, C. Arce, S. Gutierrez, Gender differencesm in the eeg during cognitive activity, *Int. J. Neurosci.*, Vol. 72, Issues 3-4, January 1993, pp. 257-264.

[11]. S. E. Kober, J. L. Reichert, C. Neuper, G. Wood, Interactive effects of age and gender on EEG power and coherence during a short-term memory task in middle-aged adults, *Neurobiol. Aging*, Vol. 40, April 2016, pp. 127-137.

[12]. B. Rescher, P. Rappelsberger, Gender dependent EEG-changes during a mental rotation task, *Int. J. Psychophysiol.*, Vol. 33, Issue 3, September 1999, pp. 209-222.

[13]. D. J. Thomson, Spectrum estimation and harmonic analysis, *Proceedings of IEEE*, Vol. 70, Issue 9, 1982, pp. 1055-1096.

[14]. M. Niknazar, S. R. Mousavi, B. Vosoughi Vahdat, M. Sayyah, A new framework based on recurrence quantification analysis for epileptic seizure detection, *IEEE J. Biomed. Heal. Informatics*, Vol. 17, Issue 3, May 2013, pp. 572-578.

[15]. S. Georgiev, Z. Minchev, C. G. Christova, D. Philipova, Gender event-related brain oscillatory differences in normal elderly population EEG, *Int. J. Bioautomotion*, Vol. 15, Issue 1, 2011, pp. 33-48.

[16]. G. Grön, A. P. Wunderlich, M. Spitzer, R. Tomczak, M. W. Riepe, Brain activation during human navigation: gender-different neural networks as substrate of performance, *Nat. Neurosci.*, Vol. 3, Issue 4, April 2000, pp. 404-408.

[17]. C. Kamarajan, *et al.*, Theta oscillations during the processing of monetary loss and gain: A perspective on gender and impulsivity, *Brain Res.*, Vol. 1235, October 2008, pp. 45-62.

[18]. W. Klimesch, EEG alpha and theta oscillations reflect cognitive and memory performance: a review and analysis, *Brain Res. Rev.*, Vol. 29, Issues 2-3, April 1999, pp. 169-195.

[19]. S. E. Kober, C. Neuper, Sex differences in human EEG theta oscillations during spatial navigation in virtual reality, *Int. J. Psychophysiol.*, Vol. 79, Issue 3, March 2011, pp. 347-355.

[20]. M. Thordstein, N. Löfgren, A. Flisberg, K. Lindecrantz, I. Kjellmer, Sex differences in electrocortical activity in human neonates, *Neuroreport*, Vol. 17, Issue 11, July 2006, pp. 1165-1168.

[21]. J. B. Caplan, J. R. Madsen, A. Schulze-Bonhage, R. Aschenbrenner-Scheibe, E. L. Newman, M. J. Kahana, Human theta oscillations related to sensorimotor integration and spatial learning, *J. Neurosci.*, Vol. 23, Issue 11, Junuary 2003, pp. 4726-4736.

[22]. A. M. Owen, A. C. Evans, M. Petrides, Evidence for a two-stage model of spatial working memory processing within the lateral frontal cortex: A positron emission tomography study, *Cereb. Cortex*, Vol. 6, Issue 1, January 1996, pp. 31-38.

[23]. E. Salmon, *et al.*, Regional brain activity during working memory tasks, *Brain*, Vol. 119, Issue 5, 1996, pp. 1617-1625.

[24]. J. O'Keefe, L. Nadel, The Hippocampus as a Cognitive Map, *Oxford University Press,* 1978.

[25]. U. R. Acharya, S. V. Sree, S. Chattopadhyay, W. Yu, P. C. A. Ang, Application of recurrence quantification analysis for the automated identification of epileptic eeg signals, *Int. J. Neural Syst.*, Vol. 21, Issue 3, June 2011, pp. 199-211.

(054)

A Comparative Study of Sequence Identification Algorithms in IoT Context

P.-S. Gréau-Hamard [1,2], **M. Djoko-Kouam** [1] **and Y. Louet** [2]
[1] Informatics and Telecommunications Laboratory, ECAM Rennes Louis de Broglie, Bruz, France
[2] Signal, Communication, and Embedded Electronics (SCEE) team, Institute of Electronic and Telecommunications of Rennes (IETR), CentraleSupélec, Rennes, France
E-mails: {pierre-samuel.greau-hamard, moise.djoko-kouam}@ecam-rennes.com, Yves.Louet@centralesupelec.fr

Summary: In the fast developing world of telecommunications, it may prove useful to be able to analyse any protocol one comes across, even if it is unknown. To that end, one needs to get the state machine and the frame format of the protocol. These can be extracted from network and/or execution traces via Protocol Reverse Engineering (PRE). In this paper, we aim to evaluate and compare the performance of three algorithms used as part of three different PRE systems of the literature: Aho-Corasick (AC), Variance of the Distribution of Variances (VDV), and Latent Dirichlet Allocation (LDA). In order to do so, we suggest a new meaningful metric complementary to precision and recall: the fields detection ratio. We implemented and simulated these algorithms in an Internet of Things (IoT) context, and more precisely on ZigBee Data Link Layer frames. The results obtained clearly show that the LDA algorithm outperforms AC and VDV.

Keywords: Protocol reverse engineering, AC, VDV, LDA, ZigBee, IoT, Data link layer, Performance comparison.

1. Introduction

With the ever growing development of telecommunications, and especially Internet of Things (IoT), a lot of new protocols are constantly appearing. In order to know what they are used for, we need to understand how they work.

In this paper, we place ourselves in the context of a communicating object coming into an unknown environment and wanting to establish a communication with the existing networks. To that end, the object needs to have 'generic', or 'multi-standard' behavior, i. e. to be able to adapt itself to whichever standard is used in the target environment. It is the same goal as the one pursued by Software Defined Radio, except that in our case, we propose to learn the unknown protocol of the environment, and not just identify it from a database.

This is the goal of Protocol Reverse Engineering (PRE), a family of techniques which aims at reconstructing the frame formats and/or the state machine of a target unknown protocol through analyzing execution traces and/or network traces.

There is no precisely defined procedure to perform PRE, but the most encountered one [1] is a five-step process. (i) Firstly, the radio traffic is intercepted and the frames issued by the targeted protocol are isolated. (ii) Next, the meaningful binary sequences (features) of these frames are identified, (iii) and then the frames are grouped by format via the use of these features. (iv) Within each group, sequence alignment is performed, and, finally, (v) the frame formats and/or the state machine of the targeted protocol are reconstructed.

In this paper, we focus solely on the second step, the identification of remarkable sequences. This step aims at reducing the quantity of information needed to label a frame. This is achieved by identifying the remarkable sections of the frames, i. e. in our case by spotting the recurring sequences and their positions. Such sequences are most probably keywords. Our goal is to evaluate and compare the performance of different techniques achieving this, in order to obtain useful data for choosing a technique or a family of techniques to be used in a real-life system. To this end, we selected the Variance of the Distribution of Variances (VDV) [2], Aho-Corasick (AC) [3], and Latent Dirichlet Allocation (LDA) [4] techniques.

The simulation context in which we will simulate the performance of these techniques lies in the analysis of Data Link Layer (DLL) frames of the ZigBee protocol.

Most of the surveys in the PRE domain involve comparing a rather narrow range of tools and their approaches without delving into the exact mechanics or presenting their performance, like in [5]. However, some of them are more exhaustive, and present in detail the techniques used by the tools [6] and the protocols they are able to reverse engineer [7].

Nevertheless, these surveys do not refer to the performance of the different tools in a quantifiable way, and they also do not present the individual performance of the techniques used in each tool. Such an approach is legitimate, as they browse a wide range of PRE tools, but this is where the particularity of our paper stands. We select only three techniques as opposed to the dozens present in the previous surveys, and we evaluate their performance through simulations, which has not been done in the previous papers.

The rest of this paper is organized as follows: Section 2 presents the theory related to the three techniques studied; in Section 3, we simulate and compare them; and finally, we conclude in Section 4.

2. State of the Art of the Three Techniques

In this section, we present the principle and mechanisms of each of the sequence identification techniques, as well as the practical algorithms designed from them to fit our context.

2.1. Variance of the Distribution of Variances

This technique aims at statistically identifying in a population the parts which offer the least variability. The following presentation is based on the approach proposed by A. Trifilò et al [2].

The VDV technique considers a population formed of groups of individuals. The latter are themselves composed of elements which can take different numerical values. The technique unfolds in five steps:

- For each group, calculating the average, then the variance of the value of each element across all the individuals in a given group;
- Across groups, calculating the average, then the variance of these variances;
- Retaining the elements whose variance of the variances is less than a given filtration threshold.

The actual algorithm used in our context derives from the technique above, with some modifications.

The groups of individuals previously considered are now replaced by flows composed of DLL frames to be analysed, and the base unit is switched from element to 'token', an *n*-bit long position slot on the frames which can assume different sequences of *n* consecutive bits.

To be able to detect fields regardless of their position, all the possible tokens obtainable from a frame are created.

The filtration threshold actually used for filtering (FT_{VDV}) is not a fixed value, but a value proportional to the average variance of the variances. The proportionality coefficient is called filtration threshold coefficient (FT^{c}_{VDV}), and the formula linking FT_{VDV} and FT^{c}_{VDV} is:

$$FT_{VDV} = \overline{V_V(i)} \times FT^{c}_{VDV}, \quad (1)$$

with $V_V(i)$ the variance of the variances of token i.

The frames being collected on a radio link, it is not possible to clearly identify flows, so we create them by randomly attributing frames to flows following a discrete uniform law.

To enable the detection of fields of different lengths, the algorithm is executed many times, for different values of *n*, i.e. token lengths, and all the single sequences extracted from these runs are kept for metrics computation.

2.2. Aho-Corasick

This technique was designed by A. Aho and M. Corasick in order to identify a string of characters in a text [3]. However, its use can be extended to identify any pattern composed of a sequence of elements taking values from a discrete finite space. The search is then run on a sequence of these elements whose length is superior or equal to the targeted pattern. The following presentation is based on the approach proposed by Y. Wang et al. [8].

The particularity of AC is that it is based on a state machine to optimize the processing speed.

The technique operates in two major steps:

- Constructing the state machine based on the strings to search in the text;
- Scanning the whole text character by character, and notifying, for each character, the strings ending on that character.

The actual algorithm used in our context derives from the one above, with some modifications.

The text considered in the AC technique is now replaced by the DLL trace to be analysed, and the base unit is switched from character to bit. Moreover, the strings to be identified are now all the possible *n*-bit sequences.

An occurrence counter of the sequences was added, in order to perform filtering. The sequences under a threshold FT_{AC} proportional to the average number of appearances of any sequence considering a uniform distribution are filtered out. FT_{AC} is given by:

$$FT_{AC} = \frac{n-L+1}{2^L} \times FT^{c}_{AC}, \quad (2)$$

with *n* the number of bits of the trace, *L* the length of the searched sequences, and FT^{c}_{AC} the proportionality coefficient called filtration threshold coefficient. This filtering is done to keep only the frequent enough sequences.

The sequences with a similarity level superior to a given threshold are fused. By fusion, we mean that in a group of similar enough sequences, we retain the one best representing all the other ones. We achieve that through unsupervised ascendant hierarchical clustering of the sequences, using the similarity as the distance metric, defined by:

$$\mathrm{Sim}(X,Y) = \frac{l(X,Y) - ed(X,Y)}{l(X,Y)}, \quad (3)$$

with *X* and *Y* representing any two sequences, *l(X,Y)* the average length of *X* and *Y*, and *ed(X,Y)* the minimal edition distance between *X* and *Y*, i. e. the minimal number of operations to apply on one of the sequences to obtain the other one. All the sequences being the same length, the average length of X and Y, *l(X,Y)*, equals those of X and Y.

To enable the detection of fields of different lengths, the algorithm is executed many times, for different values of *n*, i.e. lengths of sequences, and all the single sequences extracted from these runs are kept for metrics computation.

2.3. Latent Dirichlet Allocation

This technique comes from the machine learning domain of Information Retrieval (IR), which aims at modeling a text mathematically, in order to extract its meaning. It was designed with the objective to identify topics from a document corpus, and to associate terms coming from a dictionary with them. However, its use can be extended to regrouping sequences of single elements taking values in a finite discrete space, from a collection of data. The following presentation is based on the approach proposed by Y. Wang et al [9].

The LDA technique is first and foremost a generative model for a corpus based on a Bayesian network; the actual implemented algorithm is deduced from it upon inference.

Let us introduce the necessary notions and parameters needed to understand the generative model and the inference based on it:

- A word w is an element taking value from a dictionary v gathering all the known vocabulary;
- A document m is a set of words w, modeled by a vector;
- A corpus W is a set of documents m, modeled by a vector;
- A term t is the base element of the vocabulary;
- V is the set of terms of the dictionary or its cardinal;
- K is the set of topics desired or its cardinal;
- M is the set of documents in the corpus or its cardinal;
- α and β are the Dirichlet prior parameters of the topics over documents and the words over topics distributions, respectively;
- ξ is the parameter of the Poisson law determining the number of words in each document;
- $\overrightarrow{\theta_m}$ is the vector characterizing the topics distribution for the document m. $\Theta = \{\overrightarrow{\theta_m}\}_{m=1}^{M}$ is the matrix $M \times K$ characterizing the topics distribution over the documents;
- $\overrightarrow{\varphi_k}$ is the vector characterizing the terms of v distribution for the topic k. $\Phi = \{\overrightarrow{\varphi_k}\}_{k=1}^{K}$ is the matrix $K \times V$ characterizing the terms distribution over the topics;
- N_m represents the number of words in document m;
- $w_{m,n}$ represents the nth word of document m. The vector $\overrightarrow{w_m}$ represents the words of document m. The vector of vectors $M \times N_m\ \vec{w}$, represents the words of the corpus;
- $z_{m,n}$ represents the topic associated to the nth word of document m. The vector $\overrightarrow{z_m}$ represents the topics respectively attibuted to each word of document m. The vector of vectors $M \times N_m\ \vec{z}$, represents the topics respectively attributed to each word of the corpus.

In LDA, we consider that a corpus is a set of documents, each of those being composed of a random number of words, where the number is drawn following a Poisson law of parameter ξ. Each of the words takes a value within the dictionary.

In the generative model, to begin, Θ *and* Φ are randomly generated following a Dirichlet law of parameters α *and* β, respectively.

Firstly, for each word to be generated of each document to be generated, the topic associated to it is randomly drawn following a multinomial law parameterized by Θ, knowing the document the word is in. Next, the value of the word is drawn from the dictionary, following a multinomial law parameterized by Φ, knowing the previously drawn topic associated with the word.

The goal of the LDA technique is to infer the words over topics and topics over documents distributions, i. e. the matrices Θ and Φ, from the corpus of documents.

These distributions are intractable, so they will be estimated through Gibbs sampling [10].

The Gibbs sampling technique comes from observing that it is impossible to simultaneously infer all the latent variables of the model (i. e. the topics). So, instead, one at a time, their distributions are inferred conditionally to all the other ones, then a new realization of the inferred distribution is drawn. When repeating this operation over all the variables a large number of times, theory shows that the realizations drawn (i. e. the sample) eventually converge towards what would be sampled from the target distribution. Then, the properties of the distribution can be statistically computed from the sample.

The actual algorithm used in our context derives from the above, with some modifications.

The documents considered in the LDA technique are replaced by the DLL frames to be analysed, so the corpus consequently becomes the DLL trace. The topics are replaced by keywords of the protocol, and the words by n-grams, groups of n consecutive bits. The n-grams having no natural delimiters, like spaces for words, all the possible n-grams obtainable from a frame are created. The terms become the different possible sequences of n bits.

The dictionary is composed of all the possible n-grams with n bits.

The gradient of perplexity is used as the stopping criterion of the Gibbs sampler. The perplexity [11] expresses the ability of a model to generalize to unknown data. The perplexity P of a learning corpus W is calculated as follows:

$$P(W) = e^{-\frac{\sum_{m \in M} \ln p(\overrightarrow{w_m})}{\sum_{m \in M} N_m}}, \quad (4)$$

with M the set of frames from the learning DLL trace, N_m the number of n-grams in the DLL frame m, and

$$p(\overrightarrow{w_m}) = \prod_{t \in V} \left(\sum_{k \in K} \theta_{m,k} \varphi_{k,t}\right)^{N_m^t}, \quad (5)$$

with V the set of the single n-grams, K the set of the keywords, and N_m^t the number of occurrences in document m of the single n-gram t.

We calculate the perplexity gradient ∇P between two consecutive time indexes *n-1* and *n* as follows:

$$\nabla P(n, n-1) = \frac{|P(n) - P(n-1)|}{P(n)} \quad (6)$$

The sampling continues as long as the perplexity gradient is above a threshold defined as the maximal perplexity gradient divided by the number of frames in the DLL trace.

Once the matrices Θ and Φ are calculated, for each keyword, the *n*-grams with the highest appearance probabilities are selected. For that purpose, the *n*-grams are ordered by descending probabilities, then iterated through, calculating the gradient within each pair of consecutive *n*-gram probabilities. Mathematically, if we consider a keyword k, and its associated *n*-gram distribution vector, $\overrightarrow{\varphi_k}$, in descending order, the probability gradient ∇p_k of an *n*-gram in position $n \in [2, V]$ is:

$$\nabla p_k(n) = \frac{|\varphi_k(n) - \varphi_k(n-1)|}{\varphi_k(n)} \quad (7)$$

The first *n*-gram is always selected, and the others are selected if their probability gradient is under the threshold defined as the maximal probability gradient.

To enable the detection of fields of different lengths, the algorithm is executed many times, for different values of *n*, i.e. *n*-gram lengths, and all the single sequences extracted from these runs are kept for metrics computation.

3. Comparative Simulations

In this section, we present the metrics (including new ones proposed in this paper) used to quantify the performance of the algorithms, as well as the parameterization for the simulations. We then discuss the results produced.

3.1. Performance Metrics

In order to define the metrics quantifying the performance of the algorithms, we introduce the notions of sequence, field, and matching condition as follows:

- **Sequence**: a sequence s is characterized by its length l, value v, and the set of its positions $p = \{p_i\}_{i \in \mathbb{N}}$. A sequence is then represented by $s(l, v, p)$. The list of the detected sequences $S = \{s\}$ is given by the identification algorithms.
- **Field**: a field c is characterized by its possible lengths L, characteristic values V (null if absent), and possible positions $P = \{P_i\}_{i \in \mathbb{N}}$. A field is then represented by $c(L, V, P)$. The list of the fields $C = \{c\}$ is obtained from the Zigbee specification. A field can be either detectable ($V \neq \emptyset$) or not detectable ($V = \emptyset$).
- **Matching condition**: the sequence $s(l, v, p)$ and the field $c(L, V, P)$ match if the following property is verified:

$$\begin{cases} l \in L, v \in V, p \cap P \neq \emptyset, if\ V \neq \emptyset \\ l \in L, p \cap P \neq \emptyset, if\ V = \emptyset \end{cases} \quad (8)$$

As metrics, we first use a tradeoff between precision and recall, the F score [12] which is the harmonic mean of the two. This metric quantifies the quality of the sequence detection, i. e. the performance of the algorithm. It is given by:

$$F = \frac{2 \times P \times R}{P + R}, \quad (9)$$

with P the precision, quantifying the part of what was correctly detected from the totality of what was detected, given by:

$$P = \frac{T_P}{T_P + F_P}, \quad (10)$$

with T_P the true positives, which are the sequences correctly detected, and F_P the false positives, which are the sequences incorrectly detected.

R is the recall, quantifying the part of what was correctly detected from what was supposed to be detected, given by:

$$R = \frac{T_P}{T_P + F_n}, \quad (11)$$

with F_n the false negatives, which are the sequences incorrectly not detected.

Each sequence counts as one true positive if its properties match at least one detectable field, it counts as one false positive in all other cases.

The number of false negatives is equal to the difference between the number of remarkable sequences across all fields and the number of true positives.

In addition to the quality of the sequence detection, we want to quantify the quality of the field detection, as it is more reprensentative of the usefulness of the algorithm.

To the best of our knowledge, a metric serving that purpose does not exist, so we introduce our own, the **fields detection ratio**. It quantifies the detected information of a field, and comes in three different forms: q_l for lengths, q_v for values, and q_p for positions.

Let us consider $S' = \{s \in S | eqn(8)\}$ the set of sequences matching at least one field, and $c_i(L_i, V_i, P_i)_{i \in I}$, a generic field, with $L_i = \{L_{ij}\}_{j \in \mathbb{N}}$, $V_i = \{V_{ij}\}_{j \in \mathbb{N}}$, $P_i = \{P_{ij}\}_{j \in \mathbb{N}}$, and I the set of all existing fields, and $s_k(l_k, v_k, p_k)$ a generic sequence.

$$q_{l_i} = \frac{Card(L_i')}{Card(L_i)}, q_{v_i} = \frac{Card(V_i')}{Card(V_i)}, \quad (12)$$
$$q_{p_i} = \frac{Card(P_i')}{Card(P_i)}$$

are, respectively, the ratios between the number of possible lengths, values, and positions of c_i detected and the total number of possible lengths, values, and positions of c_i, with $L_i' = \{L_{ij} | \exists s_k \in S' | l_k = L_{ij}\}$, $V_i' = \{V_{ij} | \exists s_k \in S' | v_k = V_{ij}\}$, $P_i' = \{P_{ij} | \exists s_k \in S' | \exists p_k | P_{ij} \in p_k \cap P_i\}$.

For each of the previous ratios, the average over all fields is calculated as follows:

$$\mu_q = \sum_{i \in I} \frac{q_i}{Card(I)}, \quad (13)$$

with q_i representing the different ratios presented in (12).

These averages are the metrics we use for our simulations.

3.2. Simulation Context

In order to evaluate the performance of the algorithms VDV, AC, and LDA, we simulate them with a DLL trace of a protocol widespread in the IoT: ZigBee [13]. This protocol is based on the standard IEEE 802.15.4 [14], widely used in the IoT for physical and data link layers.

The DLL traces to be analysed are generated by randomly creating frames from a data frame formats base we created according to ZigBee specification. The trace generation process is run at each single simulation, so the traces analysed are never the same (although they respect the same statistical properties). The traces are then processed by the algorithms in an offline procedure.

The comparative simulation was done in two steps. (i) Observing the influence of each of the algorithms parameters by simulating them over an arbitrary but wisely chosen parameters set domain. (ii) Choosing the best performing parameter set among all the ones simulated, and comparing the performance achieved.

This method allowed us to get parameter sets yielding good performance, but not the best that could be achieved by the algorithms. This is due to the fact that we used a simple optimization approach, considering that all the parameters influence the algorithms in an independent manner.

We chose to simulate all the algorithms with a number of frames varying from 1 to 1000 with a logarithmic step, and with a maximal length of the searched sequences of 4.

For the VDV algorithm, we set the number of flows randomly generated to 10 and the filtration threshold coefficient to 1.

For the AC algorithm, we set the fusion threshold and the filtration threshold to 1.

For the LDA algorithm, we set the number of keywords to 10, the maximal perplexity gradient to 1, the maximal probability gradient to 0.1, alpha to 1, and beta to 0.0001.

Note that each curve point is calculated by averaging over 100 runs of the simulation corresponding to this point parameter set.

We limited ourselves to 1000 frame traces for processing power and memory usage limitations of our simulating hardware.

3.3. Simulation Results

We first get the F score graph of the Fig. 1.

The F score synthesizing the precision and recall shows that VDV grows quickly until around 10 frames, then stabilizes around 25-30 % of F score, and drops after 100 frames in the trace. On the other hand, we can observe that AC and LDA both have very near curves displaying slow linear growth, capping around 45-50 % of F score, which is the best performance achieved. LDA is apparently slightly better by a small margin, but it presents a slow decrease above 400 frames.

The performances of all the algorithms grow at first because they are based on laws of large numbers, so they perform better with larger data sets to analyse.

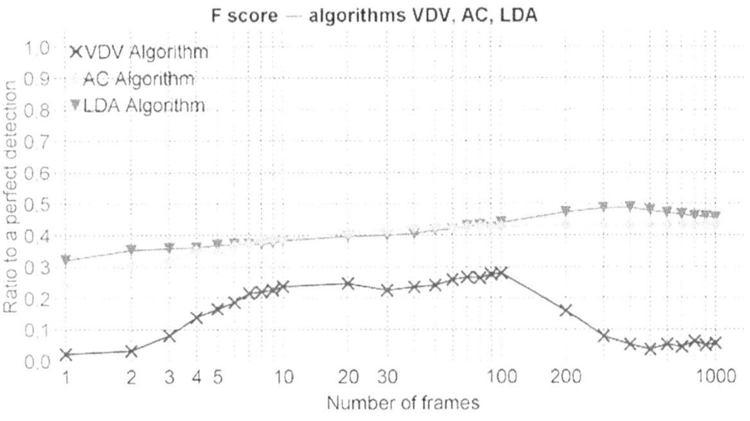

Fig. 1. Best F score of the algorithms VDV, AC, and LDA.

The VDV algorithm performance drop is due to the actual filtration threshold being a value depending only on the average variance of variances, and not on the trace size, so it is appropriated only for an interval of a given number of frames. On the other hand, the AC algorithm threshold FT_{AC} depends on the number of bits in the trace, and the LDA does not use a frequency threshold to filtrate sequences, so their performances do not display a sudden drop after a certain number of frames.

The LDA slow decrease can be explained by an insufficient number of keywords, which tends to make the algorithm converge towards a smaller number of different sequences when provided with large traces, hence lower recall, so lower F score.

Let us now switch from the quality of the sequence detection to its usefulness for field detection. We draw the average fields detection ratios of the lengths, on the graph of Fig. 2.

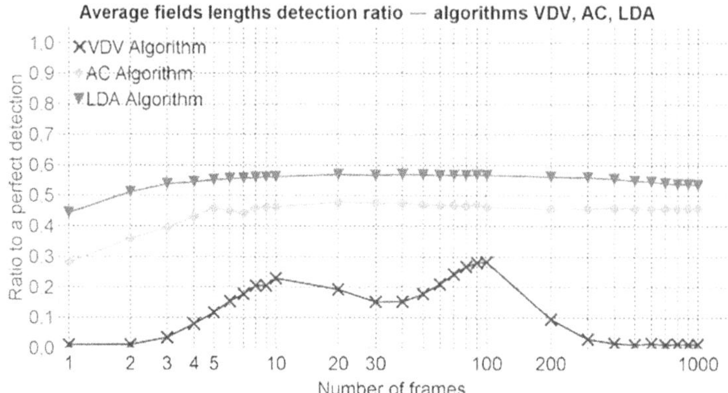

Fig. 2. Best average fields lengths detection ratio of the algorithms VDV, AC, and LDA.

We omit the other fields detection ratios as they present an identical behavior.

We can see that the VDV algorithm average fields length detection ratio presents the same behavior as its previous curve. The AC algorithm performance presents the same linear growth then stabilization behavior as its F score curve, while capping earlier, around 10 frames. LDA has the exact same behavior as its F score curve as well, with the decreasing phase beginning around 100 frames. It shows the best performance, with an average fields length detection ratio slightly less than 60 %.

We summarize the relative performance of the three algorithms in Table 1. The number of stars stands, by decreasing order, for the best, average, and worst.

Table 1. Relative performance summary of the algorithms VDV, AC, and LDA.

Algorithms	VDV	AC	LDA
F score	*	***	***
Average fields length detection ratio	*	**	***
Average fields values detection ratio	**	**	***
Average fields positions detection ratio	*	**	***
Total	5	9	12

We clearly see that the LDA algorithm offers the best performance, followed by the AC algorithm, and lastly the VDV algorithm.

4. Conclusion

We wanted a communicating object to be able to communicate in an unknown environment, so we needed it to learn the protocols in that environment. We chose to study and evaluate the performance of three possible sequence identification techniques which could be used in that learning procedure: VDV, AC, and LDA. To that end, we simulated them applied to the analysis of ZigBee DLL traces, and compared them.

For the purpose of comparison, in addition to the classic metric F score, we defined our own, the fields detection ratio.

From the simulations results, we can clearly state that in this context the LDA technique offers the best results, followed by the AC technique, and eventually the VDV technique.

A more powerful hardware could have allowed us to see if we could push further the performance of the LDA algorithm, and a more formal parameter optimization would have given us more precise maximal performance of the algorithms.

Nonetheless, with the results of the comparative simulation, we can now state that a technique based on Bayesian networks performs better than ones simply based on statistics or occurrences counting. This encourages us to further engage in Bayesian theory in the future.

References

[1]. O. Esoul, N. Walkinshaw, Finding clustering configurations to accurately infer packet structures from network data, *ArXiv Preprint*, October 2016.

[2]. A. Trifilò, S. Burschka, E. Biersack, Traffic to protocol reverse engineering, in *Proceedings of the IEEE Symposium on Computational Intelligence in Security and Defense Applications (CISDA'09)*, July 2009, pp. 1-8.

[3]. A. V. Aho, M. J. Corasick, Efficient string matching: An aid to bibliographic search, *Commun. ACM*, Vol. 18, Issue 6, June 1975, pp. 333-340.

[4]. D. M. Blei, A. Y. Ng, M. I. Jordan, Latent Dirichlet allocation, *Journal of machine Learning research*, Vol. 3, May 2003, pp. 993-1022.

[5]. A. Li, C. Dong, S. Tang, F. Wu, C. Tian, B. Tao, H. Wang, Demodulation-free protocol identification in heterogeneous wireless networks, *Computer Communications*, Vol. 55, September 2014, pp. 102-111.

[6]. S. Kleber, L. Maile, F. Kargl, Survey of protocol reverse engineering algorithms: Decomposition of tools for static traffic analysis, *IEEE Communications Surveys and Tutorials*, Vol. 21, August 2018, pp. 526-561.

[7]. B. Sija, Y.-H. Goo, K.-S. Shim, H. Hasanova, M.-S. Kim, A survey of automatic protocol reverse engineering approaches, methods, and tools on the inputs and outputs view, *Security and Communication Networks*, Vol. 2018, February 2018, pp. 1-17.

[8]. Y. Wang, N. Zhang, Y.-M. Wu, B.-B. Su, Y.-J. Liao, Protocol formats reverse engineering based on association rules in wireless environment, in *Proceedings of the 12th IEEE International Conference on Trust, Security and Privacy in Computing and Communications (TrustCom'13)*, July 2013, pp. 134-141.

[9]. Y. Wang, X. Yun, M. Shafiq, L. Wang, A. Liu, Z. Zhang, D. Yao, Y. Zhang, L. Guo, A semantics aware approach to automated reverse engineering unknown protocols, in *Proceedings of the 20th IEEE International Conference on Network Protocols (ICNP'12)*, October 2012, pp. 1-10.

[10]. E. I. George, G. Casella, Explaining the Gibbs sampler, *The American Statistician*, Vol. 46, Issue 3, August 1992, pp. 167-174.

[11]. G. Heinrich, Parameter Estimation for Text Analysis, Technical Note, *University of Leipzig*, Germany, 2008.

[12]. C. A. Haydar, Trust-based recommender systems, PhD Thesis, *Université de Lorraine*, September 2014.

[13]. ZigBee Specification, *ZigBee Standards Organization*.

[14]. IEEE Std. 802.15.-2003, *IEEE*, 2003.

(056)

Multi-objective Optimization of Meta-learning Scheme for Context-based Fault Detection

M. Kalisch, A. Timofiejczuk and P. Przystałka
Silesian University of Technology, Faculty of Mechanical Engineering,
18A Konarskiego Street, 44-100 Gliwice, Poland
Tel.: +48 32 237 14 67, fax: +48 32 237 13 60
E-mails: mateusz.kalisch@gmail.com, anna.timofiejczuk@polsl.pl, piotr.przystalka@polsl.pl

Summary: The paper deals with the problem of performance optimization of a meta-learning scheme for context-based fault detection. The context-based ensemble classifier is proposed to increase the performance of the fault diagnosis system. The most important problem to solve in this approach is to find optimal structures as well as optimal values of behavioral parameters of component classifiers. This problem has been elaborated as a multi-objective optimization task taking into account different objectives obtained from a confusion matrix. It was decided to make use of the NSGA-II algorithm in order to search for the optimal solution. A case study is based on the laboratory stand for simulation of hydraulic industrial processes. Common machine learning methods such as decision tree, naive Bayes, Bayesian network and k-nearest neighbors were taken into account in the meta-learning scheme for context-based fault detection. The obtained results prove that the proposed approach has practical relevance.

Keywords: Fault detection, Context-based reasoning, Machine learning, Multi-objective optimization, Soft computing optimization.

1. Introduction

Nowadays model-free and model-based fault detection and isolation methods play an important role in the industrial systems [1]. The paper deals with the first group of the methods only. In this case, it can be seen that faults are detected and distinguished using primary and redundant process variables. In such a system two separated classifiers must be created. The first classifier uses the subset of process variables as its input and it is dedicated for generating diagnostic signals, whereas the second one has the same set of input variables but its task is to yield a fault signature. This classifier is triggered in case when the diagnostic signal indicates a fault scenario. The algorithms corresponding to such approach can be designed using different classification methods. Generally, it is possible to apply so-called classical (e.g. decision trees, k-nearest neighbor, naive Bayes, etc.) or soft computing approaches (e.g. neural networks, Bayesian networks, fuzzy systems, neuro-fuzzy systems, etc.).

In many cases basic classifiers are not good enough to achieve satisfying results. It is possible to combine basic classifiers into committees of classifiers using methods such as Bagging or AdaBoost. Ensemble classifiers allow us to build more complex classification models containing more basic classifiers. In this approach the final result can be obtained using either voting mechanism or another classifier to create metaclassifier [2]. Another way to achieve more satisfying results is meta-learning which allows learning algorithm to find optimal parameters of the final classification model. Meta-learning extends capabilities of the machine learning processes by using metadata available during learning process to increase classification efficiency. The machine learning process can be implemented as optimization process based on e.g. multi-objective evolutionary algorithms [3]. The third option is based on that additional data like e.g. contextual features can be introduced into dataset like e.g. contextual features. Contextual features cannot be used directly by a classifier but can be useful when they are combined with other features [4]. Authors of this paper connected all three approaches in one algorithm to prepare a fault detection system for the hydraulic industrial process.

2. Meta-learning Scheme for Context-based Fault Detection

In a classification task, it is possible to distinguish three types of features: primary, contextual and irrelevant [2]. Primary features are useful for classification, without regard to the other features. The irrelevant features are not useful for classification, either when combined with the other features or when they are considered alone. Contextual features cannot be used directly by a classifier, but can be useful when they are combined with other features. The primary features can be also divided into context-sensitive and context-insensitive features. In the case of fault diagnosis process, the context variable could be connected with a number of factors e.g. weather conditions, the time of the day, etc.

In the literature some of the concepts for the usage of the context with machine learning algorithms are described. Peter Turney described five strategies which show how context can be used [5]: *Contextual normalization, Contextual expansion, Contextual classifier selection, Contextual classification adjustment and Contextual weighting*. The authors of this paper took into account the contextual classifier selection, which main task is to divide input dataset into groups, where each group is connected with a different value of the contextual feature. In the next step each subset of data is used to train the separated classifier. The diagram of the committee of classifiers with a context-based switching block is presented in Fig. 1 [6].

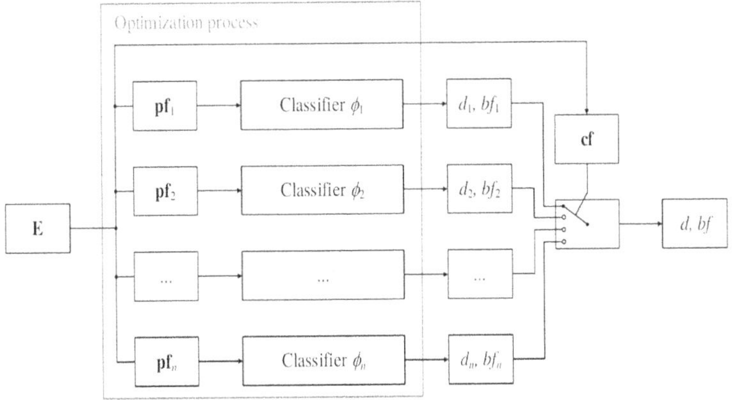

Fig. 1. Multiple classifiers with context-based switching block.

Complete model of a context-based ensemble classifier contains as many classifiers as number of unique values of a discrete contextual feature. As one can observe, the proposed meta-classifier is composed of component classifiers (ϕ_i) that are switched using contextual feature cf. The data model is formulated as follows:

$$E = \begin{bmatrix} pf_1(1) & pf_2(1) & \cdots & pf_N(1) & cf(1) & td(1) \\ pf_1(2) & pf_2(2) & \cdots & pf_N(2) & cf(2) & td(2) \\ \vdots & \vdots & \ddots & \vdots & \vdots & \vdots \\ pf_1(K) & pf_2(K) & \cdots & pf_N(K) & cf(K) & td(K) \end{bmatrix}, \quad (1)$$

where pf_n is the n-th primary feature, N is the number of primary features, cf is the contextual feature, pf_n and cf are conditional attributes, td is the target decision attribute, K is the number of learning patterns (pf/cf denotes a row vector of primary/contextual features). The inputs of base classifiers are created by means of the subsets of primary features (pf_i), whilst the outputs are computed using the following relation:

$$[d, bf] = [d_{[i]}, bf_i] = \phi_i(pf_i), \quad (2)$$

where d_i is the decision of the i-th classifier, bf_i denotes the belief factor corresponding to the decision d_i the index $i \in \{1,2,\dots,n\}$ is related to a variant of the contextual feature ($V_1, V_2, \dots, V_S$) and it is used to select the relevant classifier for a given input sample. Component classifiers are created by means of dedicated learning methods:

$$\chi_i: \{d_i, bf_i\} = \phi_i(pf_i), \quad (3)$$

where χ_i is learning function that is needed for creating the i-th component classifier, p_i is a vector of behavioral parameters corresponding to the i-th learning function, E_i is the subset of learning examples which are filtered from E applying contextual features.

The last step of the method is to formulate the multi-objective optimization problem in order to search for the best parameters (p) and structure (M) of learning methods. These methods with optimal values of behavioral parameters are used to train component classifiers. The main purpose of the optimization process is to search for the optimal structure of the learning scheme and the optimal values of learning parameters $p_1, p_2, \dots, p_d$ as well as the optimal lengths $p_{d+1}, p_{d+2}, \dots, p_{d+n}$ of vectors $pf_1, pf_2, \dots, pf_n$ in order to obtain the highest efficiency of the fault detection system. This issue is often viewed as a multi-objective optimization problem and hence it can be stated as follows:

$$\begin{gathered} MinimizeC(M,p) = \\ = min[c_1(M,p), c2(M,p), \dots, c_k(M,p)] \quad (4) \\ \text{subject to} \Omega(M,p,C), \end{gathered}$$

where c_i is the i-th criterion function that is being used to express the performance of the fault detection scheme, Ω is related to constraints and boundaries which should be chosen taking into account the properties of learning methods, training and testing datasets, etc. To reduce the complexity of the problem it is noted that in some cases the structure of meta-learning scheme (M) can be determined using a part of decision variables included in (p). Nevertheless, it must be highlighted that even in these cases the number of learning parameters corresponds to the types of component classifiers and, thus to the structure of the whole scheme.

As to be expected, the form of the function C can be elaborated taking into consideration different criteria. In this study, the authors propose to adopt statistical measures of a binary classification test that can be directly derived from a table of confusion. A general view of confusion matrix for fault detection problem is presented in Table 1.

Table 1. Confusion matrix for fault detection problem.

True state	Predicated state	
	Faulty (FX)	Faultless (F0)
Faulty (FX)	True positive (TP)	False negative (FN)
Faultless (F0)	False positive (FP)	True negative (TN)

True positive rate (TPR) and True negative rate (TNR) are two basic measures considered in the next part of the article. Both measures can be obtained from confusion matrix using following formulas:

$$\begin{aligned} TPR &= \frac{TP}{TP+FN} \\ TNR &= \frac{TN}{FP+TN} \end{aligned} \tag{5}$$

In case of fault detection problem TPR is interpreted as number of correctly classified faulty states and TNR is interpreted as number of correctly classified faultless states. In the previous paper of the authors [6] the problem (4) was solved using an indirect utility function in the simplest form at the weighted sum of objectives. In this paper Non Dominated Sorting Genetic Algorithm II (NSGA-II) [7] is employed.

3. A Case Study

The experiment was carried out on the laboratory plant dedicated for simulation of hydraulic industrial processes. This stand consists of three tanks (T1, T2, T3) connected with pipes. The scheme of the stand is presented in Fig. 2. Several pipes are equipped with manual valves (V1 to V10) which allow us to control the direction of fluid flow. It has one pomp (P) and contains number of sensors. Manual valves can be used to simulate different faults during the operation of the industrial process. The experiment was divided into 9 steps called functional states.

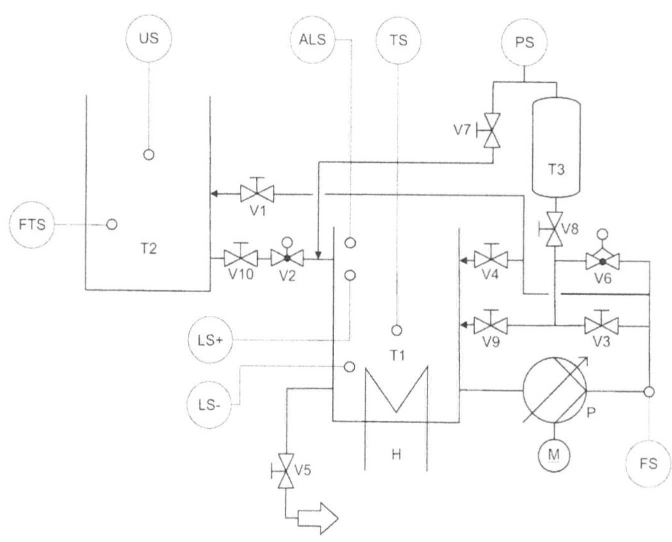

Fig. 2. Schema of FESTO laboratory station.

Each functional state was connected with one specific operation lasting a certain period of time e.g. in one of the functional state water was pumped from tank 1 (T1) to tank 2 (T2) for 1 minute. Identifiers of functional states were considered as values of contextual feature. Data has been collected from three process signals measured by three sensors: ultrasonic sensor (US) of fluid level in tank 2 (T2), pressure sensor (PS) in tank 3 (T3) and flow sensor (FS). Authors used the laboratory station to simulate industrial process under nominal conditions and with 5 different faults such as:

- Clogged pipe between tank T1 and tank T3 (simulated by partially closed valve V8),
- Leakage in tank T3 (simulated by partially open valve V7),
- Clogged pipe between tank T2 and tank T2 (simulated by partially closed valve V1),
- Clogged pipe between pump P and tank T1 (simulated by partially closed valve V4),
- Faulty sensor US (simulated by covering the work area of the sensor).

The experiment was repeated 10 times for each fault. The final number of experiments was 50 experiments for faulty state and 50 experiments for faultless state. In the next step the algorithm calculates scalar features of all available signals (raw signals of sensors). The authors choose a few time domain features often used in fault diagnosis [8], such as: average, maximum and minimum values, standard deviation, root mean square, shape factor, kurtosis, time-domain energy, skewness and entropy. The width of the window was dependent on the duration of the functional state. Prepared dataset was used to train and test ensemble classifiers. NSGA-II algorithm was used to adjust values of parameters of classifiers. The size of population for each generation was equal to 100 individuals. Complete optimization process contained 60 generations which gives 6000 evaluations of the fitness function. The probability of mutation for selected optimization algorithm was set to 10 % and 80 % of individuals of each generation were crossovered. Each evaluation of the fitness function executed training and testing processes 10 times (using cross-validation method) in order to obtain information on the repeatability of results for specific parameters of the classifiers. Average and standard deviation values of TPR and TNR measures where used in the fitness function in order to obtain fitness values for individual. The following objectives of the fitness functions were used:

$$\begin{aligned} c_{TPR} &= \frac{1}{N}\sum_{i=1}^{N}(1 - TPR_i) + t_\alpha \sigma_{TPR} \\ c_{TNR} &= \frac{1}{N}\sum_{i=1}^{N}(1 - TNR_i) + t_\alpha \sigma_{TNR} \end{aligned}, \quad (6)$$

where N is the number of classification training and testing processes in one fitness function evaluation, TPR_i/TNR_i are true positive rate / true negative rate measures obtained from one iteration, $\sigma_{TPR}/\sigma_{TNR}$ are standard deviations calculated from results obtained from all iterations for single individual and t_α is a factor determining the importance of the standard deviation. Higher value of t_α factor means higher influence of the standard deviation value on the result of the fitness function. Authors decided to use factor t_α equal to 3. The values of parameters TPR and TNR need to be maximized and the fitness function tends to be minimized so it was necessary to invert TPR and TNR values using following formulas $1 - TPR$ and $1 - TNR$.

Fig. 3 presents visualization of the Pareto front obtained during optimization process with use of the contextual classifier containing kernel based naive Bayes component classifiers. Each point on the Pareto front is connected with set of classifier parameters and each point contains information about average and standard deviation values calculated separately for faulty and faultless state. It is possible to select one point on the Pareto front, get classifier parameters connected to this point and use this parameters to create the final classifier implemented in the target solution.

Values received from the fitness function does not fully reflect the real efficiency of classifier. Fig. 4 presents final results using basic components of the fitness function (average value and standard deviation).

Each point presents average value calculated for TPR and TNR and their standard deviations as line ranges. The values of standard deviation are too small to show them on the full scale chart so the selected fragment of the chart was shown enlarged. One of the results was selected and its parameters were used to create the final classifier. It was tested using cross-validation method and compared to the classifier whose parameters have been determined by an expert.

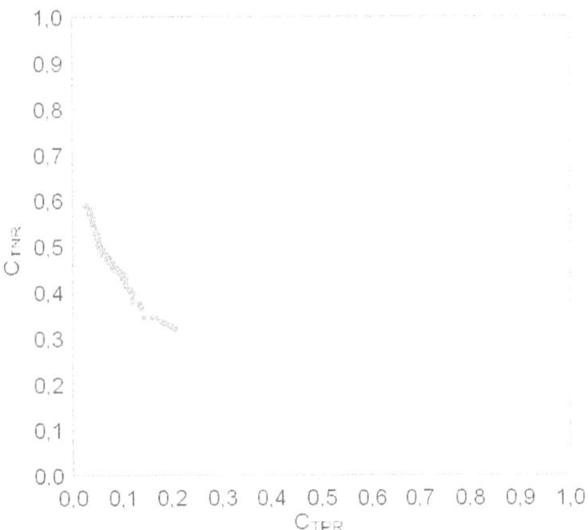

Fig. 3. Visualization of the Pareto front.

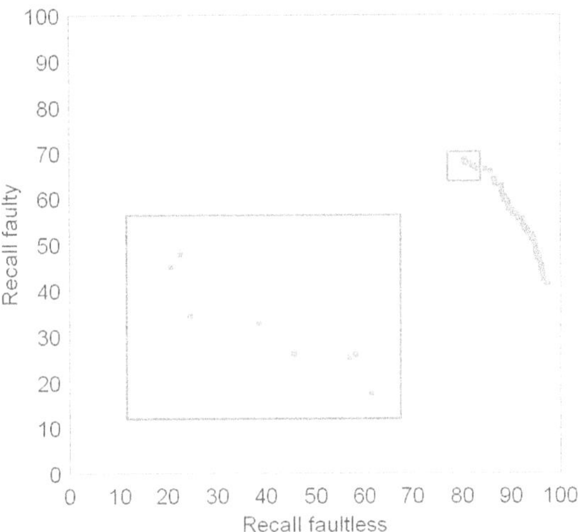

Fig. 4. Optimal results presented as average value and standard deviation.

Table 2 presents comparison between selected results of context based classifiers (average percentage of correctly classified samples for faultless and faulty with standard deviation). In both cases context-based classifier contained the same type of classifiers (naive Bayes classifier with kernel function) but in case of experiment without optimization method all primary classifiers had the same parameters adjusted by the expert.

Table 2. Examples of fault detection results.

State	With optimization	Without optimization
Faultless	78.9 (±0.36)	70.2 (±1.07)
Faulty	67.1 (±2.5)	64.5 (±4.33)

It can be seen that context-based ensemble classifier which used the optimization algorithm was able to find better solution and increase detection efficiency of both states (faultless and faulty state). Another advantage is reduced diversity between results obtained by the same classifier for different datasets.

4. Conclusions

In this paper, the authors propose and verify a multi-objective optimization method for tuning values of behavioral parameters of meta-learning scheme for context-based fault detection. The experimental tests were conducted using the laboratory stand for simulation an industrial processes. The classification results confirm that the proposed NSGA-II optimization algorithm can be extensively applied in the design of meta-learning schemes for context-based fault detection.

References

[1]. J. Korbicz, J. M. Kościelny, Z. Kowalczuk, W. Cholewa (Eds.), Fault Diagnosis, Models, Artificial Intelligence, Applications, *Springer*, Berlin, Heidelberg, 2004.

[2]. J. Han, M. Kamber, Data Mining. Concepts and Techniques, 2nd Ed., *Morgan Kaufmann*, 2006.

[3]. N. Jankowski, Meta-uczenie w Inteligencji Obliczeniowej, *Akademicka Oficyna Wydawnicza EXIT*, Warszawa, 2011 (in Polish).

[4]. P. Turney, The management of context-sensitive features: A review of strategies, in *Proceedings of the 13th International Conference on Machine Learning (ICML'96), Workshop on Learning in Context-Sensitive Domains,* Bari, Italy, 3-6 July 1996, pp. 60-66.

[5]. P. D. Turney, Exploiting context when learning to classify, in *Proceedings of the European Conference on Machine Learning (ECML'93),* Vienna, Austria, 5-7 April 1993, pp. 402-407.

[6]. P. Przystałka, M. Kalisch, A. Timofiejczuk, Genetic optimization of meta-learning schemes for context-based fault detection, in *Proceedings of the International Congress on Technical Diagnostic (ICDT'16)*, 2016, pp. 287-297.

[7]. K. Deb, et al, A fast elitist multi-objective genetic algorithm: NSGA-II, *IEEE Transactions on Evolutionary Computation*, Vol. 6, 2000, pp. 182-197.

[8]. P. Jigar, P. Vaishali, P. Amit, Fault diagnostics of rolling bearing based on improve time and frequency domain features using artificial neural networks, *International Journal for Scientific Research & Development*, Vol. 1, 2013, pp. 781-788.

(058)

Training Capsule Networks with Virtual Dataset for Object Segmentation

J. Hollósi [1] **and Á. Ballagi** [2]
[1] Széchenyi István University, Department of Information Technology, 1. Egyetem square, 9026 Győr, Hungary
[2] Széchenyi István University, Department of Automation, 1. Egyetem square, 9026 Győr, Hungary
E-mail: hollosi.janos@sze.hu

Summary: The classical convolutional neural networks performance looks exceptionally great when the test dataset are very close to the training dataset. But when it is not possible, the accuracy of neural networks may even be reduced. The capsule networks are trying to solve the problems of the classical neural networks. Capsule networks are a brand new type of artificial neural networks, introduced by Geoffrey Hinton and his research team. In this work we would like to training capsule based neural networks for segmentation tasks, when the training set and test set are very different. For the training we use only computer generated virtual data, and we test our networks on real world data. We created three different capsule based architectures, based on classical neural network architectures, such as U-Net, PSP Net and ResNet. Experiences show how capsule networks are efficient in this special case.

Keywords: Capsule network, Capsnet, Neural network, Object segmentation, Virtual dataset.

1. Introduction

Shell Eco-marathon is a unique international competition for university students to design, develop, build and drive the most energy-efficient race car. Our University's race team, the Szenergy Team has been a successful participant of the Shell Eco-marathon for over 10 years. Two years ago, Shell introduced the Autonomous Urban Concept (AUC) additional competition for self-driving vehicles at the Shell Eco-marathon. AUC competition participants have to complete five different autonomous challenges, like parking on a dedicated parking rectangle, obstacle avoidance on a straight track and so on. One of our main tasks is to create a neural network based intelligent system for this challenge, which perceives the environment of our race car, like the other vehicles, the surface of the road and other special components of the race track. Neural networks are one of the best tools for visual information-based detection and segmentation problems, like image segmentation. Nowadays, many high-performance neural network architectures are available, such as AlexNet by Krizhevsky et al. [1], VGG Net by Simonyan and Zisserman [2], GoogleNet by Szegedy et al. [3], Fully Convolutional Network by Shelhamer et al. [4], U-Net by Ronneberger et al. [5], ResNet by He et al. [6] and Pyramid Scene Parsing Network by Zhao et al. [7]. However, in this case, we do not have a sufficient number of training samples. For example, we do not have any training image about the protective barriers or the obstacles and it takes a lot of time and energy to generate and annotate real world data. Our idea is to use computer simulation environments to generate training data for this task. In this work a brand new and special type of artificial network is used, it is called capsule network [8].

2. Capsule Network

The capsule network [8, 9] (or CapsNet) is very similar to the classical neural network. We can find the main difference in the basic building block. In neural network we use neurons, but in the capsule network we can find capsules. Table 1 shows the main differences between the classical artificial neurons and the capsules. The capsule is a group of neurons that perform a lot of internal computation and encapsulate the results of the computations into an n-dimensional vector, which is the output of the capsule. The length of this output vector is the probability and the direction of the vector indicates some properties about the entity. The capsules network uses the dynamic routing algorithm, which calculates the output of the i-th (lower level) capsule for the (i+1)-th (higher level) capsule. In the routing algorithm use a novel non-linear activation function, it is called the Squash function.

Fig. 1. Sample from our dataset (top: real world test sample, bottom: virtual world training sample).

Table 1. Differences between capsule and neuron.

		Capsule	Neuron
Input		Vector($\boldsymbol{u}_i$)	Scalar (x_i)
Operations	Affine transform	$\widehat{\boldsymbol{u}}_{j\vert} = \boldsymbol{W}_{ij}\boldsymbol{u}_i$	-
	Weighting Sum	$s_j = \sum_i c_{ij}\widehat{\boldsymbol{u}}_{j\vert i}$	$a_j = \sum_i w_i x_i + b$
	Non-linear activation	$\boldsymbol{v}_j = \frac{\lVert s_j \rVert^2}{1 + \lVert s_j \rVert^2} \frac{s_j}{\lVert s_j \rVert^2}$	$h_j = f(a_j)$
Output		Vector ($\boldsymbol{v}_j$)	Scalar (h_j)

3. Virtual Dataset

Our aim is to create highly realistic image sets depicting racetracks which follow the rules defined by the Shell Eco-marathon Autonomous Urban Concept rulebook. In order to ensure repeatability and simple parameter setup it is advised to create complete, textured 3D-models of the racetracks. These simulated environments can be used to create images with desired weather and lighting conditions by scanning the track environment with a camera moving at a previously defined constant speed. The images created using this method can be processed further, including segmentation and the clustering of different object types, such as road surface, protective barrier elements, obstacle elements and other special components of the race track. The virtual environment was created with the Unreal Engine. Our model includes road surface defects and different road surface textures, which makes it possible to make road surface detection robust. In order to create image sets based on this environment model, a vehicle model equipped with a camera travelled around the racetrack on a pre-defined path. The camera was set to take pictures at pre-defined time intervals. The image set was annotated by an algorithm. Fig. 2 shows a sample from the training and the test set.

4. Network Architectures

In this work three different capsule based neural network architectures are created. The first capsule network is based on a U-Net [5] architecture, the second contains a pyramid pooling module, based on the PSP Net [7] architecture, and the last one is a residual network based capsule architecture, like ResNet [6].

U-Net

The U-Net [5] neural network architecture was originally created for biomedical image segmentation. It is based on Fully Convolutional Network, where the network can be divide into two main parts: the downsampling and the upsampling block. Fig. 2 shows our U-net style capsule network architecture.

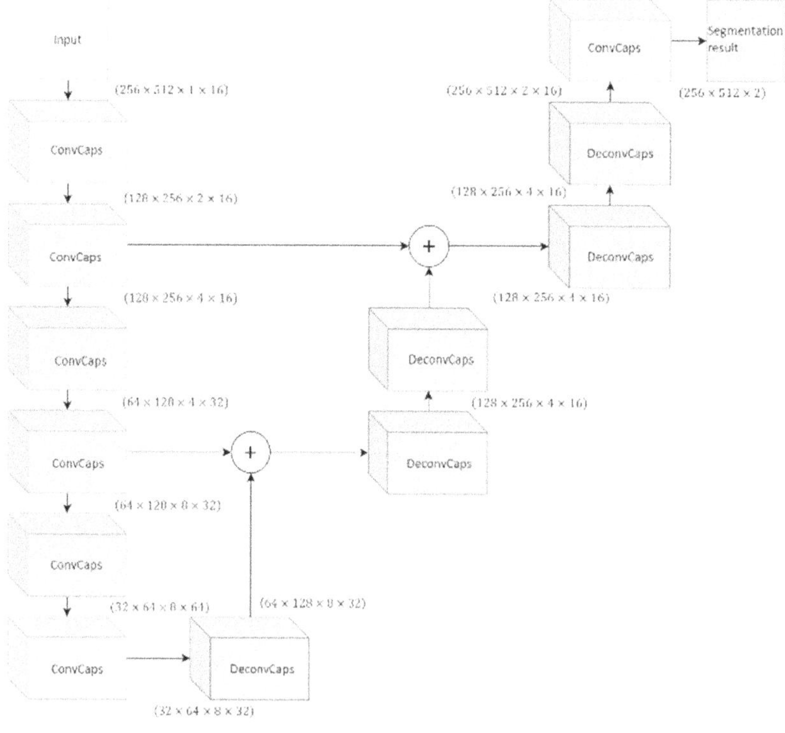

Fig. 2. U-Net architecture.

ResNet

The ResNet is a very deep neural network, created by He et al. in 2015 [6]. ResNet won the ILSVRC in 2015 with 3.6 % of error rate. The main idea of the Resnet is a residual block. Our ResNet based capsule network architecture consists of two main block: the convolutional block and the identity block. Figs. 3 and 4 shows this two blocks, where h is the height, w is the width of the input capsule, c is the number of capsules and a is the number of atoms in every capsule. Fig. 5 shows our ResNet based network.

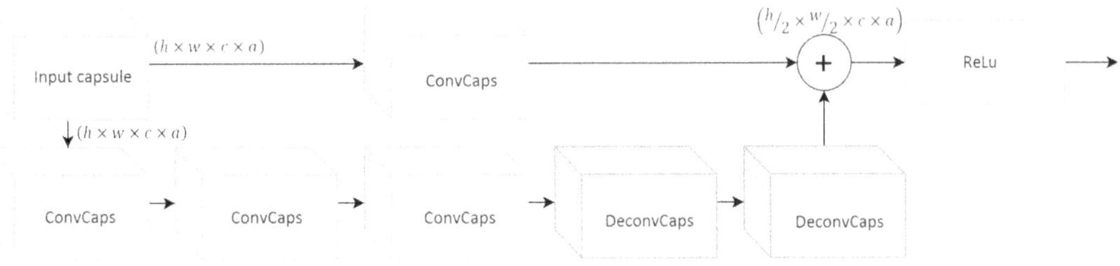

Fig. 3. Capsule based convolutional block.

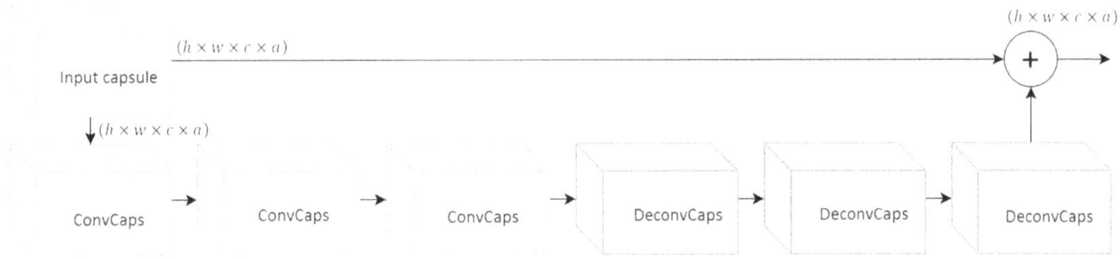

Fig. 4. Capsule based identity block.

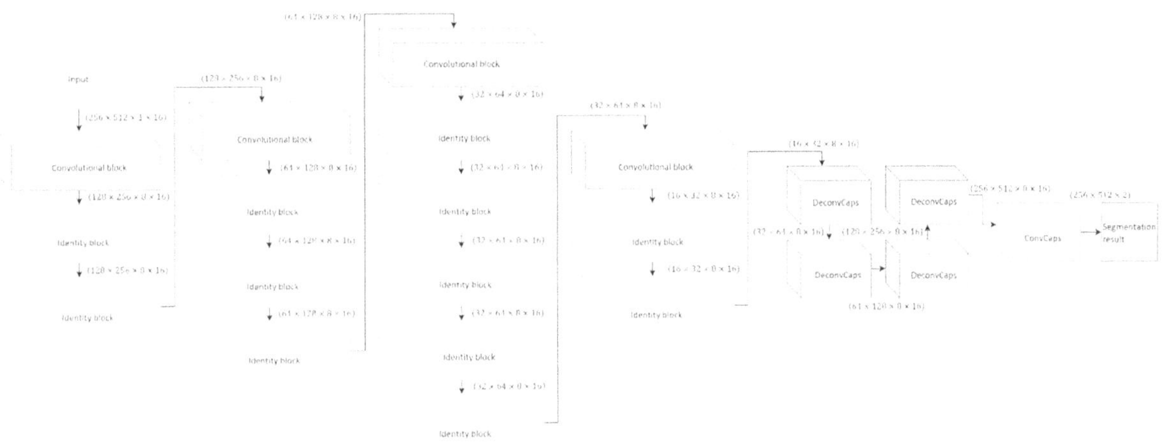

Fig. 5. ResNet Architecture.

PSP Net

The Pyramid Scene Parsing Network [7] is the best architecture on the ImageNet [10] Scene Parsing Challenge in 2016. The main building block of the PSP network is a pyramid pooling module, where the network fuses features under four different pyramid scales. The first phase of our network is built up with the same convolutional block and identity block, which used in ResNet. This is followed by a four stage pyramid block. Fig. 6 shows our PSP Net based capsule network.

5. Results

In this work we created a virtual image based dataset for the protective barrier and road surface segmentation. In our dataset the train samples comes from the virtual city environment, which is presented in 3 and we use only real world images for testing the accuracy of the networks. Our training dataset contains 1572 computer-generated virtual training samples and 131 real world images for validation. The three capsule based networks are trained on this dataset. Fig. 7 shows our results of the U-Net, ResNet and PSP Net based capsule networks. In the training phase Adam optimizer is used with 10^{-1} learning rate and 2×10^{-1} learning decay. The accuracy of the capsule based networks is calculated with dice coefficient

$$dc(y,\hat{y}) = \frac{2 \times y \times \hat{y}}{y+\hat{y}}, \quad (1)$$

where $y \in \{0,1\}$ is the ground truth and $0 \leq \hat{y} \leq 1$ is the result of the neural network.

6. Conclusions

In this work we training capsule based networks with virtual training data for real world objects segmentation, where our virtual dataset contains computer generated images from a virtual city environment. The results indicate that capsule networks can be used with high reliability in some cases when the size of available dataset is minimal or the training dataset is different from the test dataset. The best results we achieved with the U-Net based capsule network, followed by the residual capsule network, and the last one is the PSP Net. Our experiences shows that in the world of capsule networks, less is more. The U-Net style capsule network architecture is simple but robust. The other two network are more complex, which means lower efficiency in this case. In the future, we would like to achieve higher accuracy in image segmentation tasks with complex capsule based networks. To do this, we would like to examine the effectiveness of the routing algorithm in more detail.

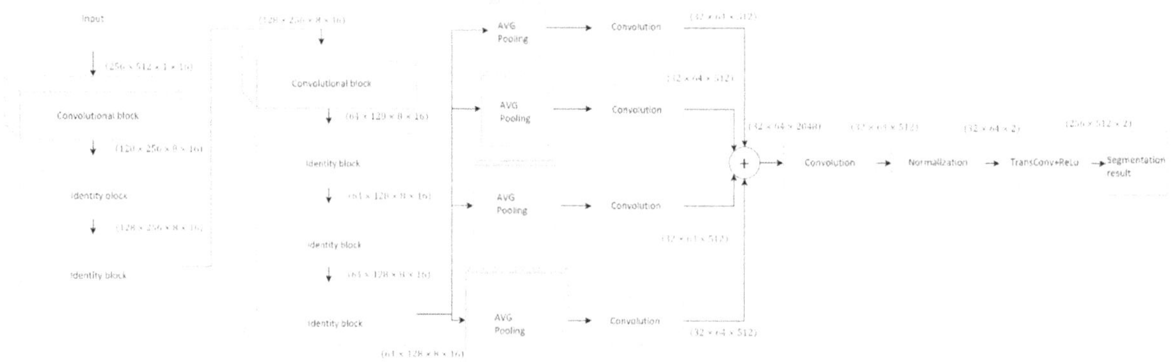

Fig. 6. PSP Net architecture.

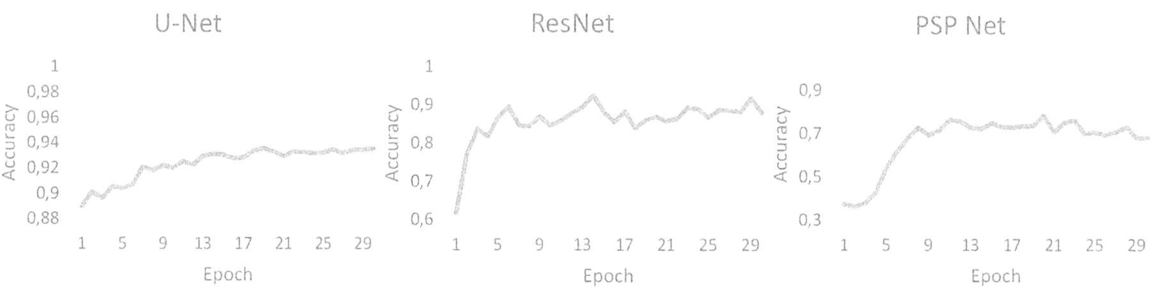

Fig. 7. Accuracy of the capsule based networks.

Acknowledgements

Supported by the ÚNKP-19-3-I-SZE-17 New National Excellence Program of the Ministry for Innovation and Technology.

References

[1]. G. A. Krizhevsky, I. Sutskever, G. E. Hinton, Imagenet classification with deep convolutional neural networks, in *Proceedings of the 25th International Conference on Neural Information Processing Systems (NIPS'12)*, Vol. 1, Nevada, USA, 2012, pp. 1097-1105.

[2]. K. Simonyan, A. Zisserman, Very deep convolutional networks for large-scale image recognition, in *Proceedings of the 3rd International Conference on Learning Representations*, San Diego, USA, 2015.

[3]. C. Szegedy, W. Liu, Y. Jia, P. Sermanet, S. Reed, Going deeper with convolutions, in *Proceedings of the IEEE Conference on Computer Vision and Pattern Recognition (CVPR'15)*, Boston, MA, USA, 2015, pp. 1-9.

[4]. E. Shelhamer, J. Long, T. Darrell, Fully convolutional networks for semantic segmentation, *IEEE Transactions on Pattern Analysis and Machine Intelligence*, Vol. 39, Issue 4, 2017, pp. 640-651.

[5]. O. Ronneberger, P. Fischer, T. Brox, U-Net: Convolutional networks for biomedical image segmentation, *Lecture Notes in Computer Science*, Vol. 9351, 2015, pp. 234-241.

[6]. K. He, X. Zhang, S. Ren, J. Sun, Deep residual learning for image recognition, in *Proceedings of the IEEE*

Conference on Computer Vision and Pattern Recognition (CVPR'16), Las Vegas, NV, USA, 2016, pp. 770-778.

[7]. H. Zhao, J. Shi, X. Qi, X. Wang, J. Jia, Pyramid scene parsing network, *IEEE Conference on Computer Vision and Pattern Recognition (CVPR'17)*, Honolulu, USA, 2017, pp. 6230-6239.

[8]. S. Sabour, N. Frosst, G. E. Hinton, Dynamic routing between capsules, in *Proceedings of the 31st Conference on Neural Information Processing Systems (NIPS'17)*, Long Beach, CA, USA, 2017, pp. 3856-3866.

[9]. G. E. Hinton, S. Sabour, N. Frosst, Matrix capsules with EM routing, in *Proceedings of the Sixth International Conference on Learning Representations*, Vancouver, BC, Canada, 2018, pp. 1-15.

[10]. O. Russakovsky, J. Deng, H. Su, et al, Imagenet large scale visual recognition challenge, *International Journal of Computer Vision*, Vol 115, 2015, pp. 211-252.

(060)

CT Scanner Classification with Neural Nets and Sensor Noise

M. Gerlofsma [1], M. Petkovic [1,2], P. van Liesdonk [2] and V. Menkovski [1]
[1] Eindhoven University of Technology, Eindhoven, The Netherlands
[2] Royal Philips Research Laboratories, Eindhoven, The Netherlands
E-mail: m.petkovic@tue.nl

Summary: The acquisition of Computed Tomography (CT) images has shown to be affected by the scanning device which acquires the image. Specifically, the same subject, scanned by a variety of CT devices, holds different properties depending on the device which acquired the image. This variance consequently has an impact on the medical analysis of the images. Therefore, the ability to determine the acquiring CT device based on the produced CT images may lead to improved diagnoses. In addition, knowledge of the CT device may furthermore provide a means to ensure verification of provenance without the necessity to rely on potentially corrupt or missing DICOM metadata. In this work, we apply a Convolutional Neural Network (CNN) to classify 4 manufacturers of CT scanners, based on the CT images which their devices generate. We apply our experiments on a large, publicly available dataset, and additionally apply previous classification techniques on the same dataset. With an accuracy of up to 93.6 %, our approach significantly outperforms existing work.

Keywords: CT scanners, CT device manufacturers, CT image classification, Convolutional neural networks, Sensor noise.

1. Introduction

Computed Tomography (CT) has become a vital asset in medical imaging. The CT images acquired during the scanning process are predominantly stored in the DICOM imaging format [1]. This storage format also provides additional metadata, such as the manufacturer of the scanning device which acquired the image. Such information may be exceptionally valuable as, for example, the estimation of lung density using CT images has shown to vary among CT scanner devices from different device manufacturers, which consequently affects the diagnosis of Emphysema [2], [3]. As such, knowledge of the scanning device may improve medical diagnoses.

However, to facilitate a painless data exchange between parties, DICOM metadata is predominantly implemented without any security checks, and requires only a few mandatory fields to produce a valid file. This leniency causes the metadata to be often incomplete and susceptible to modifications, which limits their benefits. To attribute CT images to specific devices without DICOM metadata, the authors of [4] extracted Sensor Pattern Noise (SPN) from the images to obtain distinct device fingerprints for a series of CT scanner devices, and performed device classification based on these fingerprints, using correlation. In addition to precise device identification, these noise patterns may also be leveraged to determine the integrity of the images themselves, which furthermore make them an attractive security control to e.g. detect image tampering [5].

Despite the initial success, the work in [4] exclusively applied an elemental classification approach based on image correlation, which consequently provides an opportunity for potential improvement. Convolutional Neural Networks (CNN) [6] have shown excellent performance for image classification and representation learning in several domains, including applications on medical images. As such, they may also prove to be an excellent tool to learn precise device fingerprints, and classify CT device manufacturers based on CT images. As such, different from the related work, we apply a CNN to classify 4 CT manufacturers based on the CT images produced by their respective CT scanners. In our paper we demonstrate the remarkable capability of neural networks to perform CT scanner classification based on CT images as well as sensor noise. We furthermore provide novel insights, and show how the extraction of distinct noise patterns has a significantly varying effect on the classification. Finally, we demonstrate the importance of sensible data processing for a task such as CT device classification.

2. Related Work

To attribute images to specific devices, in the seminal work of [7], the authors leveraged the Photo Response Non Uniformity noise (PRNU) present in the Sensor Pattern Noise (SPN) of pictures taken by photo cameras to attribute images to specific camera models. To extract the noise component of an image, the approach uses a denoising filter based on the work of [8]. This filter is applied on several images from the same, known camera model, and are subsequently averaged to obtain a reference pattern for a specific camera model. This reference pattern then serves as the fingerprint for the device, which enables attribution of future images.

This same denoising and classification procedure has been applied in [4] and later improved in [9, 10] to identify CT scanners. Therein, the authors consider a total of 3 scanners from 2 manufacturers to perform CT scanner device identification based on the CT images produced by the corresponding scanner.

Aside from specific CT device identification, other works aim to classify a group of devices instead [11], [12]. These works rely on alternative pre-processing steps, supplemented with an SVM [13] to perform the final classification. In [11], an alternative denoising technique is applied to account for the unique image acquisition and reconstruction process of CT images. Differently, the work in [12] distinguished 3 CT scanner manufacturers by performing a quantitative analysis based on the density distribution of Hounsfield Unit (HU) values within the CT images. The authors fit an SVM on the found distributions, and achieve an accuracy of 91.1 %.

Different from the related work, this work is the first to apply a deep learning method to classify CT scanner manufacturers based on the acquired CT images. In addition, we use a larger dataset, containing images from a wider array of devices, and thereby provide a better indication for the generalizability of CT scanner classification. Finally, this is the first work to perform the classification on both unprocessed CT images and extracted noise patterns, which will indicate the potential benefit of noise extraction when performing device classification.

3. Approach

To adequately evaluate and compare our approach, we first establish a baseline by applying the classification technique initially performed in [4], but on a significantly larger dataset than the initial work. We apply this approach on the unprocessed CT slices, as well as on the extracted sensor noise patterns.

For the classification using neural networks, we construct and train two convolutional neural networks (CNN) [6] to classify the slices of CT images. Here, the setup is again twofold. One CNN is trained and tested on unprocessed slices, while the second network is trained to classify the extracted sensor noise of the CT slices.

Finally, we split our training and test set by two different procedures to highlight the importance of a sensible split of CT images.

3.1. Noise Extraction Algorithm

The sensor noise components (Fig. 1) from a CT slice is extracted by applying the approach proposed in [7]. Although this approach has been initially proposed for the identification of photo cameras, the technique has also shown success in identifying CT scanners by the images which they produce [4, 9, 10].

To denoise a slice, a denoising filter F is applied. The denoised image is subtracted from the original slice to obtain the desired noise component w:

$$w = s - F(s) \tag{1}$$

The denoising filter F is the same as applied in [7], [8]. Specifically, the work applies a Wiener filter in the wavelet domain, which is applied in two stages as follows. First, the local variance of the image within the wavelet domain is estimated. Then, in the second stage, the estimated variance is applied in a Wiener filter to obtain the denoised image. These two stages are performed using the steps described below:

1) The fourth-level wavelet decomposition is calculated for the slice.

2) For each level, the three high frequency-bands are used for further processing. These are the vertical, horizontal and diagonal sub-bands, respectively.

3) For each wavelet coefficient in the sub-bands, the local variance $\hat{\sigma}^2(i,j)$ is estimated within a $W \times W$ square neighbourhood, for $W \in \{3,5,7,9\}$. The minimum of these 4 variances is chosen as the final estimate for the image variance:

$$\hat{\sigma}_W^2(i,j) = \max\left(0, \frac{1}{W^2}\sum_{(i,j)\in N} h^2(i,j) - \hat{\sigma}_0^2\right), \tag{2}$$

$$\hat{\sigma}^2(i,j) = = \min\left(\hat{\sigma}_3^2(i,j),\ \hat{\sigma}_5^2(i,j),\ \hat{\sigma}_7^2(i,j),\ \hat{\sigma}_9^2(i,j)\right), \tag{3}$$

where $(i,j) \in J$ denotes the index set for decomposition level J, and $\hat{\sigma}_0^2$ is a manually tuned parameter which has been set to $\hat{\sigma}_0^2 = 5$ to follow the original work [7].

4) After the variance estimation, the Wiener filter is applied to obtain the denoised wavelet coefficients:

$$X_{den}(i,j) = X(i,j)\frac{\hat{\sigma}^2(i,j)}{\hat{\sigma}^2(i,j) + \hat{\sigma}_0^2} \tag{4}$$

5) The above steps 2-4 are repeated for each wavelet sub-band, on each level of the decomposition.

6) The final, denoised image $F(s)$ is then obtained by applying the inverse wavelet transform.

Fig. 1. Example of extracted noise patterns from several CT slices.

3.2. Reference Pattern and Correlation

The baseline classification approach, based on correlation with a reference pattern, is performed by applying the same technique as [4]. This approach is performed in two stages. First, a reference pattern is computed for each class of CT scanners by averaging a random selection of slices from a particular class of scanners. The original process, illustrated in Fig. 5, applies this technique exclusively on the extracted noise patterns. However, since we additionally evaluate this approach on the unprocessed slices, we skip the noise extraction step in one instance of our experiments. The classification stage, illustrated by Fig. 6, then performs the classification by calculating the correlation of a CT slice, or its extracted noise component *w*, with each of the computed reference patterns *RP*:

$$\mathrm{corr}(\mathrm{s}, \mathrm{RP}) = \frac{(s-\bar{s})\left(RP-\overline{RP}\right)}{||s-\bar{s}||\ ||RP-\overline{RP}||} \quad (5)$$

The resulting correlation with a reference pattern indicates the likelihood that the image originates from the same device. Although the original work [4] accomplished this by establishing a certain threshold for the correlation value, we base the decision on the pattern that exhibits the highest correlation.

3.3. Data Split

In our experiments, we consider two approaches to split the data into the respective training and test sets. The first approach, presented in Fig. 2, accumulates the 2D CT slices from the dataset, and subsequently divides them into separate sets for training and testing. Differently, the second approach, illustrated by Fig. 3, accumulates the slices per volume, and subsequently divides the slices of entire volumes into the respective sets.

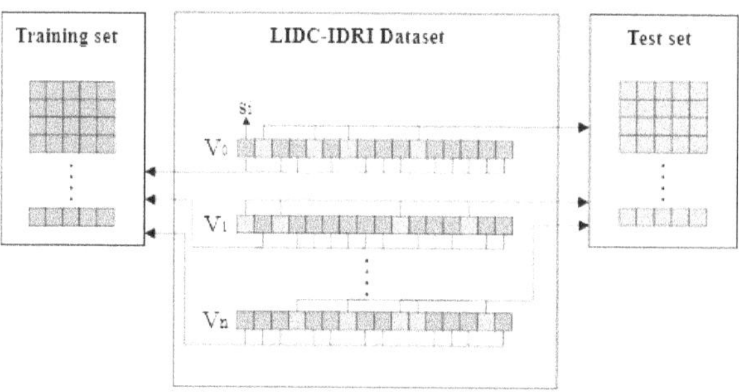

Fig. 2. A split based on individual CT slices. Neighbouring slices may end in either split.

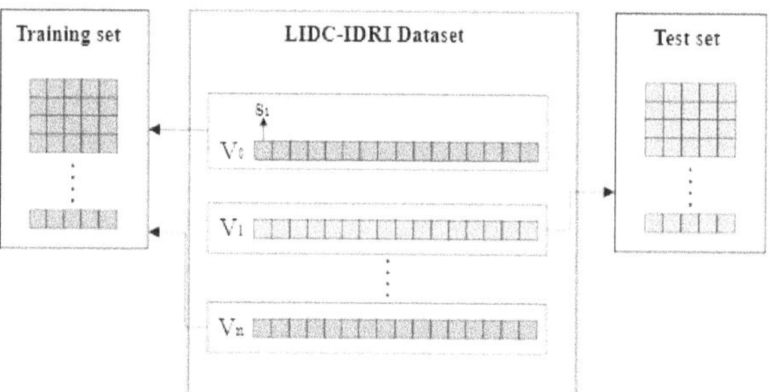

Fig. 3. A split based on CT Volumes. This type of split will keep several potential relationships among slices within a single side of the split.

So far, the related works [4, 9-11] have solely considered the first approach. As such, no volume is excluded during the training phase and computation of the reference patterns. This may lead to optimistic results as the test is likely affected by undesired relationships between individual slices which have been generated during the same scanning session of a patient. Specifically, successive, neighbouring slices from the same volume depict nearly identical content. As such, the first approach to split the data, shown in Fig. 2, assigns nearly identical slices into both train and test set.

Therefore, in our experiments, we primarily consider data splits based on the second, volume-based approach illustrated in Fig. 3. However, we also perform the alternative, first approach a single time to highlight the significance of a sensible data split.

4. Dataset

All experiments in our work are performed on samples from the anonymized and publicly accessible collection of CT imagery from the Lung Image Database Consortium and Image Database Resource Initiative (LIDC-IDRI) [14]. This dataset contains a total of 1,018 CT volumes, amounting to a total of 244,527 slices. The volumes in this dataset are represented by a total of 4 manufacturers: Philips, GE Healthcare, Siemens, and Toshiba. These manufacturers consequently form the 4 classes for the experiments. Table 1 illustrates the representation of each class within the LIDC-IDRI dataset. The CT scans in this dataset are stored in the 'Digital Imaging and Communications in Medicine' (DICOM) file format[1] which, besides the image data and device manufacturer, contains useful metadata related to the image scanning process itself. In this work, we make use of the metadata to determine the true label (device manufacturer) of the CT slices.

Table 1. CT volume representation within the LIDC-IDRI dataset.

Manufacturer	No. of Volumes
Philips	75
Siemens	206
GE healthcare	671
Toshiba	70

5. Experimental Setup

In each experiment, the manufacturer classification is performed on the slices from the LIDC-IDRI [14] dataset. To account for the class imbalance in the LIDC-IDRI dataset, the classes have been balanced by under sampling over-represented classes. As such, the final dataset used in the experiments contained 6,000 slices per class. To extract the noise patterns (Section 3.1) from the CT images, the implementation from [5] has been applied, who have kindly published their source code[2].

To perform the experiments based on the reference pattern and correlation metric (Section 3.2), we continue to primarily follow the work of [4]. Specifically, the reference patterns for the manufacturers are computed using the average of 120 slices per class. However, differently from the initial work, we explicitly split the data as visualized in Fig. 3. As such, slices from volumes which are used to calculate the reference pattern, are entirely separated from the volumes that are classified during the test phase. During classification, each slice from the test set will be compared to each of the reference patterns by calculating the correlation (Equation (5)), where the highest correlation value determines the class.

For the classification using a CNN, a simple, common architecture for image classification has been applied. Specifically, this architecture contained three convolutional layers, with a number of 8, 16 and 32 3×3 filters, respectively, with each convolutional layer being followed by a Batch normalization layer [15] and ReLU activation function. The first two convolutional blocks are furthermore followed by a 2×2 max pooling layer, while the last block contains an additional dropout layer to avoid overfitting. Finally, to increase the computational speed, input dimensions have been reduced from the original 512×512 to 299×299. An overview of the architecture is presented in Fig. 4. This architecture performed well on all tasks, and has been applied for both networks which classify based on noise patterns and unprocessed slices, respectively. The networks were trained for 10 epochs, on batches of size 128.

6. Results

6.1. Reference Pattern and Correlation

Table 2 presents the classification accuracies on extracted noise patterns using the reference pattern and correlation metric, initially applied in the work of [4]. The results show that slices from Toshiba and General Electric are classified perfectly, while CT slices from both Siemens and Philips are classified significantly worse. It is also peculiar that Philips and Siemens are most often misclassified amongst each other, which may indicate that these devices share certain software or hardware components, or share similarities in the physical acquisition process of the images which consequently affect the device fingerprint.

For the classification on the original, unprocessed slices, the result presented in Table 3 shows that predictions are significantly more distributed compared to the accuracies on noise patterns. However, the overall accuracy remains similar to the previous result, with a slight increase to 66.8 %, up from the previous 66.4 %. Moreover, predictions for General Electric and Toshiba devices have become split amongst each other and are classified significantly worse. However, Philips and Siemens devices are predicted more accurately on the original images. Interestingly, prediction mistakes for a certain class often fall into just one single, other class.

Nevertheless, the relatively low accuracy on either type of input image indicates that classification based on image correlation with a reference pattern may be insufficient to make accurate predictions on extensive datasets.

Table 2. Classification accuracy by correlation on extracted noise patterns of CT images.

	Philips	Siemens	GE	Toshiba
Philips	**29.55 %**	33.9 %	22.4 %	14.15 %
Siemens	37.78 %	**35.92 %**	14.58 %	11.72 %
GE	-	-	**100 %**	-
Toshiba	-	-	-	**100 %**
Average	**66.4 % accuracy**			

[1] https://www.dicomlibrary.com/dicom/

[2] Available at: http://dde.binghamton.edu/download/camerafingerprint/

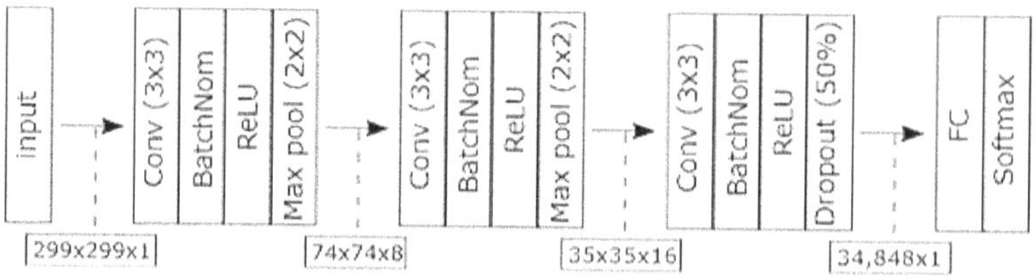

Fig. 4. The CNN architecture used for the classification of CT scanners.

6.2. Classification with Neural Networks

As can be seen in Table 5, the CNN reaches significantly better results and achieves up to 93.6 % classification accuracy on the noise patterns of CT slices. This is a significant improvement over the correlation-based experiments which achieved a maximum accuracy of 66.8 %. In addition, the neural network also outperforms the work of [12] which performed classification on just 3 manufacturers. Moreover, the deep learning classifier reached 1.1 % higher accuracy on the classification of noise patterns as opposed to the classification on original, unprocessed CT slices, presented in Table 4. This result suggests that the extraction of device fingerprints does not interfere with the capability of the neural network to learn its own features. Interestingly, the misclassifications shown in Table 4 also continue to support the apparent similarity between Siemens and Philips devices already highlighted in Section 6.1.

Table 3. Classification accuracy by correlation on unprocessed CT images.

	Philips	Siemens	GE	Toshiba
Philips	**77.85 %**	22.15 %	-	-
Siemens	29.66 %	**53.91 %**	13.43 %	3.00 %
GE	-	-	**76.5 %**	23.5 %
Toshiba	-	-	40.97 %	**59.03 %**
Average	**66.8 % accuracy**			

Table 4. Classification accuracy on unprocessed CT images with a neural network.

	Philips	Siemens	GE	Toshiba
Philips	**72.63 %**	27.37 %	-	-
Siemens	1.27 %	**98.73 %**	-	-
GE	-	-	**100 %**	-
Toshiba	-	-	-	**100 %**
Average	**92.5 % accuracy**			

Table 5. Classification accuracy on extracted noise patterns of CT images with a neural network.

	Philips	Siemens	GE	Toshiba
Philips	**98.55 %**	1.45 %	-	-
Siemens	8.40 %	**77.82 %**	-	13.78 %
GE	-	-	**100 %**	-
Toshiba	-	-	-	**100 %**
Average	**93.6 % accuracy**			

6.3. Effect of Data Split

Finally, the CNN has also been evaluated on the naive train/test split in which data is solely separated based on individual slices (Fig. 2). Table 6 shows that this approach indeed significantly favours the classification. The classifier reaches an accuracy of 99.8 % which even outperforms the much smaller setting presented in [4]. This result consequently confirms the hypothesis that the classification of CT scanner manufacturers still requires careful consideration when the data is split into separate sets.

7. Conclusion

In this paper, we presented several experiments aimed to classify CT scanner manufacturers based on individual, 2D CT image slices. We evaluated an existing approach, based on the work of [4], on a larger dataset and under stricter conditions. Next, in our approach, we evaluated a CNN on the same task. For both approaches, we performed an additional pre-processing step which extracts the noise component from a CT slice to obtain a representation of the underlying device fingerprint. We compared this pre-processing step to the classification based on the original, unprocessed images. Finally, we showed that this classification task requires careful consideration when splitting the data in respective train and test set.

The results have shown that the classification approach based on reference patterns is not suitable for larger datasets, which naturally carry more variation. In addition, the extraction of the SPN had no significant impact on the performance of this approach. Conversely, the CNN showed outstanding accuracy, and with an accuracy of up to 93.6 %, even out-performed existing work. The classification on the SPN-fingerprint performed only slightly better than the unprocessed images. However, the gained performance is only marginal and may become less significant in fully optimized networks.

Table 6. Classification of CT images using a slice-based data split.

	Philips	Siemens	GE	Toshiba
Philips	**99.57 %**	0.43 %	-	-
Siemens	-	**100 %**	-	-
GE	-	0.14 %	**99.64 %**	0.21 %
Toshiba	-	-	-	**100 %**
Average	**99.8 % accuracy**			

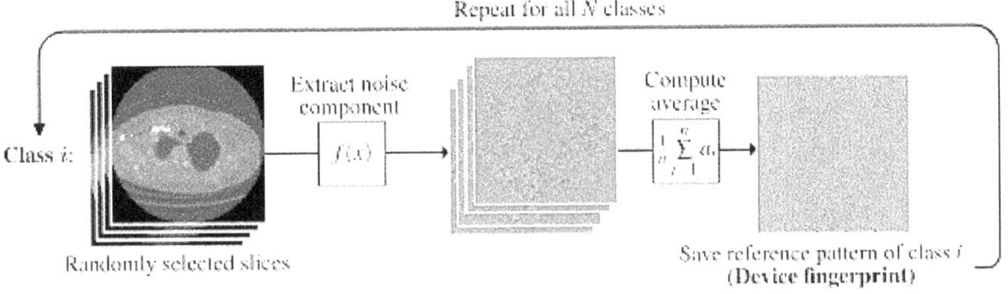

Fig. 5. Creation of reference patterns for a certain amount of devices, given a set of slices from known devices.

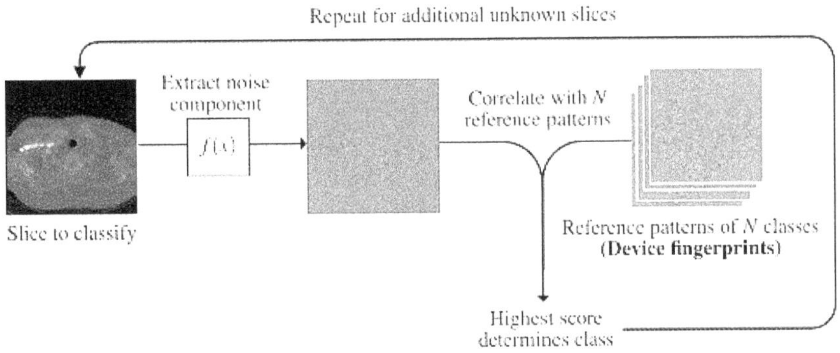

Fig. 6. The process to determine the class of unknown slices, given a precomputed set of reference patterns.

8. Discussion and Future Work

The results of the experiments have shown that CNNs are an effective method to classify scanner devices based on CT imagery. Nevertheless, this work primarily serves as a first step towards scanner classification based on neural nets. As such, the methods used in this work may still be optimized. The neural networks applied in the experiments are based on existing architectures and setups, with slight modifications to suit the dimensions and the amount of data. As such, there is still ample opportunity to improve the existing classifiers based on additional domain expertise. In addition to the network optimization, the extracted noise pattern may also be substantially optimized. The current noise pattern to establish the fingerprint was originally intended for ordinary photo cameras, yet has also shown applicability for CT scanners. However, in [11], improvements have already been made by applying more sophisticated device fingerprint based on the reconstruction algorithm of CT scanners. In addition, denoising of CT images is an extensively explored topic, and existing methods in this field may also benefit the extraction of more accurate device fingerprints.

Acknowledgements

The work presented in this paper is funded by the EC Horizon 2020 research and innovation programme under grant agreement No 780495 (BigMedilytics).

References

[1]. W. D. Bidgood Jr, S. C. Horii, F. W. Prior, D. E. Van Syckle, Understanding and using DICOM, the data interchange standard for biomedical imaging, *Journal of the American Medical Informatics Association*, Vol. 4, Issue 3, 1997, pp. 199-212.

[2]. R. Yuan, J. R. Mayo, J. C. Hogg, P. D. Pare, A. M. McWilliams, S. Lam, H. O. Coxson, The effects of radiation dose and CT manufacturer on measurements of Lung densitometry, *Chest*, Vol. 132, Issue 2, 2007, pp. 617-623.

[3]. B. C. Stoel, M. E. Bakker, J. Stolk, A. Dirksen, R. A. Stockley, E. Piit-ulainen, E. W. Russi, J. H. Reiber, Comparison of the sensitivities of 5 different computed tomography scanners for the assessment of the progression of pulmonary emphysema: a phantom study, *Investigative Radiology*, Vol. 39, Issue 1, 2004, pp. 1-7.

[4]. A. Kharboutly, W. Puech, G. Subsol, D. Hoa, Ct-scanner identification based on sensor noise analysis, in *Proceedings of the 5th European Workshop on Visual Information Processing (EUVIP'14)*, 2014, pp. 1-5.

[5]. M. Chen, J. Fridrich, M. Goljan, J. Lukâs, Determining image origin and integrity using sensor noise, *IEEE Transactions on Information Forensics and Security*, Vol. 3, Issue 1, 2008, pp. 74-90.

[6]. Y. LeCun, Y. Bengio, et al., Convolutional networks for images, speech, and time series, *The Handbook of Brain Theory and Neural Networks*, Vol. 3361, Issue 10, 1995.

[7]. J. Lukâs, J. Fridrich, M. Goljan, Digital camera identification from sensor pattern noise, *IEEE Transactions on Information Forensics and Security*, Vol. 1, Issue 2, 2006, pp. 205-214.

[8]. M. K. Mihcak, I. Kozintsev, K. Ramchandran, Spatially adaptive statistical modeling of wavelet image coefficients and its application to denoising, in *Proceedings of the IEEE International Conference on Acoustics, Speech, and Signal Processing (ICASSP'99)*, Vol. 6, 1999, pp. 3253-3256.

[9]. A. Kharboutly, W. Puech, G. Subsol, D. Hoa, Improving sensor noise analysis for CT-scanner identification, in *Proceedings of the 23rd European Signal Processing Conference (EUSIPCO'15)*, 2015, pp. 2411-2415.

[10]. A. Kharboutly, et al., Advanced sensor noise analysis for CT-scanner identification from its 3d images, in *Proceedings of the International Conference on Image Processing Theory, Tools and Applications (IPTA'15)*, 2015, pp. 325-330.

[11]. Y. Duan, D. Bouslimi, G. Yang, H. Shu, G. Coatrieux, Computed tomography image origin identification based on original sensor pattern noise and 3-d image reconstruction algorithm footprints, *IEEE Journal of Biomedical and Health Informatics*, Vol. 21, Issue 4, 2017, pp. 1039-1048.

[12]. S.-B. Lee, E.-J. Jeong, Y. Son, D.-J. Kim, Classification of computed tomography scanner manufacturer using support vector machine, in *Proceedings of the 5th International Winter Conference on Brain-Computer Interface (BCI'17)*, 2017, pp. 85-87.

[13]. C. J. Burges, A tutorial on support vector machines for pattern recognition, *Data Mining and Knowledge Discovery*, Vol. 2, Issue 2, 1998, pp. 121-167.

[14]. LIDC-IDRI, https://wiki.cancerimagingarchive.net/display/Public/LIDC-IDRI

[15]. S. Ioffe, C. Szegedy, Batch normalization: Accelerating deep network training by reducing internal covariate shift, *ArXiv Preprint*, arXiv:1502.03167, 2015.

(064)

Comparative Analysis of Various Machine Learning Approaches for Bitcoin Price Prediction

Abhishek Muvvala [1], Rohit Chivukula [2] and T. Jaya Lakshmi [3]
[1] Associate Product Developer, DXC Technology, Chennai, India
[2] School of Computing and Engineering, University of Huddersfield, Huddersfield, United Kingdom
[3] Department of Computer Science and Engineering, SRM University, AP, Andhra Pradesh, India
E-mail: jaya.phd.hcu@gmail.com

Summary: Bitcoin is used worldwide for digital payment or simply for investment purposes. Bitcoin price prediction is an interesting research problem in current scenario. In this paper, we have studied the application of machine learning approach in predicting the future price of bitcoin. Many dynamic factors effect Bitcoin prices and accurate predictions form strong base for investment decisions. In this study, we have collected the live data corresponding to bitcoin from quindle.com containing 8 features. Then we have compared the prediction performance of 11 regression algorithms. It is found that Lasso regression with a combination of generalised linear regression outperformed others with an improvement of 9 % accuracy over other regression algorithms.

Keywords: Machine learning, Regression, Bitcoin price prediction.

1. Introduction

Bitcoin is a novel digital currency system which functions autonomously without any central governing authority. Bitcoin is used worldwide for digital payment and for investment purposes. Bitcoin is decentralized i.e. it is not owned by anyone. Bitcoin trades enable individuals to sell/purchase bitcoins utilizing various currencies. The largest Bitcoin exchange is Mt Gox [13].

Exchanges made by bitcoins are simple as they are not attached to any nation. The record of all the transactions, the timestamp data is stored in a specific kind of distributed ledger called Blockchain. Each record in a blockchain is called a block. Every block stores digital information pertaining to the transaction viz. date, time and amount involved in transaction. Every block is connected to its previous block to form blockchain. During transactions the user's identity is maintained private strictly, but only their wallet ID is made public. Payments are processed by a peer-to-peer network of users over the web. Bitcoins can be exchanged with other currencies in the exchange office, where all transactions are stored on the order book. The Bitcoin's value changes dynamically. The parameters affecting Bitcoin price prediction are different from those used in stock market price prediction. Therefore, it is necessary to predict the value of Bitcoin so that correct investment decisions can be made. Bitcioin price can be predicted efficiently using Machine learning algorithms.

In this work, we focus on the short-term price prediction of bitcoin from machine learning perspective.

2. Literature

Given a training set $\{(X_1,y_1), (X_2,y_2)\ldots(X_m, y_m)\}$, where each $X_i \in R^n$ representing the input space and $y_i \in R$ denoting the target value, the aim of the regression problem is to fit a function that can approximate the value of y for an X not in the training set. Bitcoin price prediction can use this model efficiently in which X_i representing the vector of features affecting price of bitcoin, based on which the future price y_i can be predicted.

Ciaian et al., [1] studied the conventional as well as specific factors that contribute to the future BitCoin price formation such as market forces and Bitcoin attractiveness for investors and users. Their framework is rooted on the popular Barro model. The authors extract daily data for a period of five years and apply time-series based mechanisms. McNally et al, [2] have quantified the accuracy by considering Bitcoin Price Index using Bayesian recurrent neural network (RNN) and Long Short Term Memory (LSTM) network. Another model based on deep learning found in literature is ARIMA model. The non-linear deep learning methods outperform the ARIMA. Madan et al., [4] used machine-learning approach to predict Bitcoin price. The authors predict the sign of the daily price change using the data with 25 features corresponding to the Bitcoin price as well as payment network for a duration of five years. Further, the authors focus on the Bitcoin price data alone during different time durations. Katsiampa et al, [3] have studied optimal conditional heteroskedasticity model with regards to goodness-of-fit to Bitcoin price data. They found that the AR-CGARCH model emphasised the need of both short-run as well as long-run component of the conditional variance in price prediction.

Dyhrberg et al [5] have explored the hedging capabilities of bitcoin. Their work applies asymmetric GARCH methodology. The outcomes show that bitcoin can be utilized as a support against stocks in the Financial Times Stock Exchange Index. In their investigation, they have found that Bitcoin and gold stocking have similar hedging abilities. More recent works on bitcoin price prediction can be found in [8] and [9]. The summary of literature is tabulated in Table. 1.

Table 1. Summary of literature.

Name/Author/Year	Techniques Used	Limitations
Predicting the price of Bitcoin using machine learning, S. McNally, 2016.	Price prediction using recurrent neural networks (RNNs) and long short-term memory (LSTM)	A machine trained only with Bitcoin price index and transformed prices exhibits poor predictive performance.
The economics of Bitcoin price formation, P. Ciaian, M. Rajcaniova, D. Kancs, 2016.	Linear model by considering related information that is categorized into several factors of market forces, attractiveness for investors, and global macro-financial factors.	They assume that market forces and attractiveness for investors influence Bitcoin prices but with variation over time.
Automated Bitcoin trading via machine learning algorithms, I. Madan, S. Saluja, A. Zhao, Dept. Comput. Sci., Stanford Univ., Stanford, CA, USA, Tech. Rep., 2015	Price prediction problem as a binary classification task.	Does not explore or disclose the relationship between Bitcoin price and other features in the space, such as market capitalization.
Volatility estimation for Bitcoin: A comparison of GARCH models, P. Katsiampa, Econ. Lett., Vol. 158, pp. 3-6, Sep. 2017	Optimal conditional hetero skedasticity model with regards to goodness-of-fit to Bitcoin price data.	Considers only volatility and not price prediction
Hedging capabilities of Bitcoin. Is it the virtual gold?, A. H. Dyhrberg, Finance Res. Lett., Vol. 16, pp. 139-144, Feb. 2016.	Hedging capabilities of bitcoin by applying the asymmetric GARCH methodology used in investigation of gold.	Only hedging is discussed, no price prediction is done

3. Proposed Approach

The proposed approach acquires time-series data recorded daily for five certain time period at different time instances, and normalizes and smoothens. Then from the pre-processed data, the features and parameters are extracted. The accuracy is compared with different models after the final prediction.

The execution is carried out in the following steps.

3.1. Dataset Collection and Preprocessing

As Bitcoin is a kind of stock traded in stock market, dataset is available in plenty with all-time intervals. We have collected live data from quandl.com during the period 2011 to till date. This provided us the most comprehensive bitcoin price in date wise data. Dataset is extracted to CSV file. The features Time_stamp, Open, High, Low, Close, Volume_btc, Volume_currency, Weighted_price are extracted and used in the prediction task.

3.2. Split Dataset as Train and Test Set

10-fold cross validation is used for evaluating the prediction performance. 80 % of the of data is taken as training input for constructing the machine learning model and the remaining 20 % of data is considered as test set for performance prediction. The process is repeated for 10 times and the average of 10 iterations are reported.

3.3. Machine Learning Algorithms Used to Predict Price of Bitcoin

The standard regression techniques of Linear regression (LR), Logistic regression (LGR), Support Vector Machine(SVM), Multivariate Regression and, Multiple Linear Regression (MLR), Partial Least Squares (PLS), Support Vector Regression (SVR), Back-Propagation Neural Network (BPNN), K Nearest Neighbours (kNN), Decision Trees (DT), Gradient Boosted Machine(GBM), Random Forest (RF) and LOSSO are applied on train data and evaluated on test set. The Lasso Regression algorithm introduces the L1 regularization term that plays a vital role in feature selection. The Grid Search logic is applied in this model for hyperparameter tuning in order to achieve optimum performance. A maximum of 100000 iterations are computed using the LASSO regression model. The model performed well with high accuracy.

3.4. Evaluation Measures

It is a common practice to evaluate the prediction performance of a regression problem using MAE,

RMSE and Accuracy [10]. Let y and ŷ be vector of actual and predicted values and n be the number of samples. The measures are given below.

RMSE: Root Mean Square Error is normalized distance between predicted and actual values.

$$\mathrm{RMSE} = \sqrt{\frac{1}{n}\sum_{j=1}^{n}(y_j - \hat{y}_j)^2} \quad (1)$$

MAE: Mean Absolute Error is the average of the absolute difference between the predicted values and observed value.

$$\mathrm{MAE} = \frac{1}{n}\sum_{j=1}^{n}|y_j - \hat{y}_j| \quad (2)$$

Accuracy: Accuracy is another evaluation measure to evaluate the performance. Accuracy is defined as follows:

$$Accuracy = \frac{Number\ of\ Correct\ predictions}{Total\ number\ of\ predictions\ made} \quad (3)$$

. Results

The proposed work is implemented in Python 3.6.4 with libraries scikit-learn, pandas, matplotlib and other mandatory libraries. We have downloaded dataset from quandl.com with necessary authentication keys. The data downloaded contains up-to date data. The dataset is 80 % considered as train set and 20 % considered as test set. Five days forecast price prediction is done. The experimental results are shown in Fig. 1. It is observed that all the regression algorithms produced a minimum accuracy of 50 %. LASSO in combination with GLM has given highest prediction accuracy with an improvement in terms of RMSE, MAE as well as accuracy. Neural Network based algorithms performed well over other methods.

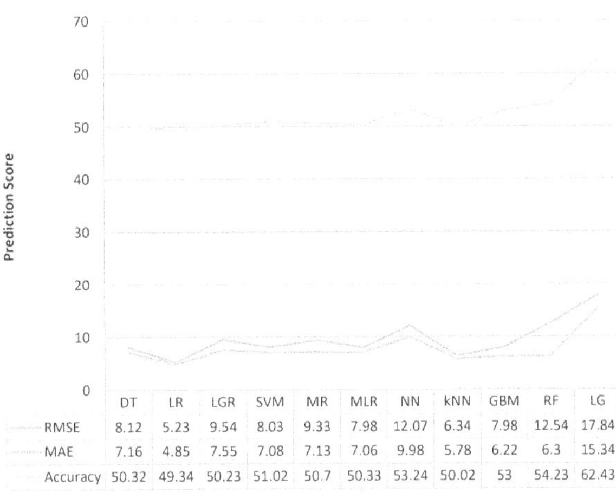

	DT	LR	LGR	SVM	MR	MLR	NN	kNN	GBM	RF	LG
RMSE	8.12	5.23	9.54	8.03	9.33	7.98	12.07	6.34	7.98	12.54	17.84
MAE	7.16	4.85	7.55	7.08	7.13	7.06	9.98	5.78	6.22	6.3	15.34
Accuracy	50.32	49.34	50.23	51.02	50.7	50.33	53.24	50.02	53	54.23	62.43

Fig. 1. Results of Bitcoin Price Prediction.

5. Conclusion

Bitcoin is a popular cryptocurrency, and it has been studied in depth in financial and computer science fields. In this work, we analyze the time series of Bitcoin price with various regression models for forecasting price for five days. The experimental results show that Lasso regression in combination with generalized linear regression outperforms the other by high accuracy on price prediction.

6. References

[1]. P. Ciaian, M. Rajcaniova, d'Artis Kancs, The economics of BitCoin price formation, *Applied Economics*, Vol. 48, Issue 19, 2016, pp. 1799-1815.

[2]. S. McNally, J. Roche, S. Caton, Predicting the price of bitcoin using machine learning, in *Proceedings of the 26th Euromicro International Conference on Parallel, Distributed and Network-based Processing (PDP'18)*, 2018, pp. 339-343.

[3]. P. Katsiampa, Volatility estimation for Bitcoin: A comparison of GARCH models, *Economics Letters*, Vol. 158, 2017, pp. 3-6.

[4]. I. Madan, S. Saluja, A. Zhao, Automated bitcoin trading via machine learning algorithms, http://cs229.stanford.edu/proj2014/Isaac%20 Madan20

[5]. H. Dyhrberg, Hedging capabilities of Bitcoin. Is it the virtual gold?, *Finance Res. Lett.*, Vol. 16, February 2016, pp. 139-144.

[6]. D. Shah, K. Zhang, Bayesian regression and Bitcoin, in *Proceedings of the 52nd Annual Allerton Conference on Communication, Control, and Computing (Allerton'15)*, 2015, pp. 409-415.

[7]. H. Jang, J. Lee, An empirical study on modeling and prediction of bitcoin prices with Bayesian neural networks based on blockchain information, *IEEE Access*, Vol. 6, 2017, pp. 5427-5437.

[8]. F. Andrade de Oliveira, L. Enrique ZÃ¡rate, M. de Azevedo Reis, C. Neri Nobre, The use of artificial neural networks in the analysis and prediction of stock prices, in *Proceedings of the IEEE International Conference on Systems, Man, and Cybernetics (SMC'11)*, 2011, pp. 2151-2155.

[9]. M. Daniela, A. Butoi, Data mining on Romanian stock market using neural networks for price prediction, *Informatica Economica*, Vol. 17, 2013.

[10]. S. McNally, Predicting the price of Bitcoin using Machine Learning, in *Proceedings of the 26th Euromicro International Conference on Parallel, Distributed and Network-based Processing (PDP'17)*, 2017, pp. 339-343.

[11]. H. Jang, J. Lee, An empirical study on modeling and prediction of bitcoin prices with Bayesian neural networks based on blockchain information, *IEEE Access*, Vol. 6, 2018, pp. 5427-5437.

[12]. T. Chai, R. R. Draxler, Root Mean Square Error (RMSE) or mean absolute error (MAE)? – Arguments against avoiding RMSE in the literature, *Geoscientific Model Development*, Vol. 7, Issue 3, 2014, pp. 1247-1250.

[13]. E. M. Little, Bitcoin, *The Investment Lawyer*, Vol. 21, Issue 5, 2014, pp.22-27.

(065)

Improved Pixel Selection Strategy for Reversible Data Hiding in Binary Images

I. C. Dragoi and D. Coltuc
Faculty of Electrical Engineering, Electronics and Information Technology,
Valahia University of Targoviste, Romania
E-mail: catalin.dragoi@valahia.ro, dinu.coltuc@valahia.ro

Summary: In this paper, a new reversible data hiding scheme for binary images is proposed. Hidden data is embedded into the binary image by modifying pixels based on a reference block created around them. The host pixels are processed as horizontally connected pairs. The nearest neighboring pixels to each host pair are considered reference pixels, forming a reference block. The host pairs are classified based on the reference block pixel distribution. This distribution is also used to evaluate the embedding distortion caused by replacing the host pair with two hidden data bits. The proposed approach selects the distribution that provides the required capacity at the lowest embedding distortion.

Keywords: Reversible data hiding, Binary images, Block based.

1. Introduction

Reversible data hiding (RDH) algorithms embed hidden data into a host file, allowing for the exact recovery of both the host and the data. Specialized RDH approaches were developed based on the host file (see [1]): images (graylevel, color and binary), audio samples, video files and encrypted data.

Several RDH frameworks (most notably [2-4]) were developed for binary images, facilitating owner identification in a wide range of applications (most notably scanned documents and digital signatures). Both [2] and [3] split the host image into non-overlapping pixel sequences, these sequences are then classified based on their distribution [2] or by converting them into decimal values [3]. Two sequence types are selected as the host values for the hidden data. A hidden bit is inserted into each selected sequence by changing from one type to another. Ideally, one of the two selected types has no corresponding sequences in the original image and the other type has enough sequences to provide the required capacity. Otherwise, a location map is used to determine the original distribution.

The recent framework of [4] splits the host into 3×3 pixel blocks. The blocks are classified into patterns, the patterns are ordered based on the distortion produced by changing their values. A pattern that provides the required capacity is selected and a rather similar pattern with few or no image blocks is determined. If the second pattern exists, it is vacated by flipping the bit value of the central pixel of the block and a location map is used to identify such changes. The main drawback of [4] is its limited capacity, i.e., a 3×3 block can contain at most one bit of hidden data providing a theoretical maximum embedding capacity of 1/9 of the image size. Furthermore, blocks containing all white or black values cannot be used (the introduced distortion is visible) and only one primary block pattern is used for direct data hiding.

The proposed RDH corrects the above-mentioned drawback of [4] by improving the initial selection of the blocks. Thus, the theoretical maximum capacity increases 3 times, from 1/9 to 1/3 of the image size. This significantly improves the pattern value distribution, allowing for the direct bit-flipping of the host pixels, bypassing the need to find/create a similar pattern with no values. The implementation of the proposed RDH framework for binary images is discussed in the next section.

2. Improved Pixel Selection for RDH in Binary Images

The proposed RDH algorithm starts by splitting the image into two distinct regions: host and reference (shown in Fig. 1). Let x denote a pixel from the host region and r denote a reference pixel. Only x pixels can be modified by the embedding algorithm.

The host pixels are processed in pairs. Each (x_1, x_2) pair is surrounded by ten reference pixels $(r_1, r_2, \ldots, r_{10})$. In order to avoid artifacts, a block-based embedding approach derived from [4] is introduced. The ten reference pixels around the host pixels (see Fig. 1) constitute the pattern used to classify the blocks. Two patterns are also considered identical if the 180° rotation of one produces the other. Note that (contrary to [4]) the pattern blocks can overlap as long as the overlapping area contains only reference pixels (which are not influenced by the data embedding process).

The selected host pattern for the hidden data varies based on both the required embedding capacity and the pattern distribution of the host image. In order to ensure the proper extraction of the hidden data, the selected pattern must be known at the decoding stage. In other words, the data hider must transmit this information to the receiver for him/her to be able to access the hidden data. A simple reserved area approach is used to transmit the parameters required by the data extraction algorithm. The first eight non-uniform blocks of the image form the reserved area and are used to store the embedding parameters (selected pattern and location map size). The original x values of the reserved area blocks are appended to the hidden data bit-stream (in order to allow their proper restoration after the data extraction process is completed).

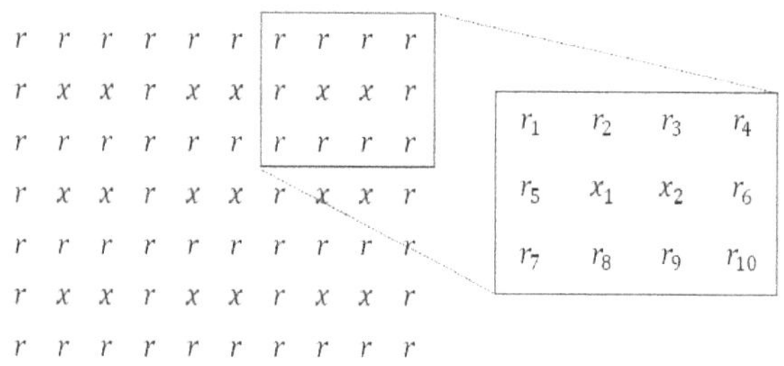

r	r	r	r	r	r	r	r	r	r
r	x	x	r	x	x	r	x	x	r
r	r	r	r	r	r	r	r	r	r
r	x	x	r	x	x	r	x	x	r
r	r	r	r	r	r	r	r	r	r
r	x	x	r	x	x	r	x	x	r
r	r	r	r	r	r	r	r	r	r

r_1	r_2	r_3	r_4
r_5	x_1	x_2	r_6
r_7	r_8	r_9	r_{10}

Fig. 1. The distribution of host pixels x and reference pixels r in the image and a reference block.

For each pattern type, the bit-flipping distortion cost is determined by first computing:

$$D_{x_1,x_2} = \sum_{i=1}^{10} w_i f(x_1, r_i) + \sum_{i=1}^{10} w_i f(x_2, r_i), \quad (1)$$

where $w_i = \begin{cases} 0.7, & \text{if } i \in \{1,4,7,10\} \\ 1, & \text{otherwise} \end{cases}$ is the weight of each reference pixel based on its proximity to the host pixels and $f(x, r_i) = \begin{cases} 0, & \text{if } r_i = x \\ 1, & \text{if } r_i \neq x \end{cases}$ is introduced to allow only values with $r_i \neq x$ to contribute to distortion estimation (see [4] for a complete description). Note that the w_i wights are determined based on the proximity of each r_i reference pixel to the (x_1, x_2) host pair. Orthogonal neighbors have $w_i = 1$, diagonal neighbors have $w_i = 0.7$.

All four possible values of (x_1, x_2) are evaluated with equation (1). Based on the original distribution of (x_1, x_2), the distortion cost of selecting a pattern is computed as:

$$D_C = \frac{n_{0,1} + n_{1,0} + n_{1,1}}{4} D_{0,0} + \frac{n_{0,0} + n_{1,0} + n_{1,1}}{4} D_{0,1} + \frac{n_{0,0} + n_{0,1} + n_{1,1}}{4} D_{1,0} + \frac{n_{0,0} + n_{0,1} + n_{1,0}}{4} D_{1,1}, \quad (2)$$

where $n_{0,0}$ is the number of blocks with the current pattern and $(x_1, x_2) = (0,0)$. In other words, there are $n_{0,0}$ pairs/blocks with (0,0) of which a quarter remains unchanged (the corresponding hidden bits are also (0,0)), a quarter becomes (0,1) producing a distortion of $D_{0,1}$ and so on. The size of the location map needed to restore the original values of the host pairs is also estimated for each pattern.

For a given embedding capacity, the optimal host pattern is the one with the lowest distortion cost that can provide space for its losslessly compressed location map, the needed capacity and the 16 original bit values of the pixel pairs in the reserved blocks.

The original (x_1, x_2) values of each block with the selected pattern are stored in a position map (which has four possible values). The map is then losslessly compressed. The compressed map is appended to the hidden data bit-stream together with the original values of reserved area blocks. The selected blocks are then used as a host for two bits of data. The (x_1, x_2) host pair is replaced with the two bits.

At the decoding stage, the receiver identifies the reserved area as the first eight non-uniform blocks of the image. The embedding parameters (the selected pattern and the location map size) are then read from the x values of the reserved area blocks. The remaining blocks of the host image are processed one-by-one. If the current block has the selected pattern, then the hidden data is read from the corresponding (x_1, x_2) host pair, otherwise the block is skipped. The extracted hidden data bit-stream is separated from the auxiliary information that was appended to it (the compressed location map and the original (x_1, x_2) values of the reserved area). Note that the auxiliary data is of known position (at the start of the initial bit-stream) and size (fixed for the reserved area and stored value for the compressed map size). The position map is decompressed and is used to indicate the original (x_1, x_2) values of each block with the selected pattern. The reserved area blocks are restored using their original stored values from the auxiliary data bit-stream.

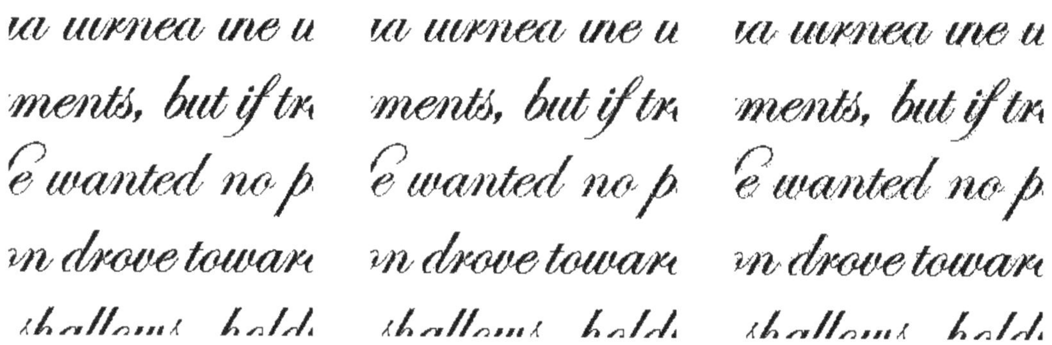

Fig. 2. RDH example on *Document*: original (left) and embedded with 128 bits (center, DRD of 0.04) and 512 bits (right, DRD of 0.17) of hidden data.

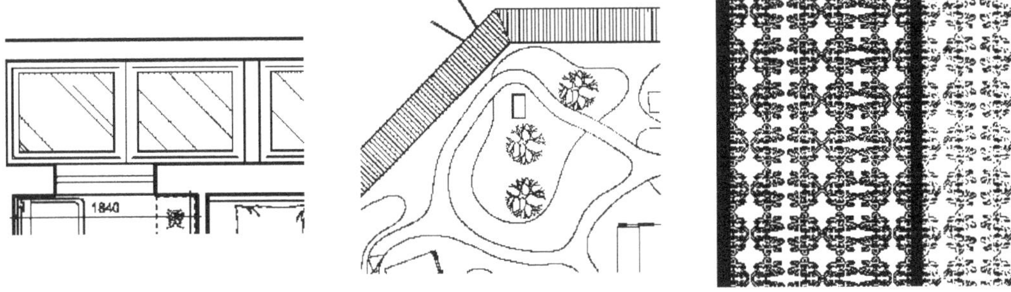

Fig. 3. Other initial test images: *CAD*, *Painting* and *Pattern*.

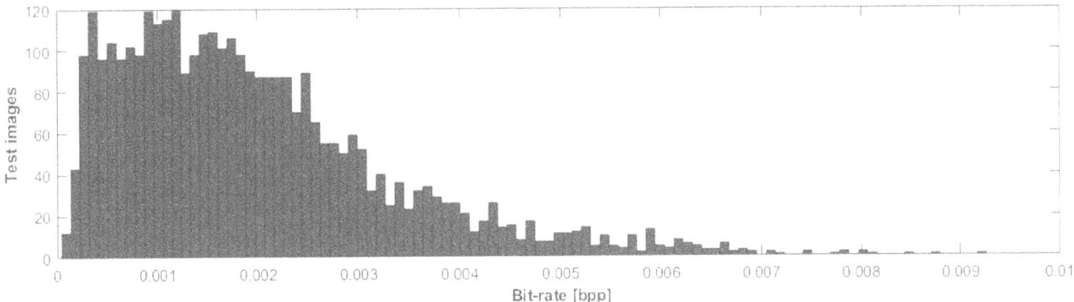

Fig. 4. Distribution of embedding bit-rates on the *Tobacco3482* test set.

3. Experimental Results

In this section, the performance of the proposed RDH approach is evaluated. The distance-reciprocal distortion (DRD) metric of [5] is used to determine the RDH embedding distortion (a lower value indicating lower distortion). The DRD value is compering the modified host image to its original counterpart. If a pixel has a different value from its original, then a block is created around it, the pixels in the block have different weights based on their proximity to the block center and their weighted values are used if they differ from the current modified pixel.

Fig. 2 shows two examples of host images containing 128 and 512 bits of hidden data. Compared to the original, the image containing 128 hidden bits has no noticeable distortion. One the other hand, the distortion on the 512 bit host is slightly visible, but it can be mistaken for scanning errors. The uniform areas remain unaffected for both examples.

The experimental results on four test images (the test set in [4], shown in Fig. 2 and 3) are presented in Table 1. The proposed approach outperformed both [3] and [4] on all test images. Under the same embedding capacity constraints, the proposed approach offers a smaller DRD value. Therefore, the proposed approach introduces a smaller distortion for a given embedding capacity. Furthermore, the proposed scheme also offers a larger maximum capacity: 1070 bits on *CAD* (DRD of 0.31), 322 bits on *Painting* (DRD of 0.08), 370 bits on *Pattern* (DRD of 0.05) and 638 bits on *Document* (DRD of 0.21).

Table 1. Results for the n-pairs scheme of [3], the SFD framework of [4] and the proposed approach.

Test Image	Capacity [bits]	DRD		
		n-pairs	SFD	proposed
CAD	101	0.08	0.05	0.04
Painting	171	0.11	0.1	0.05
Pattern	66	0.02	0.02	0.01
Document	68	0.05	0.03	0.02

The maximum embedding capacity of the proposed approach is also evaluated on the *Tobacco3482* test set (introduced in [6]). This set contains 3482 binary test images of different sizes (from 1575×1200 to 3296×2544 pixels) representing scanned forms, letters, newspaper clippings, advertisements and other such documents. In order to directly compare the results on images of different sizes, the maximum capacity results are shown in Fig. 4 as bit-rates measured in bits-per-pixel (bpp). Extremely small embedding bit-rates were only observed on 12 *Tobacco3482* images (with 0.00004 bpp, equivalent to capacities of at least 80 bits). A total of 2714 test images from the set offer a maximum bit-rate equal or higher than 0.001 bpp, offering a capacity between 1890 and 8385 bits (depending on the host image size). Bit-rates of 0.005 bpp or higher were observed on 158 test images, of which only 11 images offer more than 0.0075 bpp.

4. Conclusions

An improved pixel selection strategy for RDH in binary images was introduced. The proposed distribution of host and reference pixels allows for improved capacities at lower embedding distortion, outperforming other state-of-the-art RDH schemes.

Acknowledgements

This work was supported by UEFISCDI Romania, Grant PN-III-P1-1.1-PD-2016-1666.

References

[1]. Y. Shi, X. Li, X. Zhang, H. Wu, B. Ma, Reversible data hiding: Advances in the past two decades, *IEEE Access*, Vol. 4, 2016, pp. 3210-3237.

[2]. Y.-A. Ho, Y.-K. Chan, H.-C. Wu, Y.-P. Chu, High-capacity reversible data hiding in binary images using pattern substitution, *Computer Standards and Interfaces*, Vol. 31, Issue 4, 2009, pp. 787-794.

[3]. C. Kim, J. Baek, P. S. Fisher, Lossless data hiding for binary document images using n-pairs pattern, in *Proceedings of the International Conference on Information Security and Cryptology (ICISC'14)*, 2014, pp. 317-327.

[4]. X. Yin, W. Lu, W. Liu, J. Zhang, Reversible data hiding in binary images by symmetrical flipping degree histogram modification, in Security with Intelligent Computing and Big-data Services, *Springer*, 2020, pp. 891-903.

[5]. H. Lu, A. C. Kot, Y. Shi, Distance-reciprocal distortion measure for binary document images, *IEEE Signal Processing Letters*, Vol. 1, Issue 2, 2004, pp. 228-231.

[6]. J. Kumar, P. Ye, D. Doermann, Structural similarity for document image classification and retrieval, *Pattern Recognition Letters*, Vol. 43, 2014, pp. 119-126.

(066)

Characteristics of a Voice to Identify a Speaker

S. Kinkiri [1], B. Bakarat [1] and S. Keates [3]
[1] University of Greenwich, Medway, Kent, United Kingdom
[2] Edinburgh Napier University, Scotland, United Kingdom
E-mail: Sarithareddy99999@gmail.com

Summary: Speech is a unique way of communication among humans. Speech is a complex method of communication systems when compared to other methods. As humans, we do use non-speech, which is non-verbal communication to convey the information. Nonverbal communication does not only concentrate on the meaning of words, but it also provides information such as: what kind of emotional state the person is in. Non-verbal communication provides a higher level of information, which includes characteristics of a human voice and in this paper we will show how we can use these characteristics to identify a person.

Keywords: Human voice, Speech, Verbal/Non-verbal communication, Emotional state, Speaker identification.

1. Introduction

Human voice is extremely difficult to analyze and then recognize. There are two types of human voices: verbal and non-verbal. Human life starts with non-verbal communication with others. On average, children under the age of two, use the production of sounds instead of words, to communicate. On the other hand, people who cannot speak use nonverbal communication too. Both children and mute people can efficiently communicate, then share information and emotions without using words.

Verbal communication is one of the most common methods used for communication. It uses words to convey information to others and provides the information of a speaker [4]. Verbal communication assists in the identification of a speaker too, but not all the time. Verbal speech specifies a speaker's accent, speaking style, and pronunciation, etc. Typically, as humans, we can identify a speaker high accuracy, but we use a combination of parameters to identify a person such as a speaker accent, speaking style, and pronunciation, etc [1, 2].

Table 1 provides the variation of human speech and how verbal communication is not mandatory for identification.

Table 1. Variations of a Human Voice.

Variation in Speech	Modulation
Types of Speech	Reading a book with normal/angry mode. Giving a lecture in a classroom
Effect of Audience	With whom we are talking such as: kids/parents/friends/lectures/strangers
Emotional States	Happy/sad/angry/excitement
Life Span	Age, Kids/adults, Teenagers/elder
Types of Voices	Laugh/cry/scream

2. Production of a Human Voice

The input for human voice is air which passes through the lungs, then through vocal cords to produce a sound as shown in Fig. 1. Sound is one of the ways of communication, but it does not help us understand what a speaker is trying to convey [7, 9]. The final product, voice/sound, is produced with the help of mouth, lips, and tongue.

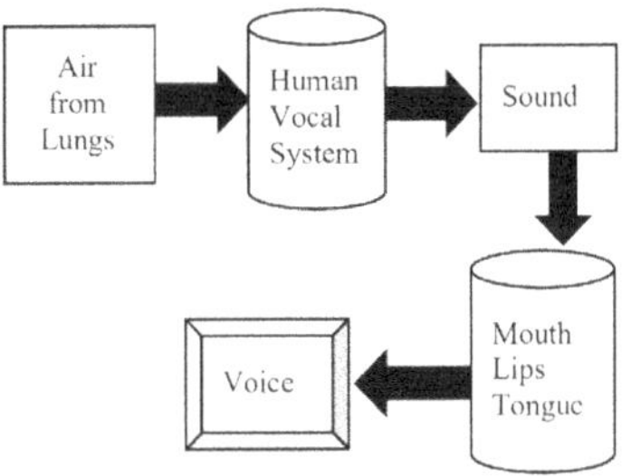

Fig. 1. Human Voice Production.

2.1. Characteristic of a Human Voice

Humans can identify a speaker, regardless of the situation. For example, imagine someone is sitting behind you. You can hear but cannot see them and cannot understand what they are talking about since you don't know the language. However, you have enough data to evaluate a speaker which includes gender, approximate age, and you can predict their emotion [5, 8]. But what necessary information is required to identify the speaker? To identify a speaker, one should be able to recognize the individual pattern of that voice [6]. There are three different characteristics of a human voice: frequency, timbre, and volume. The frequency of a voice depends on the number of vibrations of the vocal cords [10]. The vocal cords of men, who are perceived to have a lower number of vibrations per second, are normally between

100-130 vibrations per second. On the other hand, the vocal cords of women, who are perceived to have a higher number of vibrations per second, is normally between 180-220 vibrations per second. The second characteristic, the timbre, distinguishes sounds that have the same frequency and loudness (volume). Timbre is also called as tone color or tone quality. For example, each instrument has a different timbre, which is represented by comparing harmonics that are present besides the fundamental frequency. Lastly, the volume or amplitude of a voice is the vibrations that affect loudness. The higher the amplitude of the vibrations, the larger the amount of energy carried by the wave. The units of volume are measured in decibel (dB). Volume relates to how the waves, produced by the vocal cords, are amplified within the body based on factors like the speakers' mood, with whom the person is conversing, the context of the conversation, and so on.

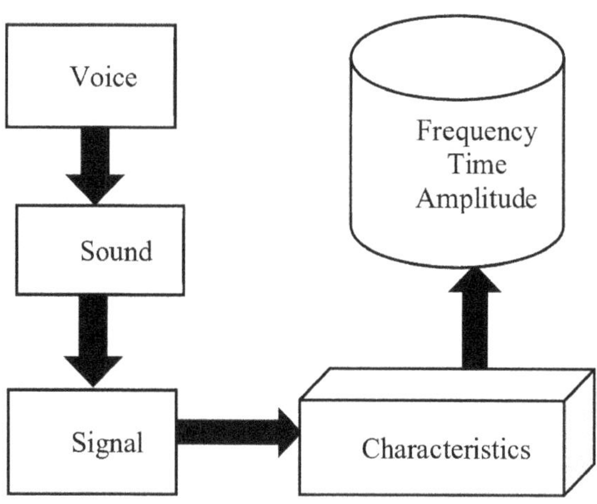

Fig. 2. Characteristics of a Voice.

3. Methodology

The experiment was conducted with the help of both female and male participants. A script was developed for participants to read a list of sentences.

The script below shows a sample of what participants will be asked to read, which will be recorded for the study. It is only an indication as further improvements may be performed before the actual running of the data gathering to improve the data set towards its final goal.

1. The boys enjoyed playing dodge ball every Wednesday;
2. Please give me a call in ten minutes;
3. I love toast and orange juice for breakfast;
4. There is heavy traffic on the highway;
5. If you listen closely, you will hear the birds;
6. My father is my inspiration for success;
7. I will be in the office in 10 minutes;
8. I will go to India to meet my parents;
9. Turn the music down in your headphones;
10. It all happened suddenly.

3.1. Initial Analysis

A proposed voice recognition system aims to generate voice patterns that are independent of spoken language. Participants voice is required to provide an input to the voice recognition system for testing and development purposes. A consent form has been prepared for the participant, explaining the purpose of research and participants are asked to go through the form before recording is started. All participants are older than 20 years and know the English language. Participants were asked to read out a script prepared by a researcher, which consists of ten sentences which include all phonemes in the English language.

3.2. Spectral Analysis

Spectrum analysis is an analysis, which provides a sound wave in terms of frequency [3]. The sound of a voice is created from vibrations produced by her/his vocal folds. By applying FFT to a participant's voice recording, the frequency of the highest peak among the participants is observed.

A person can be identified by looking at the frequency of the highest peak from the FFT waveform as shown in the table.

An additional test was performed, that is, the voice of participants were recorded at different times during the day, and on alternate days, and so on, to observe if there is any change in dominant frequency. The observed values were noted in the Table 1.

Table 1. The Frequency of highest peak per participant from Day 1 to Day 10.

Human	Min. Fre	Max. Fre	Mean	Median
1	130	140	135.5	136
2	140	145	142.8	142
3	165	170	167.2	167
4	23	28	24.9	25
5	170	177	172.3	172
6	245	272	258.1	258.5
7	410	467	436.6	444.5
8	380	430	402.5	397.5
9	340	450	368.8	363.5
10	308	350	319.9	319
11	440	510	460.8	458.5
12	660	700	675	670
13	285	346	300	290
14	220	290	246.1	235
15	45	75	57.5	57.5
16	84	90	87.7	88
17	97	124	109.5	111
18	135	160	144.8	146.5

19	195	223	202.8	196
20	123	135	128.5	127.5
21	115	150	124.7	119
22	295	345	312.5	305
23	180	220	190.6	185.5
24	207	240	214.7	210
25	95	112	100	98
26	150	181	171.2	180.5
27	250	383	332.9	361
28	254	350	299	296
29	114	320	167.1	138.5
30	243	362	305.8	312
31	173	340	231.3	212.5
32	210	2323	457	254
33	170	200	180.9	180.5
34	219	240	225.7	220
35	187	240	203.3	196
36	128	143	133.3	130
37	182	250	201.9	192.5
38	142	175	156.1	153
39	193	255	218	211.5
40	135	170	153.3	156.5
41	131	362	255.5	273
42	118	257	189.4	192
43	118	136	123.6	120.5
44	129	151	139.7	140
45	119	173	145.3	137.5
46	114	148	133.9	137
47	126	223	166.4	151
48	100	151	121	119.5
49	119	193	146	137.5
50	115	241	192.9	195
51	129	190	145.4	135
52	167	243	188.9	172.5
53	97	132	111.6	105
54	174	210	186.7	187.5
55	180	255	238.9	246.5
56	115	126	118.2	116.5
57	178	255	201.8	190
58	108	193	136.2	128.5
59	132	213	164.6	147.5
60	104	204	154.3	157.5
61	110	190	154.7	152.5
62	105	198	143.8	136.5
63	111	178	133.7	118.5
64	113	198	137.9	128.5
65	156	255	212.7	227.5
66	102	223	154.9	150
67	120	199	163.8	171
68	185	239	219.2	223
69	149	196	163	158.5
70	176	195	185.4	187
71	168	200	179.9	174
72	245	250	247.9	248
73	138	179	150	142.5
74	198	250	212.8	199.5
75	229	245	235.4	234
76	128	251	199	192.5
77	125	250	188.1	188.5
78	181	255	216.7	220.5
79	110	135	123.3	121.5
80	162	210	181.2	178.5
81	83	99	89.1	86.5
82	180	250	207.8	200.5
83	237	255	245.9	248.5
84	85	160	126.2	131.5
85	85	255	161.3	159.5
86	117	243	168.2	174
87	90	255	160.4	148.5
88	100	255	171.3	155.5
89	85	121	96.4	95
90	115	255	173.1	160
91	100	120	110.3	112
92	100	255	192.9	215.5
93	100	231	155.8	146.5
94	87	210	145.7	130.5
95	231	255	246.4	249.5
96	130	231	204.3	205.5
97	87	111	95.5	95
98	115	232	177.4	183.5
99	100	234	158.6	149
100	91	231	163.5	187

3.3. Parameters of a Human Voice

Frequency range values have been observed from Spectral anlaysis. Each person has a specific frequency range, by looking at the frequency range, we can eliminate more than half of the population. However, what if two participants have the same frequency range? What are the other parameters that one has to consider in order to identify a person.

3.3.1. Speech Rate

People communicate with each other at different speech rates. Speech rate is considered as one of the parameters to identify a speaker. A participant voice (speaking in the English language) was recorded 6 times, in a noiseless room. 100 participants were requested to read a script as shown below. However, 25 participant's speech rate was calculated and mentioned in Table 2. These observations presented which include different types of speech rates – most of them are comparatively constant and some who have varied results with each recording.

Table 2. Speech Rate per Minute.

Number of Partici-pants	Speech Rate (words per minute)					
	Recording 1	2	3	4	5	6
1	102	98	110	108	104	102
2	120	115	112	114	112	110
3	118	112	114	106	110	118
4	130	132	134	122	118	125
5	128	120	135	110	115	120
6	98	92	96	98	100	96
7	128	120	135	110	115	120
8	127	127	126	130	134	135
9	100	110	120	110	115	120
10	142	140	141	142	140	140
11	110	115	114	112	110	110
12	108	110	120	110	115	120
13	118	112	114	106	110	110
14	130	134	132	128	125	127
15	128	120	135	110	115	120
16	127	127	126	130	133	134
17	145	150	150	148	150	150
18	138	135	140	140	135	135
19	125	126	125	125	125	125
20	130	125	115	118	120	120
21	90	95	95	90	92	90
22	138	137	138	135	136	136
23	148	150	126	150	150	145
24	128	132	128	130	130	130
25	140	140	140	140	140	140

3.3.2. Accent

Accent is one of the keys to human speech to identify their locality. An accent provides various details about a speaker, such as an ethnicity, social status, and their first language. We tend to mimic a persons' accent subconsciously when they have a conversation with each other. Everyone has a unique accent in their speech community. Hence, we can use an accent to identify a speaker, however, it will be difficult if all the speakers are from the same locality.

3.3.3 Pauses

During the speech, there are two types of pauses: Pause by a user, and Natural Pause.

Pause by a user occurs:

- While giving a presentation, we make sure to give a pause in between our words to ensure the, audience is listening;
- While discussing a project topic with our supervisor/project leader;
- Depending on the context conversations.

Natural pause will occur without our knowledge or consciousness, in situations such as:

- While talking in our first language.
- Conversations with parents/family/friends.
- When giving a speech on something you are very well-versed in.

3.3.4 Speech Variation

Human voice changes over time, from birth through puberty. For example, kids/infants sound different as compared to adults. Voices sometimes change during day and night. I have recorded peoples' voices in the morning and evening time and their relative amplitude and frequency values changed based on various reasons.

- Participants are more active in the morning and they became tired by the night because of work during the daytime.
- Some participants were active in the evening since they were about to go home.
- Some participants sounded the same during morning and evening hours.

4. Results

A speaker's voice varies based on several factors and situations. However, there is a list of parameters that can be used to identify a speaker. Frequency of the highest peak is one of the parameters used to identify a speaker. Female and male participants have different frequency range. There are two ways of identifying a speaker based on frequency values. Firstly, one has to decide whether a speaker is female or male. Secondly, comparing the frequency value of a person with all the participants and, finally, eliminating the ones which do not match.

Frequency parameter helped to delete a list of people who can not be a speaker, then the next parameter would be speech rate. Participants will be eliminated based on, how many words a speaker can say in one minute and both minimum and maximum words per minute will be compared. Those who do not match will be eliminated and the list of people remaining to be compared will be narrower. Next, the accent, pronunciation and most often used words (such as some people have a tendency to use some words very often) will be compared. Eventually, the final list will contain approximately 5 people. Recogning 1 out of 100 is difficult, but identifying 1 out 5 is comparatively easy.

4. Conclusion

A speaker's voice varies in frequency, tone, and volume; enough to uniquely identify a person. However, other factors can contribute in this uniqueness: the size and shape of the mouth, throat, nose, and vocal cords. Sound is produced by air passing from the lungs through the throat, vocal cords and then mouth. A voice makes different sounds based on the position of mouth and throat.

Speaker recognition systems are already available, but their overall accuracy is limited because of several issues such as extracted features based on very short time windows of speech. Such models fail to capture useful information of a speaker since current speech recognition systems and extracted features are language-dependent. By using the voice parameters, we are able to eliminate 80 % of population to be able to identify a person.

5. References

[1]. Z. Aung, A robust speaker identification system, *International Journal of Trend in Scientific Research and Development*, Vol. 2, Issue 5, 2018, pp. 2057-2064.

[2]. N. Dehak, P. Kenny, R. Dehak, P. Dumouchel, P. Ouellet, Front-end factor analysis for speaker verification, *IEEE Transactions on Audio, Speech, and Language Processing*, Vol. 19, Issue 4, 2011, pp. 788-798.

[3]. L. Bo, Extraction of instantaneous frequency characteristic using time-frequency ridges, *Chinese Journal of Mechanical Engineering*, Vol. 44, Issue 10, 2008, 222

[4]. Y. Byelozorova, The allocation of self-similar structures in voice signals for speaker identification tasks, *Science Rise*, Vol. 5, Issue 2, 2017, pp. 22-27.

[5]. J. Přibil, A. Přibilová, J., Matoušek, Evaluation of speaker de-identification based on voice gender and age conversion, *Journal of Electrical Engineering*, Vol. 69, Issue 2, 2018, pp. 138-147.

[6]. E. Godoy, O. Rosec, T. Chonavel, Voice conversion using dynamic frequency warping with amplitude scaling, for parallel or nonparallel Corpora, *IEEE Transactions on Audio, Speech, and Language Processing*, Vol. 20, Issue 4, 2012, pp. 1313-1323.

[7]. R. Togneri, D. Pullella, An overview of speaker identification: accuracy and robustness issues, *IEEE Circuits and Systems Magazine*, Vol. 11, Issue 2, 2011, pp. 23-61.

[8]. S. Badhe Sanjay, S. R. Gulhane, S. D. Shirbahadurkar, Analysis of spectral features for speaker clustering, *International Journal of Innovative Technology and Exploring Engineering*, Vol. 8, Issue 93, 2019, pp. 134-137.

[9]. J. Ming, T. Hazen, J. Glass, D. Reynolds, Robust speaker recognition in noisy conditions, *IEEE Transactions on Audio, Speech and Language Processing*, Vol. 15, Issue 5, 2007, pp. 1711-1723.

[10]. H. Gao, Q. Ma, X. Zheng, Recognition feature extraction based on little speech data for speaker under noisy conditions, *Journal of Computer Applications*, Vol. 30, Issue 10, 2010, pp. 2712-2714.

[11]. S. Kinkiri, S. Keates, Identification of a speaker from familiar and unfamiliar voices, in *Proceedings of the 5th International Conference on Robotics and Artificial Intelligence (ICRAI'19)*, 2019, pp. 94-97.

(067)

AI in Gastronomic Tourism

G. Pavlidis [1], S. Markantonatou [1], K. Toraki [1], A. Vacalopoulou [1], C. Strouthopoulos[2], D. Varsamis [2], A. Tsimpiris [2], S. Mouroutsos [3], C. Kiourt [1], V. Sevetlidis [1] and P. Minos [1]
[1] Athena Research Centre, University Campus at Kimmeria, GR-67100, Xanthi, Greece
[2] International Hellenic University, Terma Magnisias, GR-62124, Serres, Greece
[3] Democritus University of Thrace, University Campus at Kimmeria, GR-67100, Xanthi, Greece
Tel.: + 302541078787, fax: + 302541063656
E-mail: gpavlid@athenarc.gr

Summary: Gastronomy is increasingly becoming a decisive flavour of tourists' experience. Tourists' gastronomic experience could be significantly enhanced by AI tools that provide image-based dish recognition and menu translation, thus covering the basic needs of tourists during a visit that involves culinary experiences. This paper presents and discusses solutions explored with the project GRE-Taste that deals with the enhancement of culinary tourism experience in northern Greece, for which no linguistic resources exist and where general-purpose tools fail.

Keywords: Dish recognition, Menu translation, Gastronomic tourism, AI, OCR, CNN, PureFoodNet.

---

1. Introduction

Food is both an essential commodity and a social and cultural heritage. According to [1] food is as vital to human health and well-being as all other products together and this is the main reason why so much importance is attached to it. This work also suggests that food plays a multi-functional connective role in society and that sustainable food systems support sustainable communities. Food influences peoples' lifestyle, health and habits as well as the design model for land, water, energy, transport and ecosystem services. *Gastronomy* and cooking are gradually becoming more and more important multidimensional societal factors. In 2014, the European Parliament's Committee on Culture and Education adopted a movement on "European culinary heritage: cultural and educational aspects"[1], which recognizes the importance of food and gastronomy as an artistic and cultural expression and proclaims them fundamental pillars of family and social relationships[2].

In the context of events organized by the S3 Platform[3] international experts proclaimed food an element of smart specialization in EU countries and regions and addressed food innovation issues as a driving force for smart regional development [2].

According to [3], *gastronomic tourism is a visit to primary and secondary producers of food and beverages, gastronomy festivals, dining venues and specific locations, where tasting and experience of specialty local food features are a prime motivation for the visit.*

Nowadays, the culinary aspect of tourism is prominent with a growing tendency in the next decade, whereas mass tourism seems to have reached a tipping point, as the quest of individual experiences is taking over [4]. This implies that the tourist will seek the pleasure of discovering tastes along with the cultural traits of foods in their local settings rather than being directed to pre-selected restaurants. To fully enable tourists to savour foods and experience the cultural context in local settings one has to draw on two resources, namely rich visual content [5] and knowledge of details of a foreign language and scripture. This requirement goes even further if knowledge of the materials, dietary properties, cooking techniques and, health issues come into play. Accordingly, two challenges present themselves, namely image-based content recognition and classification—*food image recognition*, and language-based knowledge mining and translation—*menu translation*. This paper presents the path followed to address these challenges within the GRE-Taste project that targets culinary tourism and food tradition in northern Greece[4].

2. Food Image Classification

Food (dish) image classification is a particular challenge due to the visual and the semantic complexity stemming from the variation in the mixing of ingredients practiced by regional communities [6], [7]. Although a multitude of applications, algorithms

---

[1] European gastronomic heritage: cultural and educational aspects, http://www.europarl.europa.eu/sides/getDoc.do?type=TA&reference=P7-TA-2014-0211&language=EN&ring=A7-2014-0127

[2] European gastronomic heritage: cultural and educational aspects, http://www.europarl.europa.eu/sides/getDoc.do?type=TA&reference=P7-TA-2014-0211&language=EN&ring=A7-2014-0127

[3] S3 Platform provides aid in the development and application of smart specialization strategies (RIS3) in Europe, http://s3platform.jrc.ec.europa.eu/s3-platform

[4] GRE-Taste project website @ http://gre-taste.ceti.gr

and systems is now available, recognizing dishes and their ingredients is a problem that has not been fully addressed by the machine learning and computer vision communities [6], basically due to the lack of distinctive spatial layout in food images. Ingredients, say of a salad, constitute mixtures that typically come in different shapes and sizes; furthermore, often the nature of a dish is defined by the different colours, shapes and textures of the ingredients [8]. Solutions to this problem have been proposed that exploit a range of innovative ideas; recently deep learning techniques produce remarkably successful results.

In GRE-Taste the problem is even more challenging, as traditional and regional Greek food and dish images have not been used to develop models in the past. Apparently, since the project targets tourism and mobile device apps, several restrictions apply regarding the storage and processing power availability. Given this context, three alternatives have been explored, (a) the development of a totally new architecture based on CNNs, (b) the application of transfer learning and fine-tuning of existing models, and (c) the usage of online deep learning platforms. The first scenario included the development of a new CNN architecture, the *PureFoodNet*, which consists of three convolutional and one classification blocks (as shown in Fig. 1) [9]. To implement the second scenario, VGG16 [10], InceptionV3 [11], ResNet50 [12], InceptionResNetV2 [13], MobileNetV2 [14], DenseNet121 [15], and NASNetLarge [16] have being used. The third scenario included the experiments on Google Vision AI[1] (VAI), Clarifai[2] (CAI), Amazon Rekognition[3] (AR) and Microsoft Computer Vision[4] (MCV) platforms.

As deep learning approaches rely heavily on existing data, the first issue to be tackled was the selection of an appropriate dataset that would aid in the recognition of Greek dishes; however, such a dataset does not exist. The most popular datasets consist of general/universal food categories, whereas some are only regional (like UECFood100/256). A relevant image collection and photo-shooting task was initiated and has not been completed yet. Thus, the results presented in this study are based on the usage of the popular Food101 dataset, which was created around 2015 and includes 101 food categories with 101,000 food images.

In the first set of experiments (scenarios a and b), PureFoodNet was tested against VGG16, InceptionV3, ResNet50, InceptionResNetV2, MobileNetV2, DenseNet121 and NASNetLarge. Fig. 2 graphically depicts the accuracy attained by each model (left) in terms of categorical top-1 and top-5 performance for training and validation ("val" denotes the validation phase), along with a graph of the number of epochs needed during training respectively (right). Apparently, most of the models performed quite well, with the worst validation accuracy observed for the VGG16 model, which was also among the slowest ones. In addition, although NASNetLarge showed an excellent performance it needed 83.33 % more time and around 92 % more time than the PureFoodNet.

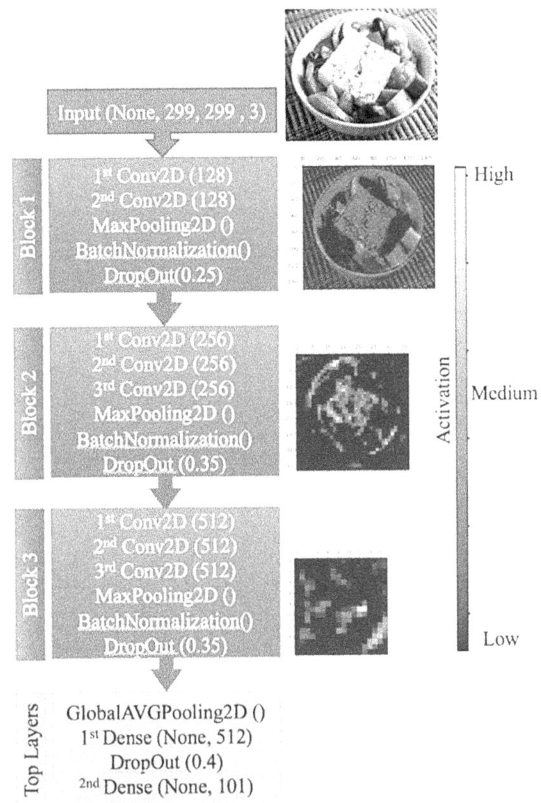

Fig. 1. The PureFoodNet architecture for traditional Greek food recognition.

PureFoodNet performed quite well even though it was not the best, but it was definitely the most light-weight, time/resource consuming approach. Furthermore, due to its low complexity, PureFoodNet is one of the most easily customisable and tuneable models for further studies.

For the second set of experiments (scenario c), two test images were selected (typical Greek salad and a fruit desert) to compare the performance of the online AI platforms; and the task also included reporting on the ingredients of the dish. The performance of each platform is shown in Fig. 3, in which green denotes an acceptable response, red denotes an unacceptable response and white an irrelevant response. Apparently, MCV and AR performed rather poorly, whereas VAI was somewhat better. CAI performed significantly better, basically because it had been designed for the specific task of food recognition.

[1] Google Vision AI @ https://cloud.google.com/vision/
[2] Clarifai @ https://clarifai.com
[3] Amazon Rekognition @ https://aws.amazon.com/recognition/
[4] Microsoft Computer Vision @ https://www.microsoft.com/cognitive-services

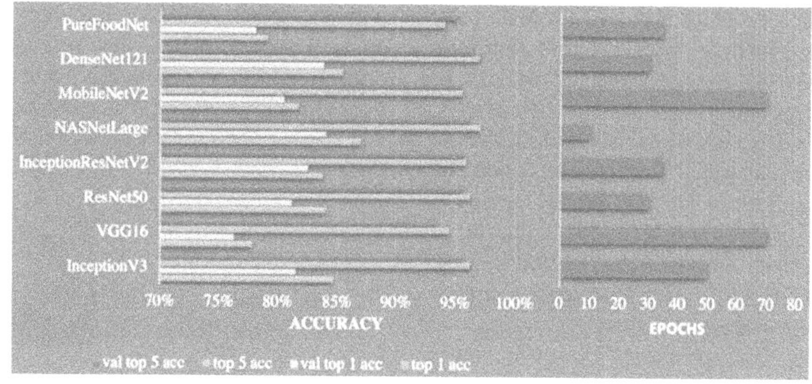

Fig. 2. Comparison of popular deep architectures with PureFoodNet in food recognition.

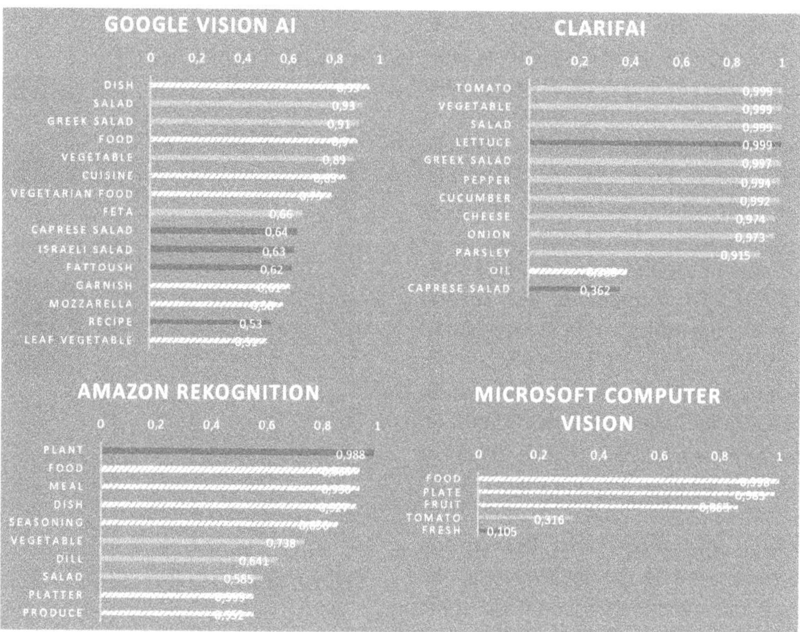

Fig. 3. Results on food recognition image A by the reviewed platforms.

3. Menu Translation

Greece boasts a wealth of local foods and drinks that form part of a rich cultural context and contribute to the gastronomic aspect of the local tourism industry. Greek, however, is not a widely spoken language and has its own alphabet that renders menu understanding difficult for the average tourist. At the moment, only some guided tours are available that focus on the gastronomy aspect while gastronomy-related tours enhanced with the cultural traits of food are even rarer. To date, no relevant electronic applications are available.

Current solutions to the linguistic problem of culinary tourist experience focus (a) on providing restaurants with on-demand menu translations [17], or (b) on machine translation of menus, such as the Word Lens [18] and the Purdue Menu Translator [19]. Nevertheless, it should be stressed that despite any technical details, machine translation approaches require special databases for each language and none of them includes Greek (yet). Eventually, Greek have to make do with solutions like Google Images, Google Translate, BabelNet and Wikipedia. In addition, understanding a menu is not a terminological problem only, it has to do with the way menus are written and on the contextual knowledge required to fully appreciate a type of food.

In GRE-Taste the workflow for the menu translation consists of two main parts, one that deals with the optical character recognition (OCR) in menu photos and another that deals with the content translation (Fig. 4). Currently, the OCR part of the workflow is explored using (a) online services, APIs and engines, like Google Vision AI, Tesseract and ABBYY and (b) in-house research. The translation part involves the development of a tri-lingual thesaurus of foods, nutritional and cultural information and the translation engine itself. The Greek food ontology will stand on top of the system to aid in the correct multi-lingual food translation, although it is currently in a form of a multi-lingual thesaurus.

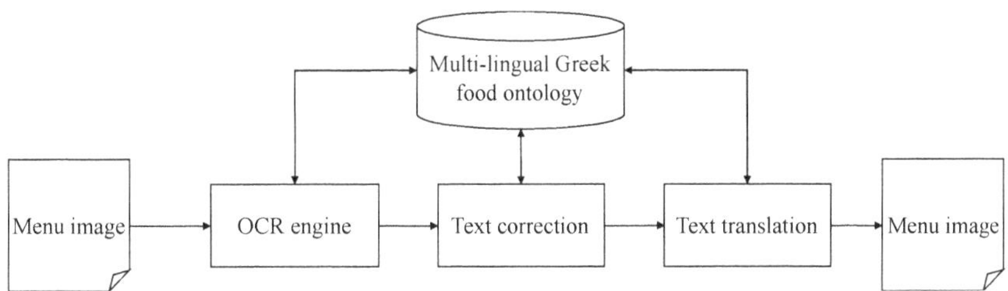

Fig. 4. The menu translation workflow in GRE-Taste.

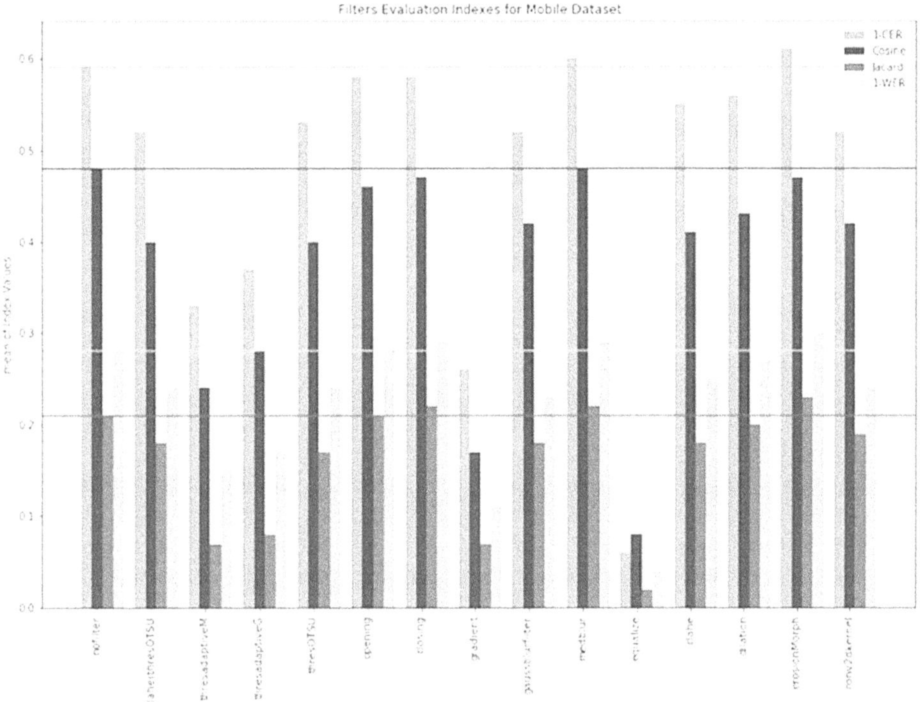

Fig. 5. Average performance results for 15 pre-filtering methods in 1-CERi, 1-WERi, cosine and Jaccard indices.

The OCR problem relates with the identification of text in images. There is a rich bibliography on this challenge and various text detection approaches have been developed that successfully identify texts of interest in complex images [20]. Recently, this research was expanded to accommodate the needs of food and meal applications by recognising text in menu images[1] [21-23]. In GRE-Taste the focus is on identifying text in menu photos shot with any mobile phone cameras, in any lighting conditions. This may include under/over-exposed photos with a partially captured menu in an arbitrary orientation, which, in many cases, includes heavy combinations of graphics, photos, printed and handwritten text. Since this is something like a worst-case usage scenario in OCR, the GRE-Taste team focused the efforts and conducted a number of experiments in this direction of devising an image pre-processing strategy whose output will feed a state-of-the-art OCR system, like the Tesseract[2] [24]. A number of filtering techniques have been compared, including several thresholding approaches, morphological operations, global and adaptive gradient approaches, Gaussian techniques and wiener filtering [25-30]. Preliminary experiments have been conducted on a mixture of general-purpose text images and Greek menu images collected and annotated by the GRE-Taste team[3]. Fig. 5 shows the cosine, Jaccard, CER and WER indices [31-33] as the average performance results of Tesseract OCR empowered with the pre-processing methods on a subset of 80 menu images. Horizontal lines denote the corresponding index value attained without any pre-filtering. Apparently, there is a slight improvement in the results for the case of erosion and median blurring in almost all indices.

[1] See for example https://apkpure.com/foodtranslator/com.foodwandering.android.foodtranslator, https://apkpure.com/foodie-for-all/com.uos.kyungimlee.myapplication based on Google Vision https://cloud.google.com/vision/.

[2] https://github.com/tesseract-ocr/

[3] It should be stressed that these tests only included a limited dataset as the data collection process is still underway.

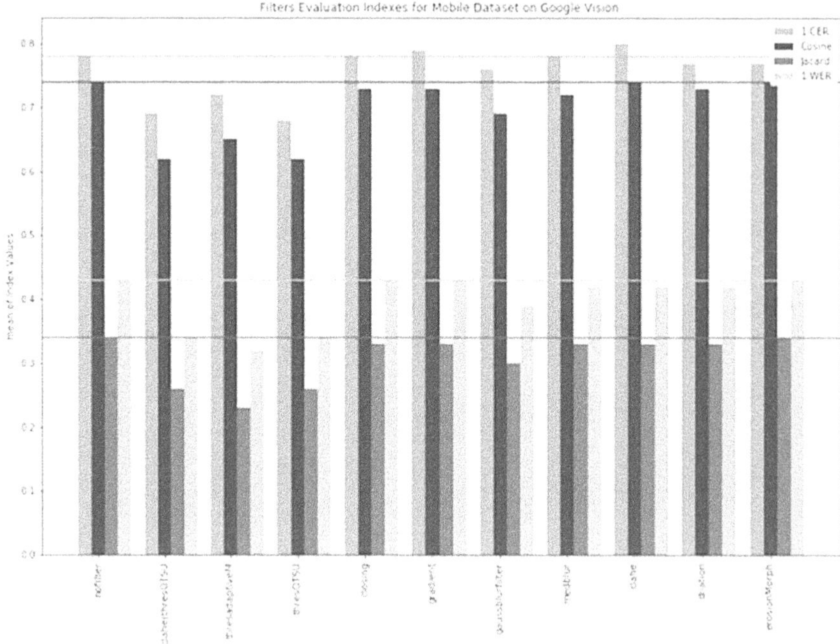

Fig. 6. Average performance results for 11 pre-filtering methods in 1-CERi, 1-WERi, cosine and Jaccard indices using the Google Vison AI.

Repeating these experiments in the Google Vision platform for the 11 pre-filtering strategies, the average results shown in Fig. 6 were obtained, again in terms of the 1-CERi, cosine, Jaccard and 1-WERi indices. It is evident that gradient-based filtering and contrast-limited adaptive histogram equalization gave a slight improvement at least in the 1-CERi index. It is also evident in both experiments that for a very limited number of pre-filtering cases only there was an improvement, basically due to the inner processes in Tesseract and Google Vision AI.

It should be mentioned that, although Google Vision AI achieved about 20 % better performance than the customized Tesseract application, its usage in relevant applications may be prohibited because of the charging policy adopted by its developers.

The core of the menu translation challenge consists in rendering the text the menus into a predetermined language; this complicated problem involves translation of the information that is explicit in the menus, namely names of dishes and their ingredients, and provision of dietary and cultural information that is implicit in the menus. The menu translation problem is mostly a terminological one and, precisely for this reason, GRE-Taste has focused on the development of a trilingual thesaurus of foods served in restaurants and taverns of northern Greece. A dedicated web terminographical environment was developed[1] that (a) accommodates texts retrieved from 120 restaurant/tavern/pastry shop menus of the study area and (b) enables the development of a thesaurus that models information on dishes, ingredients, courses in a meal, source of food and part of it, cooking methods in addition to nutritional and cultural information. Currently, the thesaurus contains 3072 Greek and English terms designating 1405 concepts that are connected with 2660 relation instances.

Overall, GRE-Taste will result in a multi-faceted thesaurus for Greek gastronomy for the first time. Some of the issues GRE-Taste takes into account are:

- Varieties in culinary language related with dialectic forms, local specialties, etc;
- Dish variations, leading to the definition of specific types of dishes, e.g. "stifado" and "rabbit/beef/cuttlefish stifado";
- Synecdoche and ambiguity, i.e. when the same word denotes both the food and its source, e.g. "lettuce", which may be used to name the vegetable as a plant, the vegetable as an ingredient of a salad or the lettuce salad;
- Categorization of dishes, i.e. some dishes may need to be classified under more than one general category (facet), e.g. "papoutsakia", literary small shoes, "eggplant with minced meat" may be classified both as meat dishes and vegetable dishes.

Dealing with the above, mainly terminological, issues ensures that users will be able to select dishes according to their liking and their specific needs and peculiarities.

The translation procedure strongly relies on the thesaurus; it also uses existing home-made multilingual dictionaries of the general language, part of speech recognition and lemmatization performed with the ILSP tools for Greek[2], whereas automata

[1] http://gretaste.ilsp.gr/

[2] http://nlp.ilsp.gr/soaplab2-axis/

implementing simple grammar rules are currently being developed. The first translation toy experiments[1] suggest that the adopted approach has a significant potential to outperform Google Translate only by using its lexical resources and lemmatising facilities (no other linguistic knowledge) provided that the thesaurus can cover the terminological demands of the menu.

4. Conclusions

Culinary and gastronomic tourism are increasingly gaining momentum in the tourism industry as food is an important factor of social life and culture. Generic AI tools, such as machine translation and image-based recognition, can provide some aid to the tourist but still with significant limitations and high levels of generalization that leads to fails in traditional, ethnic or regional settings.

GRE-Taste is a project focusing on developing new workflows and AI tools to address the main issues in this domain for a particular region of interest with rich cultural context. New methods for dish recognition and menu translation have been designed with promising results. The PureFoodNet system that was developed is able to provide accurate dish recognition with low processing and storage demands[2]. In addition, the lack of language resources has been addressed with the development of a completely new multi-faceted thesaurus for the Greek gastronomy in the general cultural context.

Acknowledgements

This research has been co□financed by the European Regional Development Fund of the European Union and Greek national funds through the Operational Program Competitiveness, Entrepreneurship and Innovation, under the call RESEARCH – CREATE – INNOVATE (project code: T1EDK-02015). We also gratefully acknowledge the support of NVIDIA Corporation with the donation of the Titan Xp GPU used for the experiments of this research.

References

[1]. K. Morgan, Local and green, global and fair: the ethical foodscape and the politics of care, *Environment and Planning A*, Vol. 42, Issue 8, 2010, pp. 1852-1867.

[2]. A. Cavicchi, K. C. Stancova, Food and gastronomy as elements of regional innovation strategies, *Institute for Prospective and Technological Studies, Joint Research Centre,* Sevilla, 2016.

[3]. C. Mitchel Hall, L. Sharples, R. Mitchel, N. Macionis, and B. Cambourne, Food Tourism Around the World: Development, Management and Markets, *Elsevier, Ltd,* Burligton, USA, 2003.

[4]. Skift Team – The Ontario Culinary Tourism Alliance, Free Report: The Rise of Food Tourism, Free Report: The Rise of Food Tourism, https://skift.com/insight/free-report-the-rise-of-food-tourism/

[5]. D. Jurafsky, The Language of Food: A Linguist Reads the Menu, *WW Norton & Company*, 2014.

[6]. M. Weiqing, J. Shuqiang, L. Linhu, R. Yong, J. Ramesh, A Survey on Food Computing, *ACM Computing Surveys*, 2019.

[7]. S. Mezgec, S. Koroušić, NutriNet: A deep learning food and drink image recognition system for dietary assessment, *Nutrients*, Vol. 9, Issue 657, 2017, E657.

[8]. G. Ciocca, P. Napoletano, R. Schettini, CNN-based features for retrieval and classification of food images, *Computer Vision and Image Understanding*, Vol. 176-177, 2018, pp. 70-77.

[9]. C. Kiourt, G. Pavlidis, S. Markantonatou, Deep learning approaches in food recognition, in Machine Learning Paradigms – Advances in Theory and Applications of Deep Learning, *Springer*, 2020.

[10]. K. Simonyan, A. Zisserman, Very deep convolutional networks for large-scale image recognition, in *Proceedings of the 3rd IAPR Asian Conference on Pattern Recognition (ACPR'15)*, 2015.

[11]. C. Szegedy, V. Vanhoucke, S. Ioffe, J. Shlens, Z. Wojna, Rethinking the inception architecture for computer vision, in *Proceedings of the IEEE Conference on Computer Vision and Pattern Recognition (CVPR'16)*, 2016, pp. 2818-2826.

[12]. K. He, X. Zhang, S. Ren, J. Sun, Deep residual learning for image recognition, in *Proceedings of the IEEE Conference on Computer Vision and Pattern Recognition (CVPR'16)*, 2016, pp. 770-778.

[13]. C. Szegedy, S. Ioffe, V. Vanhoucke, A. A. Alemi, Inception-v4, inception-ResNet and the impact of residual connections on learning, in *Proceedings of the Thirty-First Conference on Artificial Intelligence (AAAI'17)*, 2017, pp. 4278-4284.

[14]. M. Sandler, A. Howard, M. Zhu, A. Zhmoginov, C. L, and C., MobileNetV2: Inverted residuals and linear bottlenecks, in *Proceedings of the IEEE Conference on Computer Vision and Pattern Recognition (CVPR'18)*, 2018, pp. 4510-4520.

[15]. G. Huang, Z. Liu, L. van der Maaten, K. Weinberger, Densely connected convolutional networks, in *Proceedings of the IEEE Conference on Pattern Recognition and Computer Vision (CVPR'17)*, 2017, pp. 2261-2269.

[16]. B. Zoph, V. Vasudevan, J. Shlens, V. Le, Learning transferable architectures for scalable image recognition, in *Proceedings of the IEEE Conference on Computer Vision and Pattern Recognition (CVPR'18)*, 2018.

[17]. TranslateMyMenu, Translate My Menu – Menu translation service, https://translatemymenu.com/en_US

[18]. Wikipedia, Word Lens, *Wikipedia*, 20-October-2019.

[1] These experiments included the selection of a menu, the lemmatisation of the Greek text and the verbatim translation.

[2] A cross-platform online version of the system can be found in http://gre-taste.ceti.gr/webapp/. The system can be used on a mobile device as a service and can be easily ported to a native mobile app.

[19]. Purdue University, New translator app makes sense of foreign-language food menus, https://www.purdue.edu/newsroom/research/2011/110908BoutinMenutranslate.html

[20]. X. Zhou, *et al.*, EAST: an efficient and accurate scene text detector, in *Proceedings of the IEEE Conference on Computer Vision and Pattern Recognition (CVPR'17)*, 2017, pp. 5551-5560.

[21]. W. Swastika, H. Setiawan, M. Subianto, Android based application for recognition of Indonesian restaurant menus using convolution neural network, in *Proceedings of the International Conference on Sustainable Information Engineering and Technology (SIET'17)*, 2017, pp. 30-34.

[22]. W. Min, S. Jiang, L. Liu, Y. Rui, R. Jain, A survey on food computing, *ArXiv Preprint*, arXiv:1808.07202, 2018.

[23]. R. Ullah, A. Sohani, A. Rai, F. Ali, R. Messier, OCR engine to extract food-items, prices, quantity, units from receipt images, heuristics rules based approach, *International Journal of Scientific & Engineering Research*, Vol. 9, Issue 2, 2018, pp. 1334-1341.

[24]. R. Smith, Tesseract Open Source OCR Engine, GitHub, https://github.com/tesseract-ocr/tesseract

[25]. N. Otsu, A threshold selection method from gray-level histograms, *IEEE Transactions on Systems, Man, and Cybernetics*, Vol. 9, Issue 1, 1979, pp. 62-66.

[26]. B. Hunt, A matrix theory proof of the discrete convolution theorem, *IEEE Transactions on Audio and Electroacoustics*, Vol. 19, Issue 4, 1971, pp. 285-288.

[27]. C. A. Glasbey, G. W. Horgan, Image Analysis for the Biological Sciences, Vol. 1, *Wiley*, Chichester, 1995.

[28]. F. Orieux, J.-F. Giovannelli, T. Rodet, Bayesian estimation of regularization and point spread function parameters for Wiener-Hunt deconvolution, *JOSA A*, Vol. 27, Issue 7, 2010, pp. 1593-1607.

[29]. E. D. Pisano, *et al.*, Contrast limited adaptive histogram equalization image processing to improve the detection of simulated spiculations in dense mammograms, *Journal of Digital imaging*, Vol. 11, Issue 4, 1998, 193.

[30]. K. Zuiderveld, Contrast limited adaptive histogram equalization, *Graphics gems IV*, 1994, pp. 474-485.

[31]. S. V. Rice, J. Kanai, T. A. Nartker, An Evaluation of OCR Accuracy, Annual Research Report, *Information Science Research Institute*, Vol. 9, 1993.

[32]. J. W. Ratcliff, D. E. Metzener, Pattern-matching-the gestalt approach, *Dr Dobbs Journal*, Vol. 13, Issue 7, 1988, 46.

[33]. V. I. Levenshtein, Binary codes capable of correcting deletions, insertions, and reversals, *Soviet Physics Doklady*, Vol. 10, 1966, pp. 707-710.

Software Development Analysis for Energy Efficiency Using Process Metrics

A. Kruglov, D. Atonge, D. Strugar, G. Succi [1], S. Ergasheva and X. Vasquez
[1] Innopolis University, Universitetskaya st., 1, 420500 Innopolis, Russia
Tel.: + 79089094353
E-mail: a.kruglov@innopolis.ru

Summary: The InnoMetrics project aims at building and validating a quantitative framework to assess and guide the software development teams using process metrics collected non-invasively throughout the life-cycle of software systems, from the initial concept to the deployment, execution, and maintenance taking into consideration energy concerns, which play a pivotal role in the success of applications and infrastructures. In this paper, we report the early experience we have in its development together with the data of developers' activities that we have obtained so far, including running processes and applications, user actions in browser or IDE and associated energy consumption.

Keywords: Non-invasive measurement, Granular computation, Energy efficiency, Software development, Process metrics.

---

1. Introduction

An important role in the design of energy-efficient systems takes the analysis of values of the basic parameters (metrics) of energy consumption. Software metrics are quantitative measures of specific attributes of software development, including software process, product and resource metrics [1, 2]. There are several kinds of product metrics, based on the analysis of source code, developed during the past few decades for different programming paradigms such as structured programming and object-oriented programming (OOP). To provide a novelty approach on energy efficiency assessment of the software product, we focused on the development process analysis metrics [2]. However, the group of process metrics has not properly been observed yet [3]. One of the reasons for this is the absence of a tool for sufficient analysis of the development process [2]. Usually, such a process involves the participation of the developer which is called an invasive measurement collection method [4], where we faced the problem of subjective measurement. Furthermore, it in turns leads to the increase of time costs of the project as far as it requires the personal involvement of the developers where switching between tasks can be disturbing and time consuming activity. Thus, software metrics collection in a non-invasive way – where metrics are collected in an automatic way, without developers' intervention – is claimed as promising approaches in this area [5-7]. This approach allows us to track a variety of software development process factors affecting its efficiency and calculate it in real-time. The advantages of this approach can be:

- Process is analyzed continuously and not on a punctual basis;
- The granularity of the data derived can be maximized opposed to invasive metric collection method;
- Process itself will proceed without interrupting the developers from the main workflow, hence the data can be collected more reliably [2].

Moreover, the toolkit integrates with the most used software development environment and office applications. Development of the framework which provides a non-invasive way of collecting software development process metrics could result in a set of vital metrics and development effort patterns. Using effective visualization of the results of data analysis, one can get sufficient insights into the development process and its energy efficiency.

2. Energy Metrics

The InnoMetrics system is basically developed based on the monitoring of the software development process energy efficiency and the developers' teams productivity.

In general, all studies in energy-related metrics [3] were devoted to the real measurement and model-based measurement. As these kinds of measurements involve usage of third-party hardware tools to get energy metrics from various components, we considered them as out of the scope of our non-invasive software development process analysis approach. The study suggests that code analysis is thoroughly analysed, nonetheless, the group of process metrics was not properly explored. The main reason for this insufficient analysis of process measurements is the absence of the tool. Furthermore, the process cost increases since, usually it requires the developers' participation.

Application energy consumption is dependent on a wide variety of system resources and conditions. Energy consumption depends on but is not limited to, the processor, the device uses, memory architecture, the storage technologies used, the display technology used, the size of the display, the network interface that you are connected to, active sensors, and various conditions like the signal strength used for data transfer, user settings like screen brightness levels, and many more user and system settings [8].

For precise energy consumption measurements, one needs specialized hardware [9]. While they provide the best method to accurately measure energy consumption on a particular device, such a methodology is not scalable in practice, especially if such measurements have to be made on multiple devices. Even then, the measurements by themselves will not provide much insight into how the application contributes to the battery drainage, making it hard to focus on any application optimization efforts.

The InnoMetrics system aims at enabling users to estimate their application's energy consumption without the need for specialized hardware. Such estimation is made possible using a software power model that has been trained on a reference device representative of the low powered devices applications might run on.

Based on the findings of the research, metrics like following were investigated [3]:

- Software Energy Consumption (SEC) – the total energy consumed by the software;
- Unit Energy Consumption (UEC) – the energy consumed by a specific unit of the software.

Considering our profiling method and the tools available for us, the ability to attribute the energy consumption was possible only at the process level in coarse granularity. However, the hardware resource usage can fill the gap when it comes to accurately relating Energy Consumption (EC) to individual software elements hence enabling the computation of the UEC.

To evaluate the Unit Energy Consumption (UEC) the following hardware resources should be monitored:

- Hard disk: disk bytes/sec, disk read bytes/sec, disk write bytes/sec;
- Processor: percentage of processor usage;
- Memory: private bytes, working set, private working set;
- Network: bytes total/sec, bytes sent/sec, bytes received/sec;
- IO: IO data (bytes/sec), IO read (bytes/sec), IO write (bytes/sec).

Attributing some weights to elements of the UEC or by some reliable assumption such as considering the power model to be linear in nature for each individual component, the SEC Metric is computed.

The bottleneck in this situation is that it is difficult to match up constantly changing application process IDs and names. The energy consumption of the system depends on a variety of factors that are not limited to those which can be collected using the above mentioned performance classes.

3. System Description

The framework for the non-invasive approach for software metrics collection and analysis consists of three parts, which were defined in a high-level of abstraction of the general architecture from a logical point of view (see Fig. 1):

- Data Collectors, for collecting data from different OS types;
- Server, which includes the analytic module for quantitative and qualitative analysis of the obtained data;
- Dashboard, for a visual representation of information about the development process.

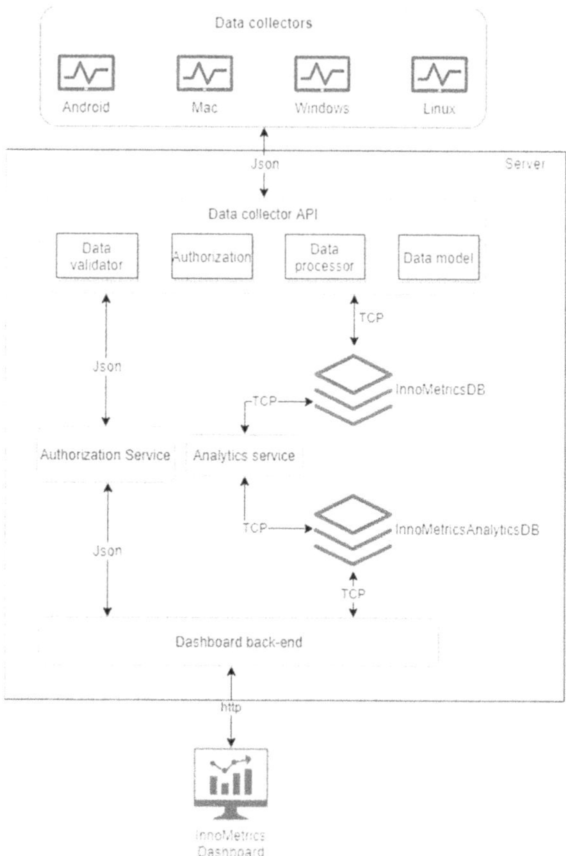

Fig. 1. System architecture. Logical view.

In general, the architecture has 3 main parts mentioned above, however, the detailed information of all components separately will be described throughout this section.

The data collectors in the architecture are a set of services developed for major operating systems, in which they have the main aim of monitoring the activities that users perform on their devices, and collect the data needed to calculate and analyze the energy consumption of the device under usage and the process efficiency.

DataCollector API is the main point of interaction for the data collection components with the centralized database, in the same way, this API handles the outgoing notifications to these components.

Innometrics Database, the information repository in which the raw information collected is stored, which will be transformed and analyzed through the Analytics service.

Analytic service is an automatic data transformation process, whose main purpose is to take the raw collected data and transform it to perform a much faster analysis process, without impacting the performance of the transactional database. Whereas in InnoMetrics Analytics Database, the analysis of the information collected is carried out, which will not have the information in real-time, but a periodic load of the information collected and transformed will be performed. Finally, the Dashboard backend component provides an interface between the presentation layer and the analysis database.

The interface of the system is a small control module where the users are in charge of a specific project have the ability to visualize information with the help of graphs, charts, and maps. InnoMetrics Dashboard is a web system, focused on visualizing the analyzed information based on the obtained data from collectors during the development process. The analyzed data can play a vital role in the Agile software development process optimization which helps in the decision-making process. In addition, it will have a small module to manage the system settings like automatic data transfer based on the time interval the user set, the users' ability to send error reports to the developers and ease of collected metrics modification.

Before analysis of the application design methods, the set of functional and non-functional requirements were established in terms of the system implementation. These requirements and the constraints under which the system should operate and be developed have distinctive features from other software metrics collection systems. The main functionality that our system defines is the energy-related metrics collection and analysis. Based on these process metrics, the energy efficiency prediction and development process optimization can be of paramount importance.

In order to provide quality attributes like scalability, fault-tolerance, and adaptability to new requirements of the system, it is based on a microservices architecture with two main access points and a series of specialized services such as Analytic services, Administration services, Authorization service, etc.

For an initial deployment of the solution, there is a server that will host all the services (see Fig. 2).

The user devices here in the figure are tracked by the data collection components that are only focused on data collection, storage, and transmission. While manager component represents the user with a manager role of each project to where they have access to a dashboard where they can easily monitor the performance of their work team from the information collected.

The DataCollector service is mainly in charge of providing an interface of communication for the different data collectors so they can store data in our data repository. Additionally, providing a notification interface to send information from the core system to these external components.

AuthorizationService component specializes in the authentication and authorization of users, generation and validation of tokens that are required to process any request that is processed by the different services within the system.

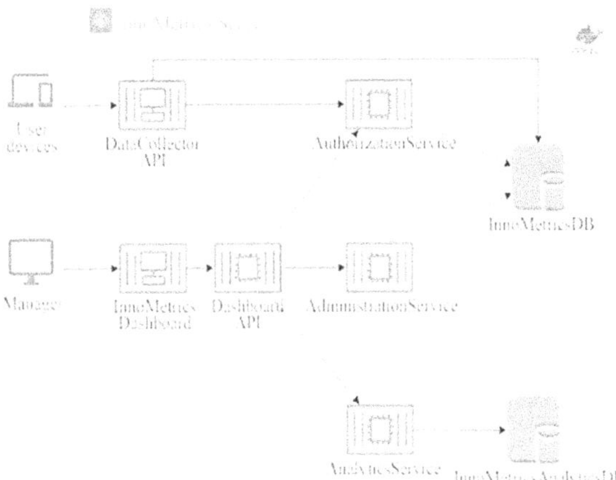

Fig. 2. System architecture. Physical view.

DashboardAPI is responsible for providing the necessary data to generate graphics within the dashboard. AdministrationService provides the functionalities that allow you to make configurations within the system, such as user and role administration, configure the frequency with which the data analysis process is executed, among others.

Administration Service provides the functionalities that allow the users to make configurations within the system, such as user and role administration, configure the frequency with which the data analysis process is executed, etc.

AnalyticsService is in charge of carrying out the data transformations to generate the information required by end-users.

With the purpose to provide an agile way to deploy and scale the system, Docker container is used as a virtualization engine, having OpenJDK as the main JVM of the services and Postgres as RDBMS.

The diagram in Fig. 3 provides a high-level perspective on the implementation of the API used by the data collector components, which is being developed under the Spring Boot framework, taking functionalities such as Spring boot security for user validation processes and authorization, Spring boot Data as a persistence engine. And additionally, there is the support of third-party libraries that will be described later.

Within the *controller* package are the classes to be exposed as REST services, which are divided into 3 classes:

- *AdminAPI* exposes those methods that are related to the administration of users, roles and system configurations;
- *AuthAPI* provides the mechanisms for user authentication and token generation;

- *DataCollectorAPI*, the controller in charge of exposing the methods that are used by the different collection modules for the transmission of data to the central repository.

Following the structure proposed in the spring boot architecture, the services layer contains the business logic needed in each of the processes exposed by the controllers and also provides an abstraction layer between the controllers that make use of DTO (Data Transfer Objects) and the persistence layer that naturally map the entities contained in the database.

Using the functionalities provided by the implementation of JPA in spring boot through the *JPARepository* interface, this layer contains the persistence interfaces of the entities modeled within the entity package.

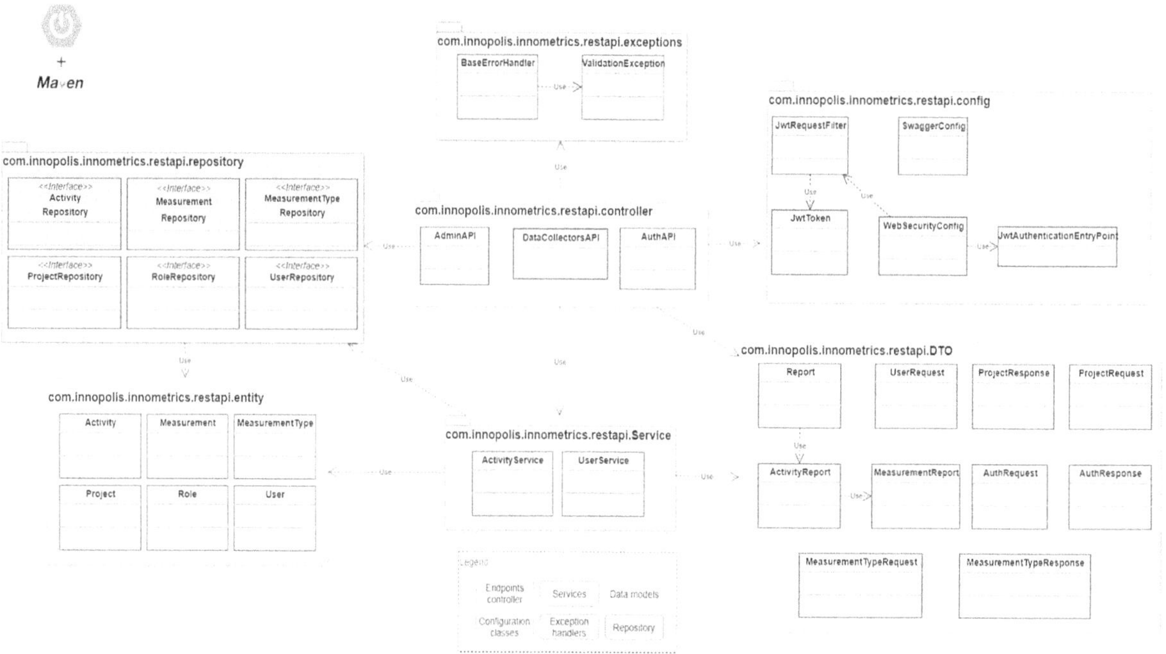

Fig. 3. System technical architecture.

In the *entity* package, we have the models of the entities that are involved in the data collection process, which are an abstraction of the database entities.

The *DTO* layer models the objects used in the request and response processes of each method exposed in the controller layer, this layer allows us to decouple the data collection components and the model that is being persisted in the database.

Within *config* layer are those classes that provide the configuration mechanisms for the libraries used, such as, spring boot security configuration to integrate it with the JsonWebToken (JWT) library, which is in charge of the generation of authentication tokens. As well as the configuration spring fox-swagger libraries for the API documentation generation.

Exception is a layer that allows us to make an extension of the RuntimeException class to provide a unified exceptions handling mechanism.

4. Data Collection Process

Data collection from the users' devices is described in detail in Fig. 4, to be able to store the information collected within the central repository. It is suggested that the components perform the data load process periodically but not in real-time because of the technology limitation in terms of real-time data collection API. Each of the requests must include an authorization token which was decided to establish as 90 days in order not to overload the users every time with the authentication process. Nevertheless, if the token is not valid or is expired, the component that performs the request will be notified with an error response. Under such conditions, the component has to request a new token or request the user access credentials.

Then, the API loads the data sequentially and returns a flag in each of the activities sent in order to notify the collection component of the status of the load. The same process follows in order to provide the components with the ability to retry the load of information that could not be processed and notify the user about these problems.

As a result of the above-mentioned sequence of activities, the following data is being collected in tabular form: process name, process id, status (app focus or idle), start time, end time, IP address, mac address, process description, battery power, memory and GPU utilization.

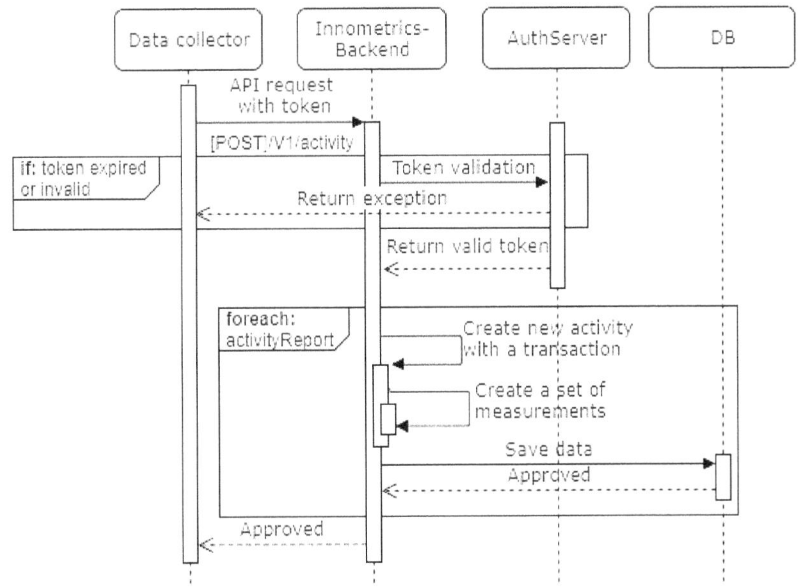

Fig. 4. Data collection sequence diagram.

Further, at the hand of these data collected, the analysis of the process is done. The time data of the development process such as start time and end time, program status are used to calculate the time spent for particular programs during the given period of time.

5. Implementation

The collector is presently an application with the following interfaces:

- Registration interface for the users;
- Login interface for the users;
- Collector Interface: Which displays data collected from the host's machine.

Registration Interface

By using this interface if the user is not signed in yet, the user has either login or create a new account of which sequence of actions is described in Fig. 5. If the user chooses to create an account, the parameters like token and user details like email, name, surname, and password should be included via the provided interface.

The user will be provided with one of the following responses as feedback (Table. 1).

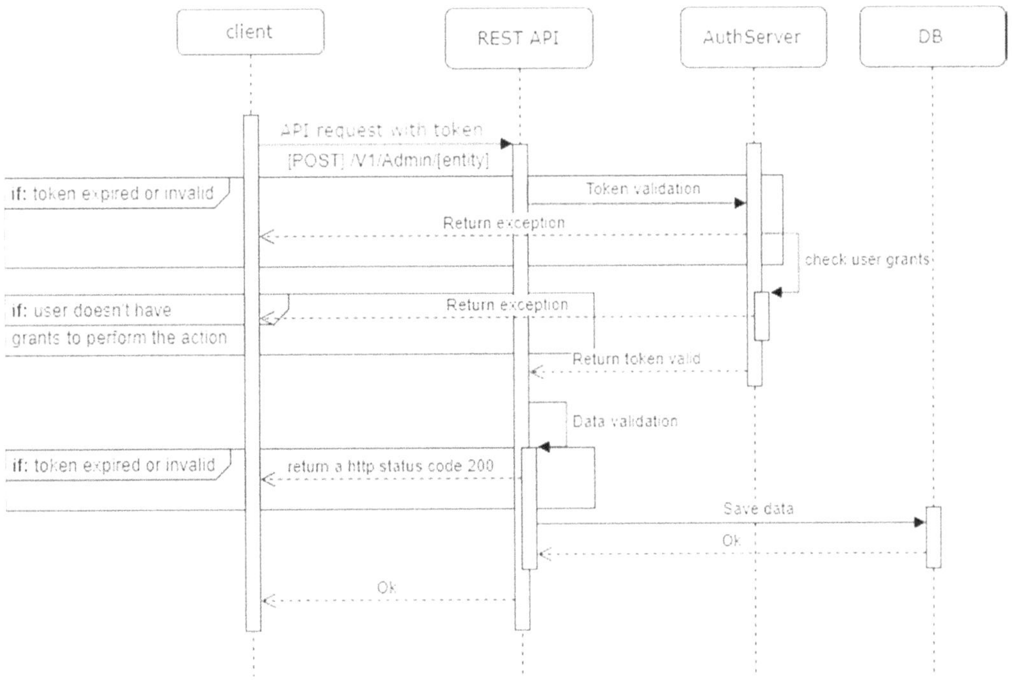

Fig. 5. User registration sequence diagram.

Table. 1. Feedback types as response.

200	OK
201	Created
401	Unauthorized
403	Forbidden
404	Not Found

Login Interface

If the user isn't signed in and wants to send the collected data to the backend at the end of the working day, the only option is first to login with the user credentials and then send. The required parameter to be provided while login in Authentication Request which contains the information about email, password and project ID fields. Otherwise, the data collected has a defined time interval that is set to send the data collected automatically without user intervention. The whole sequence of process activities is illustrated in Fig. 6 below.

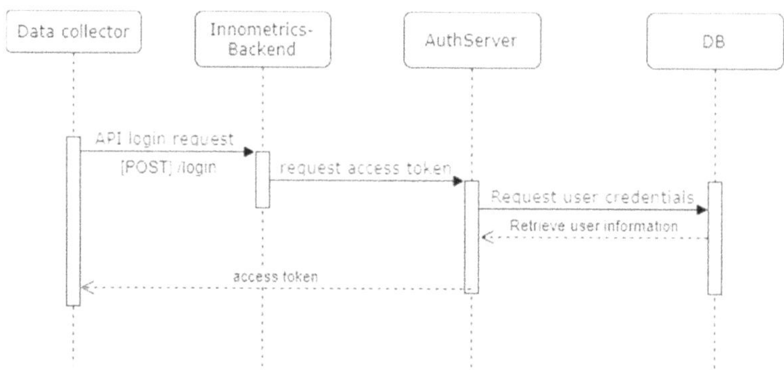

Fig. 6. User login sequence diagram.

The feedback to the AuthenticationRequest as responses are described in Table. 1.

Collector Interface

The parameters to send the collected data to the back-end should include the token and the report. Here, the token should be added to the header. The report structure should be as following:

```
{
"activities": [
{
"activityID": 0,
"activityType": "string",
"browser_title": "string",
"browser_url": "string",
      "end_time":"2019-11-28T09:30:38.470Z",
     "executable_name": "string",
     "idle_activity": true,
     "ip_address": "string",
     "mac_address": "string",
     "measurements": [
    {
"measurementTypeId": 0,
"value": 0
}
],
      "start_time":"2019-11-
      28T09:30:38.471Z",
      "userID": "string"
}
]
}
```

Here, in the data collector interface, there is minimal interaction, as sending the data collected is triggered by just one click (send). Where the token and the collected data with required parameters are sent to the backend. The response feedback is described in Table. 1. If the users' local database isn't empty, the data collected will be transferred to the backend via a REST API.

6. Testing and Results

As soon as the development of the system has been finished, the beta testing phase was arranged with the contribution of university graduates. During our beta testing phase of our system, we have been able to collect data about 50+ applications used by the participants of the test group, with a daily average of 2500 samples. Based on the information we collect on a daily basis, the development team is in charge of analyzing and assessing some relevant aspects, quality in the data collection process and data itself. Which will help us to develop a reliable and consistent data model, to subsequently move on to the next stage – experiment on the energy consumption metrics collection. Besides, starting focusing on deep data analysis and infer additional information on energy efficiency from collected data will be the main concentration.

7. Conclusion and Further Work

In this paper the new approach of measuring the software development process metrics in a non-invasive way. The architecture and implementation of this system were announced and tested with the contribution of university students. For now, all the necessary sorts of Operating system versions were developed for collecting basic process metrics mentioned above. We came up with using process metrics in combination with product metrics to reconstruct the development process.

To sum up, there are two major metrics related to energy consumption [3]:

- Software Energy Consumption (SEC). SEC is the total energy consumed by the software;
- Unit Energy Consumption (UEC). UEC is the measure for the energy consumed by a specific unit of the software.

To evaluate UEC we have to monitor the hardware parameters, which are disk (read bytes/sec, write bytes/sec), CPU usage, memory (working set, private working set), network (bytes sent/sec, bytes received/sec), IO (read bytes/sec, write bytes/sec). The extraction of reliable energy consumption data at the required level of granularity is the aspect of further investigation.

Architectural decisions of the development were justified with the non-functional requirements we are focused on. Based on the requirements and research on energy consumption process metrics, additional metrics will be added to the system to collect for more reliable results. The next step in our research is to verify the results of the collected data from industrial companies.

In addition, we will focus on energy metrics collection for different data collectors and other agents like software management systems and integrated development environments in future work.

Acknowledgments

This research project is carried out under the support of the Russian Science Foundation Grant No 19-19-00623.

References

[1]. E. Jagroep, et al., An energy consumption perspective on software architecture, *LNCS, Software Architecture*, Vol. 9278, 2015, pp. 239-247.

[2]. S. Ergasheva, et al., Metrics of energy consumption in software systems: A systematic literature review, *IOP Conference Series Earth and Environmental Science*, Vol. 431, 2019, 012051.

[3]. E. Jagroep, et al., Energy efficiency on the product roadmap: An empirical study across releases of a software product, *Journal of Software: Evolution and Process*, 2016, pp. 1-34.

[4]. A. Hayri, et al., The impact of source code in software on power consumption, *International Journal of Electronic Business Management*, Vol. 14, 2016, pp. 42-52.

[5]. A. Janes, M. Scotto, A. Sillitti, G. Succi, A perspective on non invasive software management, in *Proceedings of the Instrumentation and Measurement Technology Conference (IMTC'06)*, 2006, pp. 1104-1106.

[6]. M. Scotto, A. Sillitti, G. Succi, T. Vernazza, Non-invasive product metrics collection: An architecture, in *Proceedings of the Workshop on Quantitative Techniques for Software Agile Process (QUTE-SWAP'04)*, New York, NY, USA, pp. 76-78.

[7]. T. Vernazza, G. Granatella, G. Succi, L. Benedicenti, M. Mintchev, Defining metrics for software components, in *Proceedings of the 5th World Multi-Conference on Systemics, Cybernetics and Informatics (ISAS-SCI'2000)*, Vol. 11, Florida, 2000, pp. 16-23.

[8]. Microsoft, Shiv Prashant Sood, Energy Consumption Tool in Visual Studio 2013, https://devblogs.microsoft.com/devops/energy-consumption-tool-in-visual-studio-2013/

[9]. E. Jagroep, J. Martijn, E. M. van der Werf, S. Jansen, M. Ferreira, J. Visser, Profiling energy profilers, in *Proceedings of the 30th Annual ACM Symposium on Applied Computing (SAC '15)*, 2015, pp. 2198-2203.

[10]. Apple Inc., MetricKit documentation, https://developer.apple.com/documentation/metrickit

(073)

Learnings and Option Pricing: How Machine Learning Generates an Explainable Heavy-Tailed Solutions of Option Prices

Chansoo Kim [1, 2] and BoungSecon Choi [2]
[1] Computational Science Center & ESRI, Korea Institute of Science and Technology, Seoul, Republic of Korea
[2] Department of Economics & SIRFE, Seoul National University, Seoul, Republic of Korea
Tel.: + 82-2-880-, +82-2-958-6448, fax: + 82-2-958-5451
E-mails: eau@econ.kist.re.kr, bschoi12@snu.ac.kr

Summary: Prices of the Korean Stock Prices Index (KOSPI) option are computed through three major machine learning approaches: expectation maximization algorithm, deep learning and reinforcement learning. We compare the computed results with the generalized Black-Scholes option prices. The generalized one defines the underlying through the leptokurtic GramCharlier A series distribution. These results well explain the heavy-tailed behavior of the KOSPI in contrast to the original Black-Scholes formula. The closeness between the learning solutions and heavy-tailed analytic solution explains the machine learning result more inductively and analytically.

Keywords: Option pricing, Black-Scholes price, Gram-Charlier A series, Expectation maximization, Deep learning, Reinforcement learning, Korean Stock Prices Index (KOSPI).

1. Introduction

We analyze the index option prices using various machine learning approaches. Korea Composite Stock Price Index 200 (KOSPI 200) option prices during the fiscal years from 1994 to 2018 are used for our analysis, because it clearly shows heavy-tailed behavior such as leptokurtic.

KOSPI is the index of all common stocks traded on the Stock Market Division of the Korea Exchange, which is equivalent to the S&P 500 in the States. Especially KOSPI 200, which is one of the representative indexes in Republic of Korea, is composed of 200 big companies in the Market. Fig. 1 depicts its time-varying movement.

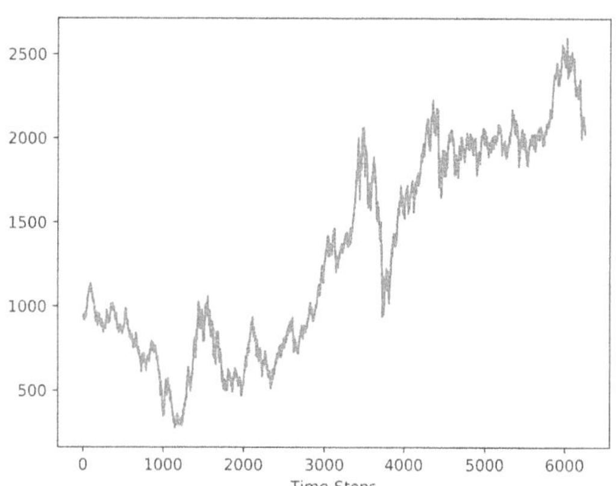

Fig. 1. KOSPI Index during a period from 1994 to 2018. Blue line depicts the time-series of the given data.

The well-known Black Scholes partial differential equation (PDE) is the call option price dynamics over time:

$$\frac{\partial V}{\partial t} + \frac{1}{2}\sigma^2 S^2 \frac{\partial^2 V}{\partial S^2} + rS\frac{\partial V}{\partial S} - rV = 0, \qquad (1)$$

where V is the option's price as a function of stock price S and time t, r is the risk-free interest rate, and σ means the volatility of the stock. This model requires the Black-Schols environment, which assumes the underlying are impractically perfect such as normality of the return rate. However, many empirical results show that a return rate of stock price is heavy-tailed since Fama [4] and Mandelbrot [8].

Recently it is shown that there exist infinitely many solutions to the boundary problem consisting BlackSchloes PDE and the call option payoff as the terminal condition [1, 2]. The analytic solutions include the ones based on heavy-tailed Gram-Charlier A type distributions, which incorporate the market data more than Gaussian assumption, as well as the famous Black-Schloes formula as a special case.

In this work, we apply three tangible machine learning techniques to evaluate its prices based on the heavy-tailed property. Our novelty comes from comparing the black-box type machine learning prices with the analytical one. It gives us some inductive reasoning to explain the learning process.

2. Data Analytics: EM, Deep and Reinforcement Learnings

Among recent popular machine learning techniques, we choose three major ones for pricing the KOSPI 200 index option: EM algorithm, deep learning and reinforcement learning. We apply KOSPI dataset as shown in Fig. 1. Each of the three machine learning approaches is performed 100 times to obtain proper random behavior.

We first apply EM learning to our data. It fits the KOSPI 200 underlying return with three Gaussian distributions to obtain a plausible heavy-tail one. Three Gaussian distributions fit the distribution as seen in Fig. 2.

$$EM = \alpha_{-1}\phi(\mu_{-1}, \sigma_{-1}) + \alpha_0\phi(\mu_0, \sigma_0) + \alpha_{+1}\phi(\mu_{+1}, \sigma_{+1}) \quad (2)$$

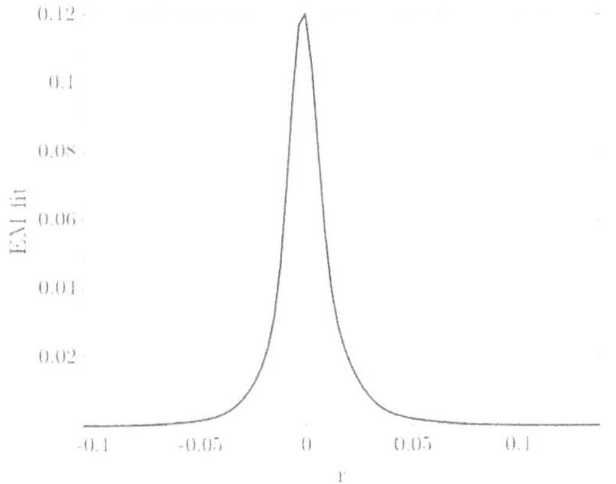

Fig. 2. EM fit of the KOSPI 200 return distribution: the distribution is drawn according to the return r in blue line.

We obtain parameters for the Eq. (2). The first term has μ_{-1} = −1.10E−3 and σ_{-1} = 4.63E−5 with weight α_{-1} = 0.457. The second and third have μ_0 = 3.69E−4 and σ_0 = 2.15E−4 with weight α_0 =0.376 and μ_{+1} = 2.30E−3 and σ_{+1} = 9.98E−4 with weight α_{+1} = 0.167, relatively. EM learning works as an important augmenting computation, in the sense that it gives a set of distribution parameters to better use the Black Scholes PDE, i.e., Eq. (1). This result can be directly compared to the explainable solution suggested in Eq. (3) below and to generate option prices.

Following Han et al. [6], we apply deep learning technique to solve the Black-Scholes PDE. As how KOSPI 200 Index option is composed, this model consider the fair price of a European claim based on these assets with each strike prices. Then we solve the Black-Scholes option pricing equation for Korean market case with specific rate r = 0.032, which is extracted from Fig. 3.

Finally, using recent work of the reinforcement learning [5], the KOSPI index option is priced. It solves the same problem, Eq. (1), in a way of dynamic programming. In other words, it learns for an optimal policy based on samples, while Black-Scholes PDE ignores risk in options. The reinforcement learning incorporates Black-Scholes pricing concept but does not assume famous 'no arbitrage conditions' and exact PDE model, which means existence of known solution [5]. KOSPI 200 option price computed from reinforcement learning, and as a result we obtain its price of 1,820.

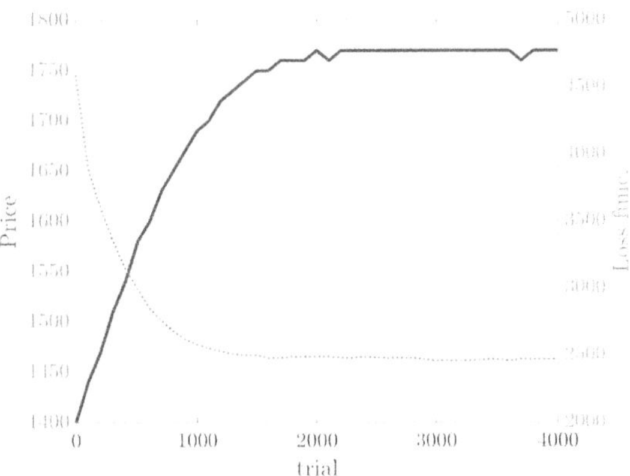

Fig. 3. The option price obtained through deep learning. Blue line depicts the price with increasing learning trials. Red dotted line means loss function value for each trial.

3. Concluding Remark: A Heavy-Tailed Explainable solution

According to Corrado & Su and Jondeau et al., [3, 7], we can model the underlying distribution, which consists of a financial option, using Gram-Charlier A series with kurtosis and leptokurtic.

$$q^{\eta}\left(x; h_t, v^2\tau\right) \equiv \left\{1 + \eta_2 \frac{(x-h_t)^2 - v^2\tau}{v^4\tau^2} + \eta_4 \frac{(x-h_t)^4 - 6v^2\tau(x-h_t)^2 + 3v^4\tau^2}{v^8\tau^4}\right\} \phi\left(x; h_t, v^2\tau\right) \quad (3)$$

Based on the underlying distribution given in Eq. (3), we possibly evaluate the options with the heavy-tailed behavior [1-3, 7-8].

The seminal Black Scholes PDE (1) gives the fair price value 1,804 of the call optimal. The fair prices at the-money due to these simulations are 1,835, 1,770, and 1,820, respectively. Our analytic solution based on Eq. (3), which uses the Gram-Charlier A series distribution for the underlying distribution, results in its optimal price 1,818 at-the-money. Among the three machine learning results, the reinforcement learning fits the most to the explainable solution.

This makes us to understand better how reinforcement learning presents the optimal price for the heavy-tailed returns of index options. Our contribution is directly related to the comparison between the machine learning with the analytic prices. It gives us inductive reasoning to explain the learning. Particularly it includes risk in options, which is ignored in "risk-neutral" Black-Scholes pricing.

References

[1]. B. S. Choi, M. Y. Choi, General solution of the Black–Scholes boundary-value problem, *Physica A*, Vol. 509, 2018, pp. 546-550.

[2]. B. S. Choi, C. Kim, H. Kang, M. Y. Choi, General solutions of the heat equation, *Physica A*, Vol. 539, 2020, 122914.

[3]. C. J. Corrado, T. Su, Implied volatility skews and stock return skewness and kurtosis implied by stock option prices, *European Journal of Finance*, Vol. 3, 1997, pp. 73-85.

[4]. E. F. Fama, The behavior of stock-market prices, *The Journal of Business*, Vol. 38, 1965, pp. 34-105.

[5]. I. Halperin, QLBS: Q-learner in the Black-Scholes (Merton) worlds, *arXiv.org*, 2017, 1712.04609.

[6]. J. Han, A. Jentzen, E. Weinan, Solving high dimensional partial differential equations using deep learning, *Proceedings of the National Academy of Sciences*, Vol. 115, 2018, 8505.

[7]. E. Jondeau, S.-H. Poon, M. Rockinger, Financial Modeling Under Non-Gaussian Distributions, *Springer-Verlag*, London, 2007.

[8]. B. Mandelbrot, The variation of certain speculative prices, The Journal of Business, Vol. 36, 1963, pp. 394-419.

(074)

On the Efficiency of Inpainting Methods for Marine Snow Removal in Underwater Images

Bogdan Smolka and **Monika Mendrela**
Silesian University of Technology, Akademicka 16, 44-100 Gliwice, Poland
E-mail: Bogdan.Smolka@polsl.pl

Summary: In this paper the problem of marine snow removal from underwater color images is investigated. The marine snow is an aggregation of biogenic material falling down from the upper layers of the water column, appearing as small bright particles which decrease the quality of the underwater images. Some efficient algorithms for the marine snow detection have been developed, however the pixels classified as marine snow have to be replaced by an estimate determined using the information from the local neighborhood. We evaluate in this work some popular image inpainting methods in terms of image quality measures and propose a fast technique of missing data substitution. We show that the proposed technique, although simple and fast, is comparable with much more advanced solutions and can be used for real time applications.

Keywords: Image enhancement, Marine snow, Noise reduction.

1. Introduction

The problem of underwater image enhancement has attracted a lot of attention due to many sources of quality deterioration. Images acquired underwater are very often affected by poor lighting conditions. They may be of low contrast, very often they are blurred, hazed and their chrominance channels can be severely distorted or the color can be even totally lost. Additionally, a big problem of underwater imaging is a natural phenomenon termed as *marine snow* (MS), which is an aggregation of biogenic material falling down from the upper layers of the water column. As plants and animals near the surface of the ocean die and decay, their remains descend toward the seabed. This marine snow grows due to the aggregation process, as the particles fall down, some reaching several centimeters in diameter.

Marine snow is composed of faecal matter, sand, soot and other inorganic material as well as some small organisms which attach to the marine snowflakes. The drifting particles of MS are reflecting light and they appear as bright spots [1, 5] occluding the underwater image scene. For image processing algorithms, marine snow is mostly considered as a source of noise, which should be removed from the image, to avoid the decrease in performance of image processing procedures like object segmentation, classification or recognition. Fig. 1 depicts two exemplary images taken from the database [15], which are affected by the marine snow, visible as small, white particles.

The problem of MS detection and removal is difficult as the floating particles very often resemble the structures of the seabed, like small stones, texture of the plants and animals. Additionally, the pixels depicting the detected snowflakes should be removed in such a way that after the restoration they are not recognizable by the human eye and do not introduce artifacts which could affect the performance of the image analysis systems.

Fig. 1. Exemplary test images used for the evaluation of the efficiency of marine snow removal.

In this paper we evaluate the usefulness of various image inpainting methods suitable for marine snow replacement. We also propose an efficient, fast technique of missing data substitution, which can be used in real time applications.

3. Proposed Fast Inpainting Methods

The aim of our work is to propose a fast method of previously detected marine snow removal, (with the use of a suitable detection technique, [2, 7, 8]) and to compare its effectiveness with image inpainting methods known from the literature in terms of suitable image restoration efficiency measures.

In the first experiment we have chosen a set of test images (see Fig. 2) and simulated the marine snow as small regions marked by black color. The black holes should be filled by an appropriate inpainting algorithm, so that the difference between the original and restored image is minimized.

We developed a set of algorithms which recursively fill in the missing pixel values with the average of the neighbors with known values, contained in the processing window W of size 3×3. The elaborated techniques can be seen as a generalization of the fast image inpainting method proposed in [11].

To properly describe the idea behind the proposed inpainting schemes we will make use of the following notation: M (Missing pixels map) – an array, in which we mark positions of the missing pixels to be filled in, NMP (Non-Missing Pixel) – pixel which is not going to be changed and has its own value, MP (Missing Pixel) – pixel with unknown value and FAIM (Fast Averaging Inpainting Method) denotes various versions of fast inpainting algorithm.

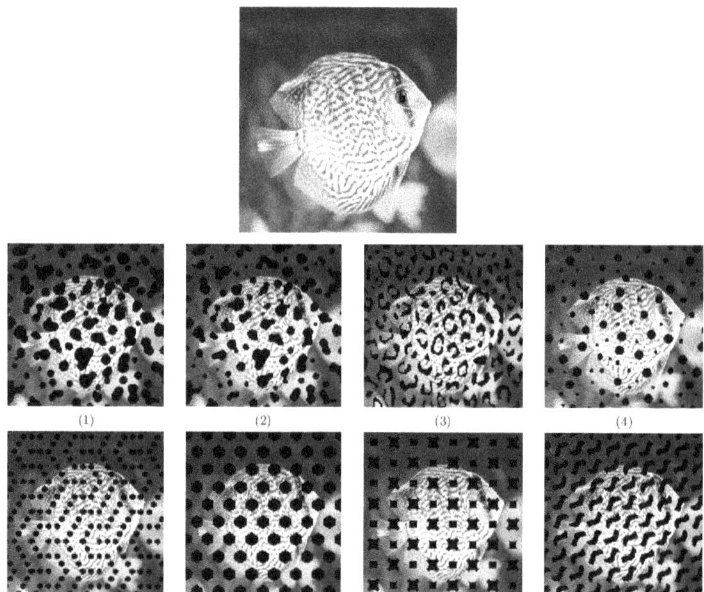

Fig. 2. Exemplary test image used for the evaluation of inpainting methods and below its distorted versions with missing regions marked with black.

The following algorithms have been tested:

- **FAIM 1** – applying a 3×3 window and using 4-neighborhood, we are searching for MPs with at least 2 neighboring NMPs. We replace them with MEAN of NMP color channel values and remove their positions from M. When considering the next MP, we use all pixels not included in M, which means that we recursively use all the already recovered MPs. We repeat the operations until all MPs are removed.
- **FAIM 2** – works as in the previous case but with the 8-neighborhood and the minimum number of NMP needed for MP replacement is increased to 3.
- **FAIM 3** – In this modification, the step of removing positions of recovered pixel from M is done after removal of all MPs, which fulfill the condition of having at least 2 NMPs as neighbors. So after M is modified, we proceed in the next iteration with the removal of the remaining MPs.
- **FAIM 4** – this scheme is the same as in FAIM 3, however 8-neighborhood is used and the condition of at least 2 NMPs is increased to 3.
- **FAIM 5** – in this modification our priority is to recover in the first place the MPs which have the highest number of known neighbors in W. For 4-neighborhood case, in the first step we are looking for MPs which are in neighborhood relation with at least 4 NMPs. Like in FAIM 3, the M map is updated after interpolating all MPs fulfilling this requirement. Then, we relax the condition and consider missing pixels having 3 NMPs in the moving window. After checking this condition and refreshing M, we come back to our first requirement of having 4 NPs. Then we decrease the required number of known pixels to 3. If there are no MPs having 3 NMPs as neighbors, we consider the missing pixels having 2 NMPs in their neighboorhood. Then we come back again to the requirement of 4, and successively to 3, 2 and eventually to 1 NMP, until all of the MPs are removed.
- **FAIM 6** – the last algorithm is the same as FAIM 5, but 8-neighborhood is used and the step of looking for MPs works using the requirement of possessing successively from 8 to 1 NMPs belonging to W in the successive algorithm sweeps.

3.1. Experiments on Artificial Images

To evaluate the effectiveness of the proposed simple and fast interpolating technique, a set of widely used inapainting methods were tested: ALOHA – Annihilating Filter-based Low-Rank Hankel Matrix [10], AMLE – Absolute Minimizing

Lipschitz Extension Inpainting [3], HARI – Harmonic Inpainting via a Discrete Heat Flow [12], INPAI – Inpaitning via Iterative Process based on DCT and IDCT [9], INAS (1, 2) – Interpolate NaN Elements based on Sparse Linear Algebra and PDE Discretizations [4], MPR – Modified Planar Rotator Model for Missing Data Prediction [14] and MSI – Mumford-Shah Inpainting with Ambrosio-Tortorelli Approximation [6].

The results of the restoration of missing regions using the distorted images depicted in Fig. 2 in terms of the PSNR, NCD and FSIM [13] image restoration quality measure are exhibited in Table 1 and Fig. 3. Additionally Fig. 4 show the visual comparison of the inpainting results using the distorted image depicted in Fig. 2 with holes from mask 4. As can be easily seen the best restoration results are delivered by the ALOHA inpainting method [10]. However, this technique is extremely slow and processing a single image with medium resolution requires several minutes, even when running the code exploiting a powerful GPU card. Therefore, this technique although excellent in performance cannot be used for practical applications. Other algorithms rendered comparable results, with the exception of MPR [14].

Table. 1. Comparison of image restoration quality in terms of PSNR [dB] obtained with various inpainting methods using 8 versions of corrupted test image, (see Fig. 2). Best results are highlighted in bold font.

	Corrupted image number							
Method	1	2	3	4	5	6	7	8
ALOHA	15.99	**17.10**	**20.81**	**19.36**	**21.21**	16.74	**19.31**	**19.20**
AMLE	16.34	16.61	17.73	17.81	18.02	16.57	16.93	17.18
HARI	15.56	16.08	17.58	17.95	17.74	16.01	17.21	17.29
INAS 1	15.54	15.85	18.25	17.37	18.18	15.41	16.57	16.79
INAS 2	16.61	16.82	17.75	18.08	17.92	**16.85**	17.36	17.38
INPAI	16.48	16.58	17.73	17.83	17.75	16.71	17.10	16.96
MPR	15.14	15.64	16.99	16.50	17.13	15.13	16.29	16.32
MSI	**16.68**	16.89	17.75	18.07	17.91	**16.85**	17.36	17.39
FAIM 1	14.69	15.16	15.77	16.23	15.88	14.70	15.26	15.46
FAIM 2	15.32	15.74	16.52	17.28	17.26	15.42	16.08	16.29
FAIM 3	14.60	15.23	15.91	16.36	16.29	14.82	15.58	15.65
FAIM 4	15.44	15.70	16.97	17.11	17.14	15.73	16.20	16.47
FAIM 5	15.33	15.75	16.55	17.28	17.27	15.42	16.08	16.31
FAIM 6	15.69	15.98	16.93	17.36	17.39	15.79	16.31	16.69

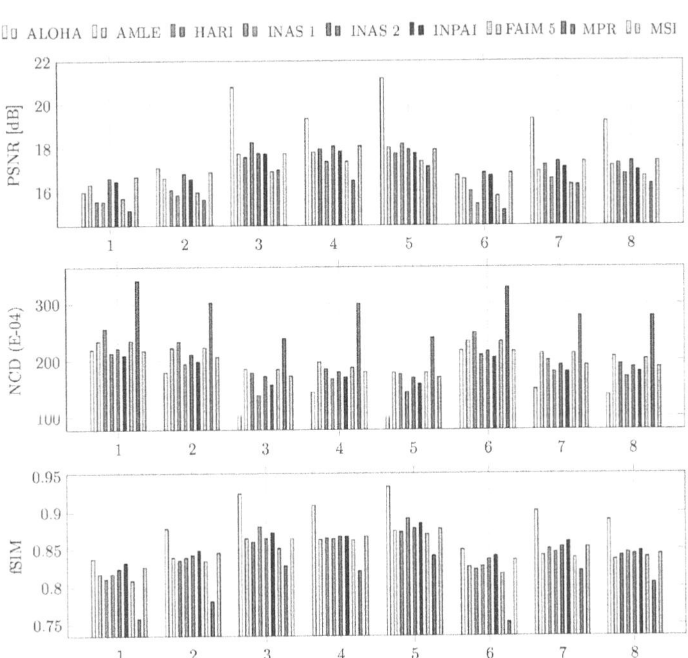

Fig. 3. Comparison of inpainting results in terms of PSNR, NCD and Feature SIMilarity (FSIM), [13] using corrupted test images depicted in Fig. 2.

As described before, in the proposed fast inpainting approach, the missing values are filled with a local average of known pixels in an iterative way, so that samples with highest number of known members always have a priority. The proposed method yields satisfactory results. Of course some blurring of details can be noticed, however the method is very fast, even when running the MATLAB, unoptimized code and yields acceptable interpolation results.

3.2. Experiments on Real Images

As the ground truth images are not available, we decided to manually mark all snow particles in 15 carefully chosen, representative color images of size 640×480, retrieved from a video sequence from a database [15], consisting of more than 1000 frames. In this way we obtained a set of 15 images with marine snow particles marked as regions of pixels with missing values. As the ground truth images, without the snow flakes, are not available, we filled the marked areas with the ALOHA inpainting algorithm, choosing the method's settings so that it provided visually pleasing results. These restored images were treated as a reference set, which enabled to perform the objective evaluation of various inpainting methods.

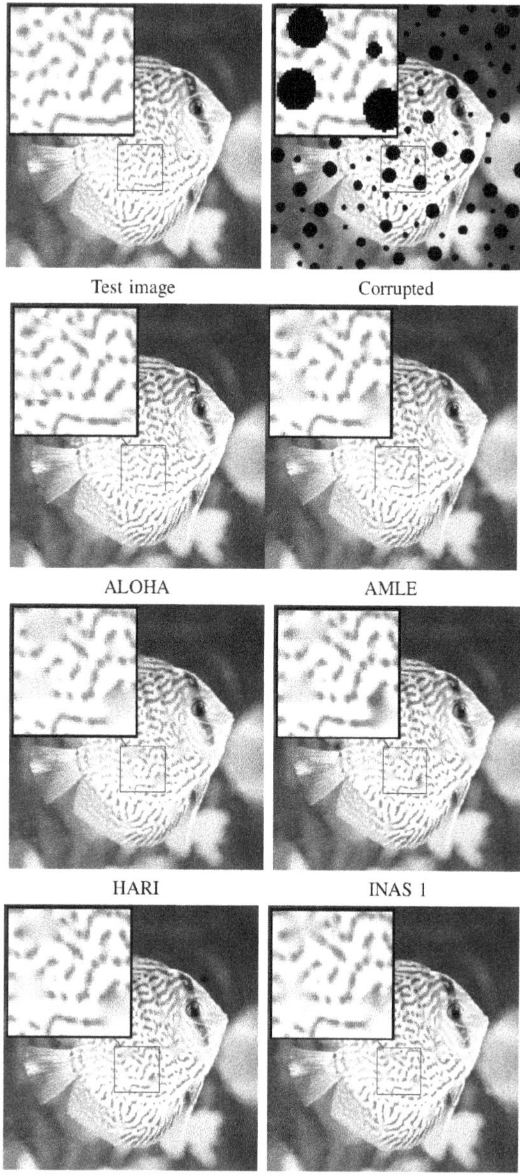

Fig. 4. Comparison of image inpainting results obtained with the selected techniques known from the literature and using the proposed method for test image depicted in Fig. 2 with holes from mask 4.

The images depicting the marked regions of MS were stored and then used to simulate images with increasing contamination intensity. To this end, the holes (marked regions) from all images from the dataset were superimposed on each of the 15 pictures restored with ALOHA. Thus we obtained $15 \times 15 = 225$ different images with marked marine snowflakes.

To further increase the presence of marine snow, we created a database consisting of images with artificial holes (snow regions) taken from 2 differing MS masks. The masks were chosen randomly 3 times for each image, so that 45 images with missing regions were prepared. Then, for each reference image, also 3 corrupted versions containing holes from 3, 4 and 5 other images were created. Thus we obtained a dataset of 5 marine snow contamination intensity levels, containing $225+4\times5=405$ images, with marked holes. Of course, having the images with marked marine snow flakes, we can transfer them to the reference images. Thus we created another database of 405 plausibly looking images contaminated with artificial snow which can be used for other experiments. Fig. 5 depicts examples of images with increasing marine snow intensity levels. In each image the superimposed snowflake regions are indicated with white color.

Table 2 shows the average time for processing a single frame from the test video sequence. The best compromise between the unpainting efficiency and computational complexity offers FAIM 5, which will be referred to simply as FAIM. The efficiency of the proposed interpolation method is presented in Fig. 6, which the performance of the fast interpolation technique in comparison with other inpainting methods using PSNR measure. The proposed algorithm is comparable with much more advanced and therefore much slower methods, which are not suitable for real time frame processing. Therefore, the proposed fast inpainting algorithm can be used for real-time marine snow removal in underwater video sequences.

Table 2. Comparison of the average processing time of the frames in the test video sequence.

Method	Time [s]	Method	Time [s]
ALOHA	6600.5	MSI	36.42
AMLE	670.5	FAIM 1	2.07
HARI	3.93	FAIM 2	2.80
INAS 1	0.55	FAIM 3	0.61
INAS 2	0.40	FAIM 4	21.03
INPAI	2.04	FAIM 5	1.14
MPR	3.62	FAIM 6	171.8

4. Conclusions

In the paper a fast interpolation method intended for the removal of marine snow in underwater image sequences has been proposed. The new technique is fast enough to be applied in real time applications in which the distortions produced by marine snow have to be eliminated. The performed experiments revealed that the new, fast technique is comparable in performance with the state-of-the-art inpainting methods. Future work will be focused on the elaboration of a robust method of marine snow detection and its replacement with the described fast inpainting technique.

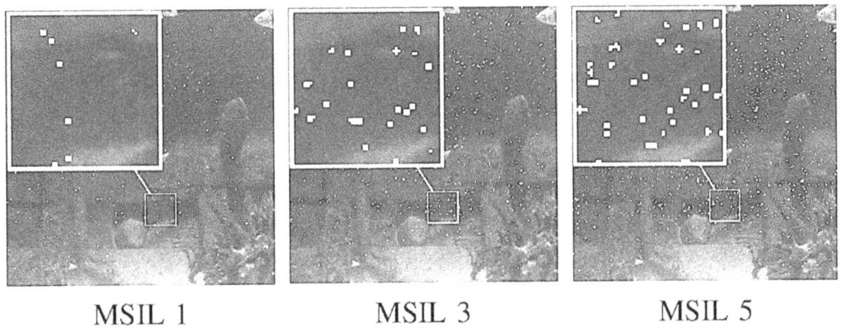

Fig. 5. Examplary images with increasing Marine Snow Intensity Level (MSIL).

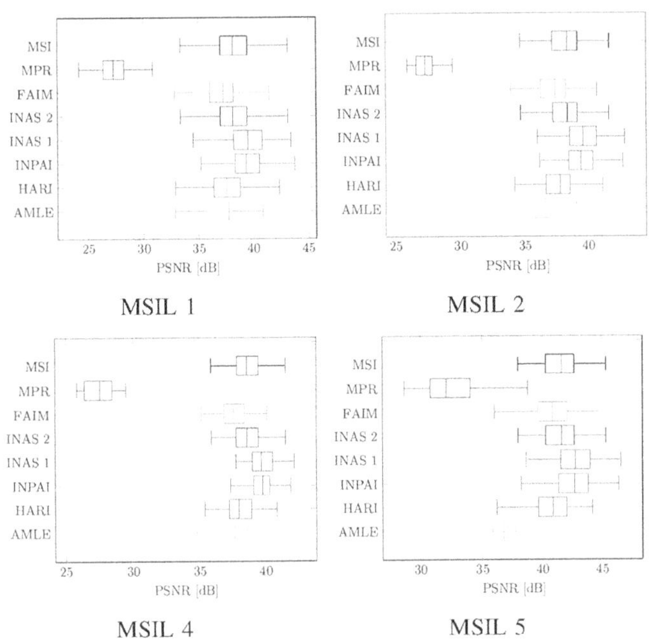

Fig. 6. Boxplots showing the performance of inpainting methods for low and high MSIL.

Acknowledgments

This work was supported by a research grant 2017/25/B/ST6/02219 from the National Science Centre, Poland and was also funded by the Silesian University of Technology, Poland, (BK/200/RAU1/2020).

References

[1]. A. L. Alldredge, M. W. Silver, Characteristics, dynamics and significance of marine snow, *Progress in Oceanography*, Vol. 20, Issue 1, 1988, pp. 41-82.

[2]. S. Banerjee, G. Sanyal, S. Ghosh, R. Ray, S. Nath Shome, Elimination of marine snow effect from underwater image – an adaptive probabilistic approach, in *Proceedings of the IEEE Students' Conference on Electrical, Electronics and Computer Science (SCEECS'14)*, 2014, pp. 1-4.

[3]. V. Caselles, J. Morel, C. Sbert, An axiomatic approach to image interpolation, in *Proceedings of the IEEE International Conference on Image Processing (ICIP'97)*, Vol. 3, 1997, pp. 376-379.

[4]. J. D'Errico, Inpaint NANs, *MATLAB Central File Exchange*, 2004

[5]. A. L. Dörgens, S. Ahmerkamp, J. Müssig, R. Stocker, M. Kuypers, A. Khalili, K. Kindler, A laboratory model of marine snow: Preparation and characterization of porous fiber particles, *Limnology and Oceanography: Methods*, Vol. 13, Issue 11, 2015, pp. 664-671.

[6]. S. Esedoglu, J. Shen, Digital inpainting based on the Mumford-Shah-Euler image model, *European Journal of Applied Mathematics*, Vol. 13, Issue 4, 2002, pp. 353-370.

[7]. F. Farhadifard, M. Radolko, U. Freiherr von Lukas, Marine snow detection and removal: Underwater image restoration using background modeling, in *Proceedings of the 25. Int. Conference in Central Europe on Computer Graphics, Visualization and Computer Vision (WSCG'17)*, 2017, pp. 81-89.

[8]. F. Farhadifard, M. Radolko, U. Freiherr von Lukas, Single image marine snow removal based on a supervised median filtering scheme, in *Proceedings of the International Joint Conference on Computer Vision, Imaging and Computer Graphics Theory and Applications (VISIGRAPP'17)*, 2017, pp. 280-287.

[9]. D. Garcia, Robust smoothing of gridded data in one and higher dimensions with missing values, *Computational*

Statistics & Data Analysis, Vol. 54, Issue 4, 2010, pp. 1167-1178.

[10]. K. H. Jin, J. C. Ye, Annihilating filter-based low-rank Hankel matrix approach for image inpainting, *IEEE Transactions on Image Processing*, Vol. 24, Issue 11, 2015, pp. 3498-3511.

[11]. M. M. Oliveira, B. Bowen, R. McKenna, Y. S. Chang, Fast digital image inpainting, in *Proceedings of the Int. Conference on Visualization, Imaging and Image Processing (VIIP'01)*, 2001, pp. 261-266.

[12]. J. Shen, T. F. Chan, Mathematical models for local nontexture inpaintings, *SIAM Journal on Applied Mathematics*, Vol. 62, Issue 3, 2002, pp. 1019-1043.

[13]. L. Zhang, L. Zhang, X. Mou, D. Zhang, FSIM: A feature similarity index for image quality assessment, *IEEE Trans. on Image Processing*, Vol. 20, Issue 8, 2011, pp. 2378-2385.

[14]. M. Žukovič, D. T. Hristopulos, Gibbs Markov random fields with continuous values based on the modified planar rotator model, *Physical Review E*, Vol. 98, Issue 6, 2018, 062135.

[15]. Comprehensive Dataset for Underwater Change Detection, http://underwaterchangedetection.eu.

(075)

Support Vector Machine with Heavy-tailed Distribution Data

Chansoo Kim [1,2] and ByoungSecon Choi [2]
Computational Science Center & ESRI, Korea Institute of Science and Technology, Seoul, Republic of Korea
[1] Department of Economics & SIRFE, Seoul National University, Seoul, Republic of Korea
Tel.: + 82-2-880-, +82-2-958-6448, fax: + 82-2-958-5451
E-mails: eau@econ.kist.re.kr, bschoi12@snu.ac.kr

Summary: As an implementation of the supervised machine learning, a Support Vector Machine (SVM) has been widely used as a powerful data discriminative classifier. It is defined by a separating hyperplane, which is obtained given labeled training data, and this hyperplane categorizes new examples. Among the parameters to compute the optimal hyperplane, the kernel plays a role to transform the problem into separable states. As a kernel trick for radial basis functions, Gaussian function is mostly used. While its popularity and analytical conciseness, it is not able to capture the heavy-tailed behavior. We apply Gram-Charlier A series to describe the heavy-tailed distribution of the given dataset. As an example, we perform simulations to classify various options with the stock underlying, which are characterized by the strike price and maturity, in Korean option market according to their underlying industries such as manufacturing business and finance industry, demonstrating the versatile applicability of our scheme.

Keywords: Support Vector Machine (SVM), Kernel trick, Heavy-tailed distribution, Classification, Outliers.

1. Introduction

Support Vector Machine (SVM) has been widely used for data classification as a supervised machine learning. It is fed by a set of labeled training data, then an optimal separating hyperplane is computed based on this dataset.

Each training data point, which is already marked as belonging to one or the other of two categories, is added to an SVM training algorithm to build a classifier model. It assigns new example data to one or the other category, making itself a non-probabilistic binary classifier.

More analytically, an SVM training algorithm finds and improves a hyperplane or set of hyperplanes in a high- or infinite-dimensional space. This 'separating' hyperplane then performs classification or outlier detection. The hyperplane in the relatively better separator has the largest distance to the nearest training datasets of any (given) classes. In other words, the larger the margin around a hyperplane, the lower the error of the SVM.

Originally this maximum-margin hyperplane algorithm is proposed by Vapnik in 1963 to construct a linear classifier [6, 7]. However, Aizerman et al. [1] proposed so-called kernel trick, in which nonlinear functions are applied to the maximum-margin hyperplanes [2], to build a nonlinear classifiers. Especially, in this scheme, every dot product is replaced by a nonlinear kernel function, then the (nonlinear) feature space of the given dataset is transformed into a hyperplane. One of the common kernels is the Gaussian radial basis function

$$k(\vec{x}_i, \vec{x}_j) = exp\left(-\gamma|\vec{x}_i - \vec{x}_j|^2\right) \quad (1)$$

While its popularity and analytical conciseness, this Gaussian type kernel function is not able to capture the heavy-tailed behavior of the given dataset.

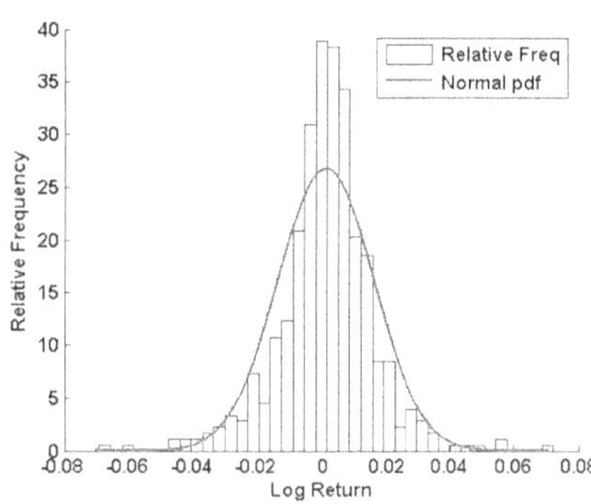

Fig. 1. Failure of Gaussian (Normal) Probability Density Function (PDF). Density distribution of the log-return of KOSPI (Korea Composite Stock Price Index) is plotted in histogram, and the Normal fit is drawn in red solid line.

Fig. 1 shows the distribution of the log-return of KOSPI (Korea Composite Stock Price Index) and its Gaussian fit. One can clearly observe that the Gaussian distribution fails to fit the KOSPI log-return. This result implicates the characteristics of outliers cannot be well captured by the SVM with Gaussian kernel.

We, in this research, suggest a modified SVM with the heavy-tailed distribution function form. Then, as an example, we perform simulations to classify various (financial) stock options in Korean option market according to their underlying industries. They are characterized by the strike price S and the time to maturity τ. And the underlying industries are manufacturing industry and finance, insurance, real-estate (FIRE) businesses. The result may well demonstrates the versatile applicability of our scheme.

2. A Modified Support Vector Machine with Heavy-Tailed Distribution Function Form

Generally, we have a SVM learn a nonlinear classification rule, then it applies the linear one for the transformed datasets, ($\vec{x}_i$) . In kernel trick, we provide a kernel function, which should satisfies,

$$k(\vec{x}_i, \vec{x}_j) = \varphi(\vec{x}_i) \cdot \varphi(\vec{x}_j) \tag{2}$$

If we apply Gaussian-type kernel function, Eq. (1) is utilized to construct Eq. (2) with the strong normality (Gaussian property). Regardless of the specific kernel function, Eq. (2) is used to derive the classification vector $\vec{w}$,

$$\vec{w} = \sum_{i=1}^{n} c_i y_i \varphi(\vec{x}_i) \tag{3}$$

In the above equation, the coefficients c_i are computed from the optimization problem in Eq. (4).

$$\begin{aligned} \max \sum_{i=1}^{n} c_i - \frac{1}{2}\sum_{i=1}^{n}\sum_{j=1}^{n} y_i c_i \left(\varphi(\vec{x}_i) \cdot \varphi(\vec{x}_j)\right) y_j c_j = \\ = \max \sum_{i=1}^{n} c_i - \frac{1}{2}\sum_{i=1}^{n}\sum_{j=1}^{n} y_i c_i \mathrm{k}(\vec{x}_i, \vec{x}_j)\, y_j c_j \end{aligned} \tag{4}$$

which is subject to $\sum_{i=1}^{n} c_i y_i = 0$ and $0 < c_i < \frac{1}{2n\lambda}$ for all data points.

To capture the outlier behavior, we consider the Gram-Chalier series A expansion of the Gaussian kernel function. A modified kernel function, which can incorporate the heavy-tailed distribution, is then written with polynormials,

$$\begin{aligned} k(\vec{x}_i, \vec{x}_j) \approx exp\left(-\gamma|\vec{x}_i - \vec{x}_j|^2\right)\Big[1 + \frac{\beta}{3!}\left(|\vec{x}_i - \vec{x}_j|^3 - \right. \\ \left. -|\vec{x}_i - \vec{x}_j|\right) + \frac{\alpha}{4!}\left(|\vec{x}_i - \vec{x}_j|^4 - 6|\vec{x}_i - \vec{x}_j|^2 + 3\right)\Big] \end{aligned} \tag{5}$$

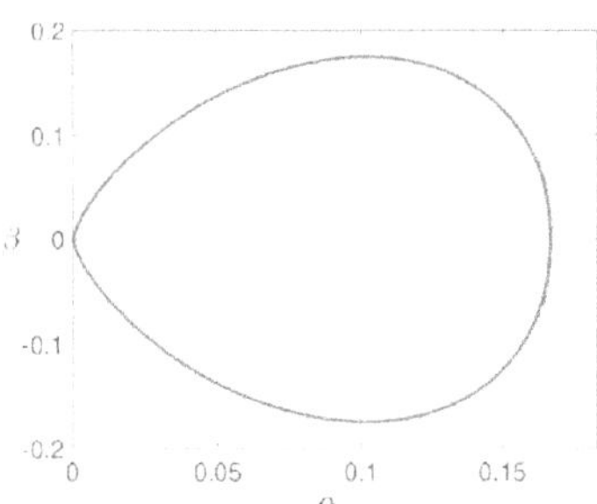

Fig. 2. Parameter region $\mathfrak{R}$ to have positivity of the GramCharlier-type function. One can choose a parameter set of (β,) from this region $\mathfrak{R}$.

The expression in Eq. (5) is not guaranteed to be positive, therefore we need to consider a specific region, which make it a valid probability distributional form. According to our researches [3, 5], we are able to find a parameter sets of in the region Fig. 2.

We choose parameters (β,) from the positivity region as drawn in Fig. 2. Then it enables us to apply the modified kernel function into the kernel trick of an SVM.

This makes us to improve the SVM better with outlier dataset. According to Corrado & Su [4], we can model the distribution, which has fat-tail characteristic, using Gram-Charlier A series with kurtosis. Also it allows the SVM to be applied to heavy-tailed or outlier dataset such as Fig. 1, which are originally failed in being described under the SVM with Gaussian kernel trick.

3. Concluding Remark: Simulation Result

As an example, we perform simulations to classify various options based the stock underlying according to their industries. Those options are two dimensional data, which are strike price S and the time to maturity τ. And the industry of specific options works as its label ('correct answer' of the supervised learning): manufacturing and FIRE.

A set of simulations are under the process, and results are updated upon at being public in an oral or poster session. This result clearly demonstrates the versatile applicability of our scheme due to intrinsic data feature.

This makes us to build a better classifier. Our contribution is directly related to the improvement of SVM. Particularly it includes heavy-tailed features such as outliers and kurtosis, which are ignored before.

References

[1]. M. A. Aizerman, E. M. Braverman, L. I. Rozonoer, Theoretical foundations of the potential function method in pattern recognition learning, *Automation and Remote Control*, Vol. 25, 1964, pp. 821-837.

[2]. B. E. Boser, I. M. Guyon, V. N. Vapnik, A training algorithm for optimal margin classifiers, in *Proceedings of the 5th Annual Workshop on Computational Learning Theory (COLT'92)*, 1992, pp. 144-152.

[3]. B. S. Choi, C. Kim, H. Kang, M. Y. Choi, General solutions of the heat equation, *Physica A*, Vol. 539, 2020, 122914.

[4]. C. J. Corrado, T. Su, Implied volatility skews and stock return skewness and kurtosis implied by stock option prices, *European Journal of Finance*, Vol. 3, 1997, pp. 73-85.

[5]. C. Kim, B. S. Choi, A generalized central limit theorem for skewed and heavy-tail distributions, mimeograph, 2020.

[6]. V. Vapnik, A. Chervonekis, On a class of algorithms of learning pattern recognition, *Automation and Remote Control*, Vol. 25, 1964, pp. 937-945 (in Russian).

[7]. V. Vapnik, A. Lerner, Pattern recognition using generalized portrait method, *Automation and Remote Control*, Vol. 24, 1963, pp. 774-780 (in Russian).

Exploring and Exploiting the Implicit Language Model in Recurrent Neural Networks for Handwriting Recognition

Arseniy Nerinovsky and **Andrey Filchenkov**
ITMO University, Machine Learning Lab, 49 Kronverkskiy pr., St. Petersburg, Russia
Tel.: + 79626822493
E-mail: nerinovsky.arseny@gmail.com

Summary: The gated convolutional recurrent neural network (GCRNN) is a state-of-the-art model for offline handwriting recognition. GCRNNs follow the encoder-decoder architectural pattern. Features obtained from the convolutional encoder are passed to the recurrent decoder. Our examination reveals an implicit language model in the decoder. Based on this knowledge, we apply decoder pretraining in order to explicitly train the implicit language model. We also examine the structure of the model output, which reveals sparsity in the encoder features – character related information is duplicated and interleaved with uninformative noise. In order to circumvent such failures and aid the usage of the implicit language model, we propose several methods of information compression, one of them being a novel technique we call ``grouping''. Results show WER 13.4 improvements over our GCRNN implementation.

Keywords: Handwriting recognition, Encoder-decoder, Information compression, Gated convolutional recurrent neural network, Implicit language model.

1. Introduction

Offline handwriting text recognition is the task of extracting text from images containing this text written by hand. Currently, text recognition is done mainly by neural networks on the line level. We follow this trend by adopting the Gated Convolutional Recurrent Neural Network (GCRNN) [1] that is a state-of-the-art solution for offline handwriting recognition.

The contribution of our work includes the following: we investigate the GCRNN model and find evidence of an implicit language model in the decoder, we also identify data specific patterns degrading the model performance. We develop several techniques of information compression in order to aid the implicit language model by battling the identified patterns.

2. Related Work

Multi-dimensional recurrent neural networks (MDRNN) [2] are one of the most widely used architectures for handwriting recognition. MDRNNs are a generalization of recurrent neural networks (RNN) to a multidimensional case. The sequential nature of RNNs makes MDRNNs quite slow to train and to infer.

To overcome the limitations of MDRNN based techniques, Bluche and Messina introduced gated convolutional recurrent neural networks (GCRNN) [1]. The proposed model is an enriched variant of a CNN-LSTM architecture composed of a convolutional encoder, a pooling layer, and a recurrent decoder. The pooling is performed with a kernel of $1 \times H$, where H is the height of the encoder feature. The pooling layer serves as a layer that maps a 2-D image representation to 1-D. Such configuration allows for capturing handwritten letters features.

3. GCRNN Exploration

3.1. Exploration by Dataset Generation.

GCRNN uses a recurrent neural network as a decoder. In order to explore what is being modeled by the decoder, we generated synthetic datasets. Our methodology was as follows: 1) We synthesized a dataset lacking a certain property; 2) We trained the model on the synthetic dataset; 3) We tested the model on the reference and synthetic datasets. If the model scores remained the same then we conclude that the tested property is not modeled.

We generated 3 datasets apart from the reference one. In the **semantic dataset**, we tested whether the text semantics is modeled, we removed it by randomly swapping words. In the **n-gram dataset** we tested whether n-grams are modeled, we removed them by substituting the words with random strings. In the **random dataset** we tested whether the word lengths matter. The dataset was created by sampling uniformly distributed strings of random characters. We also tested the models on the IAM dataset for reference. The results of the experiments may be found in Table 1.

Table 1. The results of the model testing.

Training ds.→ Test ds. ↓	IAM	Ref. ds.	Sem. ds.	N-g. ds.	Rnd. ds.
Reference ds	96.0	7.9	8.4	85.8	96.0
Semantic ds	94.8	7.9	7.7	86.0	96.7
n-gram ds	97.8	52.3	51.7	50.6	79.0
Random ds	100	61.4	62.9	64.0	75.8

From the results, we see that semantics is not modeled since the semantic model performs equally well on the reference dataset and the reference model experienced no problem with the semantic dataset. In contrast, n-grams and word length play quite a big role. Both the n-gram and the random model score poorly on the semantic and reference datasets. We may conclude that the decoder contains an implicit language model that models n-grams. The decreasing of IAM scores also supports our findings.

3.2. Exploration by Model Output Analysis

We analyzed the outputs of the GCRNN model trained on IAM. We counted the number of consecutive duplications and single occurrences of the blank symbol. It was duplicated 552,934 and appeared just once 1,593 times. Long strings of blank characters hurt the implicit language model since the decoder should also learn to ignore such sequences.

4. Proposed Approach

4.1. Grouping

As we just noted, the data fed to the decoder contains a lot of duplication and non-informative noise. The decoder input is a tensor that has a width and channel dimensions, the height dimension is removed by pooling. In order to increase the informativeness of the encoder output, we split the decoder input tensor into equal chunks across the width dimension, then we rearrange the elements of each chunk across the channel dimension. We call this grouping. We also tweak the pooling layer between the encoder and decoder as an alternative to grouping. Such methods decrease dimensionality and increase information density in the features fed to the decoder thus aiding the implicit language model.

4.2. Decoder Pretraining

As another way to aid the implicit language model we pretrain the decoder on the synthetic data as a language model in a way proposed by Dai [3]. In order to match the dimensionality of the input, we use a vector embedding for the characters. We also apply augmentations form [5]: we randomly shuffle letters in source embedding leaving the target embedding untouched.

5. Experimental Evaluation

We use Word Error Rate (WER) as a metric. We use our implementation of GCRNN as a baseline. Because of lack of the data we failed to achieve results described in [1], but our best model performs on par with the state-of-the-art models described in [4].

5.1. Pooling and Grouping Evaluation

The baseline model performed at 50.79 WER increasing the pooling window allowed us to get to 43.41 WER. Adding grouping allowed us to achieve 39.34 WER. A combination on both the techniques gave 37.34 WER.

5.2. Decoder Pretraining Evaluation

Pretraining of the decoder allowed us to achieve 43.52 WER. Adding noise or grouping degraded the result but still resulted in improvements above the baseline model. The results were namely 45.51 and 45.76 WER.

6. Conclusions

In this paper, we study the possibilities of the GCRNN model [1]. We find out that the model does not capture any high-level notion of the language and only models the language of n-grams. We also note the fact that informative signal appears in small clusters padded on both sides with blank characters. In order to improve the results, we develop several techniques: a technique we call grouping, tuning the pooling layer, and applying decoder pretraining. All the introduced techniques result in loss improvements.

Acknowledgements

The research was supported by the Government of the Russian Federation, Grant 08-08 and by the Russian Ministry of Science and Higher Education by the State Task 2.8866.2017/8.

References

[1]. T. Bluche, R. Messina, Gated convolutional recurrent neural networks for multilingual handwriting recognition, in *Proceedings of the 13th International Conference on Document Analysis and Recognition (ICDAR'17)*, Kyoto, Japan, 2017, pp. 13-15.

[2]. G. Leifert, et al., Cells in multidimensional recurrent neural networks, *The Journal of Machine Learning Research*, Vol. 17, Issue 1, 2016, pp. 3313-3349.

[3]. A. M. Dai, Q. V. Le, Semi-supervised sequence learning, in Advances in Neural Information Processing Systems, Vol. 28, *Curran Associates Inc.*, 2015, pp. 3079-3087.

[4]. C. Kermorvant, et al., Dropout improves recurrent neural networks for handwriting recognition, *CoRR*, abs/1312.4569, 2013.

[5]. M. Artetxe, et al., Unsupervised neural machine translation, *ArXiv Preprint*, arXiv:1710.11041, 2017.

(077)

Industrial Field Autonomous Systems: AI-assisted Distributed Applications at Edge

Y. Fourastier [1], C. Baron [1], H. Chaouchi [2], C. Thomas [3], P. Esteban [1], V. Lehonov [4], J.-P. Smet [5]
[1] Université de Toulouse, INSA, LAAS-CNRS, 7 Av. Colonel Roche, 31200 Toulouse, France
[2] IMT Telecom SudParis, 9, rue Charles Fourier, 91011, Evry, France
[3] HTW Berlin, Treskowalee 8, 10318, Berlin, Germany
[4] Odessa National Academy, MiRoNAFT Laboratory, Kanatnaya St. 12, 65039 Odessa, Ukraine
[5] Nexedi SAS, 147 rue du Ballon, 59110, La Madeleine, France
Tel.: + 33561336200
E-mail: yannick.fourastier@laas.fr

Summary: Complex industrial systems are increasingly software driven, rapidly evolving into autonomous, self-adaptive processing at industrial field. Artificial intelligence technologies are spreading fast at industrial Edge, improving the industrial operations efficiency. However Edge computing systems involving artificial intelligence must also continuously ensure the safe operations. This paper assesses the state of the art of cognitive technologies with their relevance for artificial intelligence implementation at industrial safety critical systems. It introduces then a state of the art for artificial intelligence safety assurance practices. Implementation at the industrial application stack is illustrated with the edge virtual operating system that operates the industrial fog. Edge operating system is evolving fast as kind of an AI intensive software. Industrial developments are illustrated with Slap OS, real case examples of swarm computing and advanced robotic.

Keywords: Artificial intelligence, Industrial edge computing, State of the art, Cyber-physical system, Edge virtual operating system, Safety, Assurance engineering, Industry cases, Swarm processing.

Complex industrial systems are increasingly software driven, rapidly evolving into autonomous and to some extent, self-adaptive processing at field. Edge computing applied in industrial context is embedding cognitive algorithms. This edge embedded artificial intelligence supports local decisions and actions which often influence safety critical operations at field level. The industrial internet of things composes a virtual platform at field. It interacts with business orchestration, such as the manufacturing execution system in the production context, the signalling systems in the transport mobility context, etc. Cognitive technologies are spreading fast at industrial Edge. Such digitized industrial platform brings more automatic decisions locally and actions.

This paper assesses the state of the art of cognitive technologies with their relevance for artificial intelligence implementation at industrial safety critical systems. Distinguishing from genetic algorithms and robotized process automation, also briefly introduced, we structure four families of techniques: machine learning, hybrid neural networks, deep neural networks, and generative adversarial networks. Cognitive technologies are presented with illustration of their purpose at the industrial application stack. The industrial cloud is beyond the field digital fog, which capacity is increasing fast. Edge Computing moves the industrial internet of thinks as virtually distributed swarm computing in near proximity. Fig. 1 illustrates possible placements of cognitive technologies closer to the industrial field.

While edge processing and storage capacities are increasing at fog, this one can also provide available resources opportunistically. Assisted with artificial intelligence, the edge virtual operating system organizes dynamically the sharing at fog, of pseudo available resources for virtual functions or services at the cyber physical system. That raises cybersecurity issues which need to be well addressed in order to partition securely the devices architecture. Meanwhile, the primary function of the installation is to run a mission critical process, which shall comply with safety requirements. This paper assesses state of the art of safety assurance for artificial intelligence to be embedded into safety critical cyber-physical systems.

We illustrate with three actual cases of industrial applications based on SlapOS, an open source edge computing framework in the context of artificial intelligence-assisted control. First case demonstrates the use of GPUs at edge to support real-time anomaly detection of the structural health of wind turbines based on models calculated on a cloud-hosted data lake using Keras deep learning. The second case demonstrates industrial control implementation based on virtualised PLCs' interconnected with IoTs at field and business orchestration in the cloud. The third case demonstrates a drone guidance implementation based on artificial intelligence deployed locally at IoT, with navigation at Edge and path planning in the cloud.

We conclude with summarizing challenges for the implementation of auto-adaptive autonomous industrial systems in safety critical applications, and future work.

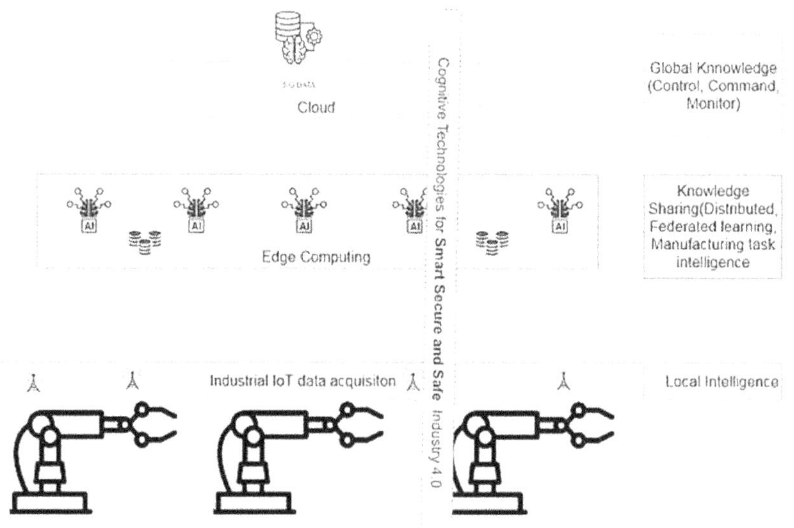

Fig. 1. IIoT and Cognitive technologies over the edge and the cloud in Future Smart Secure and Safe (3S) Industry 4.0 systems.

References

[1]. H. Tian, S. C. Chen, M. L. Shyuy, S. H. Rubin, Automated neural network construction with similarity sensitive evolutionary algorithms, in *Proceedings of the 20th IEEE Int. Conference on Information Reuse and Integration for Data Science (IRI'19)*, Los Angeles, CA, USA, July 30-August 1, 2019, pp. 283-290.

[2]. Y. Tao, Y. Tu, M. L. Shyu, Efficient incremental training for deep convolutional neural networks, in *Proceedings of the IEEE 2nd International Conference on Multimedia Information Processing and Retrieval (MIPR'19)*, San Jose, CA, USA, March 28-30, 2019, pp. 286-291.

[3]. M. Satyanarayanan, The emergence of edge computing, *Computer*, Vol. 50, Issue 1, 2017, pp. 30-39.

[4]. F. Bonomi, R. Milito, J. Zhu, S. Addepalli, *Fog computing and its role in the Internet of Things*, in *Proceedings of the 1st Ed. MCCWorkshop Mobile Cloud Comput. (MCC'12)*, New York, NY, USA, 2012, pp. 13-16.

[5]. G. Premsankar, M. Di Francesco, T. Taleb, Edge computing for the Internet of Things: A case study, *IEEE Internet Things Journal*, Vol. 5, Issue 2, Apr. 2018, pp.1275-1284.

[6]. Z. Tao, Q. Xia, Z. Hao, C. Li, L. Ma, S. H. Yi, Q. Li, A survey of virtual machine management in Edge Computing, *Proceedings of the IEEE,* Vol. 107, Issue 8, August 2019, pp. 1482-1499.

[7]. OpenStack, Build the Future of Open Infrastructure, https://www.openstack.org/

[8]. Openstack, Openstack and Edge Computing: Uses Cases and Community Collaboration, https://www.openstack.org/edge-computing/

[9]. I. Stojmenovic, S. Wen, The fog computing paradigm: Scenarios and security issues, in *Proceedings of the Federated Conference on Computer Science and Information Systems (FedCSIS'14)*, 2014, pp. 1-8.

[10]. Kubernetes, Production Grade Container Orchestration, https://kubernetes.io/

[11]. Y. Xiong, Y. Sun, L. Xing, Y. Huang, Extend cloud to edge with kubeedge, in *Proceedings of the IEEE/ACM Symposium Edge Computing (SEC'18)*, October 2018, pp. 373-377.

[12]. CoreOS, Using ETCD, https://coreos.com/etcd/

[13]. OpenEdge, https://openedge.tech

[14]. P. Liu, D. Willis, S. Banerjee, ParaDrop: Enabling lightweight multi-tenancy at the network's extreme edge, in *Proceedings of the IEEE/ACM Symposium Edge Computing (SEC'16)*, October 2016, pp. 1-13.

[15]. K. Bhardwaj, M.-W. Shih, P. Agarwal, A. Gavrilovska, T. Kim, K. Schwan, Fast, Scalable and secure on loading of edge functions using airbox, in *Proceedings of the IEEE/ACM Symposium Edge Computing (SEC'16)*, October 2016, pp. 14-27.

[16]. S. Nastic, H. Truong, S. Dustdar, A middleware infrastructure for utility-based provisioning of IoT cloud systems, in *Proceedings of the IEEE/ACM Symposium Edge Computing (SEC'16)*, October 2016, pp. 28-40.

[17]. Y. Jararweh, A. Doulat, A. Darabseh, M. Alsmirat, M. Al-Ayyoub, E. Benkhelifa, SDMEC: Software defined system for mobile edge computing, in *Proceedings of the IEEE International Conference Cloud Engineering Workshop (IC2EW'16)*, April 2016, pp. 88-93.

[18]. Y. Xiong, D. Zhuo, S. Moon, M. Xie, I. Ackerman, Q. Hoole, Amino – A distributed runtime for applications running dynamically across device, edge and cloud, in *Proceedings of the IEEE/ACM Symposium Edge Computing (SEC'16)*, October 2018, pp. 361-366.

[19]. S. Simanta, G. A. Lewis, E. Morris, K. Ha, M. Satyanarayanan, A reference architecture for mobile code offload in hostile environments, in *Proceedings of the Joint Workshop IEEE/IFIP Conference Software Architecture (WICSA'12)*, August 2012, pp. 282-286.

[20]. CRIU, Checkpoint/Restore in Userspace (CRIU), https://www.criu.org/Main_Page

[21]. J. Hwang, K. K. Ramakrishnan, T. Wood, NetVM: High performance and flexible networking using virtualization on commodity platforms, *IEEE*

Transactions Network Service Management, Vol. 12, Issue 1, Mars 2015, pp. 34-47.
[22]. S. Echeverría, D. Klinedinst, K. Williams, G. A. Lewis, Establishing trusted identities in disconnected edge environments, in *Proceedings of the IEEE/ACM Symposium Edge Computing (SEC'16)*, October 2016, pp. 51-63.
[23]. D. Boneh, M. Franklin, Identity-based encryption from the Weil pairing, in *Proceedings of the Annual International Cryptology Conference (Crypto'01)*, Berlin, Germany, 2001, pp. 213-229.
[24]. G. Wang, Q. Liu, J. Wu, Hierarchical attribute based encryption for fine-grained access control in cloud storage services, in *Proceedings of the 17th ACM Conference Computing Commun. Security (CCS'10)*, 2010, pp. 735-737.
[25]. M. Hussain, B. M. Almourad, Trust in mobile cloud computing with LTE-based deployment, in *Proceedings of the IEEE 11th International Conference Ubiquitous Intelligent Computing (UIC'14)*, December 2014, pp. 643-648.
[26]. D. Satria, D. Park, M. Jo, Recovery for overloaded mobile edge computing, *Future Generation Computer System*, Vol. 70, May 2017, pp.138-147.
[27]. A. Aral, I. Brandic, Dependency mining for service resilience at the edge, in *Proceedings of the IEEE/ACM Symposium Edge Computing (SEC'18)*, October 2018, pp. 228-242.
[28]. S. Seshia, D. Sadigh, Towards verified artificial intelligence, *ArXiv*, arXiv:1606.08514, 2016
[29]. T. Dreossi, et al., VerifAI: A toolkit for the formal design and analysis of artificial intelligence-based systems, *ArXiv*, arXiv:1902.04245, 2019.
[30]. S. M. Veres, et al., Control engineering of autonomous cognitive vehicles – A practical tutorial, Faculty of Engineering and the Environment, *University of Southampton*, Highfield, UK, 2011.
[31]. L. Briand, Automated testing of autonomous driving assistance systems, in *Proceedings of the LAAS-CNRS TrusMeIA Workshop*, Toulouse, France, July 5, 2019.

(080)

VALIS, a Novel Immune-inspired Supervised Learning Algorithm with Applications to Soft Measurements

A. N. Averkin [1] and P. M. Karpov [1]
[1] Federal Research Centre of Computer Science and Control, Moscow, Russian Federation
Tel.: +7 910 422 7182
E-mail: PeterKarpov@inversed.ru, averkin2003@inbox.ru

Summary: We present VALIS (Vote-Allocating Immune System), a supervised learning algorithm based on the principles of the immune system. Classification is performed by a population of artificial antibodies that can bind to the input data and vote for their classes. The training is performed in evolutionary manner, with new antibodies being created by means of crossover and mutation. Tests on multiple problems demonstrate that VALIS is competitive with established classification methods. Based on VALIS, a system protecting the wireless sensor networks from attacks by mutating viruses can be developed. To this end, intelligent (soft) sensors which can be trained by the evolutionary algorithm to determine the type of attack and neutralize it are employed. The machine learning technology considered belongs to the area of soft measurement methods.

Keywords: Artificial immune systems, Bioinspired computations, Machine learning, Supervised learning, Soft measurements.

1. Introduction

Artificial immune systems (AIS) are a class of algorithms based on principles found in the immune system. Depending on which features of the natural system are modelled, they fall into one of the four categories: negative selection [1], clonal selection [2, 3], immune networks [4, 5] and danger theory [6]. Various types of AIS perform different tasks such as supervised learning, unsupervised learning or optimization. We propose a new supervised learning algorithm called VALIS, which stands for VoteAllocating Immune System. The algorithm uses a population of artificial antibodies that can bind to the input data and vote for their classes, with votes of bound antibodies determining the classification result. The training process resembles a genetic algorithm with niching. New antibodies are created by means of crossover and mutation, and fitness sharing ensures that the antigen space is covered evenly. However, in contrast to the traditional evolutionary algorithms, the end result is a population that acts as a whole, collectively solving the classification problem.

2. Proposed Approach

Following the immunological metaphor, VALIS maintains a population of *antibodies*, and the data samples represent *antigens*. Both the antigens and antibodies (referred to as the *molecules*) are specified by a number of parameters called their *generalized shapes*. The degree of antibody-antigen interaction is quantified by the distance function defined over the space of generalized shapes. The exact molecule representation and the distance function depend on a particular problem. However, in many practical cases involving continuous variables, the antibodies can be represented as spheres and the distances can be measured with the usual Euclidean metric.

The classification process is analogous to the immune response of a real immune system. Depending on its distance to a particular antigen, an antibody can bind to it. Each antibody bound to the input antigen votes with its class distribution and the total votes are used to determine the classification result. Fig. 1 depicts the population trained on a test problem.

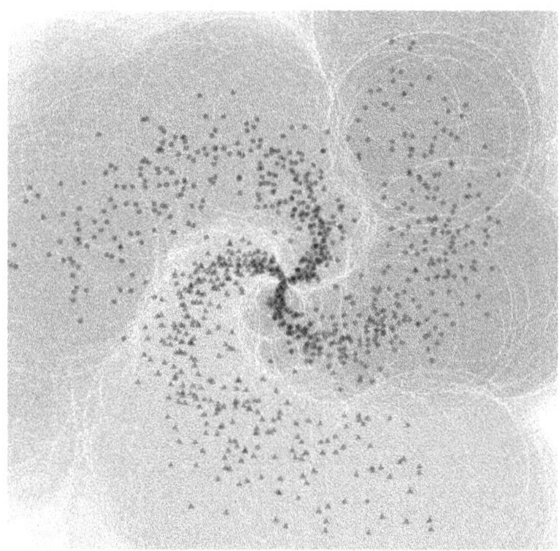

Fig. 1. Visualization of antibody population trained on a synthetic 2D dataset with three classes. Training data samples are marked in black, with class indicated by shape. Antibodies are shown as circles with colors determined by class distributions.

The training is performed in steps called generations. During each generation, new antibodies are created by means of crossover and mutation and replace the worst performing fraction of the population. An antibody's fitness is calculated based on its local classification accuracy and a sharing factor which quantifies its degree of overlap with other antibodies. When a large number of antibodies starts to accumulate in a particular area, their sharing factors drop and make other regions of the search space more attractive. This mechanism maintains the population diversity and drives the exploration, resulting in emergent training dynamics.

VALIS was compared to 9 popular classification algorithm implemented in the scikit-learn Python package [7]: k nearest neighbours (kNN), logistic regression (LR), linear and quadratic discriminant analysis (LDA, QDA), naive Bayes (NB), AdaBoost (AB), decision trees (CART), random forests (RF) and support vector machines (SVM). The algorithms were tested on six datasets from UCI repository and MASS package. The performance of each algorithm was measured using 6 repetitions of a 10-fold cross validation. The results are summarized in Table 1.

Table 1. Geometric means and minimums of relative classification accuracies.

Algorithm	Geometric mean	Minimum
VALIS	0.956	0.926
SVM	0.956	0.855
kNN (k = 1)	0.953	0.918
RF	0.940	0.817
kNN (k = 3)	0.938	0.870
LDA	0.933	0.838
LR	0.922	0.832
kNN (k = 5)	0.920	0.863
kNN (k = 7)	0.907	0.831
CART	0.883	0.778
AB	0.820	0.600
NB	0.747	0.394
QDA	0.722	0.174

3. Conclusions

We have presented VALIS, a novel immune inspired supervised learning algorithm. Compared to other AIS, VALIS is different in terms of population structure and learning dynamics. The training procedure resembles a genetic algorithm with niching, with fitness sharing ensuring antibody diversity. The system exhibits global emergent behavior as the result of local interactions, with population as a whole converging towards higher collective classification accuracy. Experiments demonstrate that VALIS is competitive with other established classification methods.

References

[1]. S. Forrest, A. S. Perelson, L. Allen, R. Cherukuri, Self-nonself discrimination in a computer, in *Proceedings of the IEEE Symposium on Security and Privacy (SP'94)*, Washington, DC, USA, 1994, pp. 202-212.

[2]. L. N. de Castro, F. J.V. Zuben, Learning and optimization using the clonal selection principle, *IEEE Transactions on Evolutionary Computation*, Vol. 6, Issue 3, 2002, pp. 239-251.

[3]. J. Brownlee, Clonal selection theory & CLONALG – The clonal selection classification algorithm (CSCA), *Swinburne University of Technology*, 2005.

[4]. L. N. de Castro, F. J. Von Zuben, AINET: An artificial immune network for data analysis, *Data Mining: A Heuristic Approach*, Vol. 1, 2001, pp. 231-259.

[5]. J. Timmis, M. Neal, J. Hunt, An artificial immune system for data analysis, *Biosystems*, Vol. 55, Issue 1, 2000, pp. 143-150.

[6]. J. Greensmith, U. Aickelin, S. Cayzer, Detecting Danger: The Dendritic Cell Algorithm, *Springer*, London, 2008, pp. 89-112.

[7]. F. Pedregosa, G. Varoquaux, et al., Scikit-learn: Machine learning in Python, *Journal of Machine Learning Research*, Vol. 12, 2011, pp. 2825-2830.

(083)

Intelligent Agents for Industry 4.0: Architecture of Hybrid Knowledge Formation System

Valery B. Tarassov [1] **and Maria N. Koroleva** [1]
[1] Bauman Moscow State Technical University, 5 b.1 2nd Baumanskaya st., 105005 Moscow, Russia
E-mail: vbulbov@yahoo.com

Summary: The near future of Industry 4.0 will be related on making these components both cognitive and collaborative and situation aware («understanding») agents. In this case shown the problems of developing hybrid knowledge formation system. A crucial role of measurement in acquiring and discovering knowledge for intelligent systems is shown. The Russian scientific tradition of considering measurement as a cognitive process is discussed. The architecture of hybrid knowledge formation system is presented. The paper consider the operation principle and structure of cognitive measurement information device.

Keywords: Intelligent system, Intelligent agents, Knowledge-based systems, Cognitive measurements, Industry 4.0.

1. Introduction

Nowadays the world-wide initiative called Industry 4.0 [1-3] becomes a main challenge for developing advanced technologies in modern Artificial Intelligence. The most important idea of Industry 4.0 is the fusion of the physical and virtual worlds [1] provided by Cyberphysical Systems (CPS). The emergence of CPS supposes the inclusion of computational resources into physical-technical processes.

Basic platforms for Industry 4.0 are Smart Factories viewed as systems of CPS. Within modular smart factories, physical processes are monitored, virtual copy of physical world is created, and well-timed decentralized decisions are made. So their basic components are advanced sensors and sensor networks, robots, instruments, monitoring tools, control systems, human-machine interface. The near future of Industry 4.0 will be related on making these components both cognitive and collaborative and situation aware («understanding») agents.

Moreover, the problems of growing both mixed human-robot societies and societies of artificial cognitive agents and smart objects will be of special concern [4].

2. Hybrid Knowledge Formation System

In this context we face the problem of constructing hybrid knowledge formation system (3rd generation knowledge acquisition system) to develop intelligent systems for Industry 4.0. First generation knowledge acquisition systems were focused on acquiring knowledge from unique human expert during his/her communication with knowledge engineer and provided the development of expert system shells. Second generation knowledge acquisition and management systems are based on a hierarchy of ontologies and ontological engineering techniques and tools. They are mainly oriented to achieving mutual understanding in a community of artificial agents (or both human and artificial agents) and enabling their joint work. Finally, third generation knowledge systems are hybrid: they suppose the joint use of various explicit and implicit knowledge sources, in particular, expert estimation and measurement techniques. For such systems, we propose to use the term *hybrid system of knowledge formation*, as combining the processes of knowledge acquisition and knowledge discovery. A possible architecture of hybrid knowledge formation system is presented in Fig. 1.

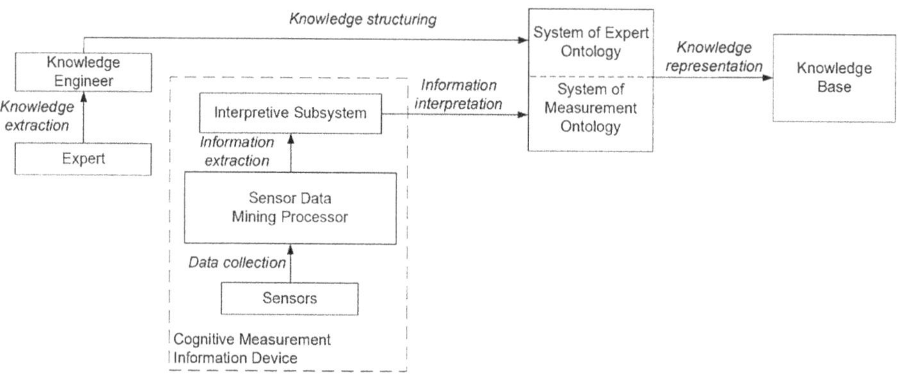

Fig. 1. Architecture of hybrid knowledge formation system.

Fig. 2. Representation of transitions «Data–Information– Knowledge–Meta-Knowledge» in «Understanding – Activities» coordinates.

Conventional knowledge extensive technologies based on ready expert knowledge elicitation and transfer have to be completed by knowledge intensive technologies supposing sensor mining, i.e. the transitions «data-information-knowledge» (Fig. 2) [5].

Acknowledgements

The research work is supported by Russian Foundation for Basic Research, Projects No. 20-0700506 and No 20-07-00770.

References

[1]. H. Kagermann, J. Helbig, A. Hellinger, W. Wahlster, Recommendations for Implementing the Strategic Initiative Industry 4.0: Securing the Future of German Manufacturing Industry, Final Report of the Industrie 4.0 Working Group, *National Academy of Science and Engineering*, 2014. http://forschungsunion.de/pdf/industrie_4_0_final_report.pdf

[2]. K. Schwab, The Fourth Industrial Revolution, *World Economic Forum*, Geneva, 2016.

[3]. 2016 Global Industry 4.0 Survey, Building the Digital Enterprise, *PwC, London*, 2016.

[4]. V. B. Tarassov, Enterprise total agentification as a way to Industry 4.0: Forming artificial societies via goal-resource networks, in *Proceedings of the 3rd International Scientific Conference Intelligent Information Technologies for Industry (IITI'18)*, Vol. 874, 2018, pp. 26-42.

[5]. R. Ackoff, From data to wisdom, *Journal of Applied Systems Analysis*, Vol. 16, 1989, pp. 3-9.

(081)

Monitoring and Controlling of Industrial Systems on the Basis of Bayesian Intelligent Measurements: Application to Petroleum Industry

E. Perestoronina [1]
[1] Financial University under the Government of the Russian Federation,
49 Leningradsky Prospekt., 125993 Moscow, Russia
Tel.: + 79653548801
E-mail: eamedvedeva@edu.fa.ru

Summary: Summary: Digital revolution dramatically affects different spheres of human life, creating opportunities and risks. New technologies can contribute to realizing the Sustainable Development Goals, hence the effective application of relevant technological developments for evaluating the effectiveness of various systems is important. Contemporary systems are quite complex and operate under conditions of uncertainty. This article presents the methods of monitoring and controlling of industrial systems under conditions of uncertainty on the example of petroleum industry. The methods mentioned are based on the methodology of Bayesian intelligent technologies that refers to the Bayesian intelligent measurements. Such methods allow to implement soft measurements and use soft modelling, audit and control technologies accompanied by uncertainty conditions. Number of indicators has been compiled based on foreign and domestic experience. A conceptual model has been developed for monitoring and controlling indicators of petroleum industry. Such model takes into account uncertainty and instability of internal and external factors, although it produces relevant results for making management decisions.

Keywords: soft measurements in economy, Bayesian intelligent technologies (BITs), Bayesian intelligent measurements (BIMs), complex systems, industrial systems, petroleum industry.

1. Introduction

Nowadays global economy is developing in terms of growing digital data influence. Digital information is spreading with unprecedented speed and scale and affects our lives dramatically. For example, global Internet Protocol (IP) traffic grew from about 100 gigabytes (GB) per day in 1992 to more than 45,000 GB per second in 2017. However, the world is only in the early days of the data-driven economy. Global IP traffic is projected to reach 150,700 GB per second by 2022 (Fig. 01) [1].

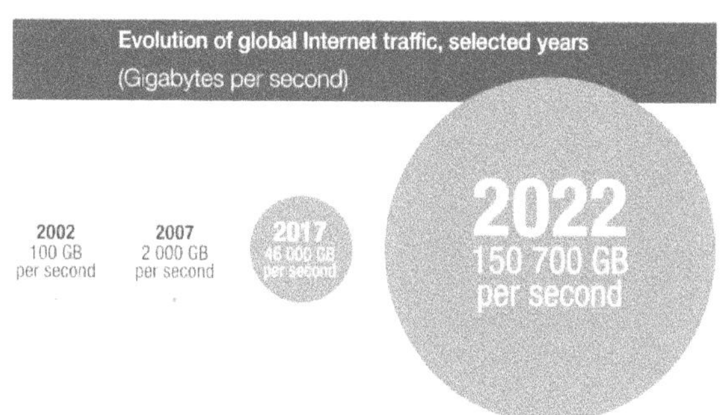

Fig. 1. Evolution of global IP [1].

In particular, information pressure has an influence on economic systems that makes them more complex. On the one hand, abundance of various information allows to study such systems more thoroughly. On the other hand, it is difficult to reveal whether such information is reliable, accurate and complete [2]. Hence, there is a need in special instruments to study complex economic systems under conditions of uncertainty but despite this fact relevant management decisions are generated.

2. Bayesian Intelligent Technologies

The role of intelligent measurements is increasing in real practice due to the informatisation of society activity. However such measurements cannot be applicable on the basis of current technological decisions.

First of all, modern complex systems contain different types and kinds of information as big data. Secondly, applicable measurements have to produce reliable results. Thirdly, the indicators observed are exposed to the environment and are under conditions of uncertainty [3].

Precisely, the methodology of Bayesian intelligent technologies (BITs) meets the specified requirements. BITs are based on Artificial Intelligence (AI) concepts, a system approach and the common theory of Bayesian intelligent measurements (BIMs). The theoretical basis of BITs refers to the regularized Bayesian approach (RBA) [4]. BITs are designed to measure complex systems and determine their properties, dynamics and trends in terms of their continuous development and active interaction with environment to generate management decisions. In practice almost all modern systems can be attributed to complex objects, therefore BITs are applicable to their measurements [5].

3. Monitoring and Controlling of Petroleum Industry

Uncertainty is an important parameter in making measurement decision [6]. Simultaneously monitoring and controlling of complex systems is being carried out under conditions of uncertainty [7]. For this reason, BITs are applicable for monitoring and controlling of such systems.

On the basis of the methodology of BITs a system of dynamic model has been developed and adapted for monitoring and controlling of petroleum industry:

$$G_t^{(MPI)} = G_t^{(IF)} * G_t^{(MiE)} * G_t^{(MaE)}, \quad (1)$$

where $Gt(MPI)$ is the dynamic general model of petroleum industry, $Gt(IF)$ is internal factors of petroleum industry, $Gt(MiE)$ is micro-environment of petroleum industry, $Gt(MaE)$ is macro-environment of petroleum industry.

All the indicators mentioned take into account internal and external factors that affect the petroleum industry such as oil prices, oil extraction, production, consumption, input-output indicators, international trade, different sanctions and barriers, Organization of the Petroleum Exporting Countries (OPEC) agreements, intergovernmental policy, etc.

The purpose for choosing this economic sphere of activity was its prevalence in the world and continuing development [8]. Petroleum industry is also the leading industrial system in the Russian economy and is gradually influenced by environment, viz. its internal and external factors (Fig. 2).

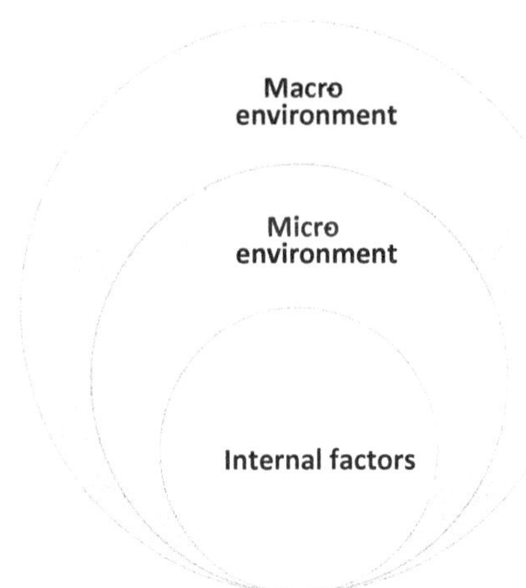

Fig. 2. Petroleum industry system [compiled by the author].

The basic indicators for calculations have been taken from open information resources, e.g. international organisations and national statistical databases [8-10].

4. Conclusions

Digital data and intelligent technologies are strongly incorporated in everyday activity as well as in economic sphere. Their influence will continue to increase, signifying new risks and opportunities. Thus, management is in search of new methods of measurements for developing suitable solutions.

The presented model allows monitoring and controlling of petroleum industry in complexity under conditions of uncertainty. The interpretation of generated indicators may be used in practice in order to make relevant decisions in management.

References

[1]. Digital Economy Report 2019 by United Nations Conference on Trade and Development (https://unctad.org/en/Pages/DTL/STI_and_ICTs/ICT4D-Report.aspx).

[2]. M. Association, Management Control and Uncertainty, Otley, D., Soin, K. (eds.), *Palgrave Macmillan*, UK, 2014.

[3]. S. V. Prokopchina, G. A. Scherbakov, Yu. V. Efimov, Modeling of socio-economic systems under conditions of uncertainty, G. A. Scherbakov (eds.), *Scientific library*, 2019 (in Russian).

[4]. S. P. Wilson, R. Dahyot, P. Cunningham, Introduction to Bayesian Methods and Decision Theory, in Machine Learning Techniques for Multimedia. Cognitive Technologies, Cord M., Cunningham P. (eds.), *Springer*, Berlin, Heidelberg, 2008.

[5]. S. V. Prokopchina, New Trends in Measurement Science. Bayesian Intelligent Measurements, in *Proceedings of the V International Conference on Sensors and Electronic Instrumentation Advances (SEIA' 2019)*, Canary Islands (Tenerife), Spain, 25-27 September 2019, pp. 317-321.

[6]. Y. Cheng, X. Chen, H. Li, Z. Cheng, R. Jiang, J. Lü, H. Fu, Analysis and Comparison of Bayesian Methods for Measurement Uncertainty Evaluation, *Mathematical Problems in Engineering*, Vol. 2018, pp. 1-10.

[7]. Z. Gao, S.K. Nguang, D.-X. Kong, Advances in modelling, monitoring, and control for complex industrial systems, *Complexity*, Vol. 2019, pp. 1-3.

[8]. Statistical Review of World Energy by British Petroleum p.l.c. (https://www.bp.com/en/global/corporate/energyeconomics/statistical-review-of-worldenergy/downloads.html).

[9]. UNECE Statistical Database (https://w3.unece.org/PXWeb2015/pxweb/en/STAT/).

[10]. Federal State Statistics Service (https://eng.gks.ru/figures/activities).

(082)

Methods and Means of Bayesian Intelligent Technologies for Management Accounting and Cost Formation

S. Mishchenko
Financial University under the Government of the Russian Federation,
49 Leningradsky Prospekt, Moscow, Russia, 125993, GSP-3
E-mail: SNMishchenko@yandex.ru

Summary: An urgent task of conducting modern business is to improve the production and financial and economic activities of organizations in order to ensure their harmonious and sustainable development. The concept of cost as an economic category is the most important in the management accounting system, since cost has a direct impact on the profit of an organization. Information about the cost price is necessary for making management decisions, as well as for choosing ways and methods to reduce it. Currently, organizations experience the strongest influence of the external environment, so the formation of the cost price is not limited only to the calculation of costs, but also includes continuous control and monitoring of factors that affect its formation. The specificity of the modern economy is the complexity and uncertainty of production environment. This is due to both rapidly changing factors of production itself, and actively influencing environmental factors, such as market changes, economic sanctions, which determine the appearance of numerous and diverse risks of production. Therefore, currently in demand are methods and tools that are focused on working in such situations. One of them is Bayesian intelligent technologies. They allow you to modernize the management accounting system, and are focused on the conditions of uncertainty and instability of factors determined in the course of the organization's activities.

Keywords: Bayesian intelligent technologies, System “Infoanalyst”, BIT-model, Factor tree, Integral factor.

1. Introduction

The cost of products (works, services) is a complex object that actively interacts with the external environment. Environmental factors cause uncertainty, characterized by vagueness, inaccuracy, and lack of information, which hinders effective solving financial and management problems [1]. Hence, it is necessary to use methods that obtain sustainable solutions as analytical assessments, recommendations, conclusions, and flexible management strategies [2]. One of them is the regularizing Bayesian approach, which has integrating and regularizing properties, based on the methodology of which, calculated data about an object can be integrated with expert estimates, by multidimensional convolution of information. Information technologies based on the regularizing Bayesian approach are called the Bayesian intelligent technologies.

2. Model for Evaluating and Monitoring the State of the Management Accounting System

The properties of a complex object and its relations to the environment are constantly changing. In this connection, it is necessary to amend the model representations of the object, evaluate its properties and criteria, as well as restrictions, assumptions, and requirements for setting the task. Depending on the information received, the target functions and criteria of the problem to be solved, the conceptual model of a complex object and its environment will change [3]:

$$G^{(O)}(t) \rightarrow G^{(M)}(t), \quad (1)$$

where $G^{(O)}(t)$ is the system of a dynamic object, $G^{(M)}(t)$ is a system of a dynamic model.

$G^{(O)}(t)$ is the Bayesian convolution of properties and relations that change with time t [3]:

$$G^{(O)}(t) = Q^{(O)}(t) * R^{(O)}(t), \quad (2)$$

where $Q^{(O)}(t)$ is the properties of a dynamic object, $R^{(O)}(t)$ is the relations of a dynamic object to environment, “*” is the Bayesian convolution symbol.

The convolution of component properties in the model is calculated using the Bayes formula [3]:

$$P(h_k|x_i|Y_i)=\frac{P(h_k|Y_{i-1})(x_i|h_k|Y_i)}{\sum_{j=1}^{K} P(h_j|Y_{i-1})l(x_i|h_j|Y_i)}, \quad (3)$$

where h_k is the estimation of a parameter, x_i is the data set, Y_i is the conditions for determining the score.

The system of the dynamic model $G^{(M)}(t)$ is the Bayesian convolution of properties and relations, as well as restrictions, assumptions, and requirements of the problem statement, also changing over time t [3]:

$$G^{(M)}(t) = Q^{(M)}(t) * R^{(M)}(t) * L^{(M)}(t), \quad (4)$$

where $Q^{(M)}(t)$ is the properties of a dynamic model, $R^{(M)}(t)$ is the relations of a dynamic model, $L^{(M)}(t)$ is the constraints, assumptions, and requirements of a dynamic model, * is the Bayesian convolution symbol.

Based on the above basic formula the system model of the costs of services of the project organization can be represented as a set of the following interrelated systems:

$$G^{PC} = G^{DC} * G^{IC} * G^{OC} * G^{E}, \quad (5)$$

where G^{CP} is the prime cost (works, services), G^{DE} is the direct costs, G^{IC} is indirect costs, G^{OE} is the other costs, G^{EF} is the environment, "*" is the Bayesian convolution symbol.

The above model in practice can be implemented by using the "Infoanalyst" software tool [4].

3. Methodology for Evaluating Cost Indicators in the Management Accounting System

To implement this task, it is necessary to build a tree of factors in the "Infoanalyst" program and enter the values of actual costs and their planned indicators to build the tree of factors (see Fig. 1). In fact, the tree of factors is the specialist's knowledge base and can be supplemented and detailed in the course of work.

Project 1
1. Cost of production (works. services')
1. Direct cost
1. Material costs
2. The cost of labor
3. Deductions on social needs
4. Depreciation of fixed assets
5. Other direct expenses
(a) expenses under contracts
6) additional costs associated with the development and p
C) payment to third-party organizations under contracts
d) payment for laboratory analysis of soil anc
e) development of tender documentation
e) expenses for payment of interest on Bank loans f
g) author's supervision
2. Indirect costs
3. Other expenses
4. Environmental factors

Fig. 1. Factor Tree.

Let's consider the indicator "expenses of construction contracts" for a specified date. The assessment of the state of this factor is on the corresponding scale (see Fig. 2).

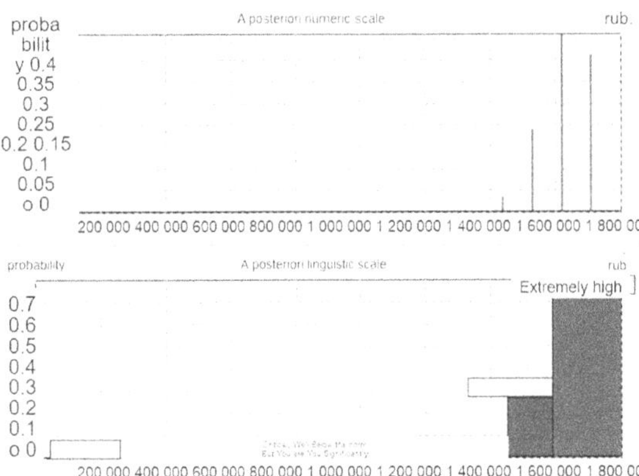

Fig. 2. Hypotheses about the state of the "expenses of construction contracts" factor.

Fig. 2 illustrates the fact that the estimate is obtained as a fuzzy set. The highest probability (0.717), has an alternative "Extremely above the norm", a possible alternative is also a score "Critically above the norm" (probability 0.271). Although each of the alternatives to this estimate has a low probability, in general, this estimate has a sufficiently high confidence approaching 1, which allows it to be used for practical purposes (see Fig. 3).

Model Metrology and risk assessment

Metrological characteristics and quality assessment of the top-level model:
The accuracy of 5.6%
the Accuracy Of 0.27
0.46 the Reliability
of the Risk model 73%

Metrological characteristics and quality assessment of the most likely model:
Accuracy 5.6% Reliability
0.461 Reliability 0.46
Risk of using the model
53.9%

Metrological characteristics and quality assessment of the lower-level model:
Accuracy 5: 5.6%
Confidence 0.269
Reliability 0.46
Risk of using the model 73.1%

Fig. 3. Metrological characteristics and risk assessment of models based on the "expenses of construction contracts".

The results obtained on the scale indicate that the factor "expenses of construction contracts"exceeded the cost rate, which requires further detailed information on it.

The results obtained on the scale indicate that the factor "expenses of construction contracts" exceeded the cost rate, which requires further detailed information on it. The system has determined that this factor is in an extremely dangerous state and tends to increase significantly. In this case, a detailed study of the documentation and a comprehensive analysis revealed that one of the subcontractors unreasonably exceeded the cost of work under the contract.

4. Conclusions

Based on the research, the following results and conclusions were obtained.

– An analytical decision support system based on the regularizing Bayesian approach can serve as an effective tool in the organization of cost management in conditions of significant information uncertainty;

– A working model based on the "Infoanalyst" computer platform was developed for the assessment and formation of costs, and the organization of management accounting under conditions of uncertainty, instability and significant influence of environment;

– The author's model can be successfully adapted to certain conditions and demands, used in practice as it meets the requirements of successful solving of the main tasks of digitalization influence of management accounting decisions.

References

[1]. O. Pavlatoa, H. Kostakis, Management accounting innovations in a time of economic crisis, *The Journal of Economic Asymmetries*, Vol. 18, 2018, e00106.

[2]. P. Rikhardsson, O. Yigitbasioglu, Business intelligence & analytics in management accounting research: Status and future focus, *International Journal of Accounting Information Systems,* Vol. 29, 2018, pp. 37-58.

[3]. S. V. Prokopchina, G. A. Scherbakov, Yu. V. Efimov, Modeling of socio-economic systems under conditions of uncertainty, G. A. Scherbakov (eds), *Scientific Library*, 2019 [in Rus.].

[4]. S. V. Prokopchina, Program "Infoanalyst" Certificate of the Federal service for intellectual property, patents and trademarks on the official registration of the computer program, No. 2004611741, dated 12th August, 2004.

Facial Expression Recognition using an Advanced Modeling of Completed Local Binary Pattern

An H. Ton-That [1] **and Nhan T. Cao** [2,3]
[1] University of Finance and Marketing, Faculty of Information Technology, Ho Chi Minh City, Vietnam
[2] University of Information Technology, Ho Chi Minh City, Vietnam
[3] Vietnam National University, Ho Chi Minh City, Vietnam
Tel.: +84 2838726789, fax: +84 2837720403
E-mail: antth@ufm.edu.vn; nhanct@uit.edu.vn

Summary: This paper proposes an improved feature modeling of Completed Local Binary Pattern (CLBP) combined with an effective image pre-processing technique for extracting features in facial expression recognition. The method has experimented on two typical kinds of dataset: medium (2040 images) and large (5130 images). Experimental results show recognition rate of the proposed method better in comparison with common modeling of Completed Local Binary Pattern feature and the Local Binary Pattern feature as well. Experiments performed on medium and large facial expression datasets obtained recognition rates are 99.95 % and 99.14 % respectively.

Keywords: Computer vision, Emotion detection, Facial expression recognition, Advanced completed local binary pattern.

1. Introduction

There are commonly two main methods to enhance the accuracy of an automatic facial expression recognition system. The first is discovering suitable features that more efficiently characterize different facial expressions, and the second is finding classifiers that better classifying facial expressions. In addition, determining a method of face image pre-process for extracting feature that is most appropriate for the kind of feature and classifier used is very useful for improving the recognition rate.

This work proposes a novel modeling of feature called the advanced modeling of completed local binary pattern or Combined Gray Local Binary Pattern (CGLBP). The feature combines the Local Binary Pattern (LBP) and Local Gray Level Difference (LGLD) of face images. This feature is extracted based on an effective method of face acquisition employed as in [1]. For emotion classification, Support Vector Machine (SVM) has been used.

2. Previous Related Works

2.1. Face acquisition

This process can be divided into two steps: basic step and enhancement step. The basic step is to detect the face region of an input face image and eliminate redundant regions. This step can carry out by manual or a real-time face detector …, and enhancement step is to optimize the face region for extracting facial expression features. This step can be made by cropping methods, image normalization or image filter processes. Then the face images are rescaled and used for feature extraction. Fig. 1 shows the process of face image preprocess.

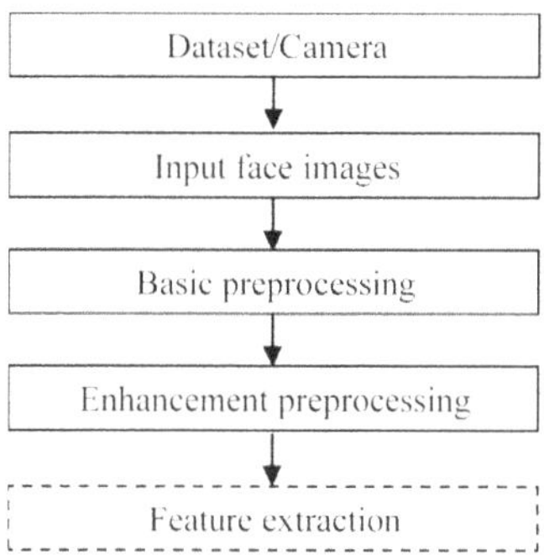

Fig. 1. The process of face image preprocess

In this work, the robust real-time face detector proposed by Viola and Jones [2] is employed to detect the face region of an input face image then a technique presented in [1] is used for cropping face images obtained from the robust real-time face detector to retain essential information and eliminate unnecessary information or pixels with little information. Fig. 2 illustrates steps for face acquisition of a face image from MUG dataset.

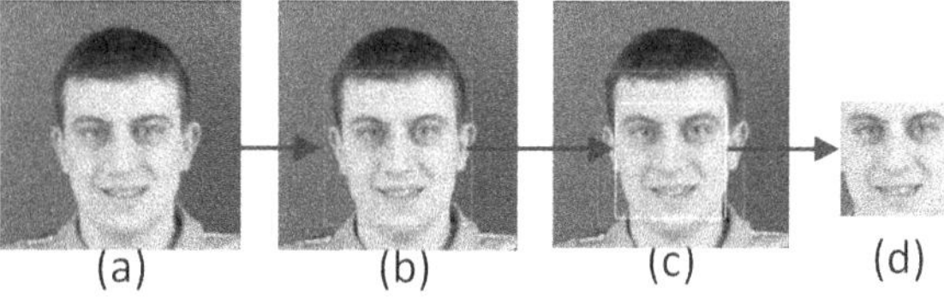

(a) Face image from image dataset
(b) Part of face image obtained from the robust real-time face detector (the red square)
(c) Part of face image obtained from the cropping technique (the yellow square or small square)
(d) Face image for extracting feature with a cropping percentage of w_2 to w_1 as in [1].

Fig. 2. The process of face acquisition.

2.2. Face Feature Extraction

Generally, there are two approaches for facial representation: geometric features as in Ref. [3] and appearance features, for example in Ref. [1]. This work uses an approach of dividing face images into non-overlap regions for extracting LBP features. Then each region is calculated LBP histogram or LBP feature. The LBP features extracted from each region are concatenated from left to right and up to down into a single feature vector of the face image as in Fig. 3.

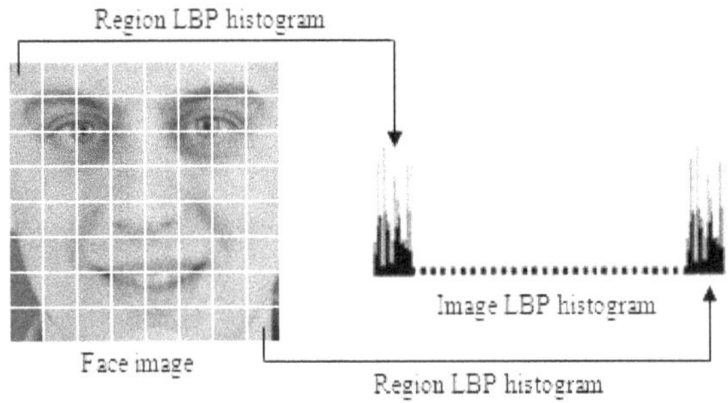

Fig. 3. Image LBP histogram or image LBP feature vector.

3. Advanced Modeling of Completed Local Binary Pattern

3.1. Local Binary Pattern (LBP)

The LBP operator was introduced as a complementary measure for local image contrast as in Ref. [4]. A local binary pattern code is computed for a pixel in an image by comparing it with its neighbors as in (3.1):

$$LBP_{P,R} = \sum_{p=0}^{P-1} s(g_p - g_c)2^p, s(x) = \begin{cases} 1, x \geq 0 \\ 0, x < 0 \end{cases} \quad (3.1)$$

with g_c is the gray value of the central pixel, g_p is the gray value of its neighbors, P is the total number of involved neighbors, and R is the radius of the neighborhood. A histogram of a labeled image $f_k(x, y)$ can be defined as following:

$$H_i = \sum_{x,y} I(f_k(x,y) = i), \quad i = 0, \ldots, n-1 \quad (3.2)$$

where n is the number of different labels produced by the LBP operator and

$$I(A) = \begin{cases} 1, & A \; is \; true \\ 0, & A \; is \; false \end{cases} \quad (3.3)$$

This histogram contains information about the distribution of the local micro-patterns, e.g. spots, edges, corners or flat areas etc., over the whole image. To represent the face efficiently, features extracted should retain spatial information. For this reason, the face image can be divided into m small regions R_0, R_1..., R_m as shown in Fig. 3. So a spatially enhanced histogram is expressed as:

$$H_{i,j} = \sum_{x,y} I(f_k(x,y) = i) \quad I\left((x,y) \in R_j\right) \quad (3.4)$$

where $i = 0,\ldots, n-1, j = 0,\ldots, m-1$.

The feature has been applied for facial expression recognition in [1]

3.2 Completed Local Binary Pattern

Local binary pattern has been used as an effective feature for facial expression recognition. But the local binary pattern only uses conventional sign component and ignores the magnitude component. However, it is also discovered that the information contained in magnitude difference or local gray level difference can provide a significant improvement to performance.

According to [5], based on a central pixel g_c and its P circularly and evenly spaced neighbors g_p, $p = 0, 1, \ldots, P-1$, the difference between g_c and g_p can be calculated as $d_p = g_p - g_c$.

The local difference vector $[d_0,\ldots, d_{P-1}]$ describes the image local structure at g_c and can be decomposed into two components:

$$d_p = s_p * m_p \quad with \begin{cases} s_p = sign(d_p) \\ m_p = |d_p| \end{cases} \quad (3.5)$$

where $s_p = \begin{cases} 1, d_p \geq 0 \\ 0, \; d_p < 0 \end{cases}$ is sign of d_p and m_p is the magnitude of d_p. Equation (3.5) is called the local difference sign-magnitude transform and it transforms the local difference vector $[d_0,\ldots, d_{P-1}]$ into a sign vector $[s_0,\ldots, s_{P-1}]$ and a magnitude vector $[m_0,\ldots, m_{P-1}]$

The model of completed local binary pattern included CLBP_S (s_p) and CLBP_M (m_p) operators. Two CLBP_S and CLBP_M operators have same binary string format, so they can be used together for pattern recognition. To form a CLBP descriptor, histograms of CLBP_S and CLBP_M codes of the image are made then they can be combined by two ways: in concatenation or jointly. In the first way, the histograms of the CLBP_S and CLBP_M codes are calculated separately, and then concatenate the two histograms together. This CLBP scheme can be represented as "CLBP_S_M". In the second way, a joint 2D histogram of the CLBP_S and CLBP_M codes are calculated. This CLBP scheme is represented as "CLBP_S/M". The feature has been research for facial expression recognition and presented in [6].

3.3. An Advanced Modeling of Completed Local Binary Pattern

The approach using CLBP_S_M in 3.2. takes much time to calculate $m_p = |d_p|$. In this work, an improved approach of modeling of completed local binary pattern is proposed called CLBP_S_G for brief. This modeling is based on the CLBP_S operator and image local gray level difference called CLBP_G for brief.

Fig. 4 shows an example of the transformation of CLBP_S and CLBP_G from a 3x3 sample block.

The sign component of CLBP_S_G is the same with the sign component of CLBP_S_M, where the CLBP_G operator is defined as in (3.6).

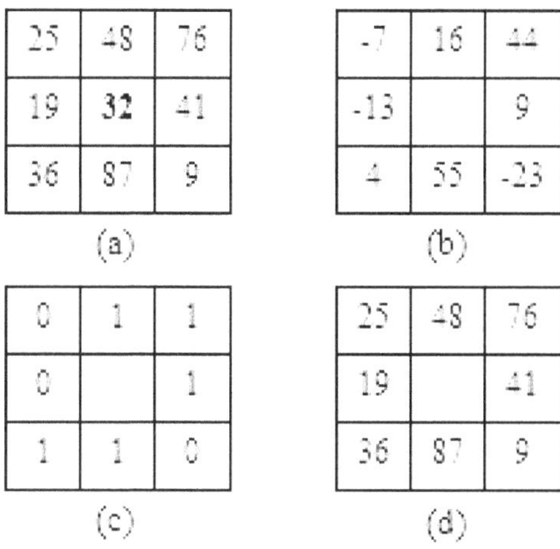

Fig. 4. The transformation of sign and magnitude components of the improved modeling of CLBP: (a) A 3x3 sample block, (b) local difference, (c) sign component and (d) gray level component.

$$CLBP\_G_{P,R} = \sum_{p=0}^{P-1} t(g_p, c)\, 2^p,\; t(x,c) = \begin{cases} 1, x \geq c \\ 0, x < c \end{cases} \quad (3.6)$$

where, the threshold c is to be determined adaptively. Here, c is taken to be the mean value of g_p over the CLBP_G operator.

Based on the idea of choosing effective threshold for CLBP_M, in order to choose an effective threshold for CLBP_G, some different thresholds were tested as following:

- The mean value of g_p from the whole image
- The mean value of g_p from the region
- The mean value of g_p from the CLBP_G operator.

Experiment results on the two datasets show that choosing the threshold as in the last case obtain the best accurate in facial expression recognition. It can be explained as following:

- One weak point of LBP operator is that it is very sensitive to noise. The label of patterns will be changed even just only one noise pixel occurred.
- So choosing threshold is the mean value of gp from the CLBP_G operator can not only make CLBP operator more tolerant of noise, but also combines the difference of magnitude component.

Two CLBP_S and CLBP_G operators also have same binary string format, so they can be used together for pattern recognition like CLBP_S and CLBP_M operators.

4. Experiments and Results

The work experimented on two typical image datasets based on the proposed method. First is Cohn-Kanade (CK) dataset including 2040 images and second is MUG dataset including 5130 images. Resolution of images is 64x64 pixels. Each region is 8x8 pixels. The 3-fold cross-validation technique has been used for estimating the performance.

4.1. The Cohn-Kanade (CK) Dataset

The Cohn-Kanade dataset is one of the most comprehensive datasets in the current facial expression research community [7]. The CK dataset consists of 100 university students aged from 18 to 30 years, of which 65 % were female, 15 % were African-American, and 3 % were Asian or Latino. Subjects were instructed to perform a series of 23 facial displays, six of which were based on description of basic emotions (i.e., anger, disgust, fear, joy, sadness, and surprise). Image sequences from neutral to target display were digitized into 640×490 pixel arrays with 8-bit precision for grayscale values.

Fig. 5 shows that accuracy rates of non-cropped images (full images obtained from the robust real-time face detection algorithm or percentage 100% of w_2/w_1) for all three kinds of feature (LBP, CLBP_S_M, CLBP_S_G) almost less than the accuracy rates of cropped images (from 80 % to 90 % of w_2/w_1) on CK dataset. The CLBP_S_G feature obtains highest accuracy at 99.95 % with cropping percentage of w_2 to w_1 being 85 % and almost better than LBP and CLBP_S_M features in remain percentages of w_2 to w_1.

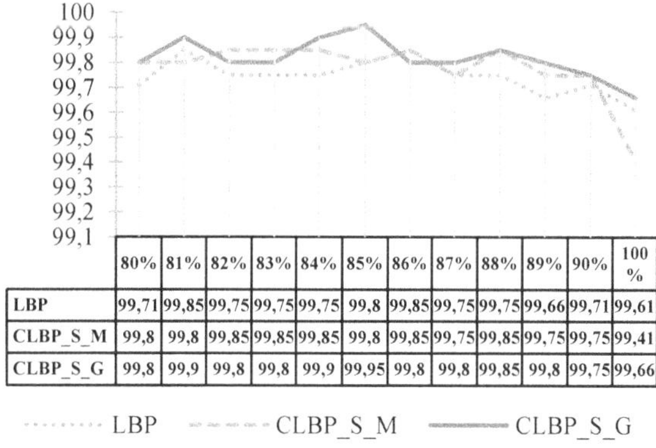

	80%	81%	82%	83%	84%	85%	86%	87%	88%	89%	90%	100 %
LBP	99,71	99,85	99,75	99,75	99,75	99,8	99,85	99,75	99,75	99,66	99,71	99,61
CLBP_S_M	99,8	99,8	99,85	99,85	99,85	99,8	99,85	99,75	99,85	99,75	99,75	99,41
CLBP_S_G	99,8	99,9	99,8	99,8	99,9	99,95	99,8	99,8	99,85	99,8	99,75	99,66

Fig. 5. Comparison of experimental results of LBP, CLBP_S_M and CLBP_S_G for CK dataset.

Table 1 shows the confusion matrix of CK dataset based on CLBP_S_G feature with cropping percentage of w_2 to w_1 being 85 %.

Table 1. Confusion matrix of CK dataset.

(%)	Anger	Disgust	Fear	Joy	Neutral	Sadness	Surprise
Anger	**100**	0.00	0.00	0.00	0.00	0.00	0.00
Disgust	0.00	**100**	0.00	0.00	0.00	0.00	0.00
Fear	0.00	0.00	**100**	0.00	0.00	0.00	0.00
Joy	0.00	0.00	0.00	**100**	0.00	0.00	0.00
Neutral	0.00	0.00	0.00	0.00	**100**	0.00	0.00
Sadness	0.00	0.00	0.00	0.00	0.00	**100**	0.00
Surprise	0.00	0.00	0.00	0.00	0.28	0.00	**99.72**

4.2. The MUG Dataset

The MUG database was created by the Multimedia Understanding Group [8]. It was created to overcome some limitations of the other similar databases that preexisted at that time, such as low resolution, uniform lighting, many subjects and many takes per subject. The aim is to help the research on the field of expression recognition. The images of 52 subjects are available to authorized internet users. This part of database includes 52 Caucasian subjects, 22 females and 30 males (with or without beards), in the 20 to 35 age range. Each image was saved with a jpeg format, 896x896 pixels and a size ranging from 240 to 340 KB.

In this work, 50 subjects (22 females and 28 males) are selected. Each expression includes 15 face images with facial expressions from less to more. Because some subjects are not enough seven facial expressions, totally 5130 human face images are selected including 750 images of anger, 735 images of disgust, 705 image of fear, 735 images of joy, 750 images of neutral, 705 images of sadness and 750 images of surprise.

Fig. 6 shows that accuracy rates of non-cropped images for all three kinds of feature (LBP, CLBP_S_M, CLBP_S_G) almost less than the accuracy rates of cropped images (from 80 % to 90 % of w_2/w_1) on MUG dataset. The CLBP_S_G feature obtains highest accuracy at 99.14 % with cropping percentage of w_2 to w_1 being 90 % and almost better than LBP and CLBP_S_M features in remain percentages of w_2 to w_1.

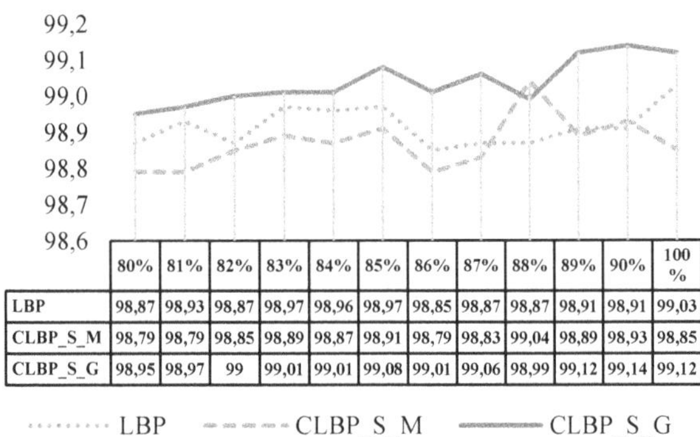

Fig. 6. Comparison of experimental results of LBP, CLBP_S_M and CLBP_S_G for MUG dataset.

Table 2 shows the confusion matrix of MUG dataset based on CLBP_S_G feature with cropping percentage of w_2 to w_1 being 90%.

Table 2. The confusion matrix of MUG dataset.

(%)	Anger	Disgust	Fear	Joy	Neutral	Sadness	Surprise
Anger	**99.07**	0.13	0.00	0.00	0.80	0.00	0.00
Disgust	0.14	**99.73**	0.00	0.00	0.14	0.00	0.00
Fear	0.00	0.00	**99.01**	0.00	0.71	0.00	0.28
Joy	0.00	0.14	0.14	**99.73**	0.00	0.00	0.00
Neutral	0.13	0.00	0.00	0.00	**99.87**	0.00	0.00
Sadness	1.13	0.00	0.28	0.00	0.14	**98.44**	0.00
Surprise	0.00	0.00	1.87	0.00	0.00	0.00	**98.13**

5. Conclusions

The research presents the facial expression recognition using an advanced modeling of completed local binary pattern with combination of face image cropping technique in preprocessing stage and the method of dividing face images into non-overlap square regions for stage of extracting features. The experimental results on CK and MUG typical datasets show that the accuracy rate of the feature based on the proposed modeling of completed local binary pattern are better than that of LBP and CLBP features. In addition, the calculating time of the proposed CLBP is better than that of original CLBP.

Acknowledgements

The authors would like to thank Professor Jeffery Cohn for authorizing us to use Cohn-Kanade dataset and Professor Anastasios Delopoulos for authorizing us to use MUG dataset in this work. This research is funded by University of Finance and Marketing, under Grant No. CS-27-20.

References

[1]. Nhan T. Cao, An H. Ton-That, Hyung-Il Choi, Facial Expression Recognition based on Local Binary Pattern and Support Vector Machine, *International Journal of Pattern Recognition and Artificial Intelligence*, Vol. 28, No. 6, 2014, 1456012.

[2] Paul Viola, Michael J. Jones, Robust real-time face detection, *International Journal on Computer Vision*, Vol. 57, No. 2, 2004, pp. 137–154.

[3] Allen Joseph, P. Geetha, Facial emotion detection using modified eyemap–mouthmap algorithm on an enhanced image and classification with tensorflow, *Visual Computer*, Vol. 36, 2020, pp. 529–539.

[4] Timo Ojala, Matti Pietikainen, Topi Maenpaa, Multiresolution gray-scale and rotation invariant texture classification with local binary patterns, *IEEE Transactions on Pattern Analysis and Machine Intelligence*, Vol. 24, No.7, 2002, pp. 971–987.

[5] Zhenhua Guo, Lei Zhang, David Zhang, A Completed Modeling of Local Binary Pattern Operator for Texture Classification. *IEEE Transactions on Image Processing*, Vol. 19, No. 6, 2010, pp. 1657-1663.

[6] Nhan T. Cao; An H. Ton-That, Hyung-Il Choi, An effective facial expression recognition approach for intelligent game systems, *International Journal of Computational Vision and Robotics*, Vol. 6, No. 3, 2016, pp. 223-234.

[7] Patrick Lucey, Jeffrey F. Cohn, Takeo Kanade, Jason Saragih, Zara Ambadar, The Extended Cohn-Kanade Dataset (CK+): A complete dataset for action unit and emotion-specified expression, in *Proceedings of the IEEE Conference on Computer Vision and Pattern Recognition Workshops*, San Francisco, CA, USA, 13-18 June 2010, pp. 94-101.

[8] N. Aifanti, C. Papachristou, A. Dolopoulos, The MUG Facial Expression Database, in *Proceeding of the 11th Interantional Workshop on Image Analysis for Multimedia Interactive Services (WIAMIS)*, Desenzano, Italy, 12-14 April 2010.

(088)

Uncertainty Estimation for Non-destructive Detection of Material Defects with U-nets

B. Lehner and **T. Gallien**
Silicon Austria Labs (SAL), Embedded AI, Altenbergerstr. 69, Science Park 3, 4020 Linz, Austria
E-mail: bernhard.lehner@silicon-austria.com

Abstract: Thermographic Imaging is a method for the detection of material defects inside the inspected specimen in a non-destructive manner. U-net was recently proposed to be used for thermographic imaging, and represents the new state-of-the-art in the field. In this paper, we propose two computationally very cheap methods to estimate the uncertainty of such u-net predictions. We demonstrate the efficacy of our method through the utilization as a loss proxy for rejection above a specific loss. For this, we use two models that differ in training data and compare with an ensemble based method.

Keywords: U-net, Uncertainty estimation, Thermographic imaging.

1. Introduction

In [5], a hybrid method for thermographic image reconstruction was proposed. Virtual wave images [1] were used as a mid-level representation and fed to very compact u-net models, significantly outperforming model based numerical methods. However, it was also shown that the reconstruction results deteriorate under low SNR conditions, and it would be useful to have an uncertainty estimate along with the output. In this paper, we propose two methods for such an estimate, which are both computationally very light-weight. Additionally, we directly infer the uncertainty by analyzing the predicted image containing the defects in a single forward pass. This is another advantage over methods that require a multitude of forward propagations in order to derive an uncertainty estimate, like e.g. dropout-based uncertainty estimation [2] or Bayesian ensembling [7].

2. Method

In this Section, we propose two methods for uncertainty estimation, and we start by describing the neural network architecture and the data that we use throughout our experiments.

2.1. Network

The u-net architecture was initially proposed for various medical image segmentation tasks [8, 3], and won the ISBI cell tracking challenge in 2015. It is basically an autoencoder with skipconnections from the contracting path to the expansive path, enabling the network to localize. For a more detailed description we refer to the original paper [8].

In this paper, we focus on the architecture from [5] with just 16 filters in the first (single channel) layer, resulting in about 1.8 million weights.

2.2. Data

We demonstrate our uncertainty estimate by the application of thermographic imaging for non-destructive material testing presented in [5] where the task is to detect material defects by reconstructing the temperature evaluation of a previously heated up specimen.

We use surface temperature profiles fed in as virtual waves [1] (as input) and target masks (representing the defects) as single channel images, both having a dimensionality of 256 by 64 pixels. An example can be seen in the 1st row of Fig. 1.

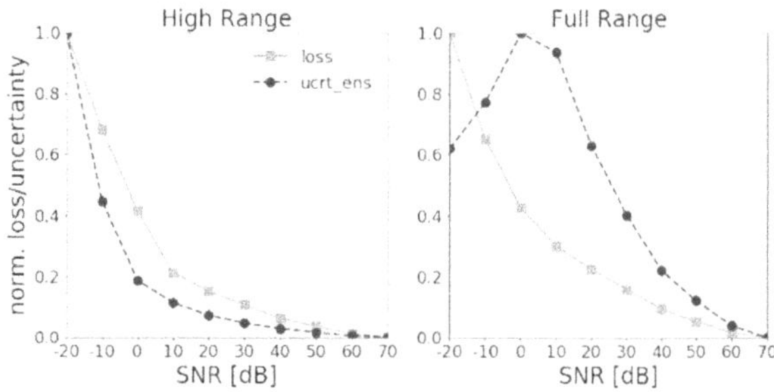

Fig. 1. Loss and uncertainty of the ensemble approach. Full Range: trained with all SNR conditions from [-20 to 70] dB; High Range: trained only with a subset ranging from [10 to 70] dB. This method reflects the decreased loss corresponding to increased SNRs only for the high range model.

For a more detailed description of the data we like to refer to [5]. For training and validating the full SNR range model, we use ten different versions of each sample, representing SNRs from -20 dB to 70 dB in 10 dB steps. All in all, we use 27,000 and 10,000 samples for training and validation of the full range model, respectively. For training and validating the high SNR range model, we use just seven SNRs, ranging from 10 dB to 70 dB in 10 dB steps. All in all, we use 18,900 and 7,000 samples for training and validation of the high range model, respectively. We evaluate both models on a separate, unseen test data set which is normalized according to the training data respectively. It consists of 1,000 samples in versions for ten different SNRs, resulting in 10,000 examples in total.

2.3. Uncertainty Estimation

First, we define a mask operator $\mathbf{g}_\theta : \mathbf{X} \in \mathbb{R}^{M \times N} \rightarrow \{0,1\}^{M \times N}$ where

$$[\mathbf{g}_\theta(\mathbf{X})]_{ij} = \begin{cases} 1 & \mathbf{X}_{ij} > \theta, 0 < \theta \leq 1 \\ 0 & \text{else} \end{cases} \quad (1)$$

We then generate the binarized predictions $\widehat{\mathbf{X}}_{\text{sens}} = \mathbf{g}_\alpha(\widehat{\mathbf{X}})$ and $\widehat{\mathbf{X}}_{\text{conf}} = \mathbf{g}_\beta(\widehat{\mathbf{X}})$, where α and β are set to 0.01 and 0.95, respectively. This leads to $\widehat{\mathbf{X}}_{\text{sens}}$ being highly sensitive with respect to the predictions, while $\widehat{\mathbf{X}}_{\text{conf}}$ involves only highly confident pixels. In Figure 1, we can see some examples of this binarization step. These two binarized masks serve then as the basis for our uncertainty estimates.

For our 1st method, we first evaluate the mean squared error (mse) of the predicted image $\widehat{\mathbf{X}}$ on only the non-zero pixels of a binarized version of $\widehat{\mathbf{X}}$. We additionally scale this by the ratio of the number of non-zero pixels of the confident to the sensitive binarized masks. Finally, we define the uncertainty estimate as

$$UCRT_1 = \frac{\text{mse}(\widehat{X} \circ \widehat{X}_{\text{sens}}, \widehat{X}_{\text{sens}})}{1 + \frac{||\widehat{X}_{\text{conf}}||_0}{||\widehat{X}_{\text{sens}}||_0}}, \quad (2)$$

where $\circ$ defines the Hadamard product and the L^0-norm is used to denote the number of non-zero pixels of the corresponding mask.

For our 2nd method, we take the relative estimated area of the defects into account as follows

$$UCRT_2 = \left(1 - \frac{||\widehat{X}_{\text{sens}}||_0}{n}\right) \frac{||\widehat{X}_{\text{conf}}||_0}{||\widehat{X}_{\text{sens}}||_0}, \quad (3)$$

where n denotes the number of pixels of the output image.

3. Setup of Experiment

We train two u-nets, a full SNR range model and a high SNR range model, as described in Section 2.2. However, we use the full validation set comprising 10.000 samples for both models for the development of our uncertainty estimates. The high SNR range model is expected to perform worse on data corresponding to untrained SNR conditions, and will be helpful to determine the capabilities of the methods.

First, we give an overview by computing the average loss and uncertainties for all SNR conditions (1,000 samples each). The monotonic decrease of the loss corresponding to increased SNRs should be reflected by the uncertainty estimates.

Second, we utilize the uncertainty estimates to implement a reject option that is supposed to reject samples with an expected loss above a specific threshold. That is, we formulate a 2-class classification problem to distinguish reject and no reject categories. The threshold for the loss is fixed so that 30 % of the validation data results fall into the category reject and shared between all methods. The corresponding uncertainty threshold is then fixed for each method and each model separately to fulfill several requirements as follows. The uncertainty is thresholded to give maximum accuracy, equal error rate, a false positive rate of 5 %, and a false positive rate of 1 %. These four requirements lead to four different uncertainty thresholds, and four evaluation results.

Finally, we take the loss and uncertainty thresholds, and evaluate on the unseen test data set.

3.1. Baseline

We compare our method with an ensemble based approach similar to the one presented by [6], comprising five models. For regression they model the prediction by means of a Gaussian mixture model and thus derive an uncertainty measure by calculating the mean of the Kullback-Leibler divergence of the individual mixture components with respect to the ensemble distribution. However, since thermographic imaging differs significantly from the proposed regression setting we do not explicitly model the predictions to be Gaussian. Instead, we derive the uncertainty measure rather from an empirical estimate of the ensemble variance instead of explicitly calculating the Kullback-Leibler divergence. That is, we take the mean of the pixelwise variances as our uncertainty baseline, and refer to it as **UCRT_ENS** for the remainder of this paper. The loss is computed on the averaged predictions of the ensemble.

Notice, that the probabilistic u-net presented by [4] is not suitable for our scenario, since our target is deterministic.

4. Results

After having described the exact setup of experiment in the previous Section, we now report on the results.

4.1. Validation Data Results

In this section we present the results on the validation data. We start by showing a weakness of the ensemble based approach in Fig. 2, where we plot the loss and uncertainty of the high SNR and the full SNR range models. For better comparison, we normalize the loss and uncertainty each to be between 0 and 1. As can be seen, the decreased loss corresponding to increased SNRs is well reflected for the high range model, but not for the full range model. This indicates, that even though the predictions are more corrupted under very low SNRs, they are getting more similar within the ensemble.

In Fig. 3, we can see that contrary to the ensemble approach, both our uncertainty methods yield results that better reflect the actual loss curves.

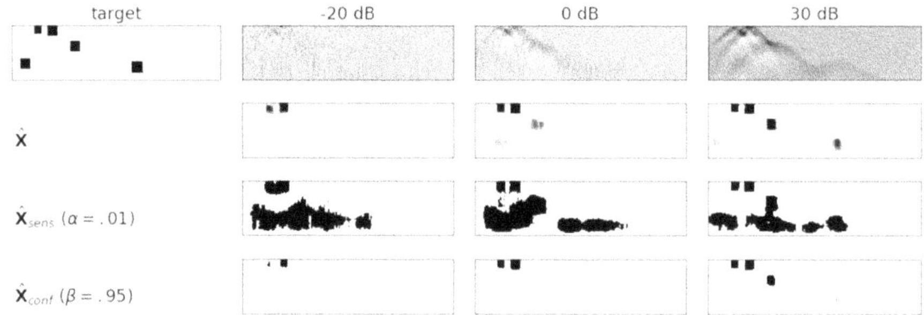

Fig. 2. The 1st row: target and input (virtual waves) to the u-net under several SNR conditions. The 2nd row: raw output of the unet. It can be seen how the quality of the output suffers as the SNR decreases. The 3rd row: the highly sensitive binarized mask used to compute the MSE. The 4th row: another binarized mask based on high confident pixles.

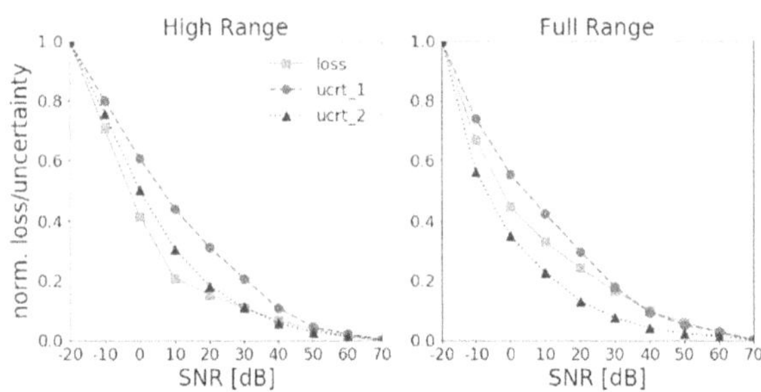

Fig. 3. Loss and uncertainty of our approaches. Compared to the ensemble approach in Figure 2, both methods better reflect the decreased loss corresponding to increased SNRs.

Next, we present the results where we use uncertainty estimates to implement a reject option as described in Section 3. In Table 1, the results of the different scenarios on the validation data are listed for all three methods. For each metric (precision, recall, f1-measure, and accuracy), the results on the full range model and the high range model are listed on the left and right column, respectively.

In general, the full SNR range model seems to be more challenging for all uncertainty based rejection methods. This makes sense, since the high SNR range models produce higher losses under the unseen, low SNR conditions (-20, -10, and 0 dB). Therefore, the average of the actual loss of the 30% that we categorize as *reject* is higher compared to the full range model, and therefore easier to be identified as such. The rejection based on method UCRT_2 from Equation 3 is the least affected by this phenomenon.

Additionally, the rejection based on UCRT_2 consistently outperforms the other methods in all regards, and on both the full and high range models. This suggests that for our specific task at hand, there is a correlation between the area of defects and the loss, since UCRT_2 factors this in.

The rejection based on method UCRT_1 from Equation 2 gives results that are comparable to the baseline method UCRT_ENS when evaluated at maximum accuracy and equal error rate. When evaluated at a limited false positive rate, UCRT_1 gives inferior results compared to UCRT_ENS, especially for the high range model.

Table 1. Results of the uncertainty based rejection on the validation set. UCRT_2 consistently outperforms the other methods.

	Precision		Recall		F1-Measure		Accuracy	
	full	high	full	high	full	high	full	high
Evaluation @Maximum Accuracy								
UCRT_ENS	.69	.85	.69	.73	.69	.79	.80	.88
UCRT_1	.75	.80	.60	.71	.67	.75	.81	.86
UCRT_2	.84	.85	.79	.81	.81	.83	.89	.90
Evaluation @Equal Error Rate								
UCRT_ENS	.63	.73	.80	.86	.71	.79	.79	.86
UCRT_1	.65	.70	.80	.85	.72	.77	.80	.84
UCRT_2	.76	.77	.88	.90	.82	.83	.87	.89
Evaluation @5% False Positives								
UCRT_ENS	.79	.87	.47	.71	.59	.78	.79	.88
UCRT_1	.80	.84	.45	.59	.58	.70	.79	.84
UCRT_2	.87	.88	.71	.78	.78	.82	.88	.90
Evaluation @1% False Positives								
UCRT_ENS	.92	.96	.19	.43	.32	.59	.74	.82
UCRT_1	.86	.89	.12	.19	.22	.31	.72	.74
UCRT_2	.96	.97	.46	.55	.62	.70	.82	.86

4.2. Test Data Results

In this section we present the results on the unseen test data, where we use uncertainty estimates to implement a reject option as described in Section 3. Notice, that since we took the loss thresholds for the reject categorization from the validation data, the relative size of the class of interest reject is not exactly 30 %, but very close with 31.5 % and 30.6 % for the full and high SNR range models, respectively.

In Table 2, the results of the different scenarios are listed for all three methods. In general, the results are very similar to the validation data results, and the rejection based on UCRT_2 consistently outperforms the other methods again.

Table 2. Results of the uncertainty based rejection on the unseen test set. In general, the results are very similar to the validation data results, and UCRT_2 consistently outperforms the other methods.

	Precision		Recall		F1-Measure		Accuracy	
	full	high	full	high	full	high	full	high
Evaluation @Maximum Accuracy								
UCRT_ENS	.70	.84	.68	.73	.69	.78	.82	.88
UCRT_1	.73	.79	.60	.71	.66	.75	.81	.86
UCRT_2	.82	.85	.78	.80	.80	.82	.88	.90
Evaluation @Equal Error Rate								
UCRT_ENS	.64	.72	.80	.86	.71	.78	.80	.86
UCRT_1	.63	.69	.80	.84	.70	.76	.80	.84
UCRT_2	.75	.76	.87	.88	.80	.82	.87	.88
Evaluation @5% False Positives								
UCRT_ENS	.80	.86	.45	.70	.58	.77	.80	.88
UCRT_1	.79	.83	.44	.59	.57	.69	.80	.84
UCRT_2	.86	.87	.71	.76	.78	.81	.88	.89
Evaluation @1% False Positives								
UCRT_ENS	.89	.95	.19	.42	.31	.58	.75	.82
UCRT_1	.84	.88	.13	.17	.22	.29	.73	.75
UCRT_2	.95	.96	.46	.54	.62	.69	.83	.86

5. Discussion

The consistency of the results even on unseen data suggests good generalization capabilities, but might be to a large degree due to the specific task at hand. The mid-level representation that we use as input (virtual waves) is designed to remove information like thermal diffusion property of the material under test. This form of data preprocessing reduces the risk of internal covariate shift, and supports generalization. However, the proposed uncertainty estimation methods could still be useful for tasks where the output can be converted into one or several binary masks as well, e.g. semantic or instance segmentation, and we intend to assess this in upcoming experiments.

Applying our approaches to other domains most likely requires the calibration of α and β hyperparameters in order to get the desired behaviour. Even so, this is just a matter of a simple grid search, or a histogram analysis of the predictions of the u-net.

Another scenario that would require the calibration of α and β is dynamic model selection, where for instance the better of two models is dynamically selected based on their uncertainty estimates. First experiments in that direction suggest that with shared α and β the difference in model performance needs to be substantial in order to reliably select the better model for each sample.

6. Conclusion

In this paper, we present two light-weight methods for uncertainty estimation of u-net predictions, and report on two experiments. First, we demonstrated the high correlation of the uncertainty with the actual loss under different SNR conditions. Second, we showed how to use uncertainty to reject predictions that exceed a specific loss. In both experiments, we managed to outperform the ensemble based baseline with one approach (UCRT_2), even though it is just based on the result of a single forward pass and computationally less expensive.

Being computationally so extremely cheap, our uncertainty estimates are best suited for applications at the edge, even in real-time scenarios.

Acknowledgements

This work has been supported by Silicon Austria Labs (SAL), owned by the Republic of Austria, the Styrian Business Promotion Agency (SFG), the federal state of Carinthia, the Upper Austrian Research (UAR), and the Austrian Association for the Electric and Electronics Industry (FEEI).

References

[1]. Burgholzer P., et al., Three-dimensional thermographic imaging using a virtual wave concept. *Journal of Applied Physics,* 121, 10, 2017, p. 105102.

[2]. Gal, Y., Ghahramani, Z., Dropout as a Bayesian approximation: Representing model uncertainty in deep learning, in *Proc. of the 33rd Int. Conf. on Machine Learning (PMLR)*, New York, USA, 2016, Vol. 48, pp. 1050–1059.

[3]. Jenkins, M. D., et al., A deep convolutional neural network for semantic pixel-wise segmentation of road and pavement surface cracks, in *Proceedings of the 26th European Signal Processing Conf. (EUSIPCO 2018)*, 2018, pp.2120–2124.

[4]. Kohl S., et al., A probabilistic u-net for segmentation of ambiguous images, in *Proceedings of the 31 Advances in Neural Information Processing Systems Conference (NIPS2018)*, 2018, pp.6965–6975.

[5]. Kovacs, P., et al., A hybrid approach for thermographic imaging with deep learning, in *Proceedings of the 45th Int. Conf. on Acoustics, Speech, and Signal Processing (ICASSP 2020)*, 2020, pp. 4277–4281.

[6]. Lakshminarayanan, B., et al., Simple and scalable predictive uncertainty estimation using deep ensembles, in *Proceedings of the 30 Advances in Neural Information Processing Systems Conference (NIPS2017)*, 2017, pp. 6402–6413.

[7]. Pearce, T., et al., Uncertainty in neural networks: Approximately bayesian ensembling, in *Proceedings of the 23rd Int. Conf. on Artificial Intelligence and Statistics* (in press).

[8]. Ronneberger, O., et al., U-net: Convolutional networks for biomedical image segmentation, in *Proceedings of the Medical Image Computing and Computer-Assisted In-tervention Conference (MICCAI 2015)*, 2015, pp. 234–241.

(090)

Deep Learning Approach for Skin Lesion Attributes Detection and Melanoma Diagnosis

Saeed Alzahrani and Waleed Al-Nuaimy
Department of Electrical Engineering and Electronics, University of Liverpool, UK
E-mail: {s.g.a.alzahrani, wax}@liverpool.ac.uk

Summary: Reliable identification of skin lesions is an important pre-requisite for diagnosing melanoma and other skin diseases. Established models of melanoma assessment suggest either methods of pattern analysis or seven-point checklist criteria for examining skin lesion. Automated and correct skin lesion identification and subsequent diagnosis of melanoma remain an unresolved challenge. In addition, the two evaluation methods have drawbacks and a trade-off. This paper proposes a method of pattern analysis combining 7-point checklist with convolution neural network for melanoma diagnosis, where the lesion features are automatically extracted. Both clinical and dermoscopic images were considered input into the established multi-input convolution neural networks (CNNs) where a separate feature extraction model was implemented from each image type. The performance of the developed algorithm is assessed using a 2000 dermoscopic image dataset. The results obtained from the proposed system show promising and competitive performance for detection of lesions and the automated diagnosis of melanoma from dermoscopic images.

Keywords: Skin lesion, Convolutional neural networks, Melanoma, Deep Learning, Dermoscopic images.

1. Introduction

The most common form of cancer is skin cancer, which can be particularly truculent. Over 100,000 new cases of skin cancer are reported in the UK annually [1]. Malignant melanoma is a minor type of skin cancer but a fetal and highly aggressive melanoma that threatens to spread to the other parts of the body causing death if not diagnosed early.

Dermatologists generally evaluate skin lesions using the seven-point checklist method [2] or the ABCD method, most widely suggested and approved skin evaluation techniques. Suspicion is stronger in the seven-point checklist rule for lesions scoring 3 points or more than 3 while low suspicion lesions should be cautiously screened and tracked for eight weeks for changes.

Argenziano et al. [2] developed a seven-point checklist for the dermoscopic distinction between benign and malignant lesions. Atypical Pigment Network (PN), Blue Whitish Veil (BWV), Vascular Structure (VS), Irregular Pigmentation (PIG), Irregular Streaks (STR), Irregular Dots and Globules (Dag), Regression Structures (RS) are the seven-point checklist lesions.

This research work is extended work of the system developed and presented in [3] by authors. Here, we present and explore the development and improvements carried out on the proposed lesion detection and melanoma diagnosis system.

2. Methodology

The proposed lesion detection and melanoma diagnosis comprises seven models (M1, M2, ..., M7). Each model purposes to detect a lesion from the seven-point checklist. Along with the other labels, the predicated lesion attribute label (P1, P2, ..., P7) is taken into consideration and their weights are summed to generate the diagnosis score according to the criteria of the 7-point checklist. If the score obtained is equal to or greater than three, the decision taken by the network will result in class 1 indicating the case of melanoma, otherwise it will result in class 0 indicating non-melanoma.

Fig. 1 shows the abstract level block diagram of proposed system.

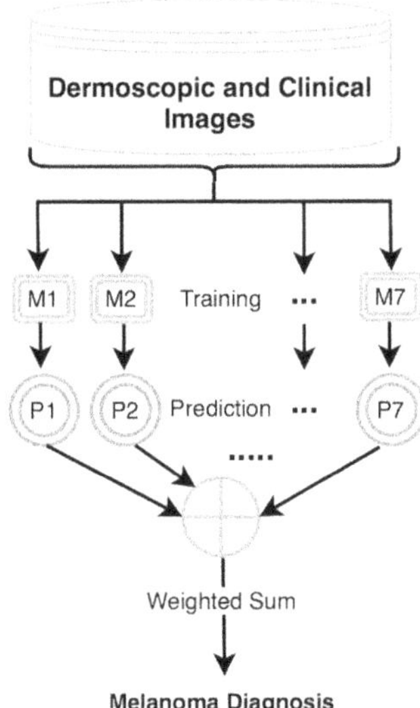

Fig. 1. Block diagram of proposed melanoma diagnosis system.

We build our system using five backbone network architectures models pretrained over ImageNet dataset. Five convolutional neural network models including AlexNet, VGG16, ResNet101, DenseNet201, Inception V3. We retrain the models on the dermoscopic and clinical images where the weights are fine-tuned. We adopt Alexnet architecture as baseline model. We apply augmentation on the training images in real-time with horizontal and vertical flipping, rotations, zooms, and random translations. As the data has imbalanced distribution of positive and negative labels, we address this issue by oversampling the minority classes in each batch of training data. We further penalised the classification by imposing an additional cost and upweighting on the minority class during model training.

3. Results and Discussions

In the experiments, a publicly accessible dataset [4] was used to test computerized image-based prediction of the 7-point skin lesion malignancy checklist. The dataset comprises over 2000 clinical and dermoscopic color images for computer-aided diagnostic system training and evaluation. The data was split randomly into 60% training and the rest for evaluation. All images were resized to $256 \times 256 \times 3$.

Table 1 and Table 2 show the performance of our proposed pipeline system for skin lesion and melanoma detection in terms of accuracy, sensitivity and specificity. Best results are obtained from Inception v3 backbone producing average accuracy, sensitivity and specificity of 0.7250, 0.6576, 0.7705; respectively, for lesion detection and 0.7253, 0.6023, 0.9071; respectively, for melanoma diagnosis.

Table 1. Lesion detection performance.

No.	Acc.	Sen.	Spe.
Baseline	0.6701	0.6387	0.7023
VGG19	0.6931	0.6473	0.7324
ResNet101	0.7067	0.6519	0.7469
DenseNet201	0.717	0.6566	0.7616
Inception V3	**0.725**	**0.6576**	**0.7705**

Table 2. Melanoma diagnsosis performance.

No.	Acc.	Sen.	Spe.
Baseline	0.643	0.5537	0.8926
VGG19	0.6722	0.5696	0.8978
ResNet101	0.6989	0.582	0.9003
DenseNet201	0.7121	0.5914	0.9055
Inception V3	**0.7253**	**0.6023**	**0.9071**

Kawahara et al. [4] presented a multi-task system for lesion detection and melanoma diagnosis achieving average accuracy of 0.7370, sensitivity of 0.6620 and specificity of 0.8060 for lesion detection and average accuracy, sensitivity and specificity of 0.7420, 0.6040, 0.9100; respectively for melanoma diagnosis on the same dataset we used to carry out the evaluation of our proposed system.

The performance of the developed separate pipelines for predicting eight different categories (melanoma diagnosis and seven-point checklist) reveals close and comparable results with the multi-task system proposed in [4]. However, the authors explained that the labels of eight categories are not mutually exclusive yet defined a multi-task loss function with eight terms for eight tasks without considering the dissimilarity among tasks. The dissimilar tasks could affect badly on the generalisation performance of the multi-task system if tested on further unseen datasets. Their method treats all eight tasks with equivalent importance and therefore it becomes crucial to find a robust strategy to choose the weighting scheme for each task in the loss function.

In future work, we aim to extend our experiments by developing a network architecture composing of a common feature pool providing task-shared features for eight tasks, along with task-specific attention modules for each task, which allows for automatic learning of both features (shared and specific) and finding the correct and suitable balance between those tasks.

4. Conclusions

A new technique for skin lesion identification and the diagnosis of melanoma from dermoscopy images was introduced and successfully implemented by integrating seven-point checklist criteria with convolution neural networks. Our approach is proven to work well and deliver favorable results.

References

[1]. Ries, Lynn AG, et al., SEER cancer statistics review, 1975-2003, *SEER*, 2006.

[2]. Argenziano, Giuseppe, et al., Epiluminescence microscopy for the diagnosis of doubtful melanocytic skin lesions: comparison of the ABCD rule of dermatoscopy and a new 7-point checklist based on pattern analysis, *Archives of Dermatology*, 134, 12, 1998, pp. 1563-1570.

[3]. Alzahrani, Saeed, et al., Seven-Point Checklist with Convolutional Neural Networks for Melanoma Diagnosis, in *Proceedings of the 8th IEEE European Workshop on Visual Information Processing (EUVIP)*, Roma, Italy, 2019.

[4]. Kawahara, Jeremy, et al., Seven-point checklist and skin lesion classification using multitask multimodal neural nets, *IEEE Journal of Biomedical and Health Informatics*, 23, 2, 2018, pp. 538-546.

(094)

Unsupervised Embedded Gesture Recognition based on Multi-objective NAS and Capacitive Sensing

J. Borrego-Carazo[1, 2], **D. Castells-Rufas**[1], **E. Biempica**[2] **and J. Carrabina**[1]
[1] CEPHIS, School of Engineering, Universitat Autònoma de Barcelona, 08193, Cerdanyola del Vallès, Spain
[2] R+D, Kostal Elétrica S.A., Notari Jesús Led 10, 08181, Senmenat, Spain
E-mail: juan.borrego@uab.cat

Summary: Gesture recognition has become pervasive in most interactive environments. Neural Networks often allow reaching higher recognition rates than competing methods at a cost of a higher computational complexity that becomes very challenging in low resource computing platforms such as microcontrollers. New optimization methodologies, such as quantization and Neural Architecture Search are steps forward for the development of embeddable networks. In addition, as neural networks are commonly used in a supervised fashion, labeling tends to include bias in the model. Unsupervised methods allow for performing tasks as classification without depending on labeling. In this work, we present an embedded and unsupervised gesture recognition system, composed of a neural network autoencoder and K-Means clustering algorithm and optimized through a state-of-the-art multi-objective NAS.

Keywords: Unsupervised Learning, Neural Networks, Neural Architecture Search, Capacitive Sensing, Embedded Electronics.

1. Introduction

Hand gestures are an efficient way of communicating. During the last two decades, with new sensors such as Kinect™, its usage has become pervasive in technology, especially in Human-Machine Interaction (HMI). Among the different sensing types, capacitive sensing stands out for its low power, highly sensitive but reliable solution for gesture recognition [1].

In parallel, Neural Networks (NNs) have achieved outstanding performance in tasks such as image classification or speech translation. In the supervised case, however, their usage is linked to the labeling, which can induce, among other factors, bias in the model and undermine its real-world use [2]. To partially solve this issue (the data collected can still be biased), unsupervised methods focus only on the information proportioned by the data to perform the task.

As an added problem, neural networks have required a certain level of computing resources preventing its deployment in low resource platforms like microcontrollers. Lately, this problem has been addressed through both optimization techniques, such as quantization and pruning. However, with the use of such techniques, the network still has to be built manually. In the case of low resource platforms, this fact imposes severe difficulties to develop NNs which are well-performing and compliant with the different memory and latency requirements of the deployment platform. To address this problem, Neural Architecture Search (NAS) [3] was developed, allowing for the automatic building of neural networks. Later, this method was extended to a multi-objective setting [4], to account for the requirements of low resource platforms and deliver functional but also minimal neural networks.

In this work, we present an autoencoder neural network that, in junction with K-Means (KM) and optimized through NAS, can perform unsupervised classification in a low resource microcontroller for recognizing gestures. Although there have been similar works with other models [5] or with other topics [6], this is the first work, as far as the authors are aware, to present a fully embedded and unsupervised solution for gesture recognition using neural networks.

2. Sensing Method and Data

2.1. Capacitive Sensing Platform

The overall sensing platform consists of a surface touch module. It has three elements: the plastic cover, the capacitive foil, and the embedded board. The touch interface is the upper part of the plastic cover, which is immediately after the capacitive foil and glued to it. The embedded board is in the lower part and connected to the capacitive foil. The sensing component, which is the capacitive foil, consists of a central sensitive surface and 24 electrodes which run through it: 9 horizontally and 13 vertically, plus a global shield electrode.

The sensing mechanism is based on the transference of charge between two capacitors: integration and measurement condensers. More details of the sensing methodology can be found at [7]. The final result of a measurement is a set of voltages sensed at the measurement capacitor, one for each electrode. Each voltage is then converted through a 10-bit ADC to obtain a final raw value for each electrode at a predefined sampling rate (in the present case, 500 Hz).

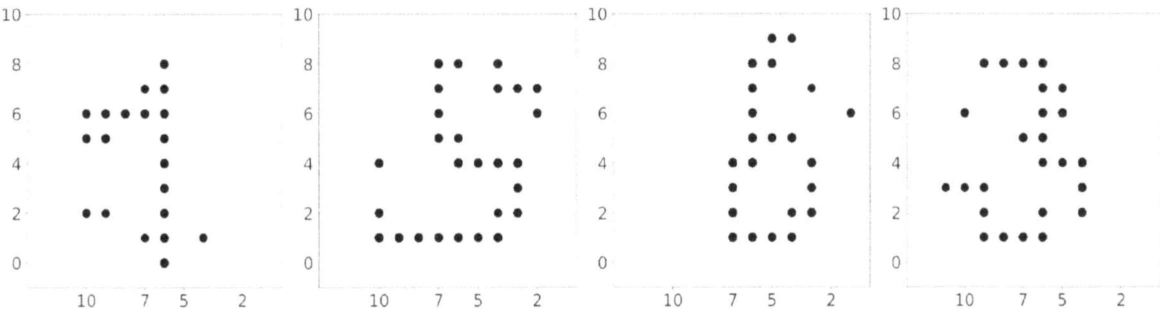

Fig. 1. Examples of numbers drawn at the sensitive surface. From left to right: a one, a five, a six and a three. The black points correspond to the electrode pairs through which the finger has passed. In an image configuration they correspond to 1s while the background is set to 0.

2.2. Data Collection and Preparation

The user enters the gestures by touching the sensing surface and, without withdrawing the finger, draws the gesture on it. We detect the touch by the method described in [8], and then we begin to collect the raw values of the electrodes as described in the previous section. By examining which electrodes, horizontally and vertically, have the highest value we can determine in which spatial coordinates the finger is placed. When the user withdraws the finger, we stop collecting data. By collapsing all the coordinates through which the finger has passed we construct a greyscale image of the figure drawn. That is, we mark the points through which the user has passed with a 1, while the rest of the untouched points remain as background with value 0. An example of such a method can be seen in Fig. 1, where different numbers drawn on the sensitive surface can be visualized as the points through which the finger has passed.

To collect the dataset, numbers from 1 to 9 were drawn a total of 100 times per number on the sensing surface. The dataset is divided in a stratified manner in training, validation, and test, with 720, 90, and 90 samples respectively.

3. Models and NAS framework

3.1. Models

We consider two autoencoder (AE) model types, that is, networks that are trained to replicate the input. The first a Convolutional Autoencoder (CAE) and the second a Dense Autoencoder (DAE), made only of fully connected layers.

In general, the architecture consists of two differentiated parts: the first, the encoder, is in charge of extracting the information and compress it in a central vector, and the second, to reconstruct the input. In the CAE case compression is performed by a succession of convolutional or pooling layers followed by ReLU activations, while the input reconstruction is performed by deconvolution layers and final upsampling. In the DE case, all the layers are fully connected followed by ReLU activations, except for the final layer which reconstructs the input by reordering the output of the network. In both cases, there is a central fully connected layer that produces the latent feature vector. An important note is that to reconstruct the input, as it is made of 0s and 1s, we have used a Binary Crossentropy Loss for training the AEs.

To provide unsupervised classification, a KM algorithm is in charge of grouping the compressed feature vectors into clusters. The choice of KM is central since it needs the number of clusters to be specified. In our case, this is precisely the number of classes.

3.1. Training and Model Optimization

To train the whole unsupervised method we divide the training into three separate steps. First, we train the AE to replicate the input. Second, once it has stopped training, we forward the entire training dataset through it and collect the latent feature vector for each input. Third, we train the KM algorithm with all the feature vectors collected. Finally, to obtain test or validation results, we forward the test or validation sets through the AE, obtain the feature vectors, and predict to which cluster they pertain.

Regarding the performance measure, we have selected a clustering supervised measure, V-Measure, for checking the actual classification capabilities of the framework. Choosing an actual unsupervised clustering metric, such as Silhouette Score would not provide direct insight into the accuracy of the predictions. The training, however, remains fully unsupervised.

As detailed as the first step, we have to build and train the network. However, building and tuning neural networks to be well-performing but also to comply with hardware requirements is a difficult task. Hence, we employ an extended implementation[20] of a NAS framework [4] oriented towards optimizing accuracy, model size, maximum feature map (working memory),

[20] https://github.com/BCJuan/SpArSeMod

and latency. An important note is that, as the search space is composed of conditional variables, we use an implementation[21] of the Arc Kernel [9], which is especially suited for conditional spaces.

The framework works, in each architecture case, CA or DE, with a configuration space composed of both training hyperparameters and architectural parameters, including post-training linear static quantization and L1-Norm based pruning. Once the search space has been defined, the framework sequentially searches for solutions which minimize the following objectives

$$Error\ (\Omega_i) = 1 - Accuracy_{Validation}(\Omega_i)$$
$$ModelSize(\Omega_i) = \sum_l \|w_l\|_0$$
$$WorkingMemory(\Omega_i) = \max_l(\|x_l\|_0 + \|w_l\|_0 + \|y_l\|_0$$
$$Latency(\Omega_i) = \frac{InferenceFLOPS}{Platform\ Frequency}$$

where Ω_i is a specific configuration of the search space, l is a specific layer of the network, w_l the weights of layer l, y_l the output of that layer and x_l the input. In our present case, the accuracy corresponds to the correct classification of each pixel of the output with regards to the input.

Once we have the best model found and trained by our NAS framework, we can proceed with the next steps of training the KM model and obtaining test results.

4. Results

The models established, CAE and DAE, are both developed in PyTorch and the NAS procedure is developed under Ax [10] and BoTorch [11].

First, we present the optimization results for the AEs, which correspond to the results for model size, maximum feature map, and latency, and detailed in Table 1. As seen, the CAE outperforms the DAE in almost all metrics, except for latency where DAE is a little bit faster. The results for the model size and maximum feature map sizes are low enough to be able to embed the model in a low resource microcontroller.

Table 1. Results for the optimization procedure with SpArSeMod. MF corresponds to maximum feature map size, MS to model size, L to latency, and V-M to the V-Measure.

Model	MF (kB)	MS (kB)	L (ms)	V-M(%)
CNN	2.69	6.13	5.53	87.18
FC	18.32	39.67	4.08	58.63

After the optimization result and after training the KM model with the feature maps obtained, we obtain the test results for the unsupervised classification. In this case, the CAE model performs much better than the DAE, achieving a good result regarding the V-Measure. This indicates the feasibility of this method to provide unsupervised classification.

As the final step of our development, we further embed the best model with CMSIS-NN in an NXP-S32K142 microcontroller to perform inference. To perform inference and obtain test results in the embedded implementation, we only need the encoder part of the CAE model and the centroids of KM. We proceed in the following manner: first and for each input, we obtain the feature vector by forwarding the input through the encoder, and second, we measure the distance to all the centroids and choose the nearest one to assign a class.

It is important to note that, in CMSIS-NN legacy API, the quantization used is the power of two based and in the case of PyTorch is linear, enforcing thus a loss of precision. This changes the accuracy of the model but not the size since in both cases we use 8-bit integers. We obtain a V-Measure of 84.08 %, hence resulting in a loss of around 3.10 % in the V-measure, but also validating our embedded deployment.

Finally, to have a visual representation of the clusters, we embed with t-SNE [12] all the obtain all the encoded features from the training set and also the centroids. As can be seen, the clusters are well separated identifying each one a group of gestures corresponding to a specific number.

Fig. 2. Cluster visualization of the different gesture numbers through t-SNE.

5. Conclusions

We have shown a full pipeline of work for unsupervised classification of gestures. We have employed a CAE plus KM as model, and a multi-objective NAS to find a proper embeddable model.

Finally, we have been able to embed that model into an embedded platform with CMSIS-NN, obtaining good performance results, and thus

[21] https://github.com/cornellius-gp/gpytorch/pull/1027

validating our approach. There are two next important steps to be able to improve the gesture recognition system. First, to change the quantization to linear instead of power of two based to reduce the drop in performance and also to improve. Second, to improve the clustering by adding a Kullback-Leibler divergence component in the loss, hence separating more the feature vectors corresponding to different numbers [13].

Acknowledgments

This project is supported by the Spanish Ministry of Science, Innovation, and Universities under grant RTI2018-095209-B-C22 and the Catalan Government industrial Ph.D. program under grant 2018-DI-3

References

[1] T. Grosse-Puppendahl *et al.*, Finding common ground: A survey of capacitive sensing in human-computer interaction, in *Proceedings of the 2017 CHI Conference on Human Factors in Computing Systems*, 2017, pp. 3293–3315.

[2] R. Binns, M. Veale, M. Van Kleek, and N. Shadbolt, Like Trainer, Like Bot? Inheritance of Bias in Algorithmic Content Moderation, in *Proceedings of the International Conference on Social Informatics*, 2017, pp. 405–415.

[3] D. Stamoulis *et al.*, Single-path nas: Designing hardware-efficient convnets in less than 4 hours, in *Proceedings of the Joint European Conference on Machine Learning and Knowledge Discovery in Databases*, 2019, pp. 481–497.

[4] I. Fedorov, R. P. Adams, M. Mattina, and P. N. Whatmough, SpArSe: Sparse Architecture Search for CNNs on Resource-Constrained Microcontrollers, in *Proceedings of the Advances in Neural Information Processing Systems Conference*, 2019, pp. 4977–4989.

[5] A. Moschetti, L. Fiorini, D. Esposito, P. Dario, and F. Cavallo, Toward an Unsupervised Approach for Daily Gesture Recognition in Assisted Living Applications, *IEEE Sens. J.*, Vol. 17, 2017, No. 24, pp. 8395–8403.

[6] C. Song, F. Liu, Y. Huang, L. Wang, and T. Tan, Auto-encoder based data clustering, *Lect. Notes Comput. Sci. (including Subser. Lect. Notes Artif. Intell. Lect. Notes Bioinformatics)*, Vol. 8258 LNCS, No. PART 1, 2013, pp. 117–124.

[7] J. Borrego-Carazo, D. Castells-Rufas, J. Carrabina, and E. Biempica, Capacitive-sensing module with dynamic gesture recognition for automotive applications, in *Proceedings of the 23rd International Symposium on Design and Diagnostics of Electronic Circuits & Systems (DDECS'20)*, 2020, pp. 1–6.

[8] U. Borgmann, Method for Detecting Contact on a Capacitive Sensor Element, *US Patent App. 16/354, 699*, 11-Jul-2019.

[9] K. Swersky, D. Duvenaud, J. Snoek, F. Hutter, and M. A. Osborne, Raiders of the lost architecture: Kernels for Bayesian optimization in conditional parameter spaces, in *Proceedings of the NIPS Workshop on Bayesian Optimization*, 2013, arXiv:1409.4011.

[10] E. Bakshy *et al.*, AE: A domain-agnostic platform for adaptive experimentation, in *Proceedings of the Neural Inf. Process. Syst. Conf.*, 2018, pp. 1–8.

[11] M. Balandat *et al.*, BoTorch: Programmable Bayesian Optimization in PyTorch, 2019, arXiv:1910.06403.

[12] L. van der Maaten and G. Hinton, Visualizing data using t-SNE, *J. Mach. Learn. Res.*, Vol. 9, Nov. 2008, pp. 2579–2605.

[13] V. Prokhorov, E. Shareghi, Y. Li, M. T. Pilehvar, and N. Collier, On the importance of the Kullback-Leibler divergence term in variational autoencoders for text generation, in *Proceedings of the 3rd Workshop on Neural Generation and Translation (WNGT'2019)*, 2019.

(095)

VPNet: Variable Projection Networks

P. Kovács [1,3], G. Bognár [1,3], C. Huber [2] and M. Huemer [1]
[1] Johannes Kepler University Linz, Institute of Signal Processing, Altenbergerstr. 69, 4040 Linz, Austria
[3] Eötvös Loránd University, Department of Numerical Analysis, Egyetem tér 1-3, 1053 Budapest, Hungary
[2] Silicon Austria Labs GmbH, Altenbergerstr. 69, 4040, Linz, Austria
E-mail: {peter.kovacs,gergoe.bognar,mario.huemer}@jku.at
christian.huber@silicon-austria.com

Summary: In this talk, we introduce VPNet, a novel model-driven neural network architecture based on variable projections (VP). The application of VP operators in neural networks implies learnable features, interpretable parameters, and compact network structures. This talk discusses the motivation and mathematical background of VPNet as well as experiments. The concept was evaluated in the context of signal processing. We performed classification tasks on a synthetic dataset, and real electrocardiogram (ECG) signals. Compared to fully-connected and 1D convolutional networks, VPNet features fast learning ability and good accuracy at a low computational cost in both of the training and inference. Based on the promising results and mentioned advantages, we expect broader impact in signal processing, including classification, regression, and even clustering problems.

Keywords: Variable projection, Signal processing, Electrocardiogram, Model-driven neural network, Hermite functions.

1. Introduction

Despite the popularity of deep learning and the advances of model-driven neural networks (NNs), traditional ML algorithms still dominate in many 1D signal processing tasks [1], especially in biomedical signal classifications such as electroencephalogram (EEG), electromyogram (EMG), and electrocardiogram (ECG) classification. The main reason behind that lies in the nature of clinical applications, where both accuracy and explainability are important. This is where the VPNet comes into picture. The theory of variable projection (VP) provides a framework to solve nonlinear least squares problems, whose parameters can be separated into linear and nonlinear ones. In many fields of signal processing, there is a large number of linear parameters, which are driven by a smaller number of nonlinear variables (see Eq. (3)). The corresponding nonlinear parameters have a physical meaning, e.g. they can be described by frequencies, properties of the window function, free parameters of the wavelets, and so on [2]. The VPNet was designed to merge the expert knowledge used by traditional model-based approaches with the learning abilities of NNs.

2. Variable Projections

Variable Projection (VP) [3] provides a framework to address nonlinear modeling problems of the form

$$x \approx \hat{x} = \sum_{k=0}^{n-1} c_k \Phi_k(\theta) = \Phi(\theta)c \qquad (1)$$

where $x \in \mathbb{R}^m$ and $\Phi_k \in \mathbb{R}^m$ denote the input data to be approximated, and a parametric function system, respectively. The symbol $\Phi(\theta)$ will refer to both the function system itself, and to a matrix of size $\mathbb{R}^{m\times n}$. The linear parameters $c \in \mathbb{R}^n$ and the nonlinear parameters $\theta \in \mathbb{R}^p$ of function system Φ are separated as above. The least squares fit of this problem means the minimization of the nonlinear functional

$$r(c,\theta) := \|x - \Phi(\theta)c\|_2^2 \qquad (2)$$

Without nonlinear parameters (i.e. if θ is fixed), the model is linear in the coefficients c. The minimization of r with respect to c leads to the well-known linear least squares approximation. In the general case, the minimization of r can be decomposed into the minimization by the nonlinear parameters θ, while the linear parameters c are computed by the orthogonal projection. Thus, the minimization of r is equivalent to the minimization of the following VP functional:

$$r_2(\theta) := \left\|x - \Phi(\theta)\Phi^+(\theta)x\right\|_2^2 \qquad (3)$$

In [3], formulae and a gradient iteration is provided for the numerical optimization of r_2. Mathematically, VP is a formalization for adaptive orthogonal transformations that allows filtering and feature extraction by means of parametric function systems. On the other hand, if a nonlinear optimization problem can be separated to linear and nonlinear parameters, VP may act as a solver, leading to several other applications [3].

3. Variable Projection Networks

The key idea is to create a Variable Projection Network (VPNet) that combines the representation abilities of VP and the prediction abilities of NNs in form of a joint model. The basic VPNet architecture is a feedforward NN, where the first layer(s) applies a VP operator that is forwarded to a fully-connected, potentially deep NN. The construction is similar to the CNNs in the sense that the first layer(s) of the network can be interpreted as a built-in feature extraction method. Here we note, that more complex VPNet architectures are also possible, e.g. similar to U-Net and AutoEncoder, which will be investigated in our future work.

The VP layer we propose has two possible behaviors, depending on its target application. It either performs a filtering of the form

$$f^{(\mathrm{vp})}(x) := \Phi(\theta)\Phi^{+}(\theta)x = \hat{x} \qquad (x \in \mathbb{R}^{m}) \quad (4)$$

or a feature extraction of the form

$$f^{(\mathrm{vp})}(x) := \Phi^{+}(\theta)x = c \qquad (x \in \mathbb{R}^{m}) \quad (5)$$

where $\theta \in \mathbb{R}^{p}$ denotes the nonlinear system parameters of the given function system θ, as defined above. These VP operators refer to the orthogonal projection and the general Fourier coefficients of the input x by means of the parametric system $\Phi(\theta)$. The filter method may fit better for regression problems, while the feature extraction is suitable for classification problems. The nonlinear system parameter vector θ comprises the learnable parameters of the VP layer. According to [3], the gradients of the VP operators can be directly calculated, and thus the backpropagation of the VP layer can be done in a natural way. The properties and advantages of VPNet are the following:

- *Role:* A novel model-driven network architecture for 1D signal processing problems.
- *Generality:* VPNet can be built by arbitrary parameterized function systems, allowing the direct incorporation of the domain knowledge into the network.
- *Interpretability:* The VP layer can be explained as a built-in feature extraction method. Moreover, the layer parameters are the nonlinear VP system parameters that provide an interpretable meaning to them. They are usually directly connected to morphological properties of the input data.
- *Simplicity:* The VP layer is usually driven by a few system parameters only, thus VPNet may provide a compact alternative to CNNs and DNNs. Actually, the VP layer can significantly decrease the number of parameters in a DNN.

4. Experiments

VPNet is evaluated and compared to fully-connected and 1D convolutional networks in supervised classification problems, motivated by particular biomedical signal processing applications.

In order to investigate the numerical and computational properties of the proposed VPNet architecture, we generated a synthetic dataset that contains multiple signals based on the Hermite function system Φ with a random system parameter $\theta \in \mathbb{R}^{3}$, and class-specific coefficients $c \in \mathbb{R}^{3}$. In this setting we compared the three architectures increasing numbers of neurons in the hidden layers.

In this talk, an ECG heartbeat classification problem was chosen for demonstrating the efficiency of VPNet on real data using the benchmark MIT-BIH Arrhythmia Database [4]. We show that the VPNet performs comparable to the fully-connected and 1D convolutional networks with VPNet having significantly fewer learnable parameters.

5. Conclusions

We developed a novel model-driven NN which incorporates expert knowledge via variable projections. The VP layer is a generic, learnable feature extractor or filtering method that can be adjusted to several 1D signal processing problems by choosing an application specific function system. The proposed architecture is simple, i.e. it has only a few parameters, which are interpretable. Based on the results of our experiments, we believe that VPNet can be effectively used for various problems in 1D signal processing including classification, regression, and even clustering problems. This will be part of future work. Finally, we note that the construction of VPNet is general in nature, since the prior knowledge is incorporated via the basis functions Φ_k's and their parameterization θ. Indeed, several applications can be reformulated as a VP problem [3].

Acknowledgements

This work is supported by: the COMET-K2 "Center for Symbiotic Mechatronics" of the Linz Center of Mechatronics (LCM), funded by the Austrian federal government and the federal state of Upper Austria; and by Silicon Austria Labs (SAL), owned by the Republic of Austria, the Styrian Business Promotion Agency (SFG), the federal state of Carinthia, the Upper Austrian Research (UAR), and the Austrian Association for the Electric and Electronics Industry (FEEI).

References

[1]. S. Kiranyaz, O. Avci, O. Abdeljaber, T. Ince, M. Gabbouj, and D. J. Inman, 1D convolutional neural networks and applications: A survey, 2019. arXiv: 1905.03554.

[2]. P. Kovács, S. Fridli, and F. Schipp, Generalized rational variable projection with application in ECG compression, *IEEE Transactions on Signal Processing*, 68, 16, 2020, pp. 478–492.

[3]. G. H. Golub and V. Pereyra. Separable nonlinear least squares: The variable projection method and its applications, *Inverse problems*, 19, 2, 2003, pp. R1–R26.

[4]. G. B. Moody and R. G. Mark, The impact of the MIT-BIH Arrhythmia Database, *IEEE Eng. Med. Biol. Mag.*, 20, 3, 2001, pp. 45–50.

(096)

Radio-based Object Detection using Deep Learning

[1,2] Aditya Singh, [1] Pratyush Kumar, [1] Vedansh Priyadarshi, [1] Yash More,
[1] Aishwarya Praveen Das, [1]Bertrand Kwibuka and [1] Debayan Gupta
[1] Ashoka University, Rajiv Gandhi Education City, 131029, Sonepat, India
[2] Carnegie Mellon University, 5000 Forbes Ave, 15213, Pittsburgh, PA United States
Tel.: +91 99038 35202
E-mail: debayan.gupta@ashoka.edu.in

Abstract: We present a novel radio-signal based, short-range object detection system for controlled environments, which substitutes complex signal processing and expensive hardware with deep learning networks to detect patterns from low-quality, inexpensive sensors. The models are trained on forms of I/Q data, sampled via software defined radios. Our system operates in the less crowded low-frequency range of 433MHz in contrast to existing RF-based sensing methods, allowing us to use cheap, off-the-shelf hardware. We demonstrate a proof-of-concept prototype, in a controlled environment, which can be scaled to build more complex detection systems relying on higher frequencies. Our system can handle occlusions, and, since it does not use visual data, is not hampered by bad lighting. The core of our system is a VGG-16 based CNN architecture trained on spectrograms, obtained by transforming I/Q data via Fourier methods. We achieve an accuracy of 0.96 on a binary classification task of detecting the presence or absence of an object in an enclosed space. Our prototype demonstrates that convolutional networks can learn features important enough from spectrograms that enable it to distinguish the presence of objects, thereby eliminating the need of sophisticated signal processing methods to do the same.

Keywords: Deep learning, CNN, Object detection, Software defined radio (SDR).

1. Introduction

Over the past decade, deep learning has fuelled advances in the domain of object and human-body detection, aiding applications as diverse as healthcare, emergency handling, and industrial monitoring [6, 19]. Their ability to extract temporal and spatial features from visual data has revolutionised the field of computer vision. Images of an area can now be used to detect and localise humans [14]. This has several useful applications – e.g. virtual reality experiences can be improved without additional hardware for tracking body parts [8]; smart buildings and cities can optimise energy consumption based on the number of people in specific regions; estimation of the number of people can help ensure practice of social distancing norms amid the current coronavirus pandemic[1].

However, most of these detection and monitoring approaches have several inherent limitations. They: (1) require multiple cameras to be installed in an area to achieve an adequate performance and coverage which results in high deployment cost, (2) suffer from the same limitations as humans suffer from, i.e., both the human eyes and cameras cannot perceive visual information in the dark or see through walls and occlusions. Additionally, comprehensive facial recognition technology compromises the right to privacy of the public.

Fortunately, visible light is just one end of the frequency spectrum. Recent advances in wireless research have shown that certain radio frequency signals can traverse through walls/occlusions and span across dark and smoky environments which are difficult to monitor [2]. Radio waves are also reflected off of the human body [17] (and any other conducting material). Furthermore, since typical WiFi systems operate in the radio wave channel, their ubiquity is an added advantage for building RF-based detection systems. These properties together make radio waves a better alternative to visible light for human-body detection.

Unfortunately, most existing research projects utilising RF-waves for human body detection focus on device-based active methods that require significant instrumentation of the person/object and the environment. This limits their scalability and robustness. Furthermore, such design also impinges on the privacy of the users. Thus, there has been a push in research to build device-free methods that can overcome these restrictions. Recent advances in device-free methods have been promising. Although they rely on using expensive, state-of-the-art hardware operating in the overcrowded high frequency WiFi channel [1, 9, 18]. Here, we present a Deep Learning-based portable object-detection system, which uses low-frequency radio waves (433 MHz, via inexpensive software radios), designed to operate through occlusions [5]. Our experiments suggest that deep neural networks can be successfully used to carry out the otherwise intractable task of object detection even

[1]https://www.who.int/emergencies/diseases/novel-coronavirus-2019/advice-for-public

with low-frequency radio waves. Our approach is partly inspired by the mechanisms used by certain owls who can use very low frequency waves (around 20 kHz) to localise their prey during night-time and through occlusions. Due to its portability and cheap deployment costs, our system has the potential to be scaled to detect and track multiple objects and can be developed to perform well in different day-to-day environments.

2. Related Work

Recent applications of ANNs to signal processing show that CNNs are able to outperform decade old feature search algorithms in radio modulation recognition. Timothy et al.[10] achieve state of the art accuracy for radio modulation recognition by training a CNN on raw I/Q samples (WiFi enabled SDR operating at 900 MHz) collected across 11 different modulations (8 digital and 3 analog), and normalised to unit variance. Even for high signal to noise ratio, the CNN achieved a better accuracy over a large coverage area. They were able to improve the accuracy by leveraging deep residual networks and LSTM [7] which performed better on visual and time-series data [11].

Zhao et. al. [18] introduced RF-pose3D which provides a significant improvement in RF-based sensing by incorporating ANNs. RF-pose3D takes the 4D RF signal captured by an FMCW radio (window of 3 seconds) as input, similar to the radio used by RF-capture and WiTrack (5.4-7.2 GHz) [3, 4]. The model operates using a regular softmax loss and is able to predict the location of each key point in space as the voxel with the highest score. The model is able to accurately track the motion and presence of a single person. To scale this to multiple people, the authors operate on the output of the CNN (in the horizontal plane) from an intermediate layer (feature map). The resulting network is able to accurately detect the 3D skeleton of multiple people and simple actions (walking, sitting, standing) over a range of 40 feet in multiple environments.

Li et al. [9] further augmented this system to detect multiple actions by performing multimodal training using the obtained 3D skeleton from RF-pose3D and existing vision based action recognition data sets. The spatial-temporal attention module trained on the multimodal data is able to perform action recognition on visual and RF based data. Further, they found that transferring knowledge related to action recognition across modalities is able to empirically improve performance regardless of whether the skeletons are generated from RF or vision based data. This system, called RF-action is able to accurately recognise actions and interactions (29 single actions and 6 interactions) of multiple humans through walls and in the dark (up to 40 feet) and represents a significant improvement in action recognition capabilities.

Although above systems show promising results, they use expensive hardware which operate on high frequency radio waves (2.0 GHz $\leq f \leq$ 7.2 GHz). In the following sections we explain our approach presenting relevant differences since we deploy a low-cost, low-frequency setup which is capable of high accuracy detection.

3. System Setup and Data Collection

Our system uses a Transmitter (T_x) made out of a Raspberry Pi 3 and a receiver (R_x) based on a Realtek RTL-SDR along with an off-the-shelf dipole antenna. We use the rtlsdr and scipy Python libraries for interfacing and transmitting narrowband FM waves at 433 MHz.

Two sets of data, D_A and D_B, are collected in a closed room (8.5 m×5.5 m). For D_A, T_x and R_x are placed $1m$ apart; the distance is doubled for D_B. In both cases the object (a 1 L water bottle) is placed exactly midway. We sample the received signal in raw I/Q form, with each recorded sample being 0.5 s. D_A is sampled at 2.6 MS/s, whereas D_B is recorded at a reduced 2 MS/s to decrease computational overhead. 2000 samples are collected in D_A, and 6000 in D_B.

4. Preprocessing and Model

After the two sets of data are collected, the data is operated on, in three different representations. The first is a raw time series radio signal, and the second is a power spectral density function generated for our samples as in [12]. For the final representation we apply Short-Time Fourier Transform (STFT) to each sample to convert it into a spectrogram representation in the frequency- time domain (50% overlap in each chunk) [9, 18]. We obtain 1,000 and 3,000 samples for each case (*object*, *no object*) in D_A and D_B respectively:

We start with a baseline architecture consisting of two convolution layers and two dense layers, then progressively vary the hyperparameters to analyze their effect on performance and arrive at the final model(s). The selected CNN model is based on the VGG-16 [15] architecture which has shown remarkable success in image recognition. It contains four convolutional layers, each followed by a pooling layer using SAME padding. ReLU activation functions are used in the convolutional layers to introduce non-linearity and a Glorot uniform kernel initializer is used to initialise the convolution layers. Two fully connected layers follow the stack of convolutional layers. The final dense layer uses a softmax activation function and the model is trained using binary cross-entropy loss via Stochastic Gradient Descent. For the model used on D_A, Batch Normalisation is done before the inputs are fed into the second convolutional layer and 40 % of the neurons are dropped after the final convolutional block to prevent overfitting. In contrast, for D_B, Batch normalisation is done after every convolutional layer and the first dense layer, and 50 % of the neurons are dropped after the second and fourth convolutional layer. We evaluate the performance of our CNN classifiers using 5-fold Cross Validation technique[1].

Table 1. Comparison of performance of CNN as the distance between T_x and R_x is double from 1m to 2 m.

Dataset	Validation Accuracy	Testing Accuracy
D_A	0.94	0.96
D_B	0.91	0.87

5. Observations

Training a three layered shallow network using the raw I/Q data and PSD data did not yield useful results as the classifier was unable to generalise well on the test set. This suggests that the input data was not an adequate feature for detecting the object (or was too noisy). However, we observed that training the CNN described above using the heatmaps of the reflected signals as input yielded a high accuracy on the test set. After training the CNN on D_A for 10 epochs, the network is able to achieve a test accuracy of 0.96 (average over 10 runs). Furthermore, an accuracy of 0.87 was observed on the test set after training and evaluating the CNN on D_B *for* 20 epochs; there is a decrease in accuracy as the distance between T_x and R_x (and the distance of the object from T_x and R_x) is doubled. Still, our system is able to perform high-accuracy object detection even after the range is increased. The accuracy results are recorded in Table 1 and the confusion matrix for D_B is shown in Fig. 1. Furthermore, loss and accuracy with respect to D_A are plotted against the epochs and shown in Fig. 2.

This demonstrates that CNNs are an effective model for identifying and extracting relevant features to carry out such classification tasks link [2].

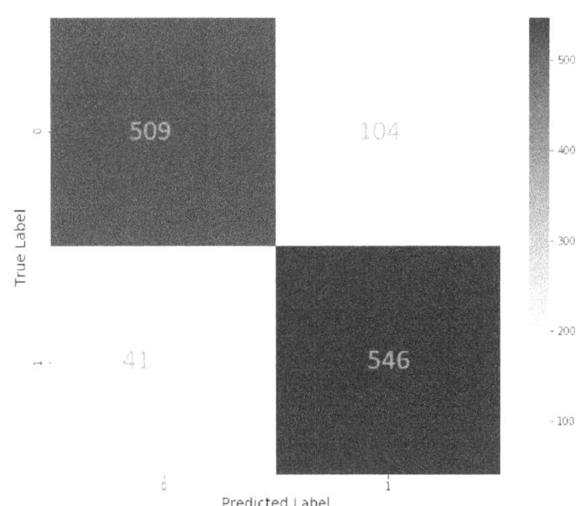

Fig. 1. Confusion Matrix for D_B.

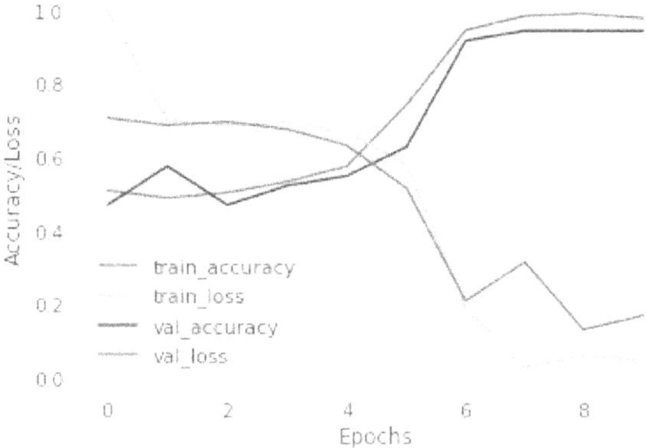

Fig. 2. Accuracy/Loss vs Epochs for D_A.

6. Conclusions

This paper proposes that it is possible to perform simple object detection with high accuracy using extremely cheap radio hardware by leveraging CNNs. We demonstrate this by developing a proof-of-concept system to detect the presence of a water bottle based on spectrograms of the received signal. Critically, we do almost no explicit signal processing or feature engineering, relying on the neural network to do the heavy lifting. This indicates the possibility of doing complex, customised object detection without expense on human capital or old-school signal processing.

In future work, we plan to scale the current system by using multiple SDRs to emit an FMCW wave, and observe how the system works in terms of detecting multiple objects (and human bodies) when it is fed more information about the surroundings. We also want to perform far more complex classifications, including locating the object, calibrating item sizes, handling more noise, and retraining or re-calibrating the system quickly for a new environment.

References

[1]. F. Adib and D. Katabi, See through walls with Wi-Fi! in *Proceedings of the Association for Computing Machinery Conference*, 2013, pp. 75–86.

[2]. F. Adib, Z. Kabelac, D. Katabi, and R. C. Miller. 3D tracking via body radio reflections, in *Proceedings of the 11th USENIX Symposium on Networked Systems Design and Implementation (NSDI 14)*, Seattle, WA, 2014, pp. 317– 329.

[3]. F. Adib, C. Y. Hsu, H. Mao, D. Katabi, and F. Durand, Capturing the human figure through a wall, *Association for Computing Machinery Transactions on Graphics*, 34, 6, Oct. 2015.

[4]. F. Adib, Z. Kabelac, and D. Katabi, Multi-person localization via RF body reflections, in *Proceedings of the 12th USENIX Symposium on Networked Systems*

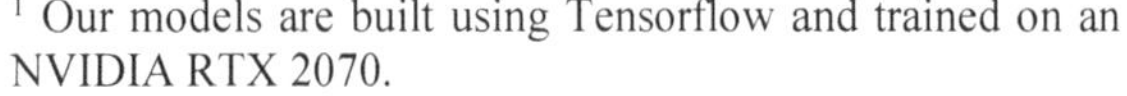

[1] Our models are built using Tensorflow and trained on an NVIDIA RTX 2070.

[2] https://github.com/pristineVedansh/radML

Design and Implementation (NSDI 15), Oakland, CA, May 2015, pp. 279– 292.

[5] P. Ali-Rantala, L. Ukkonen, L. Sydanheimo, M. Keskilammi, and M. Kivikoski, Different kinds of walls and their effect on the attenuation of radiowaves indoors, in *Proceedings of the IEEE Antennas and Propagation Society International Symposium (IEEE-APS)*, Vol. 3, 2003, pp. 1020–1023.

[6]. J. Ehrich, E. Molloy, and M. Mantovani, Conceptual design of future children's hospitals in Europe: Planning, building, merging, and closing hospitals, *The Journal of Pediatrics*, 182, 122016, pp. 411-412.

[7]. S. Hochreiter and J. Schmidhuber, Long short- term memory, *Neural Computation*., 9, 8, November 1997, pp. 1735–1780.

[8]. F. Hu, Y. Deng, W. Saad, M. Bennis, and A. H. Aghvami, Cellular-connected wireless virtual reality: Requirements, challenges, and solutions, *IEEE Communications Magazine*, 58, 5, 2020, pp. 105–111.

[9]. T. Li, L. Fan, M. Zhao, Y. Liu, and D. Katabi, Making the invisible visible: Action recognition through walls and occlusions, in *Proceedings of the International Conference on Computer Vision (IEEE/CVF- ICCV)*, 2019, pp. 872–881.

[10]. T. J. O'Shea and J. Corgan, Convolutional radio modulation recognition networks, in Jayne C., Iliadis L. (eds), Engineering Applications of Neural Networks. EANN 2016. Communications in Computer and Information Science, Vol 629, *Springer*, 2016.

[11]. T. J. O'Shea, T. Roy, and T. C. Clancy, Over the air deep learning based radio signal classification, *IEEE Journal of Selected Topics in Signal Processing*, Vol. 12, Issue 1, Feb. 2018, pp. 168 - 179.

[12]. A. Pérez-Zapata, A. F. Cardona-Escobar, J. A. Jaramillo-Garzón, and G. M. Díaz, Deep convolutional neural networks and power spectraldensity features for motor imagery classification of eeg signals, in *Proceedings of the International Conference on Augmented Cognition (AC)*, 2018, pp. 158–169.

[13]. A. F. Pérez-Zapata, A. F. Cardona-Escobar, J. A. Jaramillo-Garzón, and G. M. Díaz, Deep convolutional neural networks and power spectral density features for motor imagery classification of eeg signals. In D. D. Schmorrow and C. M. Fi-dopiastis, Eds., Augmented Cognition: Intelligent Technologies, *Springer International Publishing*, 2018, pp. 158–169.

[14]. K. Shibata and H. Yamamoto, People crowd density estimation system using deep learning for radio wave sensing of cellular communication, in *Proceedings of the International Conference on Artificial Intelligence in Information and Communication (ICAIIC'19)*, 2019, pp. 143–148.

[15]. K. Simonyan and A. Zisserman, Very deep convolutional networks for large-scale image recognition, in *Proceedings of the International Conference on Learning Representations*, 2015.

[16]. M. Zhao, S. Yue, D. Katabi, T. S. Jaakkola, and M. T. Bianchi, Learning sleep stages from radio signals: A conditional adversarial architecture, in *Proceedings of the 34th International Conference on Machine Learning (ICML 2017)*, 2017.

[17]. M. Zhao, T. Li, M. A. Alsheikh, Y. Tian, H. Zhao, A. Torralba, and D. Katabi, Through-wall human pose estimation using radio signals, in *Proceedings of the IEEE/Computer Vision Foundation Conference on Computer Vision and Pattern Recognition*, 2018, pp. 7356–7365.

[18]. M. Zhao, Y. Tian, H. Zhao, M. A. Alsheikh, T. Li, R. Hristov, Z. Kabelac, D. Katabi, and A. Torralba, Rf-based 3d skeletons, in *Proceedings of the Association for Computing Machinery conference: Special Interest Group on Data Communication (ACM-SIGCOMM)*, 2018, pp. 267–281.

[19]. Z. Zou, Q. Chen, I. Uysal, and L. Zheng, Radiofrequency identification enabled wireless sensing for intelligent food logistics, *Philosophical Transactions of the Royal Society A: Mathematical, Physical and Engineering Sciences*, 372, 2017, June 2014, 20130313.

(097)

An Effective Handwriting Text Recognizer for Historical Documents based on Convolutional Recurrent Neural Networks and Advanced Spelling Correction

P. Minos [1], L. Tsochatzidis [2], K. Markou [2], S. Symeonidis [2], X. Karagiannis [2], V. Stamou [1], S. Markantonatou [1] and I. Pratikakis [2]

[1] Institute for Language and Speech Processing / "Athena" RIC, 15125 Athens, Greece
[2] Democritus University of Thrace, Department of Electrical and Computer Engineering
67100 Xanthi, Greece
E-mail: ipratika@ee.duth.gr

Summary: This paper presents an effective Handwriting Text Recognizer for historical documents. The recognizer relies upon a recognition module based on a convolutional recurrent neural network architecture and on an advanced spelling correction module aiming to further reduce the transcription errors. The employed architecture comprises a Convolutional Neural Network serving as an encoder and several Bidirectional Long Short-Term Memory (BLSTM) modules for the decoding. The output of the network is further processed for spelling correction using a finite-state machine for the tasks of detecting spelling errors and generating candidate corrections along with a language model for the task of ranking the candidate corrections. The proposed architecture is applied to the transcription of historical Greek manuscripts that present challenging technical problems. Finally, EPARCHOS, a newly created dataset, has been made publicly available.

Keywords: Handwriting text recognition, Recurrent neural networks (RNN), BLSTMs, Spelling detection, Isolated-word error correction, Minimum edit distance, n-gram model.

1. Introduction

The potential to access our written past, which stimulates the interest of both the research community and the general public, makes Handwriting Text Recognition (HTR) a highly appealing technology, among the ones appearing in the research area of document image analysis. We propose an HTR system for offline text recognition where the input image is a textline and the key components are convolutional recurrent neural networks and a spell checking mechanism.

We work with historical texts from the Greek Byzantine literature tradition that roughly extends from the mid of 4th century to the mid of 15th century, a period that stretches between the foundation of Constantinople as the 'New Rome' and the establishment of the Ottoman Empire in Europe. Some texts of the 3rd century have been used as well as they are considered to belong to this literary tradition. In these texts a language heavily influenced by classical Greek is used that does not correspond to the spoken language at the time of the authors (neither does it correspond to the modern version of Greek). In fact, the language of these texts is not homogeneous across the centuries although a common denominator exists, namely an intended adherence to classical Greek. Consequently, our knowledge of the language used in the particular historical documents is restricted to the linguistic information contained in these texts that define the size and the contents of our, inevitably limited, corpora and lexicons.

Spell checking is the process of detecting misspelled words in a text. It provides possible corrections to these errors in order to enhance the results that are produced with the HTR model. Spelling errors can be classified as non-word errors (a non-existent word, e.g. *wrod* instead of *word*) or real-word errors (I will *meat* John instead of I will *meet* John). To this end, most techniques use a dictionary to locate non-word errors and provide candidate corrections based on a similarity metric (i.e. minimum edit distance), or a statistical language model.

In this paper we address the problem of text recognition by using a convolutional recurrent neural network architecture producing transcribed scripts that feed a second system for spelling correction. The spelling correction system uses a finite-state machine for the tasks of detecting spelling errors and generating candidate corrections along with a language model for the task of ranking the candidate corrections.

2. Methodology for the Initial Text Recognition

In this section, we present the methodology we adopted for the HTR of historical manuscripts. The CRNN-FCNN neural network architecture is motivated by the work presented in Puigcerver [1] and Sainath et al. [2] (see Fig. 1).

In the remainder of this paper we will provide a fully detailed description of the convolutional and recurrent stages, as well as of the training method.

2.1. Proposed Architecture: CRNN-FCNN Network

Three stages are implemented as explained below:

1) *Convolutional stage:* The first stage consists of a typical feed-forward convolutional network consisting of 5 consecutive blocks. Each block has a convolutional

layer with kernel size 3 x 3 and stride equal to 1 and a batch normalization layer. The leaky rectified linear function is used for neuron activation (LeakyReLU) that allows for a small, non-zero gradient when the unit is saturated and not active [4]. The first three blocks additionally incorporate a Maximum Pooling layer (with non-overlapping kernels of size 2 x 2) to reduce the dimensionality of the input image. A dropout layer (with probability 0.2) is included in the last three blocks, to improve the generalization ability of high-level features. Finally, a number of feature maps are extracted from each textline image. For the subsequent processing, the average of each column of the feature maps is calculated in order to acquire a feature vector for each time step.

2) *Recurrent stage:* A stack of recurrent blocks is applied as a decoder formed by 1-D Bidirectional LSTM (BLSTM) layers that sequentially process the extracted feature vectors corresponding to columns of the feature maps. The BLSTM layers process the information bidirectionally and lead to a separate feature vector for each direction (two in total). The feature vectors of each direction are then concatenated to form a unified representation. In each recurrent block a dropout layer is incorporated, with probability 0.5.

3) *Fully connected layers:* After the recurrent stage, two fully-connected layers are added. To deal with datasets which have a relatively large character set, we used two fully connected hidden layers with 512 hidden units each.

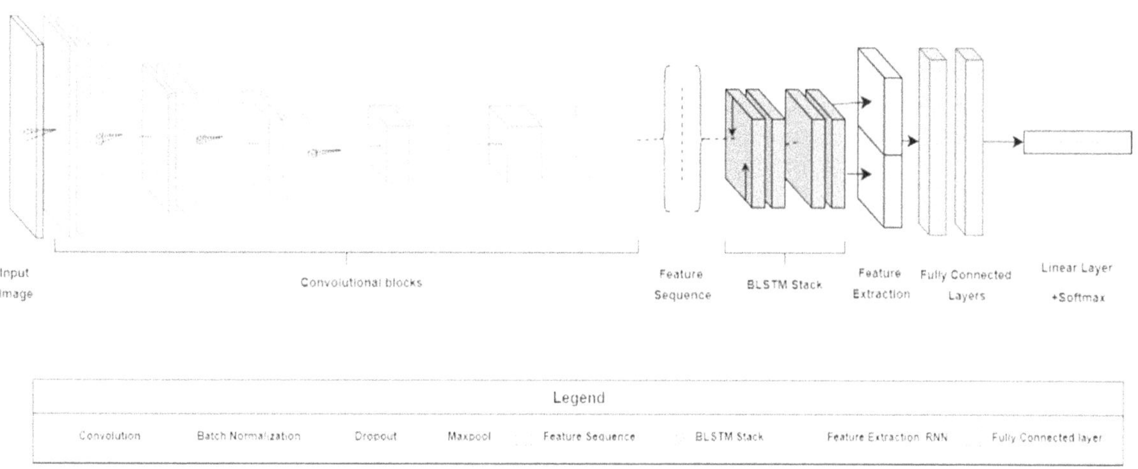

Fig. 1. Proposed RCNN-FCNN architecture.

2.3 Training

For the training of the proposed system, we used the Connectionist Temporal Classification (CTC) loss function [5], minimized by the RmsProp optimizer [6]. We used a learning rate of 0.003 and early stopping when validation loss does not improve after 20 consecutive epochs.

3. Methodology Adopted for Spelling Correction

According to Kukich [6], the isolated-word error correction can be divided into three sub-problems: detection of an error, generation of candidate corrections and ranking of candidate corrections.

3.1. Error Detection

Given a dictionary and a word, the first step is to determine whether the word exists in the dictionary. If this is not the case then the word is marked as incorrect. For efficient dictionary lookups we store the dictionary as a deterministic finite automaton (FSA). The most common types of FSA for dictionary storage are the *trie* and the *deterministic acyclic finite state automaton* (DAFSA) (see Fig. 2). Both types have the same lookup time complexity, but we opted for the latter approach because, although the creation of a DAFSA is a more complex process, a DAFSA has a smaller memory footprint. Our FSA is constructed with the algorithm presented in [11]. The worst case complexity of checking if a word of length n is accepted by the FSA (i.e. the word has been found in the dictionary) is O(n), this means that the processing time is in linear relation to the size of the word while the size of the dictionary has no effect.

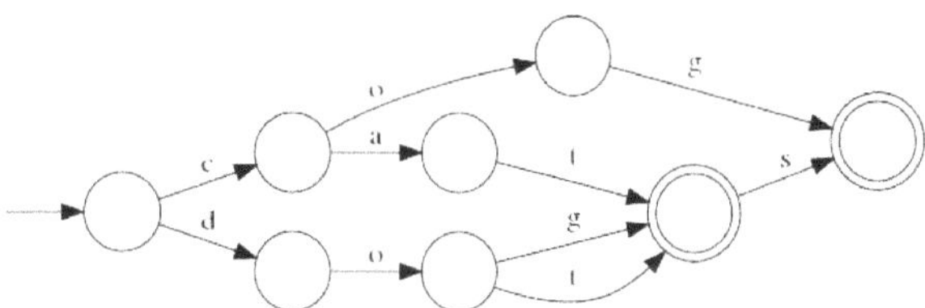

Fig. 2. A deterministic acyclic finite state automaton for the word list {cat, cats, cog, dog, dogs, dot, dots}.

3.2. Spelling Suggestion

If a word is marked as incorrect, we produce a list of suggestions similar to the word. One way to quantify the similarity of two words is to count the minimum number of editing operations that we need in order to transform the one word into the other one. Some common edit operations are:

- *insertion* of a character, e.g. wor → word (inserted at position 3)
- *deletion* of a character, e.g. worrd → word (delete r at position 2)
- *substitution* of a character, e.g. wopd → word (substitute p with r at position 2)
- *transposition* of two adjacent characters, e.g. wrod → word (exchange r at position 1 with o at position 2)

Levenstein [7] proposed a distance (Levenstein distance) that considers insertion, deletion and substitution as an edit operation while Damerau [12] presented a distance (Damerau–Levenshtein distance) that includes insertion, deletion, substitution and transposition.

Our system uses the Levenstein distance [7] to calculate the minimum edit distance between the input word and the words that exist in the dictionary. The reason why we didn't use the Damerau–Levenshtein distance is that the transposition of two adjacent characters is a common mistake when the user types a word on a keyboard, but it is unlikely to happen in OCRed input.

Although there are efficient algorithms to calculate the Levenshtein distance between two strings, their exhaustive application on every entry in a dictionary can be computationally expensive. Various techniques have been proposed to speed up this process. We draw on the algorithm proposed by Oflazer [8]. This algorithm, given an FSA, a fixed bound t and an input string w, enables the retrieval of every string s that is accepted by the FSA and the distance $D(s,w)$ is between 0 and the fixed bound t.

3.3. Ranking Candidate Corrections

Next, the candidate corrections are ranked and the best one is selected from the set of the candidates with the help of both the correction distance and of a statistical model.

First, we constructed a corpus of historical texts, mainly belonging to the Byzantine literature tradition, that contains 769895 words (99931 unique). Then we collected all the trigrams from the corpus. For each trigram we counted their frequency, i.e. the number of occurences in the corpus. The result is a word-level trigram model that can be used to assign a conditional probability to a word given previous words.

For each possible correction c of a misspelled word w_i we use the two words w_{i-2}, w_{i-1} preceding w_i in the context where the misspelled word appeared in order to estimate the probability of occurrence P of c after the bigram $w_{i-2}w_{i-1}$. As a measure of the probability of occurrence P we use the maximum likelihood estimation (MLE) that is given in (1):

$$P(c|w_{i-2}w_{i-1}) = \frac{C(w_{i-2}w_{i-1}c)}{C(w_{i-2}w_{i-1})} \tag{1}$$

In (1), C is the number of occurrences of an n-gram in our corpus. If no occurrences of the trigram $w_{i-2}w_{i-1}c$ exist, i.e. the observed frequency of the trigram is 0, we estimate the probability P of c occurring after the unigram w_{i-1} with the equation (2).

$$P(c|w_{i-1}) = \frac{C(w_{i-1}c)}{C(w_{i-1})} \tag{2}$$

Finally, if no occurences of the bigram $w_{i-1}c$ exist, we estimate the probability P of the unigram c with the equation (3):

$$P(c) = \frac{C(c)}{N} \tag{3}$$

In (3), N is the size of the training corpus (in words). The score S of the candidate c is estimated with the equation (4):

$$S(c|w_{i-2}w_{i-1}) = a\big(1/D(c,w_i)\big) + bP(c|w_{i-2}w_{i-1}) \tag{4}$$

In (4), a is a weight for the edit distance and b is the weight for the n-gram probability.

4. Experimental Results

4.1. Dataset

For our experimental work we used the Historical Greek "EPARCHOS" Dataset [9] that is publicly available. This dataset originates from a Greek handwritten codex by 2 writers, namely Antonius Eparchos and Camillos Zanettus. The codex dates from around 1500-1530. It consists of 9285 textlines containing 18809 words (6787 unique words) distributed over 120 scanned handwritten text pages. The dataset is separated into training, validation and testing partitions consisting of 1435 (63 %), 381 (17 %) and 456 (20 %) text lines respectively. The writing that appears in the dataset delivers the most important abbreviations, logograms and conjunctions cited in virtually every Greek minuscule handwritten codex from the years of the manuscript transliteration and the prevalence of the minuscule script (9th century) to the post-Byzantine years. All these particularities, as well as the 'polytonic' orthography (see below) of the miniscule writing, constitute a challenging HTR task. A page of the dataset is shown in Fig. 3.

Miniscule writing is a type of script where only lower-case characters are used. It was developed and established as a more efficient type of writing, as compared to the upper-cased script used before, because it enabled writers to inscribe multiple characters without lifting the pen from the paper, while it occupied less space. However, upper-case letters were also known and were used interchangeably with their lower-cased version, in particular when the distinction between characters was difficult. Another attribute of miniscule writing was that it followed the so-called 'polytonic orthography' in which various symbols indicated whether a change of pitch stress on the vowels occurred in classical Greek. This feature increases the number of target character classes for the HTR problem. However, particularly for the characters ϋ and ϊ, the specific diacritic marks ('diaeresis') may also be used to distinguish them from a diphthong. As a result, the transcription may vary to either solution, namely with or without the diacritic mark, depending on the word.

Abbreviations are a common attribute of miniscule writing of that era. They were used by the writers in order to increase efficiency regarding the space and time needed to write a word. Typically, multiple characters (usually two) were replaced by a special symbol while the rest of the word was kept intact. Abbreviations may appear in different positions in a word, i.e. in the beginning, middle or end of a word. A list of the most common abbreviations that appear in the dataset is given in Fig. 4 along with their corresponding translation. Fig. 5 shows two text lines and the respective transcription; the use of abbreviations is highlighted on the text lines.

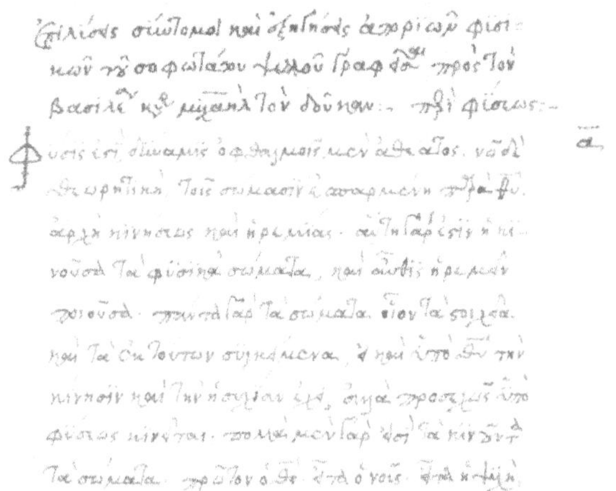

Fig. 3. A document image from the EPARCHOS dataset.

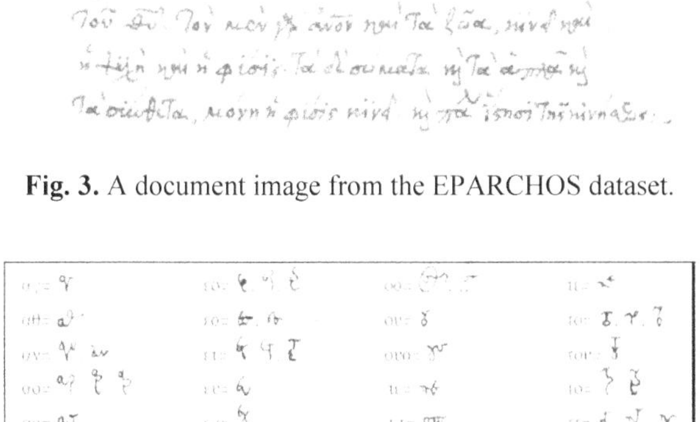

Fig. 4. List of abbreviations and their transcription.

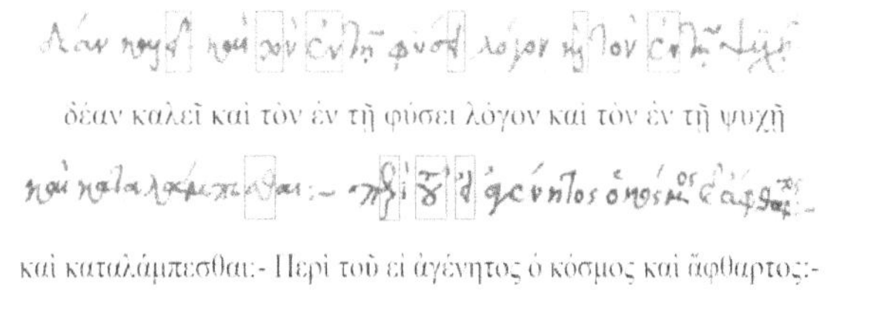

δέαν καλεῖ καὶ τὸν ἐν τῇ φύσει λόγον καὶ τὸν ἐν τῇ ψυχῇ

καὶ καταλάμπεσθαι:- Περὶ τοῦ εἰ ἀγένητος ὁ κόσμος καὶ ἄφθαρτος:-

Fig. 5. Textline images and corresponding transcription text with highlighted abbreviations.

To further increase space efficiency, the use of superscripts has been observed by the writers. Superscripts may appear in a variety of grammatical contexts including those related to the endings of inflected and uninflected words, usually at the end of a word. Often, multiple ending characters of the word appear in superscripts; these characters may also be replaced by special abbreviations in the place of the actual characters, as shown in Fig. 6.

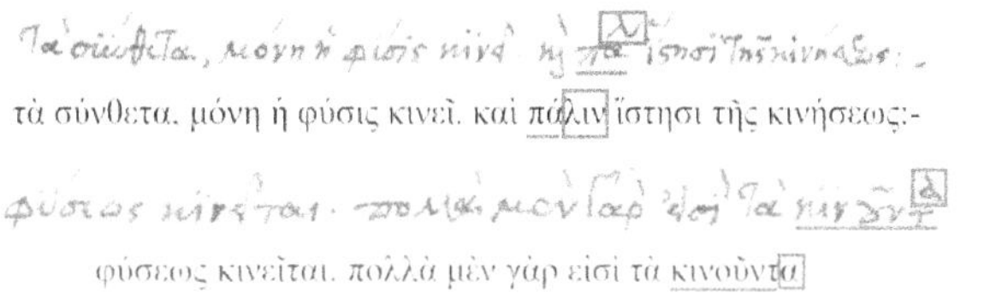

τὰ σύνθετα. μόνη ἡ φύσις κινεῖ. καὶ πάλιν ἵστησι τῆς κινήσεως:-

φύσεως κινεῖται. πολλὰ μὲν γάρ εἰσι τὰ κινοῦντα

Fig. 6. Textline images and corresponding transcription text with highlighted superscripts

4.2 CRNN-FCNN Performance

Table 1 presents the performance obtained with the proposed neural network architecture (CRNN-FCNN). For comparison purposes, the performance of the architecture of Puigcerver [1], trained and evaluated on the same dataset, is reported as well. The best-path decoder was used for CTC decoding, which is the simplest case. For each configuration, the character error rate (CER) and word error rate (WER) are reported, for both the validation and the test dataset of the "EPARCHOS" dataset. As it is shown, the proposed architecture outperforms the architecture of Puigcerver [1]. This result is attributed to the addition of the fully-connected layers that are better suited for the larger character set of the miniscule script (318 characters including all the versions of the vowels resulting from the use of pitch accent symbols).

Table 1. Text recognition performance of the proposed CRNN-FCNN architecture.

		Puigcerver [1]	Proposed
CER (%)	Val.	6.81	6.52
	Test	10.37	10.10
WER (%)	Val.	22.06	21.51
	Test	28.51	27.85

4.3. Performance of Spelling Correction

For the evaluation of the spelling correction component, we used the transcribed outcome of a manuscript containing 4203 tokens of which 3752 were words. We compared the transcribed text with the original (ground truth) and identified 1053 differences: 494 non-word errors, 248 real word errors and 311 other errors (e.g. missing or split words). Then we checked the non-word errors with our system and recorded the cases where the correct word was the first item in the list of the candidate corrections.

Our results show that the system successfully predicted the correct word as the best candidate 95 times (19.2%) when we used the distance metric combined with the statistical model ($a = 0.5$, $b = 17$) for the ranking of the candidate corrections. When we used only the edit distance for the ranking ($a = 1$, $b = 0$) the system predicted the correct word as the best candidate 65 times (13.2 %) and when we used only the language model ($a = 0$, $b = 1$) the system predicted the correct word as the best candidate 63 times (12.8 %). These results clearly show that the combined information of the distance metric and the occurrence probability improves the ranking of the candidate corrections because both lexical and contextual information is taken into account.

In future work, we plan to improve our n-gram model with smoothing and by feeding it with more data.

Acknowledgement

This research has been co-financed by the European Union and Greek national funds through the Operational Program Competitiveness, Entrepreneurship and Innovation, under the call RESEARCH-CREATE-INNOVATE (project code: T1EDK-01939).
Furthermore, we would like to thank NVIDIA Corporation, which kindly donated the Titan X GPU, to be used for this research.

References

[1] J. Puigcerver, Are multidimensional recurrent layers really necessary for handwritten text recognition? in *Proceedings of the 14th IAPR International Conference on Document Analysis and Recognition (ICDAR' 2017)*, Kyoto, Japan, November 9-15, 2017, pp. 67–72.

[2] T. N. Sainath, O. Vinyals, A. W. Senior, and H. Sak, Convolutional, long short-term memory, fully connected deep neural networks, in *Proceedings of the International Conference on Acoustics, Speech and Signal Processing (ICASSP' 2015)*, South Brisbane, Queensland, Australia, 2015, pp. 4580–4584.

[3] A. L. Maas, A. Y. Hannun, and A. Y. Ng, Rectifier nonlinearities improve neural network acoustic models, in *Proceedings of the 30th International Conference on Machine Learning*, Atlanta, Georgia, USA, 2013.

[4] A. Graves, S. Fernandez, F. J. Gomez, and J. Schmidhuber, Connectionist temporal classification: labelling unsegmented sequence data with recurrent neural networks, *ACM International Conference Proceeding Series*, Vol. 148. 2006, pp. 369–376.

[5] S. Ruder, An overview of gradient descent optimization algorithms, CoRR, Vol. abs/1609.04747, 2016.

[6] Karen Kukich, Techniques for automatically correcting words in text, *ACM Comput. Surv.*, 24, 4, December 1992, pp. 377–439.

[7] Levenshtein, Vladimir I. Binary codes capable of correcting deletions, insertions, and reversals, *Soviet Physics Doklady*. Vol. 10. No. 8. 1966.

[8] Oflazer, Kemal, Error-tolerant finite state recognition with applications to morphological analysis and spelling correction, *Computational Linguistics*, 22, 1, March 1996.

[9] Papazoglou, A., Pratikakis, I., Markou, K., Tsochatzidis, EPARCHOS - historical Greek handwritten document dataset (version 1.0) [data set], 2020.

[10] Chen, Stanley F., and Joshua Goodman, An empirical study of smoothing techniques for language modeling. *Computer Speech & Language*, 13.4, 1999, pp. 359-394.

[11] Daciuk, Jan, Bruce W. Watson, and Richard E. Watson, Incremental construction of minimal acyclic finite state automata and transducers, Finite State Methods in Natural Language Processing. 1998.

[12] Damerau, Fred J., A technique for computer detection and correction of spelling errors, *Communications of the ACM* 7.3, 1964, pp. 171-176.

(099)

Text Classification with Transformers and Reformers for Deep Text Data

Roghayeh Soleymani and Jérémie Farret
Inmind Technologies Inc., Montreal, Canada
Tel.: + 1(514) 871-0470
E-mail: esoleymani@inmindtechnologies.com

Summary: In this paper, we present experimental analysis of Transformers and Reformers for text classification applications in natural language processing. Transformers and Reformers yield the state of the art performance and use attention scores for capturing the relationships between words in the sentences which can be computed in parallel on GPU clusters. Reformers improve Transformers to lower time and memory complexity. We will present our evaluation and analysis of applicable architectures for such improved performances. The experiments in this paper are done in Trax on Mind in a Box with three different datasets and under different hyperparameter tuning. We observe that Transformers achieve better performance than Reformer in terms of accuracy and training speed for text classification. However, Reformers allow to train bigger models which cause memory failure for Transformers.

Keywords: Natural language processing, Text classification, Transformers, Reformers, Trax, Mind in a box.

1. Introduction

Text classification is one of the important natural language processing (NLP) tasks that is applicable in real-world problems such as topic tagging, question answering, spam detection, sentiment analysis, news categorization, etc. Text classification or tagging can be used in the Fog layer computions to make text data deep [1] or enrich data. This task includes an NLP step immediately after data acquisition, in Fog layer or in the cloud to organize and structure data. This strategy makes organizing, accessing, transmitting and processing the data more efficient.

Designing text classification models with classical machine learning methods follows a two-step process: feature extraction and classification. Feature extraction consists of defining some hand crafted feature vectors and designing high quality features require strong domain knowledge, tedious feature engineering and analysis, and may not be transferable between different applications.

Since 2012, deep learning models are being applied to different tasks in the world of machine learning and therefore in NLP. Neural network architectures used for text classification include recurrent neural networks (RNNs), convolutional neural networks (CNNs), Capsule Nets, Transformers, Reformers, and more (see the review by [2]). Most of these models learn feature representations automatically with less hand-engineering and allow for knowledge transfer between different applications of NLP.

In this paper, we focus on Transformers, and Reformers that rely on attention mechanism for relating different positions of a single sequence in parallel and yield state-of-the-art results on many NLP tasks [2-4]. Attention mechanism allows sequential processing of text to compute a representation of the sequence and capture meaningful relationships between words in a corpus. Transformers allow for much more parallelization than CNNs and RNNs, and make it possible to efficiently train very big models on large amounts of data on GPU clusters [2]. Reformers improve the efficiency of Transformers to train larger models on larger corpus [4].

The experiments presented in the original Reformer paper [4] are performed only on generative and language model training tasks including imagenet64, enwik8-64K, and WMT 2014 English-to-German translation task. In this paper, we experiment on text classification problems including News Classification, and Sentiment Classification. We carry out the experiments on three datasets and use different settings to compare the models in terms of performance over training and inference time. The experiments are done using Trax library, an end-to-end library for deep learning by Google Brain team with JAX backend [5].

We use for this study the integrated solution Mind in a Box Catalyst™, an On Premise and Fog computing device that features up to 4 GeForce RTX 2080 Ti for accelerated AI training and inference in its legacy version, and now up to 4 Nvidia Tesla V100 Cards.

2. Background

Transformers originally proposed by Vaswani et al. [3] are used for building language models to learn contextual text representations. These language models can then be used for text generation and classification. Each Transformer block consists of a masked multi-head attention module, followed by a layer normalization and a position-wise feed forward layer (see [3] and Fig. 1). The attention module estimate how much each word/character correlates with the other elements using an attention vector and then takes the weighted sum of the elements in this vector as the prediction of the target.

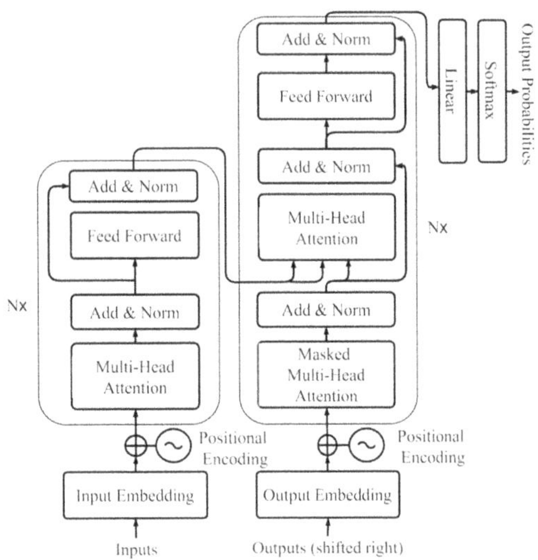

Fig. 1. The Transformer - model architecture [3].

Transformers are more efficient than RNNs for sequential processing of text in parallel, however they are memory-inefficient to train on long sequences and large models. Attempts to achieve more efficient versions of the Transformer model's self-attention mechanism include augmenting self-attention with persistent memory, adaptive attention span, factorized sparse representation of attention, and product-key attention [2]. The latest state of the art attempt is reported as Reformer model [4].

Reformer model [4] was proposed to solve the memory problem with Transformer models training using approximate attention computation based on locality-sensitive hashing and reversible layers [4]. With Locality Sensitive Hashing (LSH), nearby word embedding vectors get the same hash with high probability and the vectors that have the same hash are assigned to the same LSH bucket. Then LSH buckets are converted to sorted chunks (batches) to allow parallel processing. However, LSH buckets may be uneven in size which makes batching difficult. To tackle this, the batch size is set such that they may contain nearby hashes. Then attention is applied only to these batches and neighbor hash vectors rather than the whole input vector as being done with Transformers (see Fig. 2 and [4] for further details). In addition to LSH, Reformers use reversible layers mechanism, meaning instead of storing all the activations in memory, it recomputes the input of each layer on demand during the back propagation process. Two sets of activations are stored for each layer, one captures changes to the first layer and the other captures the last layer and then they are substracted (see [4] and [6] for further details). This model has been reported to be memory and time efficient to train on long sequences and large models.

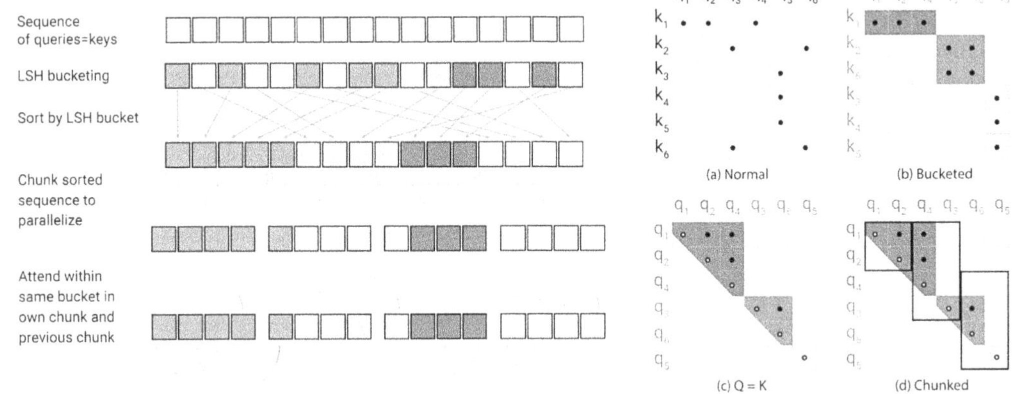

Fig. 2. Simplified depiction of LSH Attention showing the hash-bucketing, sorting, and chunking steps and the resulting causal attentions. (a-d) Attention matrices for these varieties of attention. [4].

3. Applicable Architectures

The experimental results in this paper rely on the integrated solution, Mind in a Box Catalyst™ with 4 GPU units, for balanced and accelerated training and inference capabilities in various text classification models (see Fig. 3).

The objective sought through this experimental protocol and its underlying architecture is to assess the optimization and acceleration potential of the various models and libraries, in order to seek real time and / or high performance computing capabilities. The technical common denominator here is an integration with the Python scripting language, which is currently extensively used to operate many Edge and Fog AI architectures, including the Fog AI appliance used for this experiment.

The applicable architectures for the performance considerations supported in our results are many. But the prime objective is to assess Hybrid Computing Deep Data generation strategies and in particular optimization of the choice of libraries and models depending on the data to be analyzed. Thus relevant architecture would be Cloud, Edge and Fog AI architectures applying NLP techniques to generated Deep text Data and / or Enriched Big text Data, as illustrated in Fig. 4 and Fig. 5.

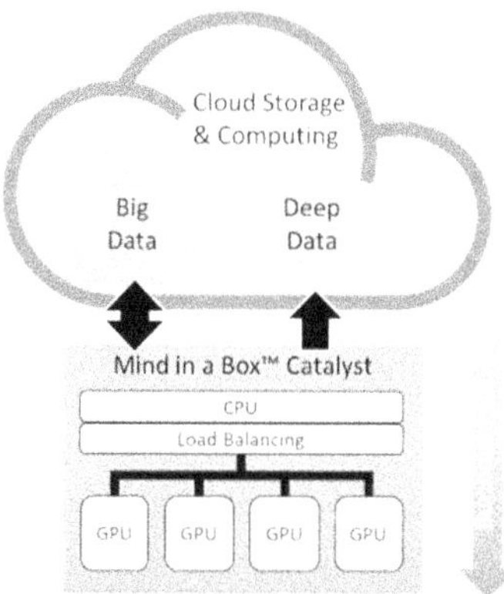

Fig. 3. On Premise/Fog AI functional architecture diagram.

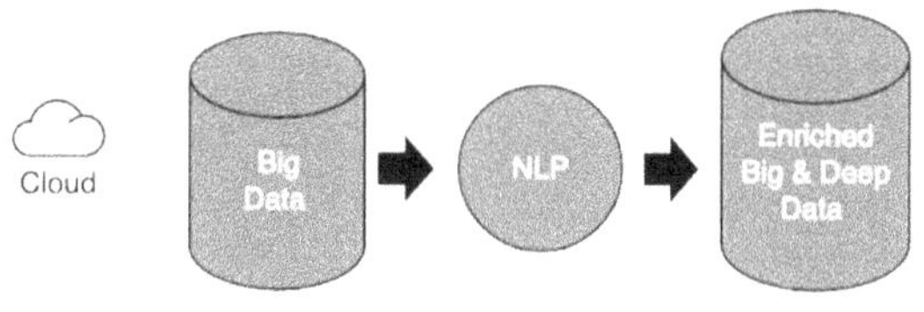

Fig. 4. Using NLP (text classification) in the cloud level to enrich big data.

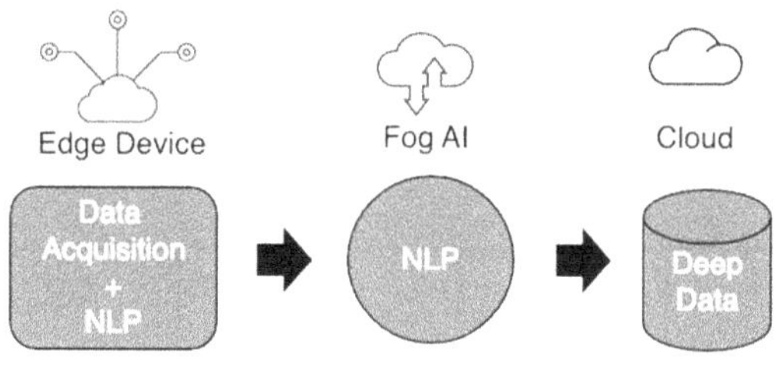

Fig. 5. Using NLP (text classification) on the edge level after data acquisition and before sending it to the fog layer. The data can be further analyzed with NLP (text classification) on the fog level before being sent to the cloud.

Fig. 4 shows a protocol to apply NLP algorithms to large amount of data (Big data) to obtain Deep data. This means that irrelevant information is removed and data is stored in a structured and organized manner. In addition, NLP text classification algorithms can be applied to add labels or tags to the stored data in order to en rich it and improve its quality for the analysis applied in the next steps of processing the data.

If data is not yet stored as Big data in the cloud, a more efficient protocol can be used for its acquisition and storage. In Fig. 5, such protocol is presented where, data is processed with NLP in the edge device immediately after acquisition, and then sent to the fog layer. In Fog layer, further text processing and classification is performed on the data and when it's sent to the cloud for storage, it is structured and organized and only the relevant information is being transmitted and stored. With this architecture, the computation is distributed over all three layers of the network and the computation load is reduced in cloud level which in turn reuses the transmition load and latency.

4. Experiments and Results

The experiments presented in the original Reformer paper [4] are performed only on generative tasks and no results of experiments have been presented for comparing Reformers with Transformers on text classification task. In this paper, three datasets are used for the experiments: IMDB and Yelp binary sentiment classification and AG News four-class topic classification dataset.

Different settings are used to tune the hyperparameters of Transformers (TR) and Reformers (RF) including: number of layers, number of attention heads, training steps, drop-out rate, learning rate, optimizers (Adam and AdaFactor [7]), and scheduled learning rate factors. Another factor is the length of attention key and value vectors that exists only for Reformer. Throughout the experiments of this paper, this length is set to 64. For all the experiments, Trax "en_8k.subword" (with 8192 vocabulary size) is used for tokenizing the texts. Final dimension of tensors at most points in the model, including the initial embedding output is 512 units and size of dense layer in the feed-forward part of each encoder block is 2048 (default setting in Trax library).

In experiments of this paper, the performance is compared in terms of average training cross entropy (train CE), testing cross entropy (test CE), test accuracy (per batch of text) and inference time (per single text) in seconds.

In Table 1, results are shown for comparing Adam and Ad factor optimizers for 2 layers of TR/FR blocks and 32 attention heads ended with a dense layer and a softmax layer.

The results show that Adafactor performs than Adam optimizer for both Transformer and Reformers. Therefore, all the results presented in Tables 2 and 3 are obtained using AdaFactor optimizer.

Comparing the results of Transformers versus Reformers in Table 2 show that Transformers outperform Reformers in terms of both accuracy and time complexity. However, further experimentation shows that in the case of Transformers, the processors run out of memory when we try to train on larger models (e.g. 3 layers and 128 heads).

In Table 1 we analyse the performance of the Transformers and reformers when changing the number of attention heads. For all cases in this table, 2 layers of TR/FR blocks are used and as shown the number of attention heads is changed from 16 to 32. These results show that increasing the number of attention heads improved the performance of these classifiers because it allows for better capturing the underlying context of the text. However, increasing the number of heads from 32 to 128 does not improve the performance.

Table 1. Results of experiments with Transformers (TR) and Reformers (RF) (2 layers of TR/FR blocks and 32 attention heads, a dense layer and a softmax layer) to compare Adam and AdaFactor optimization algorithms.

Dataset	Optimiser	Train Steps		Dropout rate		Train CE		Test CE		Test Accuracy		Train Time (sec)		Inference time(sec)	
		TR	RF	TR	RF	TR	RF	TR	RF	TR	RF	TR	RF	TR	RF
IMDB	**Adam**	3000	5000	0.3	0.3	0.308	0.377	0.347	0.395	0.833	0.868	**1491.872**	1084.734	**2.42**	**3.84**
IMDB	**AdaFactor**	3000	5000	0.3	0.3	**0.246**	**0.321**	**0.324**	**0.362**	**0.90**	**0.885**	1540.54	**1068.767**	2.726	3.853
Yelp	**Adam**	5000	10000	0.2	0.2	0.323	**0.271**	0.308	0.276	0.871	0.886	558.18	2684.084	**2.329**	**3.711**
Yelp	**AdaFactor**	5000	10000	0.2	0.3	**0.212**	0.277	**0.202**	**0.219**	**0.920**	**0.910**	**533.50**	**2158.91**	2.405	3.792
AGNews	**Adam**	10000	10000	0.2	0.2	0.271	**0.245**	0.245	0.234	0.893	0.918	1201.45	**2192.94**	**2.454**	4.087
AGNews	**AdaFactor**	10000	10000	0.2	0.2	**0.209**	0.251	**0.219**	**0.203**	**0.910**	**0.935**	**1146.337**	2307.161	2.569	**3.912**

Table 2. Results of experiments with Transformers (TR) and Reformers (RF) to compare their performance in terms of accuracy and time complexity.

Dataset	Train Steps		Number of layers	Number of heads	Dropout rate		Train CE		Test CE		Test Accuracy		Train Time (sec)		Inference time(sec)	
	TR	RF	TR RF	TR RF	TR	RF	TR	RF	TR	RF	TR	RF	TR	RF	TR	RF
IMDB	3000	5000	8 | 2	32	0.3	0.3	**0.246**	0.321	**0.324**	0.362	**0.90**	0.885	1540.54	**1068.767**	**2.726**	3.853
IMDB	1500	10000	1	128	0.4	0.2	0.291	**0.286**	**0.303**	0.330	**0.873**	0.865	**101.08**	4407.8	**2.21**	3.76
IMDB	5000	5000	2	128	0.5	0.3	**0.204**	0.327	**0.280**	0.380	**0.883**	0.854	**1216.198**	2723.7	**2.422**	3.882
Yelp	5000	10000	2	32	0.2	0.3	**0.212**	0.277	**0.202**	0.219	**0.920**	0.910	**533.50**	2158.91	**2.405**	3.792
Yelp	10000	10000	1	128	0.2	0.2	**0.211**	0.265	**0.194**	0.232	**0.923**	0.914	**1363.19**	2984.084	**2.361**	3.750
Yelp	5000	10000	2	128	0.2	0.2	**0.210**	0.261	**0.196**	0.248	**0.924**	0.895	**1191.155**	4346.708	**2.608**	4.137
AGNews	10000	10000	2	32	0.2	0.2	**0.209**	0.251	0.219	**0.203**	0.910	**0.935**	**1146.337**	2307.161	**2.569**	3.912
AGNews	5000	10000	1	128	0.2	0.2	**0.209**	0.231	**0.193**	0.232	**0.924**	0.917	**573.168**	2944.045	**2.366**	3.577
AGNews	5000	10000	2	128	0.2	0.1	**0.233**	0.298	**0.189**	0.231	**0.938**	0.911	**1129.52**	5374.905	**2.514**	4.0103

Table 3. Results of experiments with Transformers (TR) and Reformers (RF) to compare the effect of the number of attention heads in performance.

Dataset	Number of heads	Train Steps		Dropout rate		Train CE		Test CE		Test Accuracy		Train Time (sec)		Inference time(sec)	
		TR	RF	TR	RF	TR	RF	TR	RF	TR	RF	TR	RF	TR	RF
IMDB	**16**	3000	5000	0.3	0.3	0.381	**0.317**	0.366	0.399	0.847	0.864	**360.82**	**521.36**	**2.57**	**3.212**
IMDB	**32**	10000	10000	0.3	0.3	0.246	0.321	0.324	**0.362**	**0.90**	**0.885**	1540.54	1068.767	2.726	3.853
IMDB	**128**	5000	5000	0.5	0.3	**0.204**	0.327	**0.280**	0.380	0.883	0.854	1216.198	2723.7	2.822	3.882
Yelp	**16**	10000	10000	03	0.3	0.212	0.271	**0.193**	0.240	0.916	0.908	**425.42**	**1173.176**	**2.318**	**3.286**
Yelp	**32**	5000	10000	0.2	0.3	0.212	0.277	0.202	**0.219**	0.920	**0.910**	533.50	2158.91	2.405	3.792
Yelp	**128**	5000	10000	0.2	0.2	**0.210**	**0.261**	0.196	0.248	**0.924**	0.895	1191.155	4346.708	2.608	4.137
AGNews	**16**	5000	10000	0.2	0.1	0..284	0.252	0.263	0.228	0.902	0.912	**614.89**	**1699.03**	**2.129**	3.931
AGNews	**32**	5000	10000	0.2	0.2	**0.209**	**0.251**	0.219	**0.203**	0.910	**0.935**	1146.337	2307.161	2.569	**3.912**
AGNews	**128**	5000	10000	0.2	0.1	0.233	0.298	**0.189**	0.231	**0.938**	0.911	1129.52	5374.905	2.514	4.010

5. Conclusions

In this abstract, we compared Transformers and Reformers for text classification application. In literature, Reformers have shown to outperform Transformers in terms of memory and time efficiency at the similar level of accuracy on language model training and text generative tasks. However, the experiments in this paper showed that Transformers are preferred to Reformers for Text classification application. The benefit of Reformers versus Transformers was observed to be the possibility of training larger models.

Acknowledgements

This work was supported by the National Research Council through their Industrial Research Assistance Program (IRAP) and abide by their experimental research requirements.

References

[1]. Deep text analytics. (https://www.poolparty.biz/what-is-deep-text-analytics/)

[2]. S. Minaee, N. Kalchbrenner, E. Cambria, N. Nikzad, M. Chenaghlu, J. Gao., Deep learning based text

classification: A comprehensive review, *arXiv preprint arXiv*:2004.03705, 2020.

[3]. A. Vaswani, N. Shazeer, N. Parmar, J. Uszkoreit, L. Jones, A. N. Gomez, Ł. Kaiser, and I. Polosukhin, Attention is all you need, in *Advances in Neural Information Processing Systems*, 2017, pp. 5998–6008.

[4]. N. Kitaev, L. Kaiser, A. Levskaya, Reformer: The efficient transformer, in *Proceedings of the International Conference on Learning Representations*, 2020.

[5]. Trax, an end-to-end library for deep learning by Google Brain team. (https://github.com/google/trax).

[6]. A. N. Gomez, M. Ren, R. Urtasun, R. B. Grosse, The reversible residual network: Backpropagation without storing activations, in *Proceedings of the 31st Conference on Neural Information Processing Systems (NIPS 2017),* Long Beach, CA, USA, 2017, pp. 2214-2224.

[7]. N. Shazeer, M. Stern., Adafactor: Adaptive learning rates with sublinear memory cost, *Proceedings of the 35th International Conference on Machine Learning (PMLR 80),* Stockholm, Sweden, 2018.

(100)

Profiling the Performance and Energy Efficiency of Edge Accelerators in the Context of Computer Vision

R. B. Ayala Meza and **Jérémie Farret**
Inmind Technologies Inc., Montreal, Canada
Tel.: + 1(514)871-0470
E-mail: rayalameza@inmindtechnologies.com

Abstract: Deep neural networks (DNNs) are extensively used in many complex artificial intelligence (AI) applications despite of being compute-intensive and hence causing substantial energy consumption. Nowadays, with the ramping up of Internet of Things (IoT) devices, emerging Edge Computing and Edge AI practices; diverse types of embedded accelerators have appeared. These equipment come armed with multi-processor system-on-chip (MP-SoC) such as graphics processing units (GPU) and tensor processing units (TPU) accommodating requirements for different applications. However, to the wide deployment of DNNs in these constrained hardware platforms, power management needs to be improved without sacrificing application performance. This article will evaluate Google's Coral dev board and Nvidia's Jetson TX2 with benchmarks and comparison metrics from the standpoint of the process to create a model that is compatible with each edge accelerator to the thermal regulation of power through dynamic voltage and frequency scaling (DVFS).

Keywords: Convolutional neural networks, GPU, TPU, Embedded system, Hardware architecture, Edge.

1. Introduction

Neural nets were proposed in 1940 but they have seen a breakthrough in the field of computer vision in 2012, when the AlexNet system won the ImageNet challenge in image recognition [1][2]. Since then, deep neural networks (DNNs) have been successfully used in multiple applications because of its ability to extract high level features from huge amounts of raw data and state-of-the-art accuracy. Many DNNs models with different network architectures (number of layers, layer types, layer shapes, etc) have been developed. The tendency is that in order to achieve higher accuracy, the depth in number of convolutional layers must increase accordingly [3]. However, this comes at the cost of high computational complexity and hence more energy consumption [4],

DNNs processing has different computational needs. For example, training is usually done in the cloud meanwhile inference can occur in the cloud or in the edge. In applications such as industrial processes and drone navigation, real-time inference near the sensor is longed [5]. Accordingly, embedded accelerators are mainly deployed to reduce connectivity dependency, latency and security risks. Thus, they have limited energy consumption, compute and memory [5, 6]. Although these accelerators are equipped with highly-parallel compute paradigms, including both temporal (CPU, GPU) and spatial architectures (TPU) to address this issue, thermal management also has to be taken into consideration.

Dynamic voltage and frequency scaling (DVFS) is a technique which dynamically varies frequency and voltage based on the present thermal constraints on the processors, and thus optimizes energy conservation [7, 8].

This article will focus in the task of image classification, specifically in the multiple versions of GoogleNet (also known as Inception). To the best of our knowledge, this is the first work addressing DVFS to evaluate the devboards Google's Coral [9] and Nvidia's Jetson TX2 [10] (see Fig. 1) for the case of real-time applications (batching is not allowed) in low precision inference (16 bits and 8 bits). Furthermore, it will be discussed the workflow and frameworks to create a compatible model for each one.

The remainder of this article is organized as follows:

- Section 2 provides background and reviews previous works.
- Section 3 introduces the characterization methodology and discusses its results.
- Section 4 depicts the protocol adopted to this study, according to the research program overseeing it, and the hardware architectures applicable for such results.
- Section 5 presents the key insights from this work and possible future research directions.

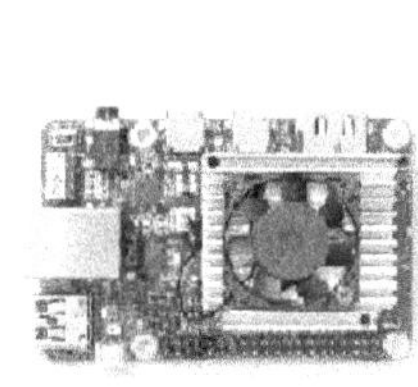

Fig. 1. Google's Coral (left) and Nvidia's Jetson TX2 (right) devboards.

2. Background and Related Work

Temporal and spatial Architectures

These are highly-parallel compute paradigms to achieve performance. Temporal architectures, can be found in CPU and GPU. Some techniques are SIMD (Single Instruction Multiple Data) which uses vectors, and SIMT (Single Instruction Multiple Thread) which employs parallel threads. The main characteristic is that the ALUs (Arithmetic Logic Units) cannot communicate directly, depend on a centralized control and can only fetch data from a memory hierarchy. In contrast, spatial architectures found in ASIC (Application Specific Integrated Circuit) and FPGA (Field Programmable Gate Array), use dataflow processing. Here, the ALUs can communicate directly and sometimes have their own control logic and local memory [3].

Dynamic Voltage and Frequency Scaling (DVFS)

It is an energy conservation technique that aims to optimize performance and power consumption (which retrospectively affects temperature) of processors during runtime. The notion behind it is to transition between different system clocks whenever needed. But, the dilemma lies in finding the right time to change frequency and the right value of the frequency itself. [8]

The manner in which the processor's frequency is scaled is determined by the scaling algorithm and the current processor's load. These algorithms can be part of the kernel code or of a specialized firmware and can be classified as proactive and reactive.

- Reactive: actions are taken when a certain state is reached.
- Proactive: actions are taken when a certain state is determined to happen in the future.

The state could be temperature (a trip_point) or workload. And the actions could be voltage and frequency control.

Optimization techniques

These aim to reduce the storage, memory requirement and computational cost by compressing the model size. And thus decrease bandwidth requirements and energy consumption, which are important in edge devices.

- Quantization: It reduces the size of weights and activation functions by converting all the 32-bit floating point (FP32) numbers to the nearest lower precision number. For example 16-bit floating point (FP16) or 8-bit fixed point (INT8). Although these representations can be less precise, the inference accuracy of DNNs is not significantly affected.
- Pruning: This technique eliminates low-weight connections between the layers by setting them to zero.
- Layer fusion: Consists in combining layers, which have similar operations and parameters, in a single one. This reduces the number of transfers from memory to registers and vice versa.

GoogleNet models

These models were heavily engineered to force performance in terms of speed and accuracy, as prior to their launch, most DNNs will just pile up many convolutional layers hoping to get better performance. Each version is a refinement over the previous one: Inception_v1 (I_v1), Inception_v2 (I_v2), Inception_v3 (I_v3) and Inception_v4 (I_v4).

The authors in [7] have investigated the impact and energy conservation of DVFS but on datacenter's GPUs. A similar analysis has been done in [11] with edge accelerators, but thermal management has been studied using a thermal camera. Finally, the investigation in [12] profiled the DVFS mechanism but only on a high-end embedded CPU (ARM Cortex-A15 available in an Odroid-XU4 board). Unlike those works, this investigation targets embedded GPU and TPU.

3. Experimental Setup and Results

The objectives are the following: (i) understand when successive inference induces temperature violations (trip points); (ii) quantify the performance (latency, inference time, memory usage) of each embedded accelerator under thermal management by DVFS and different artificial intelligence (AI) models.

For this experiment, the 4 versions of the Inception model were used. All the evaluation metrics were collected after classifying the same image (187KB) 70000 times with both devboards operating headless (no mouse, keyboard, screen, Wi-Fi were present during the inference execution).

3.1. Software Setup - Creating a Compatible Model

Both devboards are hardware-constrained. So, the models need to be compressed to run inference. Fig. 2 shows the process used to create a compatible model.

- Zoo: It depicts a repository were the state-of-the-art models are stored in different format: frozen (.pb), saved (.saved), checkpoint (.ckpt), etc. All the Inception models were downloaded from the official TensorFlow repository. [13]
- Model format: For both devboards, frozen models have been used.
- Network definition: Here, models are serialized, for efficient reading, using parsers like TFLite (Coral) and onnx (TX2).
- Optimization: Models are tuned up to increase performance and reduce memory usage. Each devboard has their own method. On one hand, the TX2 uses TensorRT, an algorithm optimizer, which will benchmark different techniques and pick the most suitable for the target GPU, batch size and other parameters (it is important to do this step within the devboard) and lower precision to FP16. On the other hand, a requirement to use Coral's TPU is to have a model with precision

INT8. Other available techniques are pruning and weight clustering.

- Save file: Models are transformed into a format to store and use at a later time for inference.

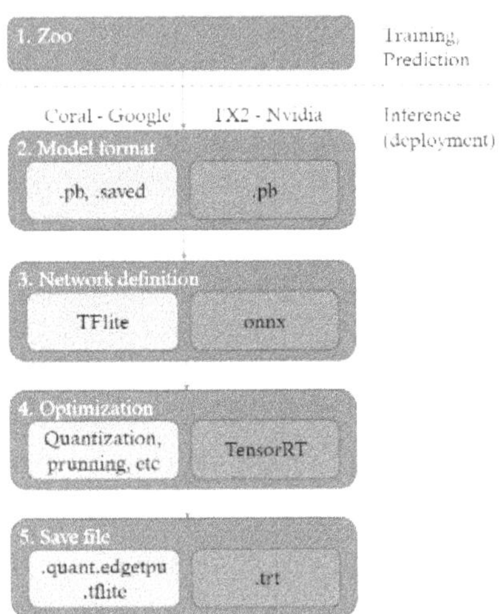

Fig. 2. Process to create a compatible model

3.2 Hardware Setup

In Table 1, each multi-processor system-on-chip (MP-SoC) is described.

3.3 Results

In Fig. 3, it is observed Coral's temperature, used memory and inference time. In Iv_1, Coral never throttles. Meanwhile in I_v4, it has throttled 10 times reaching 65.55 °C as maximum temperature. This amount of throttling is correlated to the model's size. I_v1 is the smallest one and I_v4 is the biggest one, as can be seen in Table 2. But there is a chance of throttling in I_v1 if repeating this experiment after Coral has reached its idle temperature of 59.5 C.

The biggest amount in memory usage is once again with the biggest model (I_v4 = 741.12MB). Also, all models show the highest usage at the end of the experiment.

The first inference time in all models is the slowest one because the time includes loading the model into the TPU and initializing it. Additionally, as in the other figures, it is always the biggest model (I_v4) that is more computationally expensive with 121.83ms. Finally, it seems that I_v3 and I_v4 have more fluctuations in the inference timing than the other 2 models.

In Fig. 4, it is observed that the maximum temperature reached is 63°C in I_v4. But unlike Coral it has throttled only once in this model. So, it seems that there is a type of control because temperature does not descend and ascend abruptly, which explains why the inferences are faster in TX2 than Coral. Additionally, TX2 can maintain a lower idle temperature (31.5 °C) than Coral (59.5 °C).

In term of memory usage, the TX2 uses more than Coral. It has used approximatively 3200MB in the 4 models, but this is related to the type of optimization applied to the models. TensorRT, optimizes by benchmarking different techniques and to do this it has to execute inference. When configuring TensorRT, the amount of memory to use has been set to 4096 MB. This can be reduced but it will affect to certain amount the accuracy of the model as less techniques can be benchmarked.

Table 1. Specifications of MP-SoC.

	Coral devboard	**Jetson TX2**
MP-SoC	**CPU:** Cortex-M4F, Quad Cortex-A53 **GPU:** GC7000 Lite **TPU**: edge coprocessor	**CPU:** Dual Denver2, Quad Cortex-A57 **GPU:** 256-core Nvidia Pascal
DRAM	1GB LPDDR4	8GB LPDDR4
Architecture	Spatial: ASIC	Temporal: SIMT
Frequency (MHhz)	MAX: 500	MAX-Q: 854 MAX-N: 1302
Trip_points (°C)	**CPU:** 65, 75, 80, 85, 90 **TPU:** 84.8, 89.8, 94.8	**CPU:** 95.5, 99.5, 100.5 **GPU:** -40, -5, 30, 65, 95.5, 100, 100.5, 101 **FAN:** 0, 51, 61, 71, 82, 140, 150, 160, 170, 180
Power (W)	10 -> 15	7.5 -> 15
Frameworks	a) TensorFlow b) TensorFlow Lite (optimization)	a) TensorFlow b) TensorRT (optimization)
Precision	INT8	FP32, FP16
Optimization tools	Quantization, pruning, weight clustering	Layer&Tensor fusion, quantization, kernel autotuning, dynamic tensor memory

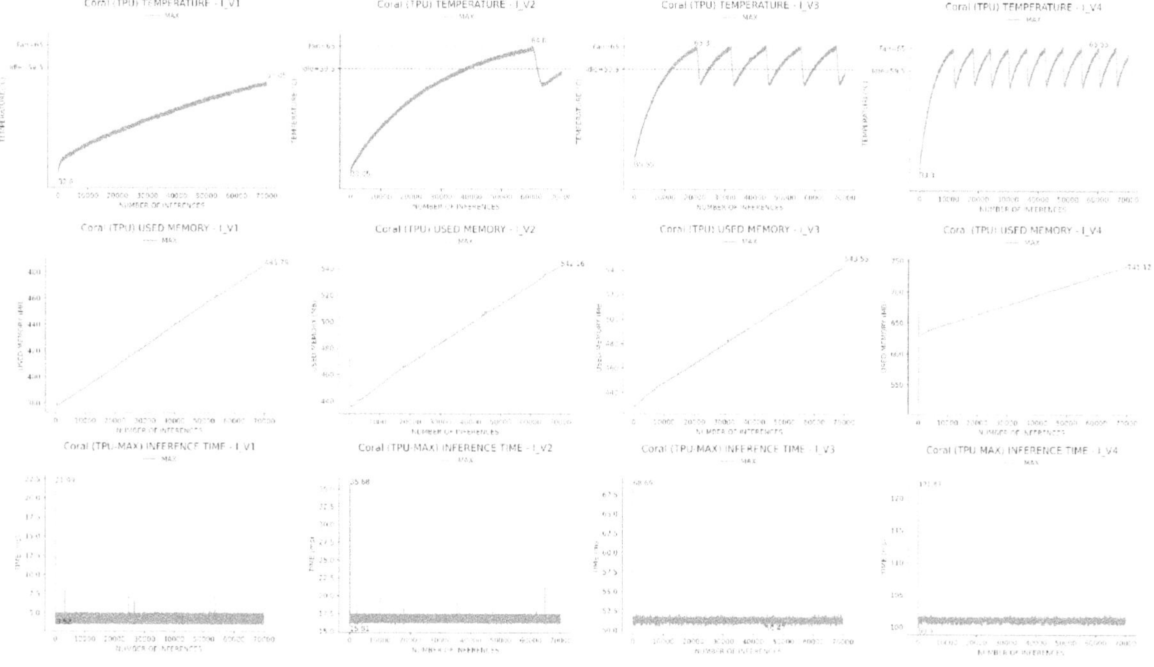

Fig. 3. Coral's evaluation metrics.

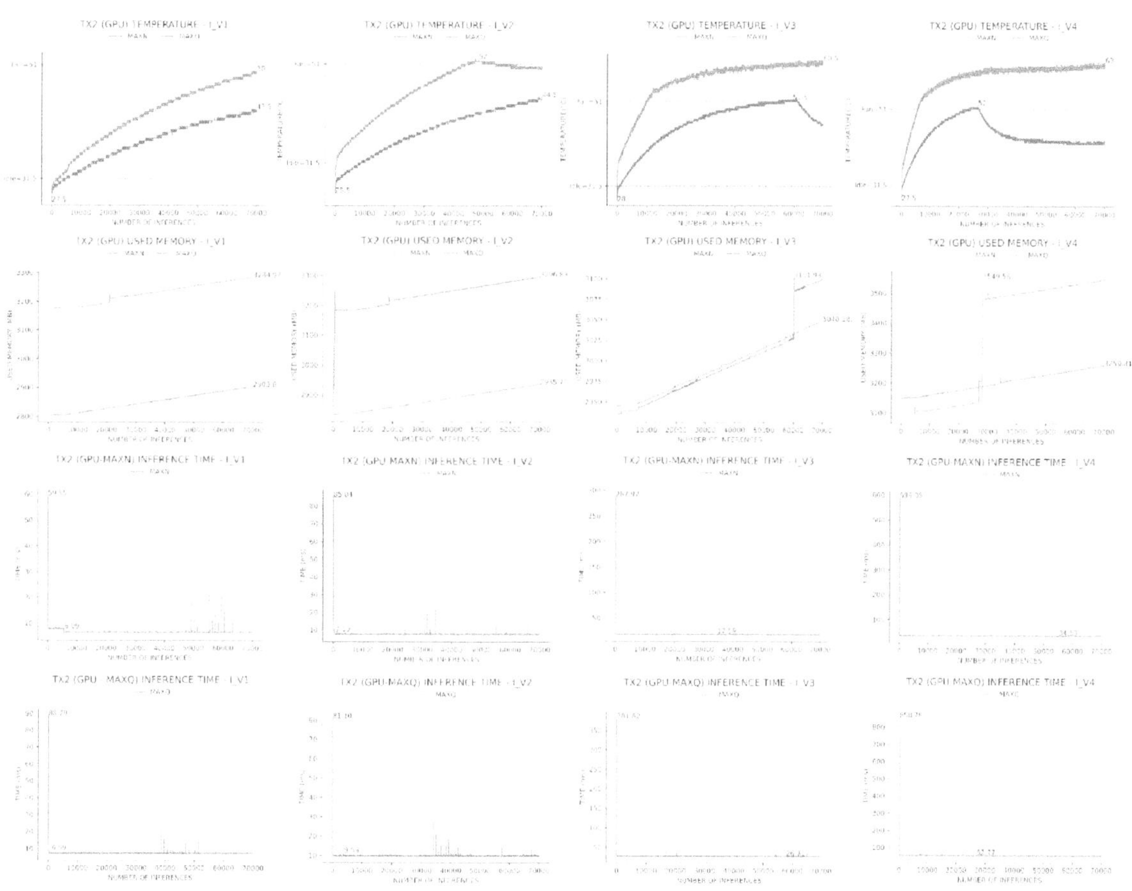

Fig. 4. TX2's evaluation metrics.

Likewise Coral, in the inference figures, it is observed that in all models the first inference is the slowest one. Also, Coral's first inference is by far faster than TX2. A possible explanation for this is that it is an ASIC and therefore it has a favorable memory hierarchy. Meanwhile, the TX2 has more data movement to do. But there is chance to reduce this timing because this devboard has a shared memory between the CPU and GPU which has not been used in this experiment because of some software limitations.

Finally, when comparing MAXN and MAXQ, it is observed that in general the former is faster because of the clock's frequency. Also I_v3 and I_v4 display less inference peaks and this is related to having a stable temperature which can be seen in these 2 models.

Table 2. Metrics.

Models (KB)	Metrics	Coral	TX2	
		MAX	MAXQ	MAXN
I_v1 (7.037)	Latency (ms)	17.97	81.58	53.11
	Score	0.64	0.65	0.65
I_v2 (12.165)	Latency (ms)	18.98	71.36	77.55
	Score	0.96	0.92	0.92
I_v3 (24.401)	Latency (ms)	17.33	354.5	270.02
	Score	1	0.99	0.99
I_v4 (43.865)	Latency (ms)	20.7	805.13	552.89
	Score	1	0.97	0.97

Fig. 5 displays the total amount of time for executing the 70000 inferences. It is observed that both devboards have used more time in I_v4 which effectively is the biggest model. But it is interesting to see that Coral, which has more compression (INT8) and is an spatial architecture, takes more time to finish the whole round of inferences than the TX2 (MAXQ and MAXN) in all models except for I_v1. This is because it uses a reactive control. By default Coral is at maximum performance all the time (500MHz) and whenever the TPU's temperature reaches the fan trip point (65°C), its clock frequency will decrease. This temperature fluctuation around the trip point affects the voltage-frequency operating point and over a sustained period of time has a negative impact on each inference as it makes their execution time more unpredictable. This can also be confirmed in Fig. 6, as once again it is seen that each inference of Coral takes more time than the TX2 in all models except for I_v1 which is the smallest one.

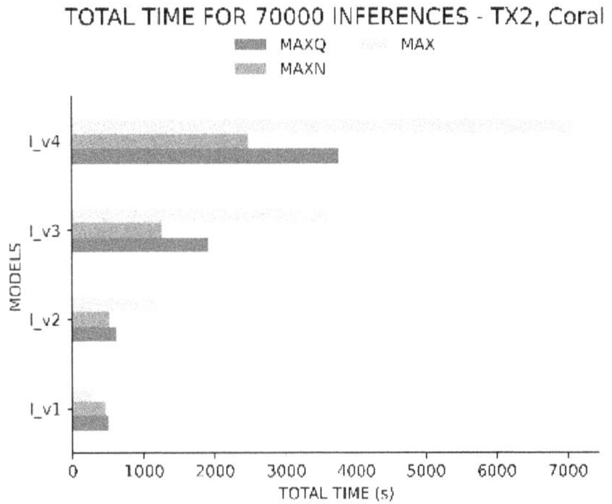

Fig. 5. Total time for 70000 inferences – TX2, Coral.

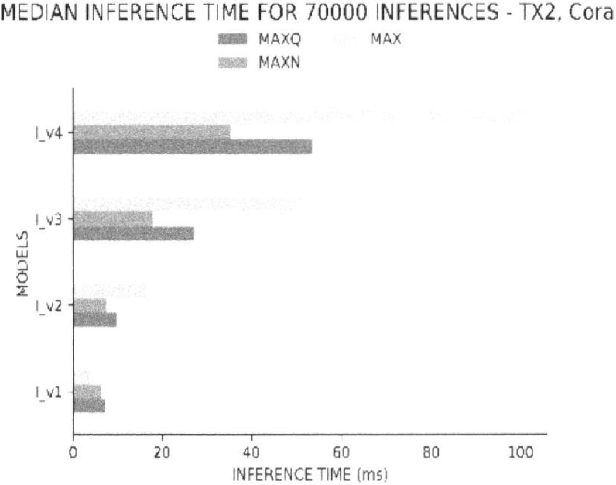

Fig. 6. Median inference time – TX2, Coral.

Coral only performs better than TX2 (MAXQ and MAXN) in Iv1 because it is the only model where it never throttles. And this proves the importance of optimizing DVFS control. Also, in both figures it is observed that the mode MAXQ takes more time than MAXN in all models. This is because it uses a lower frequency clock (from 114 MHz to 850MHZ).

4. Experimental Protocol

The experimental setup, shown in Fig. 7, includes an integrated solution, Mind in a Box (M/B), to support real time collection of the sensing data (thermal, cooling system, ...) and the computational load in Edge devices such as the two target architectures, the Google Coral (TPU) and Nvidia Jetson (GPU). This architecture, processing this information, can then prescribe load balancing and computational resources tuning. Thus optimizing the global performance of hybrid architectures leveraging Cloud, Edge and Fog Computing capabilities.

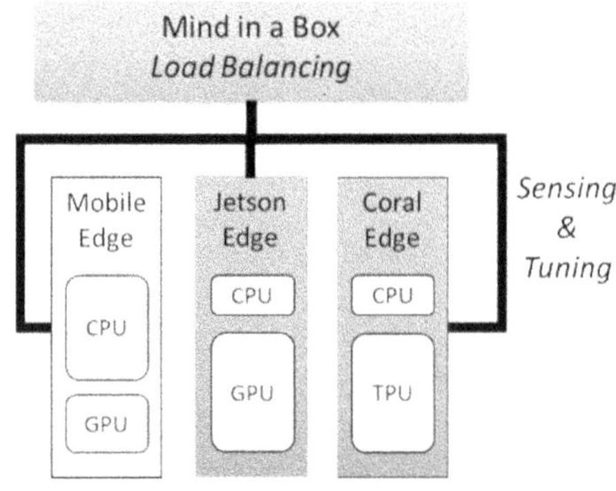

Fig. 7. Edge Computing Setup, Experimental Protocol.

This setup is typical of new Hybrid Analytics and Hybrid AI applications where Edge devices take charge of a sizeable workload in terms of local automatic processing and classification on the field, whether it is to process local information or to propose additional processing capabilities available to the architecture as a whole.

In this context, since the cost of ownership of such devices is relatively limited and their numbers can become massive, the question of optimizing performances and balancing workloads becomes an essential component which requires both current work load, multisensing consumption, and control over each Edge device computational load and hardware parametrization (such as a process unit's frequency, for instance). This experimental protocol aims at producing results which would be applicable in comparable Hybrid & Edge Computing architectures.

5. Conclusions

In this abstract, Google's Coral (TPU) and Nvidia's Jetson TX2 (GPU) edge accelerators have been compared from the angle of hardware architecture (processors, thermal regulation, etc) and software architecture (frameworks, workflow, etc) employing the multiple versions of GoogleNet (image classification) and assessing the quality of DVFS. Results suggest a great potential for further improvement in thermal regulation for the TPU. Even though it has an advantage in hardware architecture and model compression over the GPU, its performance is dismissed because of the reactive control which degrades the inference time.

References

[1]. A. Krizhevsky, I. Sutskever, and G. E. Hinton, ImageNet classification with deep convolutional neural networks, *Commun. ACM*, 60, 6, 2017.

[2]. O. Russakovsky *et al.*, ImageNet Large Scale Visual Recognition Challenge, *Int. J. Comput. Vis.*, Vol. 115, No. 3, 2015, pp. 211–252.

[3]. V. Sze, Y. H. Chen, T. J. Yang, and J. S. Emer, Efficient Processing of Deep Neural Networks: A Tutorial and Survey, in *Proceedings of the IEEE*, 2017, pp. 2295–2329.

[4]. M. Horowitz, Computing's energy problem (and what we can do about it), in *Digest of Technical Papers (ISSCC) - IEEE International Solid-State Circuits Conference*, 2014, pp. 10–14.

[5]. S. Li, L. Da Xu, and S. Zhao, The internet of things: a survey, *Inf. Syst. Front.*, Vol. 17, No. 2, 2015, pp. 243–259.

[6]. M. G. S. Murshed, C. Murphy, D. Hou, N. Khan, G. Ananthanarayanan, and F. Hussain, Machine Learning at the Network Edge: A Survey, Jul. 2019, https://arxiv.org/abs/1908.00080.

[7]. Z. Tang, Y. Wang, Q. Wang, and X. Chu, The impact of GPU DVFS on the energy and performance of deep Learning: An Empirical Study, in - *Proceedings of the 10th ACM International Conference on Future Energy Systems e-Energy'2019*, 2019, pp. 315–325.

[8]. A. K. Singh, S. Dey, K. R. Basireddy, K. McDonald-Maier, G. V. Merrett, and B. M. Al-Hashimi, Dynamic Energy and Thermal Management of Multi-Core Mobile Platforms: A Survey, *IEEE Des. Test*, Vol. 37, No. 5, pp. 25–33, 2020.

[9]. Google, Coral dev board, 2020. https://coral.ai/products/dev-board (accessed Feb. 21, 2020).

[10]. Nvidia, Jetson TX2 module, 2020. https://developer.nvidia.com/embedded/jetson-tx2 (accessed Feb. 21, 2020).

[11]. R. Hadidi, J. Cao, Y. Xie, B. Asgari, T. Krishna, and H. Kim, Characterizing the Deployment of Deep Neural Networks on Commercial Edge Devices, in *Proceedings of the 2019 IEEE International Symposium on Workload Characterization (IISWC' 2019)*, 2019, pp. 35–48.

[12]. V. Peluso, R. G. Rizzo, and A. Calimera, Performance profiling of embedded convnets under thermal-aware DVFS, *Electron.*, Vol. 8, No. 12, p. 1423, 2019.

[13]. TensorFlow Zoo. https://github.com/tensorflow/models/tree/master/research/slim

(101)

Bayesian Intelligent Measurement Technologies and Soft Measurements. Methodological Aspects and Application.

S. V. Prokopchina
Financial University under the Government of the Russian Federation,
49 Leningradsky Prospekt, 125993, Moscow, Russia
E-mail: svprokopchina@mail.ru

Abstract. This paper is devoted to description of new concept, mathematical and information-technical basis for Bayesian Intelligent Measurement and Soft Measurement. The main methodological platform is Regularizating Bayesian Approach and IT-platform is Bayesian Intelligent Technologies. As the result of these means the IT and strategy for estimation, prediction, audit of the status and characteristics of complex technogenetical objects (for example, fuel-energy enterprises) and territories are considered. The concept equations for intelligent and soft measurement, soft audit and soft management IT are given. The flexibility strategies for Bayesian Intelligent Audit and Management are suggested.

Keywords: Measurements, Regularizating bayesian approach, Uncertainty.

1. Introduction

The formation of new technological trends in the modern it industry, such as IoT, BIG DATA, DATA SCIENCE, and BI, is associated with receiving and processing different types of information flows. The distinctive properties of this information are its diversity, distribution in space and time, different physical nature, complexity of interpretability, uniqueness, which makes it difficult to process in the above technologies. One of the main types of such information is measurement information. However, most often the sources of such information are complex anthropogenic or natural objects and systems.

The specificity of complex objects and systems is their fundamental unknowability, unpredictability and unavailability for direct observations to the extent necessary for a reliable assessment of their state properties. Therefore, there is a situation of information uncertainty in which accurate values or conclusions cannot be obtained as a result of measuring parameters, evaluating properties, or auditing the States of an object or system. In such situations, the accuracy of measurements is achieved by attracting additional information in the form of knowledge about the measurement object and the factors affecting it. In this case, we use approaches that allow us to obtain not one, but a number of alternative solutions that are included in a certain interval (space) of solutions. This makes it possible to reduce the uncertainty of the result by attracting additional information from alternative solutions. The receipt of such alternatives is only possible with the use of specially tailored methods.

Taking into account the above requirements and focusing on the properties of integration, metrological and self-development of the methodological basis of the regularizing Bayesian approach (RBA) and intelligent technologies based on it (Bayesian intelligent technologies – BIT) particular Soft Bayesian measurements (SM), it seems appropriate to use them to create developing monitoring systems, polysystem audit and management under the "soft management" scheme.

2. Methodological Aspects of Bayesian Intelligent Technologies and Soft Measurements

RBA is based on the synthesis of the principles of three fundamental approaches: system, measurement and Bayesian and is intended for solving measurement problems: monitoring, rationing, auditing, and management under conditions of significant uncertainty.

To solve these problems in conditions of considerable uncertainty, the author developed the mathematical apparatus of BIT and soft measurement in the 90 - ies of the last century, which was widely used for solving applied problems. Definition of the term 'soft measurement', methodological principles of creating information technologies based on the theory of soft measurements, as well as conceptual foundations and practical applications are given in the author's works, for example, in [2-5].

So, in these works, the main provisions and definitions of new types of measurements are formulated.

Smart measurements are measurements based on the use of knowledge in the form of additional information about the measured properties and influencing factors of the environment in changing processes.

Bayesian intelligent measurements (BIM) are measurements based on probabilistic logic and a regularizing Bayesian hike as the main rule for obtaining measurement results.

Soft measurements (SM) are referred to as advanced metering, where the measurement results are obtained on the basis of the parametric logics.

System measurements are measurements of the emergent properties of complex objects that are inherent in a complex object as a complete system of interrelated properties.

If a measuring subject is included in the contour of any measurement technology, including intelligent measurement technology, as a source or receiver of information, such measurements are called **cognitive measurements** (CM).

For conditions of significant information uncertainty caused by inaccuracy, incompleteness, and vagueness of knowledge and data about the properties of an object, its functioning environment, relationships between them, goals, and task criteria, a new type of information technology for implementing measurements based on RBA was proposed.

In this approach, each solution is obtained on the corresponding measurement scale with a certain degree of probability (reliability) of solutions. For numerical data, the reliability of the solution is defined as the frequency probability, and for qualitative information, the frequency probability of the solution is replaced by a subjective, "fiducial" probability, which, unlike the frequency one, does not require long samples, stable experimental conditions, and other requirements and limitations of the postulates of probability theory and mathematical statistics. The measurement results are generated based on the principles of pattern recognition, where the images are the scale reference points. In RBA, the Bayesian decision rule is chosen as the decisive rule. The measurement problem under these conditions is solved as an inverse problem. Reference points are considered as random variables, according to the principles of the Bayesian approach. When forming a measurement solution, several scale reference points may be possible, which will form a number of alternatives to the measurement result.

Linguistic variables can be used to measure quality indicators. Weak scales are used as scales: nominal scales and order scales, that do not have computational capabilities, but have a strong semantic content that makes it possible to interpret solutions according to the goals of the measurement problem. In soft measurements, parametric logics can be implemented (the logic of Zadeh, Lukasevich, and others).

3. Basic properties of BIM and SM

The distinctive properties of BIT and SM can be summarized as follows:

1. Measurement is implemented as a decision-making process about the value of the measured object.
2. In the field of decision enter the metric space of possibilities or subjective probabilities, the values of which accompany the measurement result.
3. The measurement result can be presented in linguistic form.
4. When implementing BIM and SM, computationally weak, semantically rich scales (nominal and ordinal) are used.
5. The results of BIM and SM are a set of alternatives with metrological justification and can be interpreted as 'fuzzy' measurements.
6. The results of BIM and SM are accompanied by special complexes of metrological characteristics of accuracy, reliability, reliability, risk, entropy, amount of information on Fischer, and others.
7. The results of BIM and SM are characterized by activity, interpretability, motivating the implementation of measures
8. The results are implemented on special scales (for example, scales with dynamic restrictions of the SDR), the reference points of which are hypotheses about possible values (gradations) of the measured property.
9. The criteria of logic and inference rules are defined based on the type of the measurement task and measurement conditions
10. Scales and models of BIM and SM are dynamic objects and can be reformed during the measurement process.
11. BIM and SM are used when there is no repeatability of the conditions for the implementation of a measurement experiment, there are only individual facts, small samples of experimental data.

4. Application of BIM and SI Methodology and Technologies for Control and Management Tasks under Uncertainty

The definition of "soft rationing", "soft audit", "soft management" and formal models based on self-development schemes were given in the author's works [3-5]. Based on these formal models, information technologies and algorithms for "soft control" of complex dynamic systems of technogenic and socio-economic types were developed.

Audit and management processes for distributed technogenic systems, such as fuel and energy complexes, transport highways, or territories, are typical examples of multi-system audit and management of complex dynamic systems with properties that change over time and space. When such objects actively interact with the environment in conditions of significant information uncertainty, situations, changing restrictions (for example, according to regulatory and methodological or legal bases), criteria and requirements, the task arises of reconfiguring the models, structure and functions of monitoring, listening, and object management systems in the mode of operation of the objects themselves. During the operation of these information systems, this ensures that the models used in them are always adequate to the objects in order to ensure the effectiveness of the audit and management decisions obtained with changing properties and characteristics of both the managed systems themselves and the business landscape or natural and economic environment.

The difference from the concept of a managed system in the classical control scheme "managed object-control object" consists in the complexity of interaction and mutual influence of systems both included in the managed polysystem and in the polysystem itself. So, in the proposed concept of polysystem management, conflict situations are quite acceptable both between the systems of the control and controlled polysystems, and in these systems themselves, leading to braking and complication of management.

Management practice puts forward new tasks of polysystem management. So in the process of managing enterprises according to incomplete and inaccurate information collected by the monitoring system, it is necessary to assess and adjust in a given direction, technical condition of managed systems, sustainability of production and its impact on the environment, industrial policy , personnel, financial and market conditions and other processes of the company and the environment. It is obvious that in order to develop an effective strategy for managing such an object, it is necessary to have in the system tools for reconfiguring the object model with a sufficient degree of reliability and control over the risk of making decisions at the rate of new information about the object and the environment.

Taking into account the above requirements and focusing on the properties of integration, metrological and self-development of the methodological basis of the regularizing Bayesian approach (RBA) and information technologies based on it (Bayesian intelligent technologies - BIT), it seems appropriate to use them to create developing monitoring, audit and management systems according to the "soft control" scheme for polysystem arrows.

Obviously, all these tasks can be divided into three main groups:

- Measurement, evaluation of properties and characteristics of the control system and the controlled polysubject environment, as well as modeling their evolution, restoring the development retrospective and predicting States and situations;
- Multi-criteria control (listening) and normalization of the state of systems or their characteristics; this stage includes all tasks of various audits (product and production quality, environmental friendliness of production, personnel, energy indicators, etc.);
- Generation of optimal management decisions and management recommendations and their implementation in practice, followed by monitoring and planning.

This article discusses the possibilities of creating such self-developing systems based on models and scales with dynamic constraints (SDC).

Systems based on RBA have fields of solutions, factor trees, and their properties in the form of dynamic compacts of SDOS for the controlled environment S_t^O, the environment S_t^E, or the control polysystem interacting with the environment. When evaluating properties or situations in the process of polysystem audit based on the BIT methodology S_t^{OE}, the conceptual record of the SDC has the form:

$$S_t^{OE} = S_t^O \overset{z}{*} S_t^E \overset{z}{*} S_t^{O_L} \overset{z}{*} S_t^{O_K} \overset{z}{*} S_t^{O_U} \quad (1)$$

where $S_t^{O_L}$ – Cstrictions in space and time; t =[1;T] – time interval that determines the dynamics of the SDC; $S_t^{O_K}$ – SDC criteria base; $S_t^{O_U}$ – SDC requirements (including metrological requirements) and conditions for setting the problem; * - convolution symbol with logic z (for z = l and a parametric family of logics, the convolution corresponds to a convolution with probabilistic logic).

Due to the ability to manage not only data, but also knowledge [3-5] in systems based on RBA, as well as their openness for inclusion in information databases of new models, algorithms, and recommendations based on scales with dynamic limitations of theoretical and practical knowledge, the requirements of model reconfiguration are provided (1). Each replenishment of this type is accompanied in the system by the process of metrological justification of newly accepted information. To reflect parametric $S_t^{O_P}$, functional, or system information, a hierarchical structure of Hyper-C is constructed in the form of a composition of parametric $S_t^{O_P}$, functional $S_t^{O_F}$, and system (situational) $S_t^{O_S}$ S:

$$HS_t^O = S_t^{O_P} \overset{z}{*} S_t^{O_F} \overset{z}{*} S_t^{O_S} \quad (2)$$

Conceptual record, for the synthesis of all types of SDO, the main fundamentally important aspect of metrological justification is the Metrology of knowledge, including knowledge presented in the form of analytical dependencies, algorithms, linguistic conclusions, descriptions of situations and scenarios of their development, which is implemented on the basis of SDO. The use of SDC allows you to control the quality and metrological characteristics (MX) (accuracy, reliability, reliability), entropy and risk of the resulting solutions, as well as synthesize the technology with the required quality.

SDOS have been developed for evaluating numerical S_t^N and linguistic S_t^{lg} variables, dynamic variables $S_t^S\ (t=\overline{1,T})$ and multidimensional processes $HS_t^S\ (t=\overline{1,T})$ situations $S_t^S\ (t=ti)$, scenarios for the development of situations $HS_t^D\ (t=\overline{1,T})$, recommendations $S_t^D\ (t=f)$, and management strategies $S_t^{SS}\ (t=\overline{1,T})$ for the relationship of objects and situations . The latter type of scales allows you to create hyperscales for integral characteristics (indices, indicators), restore them, or predict them.

To conduct an audit of States or situations, reference scales of the specified types or HS hyperscales S_t^C are formed in addition to the listed ones.

The reference SDR for audit is regularized information about the norms, standards, and degrees of compliance with the established limits of indicators of object characteristics. In particular, the verification of compliance with ISO 9000 or ISO 1400 standards is implemented on the methodological and information technology base of Bayesian intelligent technologies by means of SDC. This is a necessary software tool for conducting self-audit for every enterprise, which provides significant savings in financial and time costs. The conceptual equation of such an intelligent audit, defined in this paper as an audit based on the production, use of knowledge, and management of knowledge under conditions of uncertainty (when using BIT-Bayesian intelligent audit) can be written in the following optimization form:

$$\left\{h_t^c \mid \{MX\}_t^c\right\} = \left\{\begin{matrix} \arg extrC \;\; S_t^{OE} \overset{z}{*} S_t^{CL} \overset{z}{*} S_t^{CU} \overset{z}{*} \\ S_t^{CK} \mid \left(X_t; X_t^A; \Phi_t^A; \Phi_t; \Phi_t^{CA}; \Phi_t^C\right) \end{matrix}\right\} \quad (3)$$

where $X_t ; X_t^A$ arrays of current and a priori information; $\Phi_t^A; \Phi_t$ - information technology base at the current and previous time points; $\Phi_t^{CA}; \Phi_t^C$ – calculation and methodological basis of audit, presented in the form of a set of information technologies controlling (audit) techniques that are integrated by means of Bayesian integrating technologies; S_t^{CL} – SDO of audit restrictions; SDO of audit conditions; S_t^{CU} ; $S_t^{CK} S_t^{CK}$ – SDO of the audit criteria base; C-Bayesian decision rule with flexible logic.

If the logic of a Bayesian rule other than probabilistic is applied, then such a rule is called a soft Bayesian rule. An audit method based on the application of a soft Bayesian rule CAN be defined as a "soft audit" method and used in polysystem audit tasks.

Intelligent ("soft" with flexible logic) situational or strategic management based on the RB and BIT methodology makes it possible to foresee the impact of the results of the undertaken regulation on all components of the object and ecosystem and to prevent the occurrence of crisis or emergency situations, and, if necessary, to adjust the management strategy in a timely manner, which is the basis for ensuring the sustainable functioning or development of the object. However, to ensure the stability of management in conditions of uncertainty (inaccuracy, incompleteness and vagueness) of information, it is necessary to reliably assess the situation.

The regularizing Bayesian approach (RBA) and the methodology of Bayesian intelligent technologies (BIT) provide a unique opportunity to provide such estimates and the required quality of their definition. Based on this approach, the space of situations, recommendations, or control actions is quantified, which makes it possible to form a representative set of them in the form of multidimensional and integral scales of situations, the benchmarks of which are gradations of features or typical classes of situations that are separated from each other by a given distance.

The decision-making process can be implemented as a process of transformation of such interrelated scales based on obtaining objective and reliable: knowledge about the controlled object and its environment, knowledge about their current state, dynamics of situations, trends in the evolution of the object and environment. The process of obtaining such knowledge and management based on it, obviously, can be called intelligent management based on BRA/BIT. If the logic of such control is implemented on the basis of a soft Bayesian rule with a changeable logic for obtaining solutions, then such control can be defined as "soft" control.

These technologies are implemented in the software environment of the "Infoanalyst", which is a platform developed numerous systems for monitoring, auditing and support management decision making [6-9]. Based on these technologies, audit and decision-making systems have been developed for managing energy generating complexes, resource supply networks, transport networks, housing and utilities systems, environmental protection, distributed production, territorial and socio-humanitarian development, and other tasks of multi-system audit and management.

The following figures illustrate the stages of polysystem audit of housing and communal complexes (HCS) by means of the Infoanalytic-HCS system based on RBP and soft measurement technologies.

In the process of a comprehensive polysystem audit, the state of all housing and utilities resource systems is evaluated. Moreover, the audit by means of the Infoanalytic-housing and utilities complex (the block diagram is shown in Fig. 1) can be made with the degree of detail that is necessary to obtain a reliable assessment and planning of current and major repairs, modernization and reconstruction of resource, generating and distribution systems.

Fig. 1. Audit of calculations with consumers of a residential building.

To audit the quality of functioning of the city's housing and utilities services for the supply of services to the population, information from various sources is collected and processed, including information from the population. When processing measurements, fuzzy measurement dynamic models of indicators are formed in the form of fuzzy autoregression models (Fig. 1).

During the audit, the risks and potentials of the system indicators are determined and reflected in the form of cognitive maps of risks and potentials (Fig. 2).

Fig. 2. Measurement control ("soft audit") of risks and potentials of housing and utilities indicators.

Fig. 3 shows the measuring cognitive solutions of integrated housing and utilities assessment.

As a result of a comprehensive multi-system audit of housing and utilities services, a cognitive map of the city's housing and utilities sector was obtained, which clearly reflects the current situation. Blue and green colors reflect favorable and normal, respectively, the situation with payment and provision of housing services, yellow and brown intense and critical.

A detailed explanation of the results with an explanation of the causes and influencing factors, with data and estimates on request is generated by Infoanalytic-housing and utilities.

Fig. 3. Example of measuring the quality of housing and communal services.

References

[1]. V. E. Lepsky, Evolution of ideas about management in the context of the development of scientific rationality. In the collection 'Reflexive processes and management', Edited by V. E. Lepsky, *Kognito-Center*, Moscow, 2013, p. 43-45.

[2]. D. D. Nedosekin, S. V. Prokopchina, E. A. Chernyavsky, Intellectualization of information technologies for measuring processes, *Energoatomizdat*, 1995.

[3]. Soft calculations and measurements. Edited by S. V. Prokopchina, *Scientific Library*, 2017.

[4]. Management in conditions of uncertainty, Edited by S. V. Prokopchina, *LETI Publishing House*, St. Petersburg, 2014.

[5]. Prokopchina S. V., Basic principles of the theory of soft measurements, *Soft Measurements and Computing*, No. 7, 2018.

Authors

Index

D

E

F

G

H

I

J

K

L

M

N

O

P

Q

R

S

T

U

V

W

X

Z

www.ingramcontent.com/pod-product-compliance
Ingram Content Group UK Ltd.
Pitfield, Milton Keynes, MK11 3LW, UK
UKHW061817190726
13853UKWH00006B/2197